CIVIL LIBERTIES

Second Edition

Helen Fenwick, BA, LLB,
Senior Lecturer in Law
University of Durham

Cavendish
Publishing
Limited

London • Sydney

First published in 1994 by Cavendish Publishing Limited, The Glass House, Wharton Street, London, WC1X 9PX, United Kingdom

Telephone: +44 (0) 171 278 8000   Facsimile: +44 (0) 171 278 8080

E-mail: info@cavendishpublishing.com

Visit our Home Page on http://www.cavendishpublishing.com

© Fenwick, H	1998
First edition	1994
Second edition	1998
Reprinted with amendments	1999

All rights reserved. No part of this publication may be reproduced, stored in a retrieval system, or transmitted, in any form or by any means, electronic, mechanical, photocopying, recording, scanning or otherwise, except under the terms of the Copyright Designs and Patents Act 1988 or under the terms of a licence issued by the Copyright Licensing Agency, 90 Tottenham Court Road, London W1P 9HE, UK, without the permission in writing of the publisher.

Fenwick, Helen
Civil liberties textbook – 2nd ed
1. Civil rights – Great Britain
I. Title
344.1'0285

ISBN 1 85941 199 1

Printed and bound in Great Britain by
Biddles Ltd, Guildford and King's Lynn

For Paul, Clare, Daniel and Patrick

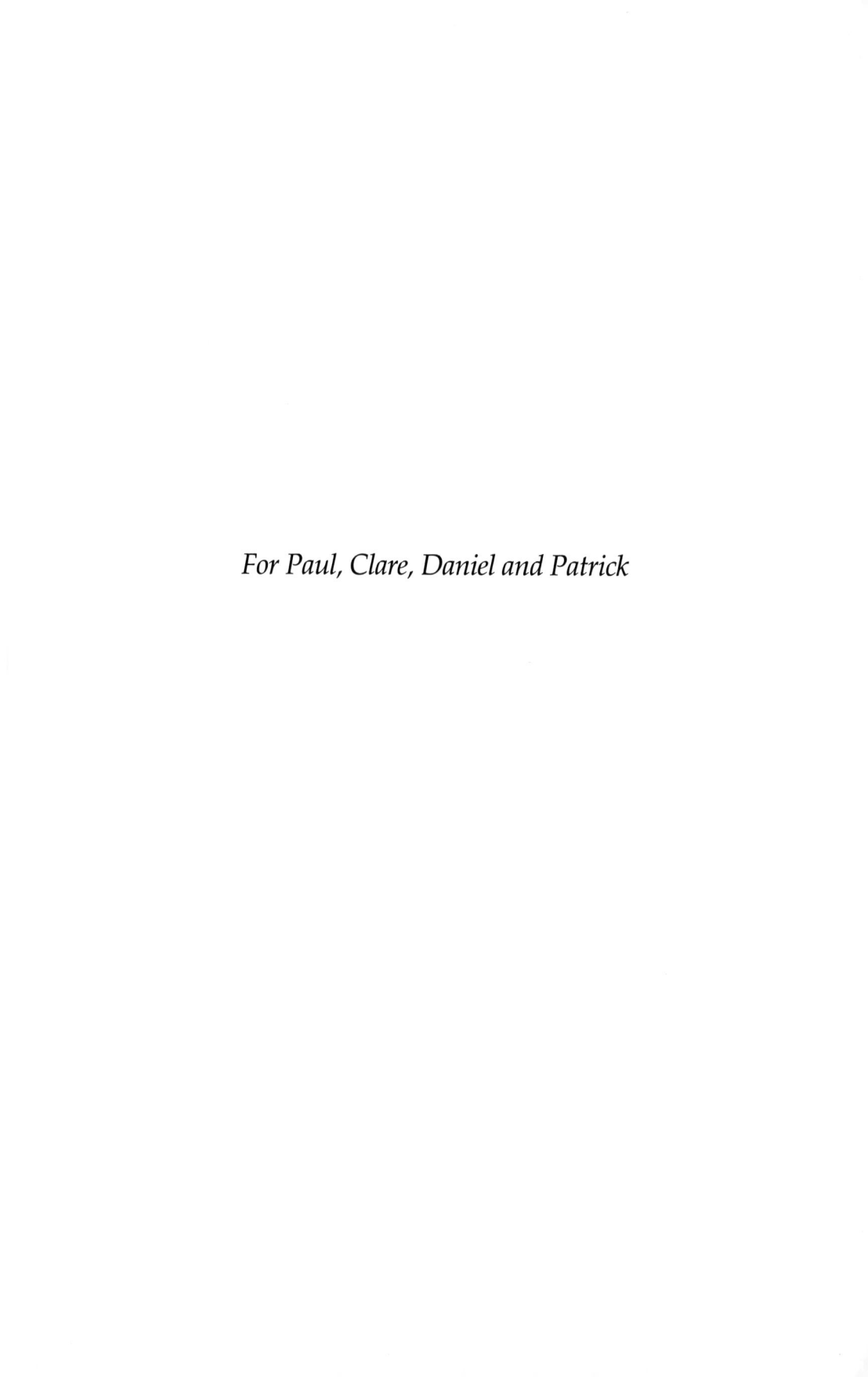

PREFACE

Protection for civil liberties in Britain at the present time is uncertain, incoherent and precarious. The last 18 years have seen a severe erosion of fundamental individual freedoms due to the burgeoning power of the state; in particular, the ancient right to silence has been curtailed as has freedom of assembly under the Criminal Justice and Public Order Act 1994. Protection for civil liberties has generally come, not from the government, but from Europe and – especially in the 1990s – from the judiciary who have begun to show a willingness to use the European Convention on Human Rights, EU law and common law principles to hold back the tide of executive power. Nevertheless, as this book suggests, the decline of civil liberties is unlikely to be reversed until the influence of the Human Rights Act 1998 becomes apparent, and possibly not even then. However, that Act, together with the Freedom of Information Act 1998, may represent an extremely significant turning point in the protection of fundamental human rights in the UK.

Despite declining protection for civil liberties, interest in the subject has never been greater in Britain than at the present time, and it is recognised that civil liberties, in so far as it can be termed a discrete subject, is not only rapidly developing but now encompasses a wide and varied area. Therefore, it is only possible for any book of this kind to deal with a selection of civil liberties: the topics chosen and the emphasis placed on them inevitably reflect my own interests. The growth in this area and its complexity has meant that in order to remain a manageable length the book is confined largely to the law in force in England and Wales.

I must acknowledge the contribution of my colleague at Durham, Professor Colin Warbrick, who offered helpful criticism of a very early draft of Chapter 3 and was a source of information in relation to the first part of Chapter 2. My thanks are also due to Gavin Phillipson of Essex University for his valuable help in researching material for Chapters 1, 3, 4, 5, 7 and 8. Kate Nicol of Cavendish Publishing has shown great patience in including my many additions at the proof stage of this book. I have drawn on certain of my articles in writing Chapters 11 and 13 and I gratefully acknowledge permission to use them here:

'Confessions, Recording Rules and Miscarriages of Justice: A Mistaken Emphasis?' [1993] *Criminal Law Review* 174–84, Sweet and Maxwell.

'Legal Advice, Videotaping and the Right to Silence' [1993] 57(4) *Criminal Law Journal* 385–89, Pageant Publishing.

'Perpetuating Inequality in the Name of Equal Treatment' [1996] 18 (2) *Journal of Social Welfare and Family Law* 263–70.

Fenwick, H and Phillipson, G, 'Confidence and Privacy: A Re-examination' (1996) 55(3) *CLJ* 447.

In particular I am grateful to my husband Paul who has supported me throughout the task of writing this book.

The law is stated as at 1 September 1997 but it has been possible to include some later material.

Helen Fenwick
University of Durham
December 1997

CONTENTS

Preface	*vii*
Table of cases	*xvii*
Table of statutes	*xliii*
Table of EU and international instruments	*li*

PART ONE
THE NATURE AND PROTECTION OF RIGHTS AND LIBERTIES — 1

1 THE NATURE OF RIGHTS AND LIBERTIES — 3
   1 WHERE DO RIGHTS DERIVE FROM? — 3
      Opposition to the liberal conception of human rights — 6
   2 WHAT IS MEANT BY A RIGHT? — 8
      Distinguishing moral and legal rights — 8
      The strength of a right: conflicts with other claims — 10
      Distinguishing rights and liberties — 13

2 THE EUROPEAN CONVENTION ON HUMAN RIGHTS — 17
   1 INTRODUCTION — 17
   2 THE SUPERVISORY PROCEDURE FOR THE CONVENTION — 20
      The role of the European Commission on Human Rights — 20
      The European Court of Human Rights — 22
      The Committee of Ministers — 24
      The right of complaint: inter-state applications — 25
      The right of complaint: individual applications — 25
   3 THE SUBSTANTIVE RIGHTS AND FREEDOMS — 35
      Article 2: Protection of life — 35
      Article 3: Freedom from inhuman treatment — 40
      Article 4: Freedom from slavery, servitude and forced or compulsory labour — 44
      Article 5: Right to liberty and security of person — 45
      Article 6: Right to a fair and public hearing — 53
      Article 7: Freedom from retrospective effect of penal legislation — 59
      Article 8: Right to respect for privacy — 61
      Article 9: Freedom of thought, conscience and religion — 64
      Article 10: Freedom of expression — 65
      Article 11: Freedom of association and assembly — 70
      Article 12: The right to marry and to found a family — 71
      Protocols to the Convention — 73
   4 ADDITIONAL GUARANTEES TO THE PRIMARY RIGHTS — 75
      Article 13: The right to an effective remedy before a national authority — 75
      Article 14: Prohibition of discrimination — 76

5	RESTRICTION OF THE RIGHTS AND FREEDOMS	78
	The system of restrictions	78
	Article 15: Derogation from the rights and freedoms in case of public emergency	78
	Article 16: Restriction on the political activity of aliens	80
	Article 17: Destruction of Convention rights	81
	Making a reservation: Article 64	81
	General restrictions on the rights and freedoms contained in Articles 8–11	81
	The doctrine of the 'margin of appreciation'	82
6	CONCLUSIONS	85

3	METHODS OF PROTECTING CIVIL LIBERTIES IN THE UK: THE BILL OF RIGHTS QUESTION	87
1	INTRODUCTION	87
2	THE POLITICAL HISTORY OF THE DEBATE	89
	Conservative support	90
	The Liberals and the Democrats	91
	The Labour position	92
3	TRADITIONAL METHODS OF PROTECTING CIVIL LIBERTIES IN THE UK	93
	The democratic process as the guardian of civil liberties	93
	Rules and judicial interpretation: current relevance of the Diceyan tradition	98
	The influence of European law	107
4	A BILL OF RIGHTS?	112
	The argument from democracy	114
	Fitness of the UK judiciary to adjudicate on human rights	119
5	ENACTING THE EUROPEAN CONVENTION ON HUMAN RIGHTS	123
	A tailor-made UK Bill of Rights?	124
	The legal status of the Convention under the Human Rights Act	125
6	ENFORCEMENT AND SCRUTINY UNDER THE HUMAN RIGHTS ACT	133
	Remedies	133
	Scrutiny	135

PART TWO
EXPRESSION 137
    The argument from moral autonomy 137
    The argument from truth 138
    The argument from participation in a democracy 140
    The argument from individual self-fulfilment 142
    Free speech protection in practice 143

Contents

4 RESTRAINING FREEDOM OF EXPRESSION TO PROTECT THE ADMINISTRATION OF JUSTICE   147
    1   INTRODUCTION   147
    2   PREJUDICING PROCEEDINGS   148
       The development of the common law   148
       The Contempt of Court Act 1981   151
       Restrictions on reporting of court proceedings   160
       Intentionally prejudicing proceedings   163
       Prejudicing proceedings: relationship between the 1981 Act and the common law   169
    3   PROTECTING JUSTICE AS A CONTINUING PROCESS   170
       Undermining the legal process in the long term   171
       Scandalising the court   173
       Victimising witnesses and others   175
    4   JURY DELIBERATIONS   176
    5   REFUSING TO DISCLOSE SOURCES   177

5 RESTRAINING FREEDOM OF EXPRESSION ON MORAL AND RELIGIOUS GROUNDS: CENSORSHIP, LICENSING AND REGULATION OF FILM AND BROADCASTING   181
    1   LAW AND PORNOGRAPHY: THEORETICAL CONSIDERATIONS   181
       The conservative position   182
       The liberal position   183
       The radical feminist position   184
    2   RESTRAINING SPEECH ON MORAL GROUNDS   189
       Statutory obscenity   190
       Statutory indecency   198
       Common law offences of indecency and obscenity   202
    3   CENSORSHIP, LICENSING AND REGULATION OF FILM AND BROADCASTING   205
       Introduction   205
       Broadcasting   206
       Satellite television   211
       Films   212
       Video   213
       The Internet   213
       Conclusions   214
    4   BLASPHEMY, SEDITIOUS LIBEL, RELIGIOUS AND RACIAL HATRED   215
       Blasphemous and seditious libel   215
       The future of blasphemy law   219
       Incitement to racial hatred   225

6	**OFFICIAL SECRECY AND ACCESS TO INFORMATION**		229
	1 INTRODUCTION		229
	2 OFFICIAL SECRECY		232
	Section 2 of the Official Secrets Act 1911		232
	The Official Secrets Act 1989		236
	Breach of confidence		250
	Defence Advisory notices		258
	Public interest immunity		259
	3 ACCESS TO INFORMATION		264
	Freedom of information abroad		264
	The Public Records Acts		265
	The Code of Practice on Access to Government Information		265
	Statutory freedom of information		272
7	**FREEDOM OF ASSOCIATION AND ASSEMBLY**		275
	1 INTRODUCTION		275
	2 FREEDOM OF ASSOCIATION		276
	Groups associated with the use of violence		276
	Trade unions		278
	3 FREEDOM OF ASSEMBLY		284
	Introduction		284
	Traditional legal recognition of freedom of assembly?		288
	Legal regulation of meetings and marches: the statutory framework		290
	Obstructing the highway and public nuisance		299
	Breach of the peace, binding over and bail conditions		300
	Criminalising public disorder		306
	Power to enter meetings on private premises		315
	Private law remedies		316

PART THREE
THE PROTECTION OF PRIVACY   317

8	**PERSONAL INFORMATION**		323
	1 MEDIA INTRUSION		323
	Breach of confidence		323
	Defamation and malicious falsehood		332
	Power of court to protect minors		333
	Media self-regulation		333
	A tort of invasion of privacy?		336
	Data protection		338
	Criminal and civil liability for intrusions		339
	2 STATE SURVEILLANCE		343
	Introduction		343

		Telephone and mail intercepts	343
		Bugging devices	349
	3	ACCESS TO PERSONAL INFORMATION	356
		Introduction	356
		Information held on computer	357
		Manually held files	360

9	**RESPECT FOR THE HOME: FREEDOM FROM ARBITRARY ENTRIES, SEARCHES AND SEIZURES**	363
	1 INTRODUCTION	363
	Legal remedies	363
	2 POLICE POWERS OF ENTRY AND SEARCH	365
	Entry without warrant	366
	Search warrants	368
	Power to enter premises at common law	369
	Voluntary searches	369
	Power of seizure	370
	3 SAFEGUARDS	372
	Code of Practice B	372
	Police accountability	374

10	**BODILY INTEGRITY AND AUTONOMY; SEXUAL EXPRESSION AND IDENTITY; FAMILY LIFE**	377
	1 BODILY INTEGRITY AND AUTONOMY	377
	Introduction	377
	Bodily integrity	377
	Bodily autonomy	379
	2 SEXUAL EXPRESSION AND IDENTITY	381
	Introduction	381
	Incest	381
	Buggery	382
	Sado-masochism	385
	Sexual identity	388
	3 FAMILY LIFE	388

PART FOUR
PERSONAL LIBERTY   391

11	**FREEDOM FROM ARBITRARY SEARCH, ARREST AND DETENTION: SUSPECTS' RIGHTS IN CRIMINAL INVESTIGATIONS**	393
	1 INTRODUCTION	393

2	THE SOURCES OF THE RULES	394
	PACE and the Codes	394
	Notes for Guidance	395
	Home Office circulars	396
3	STOP AND SEARCH POWERS	397
	The PACE stop and search power	397
	Misuse of drugs	399
	Prevention of terrorism and anticipated local violence	399
	Procedural requirements	402
	Voluntary searches	402
	Breaches of the stop and search rules	404
4	POWERS OF ARREST AND DETENTION	405
	At common law – power to arrest for breach of peace	406
	Under PACE: power of arrest without warrant	406
	Power of arrest with warrant	413
	Arrest under the Prevention of Terrorism (Temporary Provisions) Act 1989	413
	Other statutory powers of arrest	414
	Procedural elements of a valid arrest	414
	Consensual detainment	417
	Use of force	417
5	ASSAULT ON OR OBSTRUCTION OF A POLICE CONSTABLE IN THE EXECUTION OF HIS DUTY	418
	Obstruction of a constable	418
	Assault on a constable	420
6	DETENTION IN POLICE CUSTODY	421
	Time limits on detention after arrest	421
	Detention under the Prevention of Terrorism (Temporary Provisions) Act 1989	422
	Searches of detained persons	423
7	QUESTIONING AND TREATMENT OF SUSPECTS INSIDE AND OUTSIDE THE POLICE STATION	424
	General treatment inside the police station	425
	The interviewing scheme: bringing the safeguards into play	430
	The legal advice scheme	440
	Interviewing techniques and recording methods	455
	The right to silence	458
8	IDENTIFICATION OF SUSPECTS	465
	Witness identification	466
	Identification by fingerprints or bodily samples	468
9	REDRESS FOR POLICE IMPROPRIETY	468
	Introduction	468
	Exclusion of evidence	469
	Section 76(2)(a): the 'oppression' test	473

		Section 76(2)(b): the 'reliability' test	476
		Causation and the two heads of s 76	478
		Relationship between ss 76 and 78	479
		Section 78: the 'fairness' test	480
		Section 82(3): the common law discretion	498
		Mentally handicapped or ill defendants: special rules	499
		Tortious remedies	500
		Police complaints	503
	10	CONCLUSIONS	507
12	**FREEDOM OF MOVEMENT**		**509**
	1	INTRODUCTION	509
	2	FREEDOM TO TRAVEL ABROAD	510
	3	EXCLUSION ORDERS	511
		Influence on terrorism	512
		Justifications and safeguards	513
	4	THE RIGHT OF ABODE	516
		Acquired rights	518
		British citizens	519
		Proving the right of abode	520
		The position of EU and EEA nationals	521
	5	CLAIMS TO ENTER OF THOSE WITHOUT RIGHTS OF ENTRY	523
		Temporary entrants and entrants intending to remain	525
		Asylum	528
	6	ILLEGAL ENTRANTS	537
	7	DEPORTATION	538
		Deportation after conviction	539
		Deportation for the public good	540

PART FIVE
EQUALITY AND THE THEORY OF ANTI-DISCRIMINATION LAWS 547
    Phases in the movement towards equality 549
    Anti-assimilationism 551
    Discrimination and the law 552

13	**ANTI-DISCRIMINATION LEGISLATION**		**555**
	1	INTRODUCTION	555
		Discrimination on grounds of gender	555
		Discrimination on grounds of race	558
	2	DIRECT DISCRIMINATION ON GROUNDS OF SEX OR RACE	560
		Sex	560
		Race	566
		Harassment	568

3	INDIRECT DISCRIMINATION ON GROUNDS OF SEX OR RACE	570
	Sex	570
	Race	573
4	VICTIMISATION	576
5	LAWFUL DISCRIMINATION	577
	Sex	577
	Race	578
6	EQUAL PAY	579
	Choice of comparator	580
	'Same employment'	581
	The term by term approach	582
	The 'material factor' defence	583
	Conclusions	590
7	EFFICACY OF THE INDIVIDUAL METHOD	591
	Remedies	591
	Success rate of applications	593
	Reform	594
8	THE COMMISSION FOR RACIAL EQUALITY AND THE EQUAL OPPORTUNITIES COMMISSION	595
	Investigative and remedial powers	595
	Judicial review	596
	Reform	597
9	POSITIVE ACTION	598
	The theoretical basis	598
	Forms of positive action and their recognition in national law	599
	Positive action favouring women under EU law	600

14 THE CRIMINAL LAW AND THE CRIMINAL JUSTICE PROCESS; DISCRIMINATION ON GROUNDS OF SEXUAL ORIENTATION 609

1	RACIAL DISCRIMINATION	609
	Criminal law	609
	Criminal justice	609
2	GENDER DISCRIMINATION	612
	Criminal law	612
	Criminal justice	614
3	DISCRIMINATION ON GROUNDS OF SEXUAL ORIENTATION	616
	Employment and education	616
	The criminal process	619
	The European Convention on Human Rights	620

APPENDIX
THE HUMAN RIGHTS ACT 1998 621

Index 649

TABLE OF CASES

A v Austria (1963) Appl 1753/63; (1965) Yearbook VIII, p 174 65
A v Morgan Grampian Publishers and Others [1991] AC 1; [1991] 2 All ER 1 178
Abassey and Others v Metropolitan Police Commissioner [1990] 1 WLR 385, CA 415
Abbott v Refuge Assurance Co Ltd [1962] 1 QB 632 500
Abdulaziz, Cabales and Balkandali v UK (1985) 7 EHRR 471 ....77, 78, 112, 389, 525
Absolam (1989) 88 Cr App R 332 ....431, 434, 435, 485, 487
Ahaukat Ali (1991) *The Times*, 19 February 493
Air Canada v Secretary of State for Trade (No 2) [1983] 1 All ER 910 ....260, 262
Airedale NHS Trust v Bland (1993) *The Times*, 5 February 37
Aitken and Others (1971) (unreported) 233, 236
Aitken [1992] 1 WLR 1006 386
Albert v Lavin [1982] AC 546; [1981] 3 All ER 878, HL 420
Alderson v Booth [1969] 3 QB 216 414
Aldred (1909) 22 Cox CC 1 218
Alexander v Home Office [1988] 1 WLR 968 612
Ali v Secretary of State for Home Affairs [1984] 1 All ER 1009 538
Alladice (1988) 87 Cr App R 380, CA 447, 474, 479, 484, 489
Allen v Wright [1835] 8 C & P 522 409
Allen [1992] Crim LR 297 490
Ambard v Attorney General for Trinidad and Tobago [1936] AC 322;
  [1936] 1 All ER 704 174
American Booksellers Assoc, etc v Hudnitt III, Mayor, City of
  Indianapolis et al 598 F Supp 1316 185
American Cyanamid Co v Ethicon Ltd [1975] AC 396; [1975] 1 All ER 504, HL 251
Amministrazione delle Finanze dello Stato v Simmenthal Case 106/77;
  [1978] ECR 629 110
Anderson [1972] 1 QB 304 192–194
Anderson [1993] Crim LR 447 481
Andronicus and Constantinou v Cyprus (1996) 22 EHRR CD 18 ....36, 418
Anisminic [1969] 2 AC 147, HL..515
Anton Piller KG v Manufacturing Processes Ltd [1976] Ch 55;
  [1976] 1 All ER 779, CA 375
Argent (1996) *The Times*, 19 December 461, 462
Arrondelle v UK (1977) No 7889/77; 26 D and R 5 (1982) 63
Arrowsmith v Jenkins [1963] 2 QB 561; [1963] 2 All ER 210 ....289, 299
Asch v Austria (1990) Case 30/1990/221/283 59
Associated British Ports v Palmer and Others (1993) *The Times*, 5 May 283
Associated Newspapers Ltd v Wilson [1995] 2 All ER 100;
  (1993) *The Times*, 5 May 283

Associated Provincial Picture House v Wednesbury Corporation
   [1948] 1 KB 223; [1948] 2 All ER 680, CA 102, 105, 134, 209,
                                                                                                411, 412, 501, 530, 617
Association X v UK (1975) Appl 7145/75; 14 D and R 31 (1979) 36
AT&T Istel Ltd v Tulley [1992] 3 All ER 523 463
Attorney General for New South Wales v Trethowan [1932] AC 526 132
Attorney General v Antigua Times Ltd [1976] AC 16 122
Attorney General v Associated Newspapers and Others
   [1994] 1 All ER 556; (1994) 142 NLJ 1647 176
Attorney General v BBC (1987) *The Times*, 18 December 257
Attorney General v BBC [1981] AC 303; [1980] 3 WLR 109, HL 109
Attorney General v BBC, Same v Hat Trick Productions Ltd
   (1996) *The Times*, 26 July 154
Attorney General v Butterworth [1963] 1 QB 696; [1962] 3 All ER 326, CA 176
Attorney General v English (Dr Arthur's case) [1983] 1 AC 116;
   [1982] 2 All ER 903, HL 99, 156–158
Attorney General v Guardian Newspapers (No 2) [1990] 1 AC 109;
   [1990] 3 WLR 776; [1988] 3 All ER 545, HL 109, 236, 251–53,
                                                                                                267, 324, 327–29, 331
Attorney General v Guardian Newspapers [1987] 3 All ER 316;
   [1987] 1 WLR 1248 . . . . .123, 353
Attorney General v Guardian Newspapers [1992] 3 All ER 38, CA 156, 158, 162
Attorney General v Hislop and Pressdram [1991] 1 QB 514;
   [1991] 1 All ER 911; [1991] 2 WLR 219, CA 152–55, 158,
                                                                                                      163, 166–67, 169
Attorney General v Independent TV News and Others [1995] 2 All ER 370 . . . . .153, 154
Attorney General v Jonathan Cape [1976] QB 752 250
Attorney General v Leveller Magazine Ltd
   [1979] AC 440; [1979] 2 WLR 247, HL 160, 163
Attorney General v MGN [1997] 1 All ER 456 154
Attorney General v New Statesman [1981] QB 1 177
Attorney General v News Group Newspapers [1987] 1 QB 1;
   [1986] 2 All ER 833; [1986] 3 WLR 365, CA 152, 154, 155
Attorney General v News Group Newspapers plc [1989] QB 110;
   [1988] 3 WLR 163; [1988] 2 All ER 906 . . . . .163–165, 172
Attorney General v Newspaper Publishing plc
   (1990) *The Times*, 28 February 163, 167, 169, 256
Attorney General v Newspaper Publishing plc (*Spycatcher*)
   [1988] Ch 333; [1987] 3 All ER 276; [1988] 3 WLR 942, CA 99, 100, 164,
                                                                                                167, 235, 251, 253,
                                                                                                255, 257, 258, 353
Attorney General v Newspaper Publishing plc and Others
   [1997] 3 All ER 159; (1997) *The Times*, 2 May, CA 167

Table of Cases

Attorney General v Observer and Guardian Newspapers Ltd, Re
(1989) *The Times*, 9 May 163
Attorney General v Royal Society for the Prevention of Cruelty to Animals
(1985) *The Times*, 22 June 175
Attorney General v Sport Newspapers Ltd [1991] 1 WLR 1194 .... 165, 166
Attorney General v Times Newspapers Ltd [1974] AC 273;
[1973] 3 All ER 54; [1973] 3 WLR 298, HL 149, 172
Attorney General v Times Newspapers Ltd and Others (1983)
The Times, 12 February, DC 154, 158
Attorney General v Times Newspapers Ltd [1992] 1 AC 191;
[1991] 2 All ER 398; [1991] 2 WLR 994, HL 33, 167, 168, 257
Attorney General v Times Newspapers and Others
(1983) *The Times*, 12 February 153, 154, 158
Attorney General v TVS Television, Attorney General v HW
Southey & Sons (1989) *The Times*, 7 July 158
Attorney General, ex rel McWirter v IBA [1973] QB 629 199
Attorney General's Reference No 5 of 1980 [1980] 3 All ER 816, CA 190
Autronic AG v Switzerland (1990) 12 EHRR 485 83
Aziz v Trinity St Taxis [1988] WLR 79 .... 576, 577

B (a minor), Re [1981] 1 WLR 1421, CA 37
B v France (1992) 13 HRLJ 358 .... 69, 388
B v UK 34 D and R 68 (1983); (1983) 6 EHRR 354 .... 63, 617
Badham [1987] Crim LR 202 373
Bailey (1993) *The Times*, 22 March 491
Bailey v Williamson (1873) LR 8 QB 118 288
Baldry v Director of Public Prosecutions of Mauritius
[1983] 2 AC 297; [1982] 3 All ER 973 173
Barber and Others v NCR (Manufacturing) Ltd [1993] IRLR 95 588
Barbéra, Messegué and Jabardo, Judgment of 6 December 1988, A.146(2) 57
Barlow Clowes Gilt Managers v Clowes (1990) *The Times*, 2 February 162
Basher v Director of Public Prosecutions (1993) (unreported) 404
Beales [1991] Crim LR 118 .... 457, 474
Bearmans v Metropolitan Police Reciever [1961] 1 WLR 634 504
Beatty v Gillbanks (1882) 9 QBD 308 .... 304, 305
Beck, ex p Daily Telegraph [1993] 2 All ER 177 162
Belgian Linguistic Case, Judgment of 23 July 1968, A.6; (1968) 1 EHRR 252 ..... 55, 74
Belilos v Switzerland (1988) EHRR 466 81
Beldjoudi v France, A.234-A (1992); (1992) 14 EHRR 801 510
Bentley v Brudzinski [1982] Crim LR 825; (1982) *The Times*, 3 March 419, 420

Benveniste v University of Southampton [1989] IRLR 122 585
Bernstein v Skyviews & General Ltd [1978] QB 479; [1977] 2 All ER 902 363
Beycan [1990] Crim LR 185 453
Bilka-Kaufhaus GmbH v Weber von Hartz [1986] CMLR 701 .... 572, 573, 576, 585, 591
Birmingham City Council ex p, EOC [1989] AC 1155;
   [1989] 1 All ER 769 560
Birmingham Six (1991) *The Times*, 28 March 439, 451
Bishopsgate Investment Management Ltd v Maxwell [1992] 2 All ER 856 463
Black v Director of Public Prosecutions (1995) (unreported) 399
Blackledge and Others (*Ordtech*) [1996] 1 Cr App R 326, CA 168
Blake [1991] Crim LR 119 .... 457, 475
Bolam v Friern HMC [1957] 2 All ER 118 .... 379, 380
Bolger v Youngs Drug Products Ltd [1983] 103 Ct 2875 13
Bonnard v Perryman [1891] 2 Ch 269 .... 166, 252
Bonsignore v Oberstadtdirektor of the City of Cologne [1975] ECR 297 523
Bookbinder v Tebbit (No 2) [1992] 1 WLR 217 260
Bouamar v Belgium, Judgment of 29 February, A.129 (1988); [1988] 11 EHRR 1 49
Bouanimba v Secretary of State for Home Affairs [1986] Imm AR 343 522
Bouchereau [1977] ECR 1999 523
Bowers v Hardwick [1986] 478 US 186 383
Boyle v Rice, Judgment of 27 April 1988, A.131 64
Brailsford [1905] 2 KB 730 511
Brannigan and McBride v UK (1993) 17 EHRR 539; (1993) *The Times*, 28 May 51, 79, 423
Breen v Chief Constable for Dumfires and Galloway (1997) *The Times*, 24 April 514
Brezenau and Francis [1989] Crim LR 650 436
Brickley and Kitson v Police (1988) Legal Action, July 293
Bridges v California 314 US 252 (1941) 175
British Coal Corporation v Smith [1993] IRLR 308 588
British Gas v Sharma [1991] IRLR 101 591
British Steel Corporation v Granada Television [1981] AC 1096;
   [1981] 1 All ER 417, HL 330
Brixton Prison Governor, ex p Soblen [1963] 2 QB 243 541
Broadcasting Complaints Commission, ex p Barclay and Another
   (1996) *The Times*, 11 October 335
Broadcasting Complaints Commission, ex p Granada TV Ltd
   (1993) *The Times*, 31 May 324, 335
Broadcasting Complaints Commission, ex p Owen [1985] QB 1153 542
Brogan, Coyle, McFadden and Tracey v UK, Judgment
   of 29 November 1988, A.145; (1989) 11 EHRR 117 .... 50, 79, 112, 422
Broome v Cassell and Co [1972] AC 1027 501

Table of Cases

Brosch [1988] Crim LR 743, CA 415
Brown v Rentokil Ltd [1992] IRLR 302 561
Brown [1993] 2 WLR 556; [1993] 2 All ER 75, HL 385–387
Brüggemann and Schaeuten v Federal Republic of Germany (1975) 10 DR 100 389
Brutus v Cozens [1973] AC 854; [1972] 2 All ER 1297;
 [1972] 3 WLR 521; (1973) 57 Cr App R 538, HL 307, 308
Bryce [1992] 4 All ER 567; (1992) 95 Cr App R 320; (1992) NLJ 1161 492
Buchholz, Judgment of 6 May 1981, A.42 57
Buckley v UK (1997) 23 EHRR 101 63
Bugdaycay v Secretary of State for Home Affairs [1987] AC 514, HL 530, 532, 539
Burden v Rigler [1911] 1 KB 337 .... 288, 289
Burns (1886) 16 Cox CC 333 218
Burton and Another v De Vere Hotels (1996) *The Times*, 3 October 569

Caird (1970) 54 Cr App R 499 539
Calder (John) Publishing v Powell [1965] 1 QB 159 192
Calder and Boyars [1969] 1 QB 151; [1968] 3 WLR 974;
 [1968] 3 All ER 644; [1968] 52 Cr App R 706, CA 191, 193, 194
Calder v Rowntree Mackintosh Ltd [1993] IRLR 27 584
Callis v Gunn [1964] 1 QB 495 472
Cambridge Health Authority, ex p B [1995] WLR 898; (1995) TLR 159, CA 105, 515
Campbell and Another [1993] Crim LR 47, CA 467
Campbell and Cosans v UK, Judgment of 25 February 1982, A 48;
 (1982) 4 EHRR 293 .... 41, 378
Campbell and Fell v UK, Judgment of 28 June 1984, A.80 55
Canale [1990] All ER 187, CA 479
Cardiff Three case (Paris) (1993) 97 Cr App R 99 .... 394, 458, 474
Castells v Spain (1992) 14 EHRR 445 68
Castorina v Chief Constable of Surrey (1988) NLJ 180, CA 410–412
Caswell [1984] Crim LR 111 612
Caunt (1947) (unreported) 218
Central Criminal Court, ex p Francis and Francis [1989] AC 346;
 [1988] 3 All ER 375 372
Central Independent Television [1994] Fam 192 333
Chahal v UK (1997) 23 EHRR 413; (1996) *The Times*, 28 November
 (1996) *The Guardian*, 16 November 42, 47, 536, 543, 545
Chandler v Director of Public Prosecutions [1964] AC 763;
 [1962] 3 All ER 142, HL 235
Chapman v Director of Public Prosecutions (1988) Cr App R 190;
 [1988] Crim LR 843 412

xxi

Chappell & Co Ltd v Columbia Gramophone Co [1914] 2 Ch 745 340
Chief Constable of Avon, ex p Robinson [1989] All ER 15; [1989] 1 WLR 793 448
Chief Constable of Lancashire, ex p Parker and McGrath
   [1993] 2 WLR 428; [1993] 1 All ER 56 . . . . .370, 374
Chief Constable of West Midlands Police, ex p Wiley, Chief
   Constable of Nottinghamshire Police, ex p Sunderland
   [1995] 1 AC 274; [1994] 3 All ER 420; (1995) 1 Cr App R 342, HL 261, 262, 504, 505
Chief Constable of West Yorkshire Police, ex p Govell
   (1994) LEXIS transcript 350, 493
Chief Immigration Officer, Gatwick Airport ex p Kharrazi
   [1980] 3 All ER 373; [1980] 1 WLR 1396, CA 528
Chief Immigration Officer, Heathrow, ex p Salamat Bibi [1976] 1 WLR 979 . . . . .133, 524
Chief Metropolitan Magistrates' Court, ex p Choudhury
   [1991] 1 QB 429; [1991] 1 All ER 306 . . . . .109, 217, 218, 348
Choudhury v UK (1991) No 17349/1990; (1991) 12 HRLJ 172 218
Christians Against Racism and Fascism v UK (1984) 24 YBECHR 178 296
Christie v Leachinsky [1947] AC 573; [1947] 1 All ER 567, HL 414
Christie v UK [1994] 78A DRECom HR 119 . . . . .34, 349
Christou [1992] QB 979; [1992] 4 All ER 559, CA 492, 493, 498
Clarke (No 2) [1964] 2 QB 315; [1963] 3 All ER 884, CA 300
Clarke v Eley IMI Kynoch Ltd [1983] ICR 703 572
Clay Cross v Fletcher [1978] 1 WLR 1429 584
Clegg [1995] 2 WLR 80 40
Clerkenwell Metropolitan Stipendiary Magistrate, ex p The Telegraph
   and Others [1993] 2 All ER 183; (1992) *The Times*, 22 October 160
Clowser v Chaplin (1981) 72 Cr App R 342 321
Coco v AN Clark (Engineers) Ltd [1969] RPC 41 . . . . .267, 324, 328, 329
Coffin v Smith (1980) Cr App R 221 419
Collins and Wilcock [1984] 3 All ER 374; [1984] 1 WLR 1172 . . . . .396, 419
Colloza v Italy, Judgment of 12 February 1985, A.89 56
Colsey (1931) *The Times*, 9 May 174
Commission of EC v UK (1996) Case 222/94, 30 September 211
Commission v France [1988] ECR 3559 . . . . .601, 602, 605, 606, 608
Commission of European Communities v UK [1982] 3 CMLR 284 580
Condron and Another (1997) 1 Cr App R 185; (1997) 161 JP 1;
   (1996) *The Times*, 4 November, CA 460, 461, 462
Conegate Ltd v Customs and Excise Commissioners [1987] QB 254;
   [1986] 2 All ER 688 200
Coney (1882) 8 QBD 534 385
Constantine v Imperial Hotels [1944] KB 693 558

Table of Cases

Continental Can Co v Minn 297 NW 2d 241 569
Conway v Rimmer [1968] AC 910, HL 259, 261
Coolidge v New Hampshire 403 US 443 (1973) 365
Corelli v Wall (1906) 22 TLR 532 332
Cossey v UK, Judgment of 27 September 1990, A.184;
  (1990) 13 EHRR 622 ....69, 72, 120, 388
Costello-Roberts v UK, Judgment of 25 March 1993, A.247-C;
  (1993) *The Times*, 26 March 41, 378
Council of Civil Service Unions v Minister for Civil Service (*GCHQ*)
  [1985] AC 374; [1985] 3 WLR 1174; [1984] 3 All ER 935, HL 101, 103, 105,
    280–82, 511, 514
Council of Civil Service Unions v UK (1988) 10 EHRR 269 ....84, 134, 281
Cowan [1995] All ER 939 ....460, 461
Cox [1993] Crim LR 772 ....435, 440, 483
CRE v Dutton [1989] WLR 17; [1989] 1 All ER 306, CA 574
CRE, ex p Westminster City Council [1984] IRLR 230 566
Cröcher and Möller v Switzerland D and R 34 (1983); (1984) 6 EHRR 345 ....41, 83
Crown Court at Snaresbrook, ex p Director of Public Prosecutions
  [1988] QB 532; [1988] 1 All ER 315 372
Crown Court at Snaresbrook, ex p Metropolitan Police Commissioner
  (1984) 148 JP 449 196
Cyprus v Turkey (1976) Report of 10 July 63

Daily Express Case (1981) *The Times*, 19 December 158
Dallison v Caffrey [1965] 1 QB 348 409
Darbo v Director of Public Prosecutions [1992] Crim LR 56;
  (1992) *The Times*, 4 July 197
Davison [1988] Crim LR 442 474
Dawkins v Department of Environment (1993) Guardian Law Report,
  1 February 574
de Geoffre de la Pradelle v France (1993) HRLJ 276 75
De Jong, Baljet and Van de Brink, Judgment of 22 May 1984, A.77;
  (1984) 8 EHRR 20 53
De Souza v Automobile Association [1986] ICR 514 ....568, 579
De Vargattirgah v France (1981) Appl 9559/81 29
De Wilde, Ooms and Versyp v Belgium (1971) A.12 p 33 135
Dekker v VJV Centrum [1991] IRLR 27 ....562, 564
Delaney (1989) 88 Cr App R 338; (1988) *The Times*, 20 August, CA 443, 477, 490
Deputy Governor of Camphill Prison, ex p King [1985] QB 735 100
Derbyshire County Council v Times Newspapers [1993] AC 534;
  [1993] 1 All ER 1011; [1992] 3 WLR 28, HL 13, 100, 101, 104, 108,
    109, 123, 128, 140, 145

Director of Public Prosecutions v A and BC Chewing Gum Ltd
  [1968] 1 QB 159 194
Director of Public Prosecutions v Billington [1988] 1 All ER 435 483
Director of Public Prosecutions v Blake [1989] 1 WLR 432, CA 396, 427, 483
Director of Public Prosecutions v Channel Four Television Co Ltd
  and Another (1992) *The Times*, 14 September 179
Director of Public Prosecutions v Clarke [1992] Crim LR 60 309
Director of Public Prosecutions v Fidler [1992] 1 WLR 91 ....307, 308
Director of Public Prosecutions v Hawkins [1988] 1 WLR 1166;
  [1988] 3 All ER 673 415
Director of Public Prosecutions v Jordan [1977] AC 699, HL 195
Director of Public Prosecutions v Morgan [1976] AC 182 342
Director of Public Prosecutions v Orum [1988] 3 All ER 449 307
Director of Public Prosecutions v Rouse and Director of Public
  Prosecutions v Davis (1992) Cr App R 185 .... 396, 409, 483
Director of Public Prosecutions v Whyte [1972] AC 849; [1972] 3 All ER 12, HL 192, 193
Director of Public Prosecutions v Wilson [1991] Crim LR 441 ....410, 497
Director of the Serious Fraud Office, ex p Smith [1993] AC 1; [1992] 3 WLR 66 463
Djeroud v France (1991) A.191-B 390
Doe v Bolton 410 US 179 (1973) 379
Donelly v Jackman (1970) Cr App R 229; [1970] 1 WLR 562 419
Donnelly v UK (1973) Appl 5577–82/72; (1973) Yearbook XVI 26
Donovan [1934] 2 KB 498 385
Dornan v Belfast County Council [1990] IRLR 179 561
Dover Justives, ex p Dover District Council and Wells [1992] Crim LR 371 163
Duarte (1990) 65 DLR (4th) 240 349
Duchess of Argyll v Duke of Argyll [1967] 1 Ch 302 326
Dudgeon v UK, Judgment of 22 October 1981, A.45;
  (1982) 4 EHRR 149 .... 62, 317, 377, 382–84, 620
Duncan v Cammell Laird and Co [1942] AC 624 259
Duncan v Jones [1936] 1 KB 218 304
Dunford (1990) 91 Cr App R 150; (1990) 140 NLJ 517, CA 451, 484
Dunn (1990) 91 Cr App R 237; [1990] Crim LR 572, CA 488, 489

East African Asians cases (1973) 3 EHRR 76 .... 31, 42, 77, 509, 517
Ebchester v UK (1993) 18 EHRR CD 72 62
Eckle, Judgment of 15 July 1982, A.51 55
Editor of New Statesman (1928) 44 TLR 301 ....171, 173, 174
Edward Fennelly [1989] Crim LR 142 ....404, 496, 497

Table of Cases

Edwards [1991] Crim LR 45, CA 491
Edwards v Chief Constable of Avon and Somerset (1992) (unreported) 500
Edwards v Director of Public Prosecutions (1993) 97 Cr App R 301;
  (1993) *The Times*, 29 March 407–08
Edwards v UK (1992) 15 EHRR 417; (1993) *The Times*, 21 January 56
Eet [1983] Crim LR 806 424
Effick [1994] 3 WLR 583; (1994) 99 Cr App R 312, HL;
  (1992) 95 Cr App R 427; (1992) 142 NLJ 492, CA 347, 404
Ellen Street Estates Ltd v Minister of Health [1934] 1 KB 590 132
Ellis (1991) *The Times*, 31 October 513
Ellis v HO [1953] 2 QB 135 259
Emmerson [1991] Crim LR 194 455
Enderby v Frenchay [1994] 1 All ER 495; [1993] ECR I-5535, ECJ;
  [1992] IRLR 15, CA 573, 586–591
Enterprise Glass Co Ltd v Miles [1990] Ind Relations
  Review and Report 412–15C 568
Entinck v Carrington (1765) 19 St Tr 1029 ....98, 350, 351, 355, 365
Escuriaza [1989] 3 CMLR 281 523
Ex p Central Independent Television plc and Others [1991] 1 All ER 347 161
Ex p The Telegraph plc [1993] 2 All ER 971 162
Ex p United States Tobacco [1992] 1 QB 353 105

Factortame Ltd v Secretary of State for Transport [1991] 1 All ER 70, HL 111, 597
Fairnie (Dec'd) and Others v Reed and Another (1994) 20 May,
  Transcript from LEXIS, CA 326–28
Farah v Commissioner of Police for the Metropolis [1997] 1 All ER 289 611
Farrell v Secretary of State for Defence [1980] 1 All ER 1667 418
Fell [1963] Crim LR 207 233
Fernandez v Government of Singapore [1971] 2 All ER 691 531
Finley [1993] Crim LR 50, CA 467, 496
Flemming and Robinson [1989] Crim LR 658 312
Flockhart v Robinson [1950] 2 KB 498 294
Fogah [1989] Crim LR 141 ....436, 439
Forbes (1865) 10 Cox CC 362 420
Foster v British Gas [1990] 3 All ER 897 557
Foster [1987] Crim LR 821 488
Fox v Chief Constable of Kent (1984) (unreported) 303
Fox [1986] AC 281 ....404, 497
Fox, Campbell and Hartley, Judgment of 30 August 1990, A.178;
  (1990) 13 EHRR 157 ....48, 50

Francome v Mirror Group Newspapers Ltd [1984] 1 WLR 892 . . . . .327, 328
Francovich v Italy [1992] 21 IRLR 84 557
Franklin v Giddins [1978] 1 QdR 72 327
Fraser v Evans [1969] 1 QB 349 331
Friend [1997] 2 All ER 1012 460
Fulling [1987] QB 426; [1987] 2 All ER 65, CA 474
Funke v France (1993) 16 EHRR 297 . . . . .57, 464

G v Director of Public Prosecutions [1989] Crim LR 150 408
Gall (1990) 90 Cr App R 64 . . . . .467, 497
Garfinkel v MPC [1972] Crim LR 44 370
Gaskin v UK (1989) 12 EHRR 36 . . . . .62, 67, 111, 230, 317, 360, 361
Gay News v UK (1982) 5 EHRR 123 . . . . .218, 219
Geïllustreerde Pers NV v the Netherlands [1977] P & R 8 77
General Electric Co v Gilbert 429 US 126 (1976) 565
Ghani v Jones [1970] 1 QB 693 . . . . .365, 370
Gibson [1990] 2 QB 619; [1991] 1 All ER 439; [1990] 3 WLR 595, CA . . .196, 199, 203, 204, 214
Gill and Ranuana [1991] Crim LR 358 491
Gillard v Barrett (1991) 155 JP Rep 352 481
Gillick v West Norfolk and Wisbeach Area Health Authority
  [1986] AC 112; [1985] 3 WLR 830, HL 120, 396
Gillingham Borough Council v Medway Dock Co [1992] 3 All ER 931 300
Gladstone Williams (1983) Cr App R 276 420
Glasenapp v Federal Republic of Germany (1986) 9 EHRR 25 66
GLC, ex p Blackburn [1976] 1 WLR 550 . . . . .198, 199
Glinskie v McIver [1962] AC 726, HL 500
Gold v Haringey Health Authority [1987] 2 All ER 888 380
Goldberg [1988] Crim LR 678 476
Golder, Judgment of 21 February 1975, A.18 . . . . .56, 58, 84
Goldsmith and Another v Bhoyrul and Others [1997] 4 All ER 268;
  (1997) *The Times*, 20 June 101
Goodwin v UK (1994) No 17488/90 Com Rep; (1994) Guardian, 26 May 178
Goodwin v UK (1996) 22 EHRR 123 . . . . .168, 178
Goswell v Commissioner of Metropolitan Police (1996) Guardian, 27 April 502, 504
Granger v UK, Judgment of 28 March 1990, A.174 . . . . .56, 58
Grant v South West Trains Ltd (Case 249/96) (unreported) 619
Gray [1900] 2 QB 36; (1900) 69 LJ QB 502 173
Greek Case (1969) Report of 5 November; Yearbook XII, 186–510 . . . . .40, 80
Greene v Home Secretary [1942] AC 284 501

Griggs v Duke Power Company 401 US 424 (1971) 557
Guerra v Baptiste (1995) *The Times*, 8 November 122
Guildhall Magistrates' Court, ex p Primlacks Holdings Co
  (Panama) Ltd [1989] 2 WLR 841 371

H [1987] Crim LR 47 491
H v Norway (1992) 17004/90 (unreported) 37
Haase (1977) Report of 12 July; D and R 11 (1978) 57
Habermann-Beltermann [1994] ECR I-1657 ....563, 564
Hagan (1987) *The Times*, 20 May 513
Hague v Committee for Industrial Organisation 307 US 496 (1938) 284
Halford v Sharples [1992] 3 All ER 624, CA 260
Halford v UK [1997] IRLR 471; (1997) *The Times*, 3 July 349
Hamer (1979) Report of 13 December; D and R 24 (1981) 73
Hammersmith and Fulham London Borough Council, ex p M
  (1996) *The Times*, 10 October 535
Hampson v Department of Education and Science
  [1991] 1 AC 171; [1990] 2 All ER 513, HL 573, 576
Hancock and Shankland [1986] AC 455; [1986] 1 All ER 641;
  [1986] 3 WLR 1014, HL 164
Handels-og Kontorfunktionaerernes Forbund i Danmark
  v Dansk Arbejdsgiverforening (the *Danfoss* case)
  [1989] ECR 3199; [1989] IRLR 532 ....588, 589
Handyside v UK, Judgment of 7 December 1976, A.24;
  (1976) 1 EHRR 737 ....13, 68, 81, 83,
                                                              197, 214, 217, 383
Harman and Hewitt v UK (1989) 14 EHRR 657 ....62, 353
Harman v UK (1982) Appl 10038/82; (1984) Decision of 11 May;
  [1984] 38 P & R 53 60
Harris v Minister of the Interior (1952) (2) SA 428 132
Hart v Chief Constable of Kent [1983] RTR 484 414
Hashman and Harrup v UK (1996) 22 EHRR CD 184 301
Hayes v Malleable WMC [1985] ICR 703 ....561, 562
Hayward v Cammell Laird [1988] 2 All ER 257 ....100, 121, 582–84, 591
Hellewell v Chief Constable of Derbyshire [1995] 1 WLR 804 ....325, 327, 329, 331, 351
Hendrickson and Tichner [1977] Crim LR 356 294
Herbage v The Times Newspapers and Others (1981) *The Times*, 1 May 252, 332
Herczegfalvy v Austria (1992) 14 HRLJ 84; (1993) 15 EHRR 437 64
Hereford and Worcester County Council v Clayton [1996] ICR 514 568
Heron (1993) (unreported) 452, 457, 474

Hicklin (1868) 3 QB 360 .... 191, 193
Hickman v Maisey [1900] 1 QB 752 .... 297, 363, 364
Hills v Ellis [1983] QB 680; [1983] 1 All ER 667 .... 419, 420
Hinch v Attorney General for Victoria (1987) 164 CLR 15 159
Hirst and Agu v Chief Constable of West Yorkshire (1986) 85 Cr App R 143 .... 289, 300
Holgate-Mohammed v Duke [1984] 1 AC 437; [1984] 1 All ER 1054, HL 411, 421, 501
Hollandia, The [1983] 1 AC 565 123
Holmes [1981] 2 All ER 612; [1981] Crim LR 802 421
Home Secretary, ex p Westminster Press Ltd (1991) *The Guardian*, 12 February 396
Horseferry Road Metropolitan Stipendiary Magistrate, ex p Siadatan
  [1991] 1 QB 260; [1991] 1 All ER 324; [1990] 3 WLR 1006 310
Horsham Justices, ex p Farqharson [1982] 2 All ER 269, CA 161
Hoth v Secretary of State for Home Affairs [1985] Imm AR 20 522
Howell [1982] QB 416; [1981] 3 All ER 383, CA 302, 406
HRH Princess of Wales v MGN Newspapers Limited and Others
  (1993) 8 November (unreported) 324, 325, 327–29
Hsu v Commissioner of Metropolitan Police (1996) (unreported) 502, 503
Hubbard v Pitt [1976] QB 142 .... 275, 316
Huber v Austria (1971) Yearbook XIV p 548 65
Huber v Austria (1973) Report of 8 February, D and R 2 (1935) 31
Huber v Austria (1974) Appl 6821/74; 6 D and R 65 (1977) 53
Hughes v Holley (1988) 86 Cr App R 130 301
Hughes [1988] Crim LR 519, CA 446–448, 474, 481
Hurd v Jones [1986] ECR 29 522
Hutchinson (1954) (unreported) 191
Huvig v France (1990) 12 EHRR 547 356

IAT, ex p Shah (1996) *The Times*, 12 November 532
Ibrahim [1914] AC 599 .... 472, 476
Immigration Appeal Tribunal, ex p Al-Sabah [1992] Imm AR 223 521
Immigration Appeal Tribunal, ex p Antonissen [1992] Imm AR 196 522
Immigration Appeal Tribunal, ex p Bastiampillai [1983] 2 All ER 844 ... 527
Immigration Appeal Tribunal, ex p Ghazi Zubalir Ali Khan [1983] Imm AR 32 540
Immigration Appeal Tribunal, ex p Hoque [1988] Imm AR 216, CA 525, 526
Immigration Appeal Tribunal, ex p Iqbal (1992) *The Times*, 24 December 525
Immigration Appeal Tribunal, ex p Jonah [1985] Imm AR 7 531
Immigration Appeal Tribunal, ex p (Mahmud) Khan [1983] QB 790 540
Immigration Appeal Tribunal, ex p Secretary of State for Home Affairs
  [1990] 3 All ER 652 532

Table of Cases

Immigration Appeal Tribunal, ex p Singh [1973] 3 All ER 690 527
Immigration Appeal Tribunal, ex p Tamdjid-Nezhad [1986] Imm AR 396 523
Immigration Appeal Tribunal, ex p Ullah (1983) *The Times*, 14 January 540
Immigration Appeal Tribunal, ex p Yassine [1990] Imm AR 354 530
Inner London Education Authority, ex p Westminster City
  Council [1986] 1 All ER 19 542
Inquiry under the Companies Security (Insider Dealing) Act 1985,
  Re an [1988] 1 All ER 203 177
Ireland v UK (1976) 2 EHRR 25 ....40, 41
Isequilla [1975] All ER 77 472
Isgro v Italy (1991) Case 1/1990/192/252; [1993] Crim LR 261 59
Ismail [1990] Crim LR 109, CA 481

Jamel [1993] Crim LR 52..467
James and Others, Judgment of 21 February 1986, A.98 74
James v Eastleigh Borough Council [1990] AC 751; [1990] 2 All ER 607, HL 560
Jellyman (1838) 8 C & P 604 382
Jenkins v Kinsgate [1981] IRLR 388 584
Jersild v Denmark (1992) 14 HRLJ 74 66
Johnson v Whitehouse [1984] RTR 38 410
Johnstone, Judgment of 18 December 1986, A.112; (1987) 9 EHRR 203 72
Johnstone v Chief Constable of the RUC [1986] ECR 1651 ....77, 578, 601, 604, 605, 606, 608
Jones (1986) 83 Cr App R 375 385
Jones [1992] Crim LR 365 467
Jones v Chief Adjudication Officer (1990) EOR 1991 572
Jones v Manchester University (1993) *The Times*, 12 January 571
Jones and Lloyd v DPP [1997] 2 All ER 119 ....289, 297
Jordan and Tyndall [1963] Crim LR 124, CA 276
Jordan v Burgoyne [1963] 2 QB 744; [1963] 2 All ER 225 ....304, 307
Joseph [1993] Crim LR 206, CA 482

Kalanke v Freie Hansestadt Bremen [1995] IRLR 660 ....600, 601, 602, 605, 606, 607
Kamasinski (1988) Report of 5 May; (1991) 13 EHRR 36 58
Katz (1990) 90 Cr App R 456, CA 481
Kaye v Robertson and Another [1991] FSR 62;
  (1991) *The Times*, 21 March, CA 91, 321, 332,
                                                                  334, 336, 337, 339
Keenan [1989] 3 WLR 1193; [1989] 3 All ER 598, CA 395, 453, 482, 487, 488
Kelley v Post Publishing Co (Mass) [1951] 98 NE 2d 286 336

Kelly v Commissioner of Police for the Metropolis
  (1997) *The Times*, 20 August 505
Kelly v UK (1990) Appl 17579/90; (1993) 16 EHRR CD 20;
  [1993] 74 P & R 139 .... 38, 39
Kempf v Staatssecretaris van Justitie [1987] 1 CMLR 764 522
Kenlin v Gardner [1967] 2 QB 510 414
Kent v Metropolitan Police Commission (1981) *The Times*, 13 May 294, 295
Khan [1993] Crim LR 55, CA 481
Khan (Sultan) [1996] 3 All ER 289, HL; (1996) 146 NLJ 1024;
  [1995] QB 27, CA 350, 481, 494, 497
Khanna v MOD [1981] ICR 653 561
Khorasandjian v Bush [1993] 3 All ER 669 .... 341, 364, 365
Klass v Federal Republic of Germany, Judgment of 6 September 1978,
  A.28; (1979) 2 EHRR 214 .... 26, 62, 76, 281, 345
Knuller v Director of Public Prosecutions [1973] AC 435;
  [1972] 3 WLR 143; (1972) 56 Cr App R 633, HL 182, 192, 199,
                                                                        202, 203, 214, 382
Kommunistische Partei Deutschland v Federal Republic of Germany
  (1957) Appl 250/57; Yearbook 1 (1955–57) Col 6 p 222 .... 29, 125
Kosiek v FRG (1987) 9 EHRR 328 66
Kostovski v Netherlands (1989) 12 EHRR 434 59
Kowalski (1988) 86 Cr App R 339 613
Kowalska v Freie und Hansestadt Hamburg [1990] ECR I-2591 587
Kownacki v Commissioner of Metropolitan Police (1997) *The Guardian*, 30 April .. 502
Krause (1902) 18 TLR 238 294
Kruslin v France (1990) 12 EHRR 528 356

Ladlow, Moss, Green and Jackson [1989] Crim LR 219 .... 466, 496
Laker Airways v Department of Trade [1977] QB 643 281
Lam v Koo and Chiu [1992] Civil Transcript No 116 328
Lambeth v CRE [1990] IRLR 231, CA 579
Lamy v Belgium (1989) 11 EHRR 529 53
Lansbury v Riley [1914] 3 KB 229 302
Laskey, Jaggard and Brown v UK (1997) 24 EHRR 39 387
Lawless (1959) Report of 19 December, B.1 (1960–61) p 64; Judgment of 1 July 1961,
  A.3 (1960–1961); (1961) 1 EHRR 15 .... 47, 48
Lawless, A.1 (1960–61) p 360; (1961) 1 EHRR 15 32
Leander v Sweden, Judgment of 26 March 1987, A.116; (1987) 9 EHRR 443 .... 62, 75
Leech v Deputy Governor of Parkhurst Prison [1988] AC 533, HL 538
Lemon (*Gay News*) [1979] AC 617; [1979] 2 WLR 281;
  [1979] 1 All ER 898, HL 216, 218, 219, 221

Table of Cases

Letellier v France, A.207 (1991) 52
Leverton v Clwyd County Council [1989] 2 WLR 47 ....581, 584
Levin v Secretary of State for Justice [1982] ECR 1035 522
Lewis v Cox (1985) Cr App R 1 420
Lewis, ex p (1888) 21 QBD 191 288
Lewisham London Borough Council, ex p Shell UK Ltd [1988] 1 All ER 938 542
Li Shu-Ling [1989] Crim LR 58 455
Li Yau-wai v Genesis Films Limited [1987] HK LR 711 328
Lindley v Rutter [1980] 3 WLR 661 378
Lion Laboratories v Evans and Express Newspapers [1985] QB 526;
  [1984] 2 All ER 417, CA 250, 251, 267, 330, 331
Lithgow (1984) Report of 7 March, A.102; (1986) 8 EHRR 335 57
Litster v Forth Dry Dock Engineering [1989] 1 All ER 1194 129
Liverpool Juvenile Court, ex p R [1987] All ER 688 474
London United Investments, Re [1992] 2 All ER 842 463
Longman [1988] 1 WLR 619, CA 368, 374
Lord Advocate v Scotsman Publications Ltd [1990] 1 AC 812;
  [1989] 2 All ER 852, HL 238, 246, 254
Lord Chancellor ex p Witham [1997] 2 All ER 779 105
Ludi v Switzerland (1992) 15 EHRR 173 62

M and H (Minors), Re [1990] 1 AC 686; [1988] 3 WLR 485, HL 99, 108
M v Home Office [1993] 3 All ER 537 531
M v UK (1982) Appl 9907/82; [1984] P & R 35 41
Maclean and Kosten [1993] Crim LR 687 491
Maguire (1989) Cr App R 115; [1989] Crim LR 815, CA 432, 433, 439
Malik v Secretary of State for Home Affairs [1981] Imm AR 134 540
Malone v Commissioner of Police of the Metropolis (No 2) [1979] Ch 344 .....327, 343, 344
Malone v UK (1982) Report of 17 December, A.82; (1985) 7 EHRR 14 ....62, 86, 327,
                                                                      344, 345, 349, 350
Mandla v Dowell Lee [1983] 2 AC 548; [1983] 1 All ER 1062, HL 120, 224, 225, 574
Mansfield Justices, ex p Sharkey [1985] QB 613 306
Mapp v Ohio 367 US 643 (1961) 471
MAR v UK (1997) (unreported) 545
Marbury v Madison 5 US (1 Cranch) 137 (1803) 116
Marcell and Others v Commissioner of Police of the Metropolis [1992] Ch 224 327
Marckx v Belgium (1979) 2 EHRR 330 320
Marsh [1991] Crim LR 455 ....432–34, 440
Marschall v Land Nordrhein-Westfalen Case C-409/95,
  Judgment of 11 November 1997 606–08

Marshall (1992) *The Times*, 28 December 477
Marshall (No 2) [1993] 4 All ER 586 .... 111, 593
Martin Secker and Warburg [1954] 2 All ER 683; [1954] 1 WLR 1138 191
Martinez-Tobon (1993) *The Times*, 1 December 464
Martinez-Tobon v Immigration Appeal Tribunal [1988] Imm AR 319 540
Mary Quayson [1989] Crim LR 218 485
Mason [1987] Crim LR 119; [1987] 3 All ER 481, CA 457, 475, 480, 491
Masterson v Holden [1986] 3 All ER 39 620
Mathias (1989) *The Times* 24 August 477
Mats Jacobson v Sweden (1990) 13 EHRR 79 .... 54, 74, 85
Matthews (1990) Cr App R 43; [1990] Crim LR 190, CA 432–35
Matthews (1993) (unreported) 511
Matto v Wolverhampton Crown Court [1987] RTR 337 497
Maudsley v Palumbo and Others (1995) *The Times*, 19 December 328
McBrearty (1990) *The Times*, 9 January 513
McCann, Farrell and Savage v UK, A.324, Council
 of Europe Report; (1995) 21 EHRR 97 .... 38, 39, 83, 131, 418
McCluskey (1993) 94 Cr App R 216, CA 177
McEldowney v Forde [1971] AC 632 277
McGowan v Chief Constable of Kingston on Hull [1968] Crim LR 34 369
McGuigan and Cameron [1991] Crim LR 719 312
McKenzie [1993] 1 WLR 453; (1992) *The Guardian*, 29 July;
 (1992) 142 NLJ 1162, CA 499
McVeigh O'Neill and Evans v UK (1981) Report of 18 March;
 [1981] P & R 25; (1981) 5 EHRR 71 48
Meer v Tower Hamlets [1988] IRLR 399 575
Menard (1995) Cr App R 306 434
Metropolitan Police Commissioner, ex p Blackburn [1968] 2 All ER 319, CA 174
Mickleborough [1995] 1 Cr App R 297, CA 177
Mid-Glamorgan Family Health Services and Another, ex p Martin
 (1993) *The Times*, 2 June 362
Middleweek v Chief Constable of Merseyside [1992] AC 179; [1990] 3 WLR 481 500
Miller v California 413 US 15 (1973) 191
Miller v Immigration Appeal Tribunal [1988] Imm AR 358 530
Ministry of Agriculture, Fisheries and Food, ex p Hamble [1995] 2 All ER 714 102
Miranda v Arizona 384 US 436 (1996) 471
Monaghan v Corbettt [1983] 147 JP 545 410
Moran v Burbine 475 US 412 (1986) 471
Morpeth Ward Justices, ex p Ward (1992) 95 Cr App R 215 305

Table of Cases

Morris v Beardmore [1981] AC 446; [1980] 2 All ER 753 365
Morris v Duke-Cohen (1975) Sol Jo 826 556
Morse [1991] Crim LR 195 483
Moss v McLachan [1985] IRLR 76 ....99, 303
Motherwell v Motherwell (1976) 73 DLR (3d) 62 364
Moustaquim v Belgium (1991) 13 EHRR 802 390
Müller v Switzerland (1991) 13 EHRR 212 ....68, 69, 197, 204, 214, 308
Munongo v Secretary of State for Home Affairs [1991] Imm AR 616 530
Murphy v Oxford (1985) (unreported) 415
Murray (John) v UK [1996] Crim LR 370; (1996) 22 EHRR 29;
    (1996) *The Times*, 9 February 57, 58, 459, 460, 464
Murray v Ministry of Defence [1988] All ER 521, HL 416
Murray v UK (1994) 19 EHRR 193 ....49, 50, 416

Nadir, ex p (1990) *The Times*, 5 November 463
Nagy v Weston [1966] 2 QB 561; [1965] 1 WLR 280 ....289, 299
Nailie and Kanesarajah [1993] AC 674; [1993] 2 WLR 927, HL 529
Nakkuda Ali v Jayaratne [1951] AC 66 409
Nazari [1980] 3 All ER 880, CA 539
Nebraska Press Association v Stuart 427 US 539 (1976) 159, 256
Nedrick [1986] 3 All ER 1; [1986] 1 WLR 1025, CA 164
Neill [1994] Crim LR 441, CA 481
Neilson v Laugharne [1981] 1 QB 736, CA 504, 505
Neumeister Case, Judgment of 27 June 1968; (1979–80) 1 EHRR 91 ....52, 56, 57
New York Times Co v US 403 US 713 (1971) 243
News Group Newspapers Ltd v SOGAT [1986] ICR 716; [1986] IRLR 337 ....293, 300
Nicholas v Parsonage [1987] RTR 199 415
Nicol v Director of Public Prosecutions (1996) 1 J Civ Lib 75 ....304, 305
Niemietz v Germany, A.251-B (1992), para 29 ....61, 62
Nimz v Freie und Hansestadt Hamburg [1991] ECR I-297 ....587, 588
Nold v Commission [1974] ECR 481 110
Norris v Ireland (1991) 13 EHRR 186 63

O v UK (1987) 10 EHRR 82 55
O'Connor [1991] Crim LR 135 421
O'Hara v Chief Constable of the RUC [1997] WLR 1; [1997] 1 All ER 129 412
O'Leary [1988] Crim LR 827, CA 498
Observer and Guardian v UK (1991) 14 EHRR 153 ....69, 254
Ojutiku v Manpower Services Commission [1982] IRLR 418 ....572, 575

Olsson v Sweden (No 2), A.250 (1992) 34
Open Door Counselling and Dublin Well Woman v Ireland
  (1992) 15 EHRR 244 . . . . .37, 69
Oransaye [1993] Crim LR 772 432
Orphanos v Queen Mary College [1985] AC 761 575
Otto-Preminger Institut v Austria (1994) 19 EHRR 34 .68, 69, 219
Owino [1995] Crim LR 743 40
Ozturk, Judgment of 21 February 1983, A.73; (1984) 6 EHRR 409 55

P v S and Cornwall County Council, Judgment of 30 April 1996;
  [1996] ECR I-2143; [1996] IRLR 347 . . . . .110, 618, 619
Pakelli, Judgment of 25 April 1983, A.64 59
Parchment [1989] Crim LR 290 439
Paris (1993) 97 Cr App R 99; [1994] Crim LR 361, CA 394, 452, 474
Parris (1989) 9 Cr App R 68, CA 498
Pataki (1960) Appl 596/59; Yearbook III 30
Paton v UK (1980) 3 EHRR 408 37
Pearson v Immigration Appeal Tribunal [1978] Imm AR 212 .524
Pel Ltd v Modgill [1980] IRLR 142 567
Penguin Books (The *Lady Chatterley's Lover* trial) [1961] Crim LR 176 . . . . .182, 193, 195
Penny (1991) *The Times*, 17 October 466
Percy v Director of Public Prosecutions [1995] 3 All ER 124 . . . . .302, 304
Perera v Civil Service Commission [1983] IRLR 166 . . . . .573, 575
Phansopkar [1977] QB 606 133
Pickering v Liverpool Daily Post and Echo Newspapers plc
  [1991] 2 AC 370; [1991] 1 All ER 622 158
Pickstone v Freemans [1988] 2 All ER 803; [1988] 3 WLR 265 . . . . .100, 121, 129, 580
Piddington v Bates [1961] 1 WLR 162 302
Ping Lin [1976] AC 574 472
Platform 'Arzte für das Leben' v Austria (1982) Appl 1012/82;
  [1985] P & R 44; (1988) 13 EHRR 204 . . . . .70, 76, 84, 289
Podger [1979] Crim LR 524 406
Poitrimol v France, A.277-A (1993); (1993) 18 EHRR 130 58
Pollard v Photographic Company (1888) Ch 345 325
Ponting [1985] Crim LR 318 . . . . .94, 234, 235
Porcelli v Strathclyde Regional Council [1986] ICR 564 568
Prager [1972] 1 All ER 1114, CA 472
Pratt v Attorney General for Jamaica [1995] 3 WLR 995 . . . . .122, 123
Prestige Group plc, Re [1984] 1 WLR 335 . . . . .100, 595, 596

Preston [1993] 4 All ER 638; (1994) 98 Cr App R 405, HL 348, 493
Price v Civil Service Commission [1978] WLR 1417 571
Price v Rhondda Urban Council [1923] 2 Ch 372 355
Priestley (1965) 51 Cr App R 1, CA 475
Prince Albert v Strange (1849) 2 De Gex & Sm 652 321
Puttick v Secretary of State for Home Affairs [1984] Imm AR 118 523

Quinn [1990] Crim LR 581; (1990) *The Times*, 31 March, CA 496, 497

R [1992] Fam Law 108; [1991] 4 All ER 481; [1991] 3 WLR 767;
  [1992] Crim LR 207, HL 60, 115
Rainey v Greater Glasgow Health Board [1986] WLR 1017, HL 576, 585, 586
Rajakuruna [1991] Crim LR 458 482
Ramsay and Foote (1883) 15 Cox CC 231 215
Rasool [1997] 4 All ER 439; (1997) *The Times*, 17 February, CA 348
Raymond v Honey [1983] AC 1, HL 100
Rees v UK, Judgment of 17 October 1986, A.106; (1987) 9 EHRR 56 ....72, 84, 388
Rees (1986) 9 EHRR 56 ....110, 618
Registrar, Court of Appeal v Willesee [1985] 3 NSWLR 650 159
Reid [1987] Crim LR 702 ....99, 292
Rennie [1982] All ER 385, CA 472
Retail, Wholesale and Department Store Union (1986)
  33 DLR (4th) 174; [1986] 1 SCR 460 122
Riaz and Burke [1991] Crim LR 366 455
Rice v Connolly [1966] 2 QB 414; [1966] All ER 649; [1966] 3 WLR 17 ....414, 419, 420
Ricketts v Cox (1981) Cr App R 298 420
Ringeisen v Austria, Judgment of 16 July 1971, A.13; (1971) 1 EHRR 455 55
Rinner-Kuhn v FWW Spezial-Gebaudereinigung [1989] IRLR 493 572
Riyat v London Borough of Brent (1983) cited in
  IDS Employment Law Handbook 28, 1984 600
RJR MacDonald Inc v Canada (Attorney General) SCC 21 September 1995 119
Roberts (1997) 1 Cr App R 217 493
Roebuck v NUM [1977] ICR 573 175
Rookes v Barnard [1964] AC 1129 501
Royal Borough of Kensington and Chelsea, ex p Kihara
  (1996) *The Times*, 10 July 534
Rutili v Ministere de l'Interieur [1976] 1 CMLR 140 522

S v Van Niekirk [1970] 3 SA 655 171

Salabiaku v France (1988) 13 EHRR 379 57
Salamat Bibi [1977] 1 WLR 979, CA 133
Saloman v Commissioners of Custom and Excise [1967] 2 QB 116 131
Samuel [1988] QB 615; [1988] 2 All ER 135; [1988] 2 WLR 920, CA 442, 448, 451,
484, 485, 487, 497
Sang [1980] AC 402; [1979] 2 All ER 1222, HL 350, 472, 473, 480,
490–92, 494, 495, 497
Sat-Bhambra (1988) JP Rep 365; (1988) Cr App R 55 498
Saunders (1995) *The Times*, 28 November 464
Saunders v Richmond-upon-Thames London Borough Council
 [1978] IRLR 362 560
Saunders v Scottish National Camps (1981) EAT 7/80 616
Saunders v UK (1994) No 19187/91; (1997) 23 EHRR 313 ....58, 120, 465
Savundranayagan and Walker [1968] 3 All ER 439; [1968] 1 WLR 1761, CA 148, 165
Schabas (1994) 43 ICLQ 913 42
Schuler-Zgraggen v Switzerland (1993) *The Times*, 21 October 557
Schmidt and Dahlström v Sweden, Judgment of 6 February 1976, A.21;
 (1979–80) 1 EHRR 637 71
Schwabe v Austria (1992) 14 HRLJ 26 68
Scott [1991] Crim LR 56, CA 432
Seaboyer [1991] 2 SCR 577 ....119, 120
Secretary of State for Defence v Guardian Newspapers
 [1985] AC 339; [1984] 3 All ER 601, HL 177
Secretary of State for Defence, ex p Lustig-Prean, Smith and
 Others [1996] 1 All ER 257; [1996] ICR 740 ....102, 103, 105,
411, 501, 515, 617
Secretary of State for Defence, ex p Perkins [1997] IRLR 297 619
Secretary of State for Education and Science v Tameside [1977] AC 1014 294
Secretary of State for Employment, ex p Equal Opportunities
 Commission [1994] 2 WLR 409, HL 103, 123
Secretary of State for Foreign and Commonwealth Affairs, ex p Everett
 [1989] QB 891; [1989] 1 All ER 655, CA 511
Secretary of State for Home Affairs, ex p Abdi; Secretary of State for
 Home Affairs, ex p Gawe (1996) *The Times*, 17 February 533
Secretary of State for Home Affairs, ex p Binbasi [1989] Imm AR 595 529
Secretary of State for Home Affairs, ex p Brind [1991] 1 AC 696;
 [1991] 1 All ER 720; [1991] 2 WLR 588, HL; 101, 103, 104, 108,
 [1990] 1 All ER 469, CA   123, 133, 141, 145, 208
Secretary of State for Home Affairs, ex p Canbolat
 (1997) *The Times*, 24 February 533
Secretary of State for Home Affairs, ex p Chahal
 (1993) *The Times*, 12 March 534, 543, 544

Table of Cases

Secretary of State for Home Affairs, ex p Cheblak [1991] 1 WLR 890;
[1991] 2 All ER 319, CA 514, 541, 543
Secretary of State for Home Affairs, ex p Direk [1992] Imm AR 330 532
Secretary of State for Home Affairs, ex p Flynn (1995) *The Times*, 20 July 521
Secretary of State for Home Affairs, ex p Gulbache [1991] Imm AR 526 532
Secretary of State for Home Affairs, ex p Hosenball
[1977] 1 WLR 766; [1977] 3 All ER 452, CA 100, 524, 541, 543, 545
Secretary of State for Home Affairs, ex p Khawaja [1984] AC 74;
[1983] 1 All ER 765; [1983] 2 WLR 321; [1982] Imm AR 139, HL 537, 538
Secretary of State for Home Affairs, ex p Leech (No 2) [1993] 4 All ER 539 534
Secretary of State for Home Affairs, ex p Mehari [1994] 2 WLR 349 530
Secretary of State for Home Affairs, ex p P [1992] COD 295 532
Secretary of State for Home Affairs, ex p Ruddock [1987] 1 WLR 1482;
[1987] 2 All ER 518 .... 345, 353
Secretary of State for Home Affairs, ex p Sandhu [1983] 3 CMLR 131 522
Secretary of State for Home Affairs, ex p Sivakumaran
[1988] AC 958; [1988] 1 All ER 193 .... 531, 532
Secretary of State for Home Affairs, ex p Snichon Chomsuk
[1991] Imm AR 29, 32, QBD 538
Secretary of State for Home Affairs, ex p Stitt (1987) *The Times*, 3 February 101, 514
Secretary of State for Home Affairs, ex p Swati [1986] 1 All ER 717, CA 528
Secretary of State for Social Security ex p Joint Council for the
Welfare of Immigrants; Secretary of State for Social Security
ex p B [1996] 4 All ER 385; (1996) 146 NLJ 985 .... 103, 534
Secretary of State for the Home Department and Another,
ex p Norney and Others (1995) *The Times*, 6 October 103
Secretary of State for the Home Department, ex p Lancashire
Police Authority (1992) *The Times*, 26 May 396
Secretary of State for the Home Department, ex p McQuillan
[1995] 3 All ER 400; (1994) *Independant*, 23 September 102, 514, 515
Secretary of State for the Home Department, ex p Mughal [1974] QB 313 518
Secretary of State for the Home Department, ex p Northumbria
Police Authority [1989] QB 26; [1988] 2 WLR 590;
[1988] 1 All ER 556, CA 100, 287, 294
Secretary of State for Transport, ex p Factortame [1989] 2 CMLR 353 130
Security Services Tribunal, ex p Hewitt (1992) (unreported) 354
Serry (1980) 2 Cr App R 336 540
Shah v Barnet London Borough Council [1983] 2 AC 309 518
Sharpe v Director of Public Prosecutions (1993) JP 595 497
Shaw v Director of Public Prosecutions [1962] AC 220; [1961] 2 WLR 897, HL 200, 202
Shelley Films Limited v Rex Features Limited, 10 December 1993,
transcript from LEXIS 325, 327–29

Shields v E Coomes [1978] WLR 1408, CA 583
Shomer v B and R Residential Lettings Ltd [1992] IRLR 317 561
Showboat Entertainment Centre v Owens [1984] 1 WLR 384 566
Sibson v UK A.258; (1993) *The Times*, 17 May 71, 279
Sidaway v Board of Governors of the Bethlem Royal Hospital
    [1985] AC 871; [1985] 2 WLR 380, HL 379, 380
Siddiqui v Swain [1979] RTR 454 412
Silcott (1991) *The Times*, 8 December 394, 439, 451, 458
Silver v UK, Judgment of 25 March 1983, A.61; (1983) 5 EHRR 347 ....58, 64, 81, 301
Simon-Herald v Austria (1969) App 430/69 CD 38 36
Singh v British Railway Engineers [1986] ICR 22 575
Singh v Immigration Appeal Tribunal [1986] 2 All ER 721, HL 540
Skapinker [1984] 2 SCR 713 121
Skirving [1985] QB 819 ....192, 194
Smith v Gardner Merchant [1996] ICR 790; [1996] IRLR 342 616
SMS [1992] Crim LR 310 615
Smurthwaite [1994] 1 All ER 898; (1994) 98 Cr App R 437, CA 490, 491, 492
Snowball v Gardner Merchant [1987] ICR 719 568
Soering v UK, Judgment of 7 July 1989, A.161; (1989) 11 EHRR 439 ....37, 42, 43, 83, 125
Solicitor General v Radio Avon [1978] 1 NZLR 225 171
Southampton Crown Court, ex p J and P [1993] Crim LR 962 372
Sparks [1991] Crim LR 128 433
Special Adjudicator, ex p Kandasamy (1994) *The Times*, 11 March 530
Stagg (Colin) (1994) (unreported) 491
Stamford [1972] 2 WLR 1055; [1972] 2 All ER 427 ....199, 200
State, the (Lawless) v O'Sullivan and the Minister for Justice
    (1958–59) Yearbook II 107
Steel v The Post Office [1977] IRLR 288 571
Stephens v Avery [1988] Ch 449 ....325, 326, 328, 336
Stewart v UK (1982) Appl 10044/82; D and R 39 (1985); (1985) 7 EHRR 453 38
Straker [1965] Crim LR 239 ....199, 201
Strathclyde Regional Council v Wallace [1996] IRLR 672 585
Sunday Times v UK, Judgment of 26 April 1979, A.30; 67, 81–83,
    (1979) 2 EHRR 245; [1973] QB 710, CA 111, 118, 150, 157,
                                                                   159, 171, 172, 198, 301
Sutherland v UK (1996) 22 EHRR CD 182 384
SW v UK and C v UK (1995) 21 EHRR 404 60
Swanston v Director of Public Prosecutions (1997) *The Times*, 23 January 307

Taylor (1993) 98 Cr App R 361, CA 147, 155
Taylor v Anderton [1995] 2 All ER 420, CA 261
Taylor v Director of Public Prosecutions [1973] AC 964 312
Taylor's Case (1676) 1 Vent 293 ....215, 221
Thomas v NUM [1985] 2 All ER 1 99
Thomas v Sawkins [1935] 2 KB 249 ....315, 365, 369
Thomas [1990] Crim LR 269 ....404, 497
Thompson Newspapers Ltd, ex p Attorney General
  [1968] 1 All ER 268; [1968] 1 WLR 1 ....148, 166
Thompson v Commissioner of Police for the Metropolis [1997] 2 All ER 762 ......502, 503
Thorgeir Thorgierson v Iceland (1992) 14 EHRR 843 ....66, 68
Thynne, Wilson and Gunnel v UK, Judgment of 25 October 1992, A.190;
  (1990) 13 EHRR 666 ....52, 85
Tisdall (1984) *The Times*, 26 March 69, 134, 234
Tolstoy Miloslavsky v UK (1995) *The Times*, 19 July 69
Tower Boot Co v Jones [1997] ICR 254; [1997] IRLR 168 ....569, 577
Treadaway v Chief Constable of West Midlands (1994) *The Times*, 25 October 502
Trussler [1988] Crim LR 446 477
Tshuma (1981) 3 Cr App R 97 540
Turley v Allders [1980] ICR 66 561
Tyrer, Judgment of 25 April 1978, A.26; (1978) 2 EHRR 1 41

Uddin, Rahim, Ejaz Sattar v Secretary of State for
  Home Affairs [1991] Imm AR 587, CA 526
United Norwest Co-operative Ltd v Johnstone (1994) *The Times*, 24 February 464
United States v O'Brien 391 US 367 (1968) 275
Universal Thermosensors Ltd v Hibben (1992) NLJ 195 375
Uppal v UK (No 2) (1981) 3 EHRR 399 510

V, W, X, Y and Z v UK (1993) Appl No 21627/93 387
Vagrancy Cases, Judgment of 18 June 1971, A.12 49
Van der Mussele, Judgment of 23 November 1983, A.70 45
Van Duyn v Home Office (No 2) [1974] ECR 1337 ....522, 523
Van Oosterwijck v Belgium, Judgment of 6 November 1980, A.40;
  (1981) 3 EHRR 557 32
Vel v Owen (1987) JP 510 481
Vernillo v France 12 HRLJ 199 56
Vernon [1988] Crim LR 445 ....446, 447, 481
Victoria Park Racing Company v Taylor (1937) 58 CLR 479 364

Vijayanathan v France (1992) 15 EHRR 62 26
Vilvarajah and Four Others v UK (1991) 14 EHRR 248;
  A.215 (1991) 29, 43, 75
Vince and Another v Chief Constable of Dorset
  (1992) *The Times*, 7 September 425

W v Egdell [1990] Ch 359 ....267, 331
W v UK (1983) Appl 9348/81; D and R 32 (1983) 36
W, B and UK (1987) 10 EHRR 29 389
Waddington v Miah [1974] 2 All ER 377, HL 98
Wadman v Carpenter Farrer Partnership (1993) *The Times*, 31 May 570
Wales v Commissioner of Police for the Metropolis [1995] IRLR 531 577
Walsh [1989] Crim LR 822, CA 395, 482, 485, 490
Ward v Chief Constable of Somerset and Avon Constabulary
  (1986) *The Times*, 26 June, CA 410
Ward (Judith) [1993] 1 WLR 619; [1993] 2 All ER 577 439
Warwick v UK (1986) Eur Comm HR Report of 15 June 41
Webb (No 2) [1995] 1 WLR 1454 563
Webb v Emo Air Cargo (UK) Ltd [1993] 1 WLR 49;
  [1992] 4 All ER 929, HL; [1992] CMLR 793, CA 562, 564–66
Webster v Southwark London Borough Council
  [1983] QB 698; [1983] 2 WLR 217 288
Weekes [1993] Crim LR 222; (1992) *The Times*, 15 May, CA 434
Weeks, Judgment of 5 October 1988, A.145; (1987) 10 EHRR 293 ....47, 52
Weerdesteyn (1995) 1 Cr App R 405; [1995] Crim LR 239, CA 484
Welch v UK (1995) 20 EHRR 247 60
Weldon v Home Office [1991] WLR 340, CA 501
Wemhoff Case, Judgment of 27 June 1968; (1979–80) 1 EHRR 55 52
West Midlands Passenger Transport Executive v
  Jaquant Singh [1988] WLR 730, CA 567
Westminster Corporation v London and North Western
  Railway Co [1905] AC 426, HL 541
Wheeler v Leicester City Council [1985] AC 1054; [1985] 2 All ER 1106, HL 100
Whelan v Director of Public Prosecutions [1975] QB 864 278
White v Metropolitan Police Commissioner (1982) *The Times*, 24 April 501
Wiggins v Field [1968] Crim LR 50 199
Wileman v Minilec Engineering Ltd [1988] ICR 318 568
Williams (1992) *The Times*, 6 February, CA 434
Williams and O'Hare v Director of Public Prosecutions [1993] Crim LR 775 492
Williams [1987] 3 All ER 411 40

Table of Cases

Williams [1989] Crim LR 66 485
Wills v Bowley [1983] 1 AC 57, HL 410
Wilmott v Atack [1977] QB 498; [1976] 3 All ER 794 420
Wilson [1996] 3 WLR 125 386
Winder v Director of Public Prosecutions (1996) *The Times*, 14 August 314
Windisch v Austria (1990) 13 EHRR 281 59
Wingrove v UK, Judgment of 25 November 1996,
  Case 19/1995/525/611; (1997) 24 EHRR 1 219
Winn v Director of Public Prosecutions (1992) 142 NLJ 527 311
Winterwerp v Netherlands, Judgment of 24 October 1979, A.33;
  (1979) 2 EHRR 387 ....46, 545
Wise v Dunning [1902] 1 KB 167 302
Woodall and Others [1989] Crim LR 288 ....481, 491
Woodward v Hutchings [1977] 1 WLR 760, CA 330
Wright [1994] Crim LR 55 497

X and the Church of Scientology v Sweden (1977) Appl 7805/77;
  (1979) Yearbook XXII 66
X and Y v Austria (1974) Appl 7909/74; D and R 15 (1979) 58
X and Y v Netherlands (1986) 8 EHRR 235 377
X v Austria (1963) Appl 1852/63; (1965) Yearbook VIII 60
X v Austria (1970) Appl 4428/70; (1972) Yearbook XV 59, 60
X v Austria (1973) Appl 5362/72, Coll 42 56
X v Austria 18 D and R 154 (1979) 378
X v Denmark (1979) Appl 8828/79; D and R 30 (1983) 50
X v Federal Republic of Germany (1969) Appl 4045/69;
  (1970) Yearbook XIII 77
X v Federal Republic of Germany (1970) Appl 4653/70; (1974) 46 CD 22 45
X v Federal Republic of Germany (1978) Appl 8410/78; D and R 18 (1980) 45
X v Federal Republic of Germany D and R 17 (1980) 57
X v Norway (1960) Appl 867/60; Yearbook IV pp 270, 276 26
X v Spain Appl 10227/82; D and R 37 (1984) 37
X v UK (1974) Appl 6564/74; D and R 24 (1975) 73
X v UK (1978) Appl 8324/78 (unpublished) 41
X v UK (1978) Yearbook XXI; (1978) 3 EHRR 63 276
X v UK (1980) Appl 8416/79; D and R 19 (1980) 37, 389
X v UK and Ireland (1982) Appl 9829/82 (not published) 36
X v UK Appl 7990/77, D and R 24 (1981); (1981) 3 EHRR 63 ....29, 620
X v Y [1988] 2 All ER 648 ....331, 339

X, Y and Z v UK (1997) 24 EHRR 143 120

Y v Director of Public Prosecutions [1991] Crim LR 917 481
Young, James and Webster v UK, Judgment of
  13 August 1981; A.44; (1981) 4 EHRR 38 ....33, 71, 117, 275, 278
Younis [1990] Crim LR 425, CA 432

Zamir v UK (1983) Report of 11 October, D and R 40 (1983) 50
Zarczynska v Levy [1979] 1 WLR 125 566
Zaveckas (1969) Cr App R 202 ....472, 476
Zimmermann and Steiner v Switzerland (1983) 6 EHRR 17 64

TABLE OF STATUTES

UK STATUTES

Abortion Act 1967 379
Access to Health Record Act 1990 362
Access to Personal Files
   Act 1987 ....359, 360, 362
Act of Union with Scotland 1706 128
Administration of Justice Act 1970—
   s 40 365
Administration of Justice Act 1973—
   Sched 5 300
Armed Forces Act 1996—
   ss 21–28 578
Army Act 1955 280
   s 66 ....63, 617
Asylum and Immigration Act 1996—
   s 1(2) 533
   s 2 533
   s 3 533
   s 11 534
   Sched 1 534
Asylum and Immigration
   Appeals Act 1993 ....527, 533–35
   s 6 531
   s 8 533
Atomic Energy Act 1946—
   s 11 249

Bail Act 1976 306
British Nationality
   Act 1981 ....511, 517, 518, 520
   s 1(1), (3), (4) 519
   s 1(7) 519, 520
   s 2 519
   s 2(1)(d) 518
   s 2(2) 518
   s 3(1), (4), (5) 520
   s 4(2) 520
   s 5(2) 518
   s 6 520
   s 7(6), (8) 520

s 50(9)(b) 519
Sched 1 520
Broadcasting Act 1981 208
   s 29(3) 208
Broadcasting Act 1990 ....206, 207
   s 6 207
   s 6(1) 207
   s 6(1)(a) 210, 211
   s 6(2) 207
   s 10(3) 206, 208
   ss 43, 45 211
   s 142 334
   s 152 210
   s 162 205
   s 164(2), (4) 226
Broadcasting Act 1996 206
   s 89 211
   ss 106–10 210
   ss 106, 107, 152 335

Children and Young
   Persons Act 1933—
   s 39(1) 163
Cinemas Act 1985 212
Cinematograph Act 1909 ....121, 212
Cinematograph (Amendment)
   Act 1982 215
Civil Aviation Act 1942—
   s 40 ....363, 364
Companies Act 1985—
   s 432(2) 463
   s 437 464
   s 458 463
Computer Misuse Act 1990 .....359, 360
Conspiracy and Protection
   of Property Act 1875 286
   s 7 293
Contempt of Court Act 1981 ......33, 67,
                      118, 151, 163,
                  169, 170, 173, 178
   s 1 ....151, 170
   s 2(2) 152–56, 158, 170
   s 2(3) 152

s 4 160
s 4(a)–(e) 152
s 4(1) 160
s 4(2) 160–63, 167
s 5 ....99, 156–59, 169, 170
s 6(b) 159
s 6(c) 163, 169–72
s 8 ....176, 177
s 10 177–79
s 11 163
ss 12, 13 152
Sched 1 152
Courts and Legal Services Act 1990—
  s 64(1) 612
Crime and Disorder Act 1998—
  s 1 365
Criminal Justice Act 1925—
  s 47 614
Criminal Justice Act 1987 463
  s 2 463
Criminal Justice Act 1988—
  s 99 442
  s 139 397
  s 159 ....160, 161
Criminal Justice and Public
  Order Act 1994 ....95, 96,
                                 286–88, 313,
                                 315, 367, 394, 465
  ss 34–37 ....459, 460
  s 34 ....426, 456, 459,
                              461, 462, 464
  ss 36, 37 ....456, 459, 461, 464
  s 38(3) 461
  s 60 400–02
  s 61 ....313, 315
  s 68 ....313–15, 352
  s 69 ....314, 315
  s 70 ....127, 296, 351
  s 71 297
  s 81(1) 400
  s 90 213
  s 91(1) 95, 352
  s 93–97 352
  s 143 384
  s 146 617
  s 154 310
  s 168 213

Criminal Law Act 1967—
  s 2 407
  s 3 417
Criminal Law Act 1977 ....366, 405
  s 5(3) 203
  s 53 194
  s 53(6) 195
  s 62 ....430, 441
Crown Proceedings Act 1947 259
  s 28(1), (2) 259
Customs and Excise Management
  Act 1979—
  s 49 200

Data Protection Act 1984 ....111, 118,
                                 229, 266, 357,
                                 359, 360, 262
  ss 4, 5, 10, 11 358
  s 13 339
  s 21 358
  ss 22, 24 359
  Sched 1 358

Education (No 2) Act 1986 ....74, 378
  s 43 288
Employment Act 1989—
  s 3 578
Employment Rights Act 1996 616
Employment Protection
  (Consolidation) Act 1978 616
  s 23 283
  s 39(1)(b) 566
  s 58 279
  s 60 561
Equal Pay Act 1970 ....558, 577, 579
  s 1(2)(a), (b), (c) 580
  s 1(3) 573, 583, 584
  s 1(6) 581
European Communities
  Act 1972 ....123, 126, 128, 130
  s 2(1) 130
  s 2(2) 129
  s 2(4) 126, 129, 130

Fair Employment (NI) Act 1976 575
Family Law Reform Act 1987 519

Table of Statutes

Football (Offences) Act 1991—
   s 3 227

Highways Act 1980 299
   ss 27, 137 289

Immigration Act 1962 516
Immigration Act 1971 ......517, 524, 529
   s 1 517
   s 1(2) 518
   s 2 518
   s 2(2) 520
   s 3(2) 524
   s 3(5)(b) 544
   s 3(9) 520
   s 13 ....527, 533
   s 19 524
Immigration Act 1988 ......520, 542, 527
Indecent Displays (Control)
   Act 1981 ....200, 203, 215
   s 1(3)(b) 200
   s 1(4) 200
Intelligence Services
   Act 1994 ....98, 355, 356
   s 10 355
Interception of Communications
   Act 1985 ....62, 86, 98,
                    339, 343–45,
                    349, 355, 356
   s 1 346
   s 1(1) 347
   s 2 241
   s 2(2) 345, 348
   s 4(1) 345
   s 4(5) 346
   s 5(2) 347
   s 6(3) 348
   s 7 ....346, 356
   s 7(8) 345
   s 9 ....347, 348, 351

Justices of the Peace Act 1361 300
Justices of the Peace Act 1968—
   s 1(7) 300

Legal Aid Act 1982—
   s 1 441
Local Government Act 1988—
   s 28 618
Local Government (Miscellaneous
   Provisions) Act 1982 215

Magistrates' Courts Act 1980—
   s 1 413
   s 33 407
   s 43 421
Medical Reports Act 1988 361
Metropolitan Police Act 1839—
   s 54(13) 620
Misuse of Drugs Act 1971—
   s 23 ....368, 399

National Assistance Act 1948 535
Northern Ireland (Emergency
   Provisions) Act 1978 277
   s 11 48
   s 14 49
Northern Ireland (Emergency
   Provisions) Act 1991—
   s 28 277
Northern Ireland (Offences
   Against the Person) Act 1861 382

Obscene Publications Act 1959 ...68, 190,
                     191, 194, 197,
               201–06, 212–13, 215
   s 1(1) 203
   s 1(2) 205
   s 2 196
   s 2(1) 191
   s 2(4) 203
   s 3 ....196, 197, 203
   s 4 ....99, 182,
                     194, 195, 203
   s 4(1A) 212
Obscene Publications Act 1964—
   s 1(1), (2) 191, 213
   s 4(1) 219
Obscene Publications Act 1990—
   s 177 211

Offences Against the Person
  Act 1861—
  s 20 . . . . .385, 386
  s 47 385
Official Secrets Act 1889 . . . . .232, 233
Official Secrets Act 1911 . . . . .95, 232, 237,
    239, 242, 249
  s 1 . . . . .241, 242, 249
  s 2 . . . . .95, 232–36, 247–49
Official Secrets Act 1989 . . . . .134, 231,
    236, 237, 239,
    244–47, 250, 258,
    260, 266, 343, 356
  ss 1–4 . . . . .237, 242
  s 1 . . . . .245, 249, 354, 438
  s 1(1) 239, 243, 244, 247
  s 1(3) 238, 239, 241, 246–48
  s 1(4), (a) 238
  s 2 . . . . .239, 241, 248
  s 2(1) 243
  s 2(2) 239
  s 2(2)(b), (c) .240
  s 2(4) 239
  s 3 . . . . .243, 248
  s 3(1) 243
  s 3(1)(a) 240
  s 3(1)(b) 240, 243,
    244, 247, 248
  s 3(2)–(6) 240
  s 3(3) 241
  s 4 248
  s 4(2) 241, 245
  s 4(2)(a), (b) .245
  s 4(3) .241, 244,
    247, 249, 355
  s 4(4) 245
  s 4(6) 241
  s 5 236–38,
    241–43, 248, 355
  s 5(1)(a)(i)–(iii) 241
  s 5(1)(b)(ii) .242
  s 6 . . . . .236, 237, 243, 247, 248
  s 7 . . . . .237, 244

Parliament Act 1911—
  s 2 97
Parliamentary Commissioner
  Act 1967 270

s 5(1) 269
Sched 3 269
Police Act 1964—
  s 47 280
  s 48 503
  s 51 . . . . .396, 414
  s 51(3) .409, 418
Police Act 1996—
  s 67 503
  s 70 503
Police Act 1997 . . . . .96, 351,
    356, 367, 494
  s 18 367
  s 91(1) 367
  s 93(2) 367
Police and Criminal Evidence
  Act 1984 . . . . .96, 97, 365,
    366, 368, 370,
    373, 375, 393–96,
    401, 404–06, 413,
    417, 421, 422, 424–26,
    430, 431, 440, 450, 453,
    454, 457, 462, 468–70,
    472, 473, 482, 486, 489,
    494, 496, 500, 506, 507, 524
  s 1 .397–99, 402
  s 2 . . . . .399, 402
  s 2(1) 402
  s 3 . . . . .399, 402
  s 4 397
  s 8 . . . . .368, 371, 374
  s 8(1) 372
  s 8(2) 370
  s 9 371
  s 10 372
  ss 11, 14 371
  s 14(1)(b) 369
  s 16 374
  s 17 . . . . .366, 368, 398
  s 17(1)(c) 316
  s 17(2)(a) 410
  s 17(5), (6) 369
  s 18 . . . . .366, 368, 398
  s 18(1), (2) 370
  s 18(4) 373
  s 19 370
  s 22(1) .370, 371
  s 22(2)(a) 370

s 24 . . . . .316, 406, 407, 409, 413, 414, 422, 500	
s 24(4), (5), (7) 412	
s 25 . . . . .366, 406–09, 414, 500	
s 27 468	
s 28 . . . . .414, 415	
s 30(1) 481	
s 32 366	
s 36 425	
s 37(2) 421	
s 38(3) 426	
s 39(6) 426	
s 42(1) 421	
s 43(1) 421	
s 44 421	
s 51(d) 422	
s 55 . . . . .378, 430	
s 58 .15, 436, 441, 442, 469, 484, 489	
s 58(1) 448	
s 58(8) 443, 477	
s 61 468	
s 65 468	
s 67 524	
s 67(9) 425	
s 67(10) .395, 500	
s 67(11) .396, 443	
s 76 . . . . .351, 457, 473, 478, 479, 480, 495, 498	
s 76(2)(a) 473, 475, 476, 478, 479	
s 76(2)(b) 473, 475–79, 498, 499	
s 76(4) 497	
s 76(4)(a) 473	
s 76(8) 474	
s 77 499	
s 78 .97, 348, 395, 447, 453, 457, 464, 473, 475, 479–81, 484–87, 489–92, 494, 495, 497, 498, 506	
s 82(3) 473, 490, 495, 498	
s 84 503	
s 87(4) 503	
s 101(b) 609	
s 116 . . . . .407, 421	
s 117 . . . . .417, 418	
Sched 1 371	
Police and Magistrates' Court Act 1994 506	
s 37(f) 505	
Post Office Act 1953 . . . . .200, 201	
s 11 . . . . .200, 201	
s 58 344	
s 66 365	
Prevention of Terrorism (Additional Powers) Act 1996 . . . . .95, 400, 401, 535	
ss 13A, 13B 400–02	
Prevention of Terrorism (Temporary Provisions) Act 1974 95	
Prevention of Terrorism (Temporary Provisions) Act 1989 . . . . .179, 278, 366, 400, 413, 422, 425, 517	
s 1 277	
s 1(6) 277	
s 2 . . . . .277, 278	
s 3 278	
s 5 511	
s 5(4) 512	
ss 6, 7 511	
s 12 . . . . .51, 412	
s 14 . . . . .399, 413, 422, 465	
s 15(1) 369	
s 15(3) 399	
s 16C 367	
s 32 423	
s 32(2) 424	
s 36 425	
s 54 424	
Sched 1 277	
Sched 2 . . . . .421, 423, 512	
Sched 3 423	
Sched 5 . . . . .400, 421, 423, 465	
Sched 6A 367	
Sched 7 . . . . .179, 366, 368, 371	
Prison Act 1952—	
s 47 534	
Prohibition of Female Circumcision Act 1985 379	
Protection from Harassment Act 1997 . . . . .340, 365	
ss 1, 2 . . . . .338, 340	

Protection of Children Act 1978 200
Public Order Act 1936 ....225, 366
   s 1 ....278, 316
   s 2 276
   s 2(1)(a), (b) 277
   s 2(6) 315
   s 3 ....291, 295
   s 3(3) 296
   s 5 308
   s 9(3) 295
Public Order Act 1986 ....14, 99,
           224–27, 286, 292,
        294–96, 303, 312, 313
   ss 1–3 ....311, 316
   s 2 312
   s 3(1), (3) 312
   s 4 ....227, 306, 308,
               310, 311, 316
   s 4A 227, 310
   s 5 ....127, 225, 227,
            306–08, 310, 620
   s 5(3)(c) 309
   s 6(2) 311, 312
   s 6(3) 311
   s 6(4) 309
   s 7(2) 311
   s 9 311
   ss 11–14 315
   s 11 ....290, 291, 414
   s 12 ....133, 290, 291,
            293, 294, 414
   s 12(1)(b) 292
   s 12(4), (6) 294
   s 13 ....225, 290, 295–97
   s 14 ....289, 293, 303, 414
   s 14(4), (6) 294
   s 14A 127, 296–99
   s 14B 299
   s 14C 297
   s 16 ....293, 315
   ss 17–19 ....224, 225
   s 18 ....226, 227
   s 18(2), (5) 226
   ss 20, 22 226
   s 23 ....224, 226
   s 39 313
Public Records Act 1958 .....139, 264–65
   s 3(4) 265

Public Records Act 1967 264
Race Relations Act 1976 224,
              226, 559, 576
   s 1(1)(a) 566
   s 2 576
   s 4 568
   s 20 611
   ss 35–38 599
   s 53 611
Rent Act 1965—
   s 30 365
Representation of the People
   Act 1983—
   ss 95–97 288
   s 97 289
Road Traffic Act 1972—
   s 8 483
   s 8(5) 412
   s 8(7) 483
Road Traffic Act 1988—
   s 163 397

Security Services Act 1989 ...98, 249, 339,
           343, 353–56, 368
   s 1 354
   s 3 241
   s 5 ....249, 353, 356
   s 5(4) 354
Security Services Act 1996—
   ss 1, 2, 3B 355
Seditious Meetings Act 1817—
   s 3 289
Sex Discrimination Act 1975 ....556, 558,
               559, 562,
            566, 571, 577
   s 1(1)(b) 570, 572, 573
   s 4 576
   s 4(1) 577
   s 6(6)(b) 568
   ss 7, 19, 21 578
   s 41(1) 568
   s 47(3) 599
   s 51 578
   s 52 578
   s 85(4) 578

Sex Disqualification (Removal)
  Act 1919 555
Sexual Offences Act 1956 ....201, 614
  ss 10, 11 381
  s 12(1) 382, 384
  s 13 201
  s 14 384
  s 32 619
  s 44 381
  s 47 385
Sexual Offences Act 1967—
  s 1 382
  s 1(5) 617
  s 2 617
  s 4 382
Sexual Offences Act 1985 614
Sexual Offences (Amendment)
  Act 1976 615
  s 2 615
  s 4 163
Suicide Act 1961 379
Surrogacy Act 1985 379

Theatres Act 1968 ....191, 195
  s 3 ....194, 212
  s 8 201
Theft Act 1968 407
  ss 12, 15 397
Trade Union and Labour
  Relations Act 1974 ....97, 279
Trade Union Reform and
  Employment Rights
  Act 1993 ....283, 561
  ss 23–25 ....561, 566
  Scheds 2, 3 ....561, 566
Treason Act 1814 232

Unsolicited Goods and
  Services Act 1971—
  s 4 365

Video Recordings Act 1984 213
  s 4 213

COMMONWEALTH AND USA STATUTES

Access to Information Act
  1982 (Canada) 264

Bill of Rights (Canada) 127
Bill of Rights (New Zealand) 127

Civil Service Reform Act 1978 246
Constitution of the USA 143, 159,
  ....183, 365
  Art V 132
Criminal Code (Australia)—
  Arts 284, 285 289

Freedom of Information
  Act 1967 (USA) 264

Official Information Act
  (New Zealand) 269

Privacy Act 1974 (USA) 317, 356
Protection of Privacy Act
  1974 (Canada) 317

Security Service Intelligence
  Organisation Amendment
  Act 1986 (Australia) 94

TABLE OF EUROPEAN AND INTERNATIONAL INSTRUMENTS

European Convention for the Protection of Individuals with regard to the Automatic Protection of Data 1980 ....111, 118

European Convention on
Human Rights 17–26, 28–34,
37, 42, 49, 53,
72–93, 101, 103,
107–12, 119, 120, 123,
124, 126–29, 131–36,
143, 171, 179, 205, 208,
209, 214, 219, 301, 620
   Arts 1–18 124
   Art 1 ....54, 107
   Arts 2–7 18
   Arts 2–12 ....19, 26
   Art 2 ....25, 35–43, 46, 73,
74, 79, 83, 131,
389, 418, 510, 620
   Art 3 ....37, 40–43, 64, 73,
74, 77–80, 83, 134,
377, 378, 510, 544, 545
   Arts 4–6 43
   Art 4 ....44, 79, 540
   Art 4(1) 78, 79
   Art 5 ....44–54, 79,
301, 416, 544, 545
   Art 5(2) 24
   Art 5(3) 84, 422
   Art 6 ....53–59, 74, 119,
134, 464, 465, 510, 620
   Art 6(2) 78
   Art 6(3)(c) 45
   Art 6(3)(d) 84
   Art 7 ....44, 59, 60, 79, 217
   Arts 8–11 ....38, 78,
81–83, 301, 318
   Arts 8–12 18
   Art 8 ....43, 61–64, 67,
72, 76, 77, 119,
120, 134, 230, 317, 320,
327, 338, 344, 345, 349,
350, 356, 360, 361, 363,
377, 378, 383, 384, 387,
389, 416, 494, 495, 510, 620

Art 9 ....64, 65, 67, 68,
217, 218, 223, 278
Art 9(1) 217
Art 10 ....13, 33, 64–67,
69, 70, 80,
83, 101, 109,
119, 123, 128, 134,
144, 145, 149–51, 157,
168, 169, 171, 178,
197, 198, 204, 208,
214, 216–18, 220, 229,
230, 252, 255, 278, 301,
309, 310, 338, 361, 620
Art 10(1) 197
Art 10(2) 197, 198, 204,
214, 216–19, 254
Art 11 ....67, 70, 71, 80,
134, 275, 278–83,
290, 296, 298,
299, 301, 309, 310
Art 12 71–73
Arts 13–21 24
Art 13 ....43, 75–77, 281,
282, 353, 356, 545
Art 14 ....42, 67,
76–78, 80, 119,
120, 125, 218, 620
Art 15 ....28, 51, 78–80, 422
Art 15(2) 11
Art 16 80
Art 17 ....28, 64, 78,
81, 125, 278
Art 18 78
Arts 19–56 23
Art 19 20
Arts 20–23 21
Art 24 25
Art 25 ....25, 28
Art 26 ....26, 29
Art 27(b) 27
Art 27(2) 27–29
Art 27(3) 29
Art 28 30
Art 28(1)(b) 30
Arts 29, 31, 32, 34 31
Art 36 ....31, 201
Arts 38–43 22

li

Art 43 ....24, 33
Art 48 32
Arts 50–53 33
Art 50 53
Arts 53, 54 34
Art 55 32
Art 64 ....28, 78, 81

United Nations Convention on
   the Status of Refugees 1951 43

75/117 Equal Pay Directive 118

76/207 Equal Treatment Directive ...111
   Arts 2(1)(2)(3)(4) 600–08

89/552 Transfrontier Television
   Directive 211
   Arts 2(1)(2), 3(2) 211

European Social Charter 1961 18

French Civil Code—
   Art 1382 317

German Basic Law 317
   Art 1 142

Hague-Visby Rules 123

International Covenant on Civil
   and Political Rights 1966 ..17, 20, 224
   Art 12 510
   Art 17 317
   Art 18 ....222, 223
   Art 20 ....224, 225

International Covenant on
   Economic, Social and
   Cultural Rights 1966 18

United Nations Covenant on
   Civil and Political Rights 27

United Nations Declaration
   of Human Rights 1948............17

Universal Declaration
   of Human Rights 67
   Art 18 ....222, 223
   Art 20 275

Treaty of Amsterdam 110,
                              607–08, 619
Treaty of European Union
   (Maastricht Treaty) 111
   Art F2 110

Treaty of Rome 110, 615–20
   Arts 30, 36 200
   Art 48 111
   Art 119 ....129, 607
   Art 177 130
   Art 235 110

PART ONE

THE NATURE AND PROTECTION OF RIGHTS AND LIBERTIES

In many Western Democracies the rights of citizens are enshrined in a constitutional document sometimes known as a Bill or Charter of Rights. In 2000 the European Convention on Human Rights will be received into UK law under the Human Rights Act 1998. For the first time the UK will have a domestic charter of rights in the modern sense. But, traditionally, in order to discover which freedoms are protected and the extent of that protection, it has been necessary to examine the common law, statutes and the influence of Treaties to which the UK is a party, especially the European Convention on Human Rights.

Certain particular characteristics of the UK constitution have determined and will continue to determine the means of protecting fundamental freedoms in the UK. The doctrine of the supremacy of Parliament means that constitutional law can be changed in the ordinary way – by Act of Parliament. Thus Parliament has the power to abridge freedoms which in other countries are seen as fundamental rights. It follows from this that all parts of the law are equal – there is no hierarchy of laws and therefore constitutional law cannot constrain other laws.

There is no judicial review of Acts of Parliament and this will continue to be the case: a judge will not be able to declare a statutory provision invalid because it conflicts with a Convention right protected by the Human Rights Act 1998. If, for example, a statute is passed containing a provision which in some way limits freedom of speech, a judge must apply it, whereas in a country with an entrenched Bill of Rights the law might be struck down as unconstitutional. However, there are two possible constraints on this process. If the judge considers that the provision in question is at all ambiguous he or she may interpret it in such a way that freedom of speech is maintained, by relying on the incorporated European Convention on Human Rights. Further, if the domestic provision comes into conflict with an EU provision, the judge will decide to 'disapply' it, unless the conflict can be resolved. Thus, Parliamentary sovereignty has suffered some limitation but this does not mean that we can simply look to the EU to protect our civil liberties since EU instruments are not always of relevance. Where the EU does have an impact it can provide a protection which may broadly be said to remove certain fundamental freedoms or aspects of them, from the reach of Parliament, at least while the UK is a member of the EU. The Human Rights Act will provide a further constraint when it comes into force, although judges will not be able simply to strike down legislation in conflict with the Convention.

Thus, at present, civil liberties in the UK are in a more precarious position than they are in other democracies, although this does not necessarily mean that they are inevitably less well-protected: some Bills of Rights may offer only a theoretical protection to freedoms which is not reflected in practice. Civil liberties have traditionally been defined as residual, not entrenched as in other countries: they are the residue of freedom left behind after the legal restrictions have been defined.

The main purpose of this book is to identify and examine these areas of freedom but in order to do so it is necessary to say something more about the context within which they should be placed. The intention in Part I is to do this in three stages. Chapter 1 will offer an indication of the theoretical basis of rights and liberties and of the distinction between them. Chapter 2 will undertake analysis of the document which will be incorporated so as to act, in effect, as a UK Bill of Rights and which has greatly influenced the domestic protection of civil liberties – the European Convention on Human Rights. Chapter 3 will consider the nature and adequacy of the traditional domestic arrangements which protected fundamental freedoms only as liberties, with consideration of the likely impact of importing the Convention into UK law in order to provide more certain protection.

CHAPTER ONE

THE NATURE OF RIGHTS AND LIBERTIES

This book is intended to provide an analysis of the legal protection given to civil liberties in the UK.[1] The term 'civil liberties' is the name used to denote the broad class of rights known as civil and political rights as they are recognised in the UK.[2] In order to provide a coherent analysis a theoretical position will be outlined from which to mount an internally consistent critique of the state of civil liberties in the UK today. This chapter will therefore aim to outline such a position in order to provide an account of a method of deriving rights from more general political theory and criticisms of this derivation; consideration of the nature of these rights and of methods of resolving conflicts between individual rights and the claims of society; and analysis of what we may be requiring of others when we assert a right or liberty.[3] Broadly speaking, the position adopted will tend to reflect the particular brand of political liberalism expounded by John Rawls and Ronald Dworkin in so far as their theories converge. Perhaps it should be noted at this point that the liberal conception of rights which will be discussed, differs significantly from the tradition which views rights as naturally inherent in the human person.[4] By contrast, as will be seen, liberals start by devising a general political theory from which they then seek to derive a series of rights.

1 WHERE DO RIGHTS DERIVE FROM?

The liberal conception of rights can be seen to owe its antecedents to the school of so-called social contractarians which found perhaps its earliest

---

1   General reading which will be referred to throughout this book: Bailey, SH, Harris, DJ and Jones, BL, *Civil Liberties: Cases and Materials*, 4th edn, 1995; Feldman, D, *Civil Liberties and Human Rights in England and Wales*, 1993; Robertson, G, *Freedom, the Individual and the Law*, 7th edn, 1993; Ewing, KD and Gearty, CA, *Freedom Under Thatcher*, 1990; Thornton, P, *Decade of Decline: Civil Liberties in the Thatcher Years*, 1989; Sieghart, P, *Human Rights in the UK*, 1988.

2   The term 'civil and political rights' is used in contradistinction to the term 'economic and social rights' to denote first generation rights – those which have long been recognised in the Western democracies from the time of the French and American Declarations of the 'Rights of Man' in the 18th century.

3   General reading: the literature is immense but the following are of particular importance. Simmonds, NE, *Central Issues in Jurisprudence*, 1986, provides a brief but extremely lucid introduction to relevant jurisprudential issues. Substantive texts: Rawls, J, *A Theory of Justice*, 1973; Dworkin, R, *Taking Rights Seriously*, 1977, and *A Matter of Principle*, 1985; Hart, HLA, *The Concept of Law*, 1961, and *Essays in Jurisprudence and Philosophy*, 1983; Waldron, J, ed, *Theories of Rights*, 1984.

4   For a modern exposition of the Natural Law School, see Finnis, *Natural Law and Natural Rights*, 1980.

advocate in the writings of John Locke.[5] Locke imagined an actual social contract between individuals and the state at the setting up of civil society in which citizens, in order to secure the protection of their property, handed over certain powers (most importantly a monopoly of coercive force) to the government in return for the guarantee of certain rights to 'lives, liberties and estates'. Locke thus introduced the idea, which is still central to liberalism today, that the overriding purpose of the state is the securing and protection of its citizen's basic liberties. The idea of the social contract is thus clearly an immensely potent one and it is John Rawls's revival and radical revision of the idea in his *A Theory of Justice* (1972) which has almost single-handedly transformed the face of political theory; as HLA Hart has commented, rights-based theories have replaced utilitarianism[6] as the primary focus of attention.[7] Robert Nozick, a right-wing critic of Rawls whose work *Anarchy, State and Utopia* (1974) mounts a sustained attack upon Rawls's theory, has written: 'Political philosophers now must either work within Rawls's theory or explain why not'.[8]

Rawls imagines not an actual but a hypothetical social contract taking place in what he terms 'the original position'. The essential feature of this position is that the contractors (Rawls' men) are devising amongst themselves the outlines of 'the foundation charter of their society' whilst behind 'the veil of ignorance'. The men are ignorant not only of what will be their positions in the future social hierarchy but also of their skills, weaknesses, preferences and conceptions of the good life – whether, for example, they will be strict Muslims or an humanist academics. Since none of the contractors know what mode of life he will wish to pursue, he is bound (if he is rational) to choose a tolerant society and one which guarantees him the rights necessary to pursue any individual goals he may in future choose. In other words, the men will wish to put in place the means whereby they will in future be able to pursue their goals rather than adopting structures which might in future prevent them from doing so. Thus almost any conception of the good life will require, for example, freedom from arbitrary arrest, the right to a fair trial and freedom from inhuman treatment. In addition, the man who will become the Muslim might in *future* wish to restrict freedom of speech on religious matters but at *present*, self-interest dictates that he consider the possibility that his conception of the good life might necessarily include the exercise of freedom of speech. Thus Rawls's men adopt, *inter alia*, 'the first principle,' stating that 'each person is to have an equal right to the most extensive, total system of equal

---

5 *The Second Treatise of Government*, 1698.
6 See discussion below p 6.
7 See Hart's comments on this phenomena generally in 'Between Utility and Rights' in Cohen, M, ed, *Ronald Dworkin and Contemporary Jurisprudence*, 1984.
8 *Anarchy, State and Utopia*, p 183.

basic liberties compatible with a similar system of liberty for all'.[9] These basic liberties are identical with any familiar list of civil and political rights.

Although similar to Rawls in political outlook, Ronald Dworkin offers a theoretical construct which derives rights in a different manner and indeed has criticised Rawls' theory, arguing that a *hypothetical*, unlike an *actual*, contract provides no grounds for binding actual people to its terms.[10] Dworkin attempts to derive rights from the premise, which he hopes all will agree to, that the state owes a duty to treat all of its citizens with equal concern and respect – a premise which he argues persuasively is the deep assumption underlying Rawls's use of the contract device. Dworkin is not concerned with defending rights from despotic and repressive governments and indeed he sees no need to protect – by designating them as rights – those individual interests which the *majority* would like to see protected, since these will in any case be ensured by the democratic process which he assumes as a background to his theory. Dworkin's particular concern is to justify the protection of *unpopular* or minority rights – or those whose exercise may on occasion threaten the overall well-being of the community – because such rights would potentially be put at risk if their validity were to be determined through a democratic vote.

Clearly, the institution of democracy and most familiar sets of political policies such as seeking the economic betterment of the majority, seem to be satisfactorily explained by an underpinning utilitarianism.[11] Dworkin hypothesises that the great appeal of utilitarianism is owed at least in part to its appearance of egalitarianism through its promise to 'treat the wishes of each member of the community on a par with the wishes of any other',[12] taking into account only the intensity of the preference and the number of people who hold it. This appeal is evinced in the utilitarian maxim, 'everybody to count for one, nobody for more than one'. Dworkin finds, however, that raw utilitarianism betrays this promise since it fails to distinguish between what he denotes external and personal preferences. For example, if the question of whether homosexual acts should be permitted in private between adults were to be decided by a majority vote (*preference maximisation*) homosexuals would express their personal preference for freedom to perform those acts. Certain heterosexuals, however, would vote

---

9   For this reference and a brief summary of the theory, see Rawls, *op cit* pp 11–15.
10 Dworkin, *Taking Rights Seriously*, 1977, Chap 6.
11 Utilitarianism is a major political philosophy. The original conception of utilitarianism espoused by Jeremy Bentham saw the aim of government as being to promote the greatest happiness of the greatest number of people (see *Collected Works of Jeremy Bentham*, Burns, ed, 1970). A more recent and fashionable version states that an ideal society is one in which there is the maximum amount of preference satisfaction (see generally Smart and Williams, *Utilitarianism: For and Against*, 1973). References in the text will be to this latter version, known as 'preference utilitarianism'.
12 Dworkin, *Taking Rights Seriously, op cit* p 275.

against allowing this freedom because their external preference is that homosexuals should not be free to commit such acts.

Thus resolution of the question could be affected by the fact that certain citizens think that the homosexual way of life is not deserving of equal respect; a decision would therefore have been made at least partly on the basis that the way of life of certain citizens was in some way contemptible. If the government enforced this decision through the use of coercive force (the criminal law) it would clearly have failed in its central duty to treat its citizens with equal concern and respect. In other words, utilitarianism – and therefore democracy – has an in-built means of undermining its own promise of equality. Since for Dworkin protecting this promise of equality is the central postulate of political morality, he finds that homosexuals should be granted a right to moral autonomy which cannot be overridden even by a majority decision-making process.

Opposition to the liberal conception of human rights

Utilitarianism

Utilitarianism has historically been generally hostile to the idea of rights, most famously to the notion of natural and inalienable human rights as set out, for example, in the American Declaration of Independence, which was characterised by Jeremy Bentham as merely so much 'bawling upon paper'.[13] The opposition of utilitarians to the notion of *natural* rights sprang mainly from their legal positivism – their belief that a legal right only exists if there is a specific 'black letter' provision guaranteeing it. But in general, since Utilitarianism sets out one supreme goal of happiness or, in its more modern version, preference maximisation, it would clearly follow that rights under utilitarianism can have only a contingent justification. In other words, they are to be respected if they help bring about the goal of maximum satisfaction of preferences but not otherwise. It may seem odd to postulate an opposition between utilitarianism and human rights bearing in mind that JS Mill combined utilitarianism with a passionate belief in the desirability of free expression and civil rights generally. It should be noted, however, that Mill's arguments for free speech depend essentially on a belief that allowing free speech will in the long term have good effects – such as increasing the likelihood that the truth will be discovered – rather than on a belief that free expression is a good in itself or something to which human beings are entitled without reference to its likely effects. A utilitarian, confronted with a situation in which infringing a right would undeniably benefit society as a whole, would have no reason to support the inviolability of the right; for example he

---

13 Bentham, J, 'Anarchical Fallacies' in Bowring, ed, *Collected Works of Jeremy Bentham*, 1843, p 494.

or she would find it hard to explain why criminal suspects should not be tortured if it was proven that reliable evidence would be derived thereby, leading to increased convictions, deterrence of crime and substantial consequential benefit to society. A further variant of the theory which has sometimes been termed 'Rule Utilitarianism', however, states that the goals of utilitarianism can best be reached by constructing rules which it is thought will in general further the goal of happiness or 'preference maximisation' and then applying these rules to situations as absolutes rather than considering in each individual situation what can best further the goal (for discussion see Smart and Williams, note 11 above). Such rules could of course consist, at least in part, of a set of human rights. In relation to the example of torture given in the text, a rule utilitarian could plausibly maintain that a general rule of humane treatment of citizens is likely to lead to the greatest happiness. In deciding whether to torture an individual suspect this would mean that instead of considering whether in this case overall utility would be thereby increased, the state should apply the rule of humane treatment, even if in the particular case it would lead to a decrease in utility. It can be seen that for rule utilitarians the good (the goal of preference maximisation or greatest happiness) is prior to the right, in opposition to Rawls' clearly expressed conviction that the right (a system of just entitlements of citizens) is prior to any conceptions of the good – the substantive moral convictions by which individuals will live their lives.

Marxism

The former socialist bloc of states – the Soviet Union and Eastern Europe – was the driving force behind the international recognition of economic, social and cultural rights. This was at least partly due to the fact that there is a measure of hostility within Marxist thought to civil and political rights.[14] Such hostility exists mainly because Marxism advocates establishing a state which far from being neutral amongst its citizens' varying conceptions of the good and guaranteeing them the liberties necessary to pursue their private goals, instead imposes a particular conception of the good upon society. Since it regards the protection of this conception (the achievements of the revolution) as the supreme value and duty of the state, the exercise of liberties which threaten this achievement can be justifiably curtailed; hence the consistently poor record of the former Soviet bloc states and Communist China on such civil rights as freedom of speech. A theoretically related but more moderate critique of the Western liberal conception of human rights can be found in the writings of the so-called communitarians.[15]

---

14 See eg Marx, K, *On the Jewish Question*, 1843.
15 See eg Sandel, *Liberalism and the Limits of Justice*, 1982.

Critical legal studies

The Critical Legal Studies movement (CLS) attacks the whole liberal conception of law as neutral, objective and rational. It seeks to expose the value judgments, internal inconsistencies and ideological conflicts which it sees as concealed under law's benevolent exterior of impartial justice.[16] Since the whole structure of legally guaranteed human rights is a creature of the liberal conception of law, the CLS attack fastens by extension onto the liberal notion of rights. Mark Tushnet, for example, has made four main criticisms of the liberal theory of rights in what he calls 'a Schumpeterian act of creative destruction'. He asserts that rights are: first, unstable – that is, meaningful only in a particular social setting; secondly, they produce 'no determinate consequences if claimed'; thirdly, 'rights talk ... falsely converts into empty abstractions ... real experiences that we ought to value for their own sake'; and fourthly, if conceded a dominant position in contemporary discourse, rights threaten to 'impede advances by progressive social forces'.[17] It would be inappropriate to attempt a detailed refutation of the CLS position here.[18] Perhaps the most important weakness in its critique of rights is that, as many writers have pointed out,[19] it offers no guidance whatsoever as to how the interests of vulnerable minorities are to be protected without the institution of legal rights.

2 WHAT IS MEANT BY A RIGHT?

The preceding section has set out, in a very basic manner, some of the more influential liberal theories concerning the means of deriving a system of rights from a more general moral theory. In this section, two aims will be pursued. First, an attempt will be made to shed some light on what one can be taken to mean in general terms by asserting a right; secondly, a brief explanation will be given of Hohfeld's exposition of a right as an umbrella term, covering a number of more precisely delineated claims.

Distinguishing moral and legal rights

The endeavour to distinguish legal from moral rights involves a central issue in jurisprudence, namely the relationship between law and morality on which

---

16 Unger, R, *The Critical Legal Studies Movement*, 1986.
17 Tushnet, M, 'An Essay on Rights' (1984) *Texas Law Review* Vol 62, No 8 May.
18 For a general critique of the CLS attitude to rights see, for example, Price, 'Taking Rights Cynically' (1989) 48 *CLJ* 271.
19 *Ibid* note 18. See also eg Rhodes, 'Feminist Critical Theories' (1990) *Stanford Law Review* Vol 42, No 3 pp 634–38.

there is a vast literature and a number of clearly defined schools of thought. Only the barest indications of the various positions on this tendentious issue are possible here.

Legal positivism

Clearly, from a common sense point of view, if X makes a claim that she has a right to Y and there is no clear, black letter law giving her such a right, she must be taken to be asserting that she has a strong *moral* claim to Y and (probably) that this claim ought to be given *legal* force through the enactment of a specific legal right. The above point of view is – very crudely speaking – that put forward by the school of jurisprudence known as legal positivism, whose central insistence is that there is no *necessary* connection between law and morality.[20]

Natural law

To a member of the natural law school in its traditional form,[21] by contrast, the question of whether X's claim to Y was moral or legal would be decided not empirically, by consulting the statute book, but rather by examining the normative claim made by her. If her claim was supported by an abstract notion of justice then a measure purporting to deny the claim would not be accepted as a valid law since it would be unjust. The approach sounds extreme but was employed during the Nuremberg trials as the underlying justification for what might otherwise have been seen as the retrospective criminalisation of those who committed their crimes under the Nazi laws thought valid at the time.

Dworkin's theory

The views of Ronald Dworkin[22] provide a middle ground between these two theories – a 'third theory of law'.[23] His theory is highly complex but in essence is more inclusive than the positivist theory; recognising black letter legal

---

20 For a full discussion of this issue, see Hart, HLA, 'Positivism and the Separation of Law and Morals' in *Essays in Jurisprudence and Philosophy*, 1983.

21 For the classical exposition of this theory see Aquinas, *Summa Theologica* in *Selected Political Writings* (edited by D'Entreves, P, 1970).

22 For an exposition of Dworkin's account of the relationship between law and morality, see his theory of judicial adjudication in Chaps 2–4 of *Taking Rights Seriously*, in which his theory is cast mainly in the form of a critique of legal positivism. For a fuller development of the theory, see *Law's Empire*, 1986.

23 The term was coined by Mackie, 'The Third Theory of the Law' in Cohen, ed, *Ronald Dworkin and Contemporary Jurisprudence*.

rights,[24] it insists that the law may contain *further* rights which have never yet been recognised by a statute or in any judicial decision. Thus X could correctly claim she had a right to Y, on Dworkin's account, if (a) the right would be consistent with the bulk of existing law and (b) it would figure in the best possible interpretation of the area of law concerned. By this, Dworkin means that the relevant past judicial decisions would be most satisfactorily justified by showing them all to have been concerned with protecting the right at issue, even if previous individual judgments did not explicitly recognise its existence. Such a claim might well, of course, be controversial but it is precisely this that is at the root of Dworkin's disagreement with the positivists: finding out what the law is, he argues, will require not merely an empirical test of the law's *pedigree* (does it emanate from the right body?) but rather a complex enquiry which will, as he puts it, carry the lawyer 'very deep into moral and political theory'.[25]

If one is convinced by Dworkin's ingenious argument, the existence of a legal right can be adduced through interpretation (at least in common law jurisdictions). Alternatively a right could in any event be given clear explicit protection so that its legal status was not a matter for controversy.

The strength of a right: conflicts with other claims

If a legal right is conceded to exist, it must next be asked what is and should be the nature and strength of the protection thereby given? The right may come into conflict with the claims of society, such as that a certain standard of morality should be upheld. Clearly in resolving such a conflict, a judge will inevitably draw upon his or her background political theory. If, for example, a judge in the European Court of Human Rights who is a utilitarian by conviction, has to consider a convincing demonstration by a defendant government that the particular application of the right to free speech claimed by the applicant, will on balance make society worse off as a whole, he or she will be inclined to find for the government and allow the infringement of the right. Such infringement will of course be more readily allowable if the right is framed or has developed in such a way as to be open-ended in scope with in-built exceptions.

Both Dworkin and Rawls have argued persuasively against making rights vulnerable to utilitarian considerations in this way. The idea that 'Each person possesses an inviolability founded on justice that even the welfare of society

---

24 Note that in *Law's Empire* Dworkin seems to discard any reliance on recognising 'black letter' law by some means reminiscent of Hart's rule of recognition and comes to a position in which law is entirely a matter of interpretation. For criticism of this position see eg Simmonds, 'Imperial Visions and Mundane Practices' (1987) *CLJ* 465 and Cotterell, *The Politics of Jurisprudence*, 1989, pp 172–81.
25 Dworkin, *Taking Rights Seriously*, 1977, p 67.

as a whole cannot override'[26] lies at the centre of Rawls's political thought. The idea of such inviolable rights may seem extreme but is in fact accepted by all civilised countries in the case, for example, of torture. It is not thought to be a sound argument for a government to assert that it is justified in torturing certain of its citizens on the grounds that it can increase the general welfare thereby. The acceptance of this principle is attested to by the non-derogability of the right to freedom from torture in all international human rights treaties including the European Convention on Human Rights (Article 15(2)).

Dworkin has addressed the specific question as to the means of understanding a legal right in an adjudicative context in some detail. Earlier, the distinction between moral and legal rights was discussed. Here it should be noted that Dworkin also distinguishes between rights which have 'trump' status and those that do not. He gives as an example of the latter a legal right to drive either way on a two-way road: such a right is a 'weak' legal right because it is not an important human interest which is likely to be denied to certain groups through the influence of external preferences. It follows that such a right could justifiably be overridden by the government (through making the road one-way) if it thought it in the general interest to do so. By contrast, his conception of the strength of 'trump' rights leads to his insistence that an assertion of (for example) a right to free speech held by citizens 'must imply that it would be wrong for the government to stop them from speaking, even when the government believes that what they say will cause more harm than good'.[27]

It can be seen then that Dworkin gives us a very clear prescription for the approach that a judge should take in weighing strong or 'trump' rights against the general welfare of society. He roundly condemns the idea that a judge, in adjudicating upon a right or a government in framing it, should carefully weigh up the right of the citizen against the possible adverse social consequences, accepting that it is sometimes preferable to err on the side of society, sometimes on the side of the individual but on the whole getting the balance about right. 'It must be wrong', he argues, to consider that 'inflating rights is as serious as invading them'. For to *invade* a right is to affront human dignity or treat certain citizens as less worthy of respect than others, while to *inflate* a right is simply to pay 'a little more in social efficiency'[28] than the government *already* has to pay in allowing the right at all. Thus, for Dworkin, if one asserts a 'trump' right ordinary counter-arguments about a decrease in the welfare of society as a whole are simply irrelevant.

In what circumstances, then may a strong individual right be overridden? Dworkin has argued[29] that there are three general justifications for infringement and these appear to be generally accepted by liberal thought.

---

26 Rawls, J, *A Theory of Justice, op cit* p 3.
27 *Taking Rights Seriously*, p 191.
28 *Op cit* p 199.
29 *Op cit* p 200.

Competing rights

First, there is the situation in which there is a clear competing individual claim, so that the exercise of the original right will directly infringe the competing right. The paradigmatic example of such a collision of individual rights arises where one individual uses his right of free speech to prejudice the fair trial of another. Another is where one incites violence against the other, thus infringing his right to security of the person. In such cases, since both rights are, as it were, from the same class of 'strong' rights they will compete on equal terms but it may nevertheless be possible to resolve the conflict by undertaking a balancing act based on proportionality. In the case of prejudice to a trial this could be done by physically removing the trial from the area affected by the speech in question. If such avoidance of conflict was impossible a determination might be made as to the damage inflicted on each right if the other was allowed to prevail. In the case of incitement to violence, the damage inflicted if free speech was allowed to prevail might be almost irretrievable since the group affected might be placed at great risk for a period of time. In contrast, the damage to free speech created by avoidance of the risk might be of a lesser nature although undesirable: the speech could be uttered in another form or another forum so that its meaning was not lost but it was rendered less inflammatory. Alternatively, utterance of the speech could be delayed until the situation had become less volatile. The words advocating immediate violence might be perceived as outside the area of protected speech and so might be severed from the accompanying words which could be permitted.

The right is not really at stake

The second situation in which rights may be overridden is one where the values protected by the right are not at stake in this particular situation. In other words, it may be argued that most rights have a 'core', the invasion of which will constitute an actual overriding of the right but they also have a 'penumbra' – an area in which the value the right protects is present only in a weaker form.[30] An invasion of the penumbra may be said to constitute only an *infringement* of the right and may therefore be more readily justified. The argument that commercial speech should not be afforded the same protection as other kinds of speech would appear to rest precisely on the argument that it

---

30 This view is not attributed to Dworkin, although he does accept that there will be situations in which the core value of the right will not be at stake. Dworkin has comprehensively rejected Hart's theory of statutory construction and application of the rules from past cases based around the notion of a core of certainty and a penumbra of uncertainty (for Hart's position see *The Concept of Law*; for Dworkin's critique, *op cit* Chaps 2–4). Dworkin argues that the areas of a rule which form the core and those which fall in the penumbra, can only be elucidated through a judge's interpretation, which will carry him or her far from the specific words of the statute.

is in the penumbra of free speech;[31] by contrast, political speech is clearly in the 'core' of free speech.[32]

A real risk to society

The third situation justifying infringement is one in which the exercise of a right may pose a real danger to society. In such instances liberals are unwilling to take danger to mean danger to some abstract attribute to society, such as its moral health,[33] but rather insist that the danger must ultimately amount to a threat to some concrete aspect of its citizens' well-being. Thus, typically, liberals are hostile to characterising the likelihood of shocking or offending citizens as a concrete harm justifying the suppression of the right of free speech. Dworkin's own, perhaps rather unrealistically stringent test, is that the 'risk to society' justification for overriding rights is only made out if the state demonstrates 'a clear and substantial risk' that exercise of the right 'will do great damage to the person or property of others'.[34] It seems unlikely that governments would be prepared to accept such a test; the criterion laid down, for example, by the European Court of Human Rights for curtailing the right of free expression as set out in Article 10 does not even approach Dworkin's prescription either in stringency or clarity; instead it has adopted the somewhat weak and uncertain phrase, 'a pressing social need'.[35] Dworkin's rights analysis should not therefore be taken as a description of the way rights and liberties are *actually* treated in the UK and under human rights treaties but rather as an ideal against which the reality of such 'rights' protection can be measured.

Distinguishing rights and liberties

Having given an account of what may in general terms be meant by an assertion of a right in the liberal tradition, we may now turn to an analysis of the more specific claims that the assertion of a right may entail and employ this analysis to make a few general remarks about the nature of 'rights' protection in the UK.

---

31 Judgment of US Supreme Court, *Bolger v Youngs Drug Products Ltd* [1983] 103 Ct 2875, 2880–81.

32 The House of Lords appeared to recognise the central importance of free political speech in their recent decision that neither local nor central government could pursue an action in defamation: *Derbyshire County Council v The Times Newspapers* [1993] 1 All ER 1011.

33 For example, see the attacks by Hart, 'Social Solidarity and the Enforcement of Morality' in *Essays in Jurisprudence and Philosophy* and Dworkin, 'Liberty and Morality' in *Taking Rights Seriously* on Lord Devlin's view that society may justifiably use the criminal law to enforce a shared morality.

34 *Taking Rights Seriously*, p 204.

35 See *Handyside v UK* (1976) 1 EHRR 737. For further discussion of this test see Chap 4, pp 150–51.

Hohfeld's analysis

One of the more influential attempts to analyse closely the nature of a right was made by the American jurist Wesley Hohfeld.[36] Hohfeld attempted to demonstrate the way that claims of rights in everyday language can in fact be broken down into four more specific claims. First, if it is claimed that X has a right proper or 'claim right' to A then this means that persons, generally or particularly, are under some specific corresponding duty to ensure that X has access to A. Secondly, X may be said to have an immunity as against a particular person or body; this means that they are disabled from interfering with the exercise by X of the interest (A) protected by the immunity. Thirdly, if X has only a liberty (what Hohfeld calls a privilege) to do A, this far weaker claim merely means that X does no wrong in exercising his liberty – the rights of others are not thereby infringed. However, no one has a duty to allow him to exercise A or to assist him to exercise it. Fourthly, X may have a power to do B, such as to sell his property. This last category is not particularly relevant to the subject of civil liberties.

Hohfeld applied to the reality of 'rights' protection

Hohfeld's explanation is a useful analytical tool; it can be seen by utilising it that Dworkin is advocating that rights be set out as a series of immunities – areas of entitlements which even democratically elected governments are disabled from interfering with. The US Constitution and its Amendments represent such a list of immunities. In applying Hohfeld's theory to 'rights' protection in the UK it can be seen that it endows the commentator with the ability to distinguish between the different forms of protection offered towards different freedoms.

If Dworkin's analysis is used, all rights in the UK are, at present, 'weak', since all are at least theoretically subject to infringement by Parliament, whereas under Hohfeld's view the picture is more mixed. It becomes clear that most freedoms in the UK are merely liberties; one does no wrong to exercise them but there is no positive duty on any organ of the state to allow or facilitate them. For example, the Public Order Act 1986 nowhere places upon Chief Constables a duty to ensure freedom of assembly and speech. When the Human Rights Act 1998 comes into force these liberties will become rights since public authorities will be laid under a positive duty to respect them and will act unlawfully if they do not (section 6(1)), unless the only possible reading of contrary primary legislation is that the right must be infringed. At present, some of our entitlements clearly have the quality of Hohfeldian claim rights in that they are protected by a positive correlative duty. For example, arrested persons have the right of access to a solicitor

---

36 *Fundamental Legal Concepts as Applied in Judicial Reasoning*, 1920, particularly pp 35–41.

while in police custody as guaranteed by s 58 Police and Criminal Evidence Act 1984. Equal treatment in certain contexts is provided for under domestic and EU instruments.

However, even when a citizen holds a right there have been – under domestic law – no *legal* guarantees that the legislation providing the positive protection will not be repealed. Similarly, a citizen enjoying a liberty could not be certain that legislation would not be introduced into a previously unregulated area thus destroying or limiting that liberty. But this position will change under the Human Rights Act 1998. It will become much less likely that legislation will be introduced which will have the effect of limiting a liberty since such legislation might eventually be declared incompatible with the guarantees of rights under the Act (section 4). Further, when the legislation was introduced the relevant Minister would have to declare that a statement of compatibility could not be made (section 19). Similarly, existing legislative protection for a right recognised within the Act would be unlikely to be repealed since a citizen might then challenge the failure to provide the right (section 7), so long as the right was one exercisable against a public authority. Thus, in Hohfeldian terms, the 1998 Act itself does not provide a set of immunities since it can be overridden by primary legislation. But the Act clearly represents a dramatic shift in rights protection in the UK, away from residual freedoms towards positive rights.

CHAPTER TWO

THE EUROPEAN CONVENTION ON HUMAN RIGHTS

1 INTRODUCTION[1]

The European Convention on Human Rights was conceived after the Second World War as a means of preventing the kind of violation of human rights seen in Germany during and before the war. However, it has not generally been invoked in relation to large scale violations of rights, but instead has addressed particular deficiencies in the legal systems of the Member States, who on the whole create regimes of human rights in conformity with it. Drafted in 1949 by the Council of Europe, it was based on the United Nations Declaration of Human Rights,[2] and partly for that reason and partly because it was only intended to provide basic protection for human rights, it appears today as quite a cautious document, less far reaching than the 1966 International Covenant on Civil and Political Rights. Nevertheless, it has had far more effect on UK law than any other human rights treaty due to its machinery for enforcement which includes the European Court of Human Rights with the power to deliver a ruling adverse to the governments of Member States. Moreover, the Court insists upon the dynamic nature of the Convention and adopts a teleological or purpose-based approach to interpretation which has allowed the substantive rights to develop until they may cover situations unthought of in 1949. Had it been a more radical document the Convention might have been self-defeating because it might have failed to secure the necessary acceptance from Member States, both in terms of ratifying various parts of it, such as the right of individual petition, and in terms of responding to adverse judgments.

Although the European Court of Human Rights may rule against the governments of Member States, its approach – which is reflected throughout the machinery for the supervision of the Convention – is not ultimately coercive. A persuasive or consensus-based approach is evident at every stage through which an application may pass. A friendly settlement may well be reached before the case comes before the Court; even if it does not and the

---

1 General reading see Merrills and Robertson, *Human Rights in Europe*, 3rd edn, 1993; Van Dijk, P and Van Hoof, F, *Theory and Practice of the European Convention on Human Rights*, 2nd edn, 1990; Beddard, R, *Human Rights and Europe*, 3rd edn, 1980; Fawcett, JES, *The Application of the European Convention on Human Rights*, 2nd edn, 1987; Jacobs, FG, *The European Convention on Human Rights*, 1975; Nedjati, Z, *Human Rights under the European Convention*, 1978; Harris, O'Boyle and Warbrick, *Law of the European Convention on Human Rights*, 1995; Dickson, B and Connelly, A, *Human Rights and the European Convention*, 1996; Farran, S, *The UK Before the European Court of Human Rights*, 1996.
2 The Declaration was adopted on 10 December 1948 by the General Assembly of the UN.

case reaches the stage of a final ruling adverse to the government in question, the government will be free to determine the extent of the changes needed in order to respond. This approach is also reflected in the doctrine of the 'margin of appreciation' which has been developed by the Strasbourg authorities. This doctrine, to which we will return below,[3] involves allowing the domestic authorities a degree of discretion in deciding what is needed to protect various public interests in their own countries even though such interests have an impact on protection for Convention rights. The use of this doctrine allows evasion of conflict over very sensitive issues between Strasbourg and the Member State. Of course, this may lead at times to an acceptance of a lower standard of human rights than some liberal critics would advocate, but it may be suggested that it can be a reasonably appropriate influence on the dealings between Strasbourg and democracies with generally sound human rights records.

When examining the substantive rights, they may be said to fall into two groups: Articles 2–7 covering the most basic human rights and containing, broadly speaking, no express exceptions[4] or narrow express exceptions, and Articles 8–12 which may be said to cover a more sophisticated or developed conception of human rights and which are subject to a broad range of express exceptions. Thus, under Articles 2–7 argument will tend to concentrate on the question of whether a particular situation falls within the compass of the right in question, whereas under Articles 8–11 it will largely concentrate on determining whether a particular exception will apply (Article 12 only contains one exception but of a very broad nature).[5] There is an enormous amount of overlap between the Articles and it may be found that weaknesses or gaps in one can be remedied by another, although the Convention will be interpreted as a harmonious whole. It will also be found that invocation of a substantive right in order to attack a decision in the national courts on its merits may sometimes fail, but that a challenge to the *procedure* may succeed under one of the Articles explicitly concerned with fairness in the adjudicative process – Articles 5, 6 and 7.[6] The rights and freedoms are largely concerned with civil and political rather than social and economic matters; the latter are governed by the 1961 European Social Charter and the 1966 International Covenant on Economic, Social and Cultural Rights.[7]

---

3   At pp 82–85.
4   Article 6 provides that trial judgments should be pronounced publicly except where *inter alia* the interest of morals, public order or national security demand otherwise but the primary right – to a fair hearing – is not subject to these exceptions.
5   See below pp 71–72.
6   This point is developed below; see p 47. See Gearty, CA, 'The European Court of Human Rights and the Protection of Civil Liberties: An Overview' (1993) *CLJ* 89 for argument that the Convention as a whole is largely concerned with *procedural* rights.
7   (1965) Cmnd 2643; see Harris, DJ, *The European Social Charter*, 1984. The charter does not have a system of petitions. On a universal level the UK is also party to the 1966 International Covenant on Economic, Social and Cultural Rights, Cmnd 6702. It is not enforceable as regards the UK by individual petition.

The Convention has grown by way of additional protocols so that it now creates a more advanced human rights regime based on Articles 2–12 with the First Protocol[8] in conjunction with the Fourth,[9] Sixth[10] and Seventh[11] Protocols. However, the UK is not a party to any of these later Protocols, which may suggest that although there is a measure of harmony between the basic Convention regime and the UK legal system, this is not clearly the case as far as the more advanced regime is concerned.

In considering the operation of the Convention in practice it should be remembered that it was not intended to mimic the working of a domestic legal system. Thus individuals may not at present take a case directly to the European Court of Human Rights in Strasbourg[12] and in fact it is a feature of the Court that it hears very few cases in comparison with the number of applications made.[13] However, its jurisprudence has had an enormous impact, not merely through the outcome of specific cases, but in a general symbolic, educative and preventive sense. Its function in raising awareness of human rights is of particular significance in the UK since no domestic instrument is able to do so.

The enormous increase in the number of applications from the UK since the early days of the Convention suggests that more than any other institution it is coming to be seen as a guardian of human rights by UK citizens, although to an extent it may hold out a promise which it cannot fulfil. The immensely slow and difficult route to Strasbourg is becoming more so due to the number of applications despite improvements in the mechanisms for considering them.[14] The fact that an application may take at present five years to be heard is perhaps one of the main deficiencies of the Convention enforcement machinery;[15] this chapter therefore devotes some time to explaining that process and the highly significant part played in it by the European Commission on Human Rights before going on to consider the substantive rights. However, it must be remembered that the Convention does not only

---

8   Cmnd 9221. All the parties to the Convention except Switzerland are parties to this Protocol which came into force in 1954.
9   Cmnd 2309. It came into force in 1968; the UK is not a party.
10 (1983) 5 EHRR 167. It came into force in 1985. The UK is not a party.
11 (1984) 7 EHRR 1. It came into force in 1988. The UK is not a party. Note that the other Protocols are concerned with the procedural machinery of the Convention.
12 When the Eleventh Protocol comes into force individuals will have the right to take a case directly to the Court.
13 In 1991 the Commission registered 1648 applications; it referred 93 cases to the Court which gave judgment in 72. European Court of Human Rights, Survey of Activities 1959–91.
14 New procedures were introduced under the Eighth Protocol including a summary procedure for rejecting straightforward cases.
15 The *average* time is a little over four years: see 'Reform of the Control Systems', 15 EHRR 321, p 360 para 7. However, improvements, are due to be introduced under reforms discussed in this document. See below pp 22–24.

operate as an external force; as explained in Chapter 3, it can influence UK law through decisions in UK courts.

2 THE SUPERVISORY PROCEDURE FOR THE CONVENTION

Under Article 19, the Convention set up the European Commission on Human Rights (hereafter referred to as 'the Commission') and the European Court of Human Rights (hereafter referred to as 'the Court'). Thus, although the Convention may be weak in UK domestic law, the machinery for its enforcement is impressive compared to that used in respect of other Human Rights' Treaties, particularly the 1966 International Covenant on Civil and Political Rights which as far as the UK is concerned has been enforceable only through a system of assessment of national reports.[16]

Creation of the Commission, however, represented a compromise: it was thought too controversial merely to allow citizens to take their governments before the Court. There was a feeling that an administrative body might be more sympathetic to Member States' cases and the Member State might feel less on trial than in the Court. Therefore the Commission was created as an administrative barrier between the individual and the Court and is used as a means of filtering out a very high proportion of cases, thus considering far more cases than the Court. This may seem a strange device: most European Community lawyers would be horrified at the idea of creating a European Commission to keep cases out of the European Court of Justice; they would feel that for justice to be done the individual's case must be considered by the Court itself rather than by an administrative body reaching its decisions in secret.[17] Nevertheless, in human rights matters the Commission has been until recently viewed as an acceptable and useful device. That view has recently undergone a change which has led to the proposal for merger of the Commission with the Court;[18] we will return to this matter below.

The role of the European Commission on Human Rights

The main role of the Commission is to filter out cases as inadmissible, thereby reducing the work load of the Court. However, it also has another role: it tries to reach a friendly settlement between the parties and can give its opinion on the merits of the case if it is not intended that a final judgment should be

---

16 The Optional Protocol to the Covenant governs the right of individual petition; but it has not been ratified by the UK. For comment on the general efficacy of the reporting system see (1980) HRLJ, pp 136–70.

17 The Commission's sessions are held *in camera* (Article 33).

18 See 'Reform of the Control System', 15 EHRR 321.

given. It can also refer the case to the Court or the Committee of Ministers for the final judgment.

The Commission consists of one member for every Member State.[19] The members are elected by the Committee of Ministers[20] and their period of service is managed with a view to ensuring that the membership will change constantly.[21] The members of the Commission (who are unsalaried) are not government representatives; Article 23 provides that they serve 'in their individual capacity'.[22] In the UK members have tended to come from within the government, thus raising some doubt as to their neutrality. Apart from the criterion contained in Article 23, members of the Commission are in practice expected to display high moral integrity, have a recognised competence in human rights matters and have substantial legal experience.[23] The Commission decides by a majority of votes (Article 34) and the President has the casting vote.[24] As it is a part time body which usually only sits for about 14 weeks a year, it tends to build up a backlog of cases, thus contributing to the long delay in dealing with applications.

The role of the Commission has come under review for a number of reasons. It is barely able to deal with the number of applications it receives and as more states which used to be part of the Soviet Union or Yugoslavia become signatories to the Convention this problem will be exacerbated, especially as such countries do not have as developed a system for protection for human rights as the old Member States and so will use the Convention as a means of developing such protection. Thus, although a two tier system involving two part time bodies may have been an acceptable control mechanism when the Convention was drawn up, it has become much less appropriate. Moreover, although the notion of involvement of an administrative body in dealing with cases may have been acceptable in 1950 it arguably detracts from the authority of the Convention. The Parliamentary

---

19 Under Article 20 no two members of the Commission may be nationals of the same state.

20 Under Article 21 the members of the Commission were elected by the Committee of Ministers by an absolute majority of votes, from a list of names drawn up by the Bureau of the Consultative Assembly and this procedure is followed as far as it is applicable when a state becomes a party to the Convention and when vacancies have to be filled.

21 Under Article 22 the members of the Commission are elected for a period of six years and may be re-elected. However, of the members elected at the first election, the terms of seven members chosen by lot shall expire at the end of three years. In order to ensure that, as far as possible, one half of the membership of the Commission is renewed every three years, the Committee of Ministers may decide that the term of office of a member to be elected shall be for a period other than six years but not more than nine and not less than three years.

22 The members usually hold other posts in their own countries as university professors, legal advisers or judges. They are aided by the lawyers on the staff of the Commission.

23 Protocol number 8 requires that members 'must either possess the qualifications required for appointment to judicial office or be persons of recognised competence in national or international law'.

24 The Commission has drawn up its own rules of procedure (Article 36).

Assembly of the Council of Europe has therefore recommended that the Commission and the Court should be merged into one body which would sit full time – a new Court of Human Rights.[25] It was proposed[26] that the new Court would come into operation in 1995 and that there would be a transitional period from 1995 to 2000 during which the old Commission and Court would hear cases already referred to them while new cases would be referred to the new Court. On 11 March 1994 all but one of the contracting parties signed Protocol 11, which will greatly change the control mechanism when it comes into force.[27]

It may be argued that if the Court and Commission do merge the authority of the Convention will increase because its jurisprudence will no longer be influenced by the decisions of an administrative body. If the control system becomes more akin to that of a domestic legal system this might mean that UK judges will become more reluctant to rule contrary to the Convention and will seek more diligently to discover leeway in the law in order to avoid doing so.

The European Court of Human Rights[28]

Terms of membership of the Court, governed by Articles 38–43 of the Convention, are intended to ensure that the judges will act independently of their own governments. Under Article 38 each Member State will send one judge to the Court[29] who must be 'of high moral character and must either possess the qualifications required for appointment of high judicial office or be jurisconsults of recognised competence'. Rule 4 of the Rules of Procedure provides that a judge may not exercise his functions while he is a member of a government or while he holds a post or exercises a profession which is likely to affect confidence in his independence. However, this does not mean that a judge may not have served within the government and in fact UK judges have come from the Foreign and Commonwealth Office's Legal Advisers

---

25 See 'Reform of the Control Systems', 15 EHRR 321. For comment see Mowbray, A [1993] *PL* 419.

26 Recommendation 1194 adopted on 6 October 1992 by the Parliamentary Assembly of the Council of Europe.

27 Under Article 5 of the protocol it will come into force one year after it has been ratified by all the Member States. See (1994) 15 HRLJ 86. The merger procedure will be completed in November 1998 when the Commission will be abolished. Adoption of Protocol 11 represents a very radical reform. For discussion see eg Schermers, 'The Eleventh Protocol to the European Convention on Human Rights' (1994) 19 *EL Rev* 367, 378 and (1995) *EL Rev* 3; Lord Lester of Herne Hill QC [1996] *PL* 5.

28 For discussion of the role of the Court in interpreting the Convention see Gearty, CA, 'The European Court of Human Rights and the Protection of Civil Liberties' (1993) *CLJ* 89.

29 A list of persons is nominated by the Members of the Council of Europe and they are then elected by the Consultative Assembly. Under Article 39 each member shall nominate three candidates, of whom two at least shall be its nationals. Countries which are not yet parties to the Convention may have judges on the Court as have Hungary, Czechoslovakia, Poland and Bulgaria with representatives from Estonia, Latvia and Lithuania expected.

department which is responsible for defending the government in Strasbourg. The judges serve for longer than the members of the Commission (usually nine years) but the Court will not have the same composition for all that time because the terms of certain members expire earlier than those of others.[30] The form of the Court is governed by Article 43 which provides that it will consist of a Chamber composed of seven judges.[31] Like the Commission it sits temporarily[32] and its decisions are taken on a majority vote. Its hearings are, however, public.

The Court has jurisdiction under Article 45 of the Convention to consider all cases which raise issues as to the application of the Convention. Its constitution and jurisdiction were governed by the Convention Articles 19–56, but under Protocol 11 these Articles will be replaced by a revised Section II of the Convention (Articles 19–51).

The Court has increased enormously in standing and efficacy over the last 20 years, partly due to its activism and creativity in interpreting the Convention and its willingness to find that Member States have violated the rights of individuals. It has been pointed out that an explosion in the number of cases it considered occurred in the 1980s as lawyers in the different European Countries realised that it held out the possibility of a remedy for their clients and also of bringing about important legal change.[33] It may be considered the European constitutional Court as far as human rights matters are concerned. As originally set up, however, the Court did not bear a great resemblance to a domestic supreme or higher court in a number of respects. In particular, individuals could not take a case directly to it and its role was restricted due to the likelihood that the European Commission on Human Rights might find a case inadmissible. On 1 October 1994, when Protocol 9 came into force for the 13 states which consented to it, the individual or a group of individuals was added to the bodies who can refer a case to the Court, under amendments to Articles 44 and 48. The UK was not one of the consenting parties. Protocol 9 will be repealed by Protocol 11 which will in future govern the ability of individuals to refer cases to the Court. Under Protocol 9 Article 48 as amended, an individual can refer a case to the Court only after it has been screened by a panel of three members of the Court. If it

---

30 Under Article 40 the members of the Court shall be elected for a period of nine years. They may be re-elected. However, of the members elected at the first election the terms of four members shall expire at the end of three years and the terms of four more members shall expire at the end of six years chosen by lot. The Consultative Assembly may decide, before proceeding to any subsequent election, that the term or terms of office of one or more members to be elected shall be for a period other than nine years but not more than 12 and not less than six years.

31 The names of the judges are chosen by lot by the president before the opening of the case. The judge who is a national of any state party concerned will sit as an *ex officio* member of the Chamber.

32 It sits for about 80–90 days a year (see 15 EHRR 322, at p 327).

33 See Harris, O'Boyle and Warbrick, p 648.

does not raise a 'serious question affecting the interpretation or application of the Convention' and does not for any other reason warrant consideration by the Court the panel may decide that it should not be considered by the Court (Article 5(2)).

Under the present arrangements if an application is found inadmissible the case will not reach the Court. If it is found admissible but a friendly settlement is reached, the Court may not be required to decide on the application of the Convention (see below). Thus, the question of admissibility and the mechanism allowing for a friendly settlement are crucial within the system for enforcing the Convention. The possibility of avoiding judicial involvement may mean that a lower standard of human rights than that allowed by the Convention is maintained. From November 1998, under Protocol 11, admissibility and the examination of the merits with a view to reaching a friendly settlement will be undertaken by the Court . This is generally seen as likely to represent a more satisfactory arrangement since a judicial as opposed to an administrative body will be making the key decisions. Nevertheless, since the admissibility criteria remain unchanged under Protocol 11, current criticism of them will still be applicable in future.

Under Protocol 11 the Court will sit in Chambers of seven judges and in a Grand Chamber of 17 judges. Under Article 43 of Protocol 11 a party to a case may request that it be referred to the Grand Chamber within a period of three months from the date of the judgment of the Chamber. A panel of five judges from the Grand Chamber will accept the request if it raises a serious issue regarding the interpretation of the Convention or an issue of general importance. This procedure should represent a further significant improvement brought about by Eleventh Protocol since it seemed anomalous that a human rights Convention should make no provision for appeals. Nevertheless, adoption of the Eleventh Protocol will, *inter alia*, bring about quite radical changes in the role of the Court and therefore many critics view it as a risk.[34]

The Committee of Ministers

The Committee was not set up by the Convention; its composition and functions are regulated in the statute of the Council of Europe (Articles 13–21). The Committee consists of one representative from the government of each Member State of the Council of Europe, usually the Minister for Foreign Affairs.[35] The Committee is therefore a political body which is nevertheless

---

34 See eg Schermers, 'The Eleventh Protocol to the European Convention on Human Rights' (1994) 19 *EL Rev* 367, 378.

35 If an alternative is nominated he or she should also be a member of the government (Article 14).

performing a judicial role. Like the creation of the Commission, this is the result of a compromise; it was thought when the Convention was drafted that a Court of Human Rights with full compulsory jurisdiction would be too controversial and would therefore be unacceptable to all Member States. However, like the Commission, its role has been viewed with increasing dissatisfaction and once under the Protocol II reforms the new Court is established the Committee will no longer discharge an adjudicatory function.

The right of complaint: inter-state applications

Under Article 24 any contracting party may refer to the Commission, through the Secretary General of the Council of Europe, any alleged breach of the provisions of the Convention by another contracting party. The violation in question may be against any person; it need not be a national of the complainant state. Further, it can be an abstract application: one that does not allege a violation against any specified person but concerns incompatibility of a state's legislation or administrative practices with the Convention. There have been 18 inter-state applications so far but more than one complaint has sprung from the same situation; only six situations have in fact given rise to complaints. Thus this right has not proved effective; generally speaking states prefer not to sour their relations with other states if no interest of their own is involved. Therefore inter-state complaints have had a much less significant impact on human rights in the Member States than the individual's right of petition.

The right of complaint: individual applications

Article 25, widely viewed as the most important article in the Convention since it governs the right of individual complaint, enables UK citizens to seek a remedy for a breach of Convention rights by petitioning the European Commission. The Commission can receive petitions from any person, non-governmental organisation or group of individuals claiming to be the victim of a violation of one or more of the rights set forth in the Convention, provided that the state allegedly responsible for the violation has declared (as the UK has) that it recognises the competence of the Commission to receive such petitions. The individual need not be a national of the state in question but must be in some way subject to its jurisdiction.

The applicant must have been personally affected by the particular violation; it is not possible to bring an abstract complaint. Therefore an application alleging that Norwegian abortion legislation conflicted with Article 2 (guaranteeing protection of life) failed because the applicant did not allege that he had been personally affected by it (*X v Norway*).[36] However, there are two exceptions to this principle. First, the application can have a mixed nature: it can be partly abstract so long as there has been some personal impact on the applicant. In *Donnelly v UK*[37] the complaint concerned the allegation that the applicants had been tortured during their detention in Northern Ireland. They also wanted a full investigation of the whole system of interrogation employed by the security forces. It was found that so long as the applicants had been *affected*, a more wide-ranging review was possible in the public interest, and the complaint was admissible on that basis. Secondly, a potential victim may make a complaint if the circumstances are such that the complainant is unsure whether or not he or she is a victim of a violation of a Convention right. This was found to be the case in a complaint concerning the possibility that the applicants' telephones were being tapped (*Klass v Federal Republic of Germany*)[38] where by virtue of the very nature of the action complained of, it was impossible for the applicants to be certain that they had been affected.

The process of making a complaint is a long drawn out one and extremely cumbersome despite some improvement to it undertaken in 1990 under the Eighth Protocol. There are a very large number of hurdles to be overcome which arise in particular from the question of admissibility. A number of stages can be identified.

Pre-complaint

At this stage, before contacting the Commission, it must appear that:
(1) *Prima facie*, a violation of one or more of the rights or freedoms contained in the Convention has taken place. This refers to Articles 2–12 and, as far as the UK is concerned, Protocol 1.
(2) The available UK remedies have been exhausted (Article 26).
(3) The application has been made within six months of the final decision of the highest competent court or authority (Article 26).

These questions will be considered at the stage of determination of admissibility so they will not be considered now, but chronologically speaking they arise before the question of admissibility and it should be borne in mind that *prima facie* they must be fulfilled before the complaint can be set in motion. Whether they are fulfilled will be determined by the Commission.

---

36 Appl 867/60, Yearbook IV pp 270, 276; see also *Vijayanathan v France* (1992) 15 EHRR 62.
37 Appl 5577–82/72, Yearbook XVI.
38 Judgment of 6 September 1978 A.28 (1979–80); 2 EHRR 214 (see (1980) 130 *NLJ* 999).

The European Convention on Human Rights

It is worth noting that of 15,911 applications submitted to the Commission up to December 1989 only 670 were ultimately declared admissible.[39]

Registration of the complaint

Registration merely means that an application is pending before the Commission; it has no bearing on admissibility. However, the Secretary to the Commission may draw the attention of the complainant to the case law of the Commission by way of a standard letter, suggesting that the complaint had better be withdrawn. Thus not all complaints are registered. This practice is open to criticism since it appears to the applicant that the application is inadmissible, whereas formally only the Commission should rule on admissibility. It is an additional means of cutting down on the very large number of applications.

Determination of the admissibility of the complaint

Determining the question of admissibility is the Commission's main function and it is the main method of filtering out applications. The complaint must satisfy the admissibility conditions as follows:

(1) The application must not constitute an abuse of the right of complaint.[40] This condition is not often used; it concerns either the aim of applicant – it may appear that the case is obviously being brought for political propaganda purposes – or his or her conduct.

(2) The matter must not be the same as a matter already examined.[41] This means that unless it contains relevant new information, the complaint must not concern a matter which is substantially the same as a matter which has already been examined by the Commission or has already been submitted to another procedure or international investigation or settlement. The limitation in respect of complaints submitted to another international organ has not in practice been of significance; no UK complaints have been rejected on this basis. This is mainly because the UK has not accepted the individual right of complaint to the UN Covenant on Civil and Political Rights. The limitation in respect of previous complaints made to the Commission itself appears to refer to identical applications by the *same* applicant. If it referred to identical applications by another applicant that would militate against the general principle of individual petition. If the same applicant makes a complaint, new *facts* are needed if it is not to be rejected.

---

39 Noted in *Theory and Practice of the ECHR*, p 52: figures from European Commission on HR Survey of Activities and Statistics, 1989, p 16.
40 Article 27(2).
41 Article 27(b).

(3) The application must not be incompatible with the provisions of the Convention.[42] This provision encompasses a number of aspects. Incompatibility will occur if:

- (a) the application claims violation of a right not guaranteed by the Convention. This includes the substantive rights of s 1 and, as far as the UK is concerned, the First Protocol. However, it may be that the right in question does not appear in the Convention but that if the claim is not granted, violation of one of the Convention rights might then occur; the right claimed may thereby acquire indirect protection.

- (b) the application claims violation of a right which is the subject of a derogation (Article 15) or reservation (Article 64) by the relevant Member State.[43] Thus the right does appear in the Convention but the state in question is not at present bound to abide by it. A reservation is made when a state ratifies the Convention, while a derogation may be made if an emergency arises, thus suspending part of the state's Convention obligations. Some rights, as will be seen, are non-derogable, because they are viewed as particularly fundamental.

- (c) the applicant or respondent are persons or states incompetent to appear before the Commission. An application from an individual can only be directed against those states which are contracting parties and have made the declaration referred to in Article 25. Further, the complaint must be directed against an organ of government, not against individuals. However, the violation of the Convention by an individual may involve the responsibility of the state. The state may have encouraged the acts in question or failed to prevent or remedy them. Thus the condition will be fulfilled if the state is in some way responsible for the alleged violation. This is an aspect of the phenomenon known as *Drittwurkung* which means that human rights provisions can affect the legal relations between private individuals, not only between individuals and the public authorities.[44]

- (d) the application is aimed at the destruction or limitation of one of the rights or freedoms guaranteed by the Convention and therefore conflicts with Article 17. The intention is to prevent an applicant claiming a right which would enable him or her to carry out activities which ultimately would lead to the destruction of the guaranteed rights. Therefore the Commission rejected the application of the banned German communist party due to its aims (*Kommunistische*

---

42 Article 27(2).
43 These provisions are discussed below, at pp 78–81.
44 See Van Dijk and Van Hoof, Chap 1 Part 6. For commentary on *Drittwurkung* see Alkema, EA, 'The Third Party Applicability or *Drittwurkung* of the ECHR in Protecting Human Rights' in *The European Dimension*, 1988, pp 33–45.

Partei Deutschland v Federal Republic of Germany).[45] This provision suggests that the Convention adopts a teleological view of freedom; in other words, freedom is valued instrumentally as something which will lead to benefit for society as a whole, rather than being a good in itself.

(4) Domestic remedies must have been exhausted.[46] In brief, this means that the applicant must provide *prima facie* evidence of exhaustion of remedies. The burden then shifts to the state to show that a remedy was reasonably ascertainable by the applicant, that the remedy does exist and has not been exhausted and that the remedy is effective. The requirement that domestic remedies must have been exhausted refers to: the 'legal remedies available under the local law which are in principle capable of providing an effective and sufficient means of redressing the wrongs for which ... the Respondent State is said to be responsible'.[47] If there is a doubt as to whether a remedy is available, Article 26 will not be satisfied unless the applicant has taken proceedings in which that doubt can be resolved.[48] This generally means that judicial procedures must be instituted up to the highest court which can affect the decision but also, if applicable, appeal must be made to administrative bodies. The applicant only needs to exhaust those possibilities which offer an *effective* remedy, so if part of the complaint is the *lack* of a remedy under Article 13 then the application is not likely to be ruled inadmissible on this ground.[49] A remedy will be ineffective if according to established case law there appears to be no chance of success[50] and the Commission will decide whether a remedy did in fact offer the applicant the possibility of sufficient redress. If there is a doubt as to whether a given remedy is able to offer a real chance of success that doubt must be resolved in the national court itself. It has been held that judicial review is a sufficient remedy.[51] The application must have been submitted within a period of six months from the date on which the final national decision was taken (Article 26). Time runs from the decision taken by the last national authority that had to be used and after the point when the decision has been notified to the applicant and ineffective remedies will not be taken into account in assessing the point from which time runs.

(5) The application must not be manifestly ill-founded (Article 27(2)). This admissibility condition hands very significant power to the Commission.

---

45 Appl 250/57, Yearbook 1 (1955–57) Vol 6 p 222.
46 Article 26 and 27(3).
47 *Nielsen*, Appl 343/57, Yearbook II (1958–59) p 412.
48 *De Vargattirgah v France*, Appl 9559/81.
49 *X v UK* (1981) Appl 7990/77, D and R 24.
50 Appl 5874 172, Yearbook XVII (1974).
51 See *Vilvarajah and Four Others v UK* (1991) Judgment of 30 October 1991; A.12 (1991).

Formally speaking the Commission should not decide on the merits of the application. Yet when it makes a determination as to manifest ill-foundedness it is pronouncing on the merits because it is determining whether or not a *prima facie* violation has taken place. Thus this condition creates an extension of the role of the Commission behind the cloak of merely determining admissibility: it may in fact be taking the *final* decision on the merits. It will find this condition unfulfilled if the facts obviously fail to disclose a violation. In theory this ground will only operate if the ill-founded character of the application is clearly manifest. It has been said that, 'the task of the Commission is not to determine whether an examination of the case submitted by the applicant discloses the actual violation of one of the rights and freedoms guaranteed by the Convention but only to determine whether it includes any possibility of the existence of such a determination'.[52] In practice the Commission goes further: the ill-founded character of the application may not always be so manifest. This is clear from the voting procedure: it is not necessary to have unanimity on this condition; a bare majority will be sufficient. It is arguable that it should have been necessary to have unanimity or a two-thirds majority as to manifest ill-foundedness even though a bare majority would suffice in respect of the other conditions.

The examination of the merits (Article 28)

The examination is undertaken with a view to securing a friendly settlement between the parties. The Commission appoints one or more of its members to conduct the initial examination and then draft a report. After this initial stage, the Commission will have one or two hearings which are characterised by their flexibility: the Commission considers itself free to decide on a procedure which can be tailored to the nature of a particular application and this may include visiting a particular place such as a prison. This procedure may take about two years. In making an examination the Commission is not in theory bound by its own previous reports, but in practice it is generally consistent.

If both parties are willing they can reach a friendly settlement as provided for under Article 28(1)(b) straight after the application has been declared admissible.[53] The settlement is a compromise; its danger is that it could result in lower standards of human rights in particular states than the Convention allows although, under Article 28(1)(b) the settlement should be in accordance with the Convention. This may mean that, if the state party in question is prepared to pay compensation and the victim is willing to receive it, the Commission may nevertheless demand that the state should alter its law and

---

52 *Pataki*, Appl 596/59, Yearbook III (1960).
53 If a friendly settlement is reached the Commission will draw up a report stating the facts and solution reached. Up to the end of 1989, 84 friendly settlements had been reached.

administrative practice. In other words, the Commission should have regard to its general purpose of improving human rights protection and not just the particular interest of the victim. By this means it can prevent many more applications from the same state alleging the same violation.

If no settlement is reached the Commission states its opinion as to the alleged violation in the Report to the Committee of Ministers.[54] The Report will generally only go to individual applicants if the Court considers it. It should be noted that having declared the application admissible the Commission may yet, after further examination, declare it inadmissible.[55]

The decision

(1) *The role of the Committee of Ministers*

The Committee of Ministers receives the Report and this may be all it does, but if there is no move by the Commission within three months to bring the case before the Court, the Committee will take the final decision (Article 32). Oddly, the Convention is silent as to when a case should go to the Court and when to the Committee of Ministers; the matter appears to be in the discretion of the Commission. In practice non-contentious cases are usually referred to the Committee. These include those cases which do not raise significant Convention issues and/or those which raise issues which concern established Convention case law. A sub-Committee will be appointed to examine the case which will decide by a two-thirds majority.[56] If it decides that there has been a violation, it will make suggestions as to the measures to be taken by a certain period and if they are not taken it will publish the report. This is a sanction: a degree of humiliation will flow from the declaration by all the Foreign Ministers of all the other Member States that a certain state has violated international human rights norms. Also, ammunition will thereby be offered to the opposition parties in the particular state. In practice if the Commission has given its opinion that a violation has occurred, the state in question has usually taken measures to address the violation and the Committee has not had to give judgment.

It may be noted that the position of the individual applicant before the Committee is very weak; he or she has no right to appear or to make

---

54 Article 31 provides that if a solution is not reached, the Commission shall draw up a report on the facts and state its opinion as to whether the facts found disclose a breach by the state concerned of its obligations under the Convention. The opinions of all the members of the Commission on this point may be stated in the report.

55 Article 29. At this stage if it is to be rejected it must be rejected unanimously. In such a case, the decision will be communicated to the parties.

56 In *Huber v Austria*, Report of 8 February 1973, D and R 2 (1935) and the *East African Asians* cases (1973) 3 EHRR 76, the Committee could not obtain a two-thirds majority as to the determination whether there had been a violation of the Convention; its resolution in both cases was to take no further action on the applications.

representations. The individual is in an equally weak position before the Court but the role of the Commission before the Court allows the individual's interests to be represented in a way which does not occur before the Committee.

(2) *The Court*

The Court cannot hear a case unless it has gone through all the Commission's procedure and a report has gone to the Committee of Ministers. The fact, as mentioned above, that the individual in question cannot refer the case to Court[57] did not seem odd at the inception of the Convention when the right of individual petition in itself seemed controversial but it does today. However, the Commission is likely to bring the case before the Court and does bring the vast majority of cases once it has found them admissible. In exercising its discretion as to bringing a case before the Committee of Ministers or the Court the Commission will be influenced by its nature. In general a difficult question will go to the Court while if the Commission is unanimous that no breach has occurred it will go to the Committee. The trend has been to refer more cases to the Court in relation to the number of cases declared admissible.

The Court is not bound by the Report of the Commission. The function of the Commission 'is to present to the Court the issues in the case and all the relevant information which we ourselves have obtained concerning the case'.[58] The Court may disagree with points of Commission's decisions; it may consider admissibility again and then reject the application as inadmissible. In other words the Court is no more bound by the Commission on admissibility than it is on opinion. It may be argued that this procedure does not maintain equality between the parties because a negative decision on admissibility will never come before the Court while a positive one will.[59] However, in practice the Court tends to agree with the Commission on admissibility. Nevertheless this and other aspects of the proceedings before the Court and Commission do involve a duplication of function which is time consuming and so supports the argument for abolition of the Commission.

The proceedings before the Chamber of seven judges will consist of a written stage, followed by a hearing.[60] An on-the-spot inquiry can be conducted by a delegate of the Court. The Court can also order a report from

---

57 Under Article 48 the following can bring a case before the Court: the Commission; a High Contracting Party whose national is alleged to be a victim; a High Contracting Party which referred the case to the Commission; a High Contracting Party against which the complaint has been lodged. But note that Protocol 11 would give the individual a right to seize the Court.

58 *Lawless*, A.1 (1960–61), p 360; (1961) 1 EHRR 15.

59 See *Van Oosterwijck v Belgium*, Judgment of 6 November 1980, A.40; (1981) 3 EHRR 557. The Court disagreed with the Commission's decision that the application was admissible; the Court held that local remedies had not been exhausted; thus the Court's decision was not on the merits.

60 Under Article 55 the Court shall draw up its own rules and determine its own procedure.

an expert on any matter. The Commission acts as an independent and impartial advisory organ in the proceedings. As is the case with the Committee, the applicant is in a weak position in the hearing. Previously he or she did not have any right to take part in the proceedings; now after a change in the rules of procedure in 1982 an applicant can be heard as a person providing clarification. However, the issue lies between the Court and the state to establish whether a violation has occurred. If it appears established, the state must attempt to demonstrate that the case falls within an exception to the right in question. The Court is not bound by its own judgments.[61] Nevertheless, it usually follows and applies its own precedents unless departure from them is indicated in order to ensure that interpretation of the Convention reflects social change.

The procedure before the Court may conclude before the judgment on the merits if the state settles. However, the Court does not have to discontinue the procedure; it can proceed in the interests of the Convention and may give a declaratory judgment even though the state is now willing to settle. The judgment does not state what remedial measures should be taken; it is up to the state to amend its legislation or make other changes in order to conform with the judgment. Thus a response may well be in doubtful conformity with the Convention.[62] The Court is not ultimately a coercive body and relies for acceptance of its judgments on the willingness of states to abide by the Convention. Under Article 51 reasons must be given for the judgment of the Court and if the judgment does not represent in whole or in part the unanimous opinion of the judges, any judge shall be entitled to deliver a separate opinion. Under Article 52 the judgment of the Court is at present final[63] and under Article 53 it is binding on the state party involved.

The Court can award compensation under Article 50. The purpose of the reparation is to place the applicant in the position he would have been in had the violation not taken place. It will include costs unless the applicant has received legal aid. It can also include loss of earnings, travel costs, fines and costs unjustly awarded against the applicant. It can also include intangible or non-pecuniary losses which may be awarded due to unjust imprisonment or stress.[64]

---

61 Rule 51 para 1 of the Rules of the Court.
62 The Contempt of Court Act 1981 may be said to represent such a response to the ruling that UK contempt law violated Article 10 in that it preserved common law contempt, which appears, especially since the decision in *AG v Times Newspapers Ltd* (see Chap 4 p 167), to give insufficient weight to freedom of speech.
63 As noted above this will no longer be the case under Article 43 of Protocol 11.
64 For example, in the *Young, James and Webster* case (1981) Judgment of 13 August 1981, A.44; (1981) 4 EHRR 38, pecuniary and non-pecuniary costs were awarded: the Court ordered £65,000 to be paid.

Supervision of the judgment by the Committee of Ministers

Under Article 54, the Committee is charged with supervising the execution of the Court's judgment. This includes both the judgment on the merits and on compensation. The Committee notes the action taken to redress the violation on the basis of information given by the state in question. If the state fails to execute the judgment the Committee decides what measures to take: it can bring political pressure to bear including suspension or even, as a final sanction, expulsion from the Council of Europe. Doubts have been raised over the fitness of the Committee to oversee one of the key stages in the whole Convention process, namely the implementation of national law to bring it into line with the findings of the Court. It is apparent that a rigorous analysis of the changes that the offending state has made in its law would be desirable, to ensure that the judgment is fully implemented and to make future similar breaches of the Convention by that state impossible. The Committee would not *prima facie* appear to be capable of carrying out such a quasi-judicial role and indeed it appears that in practice the Committee usually merely notes the receipt of the state's explanation of the changes it has made without any attempt to conduct the kind of analysis which it is suggested should be undertaken.

The question of the full implementation of a judgment of the Court arose in *Olsson v Sweden (No 2)*.[65] The applicants complained that despite a previous judgment of the Court to the effect that a violation of the Convention had occurred, the Swedish authorities had continued the practice which was contrary to the Convention. However, the Court found that the fresh complaint raised a new issue and that therefore the question as to whether the state had fulfilled its obligations under Article 53 by implementing the judgment did not arise. Thus, this judgment avoided addressing the Article 53 issue. However, it is suggested that the Court should be able to rule on the question whether measures introduced to implement its own judgment are sufficient. If it became clear that it could do so one of the main concerns regarding the procedure for supervising its judgments would be addressed, although there seems to be a case for also requiring more of the Committee in terms of analysing the measures taken to implement the judgment. The role of the Committee under Article 53 has been retained under Protocol 11, reflecting the view that its authority has played a part in persuading states to adopt measures implementing the judgment of the Court.

---

65 A.250. Note that a similar issue arose in *Christie v UK* (No 21482/93, 78–A DR 119) which was, however, found inadmissible by the Commission.

3 THE SUBSTANTIVE RIGHTS AND FREEDOMS

In what follows, an outline will be given of the scope of the Articles covering the substantive rights and freedoms. More detailed treatment of decisions which are relevant to particular areas of UK law will be undertaken when those areas of domestic law are considered.

Article 2: Protection of life

(1) Everyone's right to life shall be protected by law. No one shall be deprived of his life intentionally save in the execution of a sentence of a court following his conviction of a crime for which this penalty is provided by law.

(2) Deprivation of life shall not be regarded as inflicted in contravention of this Article when it results from the use of force which is not more than absolutely necessary:

   (a) in defence of any person from unlawful violence;

   (b) in order to effect a lawful arrest or to prevent the escape of a person lawfully detained;

   (c) in action lawfully taken for the purpose of quelling a riot or insurrection.

Scope of the right

Article 2 provides non-derogable protection of the right to life. This might seem straightforward – governments are enjoined to refrain from the wanton killing of their subjects – but aside from that instance it is in fact hard to determine what a right to life encompasses. Clearly, it is difficult to pinpoint the stage at which it may be said that the responsibility of a state for a person's death is so clear, the causal potency between the state's action or omission and the death so strong, that the right to life has been violated.[66]

Decisions under Article 2 have not yet entirely clarified this issue but they do suggest that two distinct duties are placed on the national authorities, although their scope is unclear. First, Article 2 places the public authorities under a duty not to take life except in certain specified circumstances. Secondly, Article 2 places a positive obligation on the state authorities to protect the right to life by law. This positive obligation may take a number of forms. It requires that reasonable steps be taken in order to enforce the law in

---

66 See further Sieghart, *The Lawful Rights of Mankind*, 1986, Chap 11.

order to protect citizens (*X v UK and Ireland*).[67] It was held in *W v UK*[68] that these measures will not be scrutinised in detail. Clearly, the state may not be able to prevent every attack on an individual without an enormous expenditure of resources. Therefore the Convention will leave a wide margin of discretion to the national authorities in this regard, although the state will be under some duty to maintain reasonable public security.[69] Where state agents' actions are very closely linked to the preservation of a known individual's life as, for example, the actions of police officers during a hostage situation, the state will be under a positive obligation not only to seek to preserve life but also to act reasonably in so doing. The need to preserve life in the immediate situation would appear to override the general duty to maintain state security and prevent crime. These notions seem to underlie the findings of the Commission in *Andronicus and Constantinou v Cyprus*.[70] Article 2 was found to have been violated by Cypriot police when, in attempting to deal with a siege situation in which a hostage had been taken, they fired a number of times at the hostage taker, killing the hostage. The number of bullets fired reflected, it was found, a response which lacked caution.

The positive obligation may also entail the taking of appropriate steps to safeguard life[71] but the breadth of this duty is unclear. It seems that it will include the provision of adequate medical care in prison[72] since in this instance the state is directly responsible for the welfare of citizens during their imprisonment. However, it is unclear how far the individual should have a right to secure the expenditure of resources so that the state can save or preserve his or her life. The state may bear some responsibility in a number of instances: a person might die due to poor housing conditions or due to a failure to impose a particular speed limit in poor driving conditions but it is doubtful whether Article 2 was intended to be read so widely as to cover such situations. It is unclear how far Article 2 places states under an obligation to seek to ensure the continuance of life where the individual involved or those acting on his or her behalf, wish it to end. The Commission has found that passively allowing a person to die need not attract criminal liability in order to satisfy Article 2.[73] This might apply to allowing a handicapped baby or a patient in a persistent

---

67 Appl 9829/82 (not published).
68 Appl 9348/81, D and R 32 (1983) p 190.
69 Appl 7145/75, *Association X v UK*, 14 D and R 31 (1979).
70 (1996) 22 EHRR CD 18.
71 *X v UK*, No 7154/75, 14 D and R 31 at 32 (1978).
72 *Simon-Herald v Austria*, App 430/69 CD 38 (the application was declared admissible and a friendly settlement was later reached).
73 *Widmer v Switzerland*, No 20527/92 (1993), unreported.

vegetative state to die.[74] However, a breach of Article 2 would probably be found where a positive act had occurred in order to end life.

Express or implied exceptions

The question has arisen in the context of national legislation on abortion whether an unborn baby can fall within the interpretation of 'everyone', but it has been determined that even if the foetus can be protected, its right to life will be weighed against the mother's life and physical and mental health.[75] In *Paton v UK*[76] it was found by the Commission that Article 2 applies only to persons who have been born. Had the Commission found otherwise, all national legislation in the Member States permitting abortion would have been in breach of Article 2 since abortion even to save the mother's life would not appear to be covered by any of the exceptions. *H v Norway*[77] clarified the position. The Commission found that the lawful abortion of a 14 week foetus on social grounds did not breach Article 2. It took this stance on the basis that since the state parties' laws on abortion differed considerably from each other, a wide margin of discretion should be allowed. It appears that the wider abortion laws within the Member States probably comply with Article 2, although in *Open Door Counselling v Ireland* the Court left open the possibility that Article 2 might place some restrictions on abortion.[78]

A very significant express exception to Article 2 is in respect of the death penalty, which also includes extradition to a country where the death penalty is in force.[79] Protocol 6 has now removed the death penalty exception but it has not been ratified by the UK. However, it might be possible to challenge use of the death penalty in countries which have not ratified Protocol 6 under other Convention rights such as Article 3.[80]

Generally speaking the para 2 exceptions are reasonably straightforward and are aimed mainly at unintentional deprivation of life. This was explained

---

[74] The position under British law seems to be that failing to intervene to save the life of a handicapped baby may be acceptable in some circumstances: see Arthur (unreported) discussed by Gunn and Smith [1985] *Crim LR* 705; *Re B (a minor)* [1981] 1 WLR 1421, CA. Allowing a patient in a persistent vegetative state to die will be acceptable if it can be said, objectively speaking, to be in his or her best interests because no improvement can be expected (*Airedale NHS Trust v Bland* (1993) *The Times*, 5 February, HL).
[75] *X v UK*, Appl 8416/79, D and R 19 (1980) p 244.
[76] (1980) 3 EHRR 408. It has been argued that a woman's right to an abortion must therefore have been impliedly accepted: Rendel, M (1991) 141 *NLJ* 1270.
[77] No 17004/90 (1992) unreported.
[78] Eur Ct HR, Judgment of 29 October 1992; (1992) 15 EHRR 244. For comment see 142 *NLJ* (1696).
[79] Appl 10227/82, *X v Spain*, D and R 37 (1984) p 93.
[80] See *Soering* below p 42 in relation to Article 3.

in *Stewart v UK*[81] which concerned the use of plastic bullets in a riot. It was found that para 2 is concerned with situations where the use of violence is allowed as necessary force and may as an unintended consequence result in loss of life. On this basis the use of plastic bullets was found to fall within its terms. However, paras 2(a), (b) and (c) also cover instances where the force used was bound to endanger life and was intended to do so but was necessary in the circumstances. Thus national laws recognising the right to use self-defence are in principle in harmony with para 2(a). Also, in certain circumstances the state can sanction the use of force with the intention of killing. It can do so, however, only when such force is absolutely necessary for the fulfilment of one of the para 2 purposes. This issue was considered by the Commission in *Kelly v UK*[82] in which a young joyrider was shot dead by soldiers in Northern Ireland when he tried to evade an army checkpoint. It was found that the application was manifestly ill-founded since the use of force was justified. However, it can be argued that this finding does not represent a strict application of a strict proportionality test. Kelly was apparently shot in order to prevent him escaping but it would not appear that it was 'absolutely necessary' to shoot to kill in the circumstances, since it might well have been possible to arrest him later.

The Court addressed the question of the strictness of the 'absolutely necessary' test in *McCann, Farrell and Savage v UK*,[83] the first judgment of the Court on Article 2. The case concerned the shooting by SAS soldiers of three IRA members on the street in Gibraltar. The UK argued that this was justified on the basis that they apparently had with them a remote control device which they might have used to detonate a bomb. The Court found that para 2 primarily describes situations 'where it is permitted to use force which may result, as an unintended outcome in the deprivation of life' but that para 2 would also cover the intentional deprivation of life. However, the use of force must be no more than absolutely necessary for the achievement of one of the para 2 purposes and the test of necessity to be used was stricter than that used in respect of the test under para 2 Articles 8–11. The main question for the Court was the extent to which the state's response to the perceived threat posed by the IRA members was proportionate to that threat. The Court found that the use of force could be justified where 'it is based on an honest belief which is perceived for good reason to be valid at the time but which subsequently turns out to be mistaken. To hold otherwise would be to impose an unrealistic burden on the state and its law enforcement personnel'.

---

81 Appl 10044/82, D and R 39 (1985); (1985) 7 EHRR 453; see also *Kelly v UK* (1993) 16 EHRR 20 in which the European Commission found that the use of force to prevent future terrorist acts was allowable. For criticism of the decision in *Kelly* see (1994) 144 *NLJ* 354.
82 Appl 17579/90, (1993) 16 EHRR CD 20; 74 D and R 139 (1993).
83 (1995) 21 EHRR 97, A.324, Council of Europe Report.

Following this finding the Court found that the actions of the soldiers who carried out the shooting did not amount to a violation of Article 2.

However, the organisation and planning of the whole operation had to be considered in order to discover whether the requirements of Article 2 had been respected. The Court focused on the decision not to arrest the suspects when they entered Gibraltar. This decision was taken because it was thought that there might have been insufficient evidence against them to warrant their charge and trial. However, this decision subjected the population of Gibraltar to possible danger. The Court considered that taking this factor into account and bearing in mind that they had been shadowed by the SAS soldiers for some time, the suspects could have been arrested at that point. Further, there was quite a high probability that the suspects were on a reconnaissance mission at the time of the shootings and not a bombing mission. This possibility, the possibility that there was no car bomb or that the suspects had no detonator was not conveyed to the soldiers and since they were trained to shoot to kill, the killings were rendered almost inevitable. All these factors were taken into account in finding that the killing of the three constituted a use of force which was more than absolutely necessary in defence of persons from unlawful violence within the meaning of para 2(a) Article 2. The state had sanctioned killing by state agents in circumstances which gave rise to a breach of Article 2.

This was a bold decision which departs from the stance taken in *Kelly*. It emphasises that a strict proportionality test must be used in determining issues under para 2 of Article 2. Applying this test, it would appear that where an alternative to the deliberate use of deadly force exists it should always be taken. It would therefore seem that the use of such force to effect an arrest would never be justified except where in the circumstances there was near-certainty that the suspect would kill if allowed to escape. This might apply, for example, in situations where hostages had been taken and threats against them issued. It would also apply in circumstances similar to those arising in *McCann* but where no opportunity for apprehension had previously arisen and where there was a stronger likelihood that a bomb might be about to be detonated. In such instances, of course, both sub-paras (a) and (b) of Article 2(2) would be in question and it therefore appears that the *McCann* judgment leaves little room for the operation of sub-para (b) independently of sub-para (a).

McCann and *Kelly* make clear the partially subjective nature of the judgment as to when the use of deadly force is 'absolutely necessary'. Article 2 itself does not make it clear whether the phrase 'absolutely necessary' is to be treated objectively or subjectively. On its face it is unclear whether Article 2 would be breached where the person using such force honestly believed, due to a mistake, that it was necessary although in actuality it was not. In such a case Article 2 would not be breached if there were also reasonable grounds for believing that such force was necessary. It may be noted that this stance is not in accord with UK law which allows the use of force, including deadly force, so long as an honest (not necessarily reasonable) belief is formed that force is required,[84] and the force used is in proportion to the circumstances as the defendant believed them to be.[85] Thus, an objective test is only used in relation to the question of the proportionality between the apparent circumstances and the force used.[86]

Article 3: Freedom from inhuman treatment

> No one shall be subjected to torture or to inhuman or degrading treatment or punishment.

Article 3 contains no exceptions and it is also non-derogable. Thus, on the face of it, once a state has been found to have fallen within its terms no justification is possible.[87] However, it has been suggested that the exceptions to Article 2 must be taken as applying also to Article 3 since if the state in certain circumstances may justifiably take life, it must be justifiable *a fortiori* to inflict lesser harm on citizens in the same circumstances.[88] This may be correct but should not be taken to mean that all the exceptions to Article 2 apply to all forms of Article 3 treatment. The Article 2 exceptions suggest elements of immediacy which would be applicable to severe wounding but not usuallyto, for example, the form of torture, severe beating of all parts of the body to extract information, which occurred in the *Greek* case.[89]

Article 3 has been interpreted widely as to the forms of treatment it covers which include some not readily associated with the terms it uses. Even so, its width has not yet been fully realised; it could be used, for example, in relation to involuntary medical intervention such as sterilisation or caesarean section. In determining the standard of treatment applicable below which a state will be in breach of Article 3 a common European standard is applied, but also all the factors in the situation are taken into account.[90] Thus it does not connote an absolute standard and in its application it allows for a measure of discretion. It is clear that in order to determine this issue *present* views must be considered rather than the views at the time when the Convention was drawn up. The circumstances must include those falling within Article 2(2), since if life may be taken by the state in certain restricted circumstances it must follow that severe wounding, although not all forms of Article 3 treatment, would be

---

84 *Williams* [1987] 3 All ER 411.
85 *Owino* [1995] *Crim LR* 743.
86 This seems to be have been the basis of the decision of the House of Lords in *Clegg* [1995] 2 WLR 80 which concerned a killing of a joyrider by a soldier in Northern Ireland.
87 *Ireland v UK* (1976) 2 EHRR 25.
88 See Harris, O'Boyle and Warbrick, *Law of the European Convention on Human Rights*, 1995, p 56.
89 (1969) Yearbook XII 1 at 504 Com Rep; CM Res DH (70) 1.
90 The *Greek* case (1969), Yearbook XII 186–510.

justified in those circumstances. Similarly, state laws allowing wounding by private individuals in self-defence would not appear to be in breach of Article 3 so long as they were in accord with para 2 of Article 2.

The three forms of treatment mentioned seem to represent three different levels of seriousness. Thus, torture, unlike degrading treatment, has been quite narrowly defined to include 'deliberate inhuman treatment causing very serious and cruel suffering'.[91] Clearly, treatment which could not come within this restricted definition could still fall within one of the other two heads, especially the broad head – 'degrading treatment'. Degrading treatment will not, however, inevitably include *all* forms of physical punishment, although it will include certain forms of corporal punishment including caning[92] which has been found not to amount to torture or inhuman treatment. Corporal punishment which could be said to be of a 'normal' type may be distinguished, it seems, from degrading corporal punishment.[93] Thus, the mere fact that physical punishment is administered will not, without more, necessarily involve a breach of Article 3 and nor will the mere threat of such punishment.[94]

A number of cases have arisen concerning the position of detainees. In determining whether a particular treatment, such as solitary confinement, amounts to a violation of Article 3 a number of factors must be taken into account. These will include the stringency and duration of the measure, the objective pursued – such as the need for special security measures for the prisoner in question[95] or the fear of stirring up discontent among other prisoners[96] – and the effect on the person concerned. The applicant will need to submit medical evidence showing the causal relationship between the prison conditions complained of and his or her deterioration in mental and physical health. If the adverse treatment has been adopted as a result of the claimant's own uncooperative behaviour it is probable that no breach will be found.[97]

Article 3 can be used in a very broad way to bring rights within the scope of the Convention which are not expressly included. Thus, Article 3 could be

---

91 *Ireland v UK* above note 87.
92 *Tyrer*, Judgment of 25 April 1978, A.26; (1978) 2 EHRR 1. In *Warwick v UK*, Eur Comm HR Report of 15 June 1986, the Commission considered that corporal punishment in schools amounted to degrading treatment.
93 *Costello-Roberts v UK*, Judgment of 25 March 1993; A.247-C (1993); (1993) *The Times*, 26 March.
94 *Campbell and Cosans*, Judgment of 25 February 1982, A.48; (1982) 4 EHRR 293.
95 In *Kröcher and Möller v Switzerland* D and R 34 (1983); (1984) 6 EHRR 345 it was found that harsh conditions imposed to ensure security may not constitute a violation of Article 3.
96 Appl 8324/78 *X v UK* (not published) the ability to encourage other prisoners to acts of indiscipline was taken into account.
97 Appl 9907/82, *M v UK* D and R 35 (1984) (dangerous behaviour of detainee taken into account in considering conditions).

invoked in relation to discriminatory treatment on the basis of race and possibly on the basis of sex or sexual orientation because such treatment can be termed degrading according to the Commission in the *East African Asians* cases.[98] This possibility could help to compensate for the weakness of the Article 14 guarantee against discrimination which does not create an independent right.[99]

Other rights which otherwise would not be recognised under the Convention include the right to remain in a certain country. Violation of Article 3 may occur because of the treatment a person may receive when returning to his or her own country having been expelled or refused admission. It will have to be clearly established that the danger of such treatment is really present. The question arose in *Soering v UK*[100] whether expulsion to a country (the US) where the applicant risked the death penalty would be compatible with Article 3 because it would subject him to conditions on Death Row likely to cause him acute mental anguish. Of course, since Article 2 specifically excludes the death penalty from its guarantee, the possibility of its use cannot in itself create a violation of Article 3 because that would render those words of Article 2 otiose. The Convention must be read as a whole. However, the Court found that the manner and circumstances of the implementation of the death penalty could give rise to an issue under Article 3. The Court held that it had to consider the length of detention prior to the execution, the conditions on Death Row, the applicant's age and his mental state. Bearing these factors in mind, especially the very long period of time spent on Death Row and the mounting anguish as execution was awaited, it was found that expulsion would constitute a breach of Article 3. (In response to this ruling the UK and USA agreed to drop the charges to non-capital murder and then extradite the applicant.)

The principle laid down in *Soering* was followed in *Chahal v UK*.[101] Originally an illegal immigrant, Mr Chahal obtained leave to remain in Britain indefinitely in 1974. In 1984 he visited the Punjab for a family wedding and met the chief advocate of creating an independent Sikh state. Later he was arrested by Indian police and allegedly tortured. He escaped from India and became the founder of the International Sikh Youth Federation in the UK. In 1990 he was arrested after a meeting at a Southall temple. The Home Office accused him of involvement in Sikh terrorism and decided to deport him on national security grounds. He sought asylum on the ground that he would be tortured if sent back to India and applied to the European Commission, alleging *inter alia* a breach of Article 3. The Court found that since there were

---

98 (1973) 3 EHRR 76.
99 See below pp 76–78.
100 Judgment of 7 July 1989, A.161; (1989) 11 EHRR 439. For discussion see *Schabas* (1994) 43 ICLQ 913.
101 (1997) 23 EHRR 413; (1996) *The Times*, 28 November; (1996) *Guardian*, 16 November.

strong grounds for believing that Mr Chahal would indeed have been tortured had he been returned to India a breach of Article 3 had occurred.[102]

For a breach of Article 3 to be established in the context of deportation or extradition cases, there must be a clear risk of ill treatment; a 'mere possibility' will be insufficient. In *Vilvarajah and Four Others v the UK*[103] the applicants, Sri Lankan Tamils, arrived in the UK in 1987 and applied for political asylum under the UN Convention of 1951 Relating to the Status of Refugees, contending that they had a well-founded fear of persecution if returned to Sri Lanka. The Home Secretary rejected the applications and the applicants sought unsuccessfully to challenge the rejection by means of judicial review. The applicants were then returned to Sri Lanka where, they alleged, four of them were arrested and ill-treated. They claimed that their deportation constituted breaches of Articles 3 and 13 of the European Convention. The Court considered whether the situation in Sri Lanka at the time the applicants were deported provided substantial support for the view that they would be at risk of Article 3 treatment. The Court determined that the general unsettled situation in Sri Lanka at the time did not establish that they were at greater risk than other young male Tamils who were returning there; it established only a possibility rather than a clear risk of ill treatment. No breach of Article 3 could therefore be established.[104] Arguably, this decision suggests that although an Article 3 issue may arise in asylum cases, the Convention cannot be viewed as a substitute for an effective domestic means of determining refugee claims. (It should be noted that Article 8 issues may also arise in some immigration claims; this possibility will be discussed below.)

Soering is a very broad decision. The approach taken in the judgment may mean that a state would infringe the Convention whenever it facilitated the breach of a Convention Article by another state. However, in general, liability arises under the Convention only where a breach has already occurred, not where it is merely probable. An exception was made to that rule in *Soering* in view of 'the serious and irreparable nature of the alleged suffering risked'.[105] Thus, the *Soering* facilitation principle may apply only where the state receiving the individual in question is likely to subject him or her to treatment amounting to serious and irreparable suffering. This would include treatment in breach of Articles 3 and 2 (such as state execution without trial) and probably 5 and 6 (imprisonment without trial). Possibly it might also include deportation leading to the probability of treatment in breach of Articles 6[106] or 7 in the receiving state which would then be likely to result in the execution or

---

102 The Article 5 issue is considered below, at pp 544–45.
103 (1991) 14 EHRR 248, A.215.
104 See further on the outcome of the Tamils' asylum claim Chap 11, pp 466–67. For comment on this case see Warbrick, C, *Yearbook of European Law*, 1991, pp 545–53.
105 Judgment of 7 July 1989, A.161 para 90.
106 See *Soering*, A.161 para 113.

imprisonment of the individual. For example, if an individual committed an act in his or her own state before leaving for another state – a party to the Convention – and the act committed was then criminalised with retrospective effect, the second state might act in breach of Article 7 if it extradited the individual in order to face charges and the possibility of imprisonment under the new law.

Article 4: Freedom from slavery, servitude and forced or compulsory labour

(1) No one shall be held in slavery or servitude.
(2) No one shall be required to perform forced or compulsory labour.
(3) For the purpose of this Article the term 'forced or compulsory labour' shall not include:
   (a) any work required to be done in the ordinary course of detention imposed according to the provisions of Article 5 of this Convention or during conditional release from such detention;
   (b) any service of a military character or, in case of conscientious objectors in countries where they are recognised, service exacted instead of compulsory military service;
   (c) any service exacted in case of any emergency or calamity threatening the life or well-being of the community;
   (d) any work or service which forms part of normal civic obligations.

Article 4 provides a guarantee which is largely irrelevant in modern European democracies, although it is conceivable that as states with less developed human rights regimes become signatories to the Convention, it might prove to be of value. Due to its restrictive wording it has not proved possible to interpret Article 4 in such a way as to allow it to cover rights unthought of when it was conceived.

It is necessary to distinguish between slavery and servitude under Article 4(1) and forced or compulsory labour under Article 4(2). Slavery denotes total ownership, whereas servitude denotes less far reaching restraints; it is concerned with the labour conditions and the inescapable nature of the service. Article 4(1) has not generated much case law and the few cases which have been brought have failed. However, it would be better from the applicant's point of view, if possible, to come within Article 4(1) as opposed to 4(2) because 4(1) contains no express exceptions and is also non-derogable.

Article 4(2) is not concerned with the total situation of the claimant concerned; it covers the compulsory character of services which will usually be temporary and incidental to the claimant's main job or total situation. Forced or compulsory labour has been held to denote the following: 'first that the work or service is performed by the worker against his will and, secondly, that the requirement that the work or service be performed is unjust or oppressive or the work or service itself involves avoidable hardship'.[107] Most of the case law arises in the area of professional obligations arising from certain jobs. For example, a German lawyer complained of having to act as unpaid or poorly paid defence counsel. The Commission rejected the complaint on the basis that if a person voluntarily chooses the profession of lawyer, aware of this obligation, then he can be taken to have impliedly consented to fulfil the obligation.[108] This argument will apply if the obligations are a normal part of the profession. Less emphasis was placed on the implied consent of the applicant in *Van der Mussele*[109] which also concerned compulsory legal aid work. The Court took the view that the mere fact that the applicant had impliedly consented to the obligation was only a factor to be considered; it was not decisive. It decided that looking at all the factors including the small amount of time devoted to such work – only 18 hours – and the fact that such work enabled the obligation under Article 6(3)(c) (if necessary to have free legal advice) to be fulfilled, no breach had occurred.

Article 5: Right to liberty and security of person

(1) Everyone has the right to liberty and security of person. No one shall be deprived of his liberty save in the following cases and in accordance with a procedure prescribed by law:

(a) the lawful detention of a person after conviction by a competent court;

(b) the lawful arrest or detention of a person for non-compliance with the lawful order of a court or in order to secure the fulfilment of any obligation prescribed by law;

(c) the lawful arrest or detention of a person effected for the purpose of bringing him before the competent legal authority on reasonable suspicion of having committed an offence or when it is reasonably considered necessary to prevent his committing an offence or fleeing after having done so;

(d) the detention of a minor by lawful order for the purpose of educational supervision or his lawful detention for the purpose of bringing him before the competent legal authority;

(e) the lawful detention of persons for the prevention of the spreading of infectious diseases, of persons of unsound mind, alcoholics or drug addicts or vagrants;

---

107 Appl 8410/78, *X v Federal Republic of Germany* D and R 18 (1980), pp 216, 219.
108 *X v FRG*, Appl 4653/70 (1974) 46 CD 22.
109 Judgment of 23 November 1983, A.70.

(f) the lawful arrest or detention of a person to prevent his effecting an unauthorised entry into the country or of a person against whom action is being taken with a view to deportation or extradition.

(2) Everyone who is arrested shall be informed promptly, in a language which he understands, of the reasons for his arrest and of any charge against him.

(3) Everyone arrested or detained in accordance with the provisions of para 1(c) of this Article shall be brought promptly before a judge or other officer authorised by law to exercise judicial power and shall be entitled to trial within a reasonable time or to release pending trial. Release may be conditioned by guarantees to appear for trial.

(4) Everyone who is deprived of his liberty by arrest or detention shall be entitled to take proceedings by which the lawfulness of his detention shall be decided speedily by a court and his release ordered if the detention is not lawful.

(5) Everyone who has been the victim of arrest or detention in contravention of the provisions of this Article shall have an enforceable right to compensation.

Although Article 5 speaks of liberty *and* security as though they could be distinguished they are not treated as though there is any significant distinction between them. The presumption embodied in the Article is that liberty and security must be maintained. However, it then sets out the two tests which must be satisfied if it is to be removed. First, exceptions are set out where liberty can be taken away; secondly, under paras 2–4 the procedure is set out which must be followed when a person is deprived of liberty. Thus, if the correct procedure is followed but an exception does not apply, Article 5 will be breached, as, conversely, it will if an individual falls within an exception but in detaining him or her the correct procedure is not followed. It will be found that a number of successful applications have been brought under Article 5 with the result that the position of detainees in Europe has undergone improvement. It should be noted that Article 5 is concerned with total deprivation of liberty, not restriction of movement which is covered by Article 2 of Protocol 4 (the UK is not a party to Protocol 4.)

In general the case law of the Court discussed below suggests that the circumstances in which liberty can be taken away under para 5(1)(a)–(f) will be restrictively interpreted although the instances included are potentially wide. Article 5(1) not only provides that deprivation of liberty is only permitted within these exceptions, it also requires that it should be 'in accordance with a procedure prescribed by law'. In *Winterwerp v Netherlands*[110] the Court found that this meant that the procedure in question must be in accordance with national and Convention law, taking into account the general principles on which the Convention is based, and it must not be

---

110 Judgment of 24 October 1979, A.33; (1979) 2 EHRR 387.

arbitrary. In *Chahal v UK*[111] the applicant complained *inter alia* that he had been detained although there had been no court hearing. The Home Office decided to deport him on national security grounds but he applied for asylum. He was then imprisoned for over six years. He applied to the European Commission on Human Rights, alleging, *inter alia*, a breach of Article 5 which guarantees judicial control over loss of liberty. The Court found that a breach of Article 5 had occurred since his detention should have been subject to scrutiny in court. It had been considered by an advisory panel but that did not provide sufficient procedural safeguards to qualify as a court.

5(1)(a): Detention after conviction

This exception covers lawful detention after conviction by a competent court. Thus the detention must flow from the conviction. This calls into question the revocation of life licences because in such instances a person is being deprived of liberty without a fresh conviction. In *Weeks*[112] the Court considered the causal connection with the original sentence when a life licence was revoked after the applicant was released. The Court accepted a very loose link between the original sentence and the revocation of the life licence on the basis that the sentencing judge must be taken to have known and intended that it was inherent in the life sentence that the claimant's liberty would hereafter be at the mercy of the executive. The Court declined to review the appropriateness of the original sentence.

5(1)(b): Detention to fulfil an obligation

This exception refers to deprivation of liberty in order to 'secure fulfilment of an obligation prescribed by law'. This raises difficulties of interpretation and is clearly not so straightforward as the first form of such deprivation permitted under para 5(1)(a). It is very wide and appears to allow deprivation of liberty in many instances without intervention by a court. It might even allow preventive action before violation of a legal obligation. However it has been narrowed down; in *Lawless*[113] it was found that a specific and concrete obligation must be identified. Once it has been identified, detention can in principle be used to secure its fulfilment.

The obligation includes a requirement that specific circumstances, such as the possibility of danger to the public, must be present in order to warrant the use of detention. A requirement to submit to an examination on entering the

---

111 (1997) 23 EHRR 413; (1996) *The Times*, 28 November; (1996) *Guardian*, 16 November.
112 A.145, Judgment of 5 October 1988; (1987) 10 EHRR 293.
113 Report of 19 December 1959, B.1 (1960–61) p 64; Judgment of 1 July 1961, A.3 (1960–1961); (1961) 1 EHRR 15.

UK has been found to be specific enough.[114] Moreover, it must be apparent why detention rather than some lesser measure is needed to secure compliance with the obligation. Thus the width of Article 5(1)(b) has been narrowed down by the use of restrictive interpretation in line with furthering the aims of the Convention.

5(1)(c): Detention after arrest but before conviction

This provision refers to persons held on remand or detained after arrest. Article 5(3) requires that in such an instance a person should be brought 'promptly' to trial; in other words the trial should occur in *reasonable* time. The part of 5(1)(c) which causes concern is the ground – 'arrest or detention to prevent him committing an offence'. This is an alternative to the holding of the detainee under reasonable suspicion of committing an offence; arguably the two should have been cumulative. This ground would permit internment of persons even if the facts which showed the intention to commit a crime did not in themselves constitute a criminal offence. In *Lawless*[115] the Court narrowed this ground down on the basis that internment in such circumstances might well not fulfil the other requirement in 5(1)(c) that the arrest or detention would be effected for the purpose of bringing the person before a competent legal authority. This interpretation was warranted because all of Article 5 must be read together.

A level of suspicion below 'reasonable suspicion' will not be sufficient; in *Fox, Campbell and Hartley*[116] the Court found that Article 5(1)(c) had been violated on the basis that no reasonable suspicion of committing an offence had arisen, only an honest belief (which was all that was needed under s 11 Northern Ireland (Emergency Provisions) Act 1978). The only evidence put forward by the government for the presence of reasonable suspicion was that the applicants had convictions for terrorist offences and that when arrested they were asked about particular terrorist acts. The government said that further evidence could not be disclosed for fear of endangering life. The Court said that reasonable suspicion arises from 'facts or information which would satisfy an objective observer that the person concerned may have committed the offence'. It went on to find that the government had not established that reasonable suspicion was present justifying the arrests in question. The Court took into account the exigencies of the situation and the need to prevent terrorism; however, it found that the state party in question must be able to provide some information which an objective observer would consider justified the arrest. It was found that the information provided was insufficient and therefore a breach of Article 5 had occurred. This ruling

---

114 *McVeigh O'Neill and Evans v UK* (1981) Report of 18 March 1981, D and R 25; (1981) 5 EHRR 71.
115 Note 113 above.
116 Judgment of 30 August 1990, A.178; (1990) 13 EHRR 157.

suggests that in terrorist cases a low level of reasonable suspicion is required and this test was applied in *Murray v UK*.[117] The Court found that no breach of Article 5(1)(c) had occurred, even though the relevant legislation (s 14 Northern Ireland (Emergency Provisions) Act 1987) required only suspicion, not reasonable suspicion, since there was some evidence which provided a basis for the suspicion in question.

5(1)(d): Detention of minors

This provision confers far-reaching powers on national authorities with regard to those under 18 years of age. This has led the Court to interpret the term 'educational purpose' restrictively. In *Bouamar v Belgium*[118] it was found that mere detention without educational facilities would not fulfil Article 5(1)(d)); there had to be educational facilities in the institution and trained staff.

5(1)(e): Detention of non-criminals for the protection of society

This sub-para must of course be read in conjunction with para 5(4) – all the persons mentioned have the right to have the lawfulness of their detention determined by a Court. The width of para 5(1)(e) was narrowed down in the *Vagrancy* cases in which the question arose of the current application of the term 'vagrant'.[119] The term had been applied to the applicants who had therefore been detained. The Court considered whether the applicant was correctly brought within the ambit of the term in the relevant Belgium legislation, but it refused to conduct a more than marginal review of municipal law; the question of the interpretation of national law was separated from the application of the Convention. However the Court did then turn to the Convention and conduct a far-reaching review of the meaning of 'vagrant' in accordance with the Convention on the basis of a common European standard; it then found that the applicants had not been correctly brought within that term. Thus ultimately the margin of appreciation allowed was narrow. This stance prevents too wide an interpretation of the application of the categories of para 5(1)(e).

5(1)(f): Detention of aliens and deportees

The importance of this provision is that the Convention does not grant aliens a right of admission or residence in contracting states, but para 5(1)(f) ensures that an alien who is detained pending deportation or admission has certain

---

117 (1994) 19 EHRR 193.
118 Judgment of 29 February 1988, A.129; (1988) 11 EHRR 1.
119 *Vagrancy* cases, Judgment of 18 June 1971, A.12.

guarantees; there must be review of the detention by a court and the arrest must be in accordance with national law. Also, because the lawfulness of the detention may depend on the lawfulness of the deportation itself, the lawfulness of the deportation may often be in issue.[120]

Safeguards of paras 2–4: general

Paragraphs 2–4 reiterate the principle that the liberty of the person is the overriding concern; if one of the exceptions mentioned in para 5(1) applies the safeguards of sub-paras 2–4 must still be complied with. If they are not the deprivation of liberty will be unlawful even if it comes within the exceptions. Paragraphs 2–4 provide a minimum standard for arrest and detention.

Promptly informing of the reason for arrest

Paragraph 5(2) provides that a person must be informed promptly of the reason for arrest. This information is needed so that it is possible to judge from the moment of its inception whether the arrest is in accordance with the law so that the arrestee could theoretically take action straight away to be released. The Commission's view is that this information need not be as detailed and specific as that guaranteed by para 6(3) in connection with the right to a fair trial.[121]

In *Fox, Campbell and Hartley v UK*[122] the applicants, who were arrested on suspicion of terrorist offences, were not informed of the reason for the arrest at the time of it but were told that they were being arrested under a particular statutory provision. Clearly, this could not convey the reason to them at that time. At a later point, during interrogation, they were asked about specific criminal offences. The European Court of Human Rights found that Article 5(2) was not satisfied at the time of the arrest but that this breach was healed by the later indications made during interrogation of the offences for which they had been arrested. In *Murray v UK*[123] soldiers had occupied the applicant's house, thus clearly taking her into detention but she was not informed of the fact of arrest for half an hour. The question arose whether she was falsely imprisoned during that half hour. The Court found that no breach of Article 5(2) had occurred in those circumstances. Mrs Murray was eventually informed during interrogation of the reason for the arrest and

---

120 *Zamir v UK* Report of 11 October 1983, D and R 40 (1983) p 42.
121 It was determined in Appl 8828/79 *X v Denmark*, D and R 30 (1983), p 93 that para 5(2) does not include a right to contact a lawyer.
122 Judgment of 30 August 1990, A.182; (1990) 13 EHRR 157.
123 (1994) 19 EHRR 193.

although an interval of a few hours had elapsed between the arrest and informing her of the reason for it, this could still be termed prompt.

Both these decisions were influenced by the terrorist context in which they occurred and provide examples of the Court's tenderness to claims of a threat to national security made by governments of Member States. In both, a very wide margin of appreciation was allowed. However, it would appear that both were influenced by the crime control consideration of allowing leeway to the police to resort to doubtful practices in relation to terrorist suspects and both exhibit, it is suggested, a lack of rigour in relation to due process. Such lack of rigour might be acceptable if there was a real connection between a failure to give information to suspects and an advantage to be gained in an emergency situation, since the principle of proportionality would then be satisfied. However, in Mrs Murray's case, for example, once she was in detention and her house in effect sealed off from the outside world it is not clear that telling her of the fact of the arrest could create or exacerbate an unsettled situation. Thus, the Court has allowed some departure from the principle that there should be a clear demarcation between the point at which the citizen is at liberty and the point at which her liberty is restrained.

Promptness of judicial hearing

Article 5(3) confers a right to be brought promptly before the judicial authorities; in other words not to be held for long periods without a hearing. It covers both arrest and detention and detainees held on remand. There will be some allowable delay in both situations; the question is therefore what is meant by 'promptly'. Its meaning was considered in *Brogan v UK*[124] in relation to an arrest and detention arising by virtue of the special powers under s 12 of the Prevention of Terrorism (Temporary Provisions) Act 1989. (The UK had entered a derogation under Article 15 against the applicability of Article 5 to Northern Ireland but withdrew that derogation in August 1984. Two months later the *Brogan* case was filed.) The applicants complained *inter alia* of the length of time they were held in detention without coming before a judge, on the basis that it could not be termed prompt. The Court took into account the need for special measures to combat terrorism; such measures had to be balanced against individual rights. However, it found that detention for four days and six hours was too long. The Court did not specify how long was acceptable; previously the Commission had seen four days as the limit. Following this decision, the UK government ultimately chose to derogate from Article 5 and this decision was eventually found to be lawful by the European Court of Human Rights.[125]

---

[124] Judgment of 29 November 1988; (1989) 11 EHRR 117; A.145.
[125] *Brannigan and McBride v UK* (1993) 17 EHRR 594.

The question whether detainees on remand have been brought to trial or released in a reasonable time has also been considered. The word 'reasonable' is not associated with the processing of the prosecution and trial but with the detention itself. Obviously if the trial takes a long time to prepare for there will be a longer delay but it does not follow that detention for all that time will be reasonable. In the *Neumeister* case[126] the Court rejected an interpretation of 'reasonable' which associated it only with the preparation of the trial. Thus continued detention on remand will be reasonable only so long as the reasonable suspicion of para 5(1)(c) continues to exist. But grounds for continued detention other than those expressly mentioned in 5(1)(c) could be considered such as suppression of evidence or the possibility that the detainee will abscond. However, it is clear from *Letellier v France*[127] that such dangers must persist throughout the period of detention; when they cease, specific reasons for continued detention which have been properly scrutinised must be apparent. Once the accused has been released on bail, Article 5(3) does not apply but Article 6(1) does, as will be seen later. The question of a reasonable time for preparing for the trial can also be considered under Article 6(1).

There is no absolute right to bail under Article 5(3) but the authorities must consider whether bail can achieve the same purpose as detention on remand.[128] It is also clear that detention after demand of an excessively large sum for bail will be unreasonable if a lesser sum would have achieved the same objective.[129]

Review of detention

Article 5(4) provides a right to review of detention. The detainee must be able to take court proceedings in order to determine whether a detention is unlawful. This is an independent provision: even if it is determined in a particular case by the Commission that the detention was lawful there could still be a breach of Article 5(4) if no possibility of review of the lawfulness of the detention by the domestic courts arose. This was in issue in the cases against the UK regarding discretionary life sentences and it was found that there had to be an element in the sentence which of its nature was reviewable. Thus, a life sentence consisting wholly of a punitive element would be unreviewable since no relevant circumstance could have changed. In the *Weeks* case[130] the sentence contained a security element and therefore allowed review of the applicant's progress. In *Thynne, Wilson and Gunnel v UK*,[131] the

---

126 Judgment of 27 June 1968; (1979–80) 1 EHRR 91.
127 A.207 (1991).
128 *Wemhoff*, Judgment of 27 June 1968; (1979–80) 1 EHRR 55.
129 *Neumeister*, Judgment of 27 June 1968; (1979–80) 1 EHRR 91.
130 (1987) 10 EHRR 293.
131 Judgment of 25 October 1990, A.190; (1990) 13 EHRR 666. For comment see [1991] *PL* 34.

sentence consisted of both a punitive and a security element. When the punitive element expired, a judicial procedure for review of the sentence should have been available because there was then something to review; if it had been purely punitive there would not have been. Thus is both cases a breach of Article 5(4) was found.

Article 5(4) also applies to remand prisoners. It was found in *De Jong, Baljet and Van de Brink*[132] that it grants to a person on remand a right of access to a court after the decision (in accordance with Article 5(3)) to detain him or prolong detention has been taken. It also allows access to the files used in coming to the decision on remand.[133]

Compensation

Paragraph 5(5) provides for compensation if the arrest or detention contravenes the other provisions of Article 5. This provision differs from the general right to compensation under Article 50[134] because it exists as an independent right: if a person is found to have been unlawfully arrested under domestic law in the domestic court but no compensation is available, he or she can apply to the European Court of Human Rights on the basis of the lack of compensation. As far as other Convention rights are concerned, if a violation of a right occurs which is found unlawful by the national courts but no compensation is granted, the applicant cannot allege breach of a Convention right.

Article 6: Right to a fair and public hearing

(1) In the determination of his civil rights and obligations or of any criminal charge against him, everyone is entitled to a fair and public hearing within a reasonable time by an independent and impartial tribunal established by law. Judgment shall be pronounced publicly but the press and public may be excluded from all or part of the trial in the interest of morals, public order or national security in a democratic society, where the interest of juveniles or the protection of the private life of the parties so require or to the extent strictly necessary in the opinion of the court in special circumstances where publicity would prejudice the interests of justice.

(2) Everyone charged with a criminal offence shall be presumed innocent until proved guilty according to law.

(3) Everyone charged with a criminal offence has the following minimum rights:

---

132 Judgment of 22 May 1984, A.77 pp 25–26; (1984) 8 EHRR 20.
133 *Lamy v Belgium* (1989) 11 EHRR 529.
134 Appl 6821/74, *Huber v Austria*, 6 D and R 65 (1977) p 65.

(a) to be informed promptly, in a language he understands and in detail, of the nature and cause of the accusation against him;

(b) to have adequate time and facilities for the preparation of his defence;

(c) to defend himself in person or through legal assistance of his own choosing or, if he has not sufficient means to pay for legal assistance, to be given it free when the interests of justice so require;

(d) to examine or have examined witnesses against him and to obtain the attendance and examination of witnesses on his behalf under the same conditions as witness against him;

(e) to have the free assistance of an interpreter if he cannot understand or speak the language used in court.

Article 6 is one of the most significant Convention Articles and the one which is most frequently found to have been violated.[135] This is partly due to the width of Article 6(1) which may cover numerous circumstances in which rights are affected in the absence of a judicial hearing. This may mean that even where a substantive claim under another Article fails, the Article 6(1) claim succeeds because the procedure used in making the determination affecting the applicant was defective.[136] In order to appreciate the way it operates, it is crucial to understand the relationship between paras 1 and 3. Paragraph 1 imports a general requirement of a fair hearing applying to criminal and civil hearings which covers all aspects of a fair hearing. Paragraph 3 lists minimum guarantees of a fair hearing in the criminal context only. If para 3 had been omitted, the guarantees contained in it could have arisen from para 1 but it was included on the basis that it is important to declare a minimum standard for a fair hearing. In practice then, paras 1 and 3 may often both be in question in respect of a criminal charge.

Since para 3 contains *minimum* guarantees the para 1 protection of a fair hearing goes beyond para 3. In investigating a fair hearing the Commission is not confined to the para 3 guarantees; it can consider further requirements of fairness. Thus if para 1 is *not* violated it will be superfluous to consider para 3 and if one of the para 3 guarantees is violated there will be no need to look at para 1. However, if para 3 is not violated it will still be worth considering para 1. It follows that although civil hearings are expressly affected only by para 1, the minimum guarantees may also apply to such hearings too.

---

135 63 violations were found up to the end of 1989. The next most invoked article is Article 5 (23 violations).

136 For example, in *Mats Jacobson v Sweden* (1990) 13 EHRR 79 the applicant was prevented from making changes to his property. His substantive claim under Article 1 of Protocol 1 failed but his Article 6(1) claim succeeded since he was allowed no adequate access to a court to challenge the prohibition.

6(1): Fair trial

Besides the procedural guarantees, Article 6(1) has been found to provide a right of access to a court whether the domestic legal system allows access to a court in a particular case or not. Obviously that depends on whether an individual instance falls within Article 6(1). The meaning of 'civil rights and obligations' does not depend upon the legal classification afforded the right or obligation in question by the national legislator; the question is whether the content and effect of the right or obligation (taking into account the legal systems of all the contracting states) allows the meaning 'civil right' or 'civil obligation' to be assigned to it.[137] This wide provision allows challenge to decisions taken in the absence of legal procedures in a disparate range of circumstances.[138]

The question of what is meant by 'a criminal charge' has generated quite a lot of case law. 'Charge' has been described as 'the official notification given to an individual by the competent authority of an allegation that he has committed a criminal offence'.[139] Offences under criminal law must be distinguished from those arising only under *disciplinary* law. In order to do so the Court will consider the nature and severity of the penalty the person is threatened with.[140] In *Campbell and Fell v UK*[141] the Court had to consider whether prison discipline could fall within Article 6(1). The applicants, prisoners, were sentenced to a substantial loss of remission. This was such a serious consequence that the procedure in question could be considered as of a criminal character but the Court considered that not *all* disciplinary offences in prison which in fact had an equivalent in the ordinary criminal law would be treated as of a criminal character. Moreover, classification of a petty offence as 'regulatory' rather than criminal will not be decisive for Article 6(1) purposes; the Commission may yet determine that the offence is of a criminal character.[142] Otherwise, by reclassifying offences, the state in question could minimise the application of the Convention.

Once it has been determined that a particular instance falls within Article 6(1) it must be determined whether the right in question is covered by the right of access to a court. It seems that, for example, Article 6(1) does not confer a right of appeal to a higher court.[143] It may include access to legal advice and by implication legal aid. These issues arise in relation both to

---

137 Judgment of 16 July 1971, *Ringeisen v Austria*, A.13 p 39; (1971) 1 EHRR 455.
138 For example, *O v UK* (1987) 10 EHRR 82 concerned a decision to terminate access to a child in care although no legal procedure was in place allowing consideration of its merits.
139 Judgment of 15 July 1982, *Eckle*, A.51 (1982) p 33.
140 *Campbell and Fell*, Judgment of 28 June 1984, A.80.
141 Above note 140.
142 *Ozturk*, Judgment of 21 February 1983, A.73; (1984) 6 EHRR 409.
143 *Belgian Linguistic* cases, Judgment of 23 July 1968, A.6; (1968) 1 EHRR 252.

access to a court hearing and the *fairness* of the hearing. In *Golder* [144] it was found that a refusal to allow a detainee to correspond with his legal advisor would be contrary to Article 6(1) since in preventing him even initiating proceedings it hindered his right of access to a court.

Access to legal advice may not always imply a right to legal aid. The circumstances in which it will do so were considered in *Granger v UK*.[145] The applicant had been refused legal aid and so did not have counsel at appeal; he only had notes from his solicitor which he read out but clearly did not understand. In particular, there was one especially complex ground of appeal which he was unable to deal with. In view of the complexity of the appeal and his inability to deal with it, legal aid should have been granted. It was found that paras 6(1) and 6(3)(c) should be read together and, if it would be apparent to an objective observer that a fair hearing could not take place without legal advice, then both would be violated. *Granger* was concerned with the fairness of the hearing rather than with the ability to obtain access to a court *at all*. However, in some instances a person unable to obtain legal aid would be unable to obtain legal advice and therefore might be unable to initiate proceedings. In such instances access to a court would be the main issue.

Apart from access to legal advice and the other minimal guarantees of para 6(3), what other rights are implied by the term a 'fair hearing'? It has been found to connote equality between the parties,[146] and in principle entails the right of the parties to be present in person[147] although criminal trial *in absentia* does not automatically violate Article 6.[148] A refusal to summon a witness may constitute unfairness[149] as may a failure to disclose evidence.[150]

The hearing must take place within a reasonable time. These are the same words as are used in Article 5(3) but here the point is to put an end to the insecurity of the applicant who is uncertain of the outcome of the civil action or charge against him or her rather than with the deprivation of liberty. Thus the ending point comes when the uncertainty is resolved either at the court of highest instance or by expiry of the time limit for appeal. In determining what is meant by 'reasonable' fairly wide time limits have been applied so that in some circumstances as much as seven or eight[151] years may be reasonable.

---

144 Judgment of 21 February 1975, A.18.
145 Judgment of 28 March 1990, A.174.
146 Judgment of 27 June 1968, *Neumeister*, A.8 (1968) p 43.
147 *Colloza v Italy*, Judgment of 12 February 1985, A.89 (1985).
148 *Colloza v Italy*, above.
149 Appl 5362/72, *X v Austria*, Coll 42 (1973) p 145.
150 *Edwards v UK* (1992) 15 EHRR 417; (1993) *The Times*, 21 January (it was found that the hearing in the Court of Appeal remedied this failure).
151 In *Vernillo v France* 12 HRLJ 199, seven and a half years in respect of civil proceedings was not found too long due to the special responsibilities of the parties.

The Court has approved a period of nearly five years[152] and the Commission a period of seven and a half.[153] It will take into account the conduct of the accused (which may have contributed to the delay) and the need for proper preparation of the case, bearing in mind any special circumstances such as those which might arise in child care cases. In order to determine how long the delay has been the point from which time will run must be identified. In criminal cases it will be 'the ... stage ... at which the situation of the person concerned has been substantially affected as a result of a suspicion against him'.[154] In civil cases it will be the moment when proceedings concerned are initiated, not including pre-trial negotiations.[155]

6(2): The presumption of innocence in criminal cases

Paragraph 2 'requires *inter alia* that when carrying out their duties, members of a court should not start with the preconceived idea that the accused has committed the offence charged; the burden of proof is on the prosecution and any doubt should benefit the accused. It also follows that it is for the prosecution to inform the accused of the case that will be made against him so that he may prepare and present his defence accordingly and to adduce evidence sufficient to convict him'.[156] It follows from the presumption of innocence that the court must base its conviction exclusively on evidence put forward at trial.[157] Thus a conviction based on written statements which were inadmissible breached para 6(2).[158] This provision is very closely related to the impartiality provision of para 6(1).

The expectation that the state bears the burden of establishing guilt requires that the accused should not be expected to provide involuntary assistance by way of a confession. Thus the presumption of innocence under para 6(2) is closely linked to the right to freedom from self-incrimination which the Court has found to be covered by the right to a fair hearing under para 6(1) (*Funke v France*).[159] In *Murray (John) v UK*,[160] on the other hand, the Commission did not find that para 6(1) had been breached where inferences had been drawn at trial from the applicant's refusal to give evidence. The Court also found no breach of Article 6 due to such drawing of inferences in

---

152 *Buchholz*, Judgment of 6 May 1981, A.42.
153 Report 12 July 1977 in *Haase* D and R 11 (1978) p 78.
154 *Neumeister*, Report of 27 May 1966, B.6 (1966–69) p 81.
155 Report of 7 March 1984, *Lithgow*, A.102 (1986) p 120; (1986) 8 EHRR 335.
156 Judgment of 6 December 1988, *Barbéra, Messegué and Jabardo*, A.14 6(2) (1989) p 33. See also *Salabiaku v France* (1988) 13 EHRR 379.
157 *X v Federal Republic of Germany* D and R 17 (1980) p 231.
158 *Barbéra* above note 156.
159 (1993) 16 EHRR 297.
160 (1996) *The Times*, 9 February. For comment see Munday, R [1996] *Crim LR* 370.

the particular circumstances of the case, taking into account the fact that 'the right to silence' could not be treated as absolute, the degree of compulsion exerted on the applicant and the weight of the evidence against him.[161] However, the Court did find that Article 6(1) had been breached by the denial of access to a lawyer since such access was essential where there was a likelihood that adverse inferences would be drawn from silence. In *Saunders v UK*[162] the Commission found that the applicant's right to freedom from self-incrimination had been infringed in that he had been forced to answer questions put to him by inspectors investigating a company takeover or risk the imposition of a criminal sanction. The ruling of the Court was to the same effect, taking into account the special compulsive regime in question for Department of Trade and Industry inspections.[163]

6(3)(a), (b) and (c): legal representation in criminal cases

These sub-paragraphs are very closely related due to the word 'facilities' used in sub-para (b). Sub-paragraphs (b) and (c) may often be invoked together: (c) in respect of the assignment of a lawyer and (b) in respect of the time allowed for such assignment. It is not enough that a lawyer should be assigned; he or she should be appointed in good time in order to give time to prepare the defence and familiarise herself or himself with the case.[164] Both sub-paragraphs also arise in relation to notification of the right of access to legal advice and it has been held that an oral translation of the requisite information is insufficient.[165] As has already been noted in relation to *Granger* the legal advice provisions must be read in conjunction with the right to a fair trial. A lawyer must be assigned if otherwise an objective observer would consider that a fair hearing would not occur. In *Poitrimol v France* (1993)[166] the Court stated: 'Although not absolute, the right ... to be effectively defended by a lawyer, assigned officially if need be, is one of the fundamental features of a fair trial.' In furtherance of the notion of providing effective legal representation it has been found that para 6(3)(c) does not merely import a right to have legal assistance but rather it includes three rights:[167]

(1) to have recourse, if desired, to legal assistance;

(2) to choose that assistance;

---

161 *Murray (John) v UK* (1996) 22 EHRR 29.
162 No 19187/91 Com Rep paras 69–75.
163 *Saunders v UK* (1997) 23 EHRR 313.
164 Appl 7909/74, *X and Y v Austria*, D and R 15 (1979) p 160.
165 *Kamasinski* Report of 5 May 1988 para 138; (1991) 13 EHRR 36.
166 A.277-A; (1993) 18 EHRR 130.
167 From *Golder*, Judgment of 21 February 1975, A.18; see also *Silver v UK*, Judgment of 25 March 1983, A.61; (1983) 5 EHRR 347.

(3) if the defendant has insufficient means to pay, for that assistance to be given it free if the interest of justice so require.[168]

6(3)(d): Cross-examination in criminal cases

The Strasbourg case law has left a wide discretion to the national court[169] as to the interpretation of the first limb of para 6(3)(d) – the right to cross-examine witnesses – and so has deprived this right of some of its effect. This right would seem to be specific and unambiguous in its guarantee that witnesses against the defendant must be at the public hearing if their evidence is to be relied on. It would therefore seem to outlaw hearsay evidence. The Court has, however, shrunk at times from a straightforward assertion that this is the case.[170] The second limb – the right to call witnesses and have them examined under the same conditions as witnesses for the other side – obviously allows for a wide discretion as it only requires that the prosecution and defence should be treated equally as regards summoning witnesses.[171] So conditions and restrictions can be set so long as they apply equally to both sides. This provision relates to the concept of creating equality between parties; it is closely related to the fair hearing principle and therefore will apply in civil cases too.

Article 7: Freedom from retrospective effect of penal legislation

(1) No one shall be held guilty of any criminal offence on account of any act or omission which did not constitute a criminal offence under national or international law at the time when it was committed. Nor shall a heavier penalty be imposed than the one that was applicable at the time the criminal offence was committed.

(2) This Article shall not prejudice the trial and punishment of any person for any act or omission which, at the time when it was committed, was criminal according to the general principles of law recognised by civilised nations.

Article 7 contains an important principle and it is therefore non-derogable although it is subject to the single exception contained in para 2. It divides into two separate principles:

---

168 *Pakelli*, Judgment of 25 April 1983, A.64 (1983).
169 See eg *Asch v Austria* (1990) Case 30/1990/221/283.
170 Such an assertion was made in *Kostovski v Netherlands* (1989) 12 EHRR 434 and *Windisch v Austria* (1990) 13 EHRR 281. However, these decisions were not followed in *Isgro v Italy* (1991) Case 1/1990/192/252. For further discussion of this right see [1993] *Crim LR* 261–67.
171 Appl 4428/70, *X v Austria* (1972) Yearbook XV p 264.

(1) The law in question must have existed at the time of the act in question for the conviction to be based on it.

(2) No heavier penalty for the infringement of the law may be imposed than was in force at the time the act was committed.

As far as the first principle is concerned this also means that an existing part of the criminal law cannot be applied by analogy to acts it was not intended for.[172] Allowing such extension would fall foul of the general principle that the law must be unambiguous, which is part of the principle that someone should not be convicted if he or she could not have known beforehand that the act in question was criminal. In order to determine whether these requirements have been met the Strasbourg authorities are prepared to interpret domestic law[173] although normally they would not be prepared to do so. Although it will be cautious in this respect the Commission must take note of an allegedly false interpretation of domestic law. *Harman v UK*[174] concerned unforeseeable liability for contempt of court. It had not previously been considered to be contempt if confidential documents were shown to a journalist after being read out in court. The Commission declared the application admissible but meanwhile a friendly settlement was reached.

Article 7 was found to have been breached in *Welch v UK*.[175] Before the trial of the applicant for drug offences a new provision came into force under the Drug Trafficking Offences Act 1986, making provision for confiscation orders. This was imposed on the applicant, although the legislation was not in force at the time when he committed the offences in question. It clearly had retrospective effect and was found to constitute a 'penalty' within Article 7(1). In *SW v UK and C v UK*[176] the applicants claimed that marital rape had been retrospectively outlawed and that therefore their criminalisation for forced sexual intercourse with their wives created a breach of Article 7. Their convictions were based on the ruling of the House of Lords in *R*[177] which removed the marital exemption. The Court found that the anticipated reform of the law undertaken in *R* was almost inevitable and that therefore the applicants should have foreseen that their conduct would be found to be criminal. Thus no breach of Article 7 was found.

Paragraph 7(2) provides an exception which appears to arise if a person is convicted retrospectively for an offence recognised in other countries but not the one in question at the material time. This exception is potentially quite wide; it is not restricted to war crimes and could cover any deeply immoral

---

172 Appl 1852/63, *X v Austria* (1965) Yearbook VIII.
173 This was determined in *X v Austria* above note 172.
174 Appl 10038/82; Decision of 11 May 1984; 38 D and R 53 (1984).
175 A.307-A; (1995) 20 EHRR 247.
176 (1995) 21 EHRR 404. For comment on the ruling see Osborne, C (1996) 4 EHRR 406.
177 (1991) 4 All ER 481; [1991] 3 WLR 767; [1992] *Fam Law* 108; [1992] *Crim LR* 207, HL.

conduct generally recognised as criminal in national laws. The la[.] countries which are not Member States can be taken into determining the applicability of the exception.

Article 8: Right to respect for privacy

(1) Everyone has the right to respect for his private and family life, his home and his correspondence.

(2) There shall be no interference by a public authority with the exercise of this right except such as is in accordance with the law and is necessary in a democratic society in the interests of national security, public safety or the economic well-being of the country, for the prevention of disorder or crime, for the protection of health or morals or for the protection of the rights and freedoms of others.

Article 8 seems to cover four different areas, suggesting that, for example, private life can be distinguished from family life. However, the case law suggests that these rights usually need not be clearly distinguished from each other. There will tend to be a clear overlap between them; for example it is often unnecessary to define 'family' because the factual situation might so obviously fall within the term 'private'. The inclusion of the wide (and undefined) term 'private' means that rights other than those arising from the home, family life and correspondence may fall within Article 8.

Respect for private life

In *Niemietz v Germany*[178] the Court said: 'It would be too restrictive to limit the notion [of private life] to an "inner circle" in which the individual may live his own personal life as he chooses and to exclude therefrom entirely the outside world not encompassed within that circle. Respect for private life must also comprise to a certain degree the right to establish and develop relationships with other human beings.' As Harris, O'Boyle and Warbrick observe, 'this extends the concept of private life beyond the narrower confines of the Anglo-American idea of privacy, with its emphasis on the secrecy of personal information and seclusion'.[179] Thus, 'private life' appears to encompass a widening range of protected interests, but this development has been accompanied by a reluctance of the Court to insist on a narrow margin of appreciation when considering what is demanded of states by the notions of 'respect' for private life and by the necessity of interferences with privacy.

---

178 A.251-B para 29 (1992).
179 *Law of the European Convention on Human Rights*, 1995, p 304.

Respect for the privacy of personal information clearly falls within the notion of private life but the Court has approached this aspect cautiously, tending to be satisfied if a procedure is in place allowing the interest in such control to be weighed up against a competing interest. Thus in *Gaskin v UK*[180] the interest of the applicant in obtaining access to the files relating to his childhood in care had to be weighed up against the interest of the contributors to it in maintaining confidentiality, because this interference with privacy had a legitimate aim under the 'rights of others' exception. It was held that the responsible authority did not have a procedure available for weighing the two. Consequently the procedure automatically preferred the contributors and that was disproportionate to the aim of protecting confidentiality and therefore could not be 'necessary in a democratic society'.

The opposite result was reached but by a similar route in the *Klass* case[181] brought in respect of telephone tapping. It was found that although telephone tapping constituted an interference with a person's private life, it could be justified as being in the interests of national security and there were sufficient controls in place (permission had to be given by a minister applying certain criteria including that of 'reasonable suspicion') to ensure that the power was not abused. In the similar *Malone* case,[182] however, there were no such controls in place and a breach of Article 8 was therefore found which led to the introduction of the Interception of Communications Act 1985. A similar path was followed in *Leander v Sweden*[183] in respect of a complaint that information about the applicant had been stored on a secret police register for national security purposes and released to the Navy so that it could vet persons who might be subversive. The applicant complained that he had had no opportunity of challenging the information but the Court found that as there were remedies in place, albeit of a limited nature, to address such grievances Article 8 had not been breached because the national security exception could apply. Again, in *Harman and Hewitt v UK*[184] a breach of Article 8 was found as there was no means of challenging the secret directive which had allowed the storage of information on the applicants.

Protection for personal information may be regarded as part of the 'core' of the concept of privacy, but as the Court made clear in *Niemietz v Germany*[185] aspects of relations with others will also fall within the concept. The Court has made it clear that the choice to have sexual relations with others falls within Article 8. Here also the Court has adopted a cautious

---

180 (1989) 12 EHRR 36.
181 (1979) 2 EHRR 214; see also *Ludi v Switzerland* (1992) 15 EHRR 173.
182 Report of 17 December 1982, A.82; (1985) 7 EHRR 14. See below pp 344–45.
183 Judgment of 26 March 1987, A.116; (1987) 9 EHRR 443. See also, to similar effect *Ebchester v UK* (1993) 18 EHRR CD 72.
184 (1989) 14 EHRR 657.
185 A.251-B para 29 (1992).
186 Judgment of 22 October 1981, A.45; (1982) 4 EHRR 149.

approach. In *Dudgeon*[186] the Northern Ireland prohibition of homosexual intercourse was found to breach Article 8: clearly there had been an interference with privacy; the question was whether the interference was necessary in order to protect morals. It was found unnecessary since the prohibition had not in fact been used in recent times and no detriment to morals had apparently resulted. Northern Ireland amended the relevant legislation in consequence[187] allowing intercourse between consenting males over 21. However, this case concerned a gross interference with privacy since it allowed the applicant no means at all of expressing his sexual preference without committing a criminal offence. In 1984[188] the Commission declared inadmissible an application challenging s 66 of the Army Act 1955, which governs conviction for homosexual practices in the armed forces, on the basis that it could be justified under the prevention of disorder or protection of morals clauses.[189]

Respect for the home

There is not much case law in this area largely because the Strasbourg authorities have adopted a cautious attitude to this right and tend to practise only marginal review of the justification of restrictions. At the core of the right to respect for the home is the right to occupy the home and a right not to be expelled from it. Thus, a violation of Article 8 was established in *Cyprus v Turkey*[190] which concerned occupying forces expelling citizens and making their return to their homes impossible. This was a very clear violation of the right. In contrast, in *Buckley v UK*[191] no violation of this right was found where planning permission for retaining the applicant's caravan on her own land was refused. The refusal was partly based on the planning authority's policy in controlling the sites on which gypsies could live. The Court found that a wide margin of appreciation should be allowed to the Member State and that such margin had not been exceeded since procedural safeguards were in place which allowed for the weighing up of the interests involved: the interest of the applicant in her traditional lifestyle in a caravan and the interest of the planning authority in regulating the use of the land in the area for the benefit of the local community.

The peaceful enjoyment of the home is established as an aspect of respect for the home,[192] but it is unclear as yet how far this notion could be extended

---

187 Homosexual Offences (Northern Ireland) Order 1982. See also *Norris v Ireland* (1991) 13 EHRR 186 which followed *Dudgeon*.
188 *B v UK* 34 D and R 68 (1983); (1983) 6 EHRR 354. A.9237/81.
189 The charges had involved a soldier under 21. Note that the Select Committee on the Armed Forces Bill 1990–91 recommended that s 66 should be replaced (para 41 p xiv).
190 Report of 10 July 1976.
191 (1997) 23 EHRR 101.
192 *Arrondelle v UK*, No 7889/77; 26 D and R 5 (1982).

to the various possible forms of interference with the enjoyment of the home, such as pollution by traffic fumes. Applications in such instances might fail under Article 8 due to the caution evinced in Strasbourg when dealing with this substantive right. However, they might succeed under Article 6(1) if the procedure allowing challenge to such interference was non-existent or defective.[193]

Correspondence

The case law in this area has concerned the right of a detainee to correspond with the outside world and in the UK has led to a steady relaxation of the rules relating to preventing, stopping and censoring of prisoners' correspondence.[194] In general, the supervision *per se* of prisoners' letters is not in breach of Article 8, but particular instances such as stopping a purely personal letter may be.[195] It should be noted that an Article 10 issue may also arise in such circumstances since the detainee's right to receive or impart information is affected.[196]

Article 9: Freedom of thought, conscience and religion

(1) Everyone has the right to freedom of thought, conscience and religion; this right includes freedom to change his religion or belief and freedom, either alone or in community with others and in public or private, to manifest his religion or belief, worship, teaching, practice and observance.

(2) Freedom to manifest one's religion or beliefs shall be subject only to such limitations as are prescribed by law and are necessary in a democratic society in the interests of public safety, for the protection of public order, health or morals or for the protection of the rights and freedoms of others.

The right under Article 9 of possessing certain convictions is unrestricted. Restrictions are only placed on the *expression* of thought under Article 10 and the manifestation of religious belief in Article 9(2). Of course, in general, unless thoughts can be expressed they cannot have much impact. However, Article 9 provides a valuable guarantee against using compulsion to change an opinion[197] or prohibiting someone from entering a profession due to their convictions. In the latter instance, Article 17 (which allows restrictions where a person's ultimate aim is the destruction of Convention rights)[198] might,

---

193 See eg *Zimmermann and Steiner v Switzerland* (1983) 6 EHRR 17.
194 See eg *Silver v UK*, Judgment of 25 March 1983, A.61; (1983) 5 EHRR 347.
195 *Boyle and Rice*, Judgment of 27 April 1988, A.131.
196 See *Herczegfalvy v Austria* (1992) 14 HRLJ 84; (1993) 15 EHRR 437.
197 Such action would normally also involve a violation of Article 3.
198 See below p 81.

however, come into play if someone of fascist or perhaps communist sympathies was debarred from a profession.

Freedom of religion will include the freedom not to take part in religious services, thus particularly affecting persons such as prisoners, but it may also include the opposite obligation – to provide prisoners with a means of practising their religion. However in such instances Strasbourg has been very ready to assume that restrictions are inherent in the detention of prisoners or are justified under para 2. For example, in *Huber v Austria*[199] broad 'inherent limitations' on a prisoner's right to practice religion were accepted. Similarly in *X v Austria*[200] the Commission found no violation in respect of a refusal to allow a Buddhist prisoner to grow a beard. It is arguable, however, that inherent limitations should not be assumed in relation to a right which admits express exceptions.

Article 10: Freedom of expression

(1) Everyone has the right to freedom of expression. This right shall include freedom to hold opinions and to receive and impart information and ideas without interference by public authority and regardless of frontiers. This Article shall not prevent states from requiring the licensing of broadcasting, television or cinema enterprises.

(2) The exercise of these freedoms, since it carries with it duties and responsibilities, may be subject to such formalities, conditions, restrictions or penalties as are prescribed by law and are necessary in a democratic society in the interests of national security, territorial integrity or public safety, for the prevention of disorder or crime, for the protection of health or morals, for the protection of the reputation or rights of others, for preventing the disclosure of information received in confidence or for maintaining the authority and impartiality of the judiciary.

Article 10 obviously overlaps with Article 9 but it is broader since it protects the means of ensuring freedom of expression; even if the person who provides such means is not the holder of the opinion in question she or he will be protected. The words 'freedom to hold opinion' used in Article 10 cannot be distinguished from the phrase 'freedom of thought' used in Article 9. There is also an obvious overlap with Article 11 which protects freedom of association and assembly.

---

199 (1971) Yearbook XIV p 548.
200 Appl 1753/63 (1965) Yearbook VIII 174.

Scope of the primary right

The stance taken under Article 10 is that all speech is not equally valuable. It was found in *X and Church of Scientology v Sweden*[201] that commercial speech is protected by Article 10 but that the level of protection should be less than that accorded to the expression of political ideas, thereby implying that political speech should receive special protection. The motive of the speaker may be significant; if it is to stimulate debate on a particular subject Article 10 will be more readily applicable.[202] The Court has stressed that Article 10 applies not only to speech which is favourably received but also to speech which shocks and offends. In *Jersild v Denmark*[203] the Commission accepted that this may include aiding in the dissemination of racist ideas. In this instance, the applicant had not himself expressed such views; his conviction had arisen due to his responsibility as a television interviewer for their dissemination. This factor was also taken into account by the Court in finding that the conviction constituted an interference with freedom of expression in breach of Article 10.[204] The television programme in question had included an interview with an extreme racist group, the Greenjackets; such interviews were found to constitute an important means whereby 'the press is able to play its vital role as public watchdog' and therefore strong reasons would have to be adduced for punishing a journalist who had assisted in the dissemination of racist statements by conducting the interview, bearing in mind that the feature taken as a whole was not found by the Court to have as its object the propagation of racist views. The Court pointed out that the racist remarks which led to the convictions of members of the Greenjackets did not have the protection of Article 10.

There is some evidence that the Court is reluctant to intervene in instances which may not be perceived as constituting a *direct* interference with freedom of expression by the domestic authorities. If, as in *Glasenapp v Federal Republic of Germany*,[205] the interference can be seen as in some way indirect or as largely concerned with another interest, it may find that the Article 10 guarantee is inapplicable. The case concerned a German schoolteacher who had written a letter to a newspaper indicating her sympathy with the German Communist Party. This was found to be contrary to legislation controlling the employment of people with extreme political views and her appointment as a teacher was revoked. Her claim that this constituted an interference with her freedom of expression failed since the Court characterised the claim as largely concerned with a right of access to the civil service rather than with freedom of speech.

---

201 Appl 7805/77 (1979) Yearbook XXII.
202 See *Thorgeir Thorgeirson v Iceland* (1992) 14 EHRR 843.
203 (1992) 14 HRLJ 74; see also the *Well Woman* case (below p 69).
204 (1994) 19 EHRR 1.
205 (1986) 9 EHRR 25. See to the same effect *Kosiek v FRG* (1987) 9 EHRR 328.

Article 10 includes an additional guarantee of the freedom to receive and impart information. However, the seeking of information does not appear to connote an obligation on the part of the government to make information available; the words 'without restriction by public authority' do not imply a positive obligation on the part of the authority to ensure that information can be received. So the right is restricted in situations where there is no willing speaker. Article 10 is not therefore a full freedom of information measure.[206] In fact the freedom to seek information was deliberately omitted from Article 10 – although it appears in the Universal Declaration of Human Rights – in order to avoid placing a clear positive obligation on the Member States to communicate information.

Restrictions and exceptions

Mediums other than written publications can be subjected to a licensing system under Article 10(1) and because these restrictions are mentioned in para 1 it appears that a licensing system can be imposed on grounds other than those outlined in para 2, thereby broadening the possible exceptions. However, any such exceptions must be considered in conjunction with the safeguard against discrimination under Article 14: for example if the state has a monopoly on a medium it must not discriminate in granting air time to different groups.

The restrictions of Article 10(2) are wide and two, maintaining the authority of the judiciary and preventing the disclosure of information received in confidence, are not mentioned in Article 10's companion Articles – Articles 8, 9 and 11. The first of these exceptions was included bearing in mind the contempt law of the UK but it was made clear in the well-known *Sunday Times* case,[207] that in relation to such law the margin of appreciation should be narrow due to its 'objective' nature. In other words, what was needed to maintain the authority of the judiciary could be more readily evaluated by an objective observer than could measures needed to protect morals. The case in question concerned reporting on a matter of great public interest – the Thalidomide tragedy – and therefore only very compelling reasons for preventing the information being imparted could be justified. It was held that because Article 10 is a particularly important right and the particular instance touched on its essence, a breach could be found; in response the Contempt of Court Act 1981 was passed. The 'rights of others' exception may also receive a narrow interpretation – at least in cases of defamation against a public body or

---

206 This was supported in the *Gaskin* case (1990) 12 EHRR 36 (see above p 62): the Article 10 claim failed on this basis.
207 Judgment of 26 April 1979, A.30; (1979) 2 EHRR 245 (discussed in full in Chap 4 pp 149–51).

person where the applicant was acting in good faith and was attempting to stimulate debate on a matter of serious public concern.[208]

A very different approach was taken in the *Handyside* case[209] arising from a conviction under the Obscene Publications Act 1959 and concerning the more subjective nature of the 'protection of morals' exception. The applicant put forward certain special circumstances – that the prohibited material in question was circulating in most other countries and so suppression could not be very evidently necessary in a democratic society – but such circumstances were barely discussed. A wide margin of appreciation was left to the national authorities as to what was 'necessary'. One possible reason for this was that the authority of the judiciary is a more objective notion than the protection of morals and this may have led to a variation of the necessity test. A similar approach was taken in *Müller v Switzerland*,[210] the Court stating, 'it is not possible to find in the legal and social orders of the contracting states a uniform European conception of morals ... By reason of their direct and continuous contact with the vital forces of their countries state authorities are in a better position than the international judge to give an opinion on the exact content of these requirements'.

The lack of a uniform standard was also the key factor in the ruling in *Otto-Preminger Institut v Austria*.[211] The decision concerned the showing of a satirical film depicting God as a senile old man and Jesus as a mental defective erotically attracted to the Virgin Mary. Criminal proceedings for the offence of disparaging religious doctrines were brought against the manager of the Institute which had scheduled the showings of the film. The film was seized by the Austrian authorities while criminal proceedings were pending. The European Court of Human Rights found that the seizure of the film could be seen as furthering the aims of Article 9 of the Convention and therefore it fell within the 'rights of others' exception. In considering whether the seizure and forfeiture of the film was 'necessary in a democratic society' in order to protect the rights of others to respect for their religious views, the Court took into account the lack of a uniform conception within the Member States of the significance of religion in society and therefore considered that the national authorities should have a wide margin of appreciation in assessing what was necessary to protect religious feeling. In ordering the seizure of the film the Austrian authorities had taken its artistic value into account but had not found that it outweighed its offensive features. The Court found that the

---

208 See *Thorgeir Thorgeirson v Iceland* above note 202; *Castells v Spain* (1992) 14 EHRR 445; *Schwabe v Austria* (1992) 14 HRLJ 26.
209 Judgment of 7 December 1976, A.24; (1976) 1 EHRR 737.
210 (1991) 13 EHRR 212.
211 (1994) 19 EHRR 34.

national authorities had not overstepped their margin of appreciation and therefore decided that no breach of Article 10 had occurred. This decision left a very wide discretion to the Member State, a discretion which the dissenting judges considered to be too wide.

The stance taken in *Otto-Preminger* and in *Müller* echoes the view expressed in *Cossey v UK*[212] that where a clear European view does emerge the Court may well be influenced by it but it also suggests a particularly strong reluctance to intervene in this very contentious area. The margin of appreciation in respect of the protection of morals will not be unlimited, however, even in the absence of a broad consensus. The Court so held in *Open Door Counselling* and *Dublin Well Woman v Ireland*,[213] ruling that an injunction which prevented the dissemination of any information at all about abortion amounted to a breach of Article 10. This accords with the view expressed in *B v France*[214] that what can be termed the common standards principle is only one factor to be taken into account and must be weighed against the severity of the infringement of rights in question.

The exception in respect of confidential information overlaps with others, including national security and the rights of others, but a situation could be envisaged in which a disclosure of information did not fall within those categories and could therefore be caught only by this extra exception. This might arise in respect of a disclosure by a civil servant which did not threaten national security or any person's individual rights, such as that made in the *Tisdall* case.[215]

Actions in respect of both prior and subsequent restraints on freedom of expression may be brought under Article 10, but pre-publication sanctions will be regarded as more pernicious and thus harder to justify as necessary (*Observer and Guardian v UK*).[216] In relation to post-publication sanctions criminal actions will be regarded as having a grave impact on freedom of expression, but civil actions which have severe consequences for the individual may also be hard to justify. In *Tolstoy Miloslavsky v UK*[217] the European Court of Human Rights considered the level of libel damages which can be awarded in UK courts. Libel damages of £1.5 million had been awarded against Count Tolstoy Miloslavsky in the UK in respect of a pamphlet he had written which alleged that Lord Aldington, a high ranking British army officer, had been responsible for handing over 70,000 people to the Soviet authorities without authorisation, knowing that they would meet a

---

212 (1990) 13 EHRR 622.
213 (1992) 15 EHRR 244.
214 (1992) 13 HRLJ 358.
215 See Chap 6 p 234.
216 (1991) 14 EHRR 153.
217 (1995) *The Times*, 19 July.

cruel fate. The Count argued that this very large award constituted a breach of Article 10. Was the award necessary in a democratic society as required by Article 10? The Court found that it was not, having regard to the fact that the scope of judicial control at the trial could not offer an adequate safeguard against a disproportionately large award. Thus a violation of the applicant's rights under Article 10 was found.

Article 11: Freedom of association and assembly

(1) Everyone has the right to freedom of peaceful assembly and to freedom of association with others, including the right to form and to join trade unions for the protection of his interests.

(2) No restrictions shall be placed on the exercise of these rights other than such as are prescribed by law and are necessary in a democratic society in the interests of national security or public safety, for the prevention of disorder or crime, for the protection of health or morals or for the protection of the rights and freedoms of others. This Article shall not prevent the imposition of lawful restrictions on the exercise of these rights by members of the armed forces, of the police or of the administration of the state.

Assembly

The addition of the word 'peaceful' has restricted the scope of para 1: there will be no need to invoke the para 2 exceptions if the authorities concerned could reasonably believe that a planned assembly would not be peaceful. Thus assemblies can be subject to permits so long as the permits relate to the peacefulness of the assembly and not to the right of assembly itself. However, a restriction of a very wide character relating to peacefulness might affect the right to assemble itself and might therefore constitute a violation of Article 11 if it did not fall within one of the exceptions.

It should be noted that freedom of assembly may not merely be secured by a *lack* of interference by the public authorities; they may have positive obligations to intervene in order to prevent an interference with freedom of assembly by private individuals, although they will have a very wide margin of appreciation in this regard.[218] It has been held in respect of the guarantees of other Articles that states must secure to individuals the rights and freedoms of the Convention by preventing or remedying any breach thereof. If no duty was placed on the authorities to provide such protection then some assemblies could not take place.

---

218 Appl 1012/82, *Platform 'Arzte für das Leben' v Austria* D and R 44 (1985); (1988) 13 EHRR 204 (it was not arguable that Austria had failed in its obligation to prevent counter-demonstrators interfering with an anti-abortion demonstration).

Association

'Association' need not be assigned its national meaning. Even if a group such as a trade union is not an 'association' according to the definition of national law it may fall within Article 11. The term connotes a voluntary association, not a professional organisation established by the government. It should be noted that it is only with respect to trade unions that the right to form an association is expressly mentioned, albeit non-exhaustively. Such a right in respect of other types of association is clearly implicit – a necessary part of freedom of association.

The question whether freedom of association implies protection against compulsory membership of an association was considered in *Young, James and Webster*.[219] It was found that a measure of freedom of choice is implicit in Article 11; this amounts to a negative aspect of the right to join a trade union and is not therefore on the same footing as the positive aspect, but it is still a part of freedom of association. The Court left open the question whether a closed shop agreement would always amount to a breach of Article 11; in this instance the possibility of dismissal due to refusal to join the union was such a serious form of coercion that it affected the essence of the Article 11 guarantee. It seems that the closed shop practice may be a violation of Article 11 where there is legislation allowing it, even if the body enforcing it is not an emanation of the state (an example of *Drittwürkung*). It may be noted that the degree of freedom of choice under Article 11 is limited; it does not appear to include as a necessary component the freedom to choose between unions.[220]

The right to join a trade union involves allowing members to have a union that can properly 'protect the interests of the members'. So a union must have sufficient scope for this, although this need not mean a right to strike; this right can be subject to the restrictions of the national legislature.[221] Moreover, extra restrictions may be placed on certain groups of employees under the second sentence of para 2 and these do not expressly need to be 'necessary'. However, the purposes of the Convention imply that they should indeed be necessary.

Article 12: The right to marry and to found a family

> Men and women of marriageable age have the right to marry and to found a family, according to the national laws governing the exercise of this right.

Article 12 contains no second paragraph setting out restrictions, but it obviously does not confer an absolute right due to the words 'according to the

---

219 Judgment of 13 August 1981, A.44; (1981) 4 EHRR 38.
220 *Sibson v UK* A.258 (1993); (1993) *The Guardian*, 10 May; (1993) *The Times*, 17 May.
221 Judgment of 6 February 1976, *Schmidt and Dahlström v Sweden*, A.21 (1976); (1979–80) 1 EHRR 637.

national laws' which imply the reverse of an absolute right – that Article 12 may be subject to far-reaching limitations in domestic law. The reference to national laws also accepts the possibility that legal systems may vary among contracting states as to, for example, the legally marriageable age. However, this does not mean that the Convention has no role at all; it may not interfere with national law governing the exercise of the right but may do so where it attacks or erodes its essence. If a person was denied the right to marry due to limited mental faculties or health or poverty, the essence of the right would be eroded assuming that he or she was capable of genuine consent. However, where erosion of the essence of the right arises from the national rule that only persons of the opposite sex can marry it may be acceptable. In *Rees*[222] a woman who had had a gender re-assignment operation complained that she was unable to marry. It was held that there was no violation of Article 12 because the state can impose restrictions on certain men and women due to the social purpose of Article 12 which is concerned with the ability to procreate; marriages which cannot result in procreation may therefore fall outside its ambit. This interpretation was supported on the ground that the wording of the Article suggests that marriage is protected as the basis of the family; thus Article 12 is aimed at protecting the traditional biological marriage. In other words, what appeared to be a clear interference with the essence of the right could be found not to be so under this restricted interpretation. Therefore preventing the marriage of persons not of the opposite biological sex was not found to breach Article 12. This ruling was followed in *Cossey*[223] on the ground that changes in social values did not indicate a need to depart from the decision in *Rees*.

The principle that the Convention will not interfere with national laws which only regulate the *exercise* of the right to marry is also subject to exceptions. If a person is in general free to marry but in particular circumstances will suffer detriment flowing solely from the fact of being married, Article 12 may be breached. Thus the right to marry may include placing no sanction on marriage such as sacking a person when he or she marries. But if a priest is sacked when he ceases to be celibate that would not seem to constitute a breach since he has, in a sense, chosen freely not to marry.

The right to divorce or dissolution of marriage is not included under Article 12[224] so that the state need not provide the means of dissolving a marriage although in some circumstances Article 8 may be relevant. It seems that the state need not provide such means as the right has been deliberately left out of the Convention, and although the Convention is subject to an evolutive interpretation (in other words changes in social conditions can be taken into account), that will not apply to a right which has been totally omitted.

---

222 Judgment of 17 October 1986, A.106; (1987) 9 EHRR 56.
223 Judgment of 27 September 1990, A.184; (1990) 13 EHRR 622.
224 *Johnstone* judgment of 18 December 1986, A.112; (1987) 9 EHRR 203.

In accordance with the general Convention policy of reluctance to impose positive obligations on states, the right to found a family does not include an economic right to sufficient living accommodation for the family: it denotes an interference with the ability to found a family and thus prevents the non-voluntary use of sterilisation or abortion. Article 3 and possibly Article 2[225] would probably also apply. The national laws are again allowed to regulate the enjoyment of this right but they must not erode its essence. However, it might be argued that inherent limitations on the right in certain situations may be allowed because restrictions are not enumerated under Article 12, and therefore such limitations would not create a conflict with the general Convention doctrine governing inherent limitations which tends to reject such limitations where the restrictions are enumerated. However, it was found in *Hamer*[226] that prisoners do have the right to marry under Article 12; inherent restrictions are possible but they must not affect the essence of the right. The applicant had two years to wait; that did affect the essence of the right and therefore led to a breach of Article 12. In contrast in *X v UK*[227] it was found that denial of conjugal visits to a detainee was not a violation of Article 12 since the Article grants the general right to found a family; it does not grant that that possibility should be available at any given moment.

Protocols to the Convention

The First, Fourth, Sixth and Seventh Protocols to the Convention add to it a number of substantive rights. Only the First Protocol has been ratified by the UK.

First Protocol

Article 1

> Every natural or legal person is entitled to the peaceful enjoyment of his possessions. No one shall be deprived of his possessions except in the public interest and subject to the conditions provided for by law and by the general principles of international law.
>
> The preceding provisions shall not, however, in any way impair the right of a state to enforce such laws as it deems necessary to control the use of property in accordance with the general interest or to secure the payment of taxes or other contributions or penalties.

The property Article of the First Protocol echoes Article 12 in allowing the national authorities considerable freedom to regulate the exercise of the primary right. The case law has supported this; it was determined in *James and*

---

225 See above p 37.
226 Report of 13 December 1979; D and R 24 (1981).
227 Appl 6564/74; D and R 2 (1975).

Others[228] that the margin of appreciation open to the legislature in implementing social and economic policies should be a wide one. As mentioned above, claims of interference with property may fail under the Protocol but succeed under Article 6 where a defective procedure has authorised the interference.[229]

Article 2
> No person shall be denied the right to education. In the exercise of any functions which it assumes in relation to education and to teaching, the state shall respect the right of parents to ensure such education and teaching in conformity with their own religious and philosophical convictions.

The UK is a party to the First Protocol but has made the following reservation to Article 2: '… in view of certain provisions of the Education Acts in force in the United Kingdom, the principle affirmed in the second sentence of Article 2 is accepted by the United Kingdom only so far it is compatible with the provision of efficient instruction and training and the avoidance of unreasonable public expenditure.'

In the *Belgian Linguistic* cases[230] it was held that Article 2 does not require the contracting states to provide a particular type of education: it implies the right of persons to 'avail themselves of the means of instruction existing at a given time'.

Article 3
> The High Contracting Parties undertake to hold free elections at reasonable intervals by secret ballot, under conditions which will ensure the free expression of the opinion of the people in the choice of the legislature.

Article 3 does not imply an absolute right to vote but that elections should be held at regular intervals, should be secret, free from pressure on the electorate and the choice between candidates should be genuine.

The Fourth, Sixth and Seventh Protocols cover, broadly speaking: freedom of movement (Protocol 4), abolition of the death penalty (Protocol 6), the right of an alien lawfully resident in a state to full review of his or her case before expulsion, rights of appeal, compensation for miscarriages of justice, the right not to be subjected to double jeopardy and sexual equality between spouses as regards private law rights and responsibilities (Protocol 7). A new Protocol on Minority Rights was recommended to the Committee of Ministers in 1993 but it has not been adopted.[231] The other Protocols, including the most recent, Protocol 11, are concerned with the procedural machinery of the Convention.

---

228 Judgment of 21 February 1986, A.98.
229 *Mats Jacobson v Sweden* (1990) 13 EHRR 79. See above p 54, note 136 and associated text.
230 Judgment of 23 July 1968, A.6; (1968) 1 EHRR 252.
231 See 14 HRLJ 140.

These other procedural Protocols will be abolished when Protocol 11, discussed above,[232] comes into force.

4 ADDITIONAL GUARANTEES TO THE PRIMARY RIGHTS

Article 13: The right to an effective remedy before a national authority

> Everyone whose rights and freedoms as set forth in this Convention are violated shall have an effective remedy before a national authority notwithstanding that the violation has been committed by persons acting in an official capacity.

In *Leander v Sweden*[233] it was found that 'the requirements of Article 13 will be satisfied if there exists domestic machinery whereby, subject to the inherent limitations of the context, the individual can secure compliance with the relevant laws'. This machinery may include a number of possible remedies. It has been held that judicial review proceedings will be sufficient. In *Vilvarajah and Four Others v the UK*[234] the applicants maintained that judicial review did not satisfy Article 13 since the English courts could not consider the merits of the Home Secretary's decision in this instance, merely the manner in which it was taken. In holding that the power of judicial review satisfied the Article 13 test the Court took into account the power of the UK courts to quash an administrative decision for unreasonableness, and the fact that these powers were exercisable by the highest tribunal in the UK. Thus no violation of Article 13 was found.

Article 13 does not contain a general guarantee that anyone who considers that his or her rights have been violated by the authorities should have an effective remedy; it can only be considered if one of the substantive rights or freedoms is in question. The words do not and cannot connote a requirement that there should be domestic machinery in place to address any possible grievance. The words 'are violated' of Article 13 do not mean that the violation must have been established before the national courts because clearly it could not have been – if it could that would suggest that an effective remedy *did* exist. They mean that a person should have an arguable claim; there will be no breach of Article 13 if the complaint is unmeritorious – in other words, if it is clearly apparent that no violation of the Convention has

---

232 Pages 21–24.
233 Judgment of 26 March 1987, A.116; (1987) 9 EHRR 443. Note that if such machinery exists but is of doubtful efficacy a challenge under Article 6(1) may be most likely to succeed (*de Geoffre de la Pradelle v France* (1993) HRLJ 276).
234 Judgment of 30 October 1991, A.215.

taken place. Even if no violation of the other Article is eventually found it can still be argued that the national courts should have provided an effective means of considering the possible violation. Moreover, a claim may eventually be held to be manifestly ill-founded and yet arguable. This is an odd result but, in principle, it is what the case law appears to disclose. In *Klass*[235] it was found that 'Article 13 must be interpreted as guaranteeing an effective remedy before a national authority to everyone who claims that his rights and freedoms under the Convention have been violated'. In *Platform Arzte für das Leben*[236] it was found that the claim must be arguable. Thus Article 13 can be invoked only if no procedure is available which can begin to determine whether a violation has occurred. In theory then there could be a breach of Article 13 alone and in that sense it protects an independent right. In practice case law tends not to follow this purist approach, and if no violation of the substantive right is found it is likely that no violation of Article 13 will be found either (as it may be argued occurred in the *Arzte für das Leben* case).

In the *Klass* case it was determined that phone tapping did not breach Article 8 since it was found to be in the interests of national security. The applicants claimed that Article 13 could be considered on the basis of their assertion that no effective domestic remedy existed for challenging the decision to tap. The Court accepted that the existing remedy was of limited efficacy: it consisted only of the possibility of review of the case by a Parliamentary Committee. Nevertheless, it found that in all the circumstances no more effective remedy was possible. Thus the Court allowed the doctrine of the margin of appreciation to resolve the difficulty which arose from the fact that the tapping was done in order to combat terrorism in its attack on democracy but the means employed, which included the suspension of judicial remedies, might well be termed undemocratic.

Article 14: Prohibition of discrimination

> The enjoyment of the rights and freedoms set forth in this Convention shall be secured without discrimination on any ground such as sex, race, colour, language, religion, political or other opinion, national or social origin, association with a national minority, property, birth or other status.

Article 14 does not provide a *general* right to freedom from discrimination, only that the rights and freedoms of the Convention must be secured without discrimination. Thus, if discrimination occurs in an area which is not covered by the Convention, such as most contractual aspects of employment, Article 14 will be irrelevant. It is therefore a very limited anti-discrimination measure. However, Article 14 is not the only Convention vehicle which may be used to

---

235 Judgment of 6 September 1978, A.28; (1979) 2 EHRR 214.
236 (1988) 13 EHRR 204.

challenge discriminatory practices. Not only may discrimination be attacked though the medium of one of the other Articles, most particularly Article 3,[237] but the Convention may be of particular value as a source of general principles in sex discrimination cases before the European Court of Justice.[238] An applicant may allege violation of a substantive right taken alone and also that he or she has been discriminated against in respect of that right. However, even if no violation of the substantive right taken alone is found and even if that claim is manifestly ill-founded, there could still be a violation of that Article and Article 14 taken together so long as the matter at issue is covered by the other Article. This was found in *X v Federal Republic of Germany* (1970):[239] 'Article 14 of the Convention has no independent existence ...; nevertheless a measure which in itself is in conformity with the requirement of the Article enshrining the right or freedom in question, may however infringe this Article when read in conjunction with Article 14 for the reason that it is of a discriminatory nature'. In this sense the Court has granted more autonomy to Article 14 than appeared to be intended originally.[240]

This ruling allowed more claims to be considered than the 'arguability' principle applying under Article 13. For example, in *Abdulaziz, Cabales and Balkandali*[241] the female claimants wanted their non-national spouses to enter the UK and alleged a breach of Article 8 which protects family life. That claim was rejected. But a violation of Article 14 was found because the way the rule was applied made it easier for men to bring in their spouses. It was held that 'Although the application of Article 14 does not necessarily presuppose a breach [of the substantive provisions of the Convention and the Protocols] – and to this extent it is autonomous – there can be no room for its application unless the facts at issue fall within the ambit of one or more of the rights and freedoms'. In response to this ruling the UK government 'equalised down', placing men and women in an equally disadvantageous position as regards their non-national spouses.

Under Article 14 discrimination connotes differential treatment which is unjustifiable. The differential treatment may be unjustifiable either in the sense that it relates to no objective and reasonable aim or in the sense that there is no reasonable proportionality between the means employed and the aim sought to be realised.[242] In *Abdulaziz* the aim was to protect the domestic labour market. It was held that this was not enough to justify the differential

---

237 *East African Asians* cases (1973) 3 EHRR 76.
238 See eg *Johnstone v Chief Constable of the RUC* [1986] ECR 1651.
239 Appl 4045/69 (1970) Yearbook XIII.
240 For comment on the increasing autonomy of Article 14 see Livingstone, S (1997) 1 EHRR 25.
241 A.94; (1985) 7 EHRR 471.
242 *Geïllustreerde Pers NV v the Netherlands* D and R 8 (1977).

treatment because the difference in treatment was out of proportion to that aim. The outcome in this case illustrated the limitations of Article 14 which it shares with all anti-discrimination measures: it is concerned only with procedural fairness and can only ensure equal treatment which may be unjustifiable. Unjustifiable equal treatment is, however, unlikely to occur when the group in question is comparing itself with the dominant group since the dominant group will ensure, through the democratic process, that it does not experience a lower standard of treatment. However, where, as in *Abdulaziz*, the differentiation is occurring within a non-dominant group the way is opened for equally poor treatment. This can be averted only by comparing the group as a whole with the dominant group. However, this argument was rejected by the European Court of Human Rights which found that the treatment was not racially discriminatory.

5 RESTRICTION OF THE RIGHTS AND FREEDOMS

The system of restrictions

All the Articles except Articles 3, 4(1) and 6(2) are subject to certain restrictions, either because certain limitations are inherent in the formulation of the right itself,[243] or because it is expressly stated that particular cases are not covered by the right in question or because general restrictions on the primary right contained in the first paragraph are enumerated in a second paragraph (Articles 8–11). Certain further general restrictions are allowed under Articles 17, 15 and 64. In considering the restrictions Article 18 must also be borne in mind. It provides that the motives of the national authority in creating the restrictions must be the same as the aims appearing behind the restrictions when the Convention was drafted.

Article 15: Derogation from the rights and freedoms in case of public emergency

> (1) In time of war or other public emergency threatening the life of the nation any High Contracting Party may take measures derogating from its obligations under this Convention to the extent strictly required by the exigencies of the situation, provided that such measures are not inconsistent with its other obligations under international law.

---

243 For example, Article 14 which prohibits discrimination is inherently limited because it operates only in the context of the other Convention rights and freedoms.

(2) No derogation from Article 2, except in respect of deaths resulting from lawful acts of war or from Articles 3, 4 (para 1) and 7 shall be made under this provision.

(3) Any High Contracting Party availing itself of this right of derogation shall keep the Secretary General of the Council of Europe fully informed of the measures which it has taken and the reasons therefore. It shall also inform the Secretary General of the Council of Europe when such measures have ceased to operate and the provisions of the Convention are again being fully executed.

Article 15 allows derogation in respect of most but not all of the Articles. Derogation from Article 2 is not allowed except in respect of death resulting from lawful acts of war, while Articles 3, 4(1) and 7 are entirely non-derogable. Apart from these exceptions a valid derogation requires the state in question to show that there is a state of war or public emergency and in order to determine the validity of this claim two questions should be asked. First, is there an actual or imminent exceptional crisis threatening the organised life of the state? Secondly, is it really necessary to adopt measures requiring derogation from the Articles in question? A margin of discretion is allowed in answering these questions because it is thought that the state in question is best placed to determine the facts, but it is not unlimited; Strasbourg will review it if the state has acted unreasonably. However, the Court has not been very consistent as regards the margin allowed to the state.[244] In general if a derogation is entered it must first be investigated and if found invalid the claims in question will *then* be examined.

The UK entered a derogation in the case of *Brogan*[245] after the European Court of Human Rights had found that a violation of Article 5, which protects liberty, had occurred. At the time of the violation there was no derogation in force in respect of Article 5 because the UK had withdrawn its derogation. This might suggest either that there was no need for it or that the UK had chosen not to derogate despite the gravity of the situation which would have justified derogation.[246] However, after the decision in the European Court the UK entered the derogation stating that there was an emergency at the time. This was challenged as an invalid derogation,[247] but the claim failed on the basis that the exigencies of the situation did amount to a public emergency and the derogation could not be called into question merely because the government had decided to keep open the possibility of finding a means in the future of ensuring greater conformity with Convention obligations. The fact that the emergency measures had been in place since 1974 did not mean that the emergency was not still in being. However, it may be argued that a

---

244 See below pp 82–85.
245 Judgment of 29 November 1988; (1989) 11 EHRR 117; A.145 (1989).
246 See Chap 9 p 348.
247 *Brannigan and McBride v UK* (1993) 17 EHRR 539.

state's failure to enter a derogation need not preclude the claim that a state of emergency did exist. If whenever a state perceived the possibility that an emergency situation might exist it felt it had to enter a derogation as an 'insurance measure' this would encourage a wider use of derogation which would clearly be undesirable.

In the *Greek* case[248] the Commission was prepared to hold an Article 15 derogation invalid. Greece had alleged that the derogation was necessary due to the exigencies of the situation: it was necessary to constrain the activities of communist agitators due to the disruption they were likely to cause. There had been past disruption which had verged on anarchy. Greece therefore claimed that it could not abide by the Articles in question: Articles 10 and 11. Apart from violations of those articles violations of Article 3, which is non-derogable, were also alleged. The Commission found that the derogation was not needed; the situation at the decisive moment did not contain all the elements necessary under Article 15.

Article 16: Restriction on the political activity of aliens

> Nothing in Articles 10, 11 and 14 shall be regarded as preventing the High Contracting Parties from imposing restrictions on the political activity of aliens.

Since Article 16 applies to Articles 10 and 11, it implies that restrictions over and above those already imposed due to the second paragraphs of those Articles can be imposed on aliens in respect of their enjoyment of the freedoms guaranteed, as far as their political activity is concerned. This does not mean that aliens have *no* safeguard of freedom of expression, association or assembly; restrictions can be imposed only if they relate to political activities. Through its effect on Article 14, Article 16 affects all the rights in the Convention since it means that the national authorities can discriminate in relation to aliens as far as any of the Convention rights are concerned. Article 16 has therefore been greatly criticised as creating consequences which 'hardly fit into the system of the Convention'.[249] The fact that discrimination as regards the protection afforded to Convention rights is allowable, would not, however, preclude claims that the substantive rights – other than those arising under Articles 10 and 11 – had been violated.

---

248 Report of 5 November 1969, Yearbook XII.
249 See Van Dijk, P and Van Hoof, GJH, *Theory and Practice of the European Convention on Human Rights*, p 410.

Article 17: Destruction of Convention rights

> Nothing in this Convention may be interpreted as implying for any state, group or person any right to engage in any activity or perform any act aimed at the destruction of any of the rights and freedoms set forth herein or at their limitation to a greater extent than is provided for in the Convention.

Article 17 prevents a person relying on a Convention right where his or her ultimate aim is the destruction or limitation of Convention rights. Article 17 is dealt with on the issue of admissibility but it can be looked at a later stage too. Its 'restriction' applies to all the rights and freedoms. In general if Article 17 is violated this may well mean that one of the other restrictions on the freedom in question applies too; thus Article 17 is of importance only when it appears that some measure allows evasion of a Convention guarantee in a manner not covered by the other restrictions. Thus Article 17 must be read in conjunction with all the articles as allowing for a new exception. This is of particular importance where the guarantee in question is subject to few or no restrictions.

Making a reservation: Article 64

Article 64 provides that a state can declare when signing the Convention that it cannot abide by a particular provision because domestic law then in force is not in conformity with it. This may be done when the Convention or Protocol is ratified. The Court will review the reservation in order to see whether it is specific enough: it should not be of too general a nature.[250] The UK has only entered a reservation in respect of Protocol 1.[251]

General restrictions on the rights and freedoms contained in Articles 8–11

These Articles have a second paragraph enumerating certain restrictions on the primary right. Two general phrases are used in respect of these exceptions: 'prescribed by law'[252] and 'necessary in a democratic society'. The latter phrase was interpreted in the *Handyside* case[253] and the *Silver* case[254] as meaning that to be compatible with the Convention the interference must, *inter alia*, correspond to a pressing social need and 'be proportionate to the

---

250 In *Belilos v Switzerland* (1988) EHRR 466 it was found that the reservation did not comply with Article 64 because it was too general.
251 See above p 74.
252 This phrase includes unwritten law; see *Sunday Times* case, Judgment of 26 April 1979, A.30; (1979) 2 EHRR 245.
253 Judgment of 7 December 1976, A.24; (1976) 1 EHRR 737.
254 Judgment of 25 March 1983, A.61; (1983) 5 EHRR 347.

legitimate aim pursued'. Taken together these two phrases mean that four tests must be satisfied if a restriction is to be invoked:
(1) The restriction must be in accordance with a rule of national law which satisfies the Convention meaning of 'law'.
(2) The law on which the restriction is based is aimed at protecting one of the interests listed in para 2; in other words, the restriction falls within one of the exceptions.
(3) In the particular instance it can be said that the interference is necessary in the sense that it is concerned with a particular restriction such as the protection of morals, and in the particular case there is a real need to protect morals – a pressing social need – as opposed to an unclear or weak danger to morals.
(4) The interference is in proportion to the aim pursued; in other words, it does not go further than is needed, bearing in mind the objective in question.

The interests covered by the restrictions are largely the same: national security, protection of morals, the rights of others, public safety. The state is allowed a 'margin of appreciation' – a degree of discretion – as to the measures needed to protect the particular interest.

The doctrine of the 'margin of appreciation'[255]

Under this doctrine a degree of discretion will be allowed to Member States as to legislative, administrative or judicial action in the area of a Convention right. However, Strasbourg will finally determine whether such action is reconcilable with the guarantee in question. This doctrine was first adopted in respect of emergency situations[256] but it has gradually permeated all the Articles. It has a particular application with respect to Articles 8–11, para 2, but it can affect all the guarantees. In different cases a wider or narrower margin of appreciation has been allowed. It should be pointed out that although the doctrine is well-established it has not been applied very consistently and therefore only indications as to its application can be given.

A narrow margin may be allowed, in which case a very full and detailed review of the interference with the guarantee in question will be conducted. This occurred in the *Sunday Times* case; it was held that Strasbourg review was

---

255 For discussion of the doctrine see McDonald, RJ, 'The margin of appreciation in the jurisprudence of the European Court of Human Rights', *International Law and the Time of its Codification*, 1987, pp 187–208; Van Dijk and Van Hoof, *The Theory and Practice of the European Convention on Human Rights*, 1990, p 604; O'Donell, 'The Margin of Appreciation Doctrine: Standards in the Jurisprudence of the European Court of Human Rights' (1982) 4 *Human Rights Q* 474; Morrisson, 'Margin of Appreciation in Human Rights Law' (1973) 6 *Human Rights J* 263.

256 See the *Lawless* case, Publ ECHR B.1 (1960–61) p 408; (1961) 1 EHRR 15.

not limited to asking whether the state had exercised its discretion reasonably, carefully and in good faith; it was found that its conduct must also be examined in Strasbourg to see whether it was compatible with the Convention. If a broader margin is allowed Strasbourg review will be highly circumscribed. For example, the minority in the *Sunday Times* case (nine judges) wanted to confine the role of Strasbourg to asking only whether the discretion in question was exercised in good faith and carefully and whether the measure was reasonable in the circumstances.

It is not always easy to predict when each approach will be taken but a number of relevant factors may be identified:

(1) The nature of the right in question. The doctrine is particularly applicable to the Articles 8–11 group of rights since it is used in determining whether an interference with the right is justifiable on grounds of one of the exceptions contained in para 2 of these Articles. Within this group Article 10 may be viewed as particularly fundamental.[257] Also the particular instance will be considered: does it concern, for example, a very significant need for free expression since there is a strong public interest in the subject matter? The presence of such factors may predispose the Strasbourg authorities to conduct a wide ranging review. Such review also tends to be applicable under Articles 2[258] and 3[259] although it may be narrowed where the state claims that the demands of national security justify the measures sought to be challenged under these Articles.[260]

(2) The nature of the restriction. Some restrictions are seen as more subjective than others. It is therefore thought more difficult to lay down a common European standard and the Court and Commission have in such instances shown a certain willingness to allow the exceptions a wide scope in curtailing the primary rights. For example, Article 10 contains an exception in respect of the protection of morals. This was invoked in the *Handyside* case[261] in respect of suppression of a booklet aimed at schoolchildren which was circulating freely in the rest of Europe. It was held that the UK government was best placed to determine what was needed in its own country in order to protect morals and therefore it could make an initial assessment of those requirements, which would then be considered for compatibility with Article 10 by Strasbourg.

Some restrictions, particularly national security, appear to fall more within the state's domain than others. It is thought that the state authorities are best placed to evaluate the situation and determine what is needed. In

---

[257] See eg the judgment of the Court in *Autronic AG v Switzerland* (1990) 12 EHRR 485.
[258] *McCann, Farrell and Savage v UK* (1995) 21 EHRR 97, A.324, Council of Europe Report.
[259] *Soering v UK*, Judgment of 7 July 1989, A.161; (1989) 11 EHRR 439.
[260] *Kröcher and Möller v Switzerland* No 8463/78, 34 DR 25.
[261] (1976) 1 EHRR 737.

Civil Service Unions v UK[262] the European Commission, in declaring the Unions' application inadmissible, found that national security interests should prevail over freedom of association even though the national security interest was weak while the infringement of the primary right was very clear: an absolute ban on joining a trade union had been imposed. It is worth noting that the ILO Committee on Freedom of Association had earlier found that the ban breached the 1947 ILO Freedom of Association Convention. However, in general, if a restriction is very far-reaching the Strasbourg authorities may be prepared to make a determination as to the need to impose it which differs from that of the state party in question.[263]

(3) The Court is greatly influenced by general practice in the Member States as a body and will interpret the Convention to reflect such practice so that a state which is clearly out of conformity with the others may expect an adverse ruling. However, where practice is still in the process of changing and may be said to be at an inchoate stage as far as the Member States generally are concerned, it may not be prepared to place itself at the forefront of such changes, although it will weigh the lack of a consensus against the degree of detriment to the applicant.[264] The application of this principle, which has been termed the 'common standards' principle, clearly allows flexibility in decision-making since it may sometimes be difficult to pinpoint the time at which a common standard could be said to have emerged. It might therefore be prayed in aid to support a decision either adverse or favourable to the applicant.

(4) The wording of the requirements in question. Some, such as the requirement of promptness in Article 5(3), leave open some leeway in interpretation while others are very specific, such as the right to cross examine witnesses under Article 6(3)(d).

(5) The positive obligations placed on the state. In order to allow enjoyment of the Convention right in question the state may have to act positively. In such an instance a broad margin will be allowed.[265]

The doctrine of the margin of appreciation clearly has the power to undermine the Convention and therefore its growth has been criticised. Van Dijk and Van Hoof have written of it as 'a spreading disease. Not only has the scope of its application been broadened to the point where in principle none of the Convention rights or freedoms are excluded but also has the illness been intensified in that wider versions of the doctrine have been added to the original concept'.[266] As mentioned at the beginning of

---

262 (1988) 10 EHRR 269.
263 See eg *Golder*, Judgment of 21 February 1975; A.18. Discussed Chap 11 pp 422–23.
264 *Rees v UK* (1987) 9 EHRR 56.
265 See *Platform Artze für das Leben* (1988) 13 EHRR 204, above p 70 note 218.
266 *Theory and Practice of the European Convention on Human Rights*, p 604.

this chapter, the doctrine may sometimes be appropriate as part of a general consensus-based approach to the supervision of the Convention. However, the Strasbourg authorities need to be assertive on occasion, particularly in dealing with states which fail to uphold the rights of unpopular or minority groups, even though their general human rights record is sound.

6 CONCLUSIONS

It is clear that in one sense the Convention has been astoundingly successful in creating a standard of human rights which is perceived by so many Europeans as relevant and valuable despite the fact that almost half a century has passed since it was created. The enormous and continuing increase in the number of petitions in the late 1980s and in the 1990s suggest that its potential has only recently been understood. Its influence is likely to increase as many Eastern European states become signatories to it. Although it was only intended to create a minimum standard of human rights, it has succeeded in revealing basic flaws in UK law in relation to, for example, the decision to maintain or renew the detention of life prisoners.[267]

At the same time its ability to bring about change in the laws and practices of Member States must not be exaggerated. Arguably, the Convention may be termed a largely procedural charter in the sense that a challenge to a flawed procedure is more likely to succeed under it than a claim that a substantive right has been violated.[268] Further, it may be argued that the machinery for the enforcement of the Convention is wholly inadequate, particularly in the face of a government unashamedly prepared to breach it for long periods of time.[269] This chapter spent some time dwelling on the stages through which an application will pass if it is pursued all the way through the system. The process means that if an application which is ultimately successful takes five years before the final decision, the individual affected must suffer a violation of his or her rights for all that time. There is no formal mechanism available, such as an interim injunction, to prevent the continuing violation. When the Court and Commission eventually merge, some of the overlapping stages, such as the dual consideration of admissibility, will disappear, although it is not envisaged that the question of admissibility itself should no longer arise. If the admissibility stage were eliminated the workload of the new Court would

---

[267] See eg *Thynne, Wilson and Gunnel v UK*, Judgment of 25 October 1990; (1990) 13 EHRR 666, discussed above at p 53.

[268] See eg *Mats Jacobson v Sweden* (1990) 13 EHRR 79, above p 54.

[269] The UK government is quite frequently slow to respond to an adverse ruling; when the response comes it may be inadequate. For example, it has not yet responded to the adverse decision of the European Court of HR in *Thynne, Wilson and Gunnell* (1990) 13 EHRR 666.

presumably increase enormously, although the quality of decision-making in some individual cases might be improved. The process is still likely to be lengthy, especially as it is expected that the number of petitions will increase enormously due to the accession of Eastern European Member States.

If a petition finally comes before the European Court of Human Rights it may decide that no violation has occurred due to its invocation of the margin of appreciation. If, however, it declares that a breach has indeed occurred the violation may well subsist for some years while the Member State concerned considers the extent to which it will respond. Eventually a measure may be adopted which may still represent a violation of rights but of a less pernicious nature.[270] A challenge to such a measure would have to go through the same lengthy process in order to bring about any improvement in the protection afforded in the Member State to the right in question.

Thus it may be concluded that reliance on the Convention will tend to produce only erratic, flawed and weak protection of freedoms in the UK. However, as argued at the beginning of this chapter, the solution does not appear to be adoption of a more coercive process since that might lead to open conflict with Strasbourg and perhaps ultimately withdrawal of some state parties from the Convention. The twin problems of the slow procedure and inadequate enforcement may be addressed or at least partially alleviated, it is suggested, by the reception of the Convention into UK law. This is the issue addressed in Chapter 3.

---

270 The response of the UK government to the ruling in *Malone v UK* (1985) 7 EHRR 14 which was to place telephone tapping on a statutory footing (under the Interception of Communications Act 1985) may be an example of an inadequate implementation of a ruling since the Act does not require independent authorisation of intercept warrants even in cases unconcerned with national security. (See further Chap 8 pp 344–45.)

CHAPTER THREE

METHODS OF PROTECTING CIVIL LIBERTIES IN THE UK: THE BILL OF RIGHTS QUESTION

1 INTRODUCTION[1]

The question of whether the UK should adopt a Bill of Rights, which has been canvassed over the last 25 years, initially gained impetus due to the UK's acceptance of the right of individual petition under the European Convention on Human Rights: it rapidly came to seem anomalous to some that the Strasbourg judges should have the power to rule on the compatibility of UK law with Convention rights while domestic judges had no such power. Thus in 1968 Anthony Lester QC proposed the incorporation of the European Convention on Human Rights into national law[2] and the Charter '88 Group[3] among others recently brought the issue into prominence again. It is fair to say that support for a Bill of Rights has grown among lawyers,[4] academics and politicians[5] during the 1980s and 1990s and under the Labour government incorporation of the Convention under the Human Rights Act 1998 is now imminent. Both the present Master of the Rolls and the Lord Chief Justice indicated upon taking office that they shared in this support. However, some

---

1 General reading: Lord Scarman, *English Law – The New Dimension*, 1974; Wallington, P and McBride, J, *Civil Liberties and a Bill of Rights*, 1976; Bailey, Harris and Jones, *Civil Liberties: Cases and Materials*, 1995, Chap 1; Jaconelli, J, *Enacting a Bill of Rights*, 1980; Zander, M, *A Bill of Rights*, 1985; Dworkin, R, *A Bill of Rights for Britain*, 1990; Ewing, K, *A Bill of Rights for Britain*, 1990; Feldman, D, *Civil Liberties and Human Rights*, 1993, Chap 2; 'Do We Need a Bill of Rights?' (1976) 39 *MLR* 121; 'Should We Have a Bill of Rights?' (1977) 40 *MLR* 389; 'Britain's Bill of Rights', 94 *LQR* 512; 'Legislative Supremacy and the Rule of Law' (1985) *CLJ* 111; 'Incorporating the Convention' *LAG* April 1990 25; 'Fundamental Rights: The UK Isolated?' [1984] *PL* 46; Craig, PP, *Public Law and Democracy in the United Kingdom and the United States of America*, 1990; Waldron, J, 'A Rights-based Critique of Constitutional Rights' (1993) 13 *OJLS* 18; Adjei, C, 'Human Rights Theory and the Bill of Rights Debate' (1995) 58 *MLR* 17; Oliver, D, 'A Bill of Rights for the United Kingdom' in *Government in the United Kingdom*, 1991; Lester, A, 'The Judges as Law-makers' [1993] *PL* 269.

2 Lester, A, *Democracy and Individual Rights*, 1968, pp 13–15. For the view that the Convention does not need to be formally adopted into UK law since it is already part of it and may be directly relied upon in domestic courts, see Beyleveld, D, 'The Concept of a Human Right and Incorporation of the ECHR' [1995] *PL* 577.

3 Charter '88 advocates enshrining civil liberties by means of a Bill of Rights but it has not put forward a text. See Stanger, N (1990) 8 *Index on Censorship* 14.

4 See in particular Lord Scarman, *English Law – The New Dimension*, 1974, Parts II and VII; see also Robertson, G, *Freedom, the Individual and the Law*, 1993, Chap 12; Lester, A, 'Fundamental Rights: The United Kingdom Isolated?' [1984] *PL* 46; Lord Lester [1995] *PL* 198 note 1.

5 See Zander, M, *A Bill of Rights?*, 1997, Chap 1; Barendt, E, *Freedom of Speech*, 1987, pp 329–32.

6 For example, Lord McCluskey in his 1986 Reith Lectures.

judges[6] and academic writers remain opposed or unconvinced[7] as do a number of politicians including, it seems, most Conservative MPs.[8]

Broadly speaking, rightists and leftists among academics and politicians tend to be opposed to adoption of a Bill of Rights. As indicated in Chapter 1, certain groups on the left, in the UK and abroad, tend to view civil rights with hostility. Under the theory put forward by a number of writers on the left such instruments merely focus progressive attention on 'negative rights' which foster only formal equality since in practice they may be used by the powerful to consolidate their power over the weak. At the same time this theory finds that such attention is directed away from 'positive rights' which would lead to substantive equality through the redistribution of economic resources.[9] The liberal view has been indicated in Chapter 1: generally sympathetic to the notion of civil rights,[10] it tends to view the hostility of the left as based on a false dichotomy between 'negative' and 'positive' rights, since the notion underlying it assumes that progressive energy is limited and will be depleted rather than strengthened through use. The remarkable increase in liberal and centre-left support for adoption of a UK Bill of Rights[11] is – at least in part – attributable to the fact that one party was in power for 18 years and in particular to the effect on civil liberties of the Thatcher and Major governments.

The Bill of Rights debate will be considered here largely from the liberal point of view. From that stand-point it centres on three questions. First, if the UK has traditionally managed through its unwritten constitution to maintain a reasonable human rights record, what factors suggest that there is now a need to incorporate the Convention? Secondly, even if it is accepted that some further measure is needed to provide improved protection for civil liberties, are there sound reasons for considering that incorporation is an effective, appropriate and democratically acceptable means of achieving such improvement? The third question concerns the status and enforcement of the Convention, and these issues are now likely to become dominant. Under the Human Rights Act 1998 what will the status of the Convention be, how will it be enforced and how satisfactory are the incorporating and enforcement mechanisms?

---

7   See eg Ewing and Gearty, *Freedom Under Thatcher*, p 273 *et seq*; Waldron, 13 *OJLS* 18 pp 49–51; Loughlin, M, *Public Law and Political Theory*, 1992, especially pp 220–27.

8   The official policy of the Conservative Party is against a Bill of Rights: see Conservative Research Department Brief, *Civil Liberties*, 1990. See below for full discussion pp 109–12.

9   See Tushnet, M, 'An Essay on Rights' (1984) 62 *Texas Law Review* 1363; Herman, D, 'Beyond the Rights Debate' (1993) 2 *Social and Legal Studies* 25.

10 This is not intended to imply that all liberals support the adoption of a Bill of Rights in the UK; as discussed below a number of liberals are reluctant to trust the judges to give full weight to its provisions. For an attack on such adoption from a liberal point of view see Allan, J, 'Bills of Rights and Judicial Power – A Liberal's Quandary' 16(2) *OJLS* 337–52.

11 For a full account see Zander, M, *A Bill of Rights?*, 1997, Chap 1.

2 THE POLITICAL HISTORY OF THE DEBATE

Britain was the first Member State to ratify the European Convention[12] despite some strong feeling against it in Cabinet, particularly from Lord Chancellor Jowitt. The government recognised that it was politically necessary to accept the Convention but Jowitt described it as 'so vague and woolly that it may mean almost anything ... Any student of our legal institutions must recoil from this document with a feeling of horror ...'.[13] However, the government did not at that time accept the right of individual petition or the jurisdiction of the European Court and there was no question of incorporation of the Convention into domestic law. When the government[14] eventually accepted the right of individual petition in 1966 there appears to have been little realisation of the significance of this move but it was unsurprising that it should be followed by a call for enactment of the Convention into domestic law – though without being directly enforceable.[15] The call for a Bill of Rights was taken up by Lord Lambton (Conservative) in 1969 who sought leave to introduce a '10 minute rule' Bill 'to preserve the rights of the individual' – in other words to curb the power of the Labour government in such areas as freedom of speech and education. There was little support for the Bill and it was rejected.

From the 1970s onwards growth of support for a UK Bill of Rights became apparent outside the ranks of the Conservative Party, although certain senior Conservatives displayed some such support when in opposition. Labour, which toyed with the notion in 1975, opposed it before and during the 1992 General Election, eventually decided to espouse it as official policy in 1993, while there has been a long history of Liberal and Democrat support for it. It is notable that the years of Thatcherism eventually led the main party of opposition to accept the need to receive the Convention into domestic law. The chequered history of the debate which follows suggests two things: first, there has been a general consensus for some time that the European Convention should be incorporated into domestic law as opposed to enacting a UK Bill of Rights and, secondly, that although support for a Bill of Rights is concentrated in the centrist parties, it is not confined to them.

---

12 In March 1951.
13 CAB 130/64 xcA034022; for comment see Lester, 'Fundamental Rights: The UK Isolated?' [1984] *PL* 46, pp 50–55.
14 The Labour government headed by Harold Wilson.
15 In 1968 from Mr Anthony Lester QC. His suggestion was that a Constitutional Council should be set up with powers to preview legislation and advise Parliament of potential conflict with the Bill of Rights.

Conservative support

In 1969 Mr Quintin Hogg MP published a pamphlet, *New Charter*,[16] in which he stated, 'Parliament has become virtually an elective dictatorship. The party system makes the supremacy of a government like the present, automatic and almost unquestioned'. The solution, he thought, was to make the European Convention on Human Rights enforceable in domestic courts. Mr Hogg was opposition Front Bench Spokesman on Home Affairs and the pamphlet was published by the Conservative Political Centre but the views were stated to be the author's own and not the Party's. However, in 1970, as Lord Chancellor, he spoke against a Bill of Rights proposed by Lord Arran[17] although he did not state that he was against all Bills of Rights. In 1975, when Labour was in power, he wrote four letters to *The Times* advocating a written constitution entrenching individual rights.[18] Also in 1975, Sir Keith Joseph published a pamphlet entitled *Freedom under the Law*[19] giving his view that a Bill of Rights was needed to curb the power of Parliament.

In August 1976, Sir Michael Havers (Shadow Attorney General) gave an indication that the official view of the Conservative Party was tending towards incorporation of the European Convention when he advocated such a move in a letter to the *Daily Mail*; and, in a report entitled *Another Bill of Rights?*, the Society of Conservative Lawyers supported this proposition. In 1978 Mr Leon Brittan, opposition Front Bench Spokesman on Devolution, moved an amendment to the Scotland Bill at Committee stage which would have made the European Convention effective in Scotland. The move was opposed by the government on the ground that the question was too important to be decided in such a context; and the amendment was defeated by 251 votes to 227.[20]

When the Conservative Party came to power in 1979 it made no move to incorporate the Convention, despite some back bench interest.[21] In 1980 the government opposed Lord Wade's Bill of Rights Bill in the Commons as they did Lord Scarman's Bill in 1988 which was passed in the Lords, and Sir Edward Gardner's 1989 Bill incorporating the European Convention. An indication of future official Conservative policy was given by Margaret Thatcher in a letter to Bernard Crick[22] on 26 May 1988:

---

16 Conservative Political Centre, No 430.
17 House of Lords, *Hansard*, Vol 313 Col 243, 26 November 1970. Lord Arran had moved the second reading of his Bill.
18 In May 1975.
19 Published by Conservative Political Centre.
20 House of Commons, *Hansard*, Vol 943 Col 580.
21 107 Conservative MPs signed a motion in June 1984 calling for incorporation of the Convention.
22 Founder member of Charter '88.

> The government considers that our present Constitutional arrangements continue to serve us well and that the citizen in this country enjoys the greatest degree of liberty that is compatible with the rights of others and the vital interests of the state.

This view was reiterated in 1990[23] and remains the official view of the Conservative Party at the present time.

The Liberals and the Democrats

Lord Wade (Liberal) who had in 1969 initiated a four hour debate in the House of Lords on the question of the protection of human rights, moved a further debate in 1976 in the Lords on a new Bill designed to incorporate the European Convention into UK Law. It provided that the Convention would prevail over subsequent legislation unless the legislation specifically provided otherwise. Lord Harris, the Secretary of State at the Home Office, said that the government could not form a view until there had been wide public discussion of the issue. The House gave the Bill an unopposed second reading. When Lord Wade's Bill was debated again in 1977[24] and referred to a Select Committee, the Committee recommended that if a Bill of Rights were enacted it should be the European Convention but said that they had not reached agreement on the desirability of enacting such a Bill. Lord Wade moved an amendment, which was carried, to introduce a Bill of Rights to incorporate the Convention. He introduced his Bill again in 1978 and in 1981; each time it passed the Lords and was eventually debated in the Commons in 1981, although no second reading was secured. Lord Scarman, who has been one of the most influential supporters of adoption of a Bill of Rights, made a very significant contribution to the debate in his Hamlyn lecture in 1974 in which he concluded that certain human rights should be rendered inviolate by entrenched laws protected by a Bill of Rights. In 1988 he failed to get a Bill through the Commons – although it passed the Lords – which provided that no minister, bureaucrat or public body should do any act which infringed the rights set out in the European Convention. The Liberal Democrats continued to favour adoption of the Convention before, during and after the 1992 and 1997 General Elections.[25]

---

[23] Conservative Research Department Brief, *Civil Liberties*, 1990.
[24] House of Lords, *Hansard*, Vol 379 Col 973.
[25] *Partners for Freedom and Justice*, Liberal Democrat Federal White Paper No 2 (1989).

The Labour position

In a House of Commons Debate on the Bill of Rights question in 1975,[26] Dr Shirley Summerskill, Labour Minister of State at the Home Office, said that the government was not 'committed against a Bill of Rights' but that the question required further consideration. In 1976 the Labour government published a discussion document which had been prepared by the Human Rights sub-Committee chaired by Mrs Shirley Williams, recommending the adoption of the European Convention on Human Rights into national law. Just before its publication the Home Secretary, Mr Roy Jenkins, indicated that he was moving in the direction of favouring incorporation,[27] and in 1976 the Attorney General, Mr Sam Silkin, also gave such an indication.[28] That the government was taking this question very seriously was apparent from the composition of the Working Party which drew up the Discussion Document 'Legislation on Human Rights' published by the Home Office in 1976. Senior civil servants from a large number of different departments were involved. The document was intended only to be descriptive and explanatory: no firm conclusion on the issue was reached and official Labour party policy did not change as a result.

In 1991 and 1992 Labour officially opposed adoption of a Bill of Rights on the ground that government reforms would be endangered if power were transferred from government to the judiciary. The then Shadow Home Secretary, Mr Roy Hattersley, disassociated his party from Charter '88. He wrote 'the only method of restraining the excesses of a bad government is to replace it with a good one'.[29] However, in a speech to the Fabian Society Conference on 6 January 1990 he explained more fully Labour's proposed alternative method of protecting civil rights: 'The commitment to a series of detailed and specific Acts of Parliament – each one of which establishes rights in a specific area – is a much more practical way of ensuring the freedoms we propose'. This view was encapsulated in the Labour Party Charter of Rights 1990.[30] However, after Labour lost the general election of 1992 and Mr Hattersley resigned as Shadow Home Secretary, John Smith, the new leader of the party, announced a change in policy in March 1993 after the Labour Party Conference and committed the party to incorporation of the European

---

26 The motion was put forward by Mr James Kilfedder (Ulster Unionist) House of Commons, *Hansard*, Vol 894 Col 32, 7 July 1975.
27 In a speech to the Birmingham Law Society on 12 February 1975. In 1976, at a conference organised by the British Institute of Human Rights, he left no doubt that he was in favour of incorporation.
28 In the MacDermott lecture at Queen's University, Belfast.
29 See (1988) *Guardian*, 12 December.
30 *The Charter of Rights: Guaranteeing Individual Liberty in a Free Society*, Labour Party document 1990.

Convention using the device of a 'notwithstanding' clause for protection and with a view to the eventual adoption of a home-grown Bill of Rights.

On 11 January 1994 the Labour MP Mr Graham Allen introduced a Private Members' Bill, the Human Rights No 3 Bill, which proposed incorporation of the European Convention on Human Rights with the First Protocol and the creation of a Human Rights Commission; it received a first reading in the Commons but did not progress to a second reading. In December 1996 the Labour Party issued a Consultation Paper on the matter entitled *Bringing Rights Home: Labour's plans to incorporate the European Convention on Human Rights into UK law*. After the 1997 General Election the new Labour government committed itself in the Queen's Speech to introducing a Bill incorporating the 'main provisions' of the Convention. The Human Rights Bill was introduced into Parliament in October 1997.

3 TRADITIONAL METHODS OF PROTECTING CIVIL LIBERTIES IN THE UK

The premise behind the adoption of Bills of Rights all over the world is that citizens can never be fully assured of the safety of their liberties until they are removed out of the reach of government by identifying and enshrining them in a Bill of Rights. It is thought that government cannot be expected to keep a satisfactory check on itself; only some source of power independent of government can do so. Dworkin has argued that under a Bill of Rights a government is not free to treat liberty as a commodity of convenience or to ignore rights which the nation is under a moral duty to respect.[31] In the UK, however, it has been thought until relatively recently that the unwritten constitution, as maintained by Parliament and the judiciary, is a sufficiently effective means of ensuring that power is not abused. The opposing argument, which is now gaining ascendancy, is that the traditional checks on government power have become insufficiently effective and some consider that an assertion of human rights is needed to prevent further encroachment on them.

The democratic process as the guardian of civil liberties

It has traditionally been thought that Parliament provides a means of allowing the will of the people to influence government towards the maintenance of liberty[32] through free elections and secret ballots and aided by the operation of a free press. It can react to the needs of civil liberties by providing specific legislative safeguards and in so doing can take into account the views and

---

31 Dworkin, R, *A Bill of Rights for Britain*, 1990, p 23.
32 See eg Dicey, *The Law of the Constitution*, 1959, pp 189–90; Hume, 1906: 203.

expertise of a range of groups. Moreover, it will govern according to the rule of law which will include the notion that it will accept certain limits on its powers based on normative ideals.[33] However, commentators such as Ewing and Gearty, evaluating government in the 1980s, have considered that these traditional checks may be insufficiently effective as methods of curbing the power of a determined and illiberal governing party: 'Mrs Thatcher has merely utilised to the full the scope for untrammelled power latent in the British Constitution but obscured by the hesitancy and scruples of previous consensus-based political leaders.'[34] In particular, it is clear that when the government in power has a large majority it may more readily depart from traditional constitutional principles if it is minded to do so, because Parliament is likely to be ineffective as a check on its activities.

Birkinshaw points out[35] that the opposition is hampered by the lack of a Freedom of Information Act in scrutinising the actions of ministers. This lack means that the government can choose what and how much to reveal in response to opposition questions and therefore – as the *Ponting* case[36] made clear – is able to present a selective picture of events. Government secrecy is highly significant because, increasingly, decisions affecting civil liberties are taken not under Parliamentary scrutiny but by ministers and officials exercising discretionary powers. For example, the Australian government has accepted that there should be a Parliamentary committee charged with scrutiny of the Australian Security Service;[37] in the UK, in contrast, when the Security Service Bill 1989 was debated, the government refused an amendment which would have subjected MI5 to scrutiny by a Select Committee. It continues to be the case that questions about the operation of MI5 and MI6 will not be answered in Parliament. Britain has of course never had a Freedom of Information Act, unlike other democracies and until recently Parliament has seen no need to enact one.[38] Clearly, matters which are hidden from the public and from opposition MPs may tend to evade the checks arising from the democratic process.[39]

Aside from these issues, which have become particularly pressing over the last decade, it may also be questioned whether Parliament by its nature provides an effective forum for taking the protection of civil liberties into account in passing legislation. A number of writers[40] have noted that

---

33 See eg Wade and Bradley, *Constitutional and Administrative Law*, 1985, pp 99–100.
34 Ewing and Gearty, *Freedom under Thatcher*, 1989, p 7.
35 See *Freedom of Information*, 1996, Chap 3.
36 *Ponting* [1985] *Crim LR* 318. See further Chap 6 pp 234–35.
37 See Australian Security Service Intelligence Organisation Amendment Act 1986.
38 See Chap 6 pp 272–73.
39 See further Chap 6 for discussion of recent developments in this area.
40 eg Robertson, *Freedom, the Individual and the Law*, 1993, p 506; Walker, C, *The Prevention of Terrorism in British Law*, 2nd edn, 1992, Chap 4 p 32.

Parliament at times displays a readiness to pass emergency legislation which may go further than necessary in curtailing civil liberties and which is apt to remain on the statute book long after the emergency is over. MPs, whether in government or out of it, tend to respond in an unconsidered fashion to emergencies apparent or real. Government wants to be perceived as acting quickly and decisively while members of the opposition parties, mindful of their popularity, may not wish to oppose measures adopted in the face of scares whipped up by some sections of the media. Such reactions were seen in relation to the original Official Secrets Act 1911, passed in one day with all-party support in response to a spy scare. The far-reaching s 2, which was never debated at all, remained on the statute books for 78 years. Similarly, the Birmingham Pub Bombings on 21 November 1974 led four days later to the announcement of the Prevention of Terrorism Bill[41] which was passed by 29 November virtually without amendment or dissent.

In the 1990s Parliament quite frequently showed a marked readiness to accept claims that a number of proposed statutory measures would lead to the curbing of terrorist or criminal activity. Although such measures were likely to represent an infringement of civil liberties they did not in general encounter determined criticism from the opposition. For example, the debate in the House of Commons on the Prevention of Terrorism (Additional Powers) Act 1996, which was guillotined, failed to consider in depth either the efficacy of the measure in terms of curbing terrorist activity or its likely impact on civil liberties. The debate provided, in microcosm, a good instance of the debasement and impoverishment of Parliamentary criminal justice debate in the mid-1990s. The Labour Party supported the proposals partly on the narrow ground that they represented only a small increase on the extended police powers which were included in the Criminal Justice and Public Order Act 1994 and which were not challenged on grounds of principle at the Committee stage of that Bill.[42] Thus, issues as to the real value of these powers fell to be asked only by Labour back benchers and due to pressure of time and the stance of the leadership they could not be pressed home. Similarly, the Labour Party initially supported the proposals in the Police Bill 1997 to allow the police self-authorising powers to place bugging devices on property. Their stance was modified only after a government defeat on this matter in the Lords and severe criticism from various quarters. Jack Straw, the Shadow Home Secretary, finally agreed with Michael Howard on a compromise which would ensure that in certain serious cases the police had to seek authorisation from a judicial committee.[43] This compromise was criticised in many quarters as providing only marginally more protection for civil liberties.

---

41   *HC Debs*, Vol 882 Col 35.
42   Straw, J, *ibid* Col 221.
43   See now s 91(1) of the Act.

It may therefore be said that Parliament has demonstrated that it is willing to move quickly to cut down freedoms but it is at the same time slow to bring in measures to protect them, because civil liberties issues tend to be perceived as difficult to handle and as doubtful vote-winners. It may even be the case that the governing party would like to bring forward legislation on a civil liberties issue such as homosexual rights but be hesitant to do so due to its controversial nature. This received Parliamentary wisdom has meant that measures protecting civil liberties are vulnerable to under-funding,[44] while Parliament rarely legislates with such protection in mind as a primary purpose unless forced to do so by a ruling of the European Court of Human Rights, an EC directive or a ruling of the European Court of Justice.

Thus it is fair to ask whether the democratic process can be trusted to safeguard civil liberties. Recent examples can be found to support either side in this debate. It is generally agreed that the democratic process worked well in creating the Police and Criminal Evidence Act 1984,[45] and it is fair to say that it had at least some impact, as suggested above, on the Police Act 1997. However, the Criminal Justice and Public Order Act 1994 can be cited on the other side; many pressure groups protested against the Bill: it probably attracted more public opposition than any other measure during the Conservative years in government 1979–97, apart from the poll tax, and yet the Bill went through Parliament relatively intact. As ATH Smith observes, 'Presumably for fear of being seen to be soft on crime ... the Labour Party declined to oppose the Bill on Second Reading, leaving the serious opposition to the Bill to the Peers. Given the target of [the public order aspects] of the Act and the social make-up of their Lordships' House ... the prospects of serious opposition were negligible'.[46] It may be argued that the 1994 Act was a product of special Parliamentary conditions which are unlikely to recur. A particularly illiberal Home Secretary piloted it through Parliament and the Shadow Home Secretary supported its key provisions. However, while it is important not to allow the record of the Conservative governments of 1979–97 to distort debate as to the efficacy of the democratic process in protecting civil liberties, it is also important to bear in mind the lessons which have been learnt as to the constitutional weaknesses which those governments exposed.

The fact that the UK possesses a Second Chamber is sometimes used as an argument against a Bill of Rights. The argument runs on these lines: other countries adopted Bills of Rights for a variety of reasons – either because they were at a stage in their development when human rights were particularly at risk or because of a particular feature of their constitution, such as the lack of a

---

44 Bodies such as the Equal Opportunities Commission may be under-funded, provision of legal aid may be cut without much (or any) public outcry.

45 See Zander, M, *The Police and Criminal Evidence Act 1984*, 1995, p xi: '... there can be no denying that the whole exercise was an example of the democratic process working.'

46 Smith, ATH [1995] *Crim LR* 19, at 27.

second legislative chamber[47] to keep a check on the lower house;[48] their experience is not, therefore, analogous to that in the UK. But it must be questioned how far a second chamber can protect civil liberties. The House of Lords has had some successes, notably its influence on the incorporation into the Police and Criminal Evidence Act 1984 of a provision with great potential to safeguard the liberty of the citizen – s 78.[49] As mentioned above the Lords also passed amendments to Michael Howard's Police Bill in 1997 allowing for judicial authorisation of bugging warrants. However, the powers of the Lords to thwart the wishes of the Commons are limited. Section 2 of the Parliament Act 1911 makes various provisions for presenting a Bill for the Royal Assent against the opposition of the Lords. When a Bill has been passed by the Commons in two successive sessions and it is rejected for a second time by the Lords, it can be presented on its second rejection for the Royal Assent. The very existence of this power means that the need to invoke it is unlikely to arise because the Lords will wish to avoid the need for the Commons to use it.[50]

The Lords are, then, generally circumspect in using their powers; when they oppose a Bill sent up by the Commons they tend to propose amendments at the Committee stage rather than vote against the second reading but there is a convention that amendments at the Committee stage should not re-open matters of principle already accepted by the Commons. The Lords will rarely insist on their amendments to a government Bill, although of course they may do so when the government lacks an effective majority to ensure their rejection in the Commons. O Hood Phillips also argues[51] that there is almost a convention that the Lords will not return a government Bill to the Commons for reconsideration more than once.[52] Hereditary peers (over 750 of them) form the majority of those entitled to sit in the Lords and ensure the continuance of a Conservative majority. Although many of them are not regular attenders, they can occasionally be brought in to secure the passage of Conservative legislation which the regular attenders might be inclined to reject.[53] However, their voting rights will be abolished under Labour proposals for reform of the Lords.

---

47 New Zealand, which adopted a Bill of Rights in 1990, has no second chamber.
48 This view was put forward by Lord McCluskey in his 1986 Reith lectures.
49 House of Lords, *Hansard*, 31 July 1984, Cols 635–75. See Chap 9 p 398 *et seq*.
50 The House of Lords will, however, on occasion use its powers of suspension fully as it did in relation to the Trade Union and Labour Relations (Amendment) Bill 1974–75.
51 See *Constitutional and Administrative Law*, 7th edn, p 148.
52 Lord Hailsham said in March 1976 in relation to the Trade Union and Labour Relations (Amendment) Bill that opposition had exhausted their powers in sending the Bill back once to the Commons and so had discharged their duty.
53 This occurred in May 1988 in relation to the introduction of the Community Charge (poll tax).

Rules and judicial interpretation: current relevance of the Diceyan tradition

The Diceyan tradition holds that the absence of a written constitution in the UK is not a weakness but a source of strength. This is because the protection of the citizen's liberties are not dependent on vaguely worded constitutional documents but, rather, flow from specific judicial decisions which give the citizen specific remedies for infringement of his or her liberties.[54] He regarded one of the great strengths of the British constitution as lying in the lack of broad discretionary powers vested in the executive. Citizens could only be criminalised for clear breaches of clearly established laws and such laws also governed the extent to which individual freedoms could be infringed. Where there was no relevant law citizens could know with absolute confidence that they could exercise their liberty as they pleased without fear of incurring any sanction.

Dicey's thesis is unconvincing as an analysis of UK contemporary legal culture for a number of reasons. The Diceyan view of the law as imposing only narrow and tightly defined areas of liability is no longer representative given the use of quasi- and non-legislation authorising interference with civil liberties. Many such rules, including the Home Office Guidelines relied on by the police until 1997 in using surveillance devices, remain on a non-statutory basis for many years; they therefore receive no Parliamentary scrutiny and little or no judicial scrutiny either. When such rules are placed on a statutory basis, as they have been under the Interception of Communications Act 1985, the Security Services Act 1989 and the Intelligence Services Act 1994, judicial scrutiny of their operation is typically ousted. Thus there are a number of areas of executive action which are not open to judicial scrutiny. Where judicial interpretation of the law is significant in relation to individual liberty, a mixed picture emerges. Judicial activism in the 1990s led to a number of significant decisions protective of liberty, especially in the field of judicial review. Nevertheless, the judiciary do not seem to have developed a coherent approach to the protection of civil liberties. They have interpreted some uncertain areas of the law, such as breach of the peace and common law contempt, very broadly, to some extent undermining the safeguards for liberties provided by certain statutes.

It follows from the Diceyan thesis that judges will be concerned to construe legislation strictly against the executive if it conflicts with fundamental liberties arising from the common law[55] and will interpret the common law so that fundamental freedoms are protected.[56] A rather more modern judicial method of protecting liberties may be seen in the creation of

---

54 Dicey, AV, *Introduction to the Study of the Law of the Constitution*, 10th edn, 1987, p 190.
55 See eg *Waddington v Miah* [1974] 2 All ER 377, HL.
56 See *Entinck v Carrington* [1765] 19 State Tr 1029.

Methods of Protecting Civil Liberties in the UK: The Bill of Rights Question

the presumption that law will be interpreted in accordance with international human rights treaties where possible.[57] However, consideration of recent decisions suggests that there does not seem to be a clear conception shared by most members of the judiciary of their role as protecting liberties. For example, during the miners' strike 1984–85 striking miners shouted abuse at miners going in to work guarded by police; the working miners claimed that such action was unlawful, and it was found that although no obvious legal pigeon-hole, such as assault, could be found for it due to the circumstances, it could be termed 'a species of private nuisance' and injunctions against the striking miners were therefore granted.[58] The use of common law contempt in the *Spycatcher* litigation might provide a further example.[59]

Where an attempt has been made in a statute to seek to ensure that a particular freedom is protected, as is the case in s 4 of the Obscene Publications Act 1959 and s 5 of the Contempt of Court Act 1981, it may be found that the common law begins to take on a role which undermines the statutory provisions. This may be said of the common law doctrines of contempt and conspiracy to corrupt public morals.[60] Ewing and Gearty argue that for this reason a Bill of Rights may be undesirable since the people need Parliament to protect them from the judges, not merely the judges to protect them from Parliament.[61] However, Parliament in the instances mentioned decided to leave the common law intact, possibly due to the realisation that it might at times be convenient to invoke it. Further, because a Bill of Rights would affect all areas of the common law, in contrast to the statutes in question, it might encourage judges to adopt a more rigorous approach to vague common law provisions, testing them against the standards of the Bill of Rights. It is noticeable that when the judges are enjoined in a statute to take account of a value such as freedom of expression – as they are under s 5 of the Contempt of Court Act 1981 – they are more likely to adopt a rigorous approach than when dealing with a wide and uncertain power arising at common law.[62]

The record of the judges in some fields is more impressive than in others. A number of decisions on prisoners' rights suggest some concern to protect

---

57 See the judgment of Lord Brandon of Oakbrook in *M and H (Minors), Re* [1990] 1 AC 686; [1988] 3 WLR 485, HL at p 498; [1990] 1 AC 686.
58 *Thomas v NUM* [1985] 2 All ER 1.
59 *AG v Newspaper Publishing plc* [1988] Ch 333; [1987] 3 All ER 276; [1988] 3 WLR 942, CA. See further Chap 4 p 164.
60 See further Chap 5 p 203.
61 Ewing and Gearty, *Freedom under Thatcher*, pp 270–71.
62 Contrast the approach to freedom of speech taken in *AG v English* [1983] 1 AC 116 in relation to s 5 of the 1981 Act, with that taken in *AG v Newspaper Publishing plc* [1988] Ch 333 in relation to common law contempt; also the approach to the Public Order Act 1986 taken in *Reid* [1987] *Crim LR* 702 with that taken to breach of the peace in *Moss v McLachan* [1985] IRLR 76. See Chap 4 pp 157 and 164 and Chap 7 pp 293 and 303 respectively.

Civil Liberties

freedoms,[63] but even within a field such as this in which judges have a generally good record on civil liberties, the picture is rather mixed, and their record in the area of discrimination is even more inconsistent.[64] Street in *Freedom, the Individual and the Law* argues 'our judges may be relied on to defend strenuously some kinds of freedom. Their emotions will be aroused where personal freedom is menaced by some politically unimportant area of the executive'.[65] Decisions on discrimination or prisoners' rights may be said to lie in such an area – at least in comparison with decisions taken in the fields of national security or immigration – but nevertheless do not fully suggest a clear and general determination to protect liberty. The reluctance of judges to intervene in the politically important areas, such as public security or deportation, is evidenced by the decisions in *Secretary of State for the Home Department, ex parte Northumbria Police Authority*[66] and *Secretary of State for the Home Department, ex parte Hosenball*.[67]

Thus, when a commentator in the Diceyan tradition, such as TRS Allan, seeks to defend the record of the common law in protecting fundamental rights,[68] a rather ironic pattern emerges. Allan contends that the case law shows support for civil liberties; he quotes from cases which purportedly demonstrate his contention – and then finds himself apologising for the inadequacies of the Lords' approach. Having cited *Wheeler v Leicester City Council*[69] as an instance of the sturdy defence of free speech, he concedes that Lord Roskill did not use free speech grounds at all while Lord Templeman did, in general terms, but unfortunately 'failed to address the level of principle demanded by the freedoms at issue'.[70] When he turns to the *Spycatcher* litigation, he is forced to concede from the outset that the speeches are 'disappointing'. Having praised Lord Keith for affirming the general freedom to speak, he then goes on to admit that his Lordship failed to injunct only because 'all possible damage to the interests of the Crown had already been done' and that he was 'unwilling to ... base his decision on any considerations of freedom of the press'.[71] The Diceyan thesis could, however, find support in the recent decision of *Derbyshire v Times Newspapers*[72] which has been

---

63 See in particular *Raymond v Honey* [1983] 1 AC 1, HL which asserted the right of access to the courts. Compare this ruling with *Deputy Governor of Camphill Prison ex parte King* [1985] QB 735 in which judicial review of governors' decisions was denied.
64 Compare the decisions of the House of Lords in *Hayward v Cammell Laird* [1988] 2 All ER 257 and *Pickstone v Freemans* [1988] 2 All ER 803 with their decision in *Prestige Group plc, Re* [1984] 1 WLR 335.
65 (1982) p 318.
66 [1989] QB 26; [1988] 2 WLR 590; [1988] 1 All ER 556, CA.
67 [1977] 1 WLR 766; see further Chap 12 p 541.
68 Allan, TRS, 'Constitutional Rights and Common Law' (1991) OJLS 453–60.
69 [1985] AC 1054; [1985] 2 All ER 1106, HL.
70 *Op cit* p 459.
71 *Op cit* p 460.
72 [1993] AC 534; [1993] 1 All ER 1011; [1992] 3 WLR 28, HL.

acclaimed as 'a legal landmark'.[73] The House of Lords found, without referring to Article 10 of the European Convention, that the importance the common law attached to free speech was such that defamation could not be available as an action to local (or central) government.[74] This decision is certainly to be welcomed but perhaps it may fairly be said that the threat to free speech was so clear and substantial that any other finding would have been indefensible in a state regarding itself as a free democracy.

In the field of judicial review the judges have shown some determination, particularly in the last decade, to develop the law with the basic aim of preventing the exercise of arbitrary power. However, at present the doctrine is fundamentally limited in that as long as a minister appears to have followed a correct and fair procedure, to have acted within his or her powers and to have made a decision which is not clearly unreasonable, the decision must stand regardless of its potentially harmful impact on civil liberties. Thus, the fact that basic liberties were curtailed in the *GCHQ*[75] and *Brind* cases[76] did not in itself provide a ground for review. In other words, the courts are confined to looking back at the method of arriving at the decision rather than forward to its likely effects. In cases which touch particularly directly on national security, so sensitive are the judges to the executive's duty to uphold the safety of the realm, that they may define their powers even to look back on the decision as almost non-existent.[77]

However, outside the context of national security the judiciary will refuse to allow the decision-maker to afford little or no weight to human rights. The stance the judiciary may be prepared to take when an administrative decision infringes human rights is now very close to that explained by Lord Bridge in *Brind*.[78] He rejected the argument that state officials must take the European Convention on Human Rights into account in exercising discretionary power but he accepted nevertheless that the Convention may be relevant in reviewing the exercise of such power. He said:

> ... we are entitled to start from the premise that any restriction of the right of freedom of expression requires to be justified and nothing less than an important competing public interest will be sufficient to justify it. The primary judgment as to whether the particular competing public interest justifies the

---

73 See Laws, Sir J, 'Is the High Court the Guardian of Fundamental Constitutional Rights?' [1993] PL 67.

74 *Derbyshire* was followed and its principle extended in *Goldsmith and Another v Bhoyrul and Others* [1997] 4 All ER 268; (1997) *The Times*, 20 June. It was found that a political party cannot sue in libel although individual candidates would be able to.

75 *Council of Civil Service Unions v Minister for Civil Service* [1985] AC 374; [1985] 3 WLR 1174; [1984] 3 All ER 935, HL (the Prime Minister's decision struck directly at freedom of association).

76 *Secretary of State for Home Affairs, ex parte Brind* [1991] 1 AC 696; [1991] 1 All ER 720; [1991] 2 WLR 588, HL (political speech was directly curtailed); [1990] 1 All ER 469, CA.

77 See *Secretary of State for Home Affairs, ex parte Stitt* (1987) *The Times*, 3 February.

78 [1991] 1 All ER 720, at 723.

particular restriction ... falls to be exercised by the Secretary of State ... But we are entitled to exercise a secondary judgment by asking whether a reasonable Secretary of State on the material before him could reasonably make that primary judgment.

This argument was applied in *Secretary of State for Defence, ex parte Smith and Others*.[79] The case concerned the legality of the policy of the Ministry of Defence in maintaining a ban on homosexuals in the armed forces. The applicants, homosexuals who had been dismissed due to the existence of the ban, applied for review of the policy; their application was dismissed at first instance in the Divisional Court and the applicants appealed. Rejecting the argument of the Ministry of Defence that it had no jurisdiction to review the legality of the policy in question, the court applied the usual *Wednesbury* principles. This meant that it could not interfere with the exercise of an administrative discretion on substantive grounds save where it was satisfied that the decision was unreasonable in the sense that it was beyond the range of responses open to a reasonable decision-maker. But in judging whether the decision-maker had exceeded that margin of appreciation the human rights context was important; 'the more substantial the interference with human rights, the more the court will require by way of justification before it will be satisfied that the decision was reasonable'.[80] The Court rejected the argument of the Ministry of Defence that a less exacting test than applying *Wednesbury* principles of reasonableness was required. Applying such principles and taking into account the support of the policy in both Houses of Parliament, it could not be said that the policy crossed the threshold of irrationality. The concept of proportionality as considered by the Master of the Rolls in this instance was not viewed as a separate head of challenge but merely as an aspect of *Wednesbury* unreasonableness.[81]

The significance of this decision lies in the meaning attributed to the word 'reasonable'; it denotes only a decision which is 'within the range of responses open to a reasonable decision-maker' (*ibid*). As Fenwick and Phillipson argue:

> In other words, the decision-maker is required to take account of human rights in appropriate cases. Further, he must have a more convincing justification the more his decision will trespass on those rights. But that decision remains primarily one for the decision-maker. The courts will only intervene if the decider has come up with a justification which no reasonable person could

---

79 [1996] 1 All ER 257; [1996] ICR 740. See also *Secretary of State for the Home Department, ex parte McQuillan* [1995] 3 All ER 400; (1994) *Independent*, 23 September, in which Laws J's approach was expressly followed. Sedley J was unable to find for the applicant due to the particular statutory framework in question.

80 *Ibid* at p 263.

81 For further argument as to the notion of proportionality, see Himsworth [1996] *PL* 46; his argument that the notion of proportionality as a separate head of review remains a possibility rests on an examination of *Ministry of Agriculture, Fisheries and Food, ex parte Hamble* [1995] 2 All ER 714.

Methods of Protecting Civil Liberties in the UK: The Bill of Rights Question

consider trumped the human rights considerations – a position which seems to take us straight back to classic *GCHQ* irrationality.[82]

A further, linked, factor of significance in *Smith* was the determination as to which policy considerations were to be allowed to override rights and which were not. It appears that in making this determination easily satisfied criteria were adopted. The policy factors were not required to satisfy a test such as that of a 'pressing social need'[83] since satisfying a lesser test would nevertheless bring the decision within the range of responses open to a reasonable decision-maker. This decision echoes that of Lord Bridge in *Brind* in relation to determinations as to overriding individual rights as guaranteed in the European Convention on Human Rights.[84]

These decisions, together with a number of others of a similar nature[85] reaffirm, it is suggested, the value of judicial review as a means of ensuring that some harmony between UK executive practice and the standards laid down by the European Convention on Human Rights is maintained. However, the decision in *Smith* may also be said to demonstrate the current limitations of judicial review in this respect. Judicial review may come to play a much greater part in the protection of human rights in the UK in the areas of activity affected by EU law.[86] In such areas the merits of the decision will be relevant but in non-EU areas the main concern of judicial review seems likely to remain a procedural one[87] until the European Convention on Human Rights is received into UK law.[88] Such reception, even in the weak form currently provided for under the Human Rights Bill, would mean that proportionality would be established as a separate head of review since the need for the administrative decision or measure in question would have to be considered in relation to its impact in terms of the Convention guarantees.

Recently a persuasive thesis has been put forward by Sir John Laws[89] suggesting a method of developing judicial review so that it could afford far greater protection to liberties than it does at present. The main thrust of the

---

82 See *Sourcebook on Public Law*, 1997, p 803.
83 See below p 150.
84 See below pp 208–09.
85 See for example, *Secretary of State for Social Security, ex parte Joint Council for the Welfare of Immigrants; Secretary of State for Social Security, ex parte B* [1996] 4 All ER 385; (1996) 146 NLJ 985; *Secretary of State for the Home Dept and Another, ex parte Norney and Others* (1995) The Times, 6 October.
86 See *Secretary of State for Employment ex parte EOC* [1994] 2 WLR 409, HL.
87 For the view that the direct influence of the Convention in the UK due to its significance as a source of general principles of EU law is not confined only to those areas of activity affected by EU law see Beyleveld, D, 'The concept of a human right and incorporation of the ECHR' [1995] *PL* 577.
88 Under the Human Rights Act 1998. See below p 621.
89 Laws [1993] *PL* 59–79. See above note 73.

thesis is briefly as follows. It is proposed that review could develop such that in a case in which the exercise of discretion could have an adverse impact on fundamental rights, a two-stage test would be imposed by the courts. With respect to the first stage, the thesis notes that the courts have imposed an insistence on decision-makers that their power may be used only for the purpose for which it was granted to them, the courts being the final arbiter of the nature of that purpose. As part of this attribution of purpose the courts have consistently imposed on decision-makers the presumption that power is granted to be exercised in a rational, not a capricious manner. It is proposed that a rather more stringent presumption could be imposed – namely that no statute's purpose can include interference with fundamental rights embedded in the common law and that such interference will only be allowed if it is demonstrated that reading the statute to permit such interference is the only interpretation possible.[90] This would be the first stage of the test. The problem with this approach is that it is uncontroversial to assume that power is only granted on the understanding that it will be exercised rationally – indeed this could be said to be a basic requirement of formal justice. By contrast, to assume that power is never granted to infringe basic liberties is to make a substantive claim – and on the evidence available it appears that the courts are simply not prepared to make it. Preparedness to impose such a presumption in all cases would imply the kind of unified, purposeful determination to protect civil liberties which most commentators simply fail to perceive in the judiciary.[91]

The second stage proposed is as follows: at present the courts insist that relevant considerations should be taken into account when making a decision but hold that the weight to be given to those considerations is entirely for the decision-maker to determine. It is then argued that, on principle, while this may be a reasonable approach when the matter under consideration involves such issues as economic policy, this is far from the case where fundamental rights are at stake, since it means that the decision-maker would be free 'to accord a high or low importance to the right in question, as he chooses' which

---

90 Laws adverts to the fact that an argument very similar to his was rejected in the *Brind* case. However he considers that this was because the submission made in that case was that their Lordships should make such a presumption (in this case that free speech would not be infringed) under Article 10 of the ECHR. He argues that this is a mistaken approach as it amounts to an attempt to incorporate the ECHR through the back door which the courts rightly resist since it offends against constitutional principles. Instead he urges that the correct approach would be to argue that the norms implicit in the ECHR are already reflected in the common law – an approach which gains some support from the House of Lords decision in the *Derbyshire* case [1993] AC 534; [1993] 1 All ER 1011; [1992] 3 WLR 28, HL – and that it is the importance consequently attached by the common law to fundamental rights which provides a justification for the presumption that statutes do not intend to override them.

91 See eg Oliver, D, 'A Bill of Rights for the United Kingdom', pp 151, 163; Ewing and Gearty, *Freedom under Thatcher,* 1990, generally and pp 64, 111, 157–60, 270–71 for particular criticisms of anti-libertarian judicial decisions and attitudes; Lester, 'Fundamental Rights: The United Kingdom Isolated?' [1984] *PL* 46.

'cannot be right'. The courts would therefore insist that the right could only be overridden if an 'objective, sufficient justification'[92] existed so that the infringement was limited to what was strictly required by the situation. While such a development would undoubtedly be welcome, two objections seem inescapable. The first is simply that there appears to be no compelling reason to suppose that such a concept of proportionality (as a separate head of challenge rather than as merely an aspect of *Wednesbury* unreasonableness)[93] will not remain waiting in the wings as merely a theoretical possibility until the Human Rights Act comes into force.[94] The possibility of its development as a separate head of review was first floated in the *GCHQ* case. Little enthusiasm by the judiciary to develop it has since been evident. The second point is that even if such a head of challenge were to be developed, the really crucial factor would be the criteria the courts decided to use to determine which policy considerations were to be allowed to override rights and which were not. If easily satisfied criteria were adopted – a contingency which appears not unlikely – then the increased judicial protection offered to basic liberties might well turn out to consist rather more of theory than of substance.

The decision in *Smith* clearly fails to reflect Laws' thesis although it gives an appearance of doing so. The Laws' approach was applied in order to reach an outcome protective of individual rights in *Cambridge HA, ex parte B*[95] in which Laws J himself was presiding; his decision was immediately overturned by the Court of Appeal.[96]

Two points seem to emerge from the above discussion. First, the judiciary do not seem to be united around a clear conception of their role. No compelling evidence emerges of a common understanding that they should form a bulwark to protect the citizens' liberties against the burgeoning power of the executive. Secondly, even in the area in which such a clear idea is

---

92 *Op cit* p 14.
93 See eg the remarks of Taylor LJ in *Ex parte United States Tobacco* [1992] 1 QB 353 at p 366, to which Laws adverts.
94 For discussion of other proposals for the development of judicial review, see Jowell and Lester, 'Beyond *Wednesbury*: Substantive Principles of Judicial Review' [1987] *PL* 369.
95 [1995] *TLR* 159; [1995] WLR 898, CA.
96 It was a notable feature of the case that the Court of Appeal took a wholly different approach from Laws J, a fact which led one commentator, Mallender, to question whether judicial review, which is of course supposed to represent the practical application of the Rule of Law, is in fact offending against the doctrine by virtue of its increasing uncertainty: Mallender, R, 'Judicial Review and the Rule of Law' (1996) 112 *LQR* 182–86. Mallender goes on to find that in fact, on a more general jurisprudential level, both approaches 'reveal an intention to give effect to recognisably legal values' which restrain the discretion of both of them. Nevertheless, as Fenwick and Phillipson argue, 'given that the two courts differed so markedly as to which (legal) matters were (a) relevant and (b) determinative of the matter in hand it seems apparent that the rapidly development of this area of law will inevitably entail a period of considerable uncertainty as to the content and scope of its core principles': See *Sourcebook on Public Law*, 1997, p 805. See also *Lord Chancellor ex p Witham* [1997] 2 All ER 779.

present – judicial review – the courts seem to lack the determination to continue pushing the limits of the doctrine outwards in order to ensure greater protection for liberties.

In relation to the first point it may be persuasively argued that since judges have no 'textual anchor for their decisions' and have had to 'rely on an appeal to normative ideals that lack any mooring in the common law',[97] it is unsurprising that common practice as regards fundamental freedoms has not emerged. Dawn Oliver points out that what has been termed the 'ethical aimlessness' of the common law – its lack of a sense of clear direction – means that because the judiciary as a body has no clear conception of the way the law should develop, they have not framed any set of 'guiding principles or priorities where civil and political rights clash with public interests'.[98] Thus the judges in general may be uncertain as to what weight to give to a particular liberty, while the more executive-minded amongst them can take advantage of this uncertainty to grant it little or no weight. This may also mean that debate as to the nature of civil liberties cannot get under way and that only the most obvious instances of their infringement will receive notice. Of course, even if judges had such an 'anchor' there might not be common practice among them: judges in the US Supreme Court and in the European Court of Human Rights may differ very widely as to their conceptions of liberty. However, it seems unarguable that the introduction of the Convention will achieve an increase in unity amongst English judges; while different judges will give different weights to rights and freedoms at the very least all will be certain about when they had to be taken into account.

In relation to both points it may plausibly be argued that the judiciary as a body are not at present able to construct for themselves a clear justification for increasing their powers over government, although signs of judicial activism in the 1990s suggest that some of them consider that they should do so. The reception of the European Convention on Human Rights into domestic law, which may be viewed as a public statement from the nation as a whole of the importance which they attach to human rights, may give the judges the clear mandate for which they seem to feel the need.

---

97 Justice William Brennan of the US Supreme Court in Hart, HLA, *Lectures on Jurisprudence and Moral Philosophy*, p 12, 24 May 1989.
98 Oliver, D, 'A Bill of Rights for the United Kingdom' in *Government in the United Kingdom*, 1991, p 151.

The influence of European law

Under Article 1 of the European Convention on Human Rights, the Member States[99] must secure the rights and freedoms to their subjects but they are free to decide how this should be done.[100] Each state decides on the status the Convention enjoys in national law; there is no obligation under Article 1 to allow individuals to rely on it in *national* courts. In some states it has the status of Constitutional Law;[101] in others of ordinary law.[102]

However, in the UK it has at present no binding force. Until 1997, successive UK governments considered that it was not necessary for the Convention to be part of UK law; they always maintained that the UK's unwritten constitution was in conformity with it. Thus, at present a UK citizen cannot go before a UK court and simply argue that a Convention right has been violated. Nevertheless the influence of the Convention is rapidly becoming more significant in domestic law through rulings in UK courts and in the European Court of Justice. It may be said that the Convention has been encroaching steadily on UK law from every direction[103] and that its direct reception within the current Parliament will merely be the culmination of that process.[104] It has had an impact through domestic courts in the following ways which will still be relevant when the Human Rights Act 1998 comes into force.

Statutory construction

It is a general principle of construction that statutes will be interpreted if possible so as to conform with international treaties to which the UK is a party on the basis that the government is aware of its international obligations and would not intend to legislate contrary to them. However, as Lord Brandon of

---

99 Currently the Western European members are: Austria, Belgium, Cyprus, Denmark, Finland, France, Germany, Greece, Iceland, Ireland, Italy, Liechtenstein, Luxembourg, Malta, the Netherlands, Norway, Portugal, San Marino, Spain, Sweden, Switzerland, Turkey, the United Kingdom. Eastern European members: Bulgaria, the Czech Republic, Estonia, Hungary, Lithuania, Poland, Romania, Slovakia and Slovenia The numbers will continue to increase due to the disintegration of the Soviet Union and Yugoslavia. Applications for membership are being considered from Albania, Byelorus, Croatia, Latvia, Moldova, Russia and Ukraine.
100 This was affirmed by the Irish Supreme Court in *The State (Lawless) v O'Sullivan and the Minister for Justice*; see *Yearbook of the Convention on Human Rights* Vol II (1958–59) at pp 608–22.
101 eg Austria.
102 This includes Belgium, France, Italy, Luxembourg and Germany.
103 For the argument that the extent of such encroachment has been exaggerated, see Klug, F and Starmer, K [1997] *PL* 223.
104 See pp 126–33, 621–39.

Oakbrook made clear in *M and H (Minors), Re*[105] the English courts are under no duty to apply the Convention's provisions directly: 'While English courts may strive where they can to interpret statutes as conforming with the obligations of the UK under the Convention, they are nevertheless bound to give effect to statutes which are free from ambiguity even if those statutes may be in conflict with the Convention'. This principle was accepted by the House of Lords in *Secretary of State for the Home Department ex parte Brind*,[106] but the possibility of extending the role of the Convention in domestic law by importing it into administrative law was rejected. It was made clear that although the courts would presume that ambiguity in domestic legislation should be resolved by arriving at an interpretation in conformity with the Convention, it did not follow that where Parliament had conferred an administrative discretion on the executive without indicating the precise limits within which is had to be exercised, it could be presumed that it had to be exercised within Convention limits. It had been argued that to import such a principle must have been the legislature's intention, but the House of Lords considered that this would be an unwarranted step to take, bearing in mind that Parliament had chosen not to adopt the Convention. Thus, the decision in *Brind* reaffirmed the accepted principle that the Convention should be taken into account where domestic legislation is ambiguous. It also determined that state officials are not bound by the Convention in exercising discretionary power. Lord Bridge, reflecting the view of the majority, accepted nevertheless that the Convention might be relevant in reviewing the exercise of such powers. However, the government has subsequently accepted that state officials exercising such powers should comply with the Convention.[107]

Importation of the Convention by allowing it to override statutory provisions will not occur under the Human Rights Act 1998; rather, provisions will have to be interpreted in conformity with it 'so far as it is possible to do so'. At present, the interpretation of ambiguous provisions in conformity with it still leaves it enormous scope to influence domestic law. The width of this scope was underlined by the ruling of the Court of Appeal in *Derbyshire County Council v Times Newspapers Ltd*[108] which is considered below. It was delivered in the context of the common law rather than statute but was not expressed to be confined to the common law.

---

105 [1988] 3 WLR 485 at p 498; [1990] 1 AC 686, HL.
106 [1991] 1 AC 696; [1991] 1 All ER 720; [1991] 2 WLR 588, HL.
107 *HL Deb* 559, WA, 7 December 1994, Col 84 and WA, 9 January 1995, Vol 560 Col 1.
108 [1993] AC 534; [1993] 1 All ER 1011; [1992] 3 WLR 28, HL.

Influence on the common law

Lord Scarman in *AG v BBC*[109] considered that the Convention could also influence the common law. He said that where there was some leeway to do so, a court which must adjudicate on the relative weight to be given to different public interests under the common law should try to strike a balance in a manner consistent with the treaty obligations accepted by the government: 'If the issue should ultimately be ... a question of legal policy, we must have regard to the country's international obligation to observe the Convention as interpreted by the Court of Human Rights.' This approach was endorsed by the House of Lords in *AG v Guardian Newspapers No 2*,[110] Lord Goff stating that he considered it to be his duty where free to do so to interpret the law in accordance with Convention obligations. Similarly, in *Chief Metropolitan Magistrates' Court ex parte Choudhury*,[111] Article 10 was taken into account in reviewing the decision of the magistrates' court not to grant summonses against Salman Rushdie and his publishers for the common law offence of blasphemous libel.

The need to take the Convention into account was emphasised even more strongly by the Court of Appeal in *Derbyshire County Council v Times Newspapers Ltd*,[112] Ralph Gibson LJ ruling that where a matter 'was not clear [by reference to] established principles of our law ... the court must ... have regard to the principles stated in the Convention'. Butler-Sloss LJ put the matter even more strongly 'where there is an ambiguity or the law is otherwise unclear or so far undeclared by an appellate court, the English court is not only entitled but ... obliged to consider the implications of Article 10'. The House of Lords considered that in the particular instance, the common law could determine the issues in favour of freedom of speech[113] and that therefore recourse to the Convention was unnecessary, but this does not mean that the guidance offered by the Court of Appeal is not of value in an instance in which the common law is uncertain. That guidance suggests that judges have no choice as to whether to consider the Convention where the law is ambiguous[114] or – and this does appear to be a new development – where it is not yet settled in an appellate court. Thus, even where the law is not ambiguous but there is no appellate ruling on a particular point, a judgment should be reached which is in conformity with the Convention. It may therefore be the case that all areas of the common law which are not clearly

---

109 [1981] AC 303, 354; [1980] 3 WLR 109 at 130, HL.
110 [1990] 1 AC 109 at 283.
111 [1991] 1 QB 429; [1991] 1 All ER 306.
112 Above note 108.
113 [1993] 1 All ER 1011. For comment see Barendt, E [1993] *PL* 449.
114 See further on this point (1992) *MLR* 721.

settled in the House of Lords and which bear on Convention issues, should now reflect Convention principles.

A number of issues remain unresolved. The common law is constantly evolving to encompass new situations; it may therefore be argued that where the principles governing an area of law are settled but its application to a new area is not, it must be interpreted in conformity with the Convention. Further, if a lower court imports Convention principles into a particular area on the basis that no appellate ruling is available, a higher court might arguably no longer be at liberty to depart from that ruling. If in considering the area of law generally and leaving aside the Convention-based ruling, a higher court did consider that a different interpretation might be adopted, might it not be said that as two different interpretations were now available, the law was unclear and therefore the ruling in conformity with the Convention must be retained?

Influence of the Convention on EU law

The influence of the Convention in EU law is becoming increasingly important due to acceptance of the principle enunciated in *Amministrazione delle Finanze dello Stato v Simmenthal*[115] and *Nold v Commission*,[116] namely that respect for fundamental rights should be ensured within the context of the EU. The Convention has come into a closer relationship with EU law as the process of European integration has continued.

Article F2 of the Treaty of European Union states that the EU will respect fundamental rights as recognised by the Convention. The ECJ in Opinion 2/94 (28 March 1996)[117] has, however, held that the EU cannot accede to the Convention on the ground that an amendment to the Treaty of Rome would be required in order to bring about this change, since it would go beyond the scope of Article 235. Under the Treaty of Amsterdam Article F1 voting rights of Member States who fail to observe this principle can be suspended. The result of these developments is that, in all the Member States, implementation of EU measures in national law is clearly subject to respect for the Convention rights, although an individual cannot make an application to Strasbourg against the Union alleging that the Union has violated the Convention. Even though formal accession of the Union to the Convention has not yet occurred, the Convention will control Union conduct. Thus, the decision of the ECHR in *Rees*[118] was relied upon by the ECJ in deciding, in Case 13/14 *P v S and Cornwall CC*,[119] that transsexuals fall within the Equal Treatment Directive.

---

115 Case 106/77 [1978] ECR 629.
116 [1974] ECR 481.
117 (1996) *The Times*, 16 April.
118 (1986) 9 EHRR 56.
119 Judgment of 30 April 1996; (1996) *The Times*, 7 May.

Methods of Protecting Civil Liberties in the UK: The Bill of Rights Question

This was found on the basis that the directive is simply the expression of the principle of equality, which is one of the fundamental principles of European law.

It is therefore probable that as the influence of the Convention on EU law becomes more significant and the impact of EU law becomes greater in the UK, the Convention may also have more influence. EU law can of course have *direct* effect in UK courts and may even override a UK statute;[120] therefore certain Convention principles may come to be of limited binding force in the UK as forming part of EU law. However, the potential impact of the Convention in the UK by this means has not as yet been fully realised.[121]

European law as an external force

If, contrary to the Diceyan view, further protection for civil liberties is needed, over and above that provided by the traditional constitutional means, the influence of Europe through the European Convention on Human Rights (ECHR) and the European Union has increasingly provided it.[122] It is clear that membership of the European Community and the influence of the ECHR have had an enormous impact on civil liberties in the United Kingdom in the last two decades. The influence of the European Union will increase, especially when the Amsterdam Treaty[123] becomes part of British law; EU law has already had an important impact in the areas of sex discrimination,[124] data protection[125] and freedom of movement.[126] The rulings of the European Court of Human Rights have led to better protection of human rights in such areas as prisoners' rights,[127] freedom of expression[128] and privacy.[129]

---

120 See *Factortame Ltd v Secretary of State for Transport* [1991] 1 All ER 70, HL.

121 See further on this issue, van Dijk, P and van Hoof, G, Chap 8; Clapham, *Human Rights and the European Community: A Critical Overview*, 1991; Schermers, HG (1990) 27 CMLR 249; Grief, N [1991] *PL* 555; Coppel, J and O'Neill, A [1992] 29 CMLR 669; Foster, N (1987) 8 *HRLJ* 245; Lenaerts (1991) 16 *ELR* 367; O'Leary, S, 'Accession by the EC to the ECHR' (1996) 4 EHRR 362.

122 See Farren, S, *The UK before the European Court of Human Rights*, 1996.

123 The Treaty is expected to come into force in 1999. It extends a number of existing rights under EU law and amends the Social Charter which lays down minimum rights for workers in the Community countries. The Conservative government failed to ratify it but in the Agreement annexed to the Protocol on Social Policy in the Treaty of Maastricht the other Member States recorded their agreement to 'continue along the path' laid down in it. The Labour government has withdrawn the opt out.

124 See eg *Marshall (No 2)* [1993] 4 All ER 586.

125 The Data Protection Act 1984 derived from the European Convention for the Protection of Individuals with regard to the Automatic Protection of Data, 17 September 1980.

126 Article 48 of the Treaty of Rome, which is directly enforceable.

127 For example, *Golder*, Eur Court HR, A.18, Judgment of 21 February 1975.

128 *Sunday Times*, Judgment of 26 April 1979; (1979) 2 EHRR 245. See further Chap 4 pp 149–51.

129 For example, *Gaskin v UK* (1985) 12 EHRR 16. See further Chap 8 p 360.

However, as *external* forces both these influences, in different respects, are limited. EU law tends to be concerned more with social and economic than civil rights. Demarcation between social and civil rights is not always clear but even where EU law protects rights which might be termed either civil or social, this may not be its primary purpose. Although Community law is intended to create social benefits in addition to economic benefits, social benefits are conceived of as a by-product of or adjunct to, economic integration.[130] In contrast, the influence of the European Convention on Human Rights is procedurally rather than substantively limited. As pointed out in Chapter 2, the effect of a ruling of the European Court of Human Rights is dependent on the government in question making a change in the law. The UK government may be able to minimise the impact of an adverse judgment by interpreting defeat narrowly,[131] by avoiding implementation of a ruling,[132] or by obeying the letter of the Article in question but ignoring its spirit.[133] The impact of the Convention is also lessened because the process of invoking it, considered in Chapter 2, is extremely cumbersome, lengthy[134] and expensive.[135] It may not become less so despite the changes which will occur under the Eleventh Protocol, including merger of the European Court and Commission of Human Rights.[136] Chapter 2 concluded that while the system of the long trek to Strasbourg (starting with the exhaustion of domestic remedies) remains substantially as at present only the most exceptionally determined and resourceful litigants are likely to pursue it.[137]

4 A BILL OF RIGHTS?

In the late 1990s there is a consensus among most academic commentators that the traditional methods of providing protection for civil liberties are

---

130 This is exemplified in the case of harmonization of a minimal level of employment protection provisions in order to create a 'level playing field' of competition for employers in the Single Market. See, for example, Nielsen and Szyszczak, *The Social Dimension of the European Community*, 2nd edn, 1993, pp 15–18; Hoskyns, 'Women, European Law and Transnational Politics' (1986) 14 *Int J Soc Law*, 299–315.

131 As in *Golder*, note 127 above.

132 *Brogan, Coyle, McFadden and Tracey v UK* (1988) (Case No 10/1987/133/184–7). The government refused to implement the ruling, entering a derogation under Article 15. See further Chap 2 p 79.

133 *Abdulaziz, Cabales and Balkandali v UK* (1985) 7 EHRR 471. To implement the ruling the UK 'equalised down'. See further Chap 2 p 77.

134 The Commission makes over 3,000 provisional files a year. The average petition took five years and nine months between 1982–87 if it went all the way through the system – four years before the Commission, nearly two before the Court (15 EHRR 321 at 327). Petitions can take nine years.

135 Legal aid is not available until after the complaint has been held admissible by the Commission.

136 See Chap 2 p 24.

137 See Chap 2 pp 85–86.

Methods of Protecting Civil Liberties in the UK: The Bill of Rights Question

insufficiently effective but no clear agreement as to the means which should be adopted in order to provide further protection. A degree of suspicion and distrust is often aroused at the notion of effecting such protection by means of a Bill of Rights and this may find its roots in the traditional view that Bills of Rights are high sounding documents which are ineffective in practice but dangerous because they create complacency as to liberty and that, moreover, they are the marks of a primitive, undeveloped legal system. In 1776, Bentham described declarations of rights as merely so much 'bawling upon paper'. Dicey wrote that there is 'in the English constitution an absence of those declarations or definitions of rights so dear to foreign constitutionalists', but that this was a strength rather than a weakness because such rights may be constantly suspended, whereas the suspension of the English Constitution 'would mean with us nothing less than a revolution'. Lord Hailsham has said 'show me a nation with a Bill of Rights and I will show you a nation with fewer actual human rights than Britain because the escape clauses are used, often quite ruthlessly ...'.[138] It has also been suggested that the notion of liberty and of the need to protect it must emanate from a source outside the Bill of Rights; Judge Learned Hand has written 'Liberty lies in the hearts and minds of men and women; when it dies there no constitution, no law, no court can save it ...'.

More recently the argument that Bills of Rights *per se* are ineffective or actually inimical to the protection of liberty, has tended to give way to the argument that although some independent restraint on the excess or abuse of power is needed, it would be dangerous or pointless to enact a Bill of Rights because it would not be wise to trust UK judges with such a significant power:[139] they would invoke the exceptions in order to interpret it in an executive-minded manner, thus perhaps emasculating the freedoms it was supposed to protect. Commentators such as Lee, Ewing and Gearty argue that it would be dangerous to trust to a Bill of Rights and that there is too great a tendency to regard one as a panacea for all that is wrong with civil liberties in the UK.[140] Ewing and Gearty consider that what is needed are genuine constraints on the power of the Prime Minister and that a Bill of Rights is a merely cosmetic change. It has further been argued that whether or not UK judges in particular could be trusted with a Bill of Rights, the whole notion of endowing an unelected group with a considerable area of power removed from the reach of the legislature is incompatible with democratic theory.[141]

---

138 House of Lords, *Hansard*, Vol 369 Cols 784–85.
139 For example, Ewing and Gearty, *Freedom under Thatcher*, pp 262–75; Lord McCluskey (the Solicitor General for Scotland under the last Labour government) in his 1986 Reith Lectures, Lecture 5.
140 Lee, *Judging Judges*, p 166; Ewing and Gearty, p 275.
141 Waldron, J, 'A Rights-based Critique of Constitutional Rights' (1993) 13 *OJLS* 18.

Allan, for example, argues that '[entrenched] Bills of Rights are singularly undemocratic'.[142]

The argument from democracy

Whether or not it is acceptable in a democracy that unelected judges should wield the power of a Bill of Rights partly depends on its authority and the availability of review of legislation. The most contentious possibility would arise if judges were empowered to strike down legislation in conflict with the Bill of Rights, which was also given a higher authority than other Acts of Parliament by being entrenched, so that no possibility of correction of judicial decisions by subsequent legislation arose, except in so far as provided for by the method of entrenchment. The argument from democracy has the greatest force only if the Bill of Rights could prevail over subsequent inconsistent legislation. It obviously has much less force if, as is more likely, it was able to prevail only over prior inconsistent legislation. A further possibility is that a Bill of Rights could be protected by a so-called 'notwithstanding clause' – subsequent legislation would only override it if the intention to do so was clearly stated in the legislation. The perpetrators of the argument against trusting the judges do not always make clear whether their antipathy is to all of these possibilities or only the first. It is obviously a crucial distinction as in the second and third, Parliament clearly still retains ultimate power over the shape of the law; the third possibility merely requires candour if rights are to be interfered with, which as Dworkin has commented 'is hardly incompatible with democracy'.[143]

However, the argument that a fully entrenched Bill of Rights *would* be incompatible with democracy should not be too readily conceded. Such an argument seems to proceed from the premise that any restriction upon the freedom of legislative bodies – even those designed to protect fundamental rights – is undemocratic. It should be noted initially that a true partisan of democracy ought also to be opposed to UK membership of all international human rights treaties, since the basic premise of all of these is that certain rights of citizens should be placed beyond the power of the majority to infringe them. The contrary notion, that there should be no limits on the power of the majority, can be defended only by reference to a rather crude form of preference utilitarianism[144] and arguably amounts to an impoverished conception of democracy. Such a conception could provide no reason why the majority should not authorise the internment, torture and summary execution of all IRA suspects if it was clear that this would end

---

142 'Bills of Rights and Judicial Power – A Liberal's Quandary' [1996] 16(2) *OJLS* 337–52.
143 Dworkin, R, *A Bill of Rights for Britain*, 1990.
144 See Chap 1 pp 6–7 for discussion of utilitarianism.

Methods of Protecting Civil Liberties in the UK: The Bill of Rights Question

terrorist attacks and thus immeasurably benefit the mass of the people. Those who insist that Parliament's power should be untrammelled presumably do not think that it should use its powers in this way and their conviction that it should not do so can only be justified by a belief that there must be limits on what the majority can inflict on even profoundly anti-social individuals and minorities. Thus it may be assumed that there is general acceptance of this fundamental conviction which lies behind every Bill of Rights. Those who remain opposed to entrenched rights usually profess not to be hostile to the idea of human rights *per se* but to be concerned with other issues.

Thus, one respected commentator, Jeremy Waldron, in setting out what could be termed the 'argument from controversy',[145] is concerned not so much that the majority should have unlimited power but that any particular formulation of rights will inevitably be controversial and that entrenching it amounts to a permanent disabling of those who hold a contrary view about which rights should be protected. Thus he asks rhetorically: 'Are the formulations of one generation to be cast in stone and given precedence over all subsequent revisions?' Three objections to this position are apparent. First, to characterise a Bill of Rights as setting formulations 'in stone' seems to exhibit a failure to take cognisance of the immense diversity of interpretations which can be extracted from a broadly worded document such as the European Convention,[146] and the way in which such interpretations can develop to reflect changes in popular attitudes.[147] The fact that one document – the American Constitution – has been found at different times to support both black slavery and positive discrimination in favour of black people provides clear evidence to support this argument.

The second objection is that the 'controversy' thesis determinedly ignores the reasonable degree of consensus that exists around many basic rights. For example, when discussing the possibility of protecting the right to participate

---

[145] This term is used because the fact of controversy as to the favoured list of rights lies at the heart of Waldron's argument against entrenched rights. 'A Rights-based Critique of Constitutional Rights' (1993) 13 *OJLS* 18.

[146] Waldron's objections seem all the more strange in that prima facie they do not seem to take account of those adjudicatory theories which explain the vital part that both the judges' moral and political convictions and the mass of shared assumptions and understanding in a particular society play in the interpretation of texts. (For an extremely lucid and accessible exposition of the above point see Simmonds, N, 'Between Positivism and Idealism' (1991) *CLJ* 308.) However, Waldron does mention such theories in several places (eg at pp 41–43) where he states that his objection is not so much that judges should be able to interpret and modify citizens' rights but that democratic institutions should be disabled from doing so. But once Waldron has conceded the point that judges can radically amend the meaning of texts, his point about setting rights in stone is lost. The reason why democratic institutions should be disabled from interference with *some* fundamental rights is discussed in the text above: p 114.

[147] It is indeed arguable that judges can more readily respond to marked changes in the moral climate than politicians. For example the judiciary, in response to a growing consensus that the marital rape exemption was indefensible, abolished the immunity of husbands at a time when there were no indications that Parliament was prepared to make time for legislation (*R* [1991] 4 All ER 481).

in democracy, Waldron argues that democratic procedures themselves cannot be entrenched, because 'People disagree about how participatory rights should be understood ...'. Noticeably, however, he fails to mention the near-complete agreement on the fundamental right of universal adult suffrage. This point leads on to the third objection to the 'controversy' thesis, namely, that paradoxically enough its own implications are contrary to democracy.[148] The refusal to disable the majority by entrenchment of rights includes, as just noted, a refusal to entrench democracy itself. This refusal in effect means that Waldron will not deny the right of the majority of the day to destroy democracy by disenfranchising a group such as all non-whites or even voting democracy itself out of existence, thereby denying it to future generations. Since, by contrast, a Bill of Rights is ultimately concerned with preserving a worthwhile democracy for the future, it can be persuasively argued that entrenched basic rights show more respect for democratic principles than do the advocates of retaining the untrammelled power of the majority of the day.[149] Entrenchment of a Bill of Rights would probably be possible in the UK system only by means of a written constitution (considered below). Such a task would almost certainly not be undertaken without a referendum; if the people considered such a settlement desirable they would in effect be expressing their will to be ruled by an unelected body within certain defined areas as the price of curbing elected power.

The argument against endowing the judges with power under an entrenched Bill of Rights (assuming entrenchment was possible) should also be considered in the light of the experience of America. The most striking feature of the American system is the power of the Supreme Court to render inoperative acts of the elected representatives of the people (first asserted in *Marbury v Madison*).[150] This power seems alien to UK jurists but the justification offered for it is that the legitimacy of judicial review of legislation derives not from electoral accountability but from the particular positions of the judges within the constitution. The classic statement of this theory is that of Alexander Hamilton in *Federalist* #78:

> The executive not only dispenses the honours but holds the sword of the community. The legislature not only commands the purse but prescribes the rules by which the duties and rights of every citizen are to be regulated. The

---

[148] A further paradox in Waldron's argument, the existence of which he concedes (at p 46), is that if the majority vote in a referendum for an entrenched Bill of Rights they must, on his argument, be allowed to have one. Clearly, the only way to prevent the majority from entrenching a Bill of Rights would be to have an entrenched law forbidding the entrenchment of laws. This would obviously be impossible on its own terms. Since, as Dworkin notes (*op cit* pp 36–37), opinion polls reveal that more than 71% of the population favour an entrenched Bill of Rights, Waldron's argument appears to be self-defeating.

[149] Such a view is of course endorsed by a number of legal philosophers and civil libertarians. See Dworkin, *A Bill of Rights for Britain*, 1990; the view also clearly underpins his general political philosophy, see for example 'Liberalism' in *A Matter of Principle*, 1985. See also Hart, HLA, *Law Liberty and Morality*, 1963 and Lester, *Democracy and Individual Rights*, 1968.

[150] (1803) 5 US (1 Cranch) 137.

Methods of Protecting Civil Liberties in the UK: The Bill of Rights Question

judiciary, on the contrary, has no influence over either the sword or the purse; no direction either of the strength or of the wealth of society. [Thus it will be] the least dangerous to the political rights of the Constitution.[151]

It could be noted in this context that the UK has a constitutional precedent in the shape of the House of Lords for allowing an unelected body to influence legislation. The notion is not therefore entirely foreign to the UK system. Of course, this is not a complete analogy: the House of Lords has a much more limited role in this respect than judges under an entrenched Bill of Rights would have.If the Bill of Rights were unentrenched the argument from democracy loses some of its cogency but fastens instead on the question of policy-making under the Bill of Rights. A Bill of Rights would inevitably contain open-textured provisions which would have to be interpreted and that interpretation would often involve political choices. An obvious example is the choice before the European Court in the *Young, James and Webster* case[152] concerning the question of the closed shop. Ought judges – although finally subject to Parliament under an unentrenched Bill of Rights – be given a much broader policy-making role or ought politicians to be the sole arbiters of such questions? Of course, many questions which would have to be determined by the judges in applying the provisions of the Bill of Rights lie rather in the moral than the political arena because civil rights are rights claimed against public authorities,[153] not against particular political parties. Nevertheless, it has been argued by such opponents of a Bill of Rights as Lord McCluskey that an Act of Parliament, arrived at after full consideration of the issues involved and the likely effects and covering specific areas, is a better way to protect, for example, the right to privacy than a Bill of Rights containing a provision such as 'Everyone has the right to privacy' followed by certain exceptions. The suggestion is that UK judges due to their particular training would not be at home with an uncertain concept such as a 'right to privacy'. On the other hand, as argued above, the judges in the UK have developed certain presumptions in order to protect liberty and therefore it may be suggested that they are not incapable of handling indeterminate concepts. Lester makes a forceful point in support of this proposition in his comments on the way the courts have dealt with the task of applying broadly worded EU directives on sex discrimination, provisions which a legal traditionalist would term 'so vague and woolly that they might mean almost anything'. He considers that 'English judges have interpreted and applied these general principles in a manner which recognises their fundamental nature and which gives full effect to their underlying aims', and from this he concludes that, 'Those sceptics

---

151 *The Federalist Papers*, Mentor, ed, 1961, pp 464, 465.

152 Eur Court HR, A.44, Judgment of 13 August 1981; (1981) 4 EHRR 38. See Chap 7 pp 278–79 for discussion of the decision.

153 Or against private individuals where a public authority bears some responsibility for failure to protect a right. See discussion of *Drittwurkung*, Chap 2 p 28.

who doubt the ability of British judges to protect the fundamental rights of the [European] Convention should consider their impressive record in translating the fundamental rights of Community law into practical reality'.[154] A further point worth noting is that the provisions of a Bill of Rights would have to be supplemented by specific pieces of legislation covering certain areas. If the political will to bring forward such legislation was not evident it might be influenced in favour of doing so by decisions under the Bill of Rights.

Moreover, although there is an argument (which was put forward on behalf of the Labour Party in 1990)[155] that rather than a Bill of Rights more certain protection would be assured by creating a number of statutes, each of which would cover one area of civil liberties, it may also be argued that at present this is unlikely to occur. It would be time-consuming and might therefore be unlikely to find a place in a legislative programme mainly concerned with social and economic issues. The lack of legislation passed over the last 18 years with the sole or main intention of protecting a particular liberty supports this argument. The legislation that has been passed: the Contempt of Court Act 1981, the Equal Pay Amendment Regulations, the Data Protection Act 1984 has been Europe-driven.[156] There has clearly been a lack of legislation passed to protect civil liberties which has been enacted without such coercion; the UK, unlike other jurisdictions, has failed so far to enact a Privacy Act. If the party of government tends to abjure its policy-making role in these areas, it may be argued that the only alternative is enactment of a Bill of Rights which would largely hand such a role to the judges. Even if Parliament was prepared to legislate in these areas it could still be argued that a Bill of Rights would be of value as providing a remedy which would be more flexible than a statute and might adapt to changing social conditions more readily, although whether or not it could do so in actuality would depend on the approach of the judiciary to its interpretation. Moreover, specific pieces of legislation could have the protection they offered to liberties eroded by subsequent legislation through the operation of the doctrine of implied repeal; the protection gained would therefore be more precarious than that offered by a Bill of Rights enjoying greater consitutional protection even if only due to a convention of respect for it.

---

154 Lester, 'Fundamental Rights' [1984] *PL* 70–71.

155 See *The Charter of Rights: Guaranteeing Individual Liberty in a Free Society*, Labour Party document 1990.

156 The Contempt of Court Act 1981 was passed in response to the judgment of the European Court of Human Rights in *Sunday Times*, Judgment of 26 April 1979, A.30; (1979) 2 EHRR 245. The Data Protection Act derived from the Convention for the Protection of Individuals with regard to the Automatic Processing of Data (17 September 1980) and the Equal Pay (Amendment) Regulations from the Council Directive 75/117 of 10 February 1975.

Fitness of the UK judiciary to adjudicate on human rights

Class bias

Judges are largely drawn from a tiny minority group: upper middle class, rich, white, elderly males who were public school and Oxbridge educated. As positions of power in Britain are often filled by persons drawn from this group it might seem incongruous to suggest that they should be charged with the protection of the rights of the weak or the unpopular. John Griffiths in *The Politics of the Judiciary*[157] argues that the senior judges:

> ... define the public interest, inevitably, from the viewpoint of their own class. And the public interest, so defined, is ... the interest of others in authority. It includes the maintenance of order, the protection of private property, the containment of the trade union movement.

The Griffiths argument, which is echoed by other leftist commentators, leads the left to view incorporation of the Convention as likely to lead to a diminution in the protection of civil liberties in the UK.[158] This may occur, in their view, for a number of reasons. In particular, it is thought that the judiciary, in the UK and abroad, cannot be trusted to protect the interests of minorities and/or unpopular groups but will tend to protect commercial interests and the interests of those in authority. Therefore Convention rights may be enforced by powerful bodies, including rich individuals and large corporations. Such enforcement may be to the detriment of civil liberties or to the detriment of general public interests of a social welfare nature. This is a powerful argument even to those who do not accept the conclusion which the left draws from it.

It is not hard to find decisions made by judges under human rights documents which support the leftist thesis. For example certain decisions under the Canadian Charter might find counterparts in the UK once the Convention is received into domestic law. Examples might include the use of Article 10 of the Convention to attack bans on cigarette advertising[159] or the use of Article 6 to diminish the value of special protections for rape victims within the criminal justice system.[160] In Canada the so-called 'rape shield',

---

157 4th edn, 1991, p 327.

158 See Ewing and Gearty (1997) 2 EHRR 146 on Labour's plans to incorporate the Convention.

159 The Supreme Court of Canada struck down as an unjustifiable restriction on freedom of expression a Canadian statute prohibiting advertising: *RJR MacDonald Inc v Canada* (AG) SCC 21 September 1995.

160 In Canada the so-called 'rape shield' which prevented the defence asking questions about a complainant's sexual history or reputation was struck down by the Supreme Court under the Canadian Charter on the ground of fairness to the accused: *Seaboyer* [1991] 2 SCR 577. It is possible that the anonymity of rape complainants in the UK might be challenged on similar grounds under Article 6 or possibly under Article 8 in conjunction with Article 14 (on grounds of equal rights to privacy).

which prevented the defence asking questions about a complainant's sexual history or reputation, was struck down by the Supreme Court under the Canadian Charter on the ground of fairness to the accused: *Seaboyer*.[161] It is possible that the current anonymity of rape complainants in the UK might be challenged on similar grounds under Article 6 or possibly under Article 8 in conjunction with Article 14 (on grounds of equal rights to privacy). Various powerful figures such as Ernest Saunders have been found at Strasbourg, successfully enforcing Convention rights in an unedifying fashion.[162] At the same time, when 'weak' individuals attempt to use the Convention they may find that they are unable to do so, partly due to the problem of obtaining legal aid. Even when such individuals do use the Convention they may find that the margin of appreciation doctrine operates against them as it has done in the transsexual cases against the UK.[163]

It is unclear whether or not the margin of appreciation doctrine will be used in some form in the domestic courts. It may not be given that name but the judiciary may find that certain matters, most obviously those relating to national security, are peculiarly matters for the executive. Whether they would be prepared to use that doctrine, under whatever name, in Convention cases relating to sexual autonomy is debatable. In any event, whether discretion is exercised by the judiciary in deciding Convention cases in the UK under the name of a margin of appreciation or as an inherent part of the process of administering such a broadly worded document, the outcome, under the leftist thesis, would tend to be the same.

However, the causal link between the judges' backgrounds and their decisions may not be as clear as Griffiths suggests. Other variables may be present influencing particular decisions and judges, despite similar backgrounds, sometimes display markedly differing degrees of liberalism. As Lee points out,[164] a number of House of Lords decisions on human rights issues have been reached on a three-two majority,[165] while in others a unanimous Court of Appeal has been overturned by a unanimous House of Lords.[166]

This argument does not imply that all judges have a special facility, unknown to normal people, of rooting out in themselves all the unconscious prejudices derived from their backgrounds. Obviously judges will sometimes be influenced, unconsciously or otherwise, by the interests of their class. What is apparent, however, is that despite the fact that they largely belong to a

---

161 [1991] 2 SCR 577.
162 *Saunders v UK* (1997) 23 EHRR 313.
163 See *Cossey v UK* (1990) 13 EHRR 622; *X, Y and Z v UK* (1997) 24 EHRR 143.
164 *Judging Judges*, 1st edn, 1989, p 36.
165 eg *Gillick v West Norfolk and Wisbech Area Health Authority* [1986] AC 112; [1985] 3 WLR 830, HL.
166 *Mandla v Dowell Lee* [1983] 2 AC 548; [1983] 1 All ER 1062, HL.

Methods of Protecting Civil Liberties in the UK: The Bill of Rights Question

particular societal group, they do not always display attitudes which tend to be associated with that group. At the least it is fair to say that during the Conservative years 1979–97 the judges demonstrated on the whole a greater eagerness to protect the rights of 'weak' or minority groups than did their counterparts in government. A number of highly significant decisions taken in the 1980s and 1990s relating to the rights of, for example, poorly paid women, asylum seekers or of suspects in police custody are documented in this book in which judges may be said to have acted against the interests of their class.[167] The argument that the judges will inevitably be influenced by the interests of those in authority is not, it is suggested, fully supported by the evidence.

It might also be argued that Canadian judges, who share a similar constitutional background with UK judges and to whom some, at least, of Griffiths's comments would apply, are thought to have adjusted successfully to applying the Canadian Charter of Rights and Freedoms 1982, although it should be pointed out that there had been judicial review of legislation in Canada since before Confederation in 1867. Professor Russell of the University of Toronto wrote in 1988 (six years after the Charter was adopted):

> In *Skapinker*[168] (the first Charter decision of the Canadian Supreme Court) the Court made it clear that it was prepared to take the Charter seriously, to give its terms a liberal interpretation and to strike down laws and practices of government found to be in conflict with it.[169]

Writing on two decisions in which freedom of expression was upheld under the Charter, Judge Strayer of the Federal Court of Canada has said:

> Such vague paternalistic laws had long been recognised as posing a threat to freedom of expression and they could not survive long in a country which had so recently dedicated itself to guaranteeing that freedom. One can only speculate that such laws would long since have been amended and particularised had inertia not been the line of least political resistance.[170]

In passing it is worth noting that one of the laws in question was a provincial law dealing with film censorship which did not prescribe standards for such censorship; its counterpart can be found at present in the UK in the power of local authorities to license films which derives from legislation passed in 1909.[171] Decisions under the Charter have not, however, gone uncriticised from the political left: it has been said that 'the Charter is being used to benefit vested interest in society and to weaken the relative power of the

---

167 *Hayward v Cammell Laird* [1988] 2 All ER 257; *Pickstone v Freemans* [1988] 3 WLR 265. See Chap 13 pp 580–83, Chap 11, pp 484–90. Chap 12, pp 534–35.
168 [1984] 2 SCR 713.
169 Russell, P [1988] *PL* 385, 388.
170 [1988] *PL* 347 at 359.
171 The Cinematograph Act 1909 which was concerned with the fire risk posed by films at that time.

disadvantaged and under-privileged',[172] referring to a decision condoning restriction of the collective bargaining power of unions in *Retail, Wholesale and Department Store Union*.[173] On the other hand Russell has contended that the Supreme Court 'is sensitive to the left's concerns and is struggling to avoid an approach to the Charter which will give credence to them'.[174] These relatively early favourable evaluations of the impact of the Charter have received support in later analysis. It has been suggested that the Charter 'has transformed the rights' agenda in Canada positively and creatively – sometimes even inspirationally'.[175]

Adjustment to applying the Bill of Rights

It has been argued that the judges have already shown how they would acquit themselves under a Bill of Rights and that the results are not promising.[176] For example, the Privy Council in considering questions arising from Commonwealth Bills of Rights has sometimes given certain guarantees of rights a very restrictive interpretation. In *Attorney General v Antigua Times Ltd*[177] the Privy Council found that a constitutional guarantee of freedom of speech was not infringed by Antiguan legislation requiring a licence from the Cabinet and a large deposit as a surety against libel in order to publish a newspaper. However, the Privy Council appears recently to have adopted a more liberal approach. In *Guerra v Baptiste*[178] the Privy Council had to consider delay in carrying out an execution. Guerra was convicted of murder in the Republic of Trinidad and Tobago and sentenced to death. In 1989 he appealed against his sentence but the appeal was not heard until October 1993. The Privy Council took into account the decision in *Pratt v Attorney General for Jamaica*[179] in which it was found that where a state wishes to retain capital punishment it must accept the responsibility of ensuring that execution follows as swiftly as possible after sentence, allowing a reasonable time for appeal and consideration of reprieve. If the appeal procedure allows the prisoner to prolong appellate proceedings over a period of years, the fault lies with the appeal procedure, not with the prisoner. In *Pratt* it was found that a reasonable target would be to complete the hearings within approximately one year and to carry out the sentence of death within two years. In the

---

172 (1988) 38 *UTLJ* 278, 279.
173 (1986) 33 DLR (4th) 174; [1986] 1 SCR 460; for comment see also (1987) 37 *UTLJ* 183.
174 *Op cit* p 388.
175 Penner, R, 'The Canadian experience with the Charter of Rights' [1996] *PL* 125.
176 Ewing and Gearty, *Freedom under Thatcher*, p 274.
177 [1976] AC 16.
178 (1995) *The Times*, 8 November.
179 [1995] 3 WLR 995. Bailey Harris and Jones (1995) comment that this decision would not be open to the usual criticism that traditional methods of interpretation would be used in determinations under a Bill of Rights (p 18).

present instance there had been substantial delay amounting to nearly five years between sentence and the point at which the sentence was to be carried out. The fact that problems were created by the shortage of court resources did not justify the delay. Such problems had also been a factor in the *Pratt* case. It was therefore found that the sentence must be commuted to one of life imprisonment. This decision and that in *Pratt* suggest that UK judges are quite capable of adopting a broad approach to Bills of Rights. Thus there is some basis for the argument that the judges will take decisions under the European Convention on Human Rights once it is enacted into domestic law which would not emasculate it due to adoption of a narrow and technical approach.

Recent decisions of UK judges applying the European Convention on Human Rights may be criticised as at times adopting traditional, limiting methods of interpretation, although such decisions were taken under constitutional restraints which may be less stringent once the Convention is received into domestic law. In *Brind* (in the Court of Appeal) and in *AG v Guardian Newspapers*[180] judges applied the principles of the European Convention and then proceeded to uphold the restrictions in question. On the other hand, in *Derbyshire County Council*[181] the Court of Appeal – but not the House of Lords – relied on Article 10 to produce the 'right' result. Moreover, where an international treaty has been incorporated into domestic law the English courts have shown a willingness to adopt a broad teleological approach. In *The Hollandia* (concerning provisions of the Hague-Visby Rules which have been incorporated into UK law) Lord Diplock said that such provisions 'should be given a purposive rather than a narrow literalistic construction, particularly wherever the adoption of a literalistic construction would enable the stated purpose of the international Convention ... to be evaded ...'.[182] It should also be noted that UK judges have adapted remarkably quickly to the demands of EU law as it affects fundamental rights and have been prepared to take decisions and make pronouncements upholding such rights which were probably unthinkable when the European Communities Act 1972 was passed.[183]

5 ENACTING THE EUROPEAN CONVENTION ON HUMAN RIGHTS

In December 1996, the Labour Party issued a Consultation Paper on incorporating the European Convention on Human Rights into domestic

---

180 [1987] 3 All ER 316. See also the *Brind* case [1991] 1 AC 696.
181 [1992] 3 WLR 28; see further above p 109; HL ruling: [1993] 1 All ER 1011.
182 [1983] 1 AC 565, 572.
183 Eg, *Secretary of State for Employment, ex parte EOC* [1994] 2 WLR 409, HL.

law.[184] The paper proposed incorporation of the Convention with the First Protocol and the creation of a Human Rights Commission; it also promised review of the possibility of ratifying later Protocols. It left it unclear whether such ratification would also imply that later Protocols would subsequently be incorporated into UK domestic law. It also promised that in future, consideration would be given to the possibility of introducing a tailor made UK Bill of Rights. In October 1997 the Labour government introduced the Human Rights Bill incorporating the 'main provisions' of the Convention.

A tailor-made UK Bill of Rights?

Arguments can be put forward for and against introducing a tailor-made UK Bill of Rights, either as an alternative to incorporating the Convention, or to provide further protection in future. The overwhelming majority of human rights Bills considered by Parliament have simply advocated incorporation of the European Convention on Human Rights[185] into UK law. The House of Lords Select Committee on a Bill of Rights was unanimous on this issue: 'To attempt to formulate *de novo* a set of fundamental rights which would command the necessary general assent would be a fruitless exercise.'[186] Starting from scratch and developing a Bill of Rights for the UK would be a burdensome task because the political parties (and the various pressure groups) would have great difficulty in reaching agreement on it, while the process of hearing and considering all the representations made by interested parties would be extremely lengthy. Zander argues that it is politically and psychologically easier to incorporate the Convention since it is already binding on the UK internationally and both major parties have accepted the jurisdiction of the European Court of Human Rights and the right of individual petition.[187] However, it has been suggested that a Bill of Rights could be drawn up which would be based on the Convention but would improve upon it by using more up-to-date language and dealing with certain of the inadequacies discussed below.[188] The advantage to be gained by adopting this course would have to be weighed against the possible detriment caused if the jurisprudence of the European Court on Human Rights were

---

184 *Bringing Rights Home: Labour's plans to incorporate the ECHR into UK law.*

185 See below p 112. Reference to incorporation of the Convention will be taken to mean Articles 1–18 and the First Protocol – the course advocated by the House of Lords Select Committee on Human Rights in 1978. However, it is arguably a serious deficiency of the international record of the UK in human rights matters that it has not ratified all the Protocols; it is therefore submitted that the most satisfactory course would be their incorporation with the Convention.

186 Report of Select Committee House of Lords Paper 176 June 1978.

187 Zander, *A Bill of Rights?*, p 83.

188 By the Institute for Public Policy Research: Constitution Paper No 1 'A British Bill of Rights', 1990.

seen as less directly applicable. The British judiciary might feel that they had lost the 'anchor' of the authority of the Court and the constraint of the need to apply a uniform European standard of human rights.

Arguments against relying on the Convention alone are based on its defects of both form and content which have often been criticised.[189] It is a cautious document: it is not as open textured as the American Bill of Rights and contains long lists of exceptions to the primary rights – exceptions which suggest a strong respect for the institutions of the state. Perhaps the most outstanding examples of inadequacy are the limited scope of Article 14[190] and the dangerous potential of Article 17.[191] On the other hand, the decisions of the European Court of Human Rights documented in this book suggest that the Convention is sufficiently open-textured to be able to cover circumstances not envisaged when it was created[192] and to adapt to changing social values.

The legal status of the Convention under the Human Rights Act[193]

The constitutional status of Bills or Charters of Rights varies from jurisdiction to jurisdiction. Such instruments may have no special status or they may be afforded (or may acquire) some special protection from express or implied repeal which may at its highest involve their entrenchment. The terms 'entrenchment' and 'protection' which will be used below require explanation because both may encompass a number of possibilities. 'Protection' will be used to refer to any means of giving a statute a special status without seeking to entrench it in any sense of that word. 'Entrenchment' refers to requirements of form or manner or restrictions as to substance. A requirement of form denotes the need to use a particular form of words if a subsequent enactment is to repeal a former, rather than simply allowing the normal rules of implied repeal to operate. A requirement of manner refers to the manner in which legislation is passed if it is to repeal a previous enactment. Examples of such a requirement would include the use of a two-thirds majority in Parliament if a particular piece of legislation is to be repealed or amended. A restriction as to substance refers to the most stringent form of entrenchment: no method of repealing the legislation in question is provided in it. Parts of the German Basic Law are entrenched in this manner and therefore they can never be amended or repealed unless a break with the existing legal order occurs in Germany.

---

189 see eg Hewitt, P, *The Abuse of Power*, 1982, pp 232–40; Gearty, CA (1993) 52 *CLJ* 89.
190 Article 14 provides a guarantee of freedom from discrimination but only in the context of the substantive rights. See further Chap 2 pp 76–78.
191 It was used by the Commission to allow the banning of the German Communist party: *Kommunistische Partei Deutschland v Federal Republic of Germany* Application 250/57 Yearbook I (1955–57) Vol 6 p 222.
192 See eg *Soering v UK*, Judgment of 7 July 1989, A.161; (1989) 11 EHRR 439.
193 See Jaconelli, *Enacting a Bill of Rights*, 1980, for a full discussion of this issue.

Thus, a requirement of 'form' may be termed weak entrenchment since it is the weakest possible form of entrenchment available. A requirement of manner may be referred to as semi or partial entrenchment, while a restriction as to substance may be referred to as full entrenchment. Bearing this in mind it may be found that s 2(4) of the European Communities Act 1972 has been treated as imposing a requirement of form and possibly of manner. Unless Parliament declares in an Act of Parliament that it intends to override Community law such law will prevail over subsequent inconsistent domestic legislation. However, since no means of overriding Community Law is provided in the 1972 Act, it may even be the case that if Parliament made such a declaration the courts would not give effect to it. In that case there would be no means of escaping from the impact of Community Law except by withdrawing from the EU.

As will be found below, the form of entrenchment for the Convention most favoured by a number of commentators is by means of a so-called 'notwithstanding clause'. This is, of course, entrenchment by means of a requirement of form. Therefore, as suggested earlier in this chapter, it is not open to the objections which would be and are levelled at the adoption of a requirement of manner or a restriction as to substance. This point is often lost in debate on the Bill of Rights question and therefore it is worth emphasising here that requiring a democratically elected government to be open about its intention to infringe civil rights cannot be an affront to democracy. The most common requirements of manner – such as, that legislation repealing the Bill of Rights will not be valid unless passed by a 75% majority – are incompatible with democracy if that concept is understood to connote simple majoritarianism. A Bill of Rights protected in this manner could be preserved against the wishes of the majority of the elected representatives in the legislature, so long as that majority was less than 75%. A restriction as to substance is most obviously incompatible with democracy, unless one takes the view, which is based on a different argument,[194] that full entrenchment of Bills of Rights or at least certain fundamental provisions in them, is essential in order to maintain a healthy democracy.

Under the Human Rights Act 1998 which partly reflects Labour's Consultation Paper on the matter, entitled *Bringing Rights Home: Labour's plans to incorporate the ECHR into UK Law*,[195] the Convention will have a lower status than ordinary statutes in that it will not automatically override pre-existing law (section 3). Below, the Act is considered in conjunction with methods of affording the Convention[196] further protection (using that term as wider than 'entrenchment') from repeal. In considering these possibilities it is worth bearing in mind that the need to introduce further forms of protection

---

194 See above, pp 114–15.
195 See Straw, J and Boateng, P (1997) 1 EHRR 71. For discussion see Lyell, Sir N (1997) 2 EHRR 132; Wadham, J (1997) 2 EHRR 141; Ewing, K and Gearty, C (1997) 2 EHRR 146.
196 The term 'the Convention' will be used to refer to the European Convention on Human Rights enacted into UK law in the Human Rights Act 1998.

Methods of Protecting Civil Liberties in the UK: The Bill of Rights Question

might become apparent in future, at least for key Convention rights. Liberty has suggested that certain rights may be viewed as more fundamental than others and therefore might be entrenched while others might be afforded less protection.[197]

The Labour Party proposals in the 1996 consultative document were partly based on the New Zealand model. The New Zealand Bill of Rights 1990 was disabled from overriding pre-existing legislation and was subject to express or implied repeal by future enactments. This model was also adopted for the Canadian Bill of Rights 1960. The Human Rights Act s 3(1) reads 'So far as it is possible to do so, primary and subordinate legislation must be read and given effect in a way which is compatible with the Convention rights ...'. Section 3(2)(b) reads 'this section does not affect the validity, continuing operation or enforcement of any incompatible primary legislation; and (c) does not affect the validity, continuing operation or enforcement of any incompatible subordinate legislation if ... primary legislation prevents the removal of the incompatibility'.

Use of this model for the Convention will place protection for human rights very much at the mercy of judicial interpretation of statutes. More liberal-minded judges might be prepared to find that unless a statutory provision was unarguably unambiguous it could be modified through purposive interpretation if it was not in harmony with the Convention. The requirement to construe legislation *'so far as it is possible to do so'* consistently with the Convention[198] (emphasis added) suggests that such a stance best reflects the present intentions of the Labour Government. Certain parts of the existing law may as they stand be incompatible with the Convention. Examples may include ss 5 and 14A of the Public Order Act 1986 (s 14A was inserted into the 1986 Act by s 70 of the Criminal Justice and Public Order Act 1994). Under s 3 the possibility of impliedly repealing such provisions has been ruled out, but unless they admitted of no interpretation compatible with the Convention they could be made to conform with it. The outcome would often be the same as though implied repeal had occurred. If ambiguity could not be found in a provision incompatible with the Convention, the Convention itself would presumably be repealed to the extent of its incompatibility, at least until amending legislation could be passed (s 10) – a reversal of the normal rules of implied repeal. However, it is possible that the judiciary will be prepared to take an even more vigorous stance when interpreting existing law in the light of Convention provisions. They might be prepared to ensure that the outcome which allowed the Convention to prevail was achieved even if this involved some disregard for statutory language. Lord Lester has observed, on this point:

---

197 See Klug, F and Wadham, J, 'The democratic entrenchment of a Bill of Rights: Liberty's Proposals' [1993] *PL* 579.

198 Page 6 para 1.

> Would [the courts use the incorporating measures] to go much further than the traditional position in which the courts seek to interpret ambiguous legislation so as to be in accordance with rather than breach treaty obligations undertaken by the UK? I hope and believe that they would indeed do so ...[199]

Under clause 4(5) only higher courts can make a declaration of incompatibility – a declaration that it is not possible to construe the legislation in question to harmonise with the Convention. It is therefore likely that courts would strive to construe legislation so as to conform with the Convention since otherwise the plaintiff or defendant would have to suffer a breach of Convention rights. One danger might be that the Convention standards were diluted as courts adopted the least liberal interpretation of the Convention in order to make it harmonise with UK legislation. This would be avoided if a vigorous approach is taken not only to foisting Convention based interpretations onto statutory language, but also to ensuring that Convention standards are fully upheld by means of that interpretation. This would also mean that, where essential, a declaration of incompatibility should be made, thus triggering off amending legislation by means of the s 10 fast track procedure. This course should ensure that domestic law is eventually brought into a state of conformity with the human rights norms embodied in the jurisprudence of the European Court of Human Rights as at the time of enactment; possibly a considerable amount of repressive legislation will be swept away. A future, less liberal, government wishing to restore the provisions thus removed, although not formally constrained in any way, would do so in the face of public knowledge that it was resurrecting provisions which the courts had authoritatively determined to be in breach of Britain's obligations under the ECHR and quite possibly also of common law principle.[200] In this way, both the 'adverse publicity' and the 'manifest breach' types of protection (see below) bestowed by a 'notwithstanding clause' would be given – albeit to a lesser degree[201] – to the rights protected by the Convention.

The Human Rights Act 1998 will be subject to express repeal by subsequent enactments. However, it is a constitutional truism that Parliament never uses its power to the full; for example, although theoretically able to do so, it is inconceivable in 1998 that Parliament would limit suffrage to those with incomes over a certain level. Similarly, the Convention may acquire such prestige that although its express repeal remained theoretically possible it would never be undertaken. The Act of Union with Scotland 1706 and perhaps the European Communities Act 1972 provide precedents for this.

---

199 'First Steps Towards A Constitutional Bill of Rights' (1997) 2 EHRR 124, at 127.

200 See for example the statements in the House of Lords in *Derbyshire CC v The Times Newspapers* [1993] 1 All ER 1011 to the effect that Article 10 of the ECHR and the English common law are substantively similar.

201 Lesser, because even where no formal statement of intention to legislate in breach of the ECHR had been made (see below, p 130) the Courts would not be empowered to strike down the legislation in question.

Implied repeal would still remain a possibility. However, the purposive approach discussed above in relation to previous enactments should also be adopted in relation to subsequent ones under the Human Rights Act s 3(2)(a).[202] It seems that the Convention could only be impliedly repealed if legislation was passed which initially appeared to be compatible with the Convention but subsequently appeared not to be. At the time the legislation was passed the Minister would have made a declaration of compatibility under clause 19(a) and, as discussed above, the courts will be under a duty to ensure that the legislation is compatible if at all possible. The response of the House of Lords in *Pickstone v Freemans* (1988)[203] to EU law would provide a model to be used in this situation. The House of Lords found that domestic legislation – the Equal Pay Amendment Regulations – made under s 2(2) of the European Communities Act appeared to be inconsistent with Article 119 of the Treaty of Rome. It held that despite this apparent conflict a purposive interpretation of the domestic legislation would be adopted; in other words, the plain meaning of the provision in question would be ignored and an interpretation would be imposed on it which was not in conflict with Article 119. This was done on the basis that Parliament must have intended to fulfil its EU obligations in passing the Amendment regulations once it had been forced to do so by the European Court of Justice. The House of Lords followed a similar approach in *Litster v Forth Dry Dock Engineering*.[204]

If this purposive approach to the Convention was adopted protection from implied repeal by subsequent inconsistent statutory provisions would probably be assured. It might seem unnecessary to do so, but the matter would be placed beyond doubt if an explicit favourable rule of construction were included in future in an amendment to the Human Rights Act along the lines of that employed in Lord Wade's Bill in 1981; a later inconsistent enactment would be deemed to be subject to the European Convention 'unless such subsequent enactment provides otherwise or does not admit of any construction compatible with the Convention'.[205] This was also the method adopted – with slight rewording – by Sir Edward Gardiner's Human Rights Bill in 1986–87. At the present time, however, the Labour government is not inclined to include such a form of words. Nevertheless, they appear to sum up the status of the Convention under the Bill.

In many jurisdictions Bills of Rights are afforded a higher status than other legislation. Due to the operation of the doctrine of Parliamentary sovereignty this possibility would be constitutionally controversial in the UK. However, the status of EU law in the UK provides a precedent for adopting the course of partially entrenching the Convention. Section 2(4) of the European

---

202 Page 6 para 1.
203 [1988] 3 WLR 265.
204 [1989] 1 All ER 1194.
205 House of Lords Bill 54 1980–81.

Communities Act 1972 provides 'any enactment passed or to be passed ... shall be construed and have effect subject to the foregoing provisions of this section ...'. 'The foregoing' are those provisions referred to in s 2(1) giving the force of law to 'the enforceable Community rights' there defined. The words 'subject to' suggest that the Courts must allow Community law to prevail over a subsequent Act of Parliament. This does not, of course, mean that the European Communities Act itself cannot be repealed. It may follow that Parliament has partially entrenched s 2(1) of the European Communities Act by means of s 2(4) imposing a requirement of form (express words) on future legislation designed to override Community law. In *Secretary of State for Transport, ex parte Factortame*[206] in the Court of Appeal Bingham LJ said that where the law of the Community is clear:

> ... whether as a result of a ruling given on an Article 177 reference or as a result of previous jurisprudence or on a straightforward interpretation of Community instruments, the duty of the national court is to give effect to it in all circumstances ... To that extent a UK statute is not as inviolable as it once was.

This finding was confirmed in the House of Lords.[207]

There is also the possibility of using a so-called 'notwithstanding' clause. The Human Rights No 3 Bill introduced by the Labour MP Mr Graham Allen in January 1994 would have adopted this method of protection for the Bill of Rights. The civil rights group Liberty has supported this possibility[208] as have some other commentators.[209] Based on the model of the Canadian Charter, the clause would state that subsequent legislation would only override the Convention if the intention of doing so were expressly stated in such legislation. Under a 'notwithstanding' clause the judiciary would not be required to strike down legislation without a mandate from the democratically elected government. If that government did not include the clause in any legislative provision which subsequently was found to infringe the Convention, the government could impliedly be taken to be mandating the judiciary, by its omission, to strike down the offending legislation. Thus, although under such a model the judiciary are required to render Acts of Parliament inapplicable, a role which many of them might find constitutionally problematic, they are not required to act against the wishes of the democratically elected government. Under s 19 of the Human Rights Act a Minister must state that any future Bill is either compatible or incompatible with the Convention. This is a form of 'notwithstanding' clause, but, as discussed, the judiciary are not empowered to strike down legislation which contains no such clause but which is inconsistent with the Convention.

---

206 [1989] 2 CMLR 353.
207 [1989] 2 WLR 997.
208 See Klug, F and Wadham, J [1993] *PL* 579.
209 See eg Dworkin, *A Bill of Rights for Britain*, pp 24–29. The Labour Party supported this position at its conference in 1993 although, as its 1996 Consultative document reveals, it no longer does so.

Dawn Oliver notes that such a clause provides effective protection for the Canadian Charter and offers two reasons why a government would be unwilling to state openly that it was legislating in breach of the Bill of Rights.[210] First there would be the general political embarrassment which would be caused to the government (this may be termed the 'adverse publicity' type of protection). Secondly, if the ECHR had been adopted as a domestic Bill of Rights, a declaration of intent to infringe constitutional rights would be tantamount to a declaration of the government's intention to breach its obligations under international law; this would undoubtedly provoke widespread international condemnation which would be highly embarrassing (this may be termed the 'manifest breach' type of protection). An enactment which had incorporated the ECHR would, as Oliver notes, be further protected by the legal presumption that 'Parliament does not intend to act in breach of international law' (*per* Diplock LJ in *Saloman v Commissioners of Custom and Excise*)[211] so that a reading of the relevant legislation which did not create a breach of rights would be adopted by the courts if such a reading was possible. Oliver concludes that the above method of protection would provide 'strong protection against legislative encroachment on civil and political rights'. After noting similar arguments, Dworkin comes to a similar conclusion: 'In practice this technically weaker version of incorporation would probably provide almost as much protection as [formal entrenchment].'[212] On the other hand, the response of the Conservative government in the 1990s to certain decisions of the European Court of Human Rights, in particular to its decision in *McCann, Farrell and Savage v UK*,[213] the first judgment of the Court on Article 2, does not suggest that future governments would necessarily be deterred on 'manifest breach' or 'adverse publicity' grounds from using a notwithstanding clause. After the decision in *McCann* Michael Heseltine, the Deputy Prime Minister, declared that the government would not change the administrative policies or rules which had led to the deaths in question in that case; members of the government also loudly voiced strong disapproval of the decision and their stance was welcomed in many sections of the UK press. A future government might take the view that passing a certain measure in breach of the Convention was necessary on crime control and/or anti-terrorist grounds; it might further announce its intention in future, if necessary, to seek a derogation from the relevant article in question in order to prevent a successful challenge to the measure in the European Court of Human Rights. Alternatively, a future government might be uncertain whether a particular measure would breach the Convention but decide that a 'notwithstanding' clause was to be used on insurance grounds in order to protect it due to the

---

210 'A Bill of Rights for the UK' in *Government and the UK*, 1991.
211 [1967] 2 QB 116, 143.
212 *A Bill of Rights for Britain*.
213 (1995) 21 EHRR 97, A.324, Council of Europe Report.

necessity of passing it. Of course, a succeeding UK government of liberal tendencies could simply repeal the legislation in question, thereby also repealing its protective clause. Nevertheless, it is possible that use of such a clause might not prove to be a very effective protective device.

More effective protection for the Convention could be achieved by full entrenchment. Constitutions throughout the world adopt a number of different forms of entrenchment of codes of rights. The constitution of the USA can be amended only by a proposal which has been agreed by two-thirds of each House of Congress or by a convention summoned by Congress at the request of two-thirds of the states. The proposed amendment must then be ratified by three-quarters of the states' legislatures. The amendment procedure itself – Article V of the Constitution – can be amended only by the same method. It is generally thought that if the Human Rights Bill were enacted containing a provision that it could not be repealed except in accordance with some such procedure, the courts would not give effect to it. Parliament might expressly legislate contrary to it and there would remain the possibility of unwitting implied repeal. If, under judicial scrutiny, it was determined that a later provision did not admit of a construction which would be in accordance with the Convention, the judge would probably apply the later provision thereby repealing the Convention to the extent of its inconsistency. Authority for this can be found in the *dicta* of Maughan LJ in *Ellen Street Estates Ltd v Minister of Health*[214] to the effect that Parliament cannot bind itself as to the form of future enactments. However, De Smith suggests that Parliament could redefine itself so as to preclude itself as ordinarily constituted from legislating on a certain matter. The argument is based on the redefinition of Parliament under the Parliament Acts: if Parliament could make it easier for itself to legislate on certain matters it could equally make it harder, thereby entrenching certain legislation. This analogy has, however, come under attack from Munro (*Studies in Constitutional Law*, 1987) on the ground that the Parliament Act procedure introduces no limitation on Parliamentary sovereignty. The only authorities which would support De Smith's proposition come from other constitutions; in *AG for New South Wales v Trethowan*[215] the Privy Council upheld the requirement of a referendum before a Bill to abolish the upper House could be presented for the Royal Assent. Although, as De Smith argues, this decision may be of limited application as involving a non-sovereign legislature, it does suggest that a class of legislation exists for which it may be appropriate to delineate the manner and form of any subsequent amendment or repeal. The South African case of *Harris v Minister of the Interior*[216] is to similar effect. The point cannot be regarded as settled.

---

214 [1934] 1 KB 590 at 597.
215 [1932] AC 526.
216 (1952) (2) SA 428.

Thus, a proposal that the Convention be fully entrenched would be constitutionally controversial and – probably – impossible without a written constitution. Dicey has argued that the Bill of Rights could be entrenched within a written constitution since it would be untenable to espouse 'the strange dogma, sometimes put forward, that a sovereign power such as the Parliament of the United Kingdom, can never by its own act divest itself of authority'.[217] However, such a prospect is not at present in question and there is by no means agreement between advocates of a Bill of Rights that it would be desirable.

Aside from other objections, if the Convention could be successfully entrenched by, for example, a requirement of a two-thirds majority in Parliament in order to amend it, a constitutional precedent would be created. Politicians might come to view the device of entrenchment as a useful one which could be used, for example, to protect right wing legislation from an incoming Labour government. A future Conservative government might wish to use it, for example, to protect an opt-out from EU legislation from repeal by a Labour government coming to power after a future General Election.

6 ENFORCEMENT AND SCRUTINY UNDER THE HUMAN RIGHTS ACT

Remedies

The impact of the European Convention on Human Rights once received into domestic law, may best be explained by considering the remedies which it would make available. The scope of judicial review of administrative action would be greatly widened: administrative discretion would have to be exercised within Convention limits, thus reversing the effect of the House of Lords' decision in *Brind v Secretary of State for the Home Department*.[218] An official decision could be quashed on the existing grounds but also on the ground that a particular right had been violated. If, for example, a Chief Officer of Police imposed very far-reaching conditions on certain marches, including ones likely to be peaceful, under s 12 of the Public Order Act 1986, the conditions could be challenged in the courts on the basis that Article 11 had been violated. Immigration officials would have to take Article 8 and Articles 3 and 6 into account in discharging their duties, thus reversing the effect of *Salamat Bibi*[219] and reinstating the principle put forward by Lord Scarman in *Phansopkar*[220] that immigration officials must have regard to the

---

217 *An Introduction to the Study of the Law of the Constitution*, 10th edn, p 68.
218 [1991] 1 AC 696; [1991] 1 All ER 720; [1991] 2 WLR 588, HL.
219 [1977] 1 WLR 979, CA.
220 [1977] QB 606, 626.

Convention. Ministers and other decision-makers would no longer be able to afford little weight to human rights matters, subject only to the *Wednesbury* test. They would have to show that a breach of Convention rights flowing from the decision was justified on the basis of a pressing social need. Thus, proportionality would become a separate head of review where Convention guarantees were affected by an administrative decision. The usual remedies of *certiorari, mandamus* or a declaration would be available.

The Convention guarantees could also be used to afford a defence in civil proceedings where the plaintiff was a public authority.[221] A claim of, for instance, breach of confidence in respect of government information could be met by the argument that the Article 10 principle should prevail. At present the judges apply a loose defence of public interest in publication in a somewhat idiosyncratic manner.[222] Under Article 10 the public interest in publication would always prevail except where the interest in preserving confidentiality fell within one of the exceptions contained in para 2 of the Article and met a pressing social need.

The Convention guarantees might in certain circumstances afford a defence in criminal proceedings. If a future Sarah Tisdall or Cathy Massiter was prosecuted under the Official Secrets Act 1989, Article 10 could be pleaded as a defence. The European Court and Commission of Human Rights have always been very tender to matters of national security in response to the doctrine of allowing a wide margin of appreciation in such matters.[223] However, invocation of Article 10 would at least allow the freedom of expression argument to be heard by the jury. The 1989 Act contains no public interest defence; therefore, otherwise, such argument would be irrelevant. If it succeeded, the Official Secrets Act would be to that extent modified – to include, in effect, such a defence.

Under s 6 'it is unlawful for a public authority to act in a way which is incompatible with one or more of the Convention rights' unless it is acting under the provisions of incompatible legislation. Under s 8 damages may be awarded against the public authority if the court has power to award them. Thus avenues of challenge are afforded to those whose Convention rights are breached by public authorities and such avenues may include the creation of new torts. However, the Labour government does not wish to create a general state liability to pay damages to individuals or corporate bodies whose Convention rights have been infringed. Thus, where the state failed to remedy a breach of Convention rights which was occurring due to the actions of a

---

221 Section 6. This includes a body or person, certain of whose functions are of 'a public nature'.
222 See Chap 6 pp 251–53.
223 See eg the rejection of the application to the Commission in the *Council of Civil Service Unions v UK* (1988) 10 EHRR 269. See below Chap 6 p 234 for discussion relating to the *Tisdall* case.

non-state body, it would appear that, under the Human Rights Act, no remedy would be available. Nevertheless, the definition of 'public authority' is very wide.[224] Even where the violation was due to the act of a private body, a public body might be identifiable which bore some responsibility in the matter.

Scrutiny

A very significant aspect of incorporation will be the eventual setting up of a Human Rights Commission. Unfortunately, this is not provided for under the Human Rights Act. The Consultative Paper suggests that such a Commission would probably have a number of roles which would include: providing guidance and support to those wishing to assert their rights, along the lines of the role of the Equal Opportunities Commission; instituting proceedings in its own name; scrutinising new legislation to ensure that it conforms with the Convention and monitoring the operation of the new Act.[225]

Setting up such a Commission would be a significant step towards ensuring the efficacy of the Convention, in a number of respects. Most importantly it might to some extent obviate the problem which will arise concerning the need to exhaust domestic remedies before gaining recourse to the European Court of Human Rights. At present, the European Commission of Human Rights does not require such remedies to be exhausted where 'settled legal opinion' at the relevant time is to the effect that the available remedies do not provide redress for an applicant's complaint.[226] However, once the Convention is incorporated new remedies may come into being and will need to be tested in the courts, all the way up to the House of Lords. For obvious reasons, this will particularly be the case in the early years after the Act comes into force. Sections 18, 20 and 22 will come into force on the passing of the Act, which is expected to be in November 1998. The other sections will, it is expected, come into force in early 2000.

Under the Labour government's current plans to abolish almost all civil legal aid, the vast majority of complainants will be non-legally aided and therefore will almost certainly be unable to exhaust remedies so as to have recourse to Strasbourg. Of course, if remedies are available in domestic courts, complainants may not be disadvantaged but if they are not, complainants may be unable to reach Strasbourg, although they would have been able to do so prior to the coming into force of the Human Rights Act. This may particularly be the case in relation to liability for breaches of the Convention

---

224 Section 6 and see p 8 of the Consultative Paper.
225 Page 11 of the Consultative Paper. For discussion of the role of the Commission see Spence, S and Bynoe, I (1997) 2 EHRR 152.
226 *De Wilde, Ooms and Versyp v Belgium* (1971) A.12 p 33.

by non-state bodies which arguably have a public function. The uncertainties generated while the courts determine when liability in these circumstances should arise, may not allow complainants to argue that no remedy was available. The efficacy of the Human Rights Commission in obviating this problem in the future would, of course, depend on the level of funding accorded to it and on the extent to which it allocated funding to assisting complainants and to instituting test cases of its own motion. A further reform which would obviously be beneficial would be to extend the availability of legal aid in Convention cases, at least initially.

PART TWO

EXPRESSION

All countries which have a Bill of Rights protect freedom of expression because it is perceived as one of the most fundamental rights. But why should this particular freedom be viewed as so worthy of protection? Why, as Barendt puts it, should speech which offends the majority have any special immunity from government regulation 'while there would be no comparable inhibition in restraining ... conduct ... [such as public] love-making ... which has similar offensive characteristics?'.[1] Four main justifications for offering protection to free speech have been offered and will be considered here in turn. In each case an indication will be given as to the kinds of expression the various justifications will support because all the theories will not be relevant to all forms of expression. Initially it should be noted that three of the justifications are inherently more contingent and therefore precarious than the first. These three justifications – the arguments for the opportunity to arrive at the truth through free discussion, for the necessity of free speech to enable meaningful participation in democracy and for individual self-fulfilment – all ultimately argue that speech is to be valued not for its own sake but because it will lead to some other outcome we think desirable; thus they may be characterised as teleological justifications. If, therefore, when considering a particular form of speech, a persuasive argument can be made out that allowing the speech is likely to achieve a result *antithetical* to the desired outcome, protection will no longer be justifiable. By contrast, as will be seen below, it is inherent in the first main justification for free speech – the argument for moral autonomy – that arguments about the likely *effects* of allowing the particular speech are not relevant to the question whether the justification applies – although clearly such arguments may still be relevant in deciding whether the speech should nonetheless be abrogated.

The argument from moral autonomy

This argument was outlined in Chapter 1 as one of the most powerful justifications for human rights in general and so will only briefly be rehearsed here. Ultimately, whether the particular argument used is Rawls's hypothetical social contract[2] or Dworkin's basic postulate of the state's duty to treat its citizens with equal concern and respect,[3] this justification for free

---

[1] Barendt, E, *Freedom of Speech*, 1987, p 1.
[2] See Chap 1 p 4.
[3] See Chap 1 pp 5–6.

speech is centred around the liberal conviction that matters of moral choice must be left to the individual. In either case the conclusion reached is that the state offends against human dignity,[4] or treats certain citizens with contempt if the coercive power of the law is used to enforce the moral convictions of some upon others. The argument perhaps has a more common and conspicuous application with regard to sexual autonomy and so is often disregarded in arguments about free speech.[5]

The justification is less contingent than the others, as mentioned above, because *any* restriction on what an individual is allowed to read, see or hear, clearly amounts to an interference with her right to judge such matters for herself. Thus, the argument consistently defends virtually all kinds of speech,[6] whereas the arguments from truth and democracy[7] will tend to have a somewhat less comprehensive range of application. Since the argument *also* sets up freedom of speech as a strong 'trump' right,[8] or as part of the individual's claim to inviolability,[9] the right in both cases overrides normal utilitarian arguments about the benefit or detriment to society of the particular form of speech under consideration.[10] By contrast, the justifications from democracy and truth both set out goals for society as a whole and therefore would seem reasonably to allow abrogation of speech in the interests of other public concerns which may be immediately and directly damaged by the exercise of speech. As Barendt puts it, in discussing the argument from truth, '… a government worried that inflammatory speech may provoke disorder is surely entitled to elevate immediate public order considerations over the long term intellectual development of the man on the Clapham omnibus'.[11]

The argument from truth

The most famous exposition of this argument is to be found in JS Mill's *On Liberty*.[12] The basic thesis is that truth is most likely to emerge from free and uninhibited discussion and debate. It is worth noting that this is a proposition

---

4   Barendt makes the point, however, that unlimited speech may also assault human dignity (*ibid* at pp 16–17). This argument is considered in relation to pornography below Chap 5 pp 185–88.
5   Barendt, for example, comments (at p 16) that the 'general freedom to moral autonomy … [is] perhaps without much relevance to free speech arguments'.
6   It also covers material which could only doubtfully be classified as speech, eg photographic pornography.
7   See below pp 138–42.
8   Ronald Dworkin's phrase; see Chap 1 p 11.
9   The idea is Rawls'; see Chap 1 p 10.
10 For a discussion of justifications allowing strong rights to be overidden, see Chap 1 pp 11–13
11 *Op cit* p 10.
12 Everyman, 1972.

about a causal relationship between two phenomena – discussion and truth – which of course has never been conclusively verified. However, its general truth is taken as virtually axiomatic in the Western democracies and forms the basic assumption underpinning the whole approach of reasoned, sceptical debate which is the peculiar hallmark of Western civilisation. Nonetheless, the crude assumption that more free speech will always lead to more truth has been attacked recently by feminist writers, who consider that the free availability of pornography leads not to the revelation of truth but to the creation of false and damaging images of women or, more controversially, that pornography actually 'constructs the [sexist] social reality of gender'[13] – a claim which will be examined in detail in Chapter 5 below.

It appears that Mill envisaged his argument as applicable mainly to the expression of opinion and debate but it can equally well be used to support claims for freedom of information, since the possession of pertinent information about a subject will nearly always be a prerequisite to the formation of a well-worked out opinion on the matter. However, *prima facie* it may be thought that the theory does not immediately make clear *when* we need to know the truth about a given subject. Thus it could be argued that a delay in receiving certain information (due, for example, to government restrictions) would not greatly matter, as long as the truth eventually emerged. In response to this, it may be argued that if truth is valued substantively – a position most would assent to[14] – then any period of time during which citizens are kept in ignorance of the truth or form erroneous opinions due to such ignorance, amounts to an evil, thus giving rise to a presumption against secrecy. If, alternatively or in addition, knowledge of the truth is valued because of its importance for political participation, then clearly it will be most important to know the information at the time that the issue it concerns is most likely to affect the political climate. This rationale would thus provide a strong argument against the propensity of UK governments to attempt to conceal political secrets until revelation would no longer have a damaging effect on their interests.[15]

Clearly, whether truth is valued instrumentally – for example as essential to self-development – or as a good in itself, some kinds of truths must be regarded as more important than others.[16] Thus, in the context of a collision between free speech and privacy rights, the small intrinsic value of knowing

---

13 MacKinnon, *Feminism Unmodified*, 1987, p 166.
14 Mill, as a utilitarian, would probably not see truth as inherently valuable but rather as a very important means of ensuring the overall welfare of society.
15 As seen, for example, in the so-called 'Thirty Year Rule' now contained in the Public Records Act 1958. See below Chap 6 p 265.
16 It is outside the scope of this work to attempt a full scale normative enquiry into the relative value of different truths. A commonsensical consensus approach is all that is employed in the text, where it is suggested only that the mere satisfaction of curiosity without more is of a relatively low value compared to the ending of a deception.

the facts about (say) a film star's sexual life juxtaposed with the implausibility of the notion that such information would enable more effective political participation or individual growth, provides reasonable grounds for favouring the *privacy* interest in such a case. By contrast, revelations about corruption amongst prominent politicians will arguably not only have a more important part to play in the formation and development of individuals' general opinions, they will also play a vital role in enabling informed contribution to be made to the political process. Thus, a compelling argument for favouring free speech in this situation is readily made out. We will return to this argument in Chapter 8.

The argument from participation in a democracy

Barendt describes this theory as 'probably the most attractive ... of the free speech theories in modern Western democracies' and concludes that 'it has been the most influential theory in the development of 20th century free speech law'.[17] The argument, which is associated primarily with the American writer Meiklejohn,[18] is simply that citizens cannot participate fully in a democracy unless they have a reasonable understanding of political issues; therefore open debate on such matters is essential. Its influence can be seen in the fact that directly political speech has a special protected status in most Western democracies.

Such speech does not at present have any general legal guarantee in the UK but when the British judiciary consider the claims of free speech they seem in general to be particularly concerned to protect free criticism of the political authorities. Thus, in the recent House of Lords decision in *Derbyshire v Times Newspapers*,[19] Lord Keith, in holding that neither local not central government could sustain an action in defamation said: 'It is of the highest importance that a democratically elected governmental body ... should be open to uninhibited public criticism'. The fact that he based his decision on this justification for free speech and not on, for example, the individual right of journalists to express themselves freely, is evidence of judicial endorsement of the argument from democracy – and also, possibly, of their failure to give much consideration to other, rights-based justifications. The fact that the judiciary have mainly or even only this interest in mind when considering threats to free speech, helps to explain why they are so often prepared to allow speech to be overridden by other considerations. This is because this argument sees speech as a public interest and as justified instrumentally by reference to its beneficial effects on democracy, rather than seeing it as an individual right of

---

17   *Op cit* pp 20 and 23 respectively.
18   See for example his 'The First Amendment is an Absolute' (1961) *Sup Ct Rev* 245.
19   [1993] AC 534; [1993] 1 All ER 1011; [1992] 3 WLR 28, HL.

inherent value. Therefore, clearly, it can render speech vulnerable to arguments that it should be overridden by competing public interests which are *also* claimed to be essential to the maintenance of democracy. Hence Margaret Thatcher's well-known justification for the media ban challenged unsuccessfully in the *Brind* case:[20] 'We do sometimes have to sacrifice a little of the freedom we cherish in order to defend ourselves from those whose aim is to destroy that freedom altogether.' Clearly, to a judge who sees the value of free speech only in terms of its contribution to the political process, an argument that allowing the speech in question will do more harm than good to the maintenance of democracy will always seem compelling. This is not to argue that this justification is fundamentally flawed – clearly its basic premise is correct and offers an important reason to protect speech – but rather that one should be wary of using it as the *sole* justification even for directly political speech.

There is however an argument which does see the justification as fundamentally flawed because it would appear to allow suppression of free speech by the democracy acting through its elected representatives. However, this objection may be answered by the argument that certain values, such as protection for minorities and fundamental freedoms generally, are implicit in any mature conception of a democracy.[21] Therefore the term 'democracy' or the furtherance of democracy should not be narrowly defined to include only the decisions of the particular government in power but should also encompass the general principles mentioned; by affording respect to such principles democracy will ultimately be preserved. This argument would suggest that the justification would appear to have little direct relevance to sexually explicit forms of expression or blasphemous speech but on the other hand, since freedom of expression is arguably one of the freedoms the suppression of which would undermine democracy, protection for these forms of speech can also be argued for by the justification. It should be borne in mind, however, that as this argument depends on a separate and somewhat controversial contention about the nature of democracy it offers only an indirect defence of non-political speech.[22] Nevertheless, if the above contention is accepted, one may then conclude that the argument from

---

20 *Secretary of State for the Home Dept ex parte Brind* [1991] 1 AC 696; [1991] 1 All ER 720; [1991] 2 WLR 588, HL.

21 Such a view is in fact endorsed by a number of legal philosophers and civil libertarians and amounts to the most satisfactory reply to the charge that an entrenched Bill of Rights is undemocratic. See Dworkin, *A Bill of Rights for Britain*, 1990; the view also clearly underpins his general political philosophy, see for example 'Liberalism' in *A Matter of Principle*, 1985. See also Hart, *Law, Liberty and Morality*, 1963 and Lester, *Democracy and Individual Rights*, 1968.

22 Most commentators seem to assume that the argument from democracy has little, if any, application to pornographic material. See eg Dworkin, 'Do We Have a Right to Pornography?' in *A Matter of Principle*, 1985, p 335. Similarly, the Williams Committee did not regard the argument as pertinent to their deliberations (*Report of the Committee on Obscenity and Film Censorship*, Cmnd 7772 of 1979).

democracy is actually concerned to further two values: maintenance of the democracy and effective participation in it. The two values are distinct in that although effective as opposed to passive or inert participation may help to secure maintenance of the democracy, nevertheless some of its members, while wishing to see its continuance, might not wish to participate actively in it. Thus political speech would contribute to the maintenance of both the values, while other forms of speech would contribute only to the first, confirming what was suggested at the outset, namely that this justification argues for special protection of political speech.

The argument from individual self-fulfilment

Finally, we may turn to the thesis that freedom of speech is necessary in order to enable individual self-fulfilment. It is argued that individuals will not be able to develop morally and intellectually unless they are free to air views and ideas in free debate with each other. However, as Barendt notes,[23] it may be objected that free speech should not be singled out as especially necessary for individual fulfilment; the individual might also claim that, for example, foreign travel or a certain kind of education was equally necessary. On the other hand, freedom of speech represents a means of furthering individual growth which it is possible to uphold as a 'negative freedom'; other methods of furthering individual freedom would require positive action on the part of the government.

This justification is clearly rights-based and as such, in theory at least, is less vulnerable to competing societal claims; however, it does not value speech in itself but rather instrumentally, as a means to individual growth. Therefore, in situations where it seems that allowing free expression of the particular material will be likely to retard or hinder the growth of others or of the 'speaker', the justification does not offer a strong defence of speech.[24] Precisely this argument has been used by feminist commentators to justify the censorship of pornography. Thus, MacKinnon asserts that far from aiding in the growth of anyone, 'Pornography strips and devastates women of credibility'[25] through the images of women it constructs in its readers' minds. The thesis which forms the basis of the UK law on obscenity – that certain kinds of pornography actually damage the moral development of those who read it by depraving and corrupting them, similarly fastens onto the argument

---

23 *Op cit* p 15.
24 Barendt argues (pp 16–17) that justifications for suppressing some forms of speech could be advanced on the basis that human dignity (the value promoted by allowing self development) would thereby receive protection. He cites the finding of the German Constitutional Court that there was no right to publish a novel defaming a dead person as such publication might violate the 'dignity of man' guaranteed by Article 1 of the German Basic Law (*Mephisto* (1971) BVerfGE 173).
25 MacKinnon, *op cit* p 193.

that this kind of material achieves the opposite of the outcome which allowing freedom of expression is designed to ensure.[26] The apparent vulnerability of the argument from self-development when used to justify the protection of material which is arguably degrading[27] leads Barendt to suggest[28] that a sounder formulation of the theory is one which frames it in terms of the individual's right to moral autonomy. It is submitted that moral autonomy *does* provide the most persuasive defence of sexually explicit 'speech' and this argument will be developed when obscenity law is discussed. However, it will also be argued that autonomy is conceptually distinct from the notion of self-fulfilment and that nothing is to be gained by conflating the two concepts.

Free speech protection in practice[29]

In the USA, the country with perhaps the greatest commitment to freedom of speech, the First Amendment to the Constitution provides: 'Congress shall make no law ... abridging the freedom of speech or of the press.' This stricture is not interpreted absolutely literally but it does mean that US citizens can challenge a law on the sole ground that it interferes with freedom of expression. However, freedom of expression is not absolute in any jurisdiction; other interests can overcome it including the protection of morals, of the reputation of others, national security and protecting the interest in a fair trial. In fact, freedom of speech comes into conflict with a greater variety of interests than any other liberty and is therefore in more danger of being squeezed out. Most Bills of Rights list these interests as exceptions to the primary right of freedom of speech, as does the European Convention on Human Rights Article 10. This does not mean that the mere invocation of the other interest will lead to displacement of freedom of speech; it is necessary to show that there is a pressing social need to allow the other interest to prevail.[30]

Although the UK has had no Bill of Rights protecting freedom of speech, the European Convention on Human Rights has been taken into account by

---

26 It should be noted first that radical feminists deny that their arguments have anything in common with conservative objections to pornography, eg MacKinnon, *op cit* p 175, and secondly that the feminist thesis on pornography is far more complex than this. It will be explored in more detail in Chap 5 below.

27 Dworkin also concludes that the argument from self-fulfilment fails to defend pornographic speech: 'Do We Have a Right to Pornography?' in *A Matter of Principle*; he founds his defence on moral autonomy and like the present writer clearly regards this concept as offering a separate head of justification.

28 *Op cit* p 17.

29 For comment see Marshall, G, 'Freedom of Speech and Assembly' in *Constitutional Theory*, 1971, p 154; Barendt, E, *Freedom of Speech*, 1987; Gibbons, T, *Regulating the Media*, 1991; Robertson, G and Nichol, AGL, *Media Law*, 1991; Boyle, A, 'Freedom of Expression as a Public Interest in English Law' [1982] *PL* 574; Singh, R, 'The Indirect Regulation of Speech' [1988] *PL* 212.

30 See Chap 2 p 67 for discussion of this point.

the courts in construing ambiguous legislation on the basis that as Parliament must have intended to comply with its Treaty obligations, an interpretation should be adopted which would allow it to do so.[31] Article 10 provides a strong safeguard for freedom of speech in relation to competing interests, since its starting point is the primacy of freedom of expression. Article 10 has had some impact on UK law through decided cases in Europe or because it has been taken into account where there is ambiguity in a statute or in common law. It has perhaps not had as much impact in this area as might be expected, particularly as far as considering the need for the protection of morality is concerned. The reasons why this may be so will be considered below.

There are two methods of protecting the other interests mentioned: prior and subsequent restraints on freedom of speech. Prior restraints are seen as more pernicious and therefore countries with a Bill of Rights either outlaw them or keep them to a minimum. They are particularly inimical to free speech since they operate outside the public domain and therefore generate little or no publicity; generally nobody realises what has occurred. Decisions are taken by an administrative body with no possibility of challenge in the courts. On the other hand, subsequent restraints operate *after* publication of the article in question: the persons responsible may face civil or criminal liability. The trial may then generate publicity and the defendants may have an opportunity of demonstrating why they published the article in question. In other words, the case for allowing the speech in question is given a hearing.[32] However, the distinction between the two kinds of restraint may not be as stark as this implies. Subsequent restraints may have a chilling effect on publications; editors and others may well not wish to risk the possibility of incurring liability and may therefore themselves take the decision not to publish without reference to any outside body.

When one turns to consider UK law in this area one confronts a mass of common law and statutory restrictions on freedom of speech and activities associated with it such as marches or demonstrations. In order to determine how far freedom of speech is protected it is necessary to consider the width of these restrictions in order to determine how much of an area of freedom is left within which expression can be exercised. It will be found that the law in this area has developed in an incoherent fashion; the lack of a consistent pattern is probably due to the lack of a free speech clause against which the other interests have to be measured. The emphasis has to be on the judges' concern to strike a balance between free speech and a variety of other interests. A pervasive critical theme will be exposure of the judges' readiness to allow freedom of expression to be restricted on uncertain or flimsy grounds. It will be found in certain areas that some of the interests identified by judges as

---

31 See further Chap 3 pp 109–10.
32 See Barendt, E, 'Prior Restraints on Speech' [1985] *PL* 253.

justifying such restrictions would not qualify as sufficient grounds for outweighing the right of free expression under the liberal conception of rights outlined in Chapter 1.

In considering UK law it will be argued that statutes in this area give, in general, greater protection to freedom of speech than does the common law and that recently it has come particularly under threat, largely but not exclusively, through common law developments. This is not to argue that no English statute will have to be modified once Article 10 is given further effect in UK law under the Human Rights Act. However, it is suggested that the Diceyan view of the judges' role as guardians of freedom of speech through their application of the common law is not easy to sustain in the light of some recent developments.[33] Of course, it must be said that there is inconsistency between judges as to how far they believe free speech *should* be upheld in the face of other interests. Moreover, judges often have little room to consider the free speech cases on its merits; at times, as in the *Brind* case, which is discussed below, they can proceed only by means of judicial review. However, a theme which runs through this chapter is the extent to which the common law undermines statutory safeguards for freedom of speech.

Of course, in examining the statutory provisions considered in this chapter it will become apparent that some of them do provide extremely wide powers intended to protect other interests. It must, however, be remembered that they were framed by a Parliament which had no legal brake upon its powers; it did not have to have regard to a written constitution forcing it to take freedom of speech into account. Thus at times it has been prepared to frame laws which if fully enforced would severely damage freedom of expression. However, the laws are not always fully enforced; if they were, the consequent clash between the media and the government would bring the law into further disrepute. Thus, although by examining the provisions of these statutes an indication of the 'balance' Parliament had in mind may be gained, other more nebulous factors including public concern for media freedom must also be taken into account. This 'balance' may change once the Human Rights Act comes into force in 2000. This Part will evaluate the likely extent of any such change.

---

[33] However, the House of Lords' decision in the *Derbyshire* case [1993] AC 534; [1993] 1 All ER 1011; [1992] 3 WLR 28, provides some comfort for the Diceyan thesis, as argued above in Chap 3 p 101.

CHAPTER FOUR

RESTRAINING FREEDOM OF EXPRESSION TO PROTECT THE ADMINISTRATION OF JUSTICE

1 INTRODUCTION[34]

This chapter is concerned with two conflicting interests: the interest in protecting the administration of justice and in the free speech principle. It should be noted that protection of the administration of justice is a general aim which is not concerned only with protecting a person's right to a fair trial although it may have that effect. The fact that many aspects of the law of contempt can be seen as having as their *ultimate* rationale the protection of the right to a fair trial leads to the conclusion that since this other 'strong' right is at stake, free speech must be compromised to a certain extent.[35] However, the fact that the law of contempt does not directly protect the fair trial of specific individuals, whereas its operation clearly directly infringes the individual freedom of specific journalists, makes one reluctant to accept that the free speech principle should be readily abrogated except where a clear and severe detriment to society may otherwise occur.

The main effect of criminal contempt is to limit the freedom of the media to report on or comment on issues arising from, or related to, the administration of justice. Such restriction answers to a genuine public interest in ensuring that justice is properly administered and is unaffected by bodies who are unlikely to judge the merits of a case fairly. If, for example, a large section of the media, in pursuance of a good story, takes the view that a defendant is guilty, it may slant stories and pictures so that they seem to give that impression and clearly such coverage may affect the jury. If so, the conviction will have been influenced by the partial views of a certain group of people who do not have all the evidence available to them and are influenced by concerns other than the concern to ensure fairness in decision making. If a trial seems to have been prejudiced by unfair reporting a successful appeal may be brought on that basis[36] but this method only creates a remedy for the defendant; it does not punish the media or deter them from such behaviour in future. No-one would argue that this is a desirable method of preventing prejudice to the administration of justice since it may allow the guilty to be

---

[34] General reading: Arlidge, A and Eady, D, *Contempt of Court*, 1982; Sufrin, B and Lowe, N, *The Law of Contempt*, 3rd edn, 1996; Miller, CJ, *Contempt of Court*, 1989; Barendt, E, *Freedom of Speech*, 1987, Chap 8; Robertson, G, *Media Law*, 1992, Chap 6; Laws, J, 'Problems in the Law of Contempt' (1990) *CLP* 99; Naylor, B (1994) *CLJ* 492.

[35] See the discussion as to when 'strong' individual rights may be infringed in Chap 1 pp 11–13.

[36] See the successful appeal on this basis in *Taylor* (1993) 98 Cr App R 361, CA.

147

acquitted. Contempt law may properly deter newspapers from such behaviour but the tests employed in order to allow it to do so need to be tightly drawn if they are not to prevent fair reporting of proceedings and debate in the media on issues relevant to proceedings.

2   PREJUDICING PROCEEDINGS

The development of the common law

This particular area of criminal contempt at common law curtailed the freedom of the media to discuss and report on issues arising from criminal or civil proceedings on the basis that those proceedings might suffer prejudice. However, it went further than was necessary to deal with very clear risks of interference with the administration of justice. The media was restricted in their reporting of issues relevant to civil or criminal proceedings which were or were soon to be in being. It is important to note that *civil* proceedings can also be prejudiced, even though usually no jury is involved, but obviously this danger may be less likely to arise. It is apparent that more weight was given to protecting the administration of justice rather than free speech, from the ease with which it was possible to satisfy the common law tests.

The elements of common law contempt consisted of the creation of a real risk of prejudice (the *actus reus*) and an intention to publish; it was therefore a crime of strict liability. The *actus reus* could be fulfilled if it was shown that the publication in question had created a risk that the proceedings in question might be prejudiced; it was irrelevant whether they actually had been. This distinction was clearly illustrated by *Thompson Newspapers Ltd, ex parte AG*.[37] While the defendant was awaiting trial *The Sunday Times* published his photograph and commented on his unsavoury background as a brothel keeper. This was held to amount to contempt. He was convicted and then appealed on the ground that the trial had been prejudiced by the article, but his appeal failed on the basis that jurors had not in actuality been so prejudiced. This case further illustrates the nature of the *actus reus*: it was not necessary to publish very damaging comments in order to create the risk in question.

At common law there was a certain time before and a certain time after the action, known as the *sub judice* period, when there was a risk that any article published relevant to the action might be in contempt. The starting point of this period occurred when the proceedings were 'imminent' (*Savundranayagan and Walker*).[38] This test attracted much criticism due to its vagueness and

---

37   [1968] 1 All ER 268; [1968] 1 WLR 1.
38   [1968] 3 All ER 439; [1968] 1 WLR 1761, CA.

width; it was obviously capable of applying a long time before the trial and it therefore had an inhibiting effect on the media out of proportion to its value. In particular, it gave rise to the restriction caused by so-called 'gagging writs'. A newspaper might be discussing corruption in a company. If a writ for libel was then issued – although there was no intention of proceeding with the case – the newspaper might find itself in contempt if it continued to discuss the issues. Thus this method could be used to prevent further comment.

The need for reform which would in particular address the width of the imminence test was apparent and led to the setting up of the Phillimore Committee in 1974[39] but it might not have come about without the influence of the European Court of Human Rights. The ruling that UK contempt law breached Article 10 arose due to the decision of the House of Lords in *AG v Times Newspapers Ltd*.[40] The case concerned litigation arising out of the Thalidomide tragedy. The parents of the Thalidomide children wished to sue Distillers, the company which had manufactured the drug, because they believed that it was responsible for the terrible damage done to their unborn children. Distillers resisted the claims and entered into negotiation with the parents' solicitors. Thus the litigation was dormant while the negotiations were taking place. Meanwhile *The Sunday Times* wished to publish an article accusing Distillers of acting ungenerously towards the Thalidomide children. The article came close to saying that Distillers had been negligent, although it was balanced in that it did consider both sides.

The Attorney General obtained an injunction in the Divisional Court preventing publication of the article on the ground that it amounted to a contempt of court. The Court of Appeal then discharged the injunction in a ruling which weighed up the public interest in freedom of speech against the need to protect the administration of justice and found that the former value outweighed the latter: the article concerned a matter of great public interest and since the litigation in question was dormant it would probably be unaffected by it. The House of Lords then restored the injunction on the ground that the article dealt with the question of negligence and therefore prejudged the case pending before the court. It held that such prejudgment was particularly objectionable as coming close to 'trial by media' and thereby leading to an undermining of the administration of justice: a person might be adjudged negligent by parts of the media with none of the safeguards available in court. The confidence of the public in the courts might be undermined, thus creating a long term detriment to the course of justice generally.

---

39 See *Report of the Committee on Contempt of Court* 1974 Cmnd 5794. For comment see Dhavan, R, 'Contempt of Court and the Phillimore Committee Report' (1976) 5 *Anglo-American LR* 186–253.

40 [1974] AC 273; [1973] 3 All ER 54; [1973] 3 WLR 298, HL. For casenotes see: Miller, CJ (1974) 37 *MLR* 96; O'Boyle, M (1974) 25 *NILQ* 57; Williams, DGT (1973) *CLJ* 177 and Miller, CJ [1975] *Crim LR* 132.

This ruling seemed to create two possible new tests for the *actus reus* of contempt:

(1) The prejudgment test, which seemed to be wider than the test of real risk of prejudice, in that little risk to proceedings might be shown but it might still be possible to assert that they had been prejudged. This test was heavily criticised by the Phillimore Committee; it had a potentially grave effect on freedom of speech because it was very difficult to draw the line between legitimate discussion in the media and prejudgment.

(2) The risk of creation of a long-term effect on the course of justice. It seemed that this test could be satisfied even where it could not be shown that any particular proceedings might be affected (perhaps because they were clearly even more unlikely to be affected than those in *The Sunday Times* case); it therefore appeared that it might operate as an alternative to the first test, rather than as a definitional element of it.

Because it might be easier to satisfy these tests than the old test for the *actus reus* of common law contempt, the Phillimore Committee considered that the *Sunday Times* ruling strengthened the case for reform. Meanwhile the case was on its way to the European Court of Human Rights. The editor of *The Sunday Times* applied to the European Commission of Human Rights seeking a ruling that the imposition of the injunction breached Article 10 of the European Convention, and five years after the judgment of the House of Lords the case came before the European Court of Human Rights (*Sunday Times* case).[41]

The Article 10 guarantee of freedom of expression is subject to exceptions to be narrowly construed. The Court found that the injunction clearly infringed Article 10 para 1 and that this was not a trivial infringement; the free speech interest involved was very strong because the matter was one of great public concern. However, the injunction fell within Article 10(2) because it had an aim permitted by one of exceptions – maintenance of the authority of the judiciary.

The next question was whether the injunction was 'necessary in a democratic society' in order to achieve the aim in question: it was not enough merely to show that the injunction was covered by an exception. In order to make a determination on this point the Court considered the meaning of the term 'necessary'. It ruled that this did not mean indispensable but connoted something stronger than 'useful', 'reasonable' or 'desirable'. It implied the existence of a 'pressing social need'. Was there such a need? The Court employed the doctrine of proportionality in determining the meaning of 'need': it weighed up the strength of the free speech interest against the strength of the threat to the authority of the judiciary. It found that although

---

41 Judgment of 26 April 1979, A.30; (1979) 2 EHRR 245. Case notes see: Duffy, PJ, 5 *H Rts Rev* 17; Mann, FA (1979) 95 *LQR* 348; Wong, W-WM (1984) 17 *NY Univ JIL and Pol* 35.

courts are clearly the forums for settling disputes, this does not mean that there can be no newspaper discussion before a case. The article was couched in moderate terms; it explored the issues in a balanced way and moreover the litigation in question was dormant and therefore unlikely to be affected by the article. Thus on the one hand there was a strong free speech interest; on the other there was a weak threat to the authority of the judiciary. If the free speech interest had been weaker it might have been more easily overcome. The court therefore concluded that the interference with justice did not correspond to a social need sufficiently pressing to outweigh the public interest in freedom of expression. A breach of Article 10 had therefore taken place. (It may be noted that the Court was divided 11 to nine in reaching this determination.)

The UK government had to respond to this decision and it did so in the enactment of the Contempt of Court Act 1981[42] which was supposed to take account of the ruling of the European Court and was also influenced to an extent by the findings of the Phillimore Committee.

The Contempt of Court Act 1981

The 1981 Act was designed to modify the common law without bringing about radical change. It introduced various liberalising factors but it was intended to maintain the stance of the ultimate supremacy of the administration of justice over freedom of speech, while moving the balance further towards freedom of speech.[43] In particular it introduced stricter time limits, a more precise test for the *actus reus* and allowed some articles on matters of public interest to escape liability even though prejudice to proceedings was created. In order to determine whether liability is created the following steps must be taken.

The publication falls within s 1 of the Act

Under s 1, conduct will be contempt if it interferes with the administration of justice in particular proceedings regardless of intent to do so. Thus not all publications which deal with issues touching on the administration of justice will fall within the 1981 Act. The starting point under s 1 is to ask whether the publication touches upon particular legal proceedings. In other words, if the article appears to have a long term effect on the course of justice generally without affecting any particular proceedings, it would seem to fall outside the

---

42 See *Report of the Committee on Contempt of Court* (1974) Cmnd 5794; Green Paper Cmnd 7145 of 1978.
43 For comment on the 1981 Act see Miller [1982] *Crim LR* 71; Lowe, NV (1982) *PL* 20; Smith, JC [1982] *Crim LR* 744; Zellich, GF [1982] *PL* 343; Redmond, M (1983) *CLJ* 9.

Act and might be considered at common law. This point will be considered below.

It is important to note that it is not necessary to show that the defendant intended to prejudice proceedings: the 'strict liability rule' under s 1 continues the position as it was at common law. After establishing that the publication might affect particular proceedings, a number of other tests must be satisfied if the strict liability rule is to be established. If the publication does affect particular proceedings but one of these tests is unsatisfied, it might still be possible to consider it at common law.

The proceedings are 'active'

This test, which arises under s 2(3), is more clearly defined than the test at common law and therefore proceedings are 'active' (or *sub judice*) for shorter periods. Thus the test is intended to have a liberalising effect. The starting and ending points for civil and criminal proceedings are defined in Schedule 1. For criminal proceedings the starting point (Schedule 1 s 4(a–e)) is: the issue of a warrant for arrest, an arrest without warrant or the service of an indictment (or summons or an oral charge); the ending point is acquittal, sentence, any other verdict or discontinuance of the trial. The starting point for civil proceedings occurs when the case is set down for a hearing in the High Court or a date for the hearing is fixed (Schedule 1 ss 12 and 13). This provision was clarified in *AG v Hislop and Pressdam*:[44] it was found that s 2(3) was fulfilled because the proceedings in question (an action for defamation) had come into the 'warned' list at the time the articles in question were published. This starting point addresses the problem of gagging writs: the mere issuance of a writ would not mean that any further comment could give rise to an action for contempt because the issue of a writ is not the starting point. The end point of the active period for civil proceedings comes when the proceedings are disposed of, discontinued or withdrawn.

Perhaps surprisingly, appellate proceedings are also covered by Schedule 1. The starting point occurs when leave to appeal is applied for, by notice of appeal or application for review or other originating process; the end point occurs when the proceedings are disposed of or abandoned.

The publication creates 'a substantial risk of serious prejudice' (s 2(2))

According to the Court of Appeal in *AG v News Group Newspapers*[45] both limbs of this test must be satisfied: showing a slight risk of serious prejudice or a substantial risk of slight prejudice would not be sufficient. The question to

---

44 [1991] 1 QB 514; [1991] 1 All ER 911; [1991] 2 WLR 219, CA.
45 [1987] 1 QB 1; [1986] 2 All ER 833; [1986] 3 WLR 365, CA.

be asked under the first limb could be broken down as follows: can it be argued that there is a substantial risk that a person involved in the case in question such as a juror would (a) encounter the article, (b) remember it and (c) be affected by it so that he or she could not put it out of his or her mind during the trial? Clearly a person cannot be affected at all by something he or she has never encountered or has forgotten about. Thus a number of factors may be identified which will be relevant to one or more of these questions. Five such factors are identified below which, apart from the first, will also be relevant at the stage of considering whether serious prejudice has occurred. In considering them it should be noted that Lord Diplock has interpreted 'substantial risk' as excluding a 'risk which is only remote'.[46] If this should be taken to mean that fairly slight risks are sufficient it is open to question as seeming not to further the policy of the Act which is to narrow down the area of liability covered by criminal contempt. However, it seems to have been interpreted in later cases as excluding such risks, creating in effect a test, it is submitted, of fairly or reasonably substantial risk.[47]

(1) If an article is published in a national newspaper it is possible that jurors and others may encounter the article; however if the publication has a very small circulation this risk might be seen as too remote. This point was considered in *AG v Hislop and Pressdram*[48] which concerned the effect of an article in *Private Eye* written about Sonia Sutcliffe, wife of the Yorkshire Ripper. *Private Eye* had published two articles making serious allegations against Sonia Sutcliffe and in response she began an action for defamation. Shortly before the hearing of the action *Private Eye* published two further articles defamatory of Mrs Sutcliffe. The Attorney General brought proceedings for contempt of court in respect of the second articles and on appeal it was determined that as *Private Eye* had a large readership, many of whom might live in London where the libel action was held, it could not be said that the risk of prejudice was insubstantial. In *AG v Independent TV News and Others*[49] TV News and certain newspapers published the fact that a defendant in a forthcoming murder trial was a convicted IRA terrorist who had escaped from jail where he was serving a life sentence for murder. It was found that s 2(2) was not satisfied since the trial was not expected to take place for nine months, there had only been one offending news item and there had been limited circulation of only one edition of the offending newspaper items. The risk of prejudice was found to be too small to be termed substantial.

---

46 *AG v English* [1983] 1 AC 116; [1982] 2 All ER 903; for comment see Zellick [1982] *PL* 343 (especially on the question of the degree of risk); Ward (1983) 46 *MLR* 85; Redmond (1983) *CLJ* 9.
47 See eg Lord Lane's comments in *AG v The Times Newspapers Ltd* (1983) *The Times*, 12 February, DC.
48 [1991] 1 QB 514; [1991] 1 All ER 911; [1991] 2 WLR 219, CA.
49 [1995] 2 All ER 370.

(2) The ruling in *AG v News Group Newspapers* made it clear that the proximity of the article to the trial will also be relevant to the question of risk. The Court of Appeal held that a gap of 10 months between the two could not create the substantial risk in question because the jury would be likely to have forgotten the article by the time the trial came on. Even if the article were faintly recollected at the time of the trial it might be likely to have little impact. Similarly, in *AG v Independent TV News and Others* one of the factors founding the ruling that s 2(2) was not satisfied was that the trial was not expected to take place for nine months and therefore the risk that any juror who had seen the offending item would remember it was not seen as substantial. In contrast, in *AG v Hislop and Pressdram* a gap of three months between publication of the article and the trial of the libel action did create such a risk. Of course, this factor cannot be considered in isolation from the others: the subject matter of the publication or language used may be more likely to ensure that it is remembered even over a substantial period of time.

(3) If the case will be very much in the public eye due to the persons or issues involved (as was the case in respect of the article in *Hislop and Pressdram* concerning Sonia Sutcliffe, wife of the Yorkshire Ripper) the article is more likely to make an impact, although the mere fact that the issue attracts a great deal of media coverage will not mean that jurors will be unable to put it from their minds. In *AG v Times Newspapers*[50] it was found that jurors were able to ignore possibly prejudicial comment in newspapers; however, that case concerned a relatively trivial incident which happened to attract publicity due to the fame of one of the persons involved.

(4) The language used in the publication will clearly be relevant. An article of a relatively mild nature not couched in particularly vitriolic language might have little influence and might in any event be blotted out by the immediacy of the proceedings. However, it is also possible that very specific pieces of information soberly conveyed, such as previous convictions of the defendant, might make even more impact than a forceful opinion couched in more emotive language. In *AG v BBC, Same v Hat Trick Productions Ltd*[51] it was found that assumptions of the guilt of the defendants may create prejudice even though they arise within a humorous context. During a programme in the irreverent, satirical series *Have I Got News for You* remarks were made which assumed that the Maxwell brothers were guilty of defrauding the *Daily Mirror* pensioners. The broadcast occurred six months before the trial of the Maxwells. It was found that despite the humorous context the remarks might have been taken seriously by viewers and that therefore s 2(2) was satisfied.

---

50 (1983) *The Times*, 12 February, DC. See also *AG v MGN* [1997] 1 All ER 456.
51 (1996) *The Times*, 26 July.

(5) Photographs accompanying an article will also be relevant especially where they are used to create a misleading impression. In *Taylor*[52] certain tabloids published a photograph which was taken of one of the defendants in a murder trial giving the husband of the victim a polite kiss on the cheek; it was distorted in such a way as to give the impression that it was a passionate mouth to mouth kiss and was captioned 'cheats kiss'. It was found that this was part of 'unremitting, extensive, sensational, inaccurate and misleading press coverage' and had led to a real risk of prejudice to the trial. (This determination was not made in contempt proceedings, although it would obviously be relevant to them, but in overturning the convictions of the two defendants.)

Having established a substantial risk that jurors and others will be influenced by the article, it will be necessary to ask whether there is a substantial risk that the effect of such influence will be of a prejudicial nature. A publication which was in some way relevant to a trial might be likely to create a substantial risk that it would *influence* persons involved in the trial, bearing the factors identified in mind but without leading to prejudice to it. An article published in every national newspaper in the land on the day of the trial and discussing certain issues relevant to it in a striking and interesting but fair and impartial manner would have an influence but, it is submitted, not a prejudicial one. In considering whether it would be prejudicial the two limbs of the test must be considered together: it must be shown that the language used, the facts disclosed or sentiments expressed would lead an objective observer to conclude that a substantial risk had been established that persons involved in the proceedings would be prejudiced, before going on to consider whether that effect could properly be described as serious.

Prejudice and its seriousness can be established in a number of ways: the article (or other publication) might be likely to have the effect of influencing persons against or in favour of the defendant; it might be likely to affect either the outcome of the proceedings in question or their very existence – as where pressure is placed on one party to drop[53] or even to continue with proceedings. As noted above, the proximity in time between the article and the trial can affect *this* limb of s 2(2), as can the extent to which it may be said that the trial concerns a person in the public eye. If the article is published some time before the trial as in *AG v News Group Newspapers* its likely effect on the minds of jurors will be lessened because it may only exist there as a faint memory: any effect it has is unlikely to be of a *seriously* prejudicial nature. This might be the case even though the article would have been likely to have such an effect had it been fresh in their minds. In the *Hislop* case, however, the

---

52 (1993) 98 Cr App R 361, CA.
53 See *Hislop and Pressdram* [1991] 1 QB 514; [1991] 1 All ER 911; [1991] 2 WLR 219, CA: this aspect of the case is discussed in relation to common law contempt, below pp 166–67.

vitriolic nature of the article did suggest that it would be likely to have a seriously prejudicial effect. The serious allegations in question were held to blacken the plaintiff's character and might well have influenced the jurors against her. The fact that Peter Sutcliffe was well-known also made it more likely that the article would have an impact.

However, courts will not be quick to assume that jurors are incapable of ignoring prejudicial publications. In *AG v Guardian Newspapers*[54] the publication of the fact that one unidentified defendant out of six in a Manchester trial was also awaiting trial elsewhere was not found to satisfy s 2(2) since it was thought that it would not cause a juror of ordinary good sense to be biased against the defendant.

> *The article amounts to 'a discussion in good faith of public affairs or other matters of general public interest' and 'the risk of impediment or prejudice to particular legal proceedings is merely incidental to the discussion' (s 5)*

If it appears that s 2(2) is fulfilled it must next be established that s 5 does not apply. *AG v English*[55] is the leading case on s 5 and is generally considered to provide a good example of the kind of case for which s 5 was framed. After the trial had begun of a consultant who was charged with the murder of a Downs Syndrome baby, an article was published in the *Daily Mail* which made no direct reference to him but was written in support of a pro-life candidate, Mrs Carr, who was standing in a by-election. Mrs Carr had no arms; the article referred to this fact and continued: 'today the chances of such a baby surviving are very small – someone would surely recommend letting her die of starvation. Are babies who are not up to scratch to be destroyed before or after birth?' The trial judge referred the article to the Attorney General who brought contempt proceedings against the *Daily Mail*. First, it was determined that the article did fulfil the test under s 2(2) on the basis that jurors would be likely to take the comments to refer to the trial; therefore the assertion that babies were often allowed to die if handicapped might influence them against the consultant, Dr Arthur.

The burden then fell on the prosecution to show that s 5 did not apply. Lord Diplock adopted a two-stage approach in determining this issue. First, could the article be called a 'discussion'? The Divisional Court had held that a discussion must mean the general airing of views and debating of principles. However, Lord Diplock considered that the term 'discussion' could not be confined merely to abstract debate but could include consideration of examples drawn from real life. Applying this test, he found that a discussion

---

54 [1992] 3 All ER 38, CA.
55 [1983] 1 AC 116; [1982] 2 All ER 903.

could include accusations without which the article would have been emasculated and would have lost its main point. Without the implied accusations it would have become a contribution to a purely hypothetical issue. It was about Mrs Carr's election and also the general topic of mercy killing. The main point of her candidature was that killing of sub-standard babies did happen and should be stopped; if it had not asserted that babies were allowed to die she would have been depicted as tilting at imaginary windmills. Thus the term 'discussion' could include implied accusations.

Secondly, was the risk of prejudice to Dr Arthur's trial merely an incidental consequence of expounding the main theme of the article? Lord Diplock held that in answering this the Divisional Court had applied the wrong test in considering whether the article could have been written without including the offending words. Instead the Court should have looked at the actual words written. The main theme of the article was Mrs Carr's election policy; Dr Arthur was not mentioned. Therefore this article was the antithesis of the one considered in the *Sunday Times* case, which was concerned entirely with the actions of Distillers. Clearly, Dr Arthur's trial could be prejudiced by the article but that prejudice could properly be described as incidental to its main theme.

Thus s 5 applied; the article did not therefore fall within the strict liability rule. This ruling was generally seen as giving a liberal interpretation to s 5.[56] Had the narrow interpretation of the Divisional Court prevailed, it would have meant that all debate in the media on the topic of mercy killing would have been prevented for almost a year – the time during which the proceedings in *Arthur's* case were active from charge to acquittal. (It may be noted that Dr Arthur was acquitted; therefore the article presumably did not influence the jurors against him. That fact, however, as already pointed out, did not preclude a finding that there was a substantial risk of serious prejudice to his trial.) Lord Diplock's test under s 5 may be summed up as follows: looking at the actual words written (as opposed to considering what could have been omitted) was the article written in good faith and concerned with a question of general legitimate public interest which created an incidental risk of prejudice to a particular case? It seems that the discussion may have been triggered off by the case itself; it need not have arisen prior to the case.

This ruling gave an emphasis to freedom of speech which tended to bring the strict liability rule into harmony with Article 10 as interpreted by the European Court of Human Rights' ruling in the *Sunday Times* case. However, despite this broad interpretation of s 5 the media obviously does not have *carte blanche* to discuss issues arising from or relating to any particular case during the 'active' period.

---

56 See eg Robertson, *Media Law*, p 216.

The *AG v English* ruling did not concern a direct reference to a particular case and therefore it was uncertain until the ruling in *AG v Times Newspapers* whether s 5 would cover such direct references. *The Sunday Times* and four other newspapers commented on the background of an intruder into the Queen's bedroom, Michael Fagin, at a time when he was about to stand trial. The comments of the *Mail on Sunday* about Fagin, which included the allegation that he had had a homosexual liaison with the royal bodyguard and that he was a 'rootless penniless neurotic', satisfied the s 2(2) test as it was thought that they would affect the jury's assessment of his honesty. However, they fell within s 5 as they were part of a discussion of the Queen's safety which was a matter of general public concern. In contrast, *The Sunday Times'* allegation that Fagin had stabbed his stepson could not fall within s 5 as it was irrelevant to the question of the Queen's safety but had nevertheless been considered in detail.

Finally it must be shown that the article was written in good faith. In *AG v Hislop* the articles in question did not fall within s 5 because it could not be said that they were published in good faith: the finding – relevant to the question of contempt at common law – that the editor had intended to prejudice the relevant proceedings – was held to be incompatible with a finding of good faith under s 5.

Section 5 clearly requires some fine lines to be drawn. Where a piece merely discusses a particular case and makes no attempt to address wider issues s 5 will not apply (*Daily Express* case),[57] but where there is some discussion of wider issues this will not mean that it will *always* apply. This issue can only be resolved by looking at the subject matter of the discussion and asking how closely it relates to the trial in question. In *AG v TVS Television, AG v HW Southey & Sons*[57a] it was determined that a TVS programme concerned with the possibility that Rachmanism had arisen in the south of England but focused on landlords in Reading, which coincided with the charging of a Reading landlord with conspiring to defraud the DHSS, could not create a merely incidental risk. Similarly, in *Pickering v Liverpool Daily Post and Echo Newspapers plc*,[58] where the discussion centred on the case itself s 5 did not apply. This issue was further considered in *AG v Guardian Newspapers*[59] and it was determined that the term 'merely incidental' should receive a wide interpretation. However, it is suggested that it would be to misunderstand s 5 to say that a discussion which arose from and concerned the case itself would never be able to take advantage of s 5 protection: s 5 impliedly accepts that the *discussion* but not the risk of prejudice it creates need not be merely incidental to the trial. Obviously, given that it will already have been shown that the article in question creates a risk of serious prejudice

---

57 (1981) *The Times*, 19 December.
57a (1989) *The Times*, 7 July.
58 [1991] 2 AC 370; [1991] 1 All ER 622, HL.
59 [1992] 3 All ER 38, CA.

it might be hard to show that this is merely incidental if the article relates largely to the case. However, it might not be impossible if the thrust of the discussion could not be said to cause prejudice, while the part which did could be said to be incidental to the rest.

Due largely to the operation of s 5 the strict liability rule seems to have created a fairer balance than was the case at common law between freedom of speech and protection for the administration of justice. However, the uncertainty as to the application of s 5 where the article focuses on the case itself means that s 5 may allow some legitimate debate in the press to be stifled and therefore it might be argued that further relaxation is needed such as a general public interest defence. However, the experience of America where the existence of the First Amendment has meant that there is far less restraint, has demonstrated that a very liberal approach can give rise to problems. In *Nebraska Press Association v Stuart*[60] the Supreme Court held that adverse publicity before a trial would not necessarily have a prejudicial effect on it and therefore a prior restraint would not be granted. Barendt argues further that subsequent restraints might therefore also be unconstitutional; thus a conviction might not be obtained in respect of an already published article which created a risk of prejudicial effect.[61] Therefore witnesses' statements may be obtained pre-trial, while assertions of guilt or confessions may all be made public. In response to this stance procedural devices such as delaying the trial or changing its venue have been adopted but they are not always very effective, leaving open the possibility that defendants may appeal against conviction and obtain an acquittal due to the publicity. Nevertheless, some broadening of s 5 or, possibly, development of a public interest defence at common law[62] might be desirable which clearly allowed discussion focusing mainly on the particular case. Miller favours the Australian approach which allows a balancing exercise between the public interest in publication and the interest in a fair trial to be carried out,[63] and which does allow suppression of material where the risk it creates to a fair trial is very clear.[64]

---

[60] 427 US 539 (1976).

[61] Barendt, p 228.

[62] Section 6(b) preserves all common law defences. Support for such a defence could derive from certain Australian cases (eg *Registrar, Court of Appeal v Willesee* [1985] 3 NSWLR 650) and from the ruling of the Court of Appeal although not the House of Lords in the *Sunday Times* case, especially Lord Denning's speech [1973] QB 710 at p 741).

[63] See Miller [1992] *Crim LR* 106,114; also Walker, S, 'Freedom of Speech and Contempt of Court: The English and Australian Approaches Compared' (1991) 40 *ICLQ* 583.

[64] Miller instances *Hinch v Attorney General for Victoria* (1987) 164 *CLR* 15; see also Miller (1993) *LQR* 39.

Restrictions on reporting of court proceedings

The general principle at stake here is that justice should be openly administered.[65] Thus courts are open to the public and therefore a fair and accurate factual report of the proceedings will not amount to a contempt. This is provided for under s 4(1) of the 1981 Act. The reverse is true of private sittings, a report of which will *prima facie* amount to a contempt. However, a number of exceptions to the principle of openness have been created to allow the withholding of information either temporarily or indefinitely. For example, at common law a judge can order prohibition of a publication in order to prevent, for example, the disclosure of the identity of a witness. The leading authority is *AG v Leveller Magazine Ltd*[66] in which it was accepted that departure from the principle of openness would be warranted if necessary for the due administration of justice, and that therefore if a court made an order designed to protect the administration of justice then it would be incumbent on those who knew of it not to do anything which might frustrate its object.

Postponing reporting of information

Section 4(2) of the 1981 Act provides that during any legal proceeding held in public a judge may make an order postponing reporting of the proceedings if such action 'appears necessary for avoiding a substantial risk of prejudice to the administration of justice in those proceedings,' thus creating an exception to s 4(1).[67] This might typically involve the reporting of matters which the defence wished to argue should be ruled inadmissible. A right of appeal against such orders in relation to trials on indictment has been created by s 159 of the Criminal Justice Act 1988. The position of the media when a s 4(2) order is made in respect of reporting a summary trial is less clear; however, it was established in *Clerkenwell Metropolitan Stipendiary Magistrate, ex parte The Telegraph and Others*[68] that in such circumstances the media have a right to be heard and must be allowed to put forward the case for discharging the order. When the applicants, publishers of national newspapers, became aware of the existence of the order they were granted a hearing before the magistrate at which they submitted that the court had power to hear representations from them as to why the order should be discharged. The magistrate held that the court had no power to hear from anyone but the parties to the proceedings. The applicants sought a declaration that the court did have the power to hear

---

65 See the comments to this effect and on the need to limit use of private hearings in Preston [1993] 4 All ER 638; 143 *NLJ* 1601.
66 [1979] AC 440; [1979] 2 WLR 247, HL.
67 For comment on s 4 of the 1981 Act see Walker, C, Cram, I and Brogarth, D (1992) 55 *MLR* 647.
68 [1993] 2 All ER 183; (1992) *The Times*, 22 October.

their representations and it was determined, relying on *Horsham Justices, ex parte Farqharson*,[69] that they had sufficient standing to apply for judicial review. It was found to be implicit in s 4(2) that a court contemplating use of the section should be able to hear representations from those who would be affected if an order was made. In determining whether the order should be maintained it would be necessary to balance the interest in the need for a fair trial before an unprejudiced jury on the one hand and the requirements of open justice on the other. In performing this balancing exercise the magistrate would need to hear representations from the press as being best qualified to represent the public interest in publicity.

The ruling of the Court of Appeal in *Horsham Magistrates, ex parte Farqharson* was to the effect that such orders should be made sparingly; judges should be careful not to impose a ban on flimsy grounds where the connection between the matters in question and prejudice to the administration of justice was purely speculative. If other means of protecting the jury from possibly prejudicial reports of the trial were available they should be used. Moreover, it must be ensured that the ban covers only the matters in question.

This ruling was reinforced by the decision in *Ex parte Central Independent Television plc and Others*.[70] During a criminal trial the jury had to stay overnight in a hotel and in order that they could watch television or listen to the radio, the judge made an order under s 4(2) postponing reporting of the proceedings for that night. The applicants, broadcasters, appealed against the order under s 159 of the Criminal Justice Act 1988 on the basis that there was no ground on which the judge could have concluded that there was a substantial risk of prejudice to the administration of justice. Further, the judge had incorrectly exercised his discretion under the subsection and failed to take proper account of the public interest in freedom of expression and in the open administration of justice. The Court of Appeal found that it had not been necessary to make the order as there was little, if any, evidence of a risk to the administration of justice: the previous reporting of the case had not suggested that reporting on the day in question would be anything other than fair and accurate. Even had there been a substantial risk it might have been possible to adopt alternative methods of insulating the jury from the media. Where such alternative methods were available they should be used. Accordingly, the appeal was allowed.

The emphasis in this case on the need to restrict reporting only where clearly necessary is to be welcomed; certainly the convenience of the jury is not a sufficient reason for invoking the subsection. Similarly, in *Ex parte The*

---

69 [1982] 2 All ER 269, CA.
70 [1991] 1 All ER 347.

Telegraph plc,[71] the Court of Appeal found that even where a substantial risk to proceedings might arise this need not mean that an order must automatically be made. The court based this finding on the need to consider the two elements of s 4(2) separately; first a substantial risk of prejudice to the administration of justice should be identified flowing from publication of matters relating to the trial and, secondly, it should be asked whether it was necessary to make an order in order to avoid the risk. In making a determination as to the second limb a judge should consider whether in the light of the competing interest in open justice the order should be made at all, and if so with all or any of the restrictions sought. In the case in question the order should not have been made since the risk of prejudice was outweighed by the interest in open justice.

This decision suggests a concern on the part of the judiciary to prevent a ready use of s 4(2) orders which would be prejudicial to the principle of open justice.[72] Incidentally it is of some interest to note that this decision followed closely on that in *AG v Guardian Newspaper*[73] which concerned an article written while a ban on reporting of a major fraud trial was in force, criticising the alleged propensity of judges in such trials to impose bans. It was held that the article created too remote a risk to constitute a contempt under the strict liability rule and Justice Brooke took the opportunity of re-emphasising the importance of the news media as the eyes and ears of the general public.

This approach was developed in *R v Beck, ex parte Daily Telegraph*.[74] Beck, who had been a social worker in charge of children's homes, was charged with offences involving sexual abuse, and due to the number of charges the trial was split into three. At the first trial a s 4(2) order was made due to the risk of prejudice to the subsequent two trials. On appeal the Court of Appeal accepted that there was a substantial risk of prejudice but went on to find that the public interest in the reporting of the trial outweighed the risk. In so finding the court emphasised the concern which the public must feel due to the particular facts of the case and the right of the public to be informed and to be able to ask questions about the opportunities created for those in public service to commit such offences.

Prohibiting reporting of information

A number of statutory provisions impose restrictions such as allowing certain persons concerned in a case to remain anonymous. This is provided for in

---

71 [1993] 2 All ER 971.
72 See also Saunders (the Guinness trials) [1990] *Crim LR* 597; *Barlow Clowes Gilt Managers v Clowes* (1990) *The Times*, 2 February.
73 [1992] 2 All ER 38.
74 [1993] 2 All ER 177.

relation to complainants in rape cases under s 4 of the Sexual Offences (Amendment) Act 1976 as amended and for children under s 39(1) of the Children and Young Persons Act 1933. Section 11 of the 1981 Act allows a court, which has power to do so, to make an order prohibiting publication of names or other matters if this appears necessary. Thus s 11 does not itself confer such a power and therefore refers to existing powers.[75] At present there are signs that a robust interpretation will be given to s 11 similar to that being taken to s 4(2): the fundamental importance of open justice will be outweighed only by very clear detriment which may answer to a general public interest flowing from publication of the matters in question – economic damage to the interests of the defendant will not suffice.[76]

Intentionally prejudicing proceedings

Section 6(c) of the 1981 Act preserves liability for contempt at common law if intention to prejudice the administration of justice can be shown. 'Prejudice [to] the administration of justice' clearly includes (and may solely denote – see below) prejudice to particular proceedings. Once the requirement of intent is satisfied it is easier to establish contempt at common law rather than under the Act since it is only necessary to show 'a real risk of prejudice' and proceedings need only be imminent, not 'active'. Clearly, liability can be established at common law in instances when it might also be established under the 1981 Act as occurred in the *Hislop* case and also in instances when the Act will not apply because proceedings are inactive. Possibly it might also be established where one of the statutory tests *other than* the 'active' requirement was not satisfied. These preliminary observations are developed below.

A publication will fall within the area of liability preserved by s 6(c) if the following three elements are present.

Intention to prejudice the administration of justice

The test for intention to prejudice the administration of justice was established in *AG v Newspaper Publishing plc*[77] and *AG v News Group Newspapers plc*.[78] It was made clear that 'intention' connotes specific intent and therefore cannot include recklessness. The test may be summed up as follows: did the

---

75 See *AG v Leveller Magazine Ltd* [1979] AC 440; [1979] 2 WLR 247, HL. For comment on s 11 of the 1981 Act see Walker, C, Cram, I and Brogarth, D (1992) 55 *MLR* 647.
76 *Dover Justices, ex parte Dover District Council and Wells* [1992] *Crim LR* 371.
77 (1990) *The Times*, 28 February; for report of the Divisional Court proceedings see *Re AG v Observer and Guardian Newspapers Ltd* (1989) *The Times*, 9 May, for comment see [1989] *PL* 477; for comment on the *mens rea* issue see Laws, J, 43 *CLP* 99 105–10.
78 [1989] QB 110; [1988] 3 WLR 163; [1988] 2 All ER 906.

defendant either wish to prejudice proceedings or (and this is *oblique* intent) foresee that such prejudice was a virtually inevitable consequence of publishing the material in question?[79] Thus it is not necessary to show a *desire* to prejudice proceedings or that where there was such a desire that it was the *sole* desire. This test is based on the meaning of intent arising from two rulings on the *mens rea* for murder: *Hancock and Shankland*[80] and *Nedrick*.[81]

This is a subjective test but the Court of Appeal in *AG v Newspaper Publishing plc* (*Spycatcher* case)[82] appeared to be asking whether or not the consequences in question were 'foreseeable', suggesting not that the defendant should actually have foreseen them but that an objective observer would have done so. This would of course be an easier test to satisfy, although since in practice it will be necessary to *infer* that the defendant foresaw the consequences, the difference between the two tests may be of only theoretical importance. This may be argued on the basis that in general if an objective observer would have foreseen a risk of prejudice it will be hard for an editor to show that he or she did not, because, unlike some defendants to whom this test is applied (in other areas of criminal law), an editor must make a decision as to publication unaffected by mental incompetence (it is assumed!), emotion or the need to act in the heat of the moment. Nevertheless, a concept of 'objective intent' is not distinguishable from recklessness; as it is clear that recklessness will not suffice for common law contempt it is clear that intention should be interpreted to mean subjective intent.

A number of circumstances may allow the inference of intention to prejudice the proceedings to be made, although it is suggested that the relevance of the circumstances will depend on the form of intent – desire or oblique intent – which seems to be in question. In *AG v News Group Newspapers plc* the newspaper's support for the prosecution in its columns and in funding a private prosecution allowed the inference to be made. A Dr B was questioned about an allegation of rape made against him by an eight year old girl but eventually the county prosecuting solicitor decided that there was insufficient evidence to prosecute him. *The Sun* got hold of the story and decided that it should offer the mother financial help in order to fund a private prosecution. It published various articles attacking Dr B: 'Rape Case Doc: *Sun* acts'; 'Beast must be named says MP', etc. The Attorney General

---

79 Moreover, although this issue has not yet arisen and may be unlikely to arise, it is necessary to show that the almost inevitable effect of the article would also have been obvious to an objective observer where it is clear that the editor did not wish to prejudice proceedings. The defence could conceivably argue that the editor in question *did* foresee that the article would almost certainly have the effect in question but that an objective observer would *not* have come to that conclusion.
80 [1986] AC 455; [1986] 1 All ER 641; [1986] 3 WLR 1014.
81 [1986] 3 All ER 1; [1986] 1 WLR 1025.
82 [1988] Ch 333; [1987] 3 All ER 276; [1988] 3 WLR 942, CA.

brought a prosecution against *The Sun* for contempt. The articles could not come within the strict liability rule because the proceedings in question – the private prosecution – were not active. The contempt alleged therefore arose at common law. It was found that intention could be established, either on the basis of a desire to prejudice the proceedings (presumably in order to vindicate *The Sun's* stance) or because *The Sun* must have foreseen that Dr B would almost certainly not receive a fair trial. The judgment would support either view but probably favours the former: in his ruling Watkins LJ said: '... they could only have printed articles of such a kind if they were campaigning for a conviction as they clearly were.' However, if he had the *latter* form of intent in mind it may be said that although *The Sun* had acted reprehensibly in using its power to attempt to influence a trial it had itself become involved in, it is arguable that intent should not have been so readily established. The fact that *The Sun* was personally involved was not, it is argued, relevant to oblique intent. The proceedings were clearly not going to occur for some time; therefore, although the defendants probably foresaw some risk of prejudice to them it was not clear that such prejudice could be said to be a virtually inevitable consequence of publication. In fact Dr B was acquitted; the jury were clearly able to put out of their minds any influence the Sun articles may have had.

The Sun case may be contrasted with *AG v Sport Newspapers Ltd*[83] in which the test for intention was perhaps more strictly interpreted. One David Evans, who had previous convictions for rape, was suspected of abducting Anna Humphries. He was on the run when *The Sport* published his convictions; the proceedings were not therefore active and so the case arose at common law. It did not appear that *The Sport* wished to prejudice proceedings. Was it foreseen as a virtual certainty that prejudice to Evans's trial would occur as a result of the publication? It was held that there was a risk of such prejudice of which the editor of *The Sport* was aware but that such awareness of risk was not sufficient. Clearly, had the *mens rea* of common law contempt included recklessness it would have been established.

Imminence

At common law the *sub judice* period began when proceedings could be said to be imminent (*Savundranayagan*).[84] This test would of course be readily satisfied where proceedings were active. However, it may not always be necessary to establish imminence. In *AG v News Group Newspapers plc*[85] it was held *obiter* that where it is established that the defendant intended to prejudice proceedings it is not necessary to show that proceedings are imminent. It was

---

83 [1991] 1 WLR 1194.
84 [1968] 3 All ER 439; [1968] 1 WLR 1761, CA.
85 [1989] QB 110; [1988] 3 WLR 163; [1988] 2 All ER 906.

found that even if the trial of Dr B was too far off to be said to be pending or imminent, the conduct of *The Sun* in publishing stories at the same time as assisting the mother in the private prosecution could still amount to contempt. Bingham LJ concurred with this dilution of the imminence test in *AG v Sport*, although in the same case Mr Justice Hodgson considered that proceedings must be 'pending'. He interpreted 'pending' as synonymous with 'active', an interpretation which would have greatly curtailed the scope of common law contempt. This point therefore remains unresolved, leaving the media without a clear guide as to the period during which publication of matter relevant to proceedings will be risky. If proceedings need not even be imminent it appears that reporting of matters which may give rise to proceedings at some point in the future will be severely circumscribed. The test of imminence is itself too wide and uncertain but would be preferable to the uncertainty on this point which was exacerbated by *AG v Sport*. It is uncertain what the alternative test contemplated by Lord Bingham could be. There cannot be an intention to prejudice something which cannot even be identified as a possibility. Thus the test at its least stringent must be that proceedings can be identified as a possibility before this head of common law contempt can be in question. This development in common law contempt may significantly curtail press freedom since it clearly does nothing to help editors who wish to determine whether or not a publication might attract a criminal prosecution.

A real risk of prejudice

It must be shown that the publication amounts to conduct which creates a real risk of prejudice to the administration of justice (*Thompson Newspapers*).[86] There may be a number of different methods of fulfilling this test. In *Hislop and Pressdram*[87] it was found that the defendants, who were one party in an action for defamation, had interfered with the administration of justice because they had brought improper pressure to bear on the other party, Sonia Sutcliffe, by publishing material in *Private Eye* intended to deter her from pursuing the action. There was a substantial risk that the articles might have succeeded in their aim; had they done so the course of justice in Mrs Sutcliffe's action would have been seriously prejudiced since she would have been deterred from having her claim decided in a court. Counsel for *Private Eye* had argued that defamatory material which the defendant seeks to justify should not be restrained, because until it is clear that the alleged libel is untrue it is not clear that any right has been infringed (*Bonnard v Perryman*).[88] This argument was rejected because the question of deterrence did not depend on

---

86 [1968] 1 All ER 268; [1968] 1 WLR 1.
87 [1991] 1 QB 514; [1991] 1 All ER 911; [1991] 2 WLR 219, CA.
88 [1891] 2 Ch 269, 289.

the truth or falsity of the allegations. The possibility of justification was thus irrelevant. In this instance it might also be noted that the relevant tests under the 1981 Act had been satisfied; therefore it would seem that *a fortiori* common law contempt could be established, it having already been accepted that the articles had been published with the intention of putting pressure on Mrs Sutcliffe to discontinue the defamation action, thereby satisfying the *mens rea* requirement at common law.

The 'real risk of prejudice' test may also be fulfilled in certain circumstances if part of the media frustrates a court order (including orders made under s 4(2) of the 1981 Act) against another part. This highly significant extension of common law contempt arose from part of the *Spycatcher* litigation. In 1985 the Attorney General commenced proceedings in Australia in an attempt to restrain publication of *Spycatcher* by Peter Wright. The book included allegations of illegal activity engaged in by MI5. In 1986, after the *Guardian* and the *Observer* had published reports of the forthcoming hearing which included some *Spycatcher* material, the Attorney General obtained temporary *ex parte* injunctions preventing them from further disclosure of such material.[89]

While the temporary injunctions were in force the Independent and two other papers published material covered by them. It was determined in the Court of Appeal (*AG v Newspaper Publishing plc*)[90] and confirmed in the House of Lords (*AG v Times Newspapers Ltd*)[91] that such publication constituted the *actus reus* of common law contempt on the basis that publication of confidential material, the subject matter of a pending action, damaging its confidentiality and thereby probably rendering the action pointless, created an interference with the administration of justice. The case therefore affirmed the principle that once an interlocutory injunction has been obtained restraining one organ of the media from publication of allegedly confidential material, the rest of the media may be in contempt if they publish that material, even if their intention in doing so is to bring alleged iniquity to public attention. This case thus allowed the laws of confidence and contempt to operate together as a significant prior restraint on media freedom and in so doing created an inroad into the general principle that a court order should only affect the party to which it is directed as only that party will have a chance to argue that the making of the order would be wrong.

The decision in *AG v Newspaper Publishing plc and Others*[92] seems to represent an attempt to narrow down the area of liability created by the decision in *AG v Times Newspapers Ltd*. The case arose from the reporting of

---

89 For full discussion of this branch of the litigation see Chap 6 pp 251–54.
90 (1990) *The Times*, 28 February.
91 [1992] 1 AC 191; [1991] 2 All ER 398; [1991] 2 WLR 994, HL: for comment see *NLJ* 173 and 1115.
92 [1997] 3 All ER 159; (1997) *The Times*, 2 May, CA.

the appeals in the *Ordtech* case,[93] a case which bore strong similarities to the *Matrix Churchill* case.[94] The appellants appealed against their convictions for exporting arms; public interest immunity certificates were issued but the Court of Appeal ordered that the material covered by them, which was crucial to the appeal, should be disclosed in summarised and edited form to the appellants and their legal advisors. The order restricted the use of the material to the appeal and requested its return on conclusion of the appeal. In court, in directing return of the documents, the Lord Chief Justice indicated that breach of the order would result in the matter being referred to the Attorney General. In its report of the proceedings the *Independent* published a small amount of material from the documents which did not also appear in the written copy of the judgment. The Attorney General brought proceedings for contempt against the *Independent*, relying on the ruling in *AG v Times Newspapers* to the effect that if a third party with the requisite intent acted to frustrate the basis on which a court had determined that justice should be administered then he was guilty of contempt. On behalf of the *Independent* it was argued that the *Times* case represented an extension of the law as it had previously been understood and that the court should be slow to extend the law any further since any such extension represented a further encroachment on freedom of expression and inhibited the media in its function of informing the public. The court did not accept that any conduct by a third party inconsistent with a court order was sufficient to amount to the *actus reus* of contempt: it was found necessary to show that a significant and adverse effect on the administration of justice in the relevant proceedings had occurred. The Court of Appeal used the wording of Article 10 of the Convention in finding that restraints on freedom of expression should be no wider than necessary in a democratic society, and considered that a third party's conduct which is inconsistent with a court order in a trivial way should not expose him to the risk of a conviction for contempt. The application of the Attorney General was therefore dismissed.

This decision narrows down the area of liability created in the *Times* case but does not affect the extension of the law it brought about. However, that extension may be incompatible with Article 10. Although trivial or technical breaches of court orders made against others will not attract liability, the area of liability which remains is likely to create a curb on press freedom which may be incompatible with the crucial role of the press in a free society. The emphasis placed upon that role in *Goodwin v UK*[95] by the European Court of Human Rights suggests that this may be the case. The principle laid down in the *Times* case appears to be ripe for challenge under Article 10 once the Human Rights Act 1998 comes into force.

---

93   See *Blackledge and Others* (1996) 1 Cr App R 326, CA.
94   See below pp 261–63.
95   *Goodwin v UK* (1996) 22 EHRR 123.

Prejudicing proceedings: relationship between the 1981 Act and the common law

Common law contempt presents not only an alternative but also, where proceedings are active, an additional possibility of establishing liability. It presents such an alternative in all instances in which proceedings are not active, assuming, of course, that the *mens rea* requirement can be satisfied, and it has proved to be of great significance in this context due to the readiness with which it is sometimes accepted that the common law tests have been fulfilled. The doctrine has therefore attracted criticism as circumventing the 1981 Act[96] but it may also, even more controversially, present an alternative in instances where proceedings *are* active but liability under the Act could not be established, thus opening up the possibility that the Act and in particular the provisions of s 5, could be undermined. This is of particular significance given that s 5 was adopted to take account of the ruling in the European Court of Human Rights that UK contempt law breached the Article 10 guarantee of freedom of speech.

Common law contempt was established in the *Hislop* case in an instance where proceedings were active and therefore the relationship between the concept of good faith under s 5 and the question of intention under s 6(c) came under consideration. It appeared that a finding of intention to prejudice the administration of justice necessary to found liability for contempt at common law would probably preclude a finding of good faith under s 5. This finding seemed to obviate the possibility of proceeding at common law in appropriate instances in order to avoid the operation of s 5 – a course which would have undermined the policy of the Act as providing some safeguards for media freedom. However, the point is open to argument. It could be said that in the majority of cases a finding of good faith under s 5 would indeed preclude a finding of intention to prejudice proceedings, but in one instance it might not. It might be shown that where a newspaper recognised a strong risk that proceedings would be prejudiced but did not desire such prejudice (as may have been the case in *AG v Newspaper Publishing plc*) a finding of good faith might not be precluded. A publisher might argue that his or her recognition of the risk to proceedings was outweighed (in his or her own mind) by the need to bring iniquity or other matters of public interest to public attention. The good faith requirement under s 5 might cover such a situation, thereby preventing liability under statute, although it might still arise at common law. Thus, for example, the principle arising from *AG v Newspaper Publishing plc* might apply where proceedings were active and where publication of material covered by an injunction fell within s 5. Thus in this sense common law

---

96 Miller has written 'I think it is at best messy and may also be dangerous to allow the common law to outflank the Act' [1992] *Crim LR* 112.

contempt clearly has the ability to undermine the statutory protection for freedom of speech.[97]

This possibility may be unlikely to arise. However, there are other circumstances in which a prosecution at common law could succeed in an instance in which proceedings were active but prosecution under the Act failed. For example, s 5 might be irrelevant because it might be clear that the article did not concern a discussion in good faith of public affairs. However, s 2(2) might not be satisfied on the basis that, although some risk of prejudice arose, it could not be termed serious enough. In such an instance there appears to be no reason why the common law could not be used instead on the basis that the test of showing 'a real risk of prejudice' is less difficult to satisfy. If so, it would be possible to circumvent the more stringent s 2(2) requirement. Of course, it would be necessary to prove an intention to prejudice the administration of justice.

3 PROTECTING JUSTICE AS A CONTINUING PROCESS

Publications which interfere with the course of justice as a continuing process, as opposed to publications which affect particular proceedings may attract liability. The forms which a risk to justice as a continuing process might take are considered below; the first issue to be considered concerns the mental element under this form of contempt. Such publications must fall outside the Contempt of Court Act 1981, which according to s 1 is concerned only with publications which may affect particular proceedings. They must therefore arise at common law; the question is whether *mens rea* must be shown as s 6(c) seems to provide. However, it could be argued that the words 'administration of justice' used in s 6(c) could be interpreted to mean 'in particular proceedings only', in which case forms of strict liability contempt may still exist at common law. Support could be found for such an interpretation on the basis that s 6(c) is concerned to demonstrate that where intention can be shown, nothing prevents liability arising at common law. Given the context in which this statement is made (appearing to present a contrast to the strict liability rule) it might seem that the area of liability preserved by s 6(c) would cover the same ground as s 1 but only in instances in which *mens rea* could be shown. This point is not settled: there is no post-Act authority on it.

If, on the other hand, s 6(c) covers all interferences with the administration of justice at common law, whether in relation to particular proceedings or not, it would appear to cover the form of contempt known as 'scandalising the

---

[97] For comment on developments in common law contempt see: Stone, 'Common Law Contempt' (1988) *NLJ* 136; Halpin, A, 'Child's play in the Lords' (1991) *NLJ* 173; McHale, J, 'Common Law Contempt' (1991) *NLJ* 1115.

court' (considered below) which would run counter to the ruling of the Divisional Court in *Editor of New Statesman*[98] and to some persuasive authority from other jurisdictions.[99] This may be the more satisfactory approach as it would be more likely to allow the UK to fulfil its obligations under Article 10. Otherwise, common law contempt might have too wide a potential and the intention of the European Court of Human Rights in the *Sunday Times* case would not be given full effect. This would mean that liability for 'scandalising the court' would arise only where *intention* to interfere with the course of justice generally was shown. However, this point cannot yet be regarded as settled.

Undermining the legal process in the long term

It is possible to affect the course of justice in the long term in various ways. It may be possible to commit contempt by commenting on a particular case in such a way as to create a prejudicial effect on the course of justice generally[100] rather than on particular proceedings. This might occur, for example, if in commenting on the particular case, which was concluded, parts of the media prejudged issues still to be determined some time in the future. A contempt might also arise, *inter alia*, where a part of the media made a judgment on a particular issue with legal implications, although no court had made a determination on the issue or where a court had made a contrary determination. It would not be relevant whether the judgment of the media was ill- or well-informed. In most instances of prejudicial comment in the media a particular proceeding is soon to occur or at least exists as a possibility in the future. Thus, attention focuses on the effect of the comment upon that proceeding. However, if no such proceeding ever occurs it might be argued that this should make no difference to any liability incurred by a part of the media for contempt. For example, in 1997 the *Daily Mirror* published pictures of five men with the caption 'Murderers!'. Proceedings against them for a racially influenced murder had previously been dropped. At the time of the *Mirror*'s comment no proceedings which could be influenced by it were in being. It was possible that the family of the victim might bring a civil action against the men for battery; thus, the *Mirror* might possibly have been found to have caused prejudice to that action. However, if the action had been heard by a judge only, which was highly likely, it would have been improbable that a finding of such prejudice would have been made. However, whether a civil

---

98 (1928) 44 *TLR* 301.
99 *Solicitor General v Radio Avon* [1978] 1 NZLR 225; *cf S v Van Niekirk* (1970) 3 SA 655. See Miller pp 378–79 and Borrie and Lowe pp 243–44.
100 *Cf The Sun* case (above) which did concern a trial by newspaper but in which it was thought that the particular proceedings would be prejudiced.

action was or was not brought it is arguable that the *Mirror* could have been prosecuted for interfering with the course of justice by its publication.

The ruling of the House of Lords in *AG v Times Newspapers*,[101] which has not been overruled, lends this argument some support, although it may also be said that the spirit of the judgment of the European Court of Human Rights in the *Sunday Times* case[102] would be flouted if it could be used. Nevertheless, Lord Diplock in the English case appeared to think that the *Sunday Times* case would be decided in the same way if a similar issue came before the UK courts. The finding of Watkins LJ in *AG v News Group Newspapers plc*,[103] to the effect that where a newspaper intends to prejudice the course of justice proceedings need not be imminent, may also support this argument. In his judgment he approved of David Pannick's contention that 'no authority states that common law contempt cannot be committed where proceedings cannot be said to be imminent but where there is a specific intent to impede a fair trial, the occurrence of which is in contemplation'. If these comments are read in the light of the contention, also approved in that decision, that 'the purpose of the contempt jurisdiction is to prevent interference with the course of justice' it might be argued that they would also apply where no trial or other proceeding was in contemplation.

It is unclear whether this form of contempt, if it exists, requires *mens rea*. The comments of Watkins LJ might support the need for such a requirement. On the other hand, the established form of contempt concerned with interferences with the long term course of justice – scandalising the court – may not require *mens rea*. If it does not it would only be necessary to establish that the article in question created a risk that the function of the courts would in general be usurped, not that the defendant recognised that fact. This form of contempt would be able to take advantage of the width of the common law tests without the constraint represented by the need to show *mens rea*. The undesirability of such a possibility lends support to the argument that s 6(c) should apply to the whole of common law contempt. It may be desirable that sanctions should be available to punish newspapers who usurp the function of the courts in the way that the *Mirror* did. However, adapting the common law for this purpose is probably undesirable due to the uncertainty which would be created within an already uncertain area of the law. If liability for intentionally interfering with the course of justice is to arise it should be placed on a statutory basis.

---

101 [1974] AC 273; [1973] 3 All ER 54; [1973] 3 WLR 298, HL.
102 Judgment of 26 April 1979, A.30; (1979) 2 EHRR 245.
103 [1989] QB 110; [1988] 3 WLR 163; [1988] 2 All ER 906.

Scandalising the court[104]

This type of contempt arose to protect the judicial system from media attacks. The idea behind it is that it would be against the public interest if the media could attack judges and cast doubt on their decisions – suggest for example that a judge had shown bias – because the public confidence in the administration of justice would be undermined. It has not been affected by the 1981 Act because there are normally no proceedings which could be influenced; any relevant proceedings will usually be concluded. If an attack on a judge occurred during the 'active' period it would probably fall outside the Act as any risk it created would tend to be to the course of justice as a continuing process rather than to the particular proceeding. Prosecutions are rare (and in recent times unheard of in the UK) but Lord Hailsham said in *Baldry v DPP of Mauritius*,[105] a Privy Council decision, that though it was likely that only the most serious or intolerable instances would be taken notice of by courts or Attorney Generals, nothing had happened in the intervening 80 years to invalidate the analysis of this branch of contempt put forward in *Gray*.[106] Thus this branch of contempt law is probably still alive and cannot merely be disregarded by the media.

As noted above, the weight of authority is probably to the effect that this is a form of strict liability contempt arising at common law but this point cannot be regarded as settled. If the view taken in *Editor of New Statesman*[107] is correct there would be no need to show an intention to lower the repute of the judge or court in question, merely an intention to publish. The *actus reus* of this form of contempt consists of the publication of material calculated to lower the reputation of a court or judge, thereby creating a real risk of undermining public confidence in the due administration of justice.

There are two main means of fulfilling this *actus reus*. First, a publication which is held to be scurrilously abusive of a court or judge may provide the classic example of scandalising the court. The leading case is *Gray*[108] which arose from the trial of one Wells on a charge of obscene libel in which Justice Darling warned the press not to publish a full account of court proceedings (because details of obscene matter might have been included). After they were over the *Birmingham Daily Argus* published an article attacking him and referring to him as an 'impudent little man in horsehair' and 'a microcosm of conceit and empty-headedness [who] would do well to master the duties of his own profession before undertaking the regulation of another'. This article was held by the Divisional Court to be a grave contempt as it was 'not

---

104 For general comment on this head of contempt see Walker, C (1985) 101 *LQR* 359.
105 [1983] 2 AC 297; [1983] 3 All ER 973.
106 [1900] 2 QB 36; (1900) 69 LJQB 502.
107 (1928) 44 *TLR* 301.
108 Above note 106.

moderate criticism; it amounted to personal, scurrilous abuse of the judge in his capacity of judge'. On the other hand, in *Ambard v AG for Trinidad and Tobago*[109] reasoned criticism of certain sentences was held by the Privy Council not to constitute contempt on the basis that 'Justice is not a cloistered virtue: she must be allowed to suffer the scrutiny and respectful, even though outspoken, comments of ordinary men'. In a more recent case, *Metropolitan Police Commissioner, ex parte Blackburn*,[110] the Court of Appeal reaffirmed this position.

Secondly, a publication may scandalise a court if it imputes bias to a judge – even if it does so in a moderate way – on the basis that allegations of partiality will undermine confidence in the basic function of a judge. The leading case in this area is *Editor of New Statesman*.[111] The pioneer of birth control, Dr Marie Stopes, lost a libel action and an article commenting on the case stated: '... the verdict represents a substantial miscarriage of justice ... we are not in sympathy with Dr Stopes but prejudice against her aims should not be allowed to influence a Court of Justice as it appeared to influence Mr Justice Avory in his summing up. Such views as those of Dr Stopes cannot get a fair hearing in a court presided over by Mr Justice Avory.' The editor was found to be in contempt because although the article was serious and seemingly respectful, it imputed unfairness and lack of impartiality to the judge in the discharge of his judicial duties. The most notorious instance of this variety of scandalising the court occurred in *Colsey*.[112] A moderate article had imputed unconscious bias to a judge because in making a determination as to the meaning of a statute he might have been influenced by the fact that he had himself earlier, as Solicitor General, steered it through Parliament. This was the last successful prosecution for this form of contempt on the UK. Prosecutions may have been discouraged due to the attacks on the *Colsey* ruling which clearly laid itself open to the charge of amounting to an unjustified encroachment on the free speech principle.[113]

It will not be surprising to learn that this is an area of contempt law which has attracted particular criticism.[114] Some critics argue that the offence of scandalising the court should be abolished altogether on the grounds that the rationale of the offence – undermining public confidence in the administration of justice – is too vague to justify imposing restrictions on freedom of speech. They argue that a system of justice should not be so lacking in self-confidence that it must suppress attacks on itself. Harold Laski has written 'To argue that

---

[109] [1936] AC 322; [1936] 1 All ER 704.
[110] [1968] 2 All ER 319, CA.
[111] (1928) 44 *TLR* 301.
[112] (1931) *The Times*, 9 May.
[113] See eg Goodhart (1935) 48 *Harv LR* 885, 903–04; (1931) 47 *LQR* 315.
[114] See Borrie and Lowe, *The Law of Contempt*, 1983, p 243 *et seq*; Law Commission Report (No 96) 'Offences relating to Interference with the Course of Justice' pp 67–68.

the expression of doubts ... as to judicial impartiality is an interference in the course of justice because the result is to undermine public confidence in the judiciary is to forget that public confidence is undermined not so much by the comment as by the habit which leads to the comment'.[115] It may be argued that the public will have *more* confidence in the judiciary if it can be freely discussed. Moreover, because no jury sits in such cases the judicial system is in a sense prosecution and judge in the same case, thereby giving rise to a suggestion of bias. It may be asked why *only* judges and not, for example, politicians or members of the clergy, should receive this special protection from criticism? Why single out judges for such insulation? The position may be compared to that in America where this form of contempt is almost extinct due to the ruling in *Bridges v California*;[116] it was held that the evil of displaying disrespect for the judiciary should not be averted by restricting freedom of expression as enforced silence on a subject is more likely to engender resent, suspicion and contempt.

On the other hand, it might be said that allowing certain sections of the press complete *carte blanche* to attack judicial decisions and perhaps impute bias *does* create a risk of undermining public confidence and that an action for defamation is not a sufficient remedy because it would place a judge in an invidious position while the action was being held. Also it might be argued that the singling out of judges can be justified on the basis that, unlike other public figures, judges have no forum from which to reply to criticism. A compromise between these two positions could be effected by adopting the course advocated by the Law Commission – replacement of this form of liability with a narrowly drawn offence covering the distribution of false matter with intent that it should be taken as true, and knowing or being reckless as to its falsity when it imputes corrupt conduct to any judge.[117]

Victimising witnesses and others

It will be a contempt to victimise a witness or a party in proceedings because it may affect the case and it will deter others from coming forward in future. Thus, this area of contempt will arise even when the proceedings are over and therefore protects the course of justice generally as well as preventing prejudice to particular proceedings. This was affirmed in *AG v Royal Society for the Prevention of Cruelty to Animals*.[118] It appears to be necessary to show an intent to punish the person in question due to the fact that he or she has played a part in a particular case but this does not mean that this needs to be

---

115 (1928) 41 *Harv LR* 1031 at 1036.
116 314 US 252 (1941).
117 This was the view of the Law Commission in their Report (No 96) *Offences Relating to Interference with the Course of Justice*.
118 (1985) *The Times*, 22 June; see also *Roebuck v NUM* [1977] ICR 573.

the dominant motive.[119] Miller suggests that recklessness should suffice, so that if the punisher realised that the person punished believed that the punishment was due to the evidence he or she had given but made no attempt to dispel this notion this would amount to contempt.[120] In general, this form of contempt has no effect on freedom of speech. However, free speech might be in issue if a publication sought, through its columns, to victimise a witness who was giving or had given evidence in proceedings against it. If so, it may be argued that the interest of society in protecting the administration of justice and the strong interest of individuals in a fair hearing should prevail over the weak free speech interest which could be asserted.

4 JURY DELIBERATIONS

Section 8 of the 1981 Act provides that disclosure of jury deliberations will amount to a contempt of court and it is clear from the ruling in *AG v Associated Newspapers Ltd and Others*[121] that this provision must be interpreted literally. In that instance jury deliberations were not disclosed directly to the defendant newspaper but to researchers who made a transcript of them. The paper then used the transcript in order to gather information for the article in question. It was argued on behalf of the defendants that the word 'disclose' used in s 8 is capable of bearing two meanings; it could mean disclosure by anyone or it could mean disclosure by a member of the jury to the defendant. Where a statute contains an ambiguous provision and affects freedoms protected by the European Convention it should be construed so as to conform with the Convention. Thus, arguably, the narrower meaning should be adopted allowing the defendants to escape liability. However, it was found that the word 'disclose' was not ambiguous: in its natural and ordinary meaning, which Parliament clearly intended it to bear, it denoted disclosure to anyone; the defendants therefore clearly fell within its provisions. The closing up of a potential loop-hole in s 8 achieved by this ruling means that the important institution of the jury is largely immune from scrutiny at least as regards the manner in which it discharges its role.

However, jury deliberations are clearly a matter of public interest and it may be argued that s 8 should have been framed much less widely. Exceptions could have been included (as they were under the clause as originally drafted)[122] which would have allowed approaches to jurors as part

---

119 *AG v Butterworth* [1963] 1 QB 696; [1962] 3 All ER 326, CA; for comment see Williams (1962) 25 *MLR* 723; Goodhart (1963) 79 *LQR* 5.
120 Miller p 359.
121 [1994] 1 All ER 556; (1993) 144 *NLJ* 195 HL; (1994) 142 NLJ 1647; [1993] 2 All ER 535.
122 See 416 *HL Deb*, 20 January 1981.

of academic research so long as the proceedings and jurors were not identified.[123] The only current constraint is the requirement of the Attorney General's consent to a prosecution but even this is not necessary where proceedings are instituted on the motion of a court. The Royal Commission on Criminal Justice recommended that s 8 should be amended in order to allow research to be conducted into the reasoning of jurors in reaching a verdict. Possibly, s 8 will be found to be incompatible with Article 10 once the Human Rights Act is in force.[124]

The section does not prevent interviewing of jurors which does not touch upon their deliberations in the jury room but such enquiries should only be undertaken with the leave of the trial court or after verdict and sentence, by the Court of Appeal.[125]

5 REFUSING TO DISCLOSE SOURCES[126]

In general very little recognition is given in UK law to the constitutional role of the press. However, an exception to this rule is afforded by s 10 of the 1981 Act which provides that:

> ... no court may require a person to disclose ... the source of information contained in a publication for which he is responsible, unless it be established to the satisfaction of the court that disclosure is necessary in the interests of justice or national security or for the prevention of disorder or crime.

Thus s 10 creates a presumption in favour of journalists who wish to protect their sources, which is, however, subject to four wide exceptions, of which the widest arises where the interests of justice require that disclosure should be made. It was found in *Secretary of State for Defence v Guardian Newspapers*[127] that disclosure of the identity of the source would only be ordered where this was necessary in order to identify him or her; if other means of identification were reasonably readily available they should be used. On the other hand, this did not mean that all other means of inquiry which might reveal the identity of the source must be exhausted before disclosure would be ordered. The term 'necessary' was found in *Re an Inquiry under the Companies Security (Insider Dealing) Act 1985*[128] to mean something less than indispensable but something more than useful. The House of Lords clarified the nature of the balancing exercise to be carried out under s 10 in *X v Morgan Grampian Publishers and*

---

123 It is worth noting that the Divisional Court in *AG v New Statesman* [1981] QB 1 indicated that disclosure of jury-room secrets which did not identify the persons concerned could have no adverse effects on the administration of justice.
124 Cm 2263, 1993, p 2.
125 *McCluskey* (1993) 94 Cr App R 216, CA. See also *Mickleborough* (1995) 1 Cr App R 297, CA.
126 For comment on s 10 see Allan, T (1991) *CLJ* 131; Miller [1982] *Crim LR* 71, 82.
127 [1985] AC 339; [1984] 3 All ER 601, HL.
128 [1988] 1 All ER 203.

Others.[129] A confidential plan was stolen from the plaintiffs, a company named Tetra; information apparently from the plan was given by an unidentified source by phone to William Goodwin, a journalist. The plaintiffs applied for an order requiring Goodwin to disclose the source and sought discovery of his notes of the phone conversation in order to discover the identity of the source. The House of Lords had to consider the application of s 10 to these facts. It found that when a journalist relies on s 10 in order to protect a source it must be determined whether the applicant's right to take legal action against the source is outweighed by the journalist's interest in maintaining the promise of confidentiality made to him or her. The House of Lords took into account various factors in balancing these two considerations, including the threat to the plaintiffs' business and the complicity of the source in 'a gross breach of confidentiality'. Lord Bridge, with whom the other Law Lords unanimously agreed, found that the interest of the plaintiffs in identifying the source outweighed the interests of the journalist in protecting it.

Goodwin applied to the European Commission on Human Rights which gave its opinion that the order against Goodwin violated his right to freedom of expression under Article 10 of the European Convention on Human Rights.[130] The Court found[131] that there was a vital public interest in protecting journalistic sources since so doing was essential to the maintenance of a free press. Thus the margin of appreciation was circumscribed by that interest. It considered that limitations placed on the confidentiality of such sources would require the most careful scrutiny. The applicant argued that 'the law as it stood was no more than a mandate to the judiciary to order journalists to disclose sources if they were "moved" by the complaint of an aggrieved party'. Was this vital interest outweighed by Tetra's interest in eliminating the threat of damage due to the dissemination of confidential material? The injunction was already effective in preventing the dissemination of such information and therefore the additional restriction on freedom of expression entailed by the disclosure order was not supported by sufficient reasons to satisfy the requirements of Article 10(2). The disclosure order was disproportionate to the purpose in question and therefore could not be said to be necessary. Tetra's interest in disclosure, including its interest in unmasking a disloyal employee, did not outweigh the vital public interest in the protection of journalistic sources. A breach of Article 10 was therefore established. In order to comply with this ruling it would be necessary to amend s 10 by omitting or amending the 'interests of justice' head. The then Conservative government stated in response that it had no plans to amend the 1981 Act.[132] Thus, when the European Convention on Human Rights is received into UK

---

129 [1991] AC 1; [1991] 2 All ER 1, HL.
130 *Goodwin v UK* (1994) No 17488/90 Com Rep, *Guardian*, 26 May 1994.
131 *Goodwin v UK* (1996) 22 EHRR 123.
132 *Hansard* (Lords) April 13 1996 Vol 571 6147 Written Answer.

law it would seem clear that s 10 will need to be amended or, at least, reinterpreted.

It is possible to circumvent s 10 under Schedule 7 para 3(5) of the Prevention of Terrorism Act (PTA) 1989 which provides for the production of material if such production would be in the public interest: the making of such an order would seem to preclude a s 10 defence. The potential danger of Schedule 7 was shown by *Director of Public Prosecutions v Channel Four Television Co Ltd and Another*.[133] Channel 4 screened a programme in its Dispatches series called 'The Committee' which was based on the allegations of an anonymous source (Source A) that RUC and Loyalist paramilitaries had colluded in the assassination of Republicans. The police successfully applied under Schedule 7 para 3(5) for orders disclosing information which would probably uncover the identity of Source A. Channel 4 refused to comply with the orders on the ground that to do so would expose Source A to almost certain death and it was then committed for contempt of court. It attempted to rely on the public interest provision of Schedule 7 in arguing that it was in the public interest for the identity of Source A to be protected but this was rejected on the following grounds. Channel 4 should not have given an unqualified assurance of protection to the source even though had it not done so the programme could probably not have been made, because so doing was likely to lead to flouting of the provisions of the Prevention of Terrorism Act. Thus giving such assurances could inevitably undermine the rule of law and therefore, it was held, help to achieve the very result that the terrorists in Northern Ireland were seeking to bring about. Channel 4 was therefore fined for non-compliance with the orders. In determining the amount of the fine it was borne in mind that the defendants might not have appreciated the dangers of giving an unqualified assurance but a warning was given that this consideration would be unlikely to influence courts in future cases of this nature.

It may be argued that this ruling fails to accord sufficient weight to the public interest in the protection of journalistic sources in order to allow the media to fulfil its role of informing the public. The comment that the assurances given to Source A as a necessary precondition to publication of this material would undermine the rule of law, ignores the possibility that undermining of the rule of law might be most likely to flow from the behaviour alleged in the programme: it might appear that nothing would be more likely to undermine the rule of law than collusion between state security forces and terrorists. The decision not to impose a rolling fine on Channel 4 or make a sequestration order may be welcomed in the interests of press freedom but it is clear that such indulgence may be refused in future, thereby creating a significant curb on investigative journalism. Schedule 7 para 3(5) as currently interpreted may therefore also be incompatible with Article 10.

---

133 (1992) *The Times*, 14 September.

CHAPTER FIVE

RESTRAINING FREEDOM OF EXPRESSION ON MORAL AND RELIGIOUS GROUNDS: CENSORSHIP, LICENSING AND REGULATION OF FILM AND BROADCASTING

1 LAW AND PORNOGRAPHY: THEORETICAL CONSIDERATIONS

The question as to how far sexually explicit speech deserves the same protection as other forms of expression and if it does not, how far and for what reasons it should be suppressed, has as Barendt notes, '... almost certainly elicited more academic commentary than any other [free speech] topic'.[1] As striking as the amount of writing on the subject, is the failure by academics of different persuasions to reach a consensus view. Thus, for example, A Simpson, a former member of the Williams Committee appointed in 1977 to review obscenity law, recalls that the law certainly did not represent such a consensus: 'Before, during and after the Committee sat, the chorus of abuse against the law continued; virtually everyone claimed that it was unworkable.'[2] In a similar vein, conservatives,[3] liberals[4] and feminists[5] have all attacked the Committee's findings and all for different reasons. In addition, even to speak of 'feminist' and 'liberal' positions necessitates a conscious simplification, because these two opposing positions, at first sight monolithic, are in fact riven by internal debate; in particular, the feminist camp displays a conspicuous lack of unanimity.[6] Nevertheless, an attempt will be made, in what follows, to outline briefly the 'core' of each stance and evaluate the strength of their arguments, both against each other and directly on the subject of the permissibility of censorship in this area.

---

1 *Freedom of Speech*, 1987, p 245.
2 Simpson, AWB, *Pornography and Politics: the Williams Committee in Retrospect*, 1983, p 80.
3 See eg the comments of Mary Whitehouse in the *Sunday Times* that as a result of the Committee's report '... we are going from a quicksand into ... a very, very mucky quagmire ...' quoted in Simpson, *Pornography and Politics, op cit* p 44; he also quotes a *Daily Telegraph* leader which criticised the 'some would say excessively liberal principle' it endorsed, *op cit* p 45.
4 See eg the detailed analysis in Dworkin, R, 'Do We Have a Right to Pornography?' in *A Matter of Principle*, 1985, in which he broadly endorses the Committee's conclusions but argues that these cannot be supported by the arguments they deployed.
5 The whole approach of the feminists is hostile to the broadly liberal stance adopted by the Committee; see for example Brownmiller, S, *Against Our Will*, 1975, where it is asserted that all previous value systems, including the liberal tradition, have worked against the interests of women. For explicit criticism of the Committee by a more moderate feminist see Eckersley, R, 'Whither the Feminist Campaign?: An Evaluation of Feminist Critiques of Pornography', 15 *Int J Soc of Law* 149. Eckersley dismisses Williams as having 'simply fail[ed] to register the feminist objection' (p 174).
6 For comments on the divisions in the feminist critique of pornography see Eckersley, *ibid*. See also Lacey, N, 93 *Journal of Law and Society* 93.

The conservative position

The conservative position, which in the popular consciousness is probably most associated with Mary Whitehouse, finds its academic and somewhat more abstract exposition in Lord Devlin's work, *The Enforcement of Morals*, 1965. In essence, Devlin's view is that since a shared set of basic moral values are essential to society, it is as justified in protecting itself against attacks on these values (such as that mounted by pornography) as it is in protecting itself against any other phenomena which threaten its basic existence, such as violent public disorder. On this thesis, moral corruption of the individual is to be prevented in order to ensure the ultimate survival of society. By contrast, Whitehouse's concerns are presumably more with damage to individuals *per se*, a position which, as argued below, appears to reflect that taken by the case law in this area. Devlin's position, by contrast, is clearly not compatible with most existing UK law:[7] it could neither support nor even account for the existence of the public good defence in s 4 of the Obscene Publications Act 1959[8] or indeed any similar defence: it would appear somewhat absurd to argue that material which threatened the very survival of society should be allowed to circulate freely on the grounds that it was somehow also in the public good.[9]

Devlin's position also appears to have been placed in doubt on the theoretical level by Hart's incisive critique.[10] Briefly, Hart's objections are as follows: on the more favourable reading of Devlin's position, he is not assuming but trying to *establish the truth* of the proposition that a shared set of moral standards (going on Devlin's account far beyond simple prohibitions on violence, theft, etc) is an essential attribute of society. If this is the case, argues Hart, Devlin fails to establish the proposition for the simple reason that he offers no empirical evidence to support it. This leads one, Hart continues, to the suspicion that Devlin actually *assumes* the truth of the proposition and thus builds his theory on a tautology: having defined society as a system of shared beliefs he then concludes, with perfect logic but some futility, that if those shared beliefs change radically or unanimity is lost, the society has disintegrated. Devlin's position, therefore does not strike one as particularly strong.

---

7   It may find reflection in some of the more obscure common law offences such as conspiracy to corrupt public morals and outraging public decency. The Lords in *Knuller v DPP* [1973] AC 435; [1972] 3 WLR 143; (1972) 56 Cr App R 633, HL, a much criticised decision, arguably gave some support to the Devlin thesis. For discussion of the decision see below p 202.

8   For discussion of the defence see below pp 194–96.

9   Under the 1959 Act, the defence of public good only comes into play once it has been decided that the material is likely to deprave and corrupt: *Penguin Books* [1961] Crim LR 176 (the *Lady Chatterley's Lover* trial). See below pp 194–96.

10 For a summary of Hart's critique see 'Social Solidarity and the Enforcement of Morality' in *Essays in Jurisprudence and Philosophy*, 1983.

The liberal position

The liberal position on pornography is broadly united around general opposition to censorship in the absence of clear evidence of a concrete harm caused by its free availability.[11] However, unanimity does not exist as to the rationales for free speech most applicable to defending a liberty to read or view pornographic material. There is general agreement that Meiklejohn's argument from participation in democracy[12] is of little relevance; as Dworkin caustically remarks, 'No one is denied an equal voice in the political process ... when he is forbidden to circulate photographs of genitals to the public at large'.[13]

A variant of Mill's argument from truth[14] was avowedly the free speech justification adopted by the William's Committee convened in 1979 to report on obscenity; although they expressed some scepticism at Mill's perhaps rather naive conviction that in a *laissez faire* market of ideas, truth would always win out,[15] they endorsed the main thrust of his theory. Interference with the free flow of ideas and artistic endeavour was unacceptable since it amounted to ruling out in advance possible modes of human development, before it was known whether or not they would be desirable or necessary. Since they also reached the conclusion that '... no one has invented or in our opinion *could* invent, an instrument that would suppress only [worthless pornography] and could not be turned against something ... of [possibly] a more creative kind',[16] they concluded that this risk of suppressing worthwhile creative art ruled out censorship of the written word. (They regarded standard photographic pornography as not expressing anything that could be regarded as an 'idea' and so as unprotected by the argument from truth.)

Ronald Dworkin has mounted a sustained attack on this rationale;[17] it rests, he contends, on the instrumental justification that allowing the free circulation of ideas is necessary to enable individuals to make intelligent and informed choices about how they want to lead their lives and then flourish in them. He finds that such an argument is unable to support its own conclusion against censorship; for, he urges, it must be accepted that allowing the free availability of pornography will 'sharply limit' the ability of some (perhaps the majority) to shape their cultural understanding of sexuality in a way they

---

11 For a brief discussion of the possible link between pornography and the commission of sexual offences see below p 188.
12 See above p 140 and note 18.
13 Dworkin, R, 'Do We Have a Right to Pornography?', *op cit* p 336.
14 See above pp 138–39.
15 *Report of the Committee on Obscenity and Film Censorship* (Williams Committee) Cmnd 7772 of 1979, Chap 5, 5.20.
16 *Op cit* para 5.24.
17 Dworkin, R, 'Do We Have a Right to Pornography?'.

think best – a way in which sexuality has dignity and beauty. His argument appears to conclude that the justification from self-development does not argue conclusively against censorship, because of the plausible case that forbidding some pornography will for many people greatly assist in their self-development. Dworkin is surely correct when he concludes that not self-development but the straightforward argument from *moral autonomy* amounts to the strongest case against censorship in this area. This argument simply points out that judging for an individual what will and will not be beneficial for him or her to read represents a clear invasion of the strong individual right to decide moral issues concerned with one's own life for oneself.[18] Such an invasion could therefore only be justified if a serious risk of substantial damage to the concrete well-being of society was shown.[19] Since the law does not posit such a risk, censorship is unacceptable. Whether this argument also provides a convincing answer to the radical feminist objections to free access to pornography will be considered below; this position must first be sketched out.

It should finally be noted that liberals are willing to support restrictions on the outlets and public display of pornography[20] on the grounds that such restrictions do not necessarily spring from contempt for those who read pornography but may simply reflect the genuine and personal aesthetic preferences of those who would rather not have to suffer the continual and ugly spectacle of publicly displayed pornography.[21]

The radical feminist position

The views of feminist writers on the harms pornography does, on the justifications offered for allowing its free availability and on what, if anything, the law should do about it are many and varied.[22] However, the radical

---

18 See Chap 1 above pp 5–6.
19 It is submitted that neither of the other two justifications for abrogating speech (described in Chap 1 pp 11–13) are applicable here. But see below p 188 for consideration of the possible link between pornography and sexual offences.
20 Such as, for example, the recommendations of the Williams Committee; see their 'Summary of Our Proposals' above note 15.
21 See Dworkin, 'Do We Have a Right to Pornography?', *op cit* pp 355–58, where he broadly endorses the Williams Committee's proposals.
22 For feminist writers who take a different stance on pornography from that broadly examined here, see any of the following: the chapters on pornography in *Smart, Feminism and the Power of Law*, 1989, in which the author expresses distrust of using the law to control pornography; Rhode, *Justice and Gender*, 1989, in which the extent to which feminism has framed a puritanical ideology of sexuality and pornography is deplored: it is argued that women who find explicit depictions of eg bondage or anonymous sex don't 'need more sexual shame, guilt and hypocrisy, this time served up as feminism'. See also Jackson, E, 'Catherine MacKinnon and Feminist Jurisprudence: A Critical Appraisal' (1992) *JLS*, pp 195–213 for a moderate critique particularly of MacKinnon's views on the impossibility of non-coercive heterosexual activity in contemporary society.

feminist position on the possibility of legal control of pornography is generally equated with the views of Catherine MacKinnon and Andrea Dworkin, who framed an Indianapolis Ordinance giving rise to civil liability for trafficking in pornography or forcing it upon unwilling recipients; its constitutionality was successfully challenged on the grounds of incompatibility with the First Amendment.[23] The essence of this variant of feminist thought is that while pornography is regarded as causing harm to some individual women, by causing some individual men to perpetrate rape, battery and sexual abuse,[24] pornography causes a far more subtle and all-pervasive harm to all women. It is on the latter argument that the remainder of the discussion will concentrate.

In some of their more terse, dramatic statements, such as 'Pornography is violence against women',[25] and 'We define pornography as a practice of sex discrimination',[26] it sounds as if MacKinnon and A Dworkin regard the very existence of pornography as a concrete harm to women which goes far beyond mere offence and yet is not a physical harm. However, in the more precise explanations they offer, it seems clear that the harm is caused through the effect it has on men's view of women: 'Men treat women as who they see women as being. Pornography constructs who that is.' In other words, the argument does remain, as R Dworkin claims, 'a causal one'.[27] At this point, having posited a link between pornography and the way men treat women, the explanation draws in the more general radical feminist thesis that men have near total power over women and that consequently, 'the way men see women defines who women can be'.[28] Elsewhere, MacKinnon explains that this power is generated by the fact that men have managed to establish the total 'privileging' of their interests and perceptions and the concomitant complete subordination of women and then passed this off as reality or 'just the way things are'. MacKinnon calls the resulting illusion 'metaphysically nearly perfect'.[29] Several more moderate feminists have pointed out[30] that this view places feminism in the bizarre position of having to deny the possibility of its own existence because it entails assuming that all available modes of thought and perception are male, although masquerading as

---

23 For the first instance decision, see *American Booksellers Assoc, etc v Hudnitt III, Mayor, City of Indianapolis et al* 598 F Supp 1316. For the (unsuccessful) appeal see 771 F 2d 323.
24 See eg MacKinnon, *Feminism Unmodified*, pp 184–91.
25 The basic thesis of Dworkin's, A, *Pornography: Men Possessing Women*, 1979, quoted in Simpson, *Pornography and Politics, op cit* p 71.
26 MacKinnon, *op cit* p 175. The quotation given refers specifically to the Indianapolis ordinance but equally summarises MacKinnon's analysis of pornography.
27 Dworkin, R, 'Liberty and Pornography', *The New York Review of Books*, 15 August 1991, p 12.
28 MacKinnon, *op cit* p 172.
29 See 'Feminism, Marxism, Method and the State' in Bartlett and Kennedy, eds, *Feminist Legal Theory*, 1991, p 182.
30 See eg Sandra Harding's introduction to MacKinnon's 'Feminism, Marxism, Method and the State' in Harding, *Feminism and Methodology*, 1987.

neutral. If this were true, it is hard to see how women could even come to realise that they were oppressed, let alone frame proposals for affirmative action to free themselves from male dominance. MacKinnon has indeed asserted that 'Feminism affirms women's point of view by ... explaining its impossibility',[31] but since MacKinnon herself has in fact somehow managed to construct a substantive and highly influential feminist point of view – including the analysis of pornography under consideration – this reply seems rather unconvincing. It might be thought at this point that since acceptance of the radical feminist thesis on pornography is apparently only possible if one also accepts a metaphysical theory which seems both to deny its own existence and to involve acceptance of the most comprehensive conspiracy theory ever devised, the thesis can be summarily dismissed.

This, it is submitted, would be premature. The most significant feminist point with respect to pornography is the effect it is said to have on men's view of women and therefore on the way they treat them. One does not have to accept the general radical feminist thesis in order to give *some* consideration to the proposition that pornography, through the effect it has on men, oppresses women. Consequently, the discussion will now turn to considering whether the feminist thesis can still provide a justification for restrictions on the freedom to consume pornography even if the notion of total female subordination is rejected.

The oppression of women caused by pornography is claimed to manifest itself in the following three distinct ways. First, women are discriminated against, sexually harassed and physically assaulted in all walks of life; this constitutes a denial of their civil right to equality. Secondly, women are denied their positive liberty, their right to equal participation in the political process because of the image in men's minds constructed by pornography which 'strips and devastates women of credibility,'[32] and consequently prevents women's contributions from being taken seriously. Finally, pornography 'silences' women – even their negative ability to speak is denied because they are not seen as fully human agents but rather as dehumanised creatures who 'desperately want to be bound, battered, tortured, humiliated and killed'.[33] The argument that the state should therefore seek to ban pornography on the basis of furtherance of equality just as it seeks to outlaw discrimination in employment is developed in *Only Words*.[34]

---

31 MacKinnon, *Feminist Legal Theory*, p 181.

32 MacKinnon, *Feminism Unmodified, op cit* p 193.

33 MacKinnon, *op cit* p 172. *Cf* Andrea Dworkin's description of the view that rape law evinces of women as one in which rape is not really against a woman's will, 'because what she wants underneath is to have anything done to her that violates or humiliates or hurts her': *Pornography: Men Possessing Women*, 1979.

34 MacKinnon, C, 1993. For criticism of the notion that banning pornography should be viewed as an aspect of the furtherance of equality, see Sadurski, W, 'On "Seeing Speech through an Equality Lens": A Critique of Egalitarian Arguments for Suppression of Hate Speech and Pornography' (1996) 16(4) *OJLS* 713.

Two points may be made in response to the above. First, this thesis attributes to men a uniformly passive and receptive attitude to all pornographic images.[35] Nowhere in a long essay on pornography[36] does MacKinnon appear to advert to the possibility that many men may completely reject the 'message' of violent misogynistic pornography, even though some may be aroused by it. Her theory thus in effect amounts to a profound refusal to recognise the immense difference which men's backgrounds, education and life experiences will have on their responses,[37] and more generally, the enormous variety of human responses to any given phenomena which will be found even amongst those of similar backgrounds; ultimately her theory denies (male) free will and with it men's individual voices.[38]

The second point is that if one leaves aside the extreme idea of the total control of men over women described above, it then becomes impossible to accept the immense influence that is attributed to the consumption of pornography. The idea, for example, that pornography silences women in all walks of life remains quite simply, 'strikingly implausible'[39] perhaps precisely *because* it is so eloquently expressed and it is hard to take seriously the notion that pornography denies women the right to participate in political life. One could only accept such arguments if one regarded women as defined completely by the images of pornography; as has been seen, that argument in turn could only have force if one first accepted that men's view of women is almost wholly constructed by pornography and then could agree to the assertion that men's view of women is all that women are. The impossibility of accepting such counter-intuitive propositions means, it is submitted, that the radical feminist argument does not convincingly establish that the availability of pornography represents or causes actual infringements of the rights of women. In strict liberal theory therefore, the argument from moral autonomy would in the absence of competing individual rights require that the choice as to which kinds of explicit literature to read and which to shun, remains properly with the individual. However, a number of comments may be made as to this finding. First, in contrast to many other types of speech, we have found that the only convincing argument for free speech in this area rests upon the interest in moral autonomy, unbolstered by other free speech justifications. Secondly, it seems self-evident that some invasions of autonomy

---

35 A Dworkin attributes a similarly monolithic character to men; consider for example the following description of the male sex. 'Terror issues forth from the male; illuminates his essential nature and his basic purpose' (*op cit* p 74).
36 MacKinnon, *op cit* Chap 14.
37 For criticism of this characteristic failing in MacKinnon's work generally, see Jackson, E, note 22 above.
38 An ironic point, since MacKinnon often talks of men 'silencing' women.
39 Dworkin, R, 'Do We Have a Right to Pornography?', *op cit* p 14; Rhode also asks how, if women are silenced by pornography, a small group of feminists managed to mount a challenge to some of the most cherished principles of American constitutionalism and one of its most successful entertainment industries, Rhode, *Justice and Gender*.

– those which interfere with choices which go to the core of the individual's identity – must be more grave than invasions with respect to more peripheral areas. Interference with the individual's choice to view violent misogynistic pornographic films with no pretension to artistic expression is arguably less of an infringement of his autonomy than, say, interfering with the right of the individual to have homosexual relations. If this argument is accepted, it follows that the autonomy interest here is comparatively weak.

These two points, taken together, would suggest that the total case for protecting inartistic violent pornography is not a particularly strong one. This case must then be balanced against the risk that there may possibly be a link between pornography and the commission of sexual offences. The argument as to this link is still ongoing and it is submitted that a proper evaluation of the evidence in this area falls within the ambit of the social sciences rather than a study of civil liberties. *Some* evidence has been produced of a link, though this evidence is disputed by other studies;[40] what is clear is that there may be said to be a chance of a risk that pornography contributes towards the motivation of sex offenders. It is submitted that until a consensus on the evidential question emerges, the law is entitled, given the relative weakness of the argument for protecting violent hard core pornography, to take a pragmatic stance and allow narrow and selective censorship of at least violent films, subject to an artistic merits defence, rather than insist that pornography should be unrestricted until the hypothesised link with sex offences has been established beyond reasonable doubt. Further, the case for withdrawal of restrictions must also be balanced against the possibility that while a particular group of men *may* be influenced by pornography towards the commission of sexual offences, a further group may also be influenced by it towards psychologically damaging treatment of women falling short of any criminal offence. If the link discussed above were established, this further argument would come into play since it would seem strange if pornography could have a highly significant influence on one group of men but none at all on any other. Thus, this point supports the pragmatic stance advocated above although it falls well short of accepting the general radical feminist position.

As a matter of interest it is worth considering what the position would be if radical feminists scholars could somehow establish that pornography really did construct the social reality of women's identity. How would the feminist argument fare in competition with the liberal arguments for free speech? In the case of the three instrumental justifications, the arguments from

---

40 Evidence *for* a causal link is quoted in MacKinnon, *Feminism Unmodified* pp 184–91, while Dworkin, R, cites a recent UK study which finds against such a link: Cumberbatch, G and Howitt, D, *A Measure of Uncertainty – the Effects of the Mass Media*, 1989. The findings of this latter study were published in the *Daily Telegraph*, 23 December 1990. Eckersley discusses the issue, above note 5 *op cit* pp 161–63. See also *Pornography: Women, Violence and Civil Liberties*, Itzen, C, ed, 1993, which puts forward a body of evidence supporting a causal link.

Restraining Freedom of Expression on Moral and Religious Grounds

democracy, truth and self-development,[41] the feminist thesis would be able to demonstrate how in the case of pornography, each argues for restraint on speech. They would argue that free circulation of pornography hinders, even prevents women's participation in the democratic process; it assists not in finding the truth but in constructing false and all-pervading images of women; it does *not* assist in the healthy development of those who take advantage of its free availability: rather they become rapists, abusers, misogynists.

The one liberal defence of free speech not *explicitly* addressed by the feminist argument is the argument from moral autonomy, which it was suggested above[42] provides the only arguable defence of the right to choose to read pornography. How would *this* argument fare if it was shown that the basic rights to equality, political participation and speech were in reality denied to all women by the consumption of pornography? Ronald Dworkin has considered this hypothetical position, in which he does not accept that pornography causes individual men to rape and assault women but accepts the remainder of the feminist claims. One might consider that he would conclude that the massive infringements of women's strong individual rights and the concomitant loss of their moral autonomy would clearly override the comparatively minor invasions of men's free speech and autonomy represented by restrictions on pornography. Somewhat surprisingly, however, Dworkin argues that even if it were the case that the posited harms were actually visited upon all women by pornography, *still* this would provide no justification for restraining its free availability.[43] Such a view places the right to consume hard core pornography over the rights of half the population to be treated with dignity and respect, to equal participation in democratic government and to free speech itself. Such a conclusion represents, it is submitted, a complete betrayal of the premise on which Dworkin's whole theory of rights is based, namely the overriding duty of the state to treat all its citizens with equal concern and respect.

2 RESTRAINING SPEECH ON MORAL GROUNDS

That the above conclusions on pornography are not in general accepted by states, is revealed by the fact that almost all Bills or Charters of Rights contain an exception to the free speech clause allowing restraint on freedom of speech on the ground of protection of morality. The justification is the harm to be guarded against which seems to include three possibilities: the corruption of persons, particularly the more vulnerable; the shock or outrage caused by

---

41 See the Introduction to Part II, above pp 137–43.
42 See p 184.
43 'Do We Have a Right to Pornography?', *op cit* p 15.

public displays of certain material and the commission of sex crimes.[44] The development of UK law has been based on the avoidance of the first two possibilities mentioned and on those grounds the public display of certain publications can be regulated, while others can be prohibited entirely, either by punishment of those responsible after publication or by being suppressed or censored before publication.

The type of restraint used tends to depend on the type of publication in question because it seems to be accepted that the harm which may be caused will vary from medium to medium. Thus printed matter, including magazines, newspapers and books, is not subject to censorship before publication but punishment is available afterwards if indecent or corrupting material is published. Books are less likely to be punished than magazines because it is thought that something which has a visual impact is more likely to cause harm. Thus films and broadcasts are censored due to their visual nature and are also subject to punishment. The theatre, however, is in an odd position; it has not been censored since 1968 despite its visual impact. Possibly this may be due to the idea that theatre audiences are more sophisticated and less likely to be affected by what they have seen than cinema audiences.

Statutory obscenity[45]

Obscenity law operates as a subsequent restraint and is largely used in relation to books, magazines and other printed material, although theoretically it could be used against broadcasts, films or videos.[46] The harm sought to be prevented is a corrupting effect on an individual. In other words, it is thought that an individual will undergo a change for the worse after encountering the material in question. The rationale of the law is thus overtly paternalistic. Of course, if all material which might appear capable of causing corruption were suppressed, a severe infringement of freedom of speech would occur. Thus, the statute which largely governs this area – the Obscene Publications Act 1959 – takes the stance that in preventing material which may deprave and corrupt a line must be drawn between erotic literature and the truly obscene on the basis that hard core pornography does not deserve

---

[44] These were the key notions of harm considered by the Williams Committee appointed in 1977 to review obscenity and indecency law (Williams Report (1979) Cmnd 7772). Broadly speaking, the Committee endorsed regulation of pornography with a view to preventing the second of the harms mentioned.

[45] See generally: O'Higgins, P, *Censorship in Britain*, 1972; Robertson, G, *Obscenity*, 1979, and *Media Law* (with Nichol, AGL), 1992, Chap 3; MacMillan, PR, *Censorship and Public Morality*, 1983. Barendt, E, *Media Law*, 1993; Baker, R, *Media Law*, 1995; Carey, P, *Media Law*, 1996; Feldman, D, *Civil Liberties in England and Wales*, 1993, Chap 15; Bailey, SH, Harris, DJ and Jones, BL, *Civil Liberties: Cases and Materials*, 4th edn, 1995, Chap 5; Itzen, C, ed, *Pornography: Women, Violence and Civil Liberties*, 1993; MacKinnon, C, *Only Words*, 1993.

[46] In *AG's Reference No 5 of 1980* [1980] 3 All ER 816, CA it was found that a video constituted an article for the purposes of the 1959 Act.

special protection.[47] This echoes the approach in America where this form of pornography is not defined as 'speech' because it is thought that the justification for the constitutional protection for freedom of speech does not apply.[48] In fact, oddly enough, this seems to mean that pornography receives less protection in the US than in the UK.

The idea of preventing corruption had informed the common law long before the 1959 Act; it sprang from the ruling in *Hicklin*.[49] Determining whether material would 'deprave and corrupt' was problematic, especially as it was unclear to whom the test should be applied. Two cases in 1954 showed the uncertainty of the law. In *Martin Secker and Warburg*[50] it was determined that the test applied to persons who might encounter the material in question. But at the same time in *Hutchinson*[51] the court held that the test should be applied to the most vulnerable person who might conceivably encounter the material and that the jury could therefore look at the effect it might have on a teenage girl. Moreover, the jury could find that something which could merely be termed shocking could deprave and corrupt.

The 1959 Act was passed in an attempt to clear up some of this uncertainty although it failed to lay down a test for the meaning of the term 'deprave and corrupt'. The *actus reus* of the offence involves the publication for gain (s 2(1)) or having for such publication (s 1(2) of the Obscene Publications Act 1964) an article which tends, taken as a whole, (or where it comprises two or more distinct items the effect of one of the items) to deprave and corrupt a significant proportion of those likely to see or hear it (s 1(1)). This is a crime of strict liability: there is no need to show an intention to deprave and corrupt, merely an intention to publish. Once it is shown that an article is obscene within the meaning of the Act, it will be irrelevant, following the ruling of the Court of Appeal in *Calder and Boyars*,[52] that the defendant's motivation could be characterised as pure or noble. The Act does not cover live performances on stage which fall within the similarly worded Theatres Act 1968.

'Deprave and corrupt'

This test could be applied to any material which might corrupt; it is clear from the ruling in *Calder (John) Publishing v Powell*[53] that it is not confined to

---

47 See for argument on this point Dworkin, R, 'Is There a Right to Pornography?' (1981) 1 *Ox JLS* 177.
48 *Miller v California* 413 US 15 (1973). It should be noted that under the argument from moral autonomy it is irrelevant whether the material concerned is classified as 'speech' or not.
49 (1868) 3 QB 360.
50 [1954] 2 All ER 683; [1954] 1 WLR 1138.
51 (1954), unreported. For an account of the proceedings see St John Stevas, N, *Obscenity and the Law*, 1956, p 116.
52 [1969] 1 QB 151; [1968] 3 WLR 974; [1968] 3 All ER 644; (1968) 52 Cr App R 706.
53 [1965] 1 QB 159.

descriptions or representations of sexual matters and it could therefore be applied to a disturbing book on the drug-taking life of a junkie. This ruling was followed in *Skirving*[54] which concerned a pamphlet on the means of taking cocaine in order to obtain maximum effect. In all instances the test for obscenity should not be applied to the type of behaviour advocated or described in the article in question but to the article itself. Thus, in *Skirving* the question to be asked was not whether taking cocaine would deprave and corrupt but whether the pamphlet itself would.

This test is hard to explain to a jury and uncertain of meaning with the result that directions such as the following have been given: '... obscenity, members of the jury, is like an elephant; you can't define it but you know it when you see it.'[55] However, it is clear from the ruling of the Court of Appeal in *Anderson*[56] that the effect in question must be more than mere shock. The trial judge had directed the jury that the test connoted that which was repulsive, loathsome or filthy. This explanation was clearly defective since it would have merged the concepts of indecency and obscenity and it was rejected by the Court of Appeal on the basis that it would dilute the test for obscenity which, it was said, must connote the prospect of moral harm, not just shock. The conviction under the Act was therefore overturned due to the misdirection. The House of Lords in *Knuller v DPP*[57] considered the word 'corrupt' and found that it denoted a publication which produced 'real social evil' – going beyond immoral suggestions or persuasion. This was quite a strict test but it was qualified by the House of Lords in *DPP v Whyte*.[58] The owners of a bookshop which sold pornographic material were prosecuted. Most of the customers were old men who had encountered the material on previous occasions and this gave rise to two difficulties. First, the old men were unlikely to engage in anti-social sexual behaviour and therefore the meaning of 'corrupt' had to be modified if it was to extend to cover the effect on them of the material: it was found that it meant creating a depraved effect on the mind which need not actually issue forth in any particular sexual behaviour. Secondly, it was suggested that the old men were already corrupt and therefore would not be affected by the material. However, it was held that corruption did not connote a once-only process: persons could be 'recorrupted' and on this basis a conviction was obtained. (Interestingly, this finding suggests that there is a presumption that the 'deprave and corrupt' test is of universal application: no person or group of persons can be excluded in principle from its ambit. In this sense it differs from the test as put forward

---

54 [1985] QB 819.
55 Robertson, *Obscenity*, p 45.
56 [1972] 1 QB 304.
57 [1973] AC 435; [1972] 3 WLR 143; (1972) 56 Cr App R 633, HL.
58 [1972] AC 849; [1972] 3 All ER 12, HL.

in *Hicklin;* that test applied only to those whose minds were open to immoral influences). The test will not be satisfied if the material in question causes feelings of revulsion from the immorality portrayed. This theory, known as the 'aversion theory', derives from *Calder and Boyars* which concerned *Last Exit from Brooklyn*; it was found that the horrific pictures it painted of homosexuality and drug-taking in New York would be more likely to discourage than encourage such behaviour.[59]

The 'deprave and corrupt' test must be applied to those likely to see or hear the material in question and therefore the concept of relative obscenity is imported into the Act. In other words, the obscenity or otherwise of material cannot be determined merely by its consideration or analysis but, rather, will depend on the character of the consumer and in this sense the test presents a contrast with German obscenity law which absolutely prohibits hard core pornography although soft core material is quite freely available.[60] It was held in *DPP v Whyte*[61] that in order to make a determination as to the type of consumer in question the court could receive information as to the nature of the relevant area, the type of shop and the class of people frequenting it. The jury must consider the likely reader in order to determine whether the material would deprave and corrupt him or her rather than considering the most vulnerable conceivable reader. In *Penguin Books*,[62] which concerned the prosecution of *Lady Chatterley's Lover*, the selling price of the book was taken into account and the fact that being in paperback it would reach a mass audience.

The jury has to consider whether the article would be likely to deprave and corrupt a *significant proportion* of those likely to encounter it. It was determined in *Calder and Boyars*[63] that the jury must determine what is meant by a 'significant proportion' and this was approved in *DPP v Whyte*, Lord Cross explaining that 'a significant proportion of a class means a part which is not numerically negligible but which may be much less than half'. This formulation was adopted in order to prevent sellers of pornographic material claiming that most of their customers would be unlikely to be corrupted by it. The effect of the article as a whole on persons likely to encounter it should be considered, not merely the effect of specific passages of a particularly explicit nature. However, in *Anderson*[64] it was made clear that where the article consists of a number of items, each item must be considered in isolation from

---

59 Above note 52. For comment see Robertson, *Obscenity*, pp 50–53.
60 Section 184(3) of the German Criminal Code.
61 [1972] AC 849; [1972] 3 All ER 12, HL.
62 [1961] *Crim LR* 176; see Rolph, CH, *The Trial of Lady Chatterley*, 1961.
63 [1969] 1 QB 151.
64 [1972] 1 QB 304.

the others. Thus, a magazine which is on the whole innocuous but contains one obscene item can be suppressed, although a novel could not be.

It may be reasonably straightforward to identify a group, of whom a significant proportion might encounter the material but it is unclear how it can then be determined that they would be likely to experience depravity and corruption as a result. The ruling in *Anderson* was to the effect that in sexual obscenity cases and normally in other obscenity cases, the defence cannot call expert evidence as to the effect that an article may have on its likely audience. Thus, the view taken in *DPP v A and BC Chewing Gum Ltd*[65] that such evidence would be admissible may be regarded as arising only due to the very specific circumstances of that case. However, it was decided in *Skirving*[66] that in cases concerned with alleged depravity and corruption arising due to factors other than the sexual nature of the material expert evidence will exceptionally, be admissible, although the evidence can only be as to the effects of the behaviour described in the material, not as to the likely effects of the material itself. Thus, generally, where the material deals with matters within their own experience, the jury will receive little help in applying the test. However, it seems clear that a jury will be able to take into account changing standards of morality ('the contemporary standards' test from *Calder and Boyars*) in considering what will deprave and corrupt. Therefore, the concept of obscenity is, at least theoretically, able to keep up-to-date. The application of these tests at the present time was seen in the trial for obscenity of the book *Inside Linda Lovelace*[67] which suggested that a prosecution brought against a book of any conceivable literary merit would be unlikely to succeed. Thus, in December 1991 the DPP refused to prosecute the Marquis de Sade's *Juliette*, even though it was concerned (fictionally) with the torture, rape and murder of women and children.

The defence of public good

This defence, which arises under s 4 of the 1959 Act (as amended by s 53 of the Criminal Law Act 1977) and s 3 of the Theatres Act 1968, was intended to afford recognition to artistic merit. Thus it may be seen as a highly significant step in the direction of freedom of speech, acknowledging the force of a variant of the free speech argument from truth which was also used by the Williams Committee.[68] Under the 1959 Act it is a defence to a finding that a publication is obscene if it can be shown that 'the publication of the article in question is justified as for the public good in that it is in the interests of

---

65 [1968] 1 QB 159.
66 [1985] QB 819.
67 For comment see (1976) *NLJ* 126. The prosecution failed.
68 See above p 183.

science, literature, art, learning or of other objects of general concern'. Under the 1968 Act the similarly worded defence which covers 'the interests of drama, opera, ballet or any other art or of literature or learning' is somewhat narrower as omitting the concluding general words. Under s 53(6) of the 1977 Act this narrower defence applies to films. Expert evidence will be admissible to prove that one of these possibilities can be established and it may include considering other works.

It was determined in *Penguin Books* in respect of *Lady Chatterley's Lover* that the jury should adopt a two-stage approach, asking first whether the article in question is obscene and if so, going on to consider whether the defendant has established the probability that its merits are so high as to outbalance its obscenity so that its publication is for the public good. The failure of the prosecution was seen as a turning point for literary freedom and the jury allowed it to be known that the second stage of the test afforded the basis on which the novel escaped suppression. In *DPP v Jordan*[69] the House of Lords approved this two-stage approach and the balancing of obscenity against literary or other merit.

In *DPP v Jordan* the attempt was made to widen the test. The main question was whether the articles in question – hard core pornography – could be justified under s 4 as being of psychotherapeutic value for persons of deviant sexuality in that the material might help to relieve their sexual tensions by way of sexual fantasies. It was argued that such material might provide a safety valve for such persons, which would divert them from anti-social activities and that such benefit could fall within the words 'other objects of general concern' deriving from s 4. The House of Lords, however, held that these words must be construed *ejusdem generis* with the preceding words 'art, literature learning, science'. As these words were unrelated to sexual benefit the general words which followed them could not be construed in the manner suggested. It was ruled that the jury must be satisfied that the matter in question made a contribution to a recognised field of culture or learning which could be assessed irrespective of the persons to whom it was distributed.

Although the test of public good has clearly afforded protection to freedom of expression in relation to publications of artistic merit, it has been criticised: it requires a jury to embark on the very difficult task of weighing a predicted change for the worse in the minds of the group of persons likely to encounter the article, against literary or other merit. Thus an effect or process must be imagined which, once established, must be measured against an intrinsic quality. Geoffrey Robertson has written: 'the balancing act is a logical nonsense [because it is not] logically possible to weigh such disparate

---

69 [1977] AC 699.

concepts as 'corruption' and 'literary merit'.[70] The test seems to create an almost complete paradox: it assumes that an individual can be corrupted, which suggests a stultifying effect on the mind and yet can also experience an elevating effect due to the merit of an article. However, such an interpretation of the test is open to two objections. First, a person could experience corruption in the sense that her moral standards might be lowered but she might retain a sense of literary or artistic appreciation. Secondly – and this might seem the more satisfactory interpretation – the *message* of the article and its general artistic impact (through, for example, its influence on other works which followed it) might be for the public good although some individuals who encountered it were corrupted. Thus the term 'publication' in s 4 must mean publication to the public at large, not only to those who encounter the article if the test is to be workable.[71]

It should be noted that, as discussed below, the defence can be avoided by bringing a charge of indecency at common law; as *Gibson*[72] demonstrated, the merits of an obscene object may, paradoxically, prevent its suppression while the merits of less offensive objects may not.

Forfeiture proceedings

Under s 3 of the 1959 Act magazines and other material, such as videos, can be seized by the police if it is suspected on reasonable grounds that they are obscene and have been kept for gain. No conviction is obtained; if found to be obscene the material is merely destroyed; no other punishment is imposed and therefore s 3 may operate at a low level of visibility. Seizure may mean that the safeguards provided by the Act can be bypassed: consideration is not given to the possible literary merits of such material because the public good defence is not taken into account in issuing the seizure warrant. The merit of an article can be taken into account in the forfeiture hearing in determining whether it out-balances its obscenity but there is not much evidence that magistrates take a very rigorous approach to making such a determination. They do not need to read every item but need only look at samples selected by the police[73] and seem in any event more ready than a jury to find that an item is obscene.[74] It seems therefore that the protection afforded by the 1959 Act to

---

70 Robertson, *Obscenity*, p 164.
71 The House of Lords in *Jordan* [1977] AC 699 appeared to take this view. See also Robertson, *Obscenity*, on the point (pp 168–69).
72 [1990] 2 QB 619; [1991] 1 All ER 439; [1990] 3 WLR 595, CA.
73 *Crown Court at Snaresbrook, ex parte Metropolitan Police Comr* (1984) 148 JP 449.
74 Bailey, Harris and Jones note (p 328) that comment arose when forfeiture proceedings of an edition of the magazine *Men Only* coincided with the jury acquittal of the editors of *Nasty Tales* of the offence under s 2 ((1973) 127 JPN 82). Robertson argues (*Obscenity*, p 96) that as the hearing is before a tribunal which has already decided that the material is – at least – *prima facie* obscene, it is likely to have an appearance of unfairness. The bench may be unlikely to be convinced that in effect, it was wrong in the first place in issuing the summons.

freedom of speech may depend more on the exercise of discretion by the police as to the enforcement of s 3 or on the tolerance of magistrates rather than on the law itself. However, s 3 can be used only in respect of material which may be obscene rather than in relation to any form of pornography; it was held in *Darbo v DPP*[75] that a warrant issued under s 3 allowing officers to search for 'sexually explicit material' was bad on its face as such articles would fall within a much wider category of articles than those which could be called obscene.

Statutory obscenity and the protection of morals exception under Article 10(2)

It seems that the 1959 Act is broadly in harmony with Article 10 of the European Convention. In the *Handyside* case[76] the European Court of Human Rights had to consider the test of 'deprave and corrupt'. A book called *The Little Red Schoolbook*, which contained chapters on masturbation, sexual intercourse and abortion was prosecuted under the 1959 Act on the basis that it appeared to encourage early sexual intercourse. The publishers applied for a ruling under Article 10 to the European Commission. First, it was determined that the book fell within Article 10(1) since it could be characterised 'ideological obscenity' as opposed to pornography. This part of the ruling suggests that pure pornography may not fall within Article 10 at all. The court then considered the protection of morals provision under Article 10(2) – which might allow suppression of the book – in order to determine whether such suppression was necessary. It did not determine whether the protection of morals exception referred to the corruption of individuals or to an effect on the moral fabric of society. It was thought that the requirements of morals vary from time to time and from place to place and that the domestic authorities were therefore best placed to judge what was needed. The fact that the book was circulating freely in the rest of Europe was adjudged irrelevant to this issue. Thus, in finding that para 2 applied, the judgment accepted that domestic authorities would be allowed a wide margin of appreciation in attempting to secure the freedoms guaranteed under the Convention in this area, although this was not to be taken as implying that an unlimited discretion was granted. This stance was again taken in *Müller v Switzerland*[77] in respect of a conviction arising from the exhibition of explicit paintings: the fact that the paintings had been exhibited in other parts of Switzerland and abroad did not mean that their suppression could not amount to a pressing social need.

---

75 (1992) *The Times*, 4 July; [1992] *Crim LR* 56.
76 European Court HR, A.24; (1976) 1 EHRR 737.
77 (1991) 13 EHRR 212. See Chap 2 p 68.

It must be borne in mind that the scope of the domestic margin of appreciation is not the same in respect of all the aims listed in Article 10(2). The protection of morals would appear to be viewed as requiring a wide margin due to its subjective nature, in contrast with the protection of the authority of the judiciary which is seen as a more objective notion.[78] The uncertainty of the notion of the protection of morals appeared in the lack of a clearly discernible common European standard.

Statutory indecency[79]

The concept of indecency, as opposed to obscenity, is contained in certain statutes and also exists at common law. The idea of prohibiting indecency is to prevent *public displays* of offensive material. Such prohibition is aimed at protecting persons from the shock or offence occasioned by encountering certain material, rather than at preventing moral deterioration. Therefore, except perhaps in a very broad sense, it may be said not to be aimed at the protection of morals at all and so might not fall within that exception to Article 10. The general lowering of moral standards or attacks on the moral fabric of society must occur – if it is assumed that it is likely to occur at all – through the medium of individual persons who are affected by encountering obscene material;[80] it would seem therefore that the 'moral fabric of society' would be unaffected by material which only serves to shock. However, it might be very broadly argued on a conservative view that indecent material might have a corrupting effect if it was repeatedly encountered because it might lead at each encounter to less outrage as sensibilities became blunted.

If the material is not obscene and is either stored with a view to sale or offered for sale in a way that does not impinge on the general public, it will not attract liability. Indecency is easier to prove than obscenity because there is no defence of public good, there is no need to consider the whole article and there is no need to satisfy the difficult test of deprave and corrupt. Prosecuting authorities have taken note of these distinctions and have therefore tended at times to rely on the law against indecency where arguably the article in question could be said to be obscene.[81] It will be seen that the existence of these two strands of law has led to some anomalies.

---

78 See the judgment of the European Court of HR in the *Sunday Times* case (1979) 2 EHRR 245; discussed in Chap 3 pp 149–50.
79 See Robertson, *Obscenity*, 1979, Chap 7; Robertson, *Media Law*, pp 115–24.
80 For criticism of the view that preventing the lowering of the moral tone of society justifies censorship, see the introduction to this chapter p 182.
81 This trend is reflected in Lord Denning's comments in *GLC, ex parte Blackburn* [1976] 1 WLR 550 at 556.

Meaning of indecency

The test for indecency was discussed in *Knuller v DPP*;[82] it was determined by Lord Reid to be satisfied by material which creates outrage or utter disgust in 'ordinary decent-minded people'. This statement, coupled with the general tenor of Lord Reid's comments, suggested that the level of shock would have to be fairly high. In *GLC ex parte Blackburn*[83] Lord Denning approved the simple test of 'is this indecent?' since he considered that if jurors were asked the more complex question 'will it deprave and corrupt?' they would allow very offensive articles into circulation. However, Lord Bridge wondered whether asking whether something is shocking or disgusting could be a suitable test of criminality. Sir Robert Megarry has said that 'indecency' is too subjective and emotional a concept[84] to be workable as a legal test. It seems that the test is not confined to sexual material; Lord Reid in *Knuller* considered that 'indecency is not confined to sexual indecency'.[85] This is supported by the finding in *Gibson*[86] that the use of freeze-dried foetuses as earrings on a model of a head was indecent. Uncertainty arises as to whether the term 'indecency' denotes a relative concept: a concept which, like that of relative obscenity, depends on its context or on the nature of the audience or recipient. According to the ruling of the Court of Appeal in *Straker*[87] such considerations are irrelevant: indecency is an objective quality discoverable by examination in the same way that, for example, a substance might be discovered to be a certain chemical. However, *Wiggins v Field*[88] suggests otherwise; the ruling specifically demanded that the circumstances in which the alleged indecency occurred should be taken into account. A prosecution was brought in respect of a reading of Allen Ginsberg's poem 'America' on the basis of a charge of using indecent language in contravention of a local byelaw. The Divisional Court held that if the context was considered – this was the work of a recognised poet, read without any intention of causing offence – the charge of indecency could not be supported. This stance was taken by the Court of Appeal in *AG ex rel McWhirter v IBA*;[89] it was agreed that the film in question 'taken as a whole' was not offensive although a small percentage of it depicted indecent incidents. Thus it may be that the *Straker* ruling, to the effect that indecency may be treated as an objective concept, is

---

82 [1973] AC 435 at 457; [1972] 3 WLR 143; (1972) 56 Cr App R 633.
83 [1976] 3 All ER 184.
84 *A Second Miscellany at Law*, p 316.
85 [1973] AC 435 at p 458.
86 [1990] 2 QB 619; [1991] 1 All ER 439, CA.
87 [1965] *Crim LR* 239; this approach was affirmed by the Court of Appeal in *Stamford* [1972] 2 WLR 1055; [1972] 2 All ER 427.
88 [1968] *Crim LR* 50.
89 [1973] QB 629.

confined to cases arising under the Post Office Act 1953, but the point cannot yet be regarded as settled. However, it is clear that the notion of indecency will vary from generation to generation and that the jury will be expected to apply current standards.[90]

The variety of specific statutory offences

The word 'indecent' is contained in a number of statutes and bye laws. Therefore, only specific areas are covered but if no statute affects a particular area the gap may be filled by the common law. Taking an indecent photograph of a person under the age of 16 is prohibited under the Protection of Children Act 1978. Offensive displays fall under the Indecent Displays (Control) Act 1981, which covers public displays of anything capable of being displayed,[91] but is limited in its application; it does not apply to the theatre, cinema, broadcasting (which are covered by different provisions), museums, art galleries, local authority or Crown buildings (s 1(4)). Shops which display an adequate warning notice are exempted[92] as far as adults are concerned; thus, as will be seen below, art galleries are, anomalously, *more* constrained in their displays than sex shops, in that they will fall within the common law on indecency and will not be able to take advantage of this exception. Mailing of sexual literature is covered by s 11 of the Post Office Act 1953; sexual literature in luggage is covered by s 49 of the Customs and Excise Management Act 1979.

In the 1970s, customs officials interpreted the term 'indecency' widely; in 1976, for example, they seized and destroyed 114,000 books and magazines and 4,000 films. It also appeared that the test was being used in an arbitrary and indiscriminate manner. For example, in 1985 books ordered by the bookshop 'Gay's the Word' were impounded, including books by Oscar Wilde and Gore Vidal. The trial was about to commence but the proceedings were withdrawn because of the ruling of the European Court of Justice in *Conegate Ltd v Customs and Excise Commissioners*.[93] It was held under Articles 30 and 36 of the Treaty of Rome that Britain could not apply a more stringent test – indecency – to imported goods when the equivalent in terms of domestically produced ones could circulate freely because they were not obscene. Thus where obscenity or indecency existed as alternatives the easier test should not be used to favour domestic goods since that would amount to arbitrary discrimination on trade between Member States contrary to Article 36. Customs officers now apply this ruling but not just to EU imports because

---

90 *Shaw v DPP* [1962] AC 220, at 292. This approach was accepted in *Stamford* above note 87.
91 For discussion of the effect of the Act see (1982) *Stat LR* 31; (1981) 45 *MLR* 62; (1981) 132 *NLJ* 629.
92 Section 1(3)(b).
93 [1987] QB 254; [1986] 2 All ER 688. Figures quoted by Robertson, *Obscenity*, p 193.

it would be too impracticable to apply different tests to imports from different countries. This ruling has therefore resulted in a major relaxation on censorship. Hard core pornography is, however, still seized; this is justifiable under Article 36 because it would also be prohibited if disseminated internally under the Obscene Publications Act.

Anomalies have arisen from the dichotomy between the tests for indecency on the one hand and obscenity on the other in other contexts. In *Straker* obscenity charges which resulted in an acquittal were brought in respect of the sale of artistic nude studies. The defendant then sent the pictures by post to persons interested in photographic art and was prosecuted successfully under s 11 of the Post Office Act 1953. In other words, the mere fact that the articles happened to be transferred through the post meant that criminal liability could arise, although otherwise it could not have done so. The DPP has recognised the anomalies created by cases of this nature and therefore he indicated – in 1981 – that prosecutions under the Post Office Act would be confined to cases where the indecent material sent through the post was unsolicited.

Apart from statutes prohibiting the promulgation of indecent material in specific situations, the possibility also arises of using the Sexual Offences Act 1956 to prevent displays of indecency in stage plays and perhaps in the context of other live performances. A play, *The Romans in Britain*, which was staged in 1982 by the Royal National Theatre, included a depiction of the homosexual rape of a young druid priest by three Roman soldiers. Mary Whitehouse wanted to bring an action in respect of this scene but the Attorney General refused permission as required under s 8 of the Theatres Act. Under s 2 of the Act, liability at common law could not arise in respect of a stage performance. Therefore, Mary Whitehouse invoked s 13 of the Sexual Offences Act 1956 which proscribes the procurement by one male of an act of gross indecency on another. This was arguably fulfilled by the procurement by the male director of the commission of an act of gross indecency by one actor on another. Had a female director been in charge no prosecution would have been possible. It was determined on a preliminary ruling that *prima facie* liability might be established using this method.[94] At that point the prosecution was withdrawn; Mary Whitehouse had established the point in question and did not wish to take the risk that the prosecution would fail as it might have done on various grounds. In particular, it was uncertain whether it could be shown that any indecency took place: it was unclear whether the actor's penis or thumb was shown in the scene. The significance of this possibility should not be over-emphasised; nevertheless it clearly subverts the purpose of the Theatres Act which should therefore be amended to prohibit liability arising under other statutes.

---

94 *The Romans in Britain,* see [1982] PL 165–67.

Common law offences of indecency and obscenity

Prosecutions for conspiracy to corrupt morals can be brought at common law as can prosecutions for indecency. Thus common law indecency creates a much wider area of liability than is created under statute because the law is not confined to specific situations such as using the mail. In *Shaw v DPP*,[95] the House of Lords determined that the offence of conspiring to corrupt public morals existed on the basis that the law conferred a general discretion to punish immoral (not merely criminal) conduct which could injure the public. Thus any subject matter which could lead others astray – although not necessarily mounting to a criminal offence – could be the subject of a prosecution if two or more persons were involved. Lord Reid in his dissenting judgment argued that the decision offended against the principle that the criminal law should be certain; it would be very difficult to determine beforehand what a jury would consider to fall within the area of liability created. The DPP then used this form of liability in instances where the material in question appeared to fall outside the Obscene Publications Act or added a charge of conspiracy to corrupt public morals to a charge of obscenity as an alternative in case the obscenity charge failed. The decision in *Shaw* has been especially criticised on the basis that it left it unclear whether an agreement to commit adultery could amount to a criminal conspiracy.[96]

Despite such criticism the House of Lords confirmed the existence of the offence of conspiring to corrupt public morals and also the existence of the substantive offence of outraging public decency and conspiring to commit it in *Knuller v DPP*[97] which concerned publication of homosexual contact advertisements. The conviction on the latter count was, however, overturned because the trial judge had misdirected the jury as to the ingredients of the offence. The House of Lords ruled that the necessary 'public' element would be present even if the indecency was not immediately visible since it appeared on an inside page, so long as there was an express or implied invitation to penetrate the cover and partake of the lewd contents; therefore there must be a reference on the cover to the contents. Furthermore, the contents must be so offensive that the sense of decency of the public would be outraged by seeing them. Whether or not a member of the public *would* be so outraged, would be determined by reference to that section of the public likely to frequent the place where the publication in question was sold. In this respect, conspiracy to outrage public decency differs from conspiracy to corrupt public morals which requires that the public at large must be considered. The motive in offering the article will be irrelevant although it will be necessary to show that the defendant was aware both of the lewd nature of the material in question and that it was being placed on public sale.

---

95 [1962] AC 220; [1961] 2 WLR 897, HL; for comment see 24 *MLR* 626; (1964) 42 *Canadian Bar Review* 561.
96 See Robertson, *Obscenity*, p 215.
97 [1973] AC 435; [1972] 3 WLR 143; (1972) 56 Cr App R 633, HL.

Both these offences were preserved in s 5(3) of the Criminal Law Act 1977, and in *Gibson*[98] the Court of Appeal reaffirmed the ruling of the House of Lords in *Knuller* as to the ingredients of the offence of outraging public decency. The defendants were convicted of the offence after displaying in an art gallery a model of a human head with earrings made out of freeze-dried human foetuses of three to four months gestation. It may be noted that at first instance the jury was directed that they were entirely free to use their own standards in deciding whether the model was indecent. Argument on appeal centred on s 2(4) of the 1959 Act which provides that where a prosecution is brought in respect of an obscene article it must be considered within the Act, not at common law, 'where it is of the essence of the offence that the matter is obscene'. 'Obscene' could denote something which disgusted the public or something which had a tendency to corrupt; if it carried the first meaning the prosecution failed as there was no suggestion that the exhibition of the earrings had a tendency to corrupt. Moreover if the second, more restricted meaning were accepted, that would undermine the defence contained in s 4 of the Act which could be invoked if the material in question was, *inter alia*, of artistic worth. However, Lord Lane held that the words of s 1(1) were plain and clearly indicated that the *restricted* meaning of 'obscene' applied throughout the Act; he refused to depart from the normal canons of statutory construction.

If the defence argument on the meaning of obscene had been accepted, a greater number of publications would have fallen within the Obscene Publications Act and could have benefited from the s 4 defence, although this would also have meant extending the ambit of the Act, including the powers of seizure under s 3. As it is, the anomaly has been continued that the artistic merit of objects which more seriously breach normal moral standards – objects which may corrupt – can prevent their suppression while the merits of less offensive objects cannot. This anomaly should be addressed not by extending the meaning of obscenity but by introducing a defence of public good which would apply to common law indecency. A further anomaly arises due to the exclusion from the Indecent Displays (Control) Act 1981 of art galleries which, as noted above, are actually more restricted under common law. It was found in *Gibson* that the prosecution did not have to prove an intent to outrage public decency or recklessness as to the risk of such outrage; it was only necessary to prove that a defendant had intentionally done an act which in fact outraged public decency; he could not escape liability merely because his own standards were so base that he could not appreciate that outrage might be caused. This requirement may be contrasted with the full *mens rea* required for conspiracy to corrupt public morals. In *Knuller* the House of Lords found that the defendant must *intend* to corrupt morals.

---

98 [1990] 2 QB 619; [1991] 1 All ER 439; [1990] 3 WLR 595; for comment see Childs [1991] *PL* 20–29.

These two common law offences are each aimed at a distinct mischief. Conspiracy to corrupt public morals clearly stems from the same roots as the offence under the Obscene Publications Act, rather than forming a part of the laws against indecency. Its existence is therefore perhaps even less defensible than that of conspiracy to outrage public decency since it covers an area of liability which cannot be distinguished from that covered by the 1959 Act and is therefore most likely to allow escape from the statutory safeguards. It can exist only on the basis that its *actus reus* is the agreement between the parties rather than the risk of corruption of morals, whereas common law indecency can be distinguished from the offence under the 1959 Act on the more substantial basis that it is concerned in essence with indecency rather than obscenity. On the other hand, it may be argued that the protection of morals answers to a more weighty public interest than the prevention of shock or outrage and this contention is reflected in Article 10 which contains an exception expressed in terms of the former interest but not the latter. However, when the defendants in *Gibson* applied to the European Commission alleging a breach of Article 10,[99] the application was found inadmissible, suggesting either that in the particular circumstances the conviction might have appeared to have the effect of protecting morals, as opposed to merely preventing outrage, or that the protection of morals exception may sometimes cover material which merely shocks. It must be said that at present the European Court has not always drawn a clear distinction between the two mischiefs: in *Müller v Switzerland*[100] paintings found to offend morals under Swiss law fell within Article 10(2) as likely to 'grossly offend the sense of sexual propriety of persons of ordinary sensitivity'. This sounds like indecency rather than corruption but the court blurred the distinction between them in implying that the former would merge with the latter once a certain level of offensiveness was reached. That level may be reached, it is suggested, by speech which may best be termed 'very shocking'. The court made it clear that speech which would merely be termed 'shocking' or 'disturbing' would not reach it. Thus it seems that these common law offences may be in harmony with Article 10, although their abolition is nevertheless warranted due to their uncertain ambit and the anomalies they create.

It may be noted that the development of the wide ranging and flexible doctrine of common law indecency and conspiracy to corrupt public morals bears some resemblance to that of common law contempt: both doctrines work in tandem with statutes which create a more precise area of liability and which provide a defence which may ensure compatibility with Article 10 of

---

99   *Gibson v UK*, Appl No 17634.
100 (1991) 13 EHRR 212.

the European Convention on Human Rights. In both instances, therefore, the common law tends to undermine the safeguards for free speech provided by the statute.

3 CENSORSHIP, LICENSING AND REGULATION OF FILM AND BROADCASTING

Introduction

In contrast to books, magazines and other printed matter, broadcasting and films are subject to a statute-based system of licensing, regulation and censorship. This stricter system of controls seems to have been adopted in answer to the view that due to their particular impact on audiences, films and broadcasting required a system of prior restraints whereas books and other printed material did not. This was the view of the Williams Committee,[101] although it has also been argued that the evidence that films have a very different impact from books or magazines is not strong and that the difference in treatment may be due to the relative youth of the medium; it has not yet gained the acceptance accorded to traditional mediums and is still viewed with some suspicion.[102] The Williams Committee considered that in the light of some psychiatric evidence to the effect that violent films might induce violent behaviour a policy based on caution was justified.[103] Due to the availability of censorship, it is very unlikely that a film or broadcast could attract liability under the Obscene Publications Act;[104] nevertheless it provides a further possibility of restraint and can also be used as a guide as to the minimum standards censorship will observe.

Within Western Europe, the UK operates one of the strictest censorship regimes for the moving image. Until recently UK governments were free, within electoral constraints, to perpetuate that regime. However, in the 1990s the regulatory regime controlling the moving image was confronted with the dissemination of speech by methods which seemed to fall outside its compass since the speech originated from outside the UK. Thus concern has been raised that obscene material may be disseminated on the Internet and by non-terrestrial broadcasters. The difficulty of attempting to regulate the moving image when it is transmitted by these means has led to the position whereby at present they are largely outside the regulatory regime for either films or

---

101 See Simpson, AWB, *Pornography and Politics: The Williams Committee in Retrospect*, 1983, pp 35–38.
102 Barendt, *Freedom of Speech*, p 125.
103 Simpson, *Pornography and Politics*, p 37.
104 The Obscene Publications Act covers all media under s 1(2) now that s 162 of the Broadcasting Act 1990 has brought radio and television within its ambit.

broadcasting and, as discussed below, as far as the Internet is concerned can probably only be considered within the Obscene Publications Act or the law of indecency. Thus, they are subject to less stringent controls than domestic broadcasting and films. This is an anomaly which confronts any country which receives the internet and satellite broadcasting but which favours a stricter censorship than at least one other Western country. It is probable that this is a situation which Western governments may eventually seek to address by international agreement.

Broadcasting[105]

Government influence over broadcasting is of enormous significance due to the importance of broadcasting as the main means of informing the public as to matters of public interest. The openly partisan nature of the popular press means that broadcasting provides the only impartial source of information for many people. The government may exert control over broadcasting by overt means, which can include, exceptionally, use of its censorship powers under s 10(3) of the Broadcasting Act 1990 or through more subtle means such as the criteria used to determine appointments to the BBC Governors. The deregulation of independent television under the 1990 Act might appear to suggest a movement away from governmental influence but it raises other questions about the influence of the new owners of broadcasting stations who may wish to use broadcasting as a means of exerting political influence. It is also misleading to speak of 'de-regulation' when the new system has led to the establishment of an overlapping and strict set of controls over broadcasting. The Broadcasting Act 1996 eased some of the restrictions on media ownership created by the 1990 Act with a view to balancing 'proper commercial demands and the wider public interest which includes plurality, diversity of opinion'.[106]

Control over broadcasting on political grounds

As part of the deregulation of television the 1990 Act set up the Independent Television Commission (ITC) to replace the Independent Broadcasting

---

105 See generally Gibbons, *Regulating the Media*, 1991; Robertson, *Media Law*, Chap 15; Munro, C, *Television, Censorship and the Law*, 1979; Reville, N, *Broadcasting*, 1991; Horrie, C and Clarke, S, *Fuzzy Monsters: Fear and Loathing at the BBC*, 1994; Bailey, Harris and Jones, 1995, Chap 5, Part 3; Reville, N, *Broadcasting: the New Law*, 1991; Barendt, E, *Broadcasting Law: A Comparative Study*, 1995; Hitchens, L, 'Approaches to Broadcasting Regulation: Australia and the UK Compared' (1997) 17(1) *LS* 40. For discussion and criticism of the Broadcasting Act 1996 see Feintuck, M [1997] 3(2) *European Public Law* 201.

106 Virginia Bottomley, Dept of National Heritage Press Release DNH 219/96. For discussion of regulation of cross media ownership and concentrated media ownership is see Fleming, H (1997) 60(3) *MLR* 378; Hitchens, LP (1994) 57 *MLR* 585.

Restraining Freedom of Expression on Moral and Religious Grounds

Authority (IBA) as a public body charged with licensing and regulating non-BBC television services. The ITC is required, under the impartiality clause introduced by s 6(1) of the 1990 Act, to set up a code to require that politically sensitive programmes must be balanced in order to ensure impartiality. Such programmes can be balanced by means of a series of programmes (s 6(2)); it is not necessary that any one programme should be followed by another specific balancing programme. However, the requirement may mean that some politically controversial programmes are not made: the expense and difficulty of setting up balancing programmes may prove to have a deterrent effect. The ITC code makes it clear that a company cannot be heard to argue that a programme which might be said to have an anti-government bias may be balanced by programmes broadcast by other companies: the company has to achieve impartiality in its own programming. In interpreting this code, the companies may act cautiously and may interpret what is meant by 'bias' broadly. Thus, although this new provision may seek to balance a need for impartiality against the need to protect freedom of expression, it may not achieve that balance in practice.

Obviously s 6 can only affect a *positive* decision to broadcast a programme dealing with a sensitive issue; there is nothing in the arrangements for the franchising of independent television and radio to affect a decision to ignore some such issues on political grounds. The franchises went to the highest bidder once a 'quality control threshold' was satisfied. Nothing was done to attempt to ensure that a political balance between franchise holders was achieved at that stage. The function of the ITC in this respect is very similar to that of the Independent Radio Authority, which has the statutory function, under Part III of the 1990 Act, of monitoring the independent radio stations.

The impartiality requirement only affects non-BBC broadcasting, although the BBC has undertaken to comply generally with the statutory duties placed on the IBA (replaced by the ITC).[107] However, this undertaking is unenforceable although the BBC generally complies. Cases of doubt will be referred up the Corporation management hierarchy: producers may refer to middle management who may seek direction from departmental heads who may then consult the Managing Director or even the Director General. Thus censorship is largely self-imposed; the government cannot bring *direct* influence to bear. However, the Board of Governors of the BBC is appointed by the government and although they usually leave editorial matters to the Director General they may occasionally intervene; they did so in 1985 in relation to a programme about an IRA sympathiser in Belfast, *Real Lives*, after condemnation of it by the Prime Minister – an incident which was perceived

---

107 This undertaking is annexed to the Corporation's licence agreement. The BBC operates under this agreement and also under the terms of its royal charter (see Cmnd 8233 and 8313 respectively). This includes the requirement to observe due impartiality. See Gibbons, T, 'Impartiality in the Media' (1985) *Archiv für Rechts– und Sozial philosophie, Beiheft*, Nr 28 pp 71–81.

as damaging to the BBC's reputation for independence from the government.[108] On the other hand, certain incidents such as coverage of the US bombing of Libya, have led to expressions of concern from the Conservative party about BBC 'bias' against the government, although this may have been partly mollified by the banning of a documentary on the Zircon spy satellite project in 1987 and a documentary on the workings of Cabinet government. Both films were eventually shown with modification, the latter by Channel 4 in 1991.[109] Generally speaking, as Gibbons points out, the 'reference up' procedure will tend to exclude the influence of the Governors partly because thinking at the higher levels may be anticipated at the lower.[110]

The IBA, before its abolition, had acquired a reputation for determined resistance to government influence, largely due to its refusal to bow to political pressure in relation to Thames TV's investigation into the shooting of three IRA members on Gibraltar, *Death on the Rock*. An independent investigation into the making of the programme largely exonerated it of bias or of interference with the enquiry in Gibraltar.[111]

Apart from the restraints already mentioned, the government has a direct power of censorship[112] which is of the widest possible nature since it allows a ban on broadcasting 'any matter' or class of matter. It was invoked by the Secretary of state in 1988 in order to issue directives requiring the BBC and IBA to refrain from broadcasting words spoken by persons representing organisations proscribed under the Northern Ireland (Emergency Provisions) legislation and also Sinn Fein, Republican Sinn Fein and the Ulster Defence Association. The ban was challenged by the National Union of Journalists and others but not by the broadcasting organisations themselves in *Secretary of State for the Home Department ex parte Brind and Others*.[113] The applicants submitted that the Home Secretary's discretionary powers were exercisable only in conformity with Article 10 of the European Convention and that in curtailing freedom of expression where there was no pressing social need to do so the directives contravened Article 10. Article 10 must be taken into account on the basis that when legislation confers an administrative discretion on an authority which is capable of being exercised in a way which infringes human rights as protected by the Convention, it may be presumed that the

---

108 Robertson, *Media Law*, p 484.
109 See further Fiddich, P, 'Broadcasting: a Catalogue of Confrontation' in Buchan, N and Sumner, T, eds, *Glasnost in Britain: Against Censorship and in Defence of the Word*, 1989.
110 Gibbons, *Regulating the Media*, p 141.
111 Windlesham/Rampton Report on *Death on the Rock* (1989).
112 The power now arises under s 10(3); previously it arose under s 29(3) of the Broadcasting Act 1981. It also arises under Clause 13(4) of the BBC's Licence and Agreement.
113 [1991] 1 AC 696; [1991] 1 All ER 720; [1991] 2 WLR 588, HL; [1990] 1 All ER 469, CA; for comment see Jowell [1990] *PL* 149 (on the Court of Appeal ruling). For further discussion, see above pp 101–02.

intention of the enabling legislation was that the discretion should be exercised within Convention limits. As the directives did not so conform the minister had acted *ultra vires*. The House of Lords agreed that the Convention could be used as a rule of statutory construction to resolve ambiguity in subsequent primary legislation but disagreed with the submission that the issuing of the directives was therefore *ultra vires*, on the ground that it could not be presumed that discretionary powers were, by analogy, limited by the terms of the Convention. Such a presumption would go far beyond the resolution of an ambiguity as it would assume that Parliament had intended to import the text of the Convention into domestic administrative law. As Parliament had chosen not to incorporate the Convention into domestic law this, it was found, was an unwarranted assumption.

It was further submitted that administrative action can be challenged by way of judicial review if it is disproportionate to the mischief at which is aimed and that this particular exercise of power went further than was necessary to prevent terrorists increasing their standing. The House of Lords held that lack of proportionality was merely to be regarded as one aspect of *Wednesbury* unreasonableness, not as a separate head of challenge. The question to be asked was therefore whether the minister's decision was one which no reasonable minister could have made. Taking into account the fact that the directives did not restrict the reporting of information but merely the manner of its presentation – direct speech – it was found that this ground of challenge had not been made out. The House of Lords indicated that the challenge might have succeeded had the interference been more wide ranging. Nevertheless, the ban meant that a Sinn Fein or IRA member could not be forced to justify their policies and therefore it caused offence to the principle that flawed or evil speech is best combatted by further speech.[114] Moreover, as it applied equally to historical programmes it infringed the principle that the search for truth should override other interests except where a clear danger in allowing the speech may be shown. In its own terms the ban may have been ineffective and self-defeating, not only because it did not appear to prevent the dubbing of the voices of Sinn Fein leaders and others by actors, but also because, ironically, in itself it publicised them, rather than denying them 'the oxygen of publicity'. Gerry Adams, the leader of Sinn Fein, was able to publicise himself in America as the man whose voice could not be heard on UK airwaves. The ban remained in place until September 1994 when it was lifted after the IRA declared the cessation of violence. Although the ceasefire broke down in 1996, the ban was not re-imposed.

---

114 A principle which derives from Mill's argument from truth; see Chap 4 pp 138–39.

Censorship on grounds of taste and decency

Under s 6(1)(a) of the 1990 Act the ITC must attempt to ensure that every licensed television service includes nothing in its programmes 'which offends against good taste and decency' and this echoes the similar requirement imposed on the BBC by the terms of its charter. Clearly, these are terms which leave a good deal of leeway to broadcasters as regards their interpretation. Moreover, they invite consideration of explicit material in the context in which it is shown, so that what might be offensive in one setting and with one particular audience in mind, would not be so in another. The ITC published a Programme Code dealing with these matters in 1991 which attempts to strike a balance between preserving good taste and decency on the one hand and avoiding too great a restraint on freedom of speech on the other. It therefore allows sexual scenes so long as they are presented with tact and discretion. As far as films are concerned it follows the guidelines laid down by the BBFC (see below): '18' rated films may be shown but only after 10 pm. Further, the BBFC standards are to be regarded as minimum ones; the mere fact that a film has an '18' certificate is not to be taken as implying that it would be proper to broadcast it. The role of the ITC in this respect is to an extent duplicated by the Broadcasting Standards Council (BSC), set up in 1988 to monitor the standards of taste and decency being maintained in programmes. Under s 152 of the 1990 Act the BSC had a duty to draw up a Code relating to broadcasting standards covering the BBC and independent television and radio broadcasting. The BSC seemed to work on the assumption that absolute standards could be discerned and maintained as opposed to steadily changing ones.[115] Section 106 of the Broadcasting Act 1996 established the new Broadcasting Standards Commission which was made up of a merger of the Broadcasting Standards Council and the Broadcasting Complaints Commission.[116] The Broadcasting Standards Commission is charged with the duty of drawing up a code in respect of programme standards under s 107 which is based on s 152 of the 1990 Act but the code must also cover matters of fairness and privacy. Section 108 re-enacts the former s 152. Thus, as far as independent broadcasting is concerned, a dual and overlapping system is in place imposing an onerous burden on the companies. The Commission is under a duty to monitor programmes (s 109) in relation to taste and decency, especially the portrayal of sex and violence, and to consider complaints regarding these matters (s 110). If a complaint is upheld, the broadcaster is under an obligation to publish it. The main sanction is contained in the adverse publicity. Nevertheless, in some respects the current arrangements could be said to represent a slackening of restraint on what may be broadcast in the sense that the television companies no longer have to submit their

---

115 BSC Annual Report 1988–89 and Code of Practice 1989 p 41. For comment on the work of the BSC see Coleman, F [1993] *PL* 448.
116 For the work of the Commission see below pp 334–35.

controversial programmes to an outside body for preview and censorship. As the Annan Committee pointed out in 1977,[117] the old system meant that programmes might be subject to dual censorship in being considered first by the IBA and then by the company concerned. However, although such censorship is now solely in the hands of the companies themselves, the ITC has a number of sanctions to use against a company which fails to abide by the Programming Code, ranging from a requirement to broadcast an apology to the power to revoke its licence. The financial penalties available are very severe and may well tend to deter the companies from taking risks in their interpretation of what is allowed by the code.

Satellite television

The ITC Code does not apply to broadcasters who are not licence holders of the ITC. Under s 43 of the 1990 Act a satellite service is required to hold an ITC licence if it is a 'domestic satellite service' or a 'non-domestic satellite service'. A domestic service uses direct broadcasting by satellite on one of the five frequencies allocated to the UK at the World Administrative Radio Conference 1977. A non-domestic satellite service is one which either uses a lower powered satellite to transmit programmes from the UK or transmits from outside the territory of prescribed countries but a UK supplier dictates the service. Section 89 of the Broadcasting Act 1996 amended s 45 of the 1990 Act to allow for the immediate suspension of non-domestic satellite services which breach s 6(1)(a) of the 1990 Act. If a satellite falls into neither of these categories it is not regulated under the Code. If it is a service licensed from within an EU Member State it must receive freedom of reception within other Member States under the EU Directive on Transfrontier Television (89/552/EEC). However, in *Commission of EC v UK*[118] it was found that s 43 of the Broadcasting Act 1990 applies different regimes to domestic and non-domestic satellite services and that in exercising control over certain broadcasters falling under the jurisdiction of other Member States the UK had failed to fulfil its obligations under the Directive Articles 2(1)(2) and 3(2).

Under the directive it is not clear that prosecution under the Obscene Publications Act may be brought where obscene material is transmitted to the UK from a licensed service within another Member State. Such a prosecution could be brought, however, against such material from a non-EU source. So far the National Heritage Secretary has issued four proscription orders against satellite channels from EU Member States which beam hard core pornography into Britain. Such proscription orders are made under s 177 of the 1990 Act; so far the question whether they breach EU law has not been addressed by the European Court of Justice.

---

117 *Report of the Committee on the Future of Broadcasting* chaired by Lord Annan Cmnd 6753.
118 Case 222/94, 30 September 1996.

Films[119]

Censorship of films operates in practice on two levels: first the British Board of Film Classification, a self-censoring body set up by the film industry in 1912, may insist on cuts before issuing a certificate allowing the film to be screened or may refuse to issue a certificate at all. It was set up in response to the Cinematograph Act 1909 which allowed local authorities to grant licences in respect of the films to be shown in their particular area; the idea was that the film industry would achieve a uniformity of decision-making by local councils. Thus it would have a guide as to whether a film would be shown and as to where to make cuts in order to achieve a wider audience. Films are classified by age: 'U' films are open to anybody as, in effect, are 'PG' (parental guidance) classified films. After that are '12', '15' and '18' certificate films. 'R18' films (restricted viewing) may be viewed only on segregated premises. An 'R18' certificate means that the BBFC considers that the film would survive an Obscene Publications Act prosecution; it will refuse a certificate if a film is thought to fall within the Act. In coming to its decision the BBFC will take the 'public good' defence under s 4(1A) of the 1959 Act, as amended, into account. This defence is the more restricted defence under s 3 of the Theatres Act 1968; s 4(1A) provides that a film or soundtrack can be justified as being for the public good 'on the ground that it is in the interests of drama, opera, ballet or any other art or of literature or learning'. Therefore the BBFC may grant a certificate on the grounds of artistic merit to a film which contains some obscene matter.

Of course, most film distributors have no interest in achieving only a restricted publication for a film and are therefore prepared to make cuts to achieve a wider circulation. Thus, the system of control may be driven largely by commercial motives: a distributor may make quite stringent cuts in order to ensure that, for example, a film receives a '15' certificate and so reaches a wider audience.

The second level of censorship is operated by local authorities under the Cinemas Act 1985 which continues the old power arising under the Cinematograph Act 1909. The local authority will usually follow the Board's advice but may choose not to grant a licence to a film regardless of its decision. Films which have been licensed but which nevertheless have been banned in some areas include *A Clockwork Orange*, *The Life of Brian*, *The Last Temptation of Christ* and *Crash*. There is no requirement of consistency between authorities and thus discrepancies have arisen between different local authority areas. It is notable that the cinema is the only art form subject to moral judgment on a local level and it may be asked why it should be so

---

[119] See generally Robertson, *Obscenity*, pp 257–68; Robertson, *Media Law*, 1991, Chap 14; Hunnings, N, *Film Censors and the Law*, 1967.

singled out. This dual system of censorship was criticised by the Williams Committee in 1979 (see below) partly on the ground of the anomalies caused by having two overlapping levels and partly due to the inconsistency between local authorities. It considered that a unified system should be adopted. In particular, it criticised a system which allowed adult films to be censored beyond the requirements of the Obscene Publications Act.

Video

Under the Video Recordings Act 1984 the BBFC was established as the authority charged with classifying videos for viewing in the home. Videos are censored in almost the same way as films and under the Video Recordings Act 1984 it is an offence to supply an uncensored video. Section 4 of the 1984 Act requires that the BBFC should have 'special regard to the likelihood of video works being viewed in the home'. Thus, makers of videos may find that videos are censored beyond the requirements of the Obscene Publications Act. The 1984 Act places the BBFC in the position of official censors and in that role their work has often been criticised as over-strict and arbitrary.[120] Censorship of videos is likely to become stricter in future. Fears that children may be more likely to commit violence after watching violent videos led the government to include a provision in the Criminal Justice and Public Order Bill 1994 which was then before the Commons. Under s 90 of the Act the BBFC must have 'special regard' to harm which may be caused to potential viewers or through their behaviour to society by the manner in which the film deals with criminal activity, illegal drugs, violent or horrific incidents or behaviour, sexual behaviour. It should be noted that the connection between violence on film and violent behaviour in children has not yet been firmly established. If, as is possible, there is a greater likelihood not that children may perpetrate violence as immediate reaction to exposure to violent films but that they may be desensitised to violence in a long term sense if they watch a great deal of it, any such connection would be very hard to establish.

The Internet

Section 168 of the Criminal Justice and Public Order Act 1994 added the transmission of electronically stored data to the Obscene Publication Act's definition of 'publication'. The information stored on the Internet is available to any user who possesses a computer of the correct specification. Children could therefore readily gain access to Internet information and images and the question of the obscenity of the material in question would probably therefore

---

[120] See Hunnings, N, 'Video Censorship' [1985] *PL* 214; Robertson, G, *Freedom, the Individual and the Law*, 1993, pp 263–72.

have to be determined by reference to that likely audience. However, since information can be placed on the Internet by any person anywhere in the world it might well be almost impossible in most instances to identify the service provider who had placed the obscene matter on the Internet. Thus, at present the availability of hard core pornography on the Internet appears to undermine the provisions aimed at it when it arrives in this country or is disseminated within it by other means.

Conclusions

It seems that, if there is to be reform of the law relating to obscenity, indecency and censorship, the government will have to take the initiative. The decisions in *Knuller* and *Gibson* do not suggest that there is a determination on the part of the judiciary to import greater certainty and liberality into this area. Similarly, after the decisions in the *Handyside* case and in *Müller v Switzerland*,[121] it seems unlikely that there will be any UK move towards greater protection of freedom of speech in this area by recourse to the European Convention on Human Rights. The UK position in respect of restraints on freedom of speech in the name of protection of morality does not appear to breach Article 10. It may be assumed that the exception contained in Article 10(2) in respect of the protection of morals will continue to be widely interpreted because the European Court of Human Rights will continue to allow a wide margin of appreciation to Member States in this very sensitive area. It is however possible that, once Article 10 becomes part of UK law, under the Human Rights Act domestic judges will take a different stance.

The Williams Committee recommended in 1979 that the printed word should not be subject to any restraint and that other material should be restrained on the basis of two specific tests: first, material which might shock should be available only through restricted outlets; second, material should not be *prohibited* unless it could be shown to cause specific harm.[122] The moving image could be censored, it was thought, since it might be most likely to have an adverse influence on the more vulnerable members of society, including children, perhaps leading them to imitate the violent behaviour depicted. Clearly these proposals would give greater weight to freedom of speech than is currently given, in that they would allow greater differentiation between the kinds of harm which might be caused by the various media. They emphasised a fundamental difference between prohibition and restriction of the sale of pornography and other explicit material. These proposals found

---

121 See further Feingold, C, 'The Little Red Schoolbook and the European Court of Human Rights' (1978) *Revue des Droits de l'Homme* 21.

122 Williams, B, *Committee on Obscenity and Film Censorship* (1979) Cmnd 7772 (also available in paperback); Simpson, *Pornography and Politics*, 1983; for commentary see McKean, WA (1980) 39 *Camb LJ* 10; Coldham, S (1980) 43 *MLR* 306; Dworkin, R (1981) 1 *Ox JLS* 177.

partial expression in the Indecent Displays (Control) Act 1981, the provisions under the Local Government (Miscellaneous Provisions) Act 1982 for regulating 'sex establishments' and the Cinematograph (Amendment) Act 1982 which changed the classification of films and in particular introduced the 'R18' rating. The proposal as to removing the prohibition as opposed to restriction from the *written* word and from much other pornographic material has not been implemented.[123]

Various far-reaching restraints remain, including the use of forfeiture proceedings and the uncertain offence of outraging public decency, both tending to undermine the safeguards for artistic freedom contained in the 1959 Act. The complex and overlapping controls affecting broadcasting, film and videos may tend to go beyond what is allowed under the 1959 Act, although satellite broadcasting and the Internet may be able to evade the statutory standard. Review of this area should look not only at these anomalies but at the whole question whether a regulatory regime based partly on an unintelligible test created in 1868 is still supportable. Therefore it is suggested that a radical overhaul of this area of law is long overdue.

4 BLASPHEMY, SEDITIOUS LIBEL, RELIGIOUS AND RACIAL HATRED

Blasphemous and seditious libel

The existence of the offence of blasphemous libel[124] stems from the 17th century when it was tried in the Ecclesiastical courts. It was then thought to be a form of sedition due to the close relationship between the Church and the state. Therefore, it only protected the Anglican Church; other sects of the Christian Church such as Catholicism, or other religions, received no protection. Its basis, which derives from *Taylor's* case,[125] was that the defendant had aspersed the Christian religion. By the middle of the 19th century and in particular after the case of *Ramsay and Foote*,[126] it became clear that the basis of blasphemy had changed: it required a scurrilous attack on Christianity rather than merely reasoned and sober arguments against it. It

---

123 For further discussion of the Committee's position see above p 183.
124 General reading: see Robertson, *Obscenity*, Chap 8 pp 236–43; Robertson, *Media Law*, Chap 3, pp 124–27; Bailey, Harris and Jones, Chap 9 pp 591–98; Robilliard, JA, *Religion and the Law*, 1984, Chap 2; Barendt, *Freedom of Speech*, pp 167, 260; for historical discussion of the development of blasphemy law see Kenny, CS, 'The Evolution of the Law of Blasphemy' (1992) 1 *CLJ* 127–42 and Walter, *Blasphemy Ancient and Modern*, 1990. For a discussion of the theoretical issues lying behind blasphemy law see Feinberg, J, *Offense to Others*, 1985 and in the context of possible reform see Law Commission Report No 145, *Offences against Religion and Public Worship*, 1985.
125 (1676) 1 Vent 293.
126 (1883) 15 Cox CC 231.

was thought by 1950 that the offence was a dead letter.[127] However, it was resurrected in *Lemon*.[128] *Gay News* published a poem – 'The Love that dares to speak its name' – by a professor of English literature, James Kirkup. It expressed religious sentiment in describing a homosexual's conversion to Christianity and in developing its theme it ascribed homosexual practices with the Apostles to Jesus and made explicit references to sodomy. Mary Whitehouse obtained leave to bring a private prosecution against *Gay News* and the editor and publishing company were convicted of the offence of blasphemous libel.

The Court of Appeal held that the intention or motive of the defendants was irrelevant since blasphemy was a crime of strict liability. It could therefore be committed by a Christian as there was no need to show that the material had mounted a fundamental attack on Christianity (as had been thought). There was no defence of publication in the public interest; serious literature could therefore be caught. The work in question need not be considered as a whole. All that needed to be shown was that the material in question, which was published with the defendant's knowledge, had crossed the borderline between moderate criticism on the one hand and immoderate or offensive treatment of matter sacred to Christians on the other. It was only necessary to show that resentment would be likely to be aroused not that it actually was aroused. The past requirement to show that a breach of the peace might be occasioned by publication of the material was no longer necessary. The case was considered by the House of Lords on the question of the mental element required. The judgment confirmed the Court of Appeal ruling that it was only necessary to show an intent to publish the material. This decision has been much criticised[129] as it inhibits many, if not most, juxtapositions of sexuality with aspects of the Anglican religion by writers and broadcasters. In common with other parts of the common law it allows the Obscene Publications Act to be circumvented because it admits of no public good defence. Moreover, there are already various areas of liability discussed above arising at common law and under statute which could be used to prevent offence being caused to Christians.

Gay News applied to the European Commission on Human Rights on a number of grounds including that of a breach of Article 10.[130] This application was ruled inadmissible in a cautious judgment. It was found that the Article 10 guarantee of freedom of expression had been interfered with but that the interference fell within the 'rights of others' exception of Article 10(2). Was the

---

127 This was Lord Denning's description of it in *Freedom under the Law*, 1949, p 46.
128 [1979] AC 617; [1979] 2 WLR 281; [1979] 1 All ER 898, HL.
129 See Robertson, *Obscenity*, p 242; Law Commission 1985 Report.
130 (1979) 5 EHRR 123.

interference necessary in a democratic society? It was found that once it was accepted that the religious feelings of citizens may deserve protection if attacks reach a certain level of savagery, it seemed to follow that the domestic authorities were best placed to determine when that level was reached. In other words, the argument used in the *Handyside* case that a very wide margin of appreciation was required was again invoked.

It seems fairly clear that this offence will not be extended beyond Anglicanism. The Law Commission in their 1985 Report[131] concluded, rather, that it should be abolished, in finding that an offence of wounding the feelings of adherents of any religious group would be impossible to construct because the term 'religion' could not be defined with sufficient precision. The argument in favour of extension of the offence was put and rejected in *Chief Metropolitan Magistrate ex parte Choudhury*[132] a case which arose out of the publication of Salman Rushdie's *The Satanic Verses*.[133] The applicants applied for judicial review of the refusal of a magistrates' court to grant summonses against Salman Rushdie and his publishers for, *inter alia*, the common law offence of blasphemous libel. The Court of Appeal determined after reviewing the relevant decisions that the offence of blasphemy was clearly confined only to publications offensive to Christians. Extending the offence would, it was determined, create great difficulties since it would be virtually impossible to define the term 'religion' sufficiently clearly. Freedom of expression would be curtailed as authors would have to try to avoid offending members of many different sects. The applicants did not, however, rely only on domestic law; during argument that the offence should be extended it was said that UK law must contain a provision to give effect to the Convention guarantee of freedom of religion under Article 9.[134] In response it was argued and accepted by the Court of Appeal that the Convention need not be considered because the common law on the point was not uncertain. However, the respondents nevertheless accepted that in this particular instance the Convention should be considered. It was found that the United Kingdom was not in breach of the Convention because extending the offence of blasphemy would breach Articles 7 and 10; the exceptions of Article 10(2) could not be invoked as nothing in the book would support a pressing social need for its suppression. Furthermore, Article 9(1) could not be treated as absolute; implied exceptions to it must include the lack of a right to bring criminal proceedings for

---

131 Report No 145, *Offences Against Religion and Public Worship*. This was preceded by the Law Commission Working Paper No 79 of the same title (1981). See Robertson, G [1981] *PL* 295; Spencer, JR [1981] *Crim LR* 810; St J Robillard (1981) 44 *MLR* 556 for comment on the 1981 Working Paper. The direction reform might take is considered further below, pp 219–25.
132 [1991] 1 QB 429; [1991] 1 All ER 306, DC; for comment see Tregilgas-Davey, M (1991) 54 *MLR* 294–99.
133 For discussion of Muslim and Western reactions to publication of *The Satanic Verses* see Abel, R, *Speech and Respect*, 1994, Chap 1 (iii).
134 For discussion of the particular question whether blasphemy law can be defended by reference to the rights of others to freedom of religion see below, pp 222–23.

blasphemy where no domestic law had been infringed. Article 9 might be infringed where Muslims were prevented from exercising their religion but such restrictions were not in question.

On behalf of the applicants it was further argued that if Article 9 provided no protection for Muslims, they had suffered discrimination in the exercise of their freedom of religion and therefore a violation of Article 14 had occurred. This interpretation of Article 9, read alongside Article 14, had been rejected by the European Commission in the *Gay News* case.[135] In this case it also failed on the ground that the envisaged extension of UK law to protect Islam would involve a violation of Article 10 which guarantees freedom of expression. Such an extension was not therefore warranted. It seems clear from this ruling and from statements made by Lord Scarman in the House of Lords in *Lemon*,[136] which were relied upon in the *Choudhury* case, that the judiciary are not minded to extend this offence, considering that only Parliament should do so.

The applicants also argued that the crime of seditious libel would extend to the image of Islam presented by *The Satanic Verses*. This offence at one time seemed to cover any attack on the institutions of the state but in modern times it has been interpreted to require an intention to incite to violence and the words used must have a tendency to incite to violence.[137] It was not therefore apt to cover the offence caused to Muslims by the book, which could be said to be intended to arouse general hostility and ill will between sections of the community but not against the public authorities. This finding, which was contrary to the ruling in *Caunt*,[138] means that incitement to religious hatred is not covered by any part of the law, although attacks on Anglicanism would in most instances fall within blasphemy, while attacks on religious groups which are also racial groups would fall within incitement to racial hatred (see below).

An application was made to the European Commission on Human Rights by the applicants in *Choudhury*[139] but it was declared inadmissible on the ground that Article 9 does not include a positive obligation on the part of the state to protect religious sensibilities. The discriminatory application of blasphemy law therefore remains a source of discontent among Muslims. Parliament had the opportunity of abolishing the offence of blasphemy in 1994 when a Bill was put forward by Lord Lester which would have achieved this. However, it was withdrawn after the government opposed it[140] partly on

---

135 (1982) 5 EHRR 123.
136 *Ibid* p 620. Lord Scarman considered that there was a case for extension, however.
137 *Burns* [1886] 16 Cox CC 333; *Aldred* (1909) 22 Cox CC 1; *Caunt* (1947) unreported but see case note 64 *LQR* 203; for comment see Barendt, pp 152–60.
138 Unreported, above note 137.
139 *Choudhury v UK* (1991) No 17349/1990; (1991) 12 *HRLJ* 172.
140 555 *HL Deb* 16 June 1994, Cols 1891–1909.

the ground that no clear consensus as to the value of abolishing this offence could be discerned.

The future of blasphemy law

At the present time it is probable that no reform of UK blasphemy law is required in order to ensure harmony with the European Convention on Human Rights Article 10 as interpreted at Strasbourg. This is clear from the findings of the European Commission in the *Gay News* case and from recent rulings of the European Court of Human Rights. In *Otto-Preminger Institut v Austria*[141] an order for the seizure and forfeiture of a film, *Das Lieberkinzil*, which caricatured aspects of Christianity was made on the basis that it disparaged religious doctrines and was 'likely to arouse justified indignation'. The Austrian government maintained, and the Court accepted, that the seizure and forfeiture were aimed at protecting the 'rights of others' within Article 10(2). In considering whether the interference was necessary in a democratic society for protecting those rights the Court took into account the lack of a uniform conception in Europe of the significance of religion in society and therefore left a wide margin of appreciation to the Austrian government. In finding that the seizure and forfeiture were necessary the Court determined that the offensive nature of the film was not outweighed by its artistic merits. No breach of Article 10 was therefore found. In *Wingrove v UK*[142] the Court had to consider whether a refusal of the British Board of Film Classification to issue a certificate licensing a short film *Visions of Ecstasy* constituted a breach of Article 10. The film depicted St Theresa of Avila kissing Christ; had it been granted a license and shown in the UK a private prosecution for blasphemy might have been brought successfully. The Court found that the restriction was prescribed by law, taking into account the fact that the BBFC was acting within its powers under s 4(1) of the 1984 Act and that no general uncertainty was apparent as to the definition of blasphemy formulated in the *Lemon* case. The refusal of the certificate had the aim of protecting the rights of others within Article 10(2). In considering the necessity and proportionality of the restriction, the Court went on to find that while the margin of appreciation allowed to states would be narrow in relation to political speech, it would be wide in relation to offending 'intimate personal convictions within the field of morals or, especially, religion'.[143] The Court found, having viewed the video, that the decision of the BBFC that it would outrage and insult the feelings of

---

141 (1994) 19 EHRR 34.
142 Opinion of the Commission: (1994) 19 EHRR CD 54. Judgment of 25 November 1996, Case 19/1995/525/611; (1997) 24 EHRR 1.
143 Page 22 of the judgment in draft form.

believing Christians could not be said to be arbitrary or excessive. The national authorities had not overstepped their margin of appreciation: the exception applied and therefore no breach of Article 10 had occurred.

Where the European Court of Human Rights leaves a wide margin of appreciation to Member States in determining the extent of the exceptions to a Convention right this may be taken to mean that, at least until a common European conception of the width of the exception emerges, states have the main responsibility for ensuring that rigorous human rights standards are maintained. It is suggested that the ease with which publications can infringe blasphemy law in the UK does not represent a maintenance of such standards and that therefore reform of blasphemy law should be attempted once the Human Rights Act comes into force by domestic judges who need not be trammelled by the margin of appreciation doctrine. There are at least two further reasons why some change is needed in the current law. First, from a pragmatic point of view, the present situation, since it is perceived by Muslims as unfair, is a considerable source of racial tension: it both engenders feelings of anger and alienation in the Muslim community and, when these feelings are expressed through such activities as book-burning and attacks on booksellers stocking *The Satanic Verses*, increased feelings of hostility towards Muslims in certain sections of the non-Muslim population. Secondly, from the liberal point of view broadly endorsed in this book, it is indefensible that the state should single out one group of citizens and protect their religious feelings while others are without such protection. In what follows therefore, the question whether blasphemy law should be extended, abolished or replaced by an offence of incitement to religious hatred, will be considered from the point of view of the philosophical justifications which would support each alternative. The probable effect of each course of action on racial tension will also be briefly considered. This discussion is premised upon the argument outlined in Chapter 1 that free speech, as a strong individual right, should be infringed only if either a similar individual right is threatened by speech or if the values which lead us to support free speech are not at issue in the instant case, or if the speech carries a real risk of substantial damage to the well being of society.

Blasphemy law: extension or abolition?

The argument to extend blasphemy to cover other faiths will be considered first.[144] To evaluate the force of this argument, it is necessary first to identify which of the rationales for blasphemy law would provide support for extension and which would not. Three rationales will be considered in turn: the argument from the protection of society, the argument from preventing individual distress and the argument from the right to religious freedom. The point of view which sees blasphemy law as protecting those shared beliefs of a society which are essential to its survival[145] would not, it is submitted, support the extension of the law to cover other faiths; the law would then be protecting a whole set of conflicting beliefs and thus supporting religious pluralism, not the survival of religious conformity. It may be argued that the law should uphold religious pluralism as a shared belief but abolition of the offence of blasphemy would do this far more simply than extension.

The argument that blasphemy laws are justified because they protect individual believers from mental anguish immediately runs into a host of problems over extension of the law. For if one is concerned to protect individuals from the mental distress which can flow from attacks on deeply held beliefs,[146] it is not readily apparent that society should not also outlaw attacks upon deeply held non-religious beliefs, such as a deep belief in the equality of the sexes.[147] But one would then arrive at a position in which the

---

144 For general discussion of this issue, see 'Speech, Religious Discrimination and Blasphemy' (1989) *Proceedings of American Society of International Law*, p 427 *et seq* and in particular Reisman's article at 435–39: he makes out an elegant thesis that attempts such as Ayatollah Khomeni's, to punish and deter unorthodox references to the Koran amount to a 'claim of the right to exclusive control of major symbols of global culture and the prerogative of deciding how they are to be used artistically' (p 437). He expresses concern over 'the support lent by religious leaders in the West' to this claim and the criticism of Rushdie expressed by some of them. He warns that imposing censorship on artists or forcing them to internalise such censorship through insisting that free expression amounts to a form of religious intolerance will lead to the deterioration of the arts: creative endeavour will become a kind of 'communal Rubrik cube in which a limited number of approved elements are moved feverishly round in an ever decreasing number of "new" combinations' (p 439).

145 Lord Devlin is usually associated with the thesis that society may justifiably protect its shared moral beliefs through the criminal law: see his *The Enforcement of Morals*, 1965. It is arguable that the protection of society was, historically at least, one of the purposes of blasphemy law: see for example *Taylor's* case [1676] 1 Vent 293 in which it was said: 'For to say, Religion is a cheat is to dissolve all those obligations whereby civil societies are preserved.'

146 Note for example the *dicta* of Lord Scarman in *Lemon* [1979] AC 617 at 620 that 'there is a case for legislation extending [blasphemy law] to protect the religious beliefs and feelings of non-Christians'. Arguably, however, he saw protection of feelings as ultimately aimed at 'the internal tranquillity of the Kingdom'.

147 Recognising this, a number of commentators have attempted to frame definitions of 'religious belief' in which the term includes both actual religious convictions and those beliefs which hold a place in peoples minds analogous to that held by religious belief. See for example Clements, B, 'Defining 'Religion' in the First Amendment: a Functional Approach' (1989) 74 *Cornell LR* 532.

criminal law would be being used to prevent people from attacking or insulting the deep beliefs of others. Arguably such a law would be unworkable since it would require judgments to be made about indeterminable matters such as the depth at which a belief was held. More importantly, not only would such a law represent a major infringement of the individual's freedom of speech, offering only the prevention of distress as a justification, it would be philosophically indefensible besides. For, if we are really committed to the notion that free discussion is the best way to arrive at the truth,[148] it seems nonsensical to abandon that position when our most important beliefs are at stake; if anything we should be most concerned precisely to *encourage* free discussion of our deep beliefs since, almost axiomatically, it is our deepest beliefs which we most wish to be true.

It is submitted that the only justification for blasphemy law which could offer even *prima facie* support for its extension is the argument from the right to religious freedom. If one regards a blasphemy law as essential because the right to religious freedom demands it, then one clearly needs to define religion. One could not follow the path described above and define religion to include secular but deeply held beliefs, as one would then be placed in the absurd position of defending secular ideas from attack by reference to a right to *religious* freedom. Nor could one overcome this difficulty by adopting a pragmatic stance and framing a statute protecting only the five major world religions. If the individual's right to religious freedom demands protection against vilificatory attacks upon her religion,[149] and since presumably members of less well-known religions are as entitled to religious freedom as members of the major religions, it follows that they must also be entitled to protection against such attacks. Clearly, therefore, a satisfactory definition of religion would have to be arrived at. The difficulties of framing such a definition have already been noted. In this connection it is also worth recalling that the UN General Assembly *Declaration on the Elimination of All forms of Intolerance and Discrimination Based on Religion and Belief*, as one commentator notes, 'does not seek to define religion or belief'. He explains that, 'This is because no definition could be agreed upon, as none could be agreed when the texts of Article 18 of the Universal Declaration and Article 18 of the ICCPR were drafted'.[150] Since, therefore, the impossibility of framing such a definition seems to be well-attested to, it may reasonably be concluded that the project to extend blasphemy law to cover other faiths is fraught with difficulty.

---

148 For an exposition of this theory see above pp 138–39.

149 This proposition is not conceded and will be considered below. It is put forward by Poulter, S, 'Towards Legislative Reform of the Blasphemy and Racial Hatred Laws' [1991] PL 85.

150 Boyle, K, 'Religious Intolerance and the Incitement of Hatred' in Coliver, S, ed, *Striking a Balance: Hate Speech, Freedom of Expression and Non-discrimination*, 1992.

Nevertheless, leaving such practical considerations aside, it is necessary to consider the substantive contention that, as Poulter puts it:

> Freedom of religion is ... a valuable human right and it may be doubted whether it can be fully enjoyed in practice if the state allows religious beliefs to be vilified and insulted in a gratuitous manner.[151]

The first assertion made here, about the value of religious freedom, is of course readily conceded. However, the argument goes on to assume that the state is under a positive duty to facilitate the 'full enjoy[ment] in practice' of its citizens' right to freedom of religion. This is surely a mistaken view; rather, it is submitted, the right to religious freedom is violated if one is not free to choose, express and manifest one's religious beliefs:[152] the right is not so violated simply because one is not protected from mental suffering caused by verbal attacks upon one's religion.

However, even if it were to be accepted for the purposes of argument that the religious freedom of those from non-Christian faiths is threatened by the lack of a blasphemy law, it is denied that this finding would be a conclusive argument for extending such a law to cover them. For if Poulter's contention is correct, then we would be confronted by a situation in which two important individual rights – freedom of religion and freedom of speech – came into conflict with each other. In such a situation, it is surely reasonable not simply to assume that freedom of religion should override freedom of speech but rather to attempt to weigh up which right would suffer most if the other was given precedence. If this is done, the argument runs as follows: if there was no offence of blasphemy, this might mean that on occasion some distress, perhaps acute, would be associated with the practice of one's religion. If there *was* such an offence, it might mean that use of the coercive sanctions of the law would severely damage the liberty to write creatively or speak one's mind freely on religious matters.[153] Clearly, the damage done to freedom of religion if there is *no* blasphemy law is far less than the damage done to freedom of speech if there is one; it is therefore concluded that the argument that freedom of religion demands a blasphemy law, fails.

With respect to racial tension, it is by no means clear that extending blasphemy law would ease the problem. Indeed it is possible that if, for example, Muslims had been able to use an extended blasphemy law to suppress *The Satanic Verses*,[154] considerable resentment might well have been

---

151 Poulter, *op cit* p 376.

152 Thus Article 18 of the Universal Declaration of Human Rights provides that 'Everyone has the right to freedom of thought, conscience and religion; this right includes freedom to change his religion or belief and freedom ... in public or private to manifest his religion or belief in teaching, practice, worship and observance'. Both the International Covenant on Civil and Political Rights (Article 18) and the European Convention (Article 9) contain very similar provisions.

153 Poulter concedes that his proposed extension of the blasphemy law (see p 378 *et seq*) might well have caught *The Satanic Verses* (pp 384–85).

154 *Ibid.*

engendered in the non-Muslim community. The justified grievance felt by Muslims about the unfairness of the present law would to a certain extent be remedied if blasphemy was abolished altogether as an offence, since at least it would then be clear that all religions were being accorded an equal lack of protection.

Incitement to religious hatred: extending the offence of incitement to racial hatred?

The International Covenant on Civil and Political Rights to which the UK is a signatory, requires contracting states to prohibit the advocacy of 'national, racial or *religious* hatred that constitutes incitement to discrimination, hostility or violence' (Article 20, emphasis added). In practical terms, it would be fairly straightforward to amend ss 17–23 of Part III of the Public Order Act 1986 which prohibit incitement to racial hatred,[155] to include religious groups.[156] The problem of defining religion of course still remains; however, since such incitement represents a far narrower area of liability than blasphemy, the danger that a wide interpretation of 'religion' would lead to the courts being overrun by claims from obscure groups is accordingly less great. Furthermore, prosecutions in this area can only be brought with the consent of the DPP, so the possibility of frivolous prosecutions being brought would be slight. The justification sometimes put forward for abrogating free speech in this area is that prohibiting the advocacy of racial hatred does not strike at the core value of free speech because neither individual self-fulfilment, nor the opportunity to arrive at the truth through free discussion, nor the chance to participate meaningfully in democracy[157] seem to be strongly threatened by such a prohibition. It would of course, still represent an interference with the individual's moral autonomy – it amounts to judging both for him and his possible audience what is and is not fit for them to hear. However, the state is supposed to leave such judgments to the individual because to do otherwise would be to violate the individual's basic right to equal concern and respect[158] and it may be argued that the present situation, in which the

---

155 For discussion of racial hatred in the context of freedom of speech see Robertson, *Media Law*, Chap 3 pp 129–32; Barendt, pp 161–67 and generally Cotterell, R [1982] *PL* 378; Dickey, A [1968] *Crim LR* 489; Gordon, *Incitement to Racial Hatred*, 1982; Leopold, P [1977] *PL* 389; Wolffe, W [1987] *PL* 85. For the argument that the state should seek to ban racially motivated hate speech on the basis of furtherance of equality just as it seeks to outlaw discrimination in employment see MacKinnon, C, *Only Words*, 1993. For criticism of the argument see Sadurski, W, 'On "Seeing Speech through an Equality Lens": A Critique of Egalitarian Arguments for Suppression of Hate Speech and Pornography' (1996) 16(4) *OJLS* 713.

156 The definition under the Race Relations Act of 'racial group' which will be used under the Public Order Act 1986 does not include religious groups; see *Mandla v Dowell Lee* [1983] 2 AC 548; [1983] 1 All ER 1062, HL.

157 See above pp 140–42.

158 See eg Dworkin, 'Do We Have a Right to Pornography?' in *A Matter of Principle*, 1985.

advocacy of hatred against Muslims is allowed, while Sikhs and Jews are protected from such speech,[159] *itself* amounts to a denial of equal respect for Muslims.[160] Accordingly, there appears to be an arguable case that the Public Order Act provisions should be extended to cover religious hatred: the interference with moral autonomy involved is necessary to avoid discrimination and there is an argument that the free speech interest involved is relatively weak; in addition there are strong utilitarian arguments that such a measure would considerably ease racial tension. At the time of writing the Labour government has made it clear that such legislation is imminent. It will probably be put in place early in 1998.

The argument above is predicated on the assumption that the prohibition of incitement to racial hatred under the Public Order Act does not already create an unacceptable infringement of freedom of speech. However, as pointed out below, it may be argued that the offences as currently conceived go beyond the mischief that they are intended to prevent. There is an argument that some provision should be available to prevent some forms of racist speech due to its special propensity to lead to disorder and that such protection should be extended to religious groups, but it is suggested that one could comfortably support the addition of incitement to religious hatred to Public Order Act offences only once they had been reformed to encompass a narrower area of liability.

Incitement to racial hatred[161]

The 1936 Act was amended in order to include this offence but Part III (ss 17–23) of the Public Order Act 1986 extends the forms it may take. This provision and other powers to control or ban marches under the 1986 Act can be used against extreme right wing organisations attempting to use meetings or marches as a means of harassing persons belonging to ethnic minority groups. However, the Part III provisions are limited by the need to show that racial hatred is likely to be stirred up; thus insulting words addressed at members of a particular racial group will not of themselves attract liability unless the general provision of s 5 of the 1986 Act applies. The 1986 Act does not provide a power to ban processions of racialist organisations unless s 13 applies.

---

159 Muslims, unlike Sikhs and Jews, are not defined as a racial, as well as religious, group. See the definition from *Mandla v Dowell Lee* [1983] 2 AC 548; [1983] 1 All ER 1062, HL, discussed below p 574.

160 It might be argued from this that all measures prohibiting incitement to racial hatred should be repealed but this is not a practicable possibility and would involve the UK in an even clearer breach of Article 20 of the ICCPR than is currently being committed by the lack of protection for Muslims.

161 For general discussion of this offence and its background see Bindman, G (1982) 132 *NLJ* 299; Cotterell, R (1982) *PL* 378; Gordon, *Incitement to Racial Hatred*, 1982; Williams, DGT [1966] *Crim LR* 320; Leopold, P [1977] *PL* 389; Wolffe, W [1987] *PL* 85.

The s 18 provision is most likely to be used in respect of processions and assemblies; it provides that liability will arise if threatening, abusive or insulting words or behaviour are used or written material of that nature is displayed, intended by the defendant to stir up racial hatred or which make it likely that racial hatred will be stirred up against a racial group (not a religious group) in Great Britain.[162] Section 18(2) catches private or public meetings (unless held in a 'dwelling').

Sections 20 and 22 largely re-enact statutory provisions relating to the incitement of racial hatred in the public performance of plays or in certain broadcasts. Section 164(2) of the Broadcasting Act 1990 amended these sections so that they covered 'programme services' rather than broadcasts or 'cable programme' services. Section 23, as amended by s 164(4) of the Broadcasting Act 1990, creates a new offence of possessing racially inflammatory material with a view, in the case of written material to publication or distribution and, in the case of a recording, to its being distributed, shown, played or included in a programme service.

These offences have a number of elements in common. None of them require a need to show disorder or an intent to cause disorder or to stir up racial hatred and there is no need to show that racial hatred is actually stirred up. It would be sufficient to show that hatred *might* actually be stirred up, so long as the accused realised that the words used might be threatening, abusive or insulting.[163] The s 18 offence is the only public order offence which may be committed by words alone unaccompanied by the need to show any likelihood that they would cause distress. The offence could be committed by uttering words which were greeted with delight by those who heard them. However, reasoned argument of a racist nature would not incur liability; the racist words must be threatening, abusive or insulting. Further, the offence might be committed by threatening, abusive or insulting words which, objectively speaking, were incapable of stirring up racial hatred so long as the accused intended that they should do so. However, the term 'hatred' is a strong one: merely causing offence or bringing into ridicule is not enough and nor is racial harassment. If the words in question, which are intended to cause offence rather than stir up hatred, are only used to the racial group they are aimed at this will not constitute the offence because they are unlikely to be stirred to racial hatred against themselves. If a bystander of another racial group is likely to be stirred up to racial hatred against the group being attacked

---

162 'Racial group' is defined using the same terms as under the Race Relations Act; see Chap 13 p 574. The result is that, for example, hatred may be stirred up against Muslims, so long as the s 5 offence is not committed but not against Sikhs.

163 Section 18(5) governs the *mens rea* if it is *not* shown that the defendant intended to stir up racial hatred. He must intend the words etc to be or be aware that they might be, threatening abusive or insulting. Awareness as used in the 1986 Act seems to mean subjective recklessness.

that would, however, fulfil the terms of the offence. Racist chanting at football matches is now prohibited under s 3 of the Football (Offences) Act 1991.

The Commission for Racial Equality has criticised these provisions as ineffective as a means of curbing demonstrations and marches by racist groups in certain areas but the Conservative government took the view that such activities should not be prevented since this would represent too severe a curtailment of freedom of expression.[164] However, in certain circumstances, where members of a particular racial group felt threatened by a demonstration, ss 4, 4A or 5 of the 1986 Act might be applicable.[165] Parliament has declined so far to create a new crime of racial attack or harassment which might sometimes be applicable to racist marches.

It may be argued that the s 18 offence as currently conceived is unsatisfactory. It is both over – and under – inclusive in failing on the one hand to protect racial groups from intimidatory marches but on the other catching speech which has not caused offence to any person and which in the circumstances (a private meeting in a pub or club for example) will not lead to immediate disorder. In company with s 5 of the 1986 Act it therefore offends against the principle that the protection of free speech should extend to ideas which disturb or shock. It is suggested that the s 18 offence should be reframed with a view to catching grossly offensive, intimidatory public behaviour or speech, including incitement to race hatred, which may come about during a racist march or assembly, rather than more widely restraining the expression of offensive ideas.[166]

Although the 1986 Act was supposed to make it easier to obtain convictions, prosecutions are rare. No prosecution may be brought without the consent of the Attorney General, with the result that although there are a large number of complaints, very few prosecutions are brought.[167] Consent is often withheld for various reasons. Prosecutions for these offences are sometimes counter-productive since the group in question may thereby gain a publicity for its material which would otherwise be lacking. If an acquittal occurs racist groups may be encouraged. Prosecutions may persuade racist groups to present their material in a less obviously bigoted style and by expressing themselves in moderate, quasi-educational terms, may be more successful in persuading others to sympathise with their cause.[168]

---

164 For discussion of this point see Poulter, S [1991] *PL* 85; Coliver, S, ed, *Striking a Balance: Hate Speech, Freedom of Expression and Non-discrimination*, 1992.
165 See Chap 7 pp 306–11.
166 See Robertson, *Media Law*, pp 168–69 for discussion of the effect of this form of liability in relation to freedom of speech.
167 By 1993 the Attorney General had given his consent to prosecution in 13 cases and convictions had been obtained in 7: *CRE Report* 1993 p 24.
168 See the Home Office Review of the relevant law 1975, Cmnd 6234.

CHAPTER 6

OFFICIAL SECRECY AND ACCESS TO INFORMATION

1 INTRODUCTION[1]

An assertion of a right to access to information probably should be distinguished from an assertion of a free speech right, although the two are clearly linked. This distinction receives support from the wording of Article 10 of the European Convention which speaks in terms of the freedom to 'receive and impart information', thus appearing to exclude from its provisions the right to demand information from the unwilling speaker. Moreover, the phrase 'without interference from public authorities' does not suggest that governments should come under any duty to act in order to ensure that information is received.

There are two reasons why access to information is often treated as a distinct interest. First, information may be sought although it is not intended that it should be communicated. It is not clear that the free speech justifications considered in the introduction to Part II would apply to someone such as a civil servant who disclosed information in such circumstances and therefore such a situation would tend to be considered purely as a freedom of information or privacy issue. Indeed, in such instances the seeker of information might well be asserting a right not merely to gain access to the information but also to have its confidential quality maintained. Access rights under the Data Protection Act 1984 often take account of both interests (see Chapter 8) and therefore may be said to be opposed to free speech interests. Thus it is clear that many demands for access to information are not based on an assertion of free speech interests. Secondly, information intended to be placed in the public domain may be sought when there is no speaker willing to disclose it or where the body which 'owns' the information is unwilling that it should be disclosed. Whether such communication of confidential

---

1 General reading, see Hartley, T and Griffiths, J, *Government and Law*, 2nd edn, 1981, Chap 13; Williams, DGT, *Not in the Public Interest*, 1965; Leigh, D, *The Frontiers of Secrecy – Closed Government in Britain*, 1980; Michael, J, *The Politics of Secrecy*, 1982; Robertson, G, *Public Secrets*, 1982; Wilson, D, *The Secrets File*, 1984; Wass, D, *Government and the Governed*, 1984, p 81 *et seq*; Birkinshaw, P, *Freedom of Information*, 2nd edn, 1996; Ewing and Gearty, *Freedom Under Thatcher*, 1990, Chap 6; Birkinshaw, P, *Government and Information*, 1990; Feldman, D, *Civil Liberties and Human Rights in England and Wales*, 1993, Chap 14; Bailey, Harris and Jones, *Civil Liberties: Cases and Materials*, 3rd edn, 1995, Chap 7; Baxter, JD, *State Security, Privacy and Information*, 1990; Shetreet, S (ed), *Free Speech and National Security*, 1991; Gill, P, *Policing Politics: Security, Intelligence and the Liberal Democratic State*, 1994; Lustgarten, l and Leigh, I, *In From the Cold: National Security and Parliamentary Democracy*, 1994; Whitty, N, Murphy, T and Livingstone, S, *Civil Liberties Law*, 1997.

information should be regarded as 'speech' or not,[2] it is clearly a necessary precondition for the production of speech and therefore could be treated as deserving the same protection as 'speech' in that the result will be that the public will acquire information. The argument that such dissemination of information will render the government more readily accountable is indistinguishable from the justification for free speech which argues that it is indispensable to democracy since it enables informed participation by the citizenry.

However, freedom of speech does not tend to encompass the imposition of positive obligations and therefore in general is violated when a willing speaker is prevented from speaking, in contrast with the situation where information deriving ultimately from an unwilling speaker – usually the government – is sought entailing the assertion of a positive right. Thus, a distinction should be drawn between gaining access to the information and then placing it in the public domain – the second situation giving rise to a free speech interest – but because these issues tend to arise together within the present legal scheme in the UK protecting a 'closed' system of government, it is convenient to consider both within the same chapter.

Rights of access to information overlap with certain privacy interests since they may cover many situations in which a person might wish to receive information, apart from that of the individual who wishes to obtain and publicise government information. However, freedom of information is most readily associated with the demand for the receipt of information with a view to placing it in the public domain; thus the rights of the individual who wishes to receive information for his or her *private* purposes will be considered in Chapter 8.

Probably the most important value associated with freedom of information is the need for the citizen to understand as fully as possible the working of government, in order to render it accountable; the main concern of this chapter is therefore with the methods employed by government to ensure that official information cannot fall into the hands of those who might place it in the public domain and with methods of preventing or deterring persons from publication when such information has been obtained. Its emphasis is on the degree to which a proper balance is struck between the interest of the individual in acquiring government information and the interest of the state in withholding it, often on grounds of national security. Clearly there is a genuine public interest in keeping some information out of the public domain; the question is whether other interests which do not correspond with and may

---

2   The European Court of Human Rights takes the view that it should not. In the *Gaskin* case (1990) 12 EHRR 36 it viewed a demand for access for information which the body holding it did not wish to disclose as giving rise only to an Art 8 issue, not an Art 10 issue. The US Supreme Court has held that the First Amendment does not impose an affirmative duty on government to make information not in the public domain available to journalists (417 US 817). For discussion of this issue see Barendt, *Freedom of Speech*, 1987, pp 107–13.

even be opposed to the interests of the public are also at work. Initially, it may be said that in the UK the area of control over government information is one in which the state's supposed interest in keeping information secret often seems to prevail very readily over the individual interest in question; often the justifications put forward for preventing access to information could not conceivably be brought within one of the three justifications broadly accepted by liberal political theory as allowing the infringement of individual rights.[3]

It has often been said that the UK is more obsessed with keeping government information secret than any other Western democracy.[4] It is clearly advantageous for the party in power to be able to control the flow of information in order to prevent public scrutiny of certain official decisions and in order to be able to release information selectively at convenient moments. The British government has available a number of methods of keeping official information secret, including use of the doctrine of public interest immunity, the deterrent effect of criminal sanctions under the Official Secrets Act 1989, the Civil Service Conduct Code,[5] around 80 statutory provisions engendering secrecy in various areas and the action for breach of confidence. The justification traditionally put forward for maintaining a climate of secrecy, which goes beyond protecting specific public interests such as national security, is that freedom of information would adversely affect 'ministerial accountability'. In other words, ministers are responsible for the actions of civil servants in their departments and therefore must be able to control the flow of information emanating from the department in question. However, it is usually seen as essential to democracy that government should allow a reasonably free flow of information so that citizens can be informed as to the government process and can therefore assess government decisions in the light of all the available facts, thereby participating fully in the workings of the democracy. A number of groups therefore advocate freedom of information and more 'open' government in Britain, as in most other democracies. They accept that certain categories of information should be exempt from disclosure but that those categories should be as restricted as possible compatible with the needs of the interest protected, and that the categorisation of any particular piece of information should be open to challenge.

The citizen's 'right to know' is recognised in most democracies including the USA, Canada, Australia, New Zealand, Denmark, Sweden, Holland, Norway, Greece and France. In such countries the general principle of freedom of information is subject to exceptions where information falls into specific categories. Perhaps responding to the general acceptance of freedom

---

3   For an explanation of these three justifications see Chap 1 pp 11–13.
4   For example, Robertson, *Freedom, the Individual and the Law*, 1989, pp 129–31.
5   See Drewry and Butcher, *The Civil Service Today*, 1991. It should be pointed out that the Civil Service Code which came into force on 1 January 1996 contains a partial 'whistle-blowing' provision in paras 11–12.

of information, there was a shift in the attitude of the Conservative government of 1992–97 to freedom of information in the UK in 1992: that is, the principle was accepted but the traditional stance as to the role of the law hardly changed. The UK has traditionally resisted freedom of information legislation and until 1989 criminalised the unauthorised disclosure of any official information at all, however trivial, under s 2 of the Official Secrets Act 1911, thereby creating a climate of secrecy in the civil service which greatly hampered the efforts of those who wished to obtain and publish information about the workings of government. The current Labour government is, however, committed to introducing a Freedom of Information Act.

2 OFFICIAL SECRECY

Section 2 of the Official Secrets Act 1911[6]

During the 19th century, as government departments grew larger and handled more official information, the problem of confidentiality grew more acute. Internal circulars such as the 1873 Treasury minute entitled *The Premature Disclosure of Official Information* urged secrecy on all members of government departments and threatened the dismissal of civil servants who disclosed any information; a Treasury minute issued in 1875 warned civil servants of the dangers of close links with the press.[7] The need for a further safeguard was emphasised in 1878 when one Marvin, who worked in the Foreign Office, gave details of a secret treaty negotiated between England and Russia to a particular newspaper. His motive appeared to be dissatisfaction with his job. He was prosecuted but it was then discovered that no part of the criminal law covered the situation. He had memorised the information and thus had not stolen any document. He was not a spy and could not therefore be brought within the provisions of the Treason Act 1814. No conviction could be obtained and the Official Secrets Act 1889 was passed largely as a means of plugging the gap which had been discovered.

The 1889 Act made it an offence for a person wrongfully to communicate information obtained owing to his employment as a civil servant. However, the government grew dissatisfied with this measure; under its terms the state had the burden of proving both *mens rea* and that the disclosure was not in the interests of the state. It was thought that a stronger measure was needed and this led eventually to the passing of the Official Secrets Act 1911. It has often been suggested that the manner of its introduction into Parliament was disingenuous and misleading.[8] It was introduced apparently in response to

---

6 See Hooper, D, *Official Secrets*, 1987, for history of the use of s 2.
7 See Robertson, *Public Secrets*, 1982, p 53.
8 See The Franks Report para 50 (Cmnd 5104, 1972); Birkinshaw, *Freedom of Information*, p 76.

fears of espionage and by the Secretary of State for War, not by the Home Secretary, giving the impression that it was largely an anti-espionage measure. Section 1 did deal largely with espionage but s 2 was aimed not at enemy agents but at English civil servants and other crown employees. It was called, innocuously, 'an Act to re-enact the 1889 Act with amendments'. These disarming measures seem to have succeeded; it was passed in one afternoon and s 2 received no debate at all.

Section 2, which appeared to create a crime of strict liability, imposed a complete prohibition on the unauthorised dissemination of official information, however trivial. It is thought that the government clearly intended s 2 to have such a wide scope and had wanted such a provision for some time in order to prevent leaks of *any* kind of official information whether or not connected with defence or national security.[9] It lacked any provision regarding the substance of the information disclosed so that technically it criminalised, for example, disclosure of the colour of the carpet in a minister's office. It criminalised the receiver of information as well as the communicator, although there did appear to be a requirement of *mens rea* as far as the receiver was concerned; he or she had to know that the disclosure had occurred in contravention of the Act. Thus it afforded no recognition to the role of the press in informing the public.

There were surprisingly few prosecutions under s 2; it seems likely that it created an acceptance of secrecy in the civil service which tended to preclude disclosure. In one of the few cases which did come to court, *Fell* (1963),[10] the Court of Appeal confirmed that liability was not dependent on the contents of the document in question or on whether the disclosure would have an effect prejudicial to the interests of the state. The eventual demise of s 2 came about due to a number of factors, of which one appears to have been the realisation that its draconian nature was perceived as unacceptable in a modern democracy and that therefore convictions under it could not be assured. Such a realisation probably developed in response to the following three decisions.

Aitken and others[11] arose due to the disclosure by a reporter, Aitken, that the UK government had misled the British people as to the amount of aid the UK was giving Nigeria in its war against Biafra. The government had suggested that it was supplying about 15% of Nigeria's arms, whereas the figure should have been about 70%. This figure derived from a government document called the Scott Report which Aitken disclosed to the press. Aitken was then prosecuted under s 2 for receiving and passing on information but the judge at trial, Mr Justice Caulfield, clearly had little sympathy with a case seemingly brought merely to assuage government embarrassment and which

---

9   See The Franks Report para 50 (Cmnd 5104, 1972).
10 [1963] *Crim LR* 207.
11 Unreported. See Aitken, J, *Officially Secret*, 1971.

disclosed no national security interest. Furthermore, the facts obtained from the Scott Report were obtainable from other sources. The judge found that a requirement of *mens rea* was needed and, moreover, effectively directed the jury to acquit in a speech which placed weight on the freedom of the press and suggested that it should prevail given the lack of a significant competing interest. He considered that s 2 should be 'pensioned off'.

Tisdall[12] also created some adverse publicity for the government due to what was perceived as a very heavy handed use of s 2. Sarah Tisdall worked in the Foreign Secretary's private office and in the course of her duties came across documents relating to the delivery of cruise missiles to the RAF base at Greenham Common. She discovered proposals to delay the announcement of their delivery until after it had occurred and to make the announcement in Parliament at the end of question time in order to avoid answering questions. She took the view that this political subterfuge was morally wrong and therefore leaked the documents to the *Guardian*. However, they were eventually traced back to her. She pleaded guilty to an offence under s 2 and received a prison sentence of six months – an outcome which was generally seen as harsh.[13]

A similar situation arose in *Ponting*,[14] the case which is usually credited with sounding the death knell of s 2. Clive Ponting, a senior civil servant in the Ministry of Defence, was responsible for policy on the operational activities of the Royal Navy at a time when Opposition MPs, particularly Tam Dalyell, were pressing the government for information relating to the sinking of the *Belgrano* in the Falklands conflict. Michael Heseltine, then Secretary of State for Defence, decided to withhold such information from Parliament and therefore did not use a reply to Parliamentary questions drafted by Ponting. He used instead a much briefer version of it and circulated a confidential minute indicating that answers on the rules of engagement in the Falklands conflict should not be given to questions put by the Parliamentary Select Committee on Foreign Affairs. Feeling that Opposition MPs were being prevented from undertaking effective scrutiny of the workings of government, Ponting sent the unused reply and the minute anonymously to the Labour MP, Tam Dalyell, who disclosed the documents to the press.

Ponting was charged with the offence of communicating information under s 2. The relevant sub-section reads:

> ... it is an offence for a person holding Crown office to communicate official information to any person other than a person he is authorised to communicate it to or a person to whom it is *in the interests of the state* his duty to communicate it. (Emphasis added.)

---

12 (1984) *The Times*, 26 March.
13 See Cripps, Y, 'Disclosure in the Public Interest: The Predicament of the Public Sector Employee' [1983] *PL* 600.
14 [1985] *Crim LR* 318; for comment see [1985] *PL* 203, 212 and [1986] *Crim LR* 491.

The defence relied on the phrase the 'interests of the state', arguing that 'state' should be interpreted as 'the organised community' rather than the government. This interpretation seemed to be warranted by part of Lord Reid's judgment in *Chandler v DPP*.[15] Thus it could be argued that it was in the interests of the nation as a whole that Parliament should not be misled and that there was a moral duty to prevent this. The word 'duty' in s 2, it was claimed, therefore connoted a moral or public duty. However, the Crown relied upon other comments of Lord Reid in *Chandler* to the effect that where national security was a factor the government would be the final arbiter of the state's interests. The judge, McCowan J, accepted this argument, finding that the 'interests of the state' were synonymous with those of the government of the day and he therefore effectively directed the jury to convict. Despite this direction they acquitted, presumably feeling that Ponting should have a defence if he was acting in the public interest in trying to prevent government suppression of matters of public interest. The prosecution and its outcome provoked a large amount of adverse publicity, the public perceiving it as an attempt at a cover up which had failed, not because the judge showed integrity but because the jury did.[16]

The decision in *Ponting* suggested that the very width of s 2 was undermining its credibility; its usefulness in instilling a culture of secrecy due to its catch-all quality was seen as working against it. The outcome of the case may have influenced the decision not to prosecute Cathy Massiter, a former officer in the Security Service, in respect of her claims in a Channel 4 programme screened in March 1985 (*MI5's Official Secrets*) that MI5 had tapped the phones of trade union members and placed leading CND members under surveillance.[17] Section 2's lack of credibility may also have been a factor in the decision to bring civil as opposed to criminal proceedings against the *Guardian* and *Observer* in respect of their disclosure of Peter Wright's allegations in *Spycatcher*: civil proceedings for breach of confidence were in many ways more convenient and certainly less risky than a s 2 prosecution. No jury would be involved and a temporary injunction could be obtained quickly in *ex parte* proceedings. However, the government did consider that the criminal rather than the civil law was in general a more appropriate weapon to use against people such as Ponting, and therefore thought it desirable that an effective criminal sanction should be available.

---

15 [1964] AC 763; [1962] 3 All ER 142, HL.
16 For comment on the decision see Ponting, C, *The Right to Know*, 1985; Brewry, G, 'The Ponting Case' [1985] *PL* 203.
17 The IBA banned the programme pending the decision as to whether Massiter and the producers would be prosecuted. The decision not to prosecute was announced by Sir Michael Havers on 5 March 1985. An enquiry into telephone tapping by Lord Bridge reported on 6 March that all authorised taps had been properly authorised. This of course did not address the allegation that some tapping had been carried out although unauthorised.

When the government was eventually defeated in the *Spycatcher* litigation the need for such a sanction became clearer.[18]

There had already been a long history of proposals for the reform of s 2. The Franks Committee, which was set up in response to Caulfield J's comments in *Aitken*, recommended[19] that s 2 should be replaced by narrower provisions which took into account the nature of the information disclosed. The Franks proposals formed the basis of the government's White Paper on which the Official Secrets Act 1989 was based. There had been various other attempts at reform; those put forward as Private Members' Bills were the more liberal. For example, Clement Freud MP put forward an Official Information Bill[20] which would have created a public right of access to official information, while the Protection of Official Information Bill[21] put forward by Richard Shepherd MP in 1987 would have provided a public interest defence and a defence of prior disclosure.

The Official Secrets Act 1989[22]

Once the decision to reform the area of official secrecy had been taken, an opportunity was created for radical change which could have included freedom of information legislation along the lines of the instruments in America and Canada. However, it was made clear from the outset that the legislation was unconcerned with freedom of information.[23] It de-criminalises disclosure of some official information, although an official who makes such disclosure may of course face an action for breach of confidence as well as disciplinary proceedings but it makes no provision for allowing the release of any official documents into the public domain. Thus, claims made, for example, by Douglas Hurd (the then Home Secretary) that it is 'a great liberalising measure' clearly rest on other aspects of the Act. Aspects which are usually viewed as liberalising features include the categorisation of information covered which makes relevant the *substance* of the information, the introduction of tests for harm, the *mens rea* requirement of ss 5 and 6, the

---

18 *AG v Guardian (No 2)* [1990] 1 AC 109 (see below pp 251–53).
19 Report of the Committee on s 2 of the Official Secrets Act 1911 (1972) Cmnd 5104; see Birtles, W, 'Big Brother Knows Best: The Franks Report on Section 2 of the Official Secrets Act' [1973] *PL* 100.
20 1978–79 Bill 96.
21 1987–88 Bill 20.
22 For comment on the 1989 Act see Palmer, S, 'The Government Proposals for Reforming s 2 of the Official Secrets Act 1911' [1988] *PL* 523; Hanbury, W, 'Illiberal Reform of s 2' (1989) 133 *Sol Jo* 587; Palmer, S, 'Tightening Secrecy Law' [1990] *PL* 243; Griffith, J, 'The Official Secrets Act 1989' (1989) 16 *JLS* 273; Feldman, D, *Civil Liberties and Human Rights*, 1993, Chap 14.3.
23 See White Paper on s 2 (1978) Cmnd 7285; Green Paper on *Freedom of Information* (1979) Cmnd 7520; White Paper: *Reform of the Official Secrets Act 1911* (1988) Cmnd 408.

defences available and decriminalisation of the receiver of information. In all these respects the Act differs from its predecessor but the nature of the changes has led commentators to question whether they will bring about any real liberalisation.[24] Other aspects of the Act have also attracted criticism: it applies to persons other than Crown servants, including journalists; it contains no defences of public interest or of prior disclosure and no general requirement to prove *mens rea*. Thus, what is omitted from its provisions, including the failure to provide any right of access to information falling outside the protected categories, is arguably as significant as what is included.

Criminal liability for disclosing information

The general prohibition on disclosing information under the Official Secrets Act 1911 was replaced by the more specific prohibitions under the Official Secrets Act 1989. Sections 1–4 of the 1989 Act (excepting the provisions of s 1(1)) which also determine the categorisation of the information, all concern unauthorised disclosures by any present or former Crown servant or government contractor of information which has been acquired in the course of his or her employment. If a civil servant happened to acquire by other means information falling within one of the categories which he or she then disclosed, the provisions of s 5 would apply. Section 7 (below) governs the meaning of 'authorisation' while ss 5 and 6 apply when any person – not only a Crown servant – discloses information falling within the protected categories.

Security and intelligence information is covered by s 1. The category covers 'the work of or in support of, the security and intelligence services' and includes 'references to information held or transmitted by those services or by persons in support of ... those services'.[25] It is therefore a wide category and is not confined only to work done by members of the Security Services. Section 1(1) is intended to prevent members or former members of the Security Services (and any person notified that he is subject to the provisions of the subsection) disclosing anything at all relating or appearing to relate to[26] the operation of those services. All such members thus come under a lifelong duty to keep silent even though their information might reveal a serious abuse of power in the Security Service or some operational weakness. There is no need to show that any harm will or may flow from the disclosure and so all information, however trivial, is covered.

---

24 For example, Ewing and Gearty, *Freedom Under Thatcher*, p 200.
25 Section 1(9).
26 Under s 1(2) misinformation falls within the information covered by s 1(1) as it includes 'making any statement which purports to be a disclosure of such information or which is intended to be taken ... as being such a disclosure'.

Section 1(3), which criminalises disclosure of information relating to the security services by a former or present Crown servant as opposed to a member of the Security Services, does include a test for harm under s 1(4) which provides that:

... a disclosure is damaging if:
(a) it causes damage to the work of or any part of, the security and intelligence services; or
(b) it is of information or a document or other article which is such that its unauthorised disclosure would be likely to cause such damage or which falls within a class or description of information, documents or articles the unauthorised disclosure of which would be likely to have that effect.

Taken at its lowest level it is clear that this test may be very readily satisfied: it is not necessary to show that disclosure of the actual document in question has caused harm or would be likely to cause harm, merely that it belongs to a class of documents, disclosure of which would be likely to have that effect. Disclosure of a document containing insignificant information and incapable itself of causing the harm described under s 1(4)(a) can therefore be criminalised, suggesting that the importation of a harm test for Crown servants as opposed to members of the security services may not inevitably in practice create a very significant distinction between them. However, at the next level, harm must be likely to flow from disclosure of a specific document where due to its unique nature it cannot be said to be one of a class of documents and in such an instance the ruling of the House of Lords in *Lord Advocate v Scotsman Publications Ltd*[27] suggests that the test for harm may be quite restrictively interpreted: it will be necessary to show quite a strong likelihood that harm will arise and the nature of the harm must be specified. The ruling was given in the context of civil proceedings for breach of confidence but the House of Lords decided the case on the basis of the principles under the 1989 Act even though it was not then in force. The ruling concerned publication by a journalist of material relating to the work of the intelligence services. Thus the test for harm had to be interpreted, according to s 5, in accordance with the test under s 1(3) as though the disclosure had been by a Crown servant. The Crown conceded that the information in question was innocuous but argued that harm would be done because the publication would undermine confidence in the Security Services. The House of Lords, noting that there had already been a degree of prior publication, rejected this argument as unable alone to satisfy the test for harm. The case therefore gives some indication as to the interpretation the harm tests may receive.

Even taken at its highest level the harm test is potentially very wide due to its open-textured wording. It states, in effect, that a disclosure of information in this category is damaging if it causes damage to the area of government

---

[27] [1990] 1 AC 812; [1989] 2 All ER 852, HL; for criticism of the ruling see Walker [1990] *PL* 354.

operation covered by the category. No clue is given as to what is meant by 'damage'; in many cases it would therefore be impossible for a Crown servant to determine beforehand whether or not a particular disclosure would be criminal. The only safe approach would be non-disclosure of almost all relevant information; the position of Crown servants under the 1989 Act in relation to information in this category is therefore only with some difficulty to be distinguished from that under the 1911 Act. However, the fact that there is a test for harm at all under s 1(3), however weak, affirms a distinction of perhaps symbolic importance between two groups of Crown servants because the first step in determining whether a disclosure may be criminalised is taken by reference to the *status* of the person making the disclosure rather than by the nature of the information, suggesting that s 1(1) is aimed at underpinning a culture of secrecy in the Security Services rather than at ensuring that no damaging disclosure is likely to be made.

Section 2 covers information relating to defence. What is meant by defence is set out in s 2(4):

(a) the size, shape organisation, logistics order of battle, deployment, operations, state of readiness and training of the armed forces of the Crown;

(b) the weapons, stores or other equipment of those forces and the invention, development, production and operation of such equipment and research relating to it;

(c) defence policy and strategy and military planning and intelligence;

(d) plans and measures for the maintenance of essential supplies and services that are or would be needed in time of war.

It must be shown that the disclosure in question is or would be likely to be damaging as defined under s 2(2):

(a) it damages the capability of or of any part of, the armed forces of the Crown to carry out their tasks or leads to loss of life or injury to members of those forces or serious damage to the equipment or installations of those forces; or

(b) otherwise than as mentioned in para (a) above, it endangers the interests of the United Kingdom abroad, seriously obstructs the promotion or protection by the United Kingdom of those interests or endangers the safety of British citizens abroad; or

(c) it is of information or of a document or article which is such that its unauthorised disclosure would be likely to have any of those effects.

The first part of this test under (a), which is fairly specific and deals with quite serious harm, may be contrasted with (b) which is much wider. The opening words of (b) may mean that although the *subject* of the harm may fall within (a), the level of harm can be considered within (b) since it does not fall within terms denoting harm used in (a). This could occur where, for example, there had been *damage* as opposed to 'serious damage' to installations abroad.

Clearly, this interpretation would allow the harm test to be satisfied in a wider range of situations. On this interpretation, as far as disclosures concerning UK armed forces operating *abroad* are concerned, it would seem that (b) renders (a) largely redundant, so that (a) would tend to play a role only where the disclosure concerned operations within the UK. It may be noted that parts of this test are mere verbiage; it would be hard to draw a significant distinction between 'endangering' and 'seriously obstructing' the interests of the UK abroad. In fact, the overlapping of the harm tests within the categories and across the categories is a feature of this statute; the reasons why this may be so are considered below.

Information relating to international relations falls within s 3(1)(a). This category covers disclosure of 'any information, document or other article relating to international relations'. Clarification of this provision is undertaken by s 3(5) which creates a test to be used in order to determine whether information falls within it. First, it must concern the relations between states, between international organisations or between an international organisation and a state; secondly it is said that this includes matter which is capable of affecting the relation between the UK and another state or between the UK and an international organisation. The harm test arises under s 3(2) and is identical to that arising under s 2(2)(b) and (c).

Section 3(1)(b) refers to confidential information emanating from other states or international organisations. This category covers 'any confidential information, document or other article which was obtained from a state other than the United Kingdom or an international organisation'. Clearly, the substance of this information might differ from that covered under s 3(1)(a), although some documents might fall within both categories. Under s 3(6) the information will be confidential if it is expressed to be so treated due to the terms under which it was obtained or if the circumstances in which it was obtained impute an obligation of confidence. The harm test under this category contained in s 3(3) is somewhat curious: the mere fact that the information is confidential or its nature or contents 'may' be sufficient to establish the likelihood that its disclosure would cause harm within the terms of s 3(2)(b). In other words, once the information is identified as falling within this category a fiction is created that harm may automatically flow from its disclosure. This implies that there are circumstances (such as a particularly strong quality of confidentiality?) in which the only ingredient which the prosecution *must* prove is that the information falls within the category.

Section 4 is headed 'crime and special investigation powers'. Section 4(2) covers any information the disclosure of which:

(a) ... results in the commission of an offence; or facilitates an escape from legal custody or the doing of any other act prejudicial to the safekeeping of persons in legal custody; or impedes the prevention or detection of offences or the apprehension or prosecution of suspected offenders; or

(b) which is such that its unauthorised disclosure would be likely to have any of those effects.

'Legal custody' includes detention in pursuance of any enactment or any instrument made under an enactment (s 4(6)). In contrast to s 3(3) in which the test for harm may be satisfied once the information is identified as falling within the category, in s 4(2) once the test for harm has been satisfied the information will necessarily be so identified. As with s 2 parts of this test could have been omitted, such as 'facilitates an escape' which would have been covered by the succeeding general words.

Section 4(3) covers information obtained by the use of intercept and security service warrants. This applies to:

(a) any information obtained by reason of the interception of any communication in obedience to a warrant issued under s 2 of the Interception of Communications Act 1985, any information relating to the obtaining of information by reason of any such interception and any document or other article which is or has been used or held for use in or has been obtained by reason of any such interception; and

(b) any information obtained by reason of action authorised by a warrant issued under s 3 of the Security Service Act 1989, any information relating to the obtaining of information by reason of any such action and any document or other article which is or has been used or held for use in or has been obtained by reason of any such action.

There is no harm test under this category. Thus, in so far as it covers the work of the Security Services, it creates a wide exception to the general need to show harm under s 1(3) when a Crown servant who is not a member of the Security Service makes a disclosure about the work of those services.

Section 5 is headed 'information resulting from unauthorised disclosures or entrusted in confidence'. This is not a new category. Information will fall within s 5 if it falls within one or more of the previous categories and it has been disclosed to the defendant by a Crown servant or falls within s 1 of the Official Secrets Act 1911. Section 5 is primarily aimed at journalists who receive information leaked to them by Crown servants, although it could of course cover anybody in that position. It is also aimed at the person to whom a document is entrusted by a Crown servant 'on terms requiring it to be held in confidence or in circumstances in which the Crown servant or government contractor could reasonably expect that it would be so held' (s 5(1)(ii)). The difference between entrusting and disclosing is significant in that in the former instance the document – but not the information it contains – will have been entrusted to the care of the person in question.

If the Crown servant has disclosed or entrusted it to another who discloses it to the defendant this will suffice (s 5(1)(a)(i) and (iii)). These provisions are presumably aimed mainly at the journalist or other non-Crown servant who receives the information from another journalist who received it from the civil servant in question. However, this does not apply where the information has been *entrusted* to the defendant but has never been *disclosed* to him or her; in that case it must come directly from the civil servant, not from another person who had it entrusted to him or her (s 5(1)(b)(ii)). The disclosure of the information or document by the person into whose possession it has come must not already be an offence under any of the six categories.

In contrast to disclosure of information by a Crown servant under ss 1–4, s 5 does import a requirement of *mens rea* under s 5(2) which, as far as information falling within ss 1, 2 and 3 is concerned consists of three elements. The defendant must disclose the information knowing or having reasonable cause to believe that it falls within one or more of the categories, that it has come into his possession as mentioned in subsection (1) above and that it will be damaging (s 5(3)(b)). As far as information falling within s 4 and probably s 3(1)(b) is concerned, only the first two of these elements will be relevant. Under s 5(6) only the first of these elements need be proved if the information came into the defendant's possession as a result of a contravention of s 1 of the Official Secrets Act 1911. Thus, as far as disclosure of such information is concerned, the *mens rea* requirement will be fulfilled even though the defendant believed that the disclosure would not be damaging and intended that it should not be. Indeed, since the *mens rea* includes an objective element it may be satisfied under all the categories where the defendant did not in fact possess the belief in question but had reasonable cause to possess it.

The requirement of *mens rea*, although not as strict as may at first appear, represents the only means of differentiating between journalists and Crown servants. The test for damage will be determined as it would be if the information was disclosed by a Crown servant in contravention of ss 1(3), 2(1) or 3(1) above. Section 4 is not mentioned because the information will not be capable of falling within s 4(1) unless the harm test is satisfied. As already mentioned there is no harm test under s 4(3). Thus an interesting anomaly arises: if, for example, information relating to the work of MI5 is disclosed to a journalist by a Security Service agent, a distinction is drawn between disclosure by the agent and by the journalist: in general it will not be assumed in the case of the latter that the disclosure will cause harm but if the information relates to (say) telephone tapping, no such distinction is drawn. If the journalist is then charged with an offence falling within s 5 due to the disclosure of information under s 4(3) both he or she and the agent will be in an equally disadvantageous position as far as the harm test is concerned. The apparent recognition of journalistic duty effected by importing the harm test under s 1(3) into the situation where a security service member discloses information to a journalist, may therefore be circumvented where such information also falls within s 4(3).

Another apparent improvement which might tend to affect journalists more than others is the decriminalisation of the receiver of information. If he or she refrains from publishing it, no liability will be incurred. Of course this improvement might be said to be more theoretical than real in that it was perhaps unlikely that the mere receiver would be prosecuted under the 1911 Act even though that possibility did exist.

Official Secrecy and Access to Information

The fact that journalists were included at all in the net of criminal liability under s 5 has been greatly criticised on the basis that some recognition should be given to the important role of the press in informing the public about government policy and actions.[28] A comparison could be drawn with the constitutional role of the press recognised in America by the *Pentagon Papers* case:[29] the Supreme Court determined that no restraining order on the press could be made so that the press would remain free to censure the government.

Section 6 covers the unauthorised publication abroad of information which falls into one of the other substantive categories apart from crime and special investigation powers. It covers the disclosure to a UK citizen of information which has been received in confidence from the UK by another state or international organisation. Typically the section might cover a leak of such information to a foreign journalist who then passed it on to a UK journalist. However, liability will not be incurred if the state or organisation (or a member of the organisation) authorises the disclosure of the information to the public (s 6(3)). Again, since this section is aimed at journalists a requirement of *mens rea* is imported: it must be shown under s 6(2) that the defendant made 'a damaging disclosure of [the information] knowing or having reasonable cause to believe that it is such as is mentioned in subsection (1) above and that its disclosure would be damaging'. However, it is important to note that under s 6(4) the test for harm under this section is to be determined 'as it would be in relation to a disclosure of the information, document or article in question by a Crown servant in contravention of s 1(3), 2(1) and 3(1) above'. Thus, although it appears that two tests must be satisfied in order to fulfil the *mens rea* requirement, the tests may in fact be conflated as far as s 3(1)(b) is concerned because proof that the defendant knew that the information fell within the relevant category may satisfy the requirement that he or she knew that the disclosure would be damaging. The requirement that *mens rea* be established is not therefore as favourable to the defendant as it appears to be because – as noted in respect of s 5 – it may be satisfied even where the defendant believes that no damage will result. Once again, aside from this particular instance, this applies in all the categories due to the objective element in the *mens rea* arising from the words 'reasonable cause to believe'.

The requirement that the information, document or article is communicated in confidence will be satisfied as under s 3 if it is communicated in 'circumstances in which the person communicating it could reasonably expect that it would be so held' (s 6(5)). In other words, it need not be expressly designated 'confidential'.

---

28 See eg Ewing and Gearty, *Freedom Under Thatcher*, pp 196–201.
29 *New York Times Co v US* 403 US 713 (1971).

A disclosure will not lead to liability under the Act if it is authorised and so it is necessary to determine whether or not authorisation has taken place. The meaning of 'authorised disclosures' is determined by s 7. A disclosure will be authorised if it is made in accordance with the official duty of the Crown servant or a person in whose case a notification for the purposes of s 1(1) is in force. As far as a government contractor is concerned, a disclosure will be authorised if made 'in accordance with an official authorisation' or 'for the purposes of the functions by virtue of which he is a government contractor and without contravening an official restriction'. A disclosure made by any other person will be authorised if it is made to a Crown servant for the purposes of his functions as such; or in accordance with an official authorisation.

Defences

The defence available to Crown servants arises in each of the different categories and reads:

> ... it is a defence ... to prove that at the time of the alleged offence he did not know and had no reasonable cause to believe that the information, document or article in question was such as is mentioned (in the relevant subsection) or that its disclosure would be damaging within the meaning of that subsection.

Belief in authorisation will also provide a defence under s 7. Thus the Act appears to provide three defences for Crown servants: first that the defendant did not know and had no reasonable cause to believe that the information fell into the category in question; secondly that he or she did not know and had no reasonable cause to believe that the information would cause harm and thirdly that he or she believed that he had lawful authorisation to make the disclosure *and* had no reasonable cause to believe otherwise. However, it is unclear whether there are three defences or only two; the Act may be read as requiring the defendant to prove that he or she did not know that the information fell into a particular category and that it was not realised that it would cause harm. This would arise if the word 'or' which links the first and second defences is expressed conjunctively: the defendant might be able to satisfy the second requirement but not the first and therefore find no protection from this defence.

However, assuming that the word 'or' is used disjunctively and that there *are* therefore three defences, the first two may in any event be conflated in certain categories, largely because the second defence is intimately tied up with the harm tests and therefore, like them, operates on a number of levels. Where the harm test operates at its lowest level only the first defence is available. Thus a person falling under ss 1(1) or 4(3) has no opportunity at all of arguing that, for example, the triviality of the information or the fact that it was already in the public domain had given rise to an expectation that its disclosure would cause no harm at all. At the next level, under s 3(1)(b), because the test for harm *may* be satisfied merely by showing that the information falls within the subsection the second defence may be more apparent than real and should perhaps therefore be categorised along with the defence under s 1 as non-existent. Under s 1(3) the second defence is extremely circumscribed. It would not necessarily avail the defendant to prove that for various reasons it was believed on reasonable grounds before the disclosure took place that it would not cause harm. So long as the prosecution could prove a likelihood that harm would be caused from disclosure of documents falling into the same class, the harm test under the section would be satisfied and the defendant would be forced to prove that he or she had no reasonable cause to believe that disclosure of documents of that class would cause harm – a more difficult task than showing this in relation to the particular disclosure in question.

Generally speaking, under all the other categories the harm test allows for argument under both the first and second defences, assuming that they are expressed disjunctively. However, under s 4(4) the second defence alone applies to information falling within the category under s 4(2)(a) while the first alone applies to information likely to have those effects under s 4(2)(b). This is anomalous as it means that the disclosure of information which had had the effect of preventing an arrest could be met by the defence that it was not expected to have that effect, while information which had not yet had such an effect but might have in future would not necessarily be susceptible to such a defence. So long as the disclosure of the document was in fact likely to have the effect mentioned it would be irrelevant that the defendant, while appreciating that it might in general have such effects, considered that they would not arise in the particular instance. Thus a broader defence would be available in respect of the more significant disclosure but not in respect of the less significant. This effect arises because under s 4(2), the first defence is contained in the second due to the use of the harm test as the means of identifying the information falling within the section.

Thus it is clear that the Act is less generous towards the defendant in terms of the defences it makes available than it appears to be at first glance. Moreover, it is important to note that although it is a general principle of criminal law that a defendant need have only an honest belief in the existence of facts which give rise to a defence, under the Act a defendant must have an honest and reasonable belief in such facts.

The Act contains no explicit public interest defence and it follows from the nature of the harm tests that one cannot be implied into it; any good flowing from disclosure of the information in question cannot be considered, merely any harm that might be caused. Thus, while it may be accepted that the Act at least allows argument as to a defendant's state of knowledge (albeit of very limited scope in certain instances) in making a disclosure to be led before a jury, it does not allow for argument as to the good intentions of the persons concerned, who may believe with reason that no other effective means of exposing iniquity exists. In particular, the information may concern corruption at such a high level that internal methods of addressing the problem would be ineffective. Of course, good intentions are normally irrelevant in criminal trials: not many would argue that a robber should be able to adduce evidence that he intended to use the proceeds of his robbery to help the poor. However, it is arguable that an exception to this rule should be made in respect of the Official Secrets Act. A statute aimed specifically at those best placed to know of corruption or malpractice in government, should, in a democracy, allow such a defence. The fact that it does not, argues strongly against the likelihood that it will have a liberalising impact.

The situation of the civil servant in the UK who believes that disclosure as to a certain state of affairs is necessary in order to serve the public interest may therefore be contrasted with the situation of his of her counterpart in the USA, where he or she would receive protection from detrimental action flowing from whistle-blowing[30] under the Civil Service Reform Act 1978. A weak form of a public interest defence may eventually be adopted if proposals in the government White Paper on freedom of information published in July 1993 are implemented by the current Labour government.[31] It was proposed that the disclosure of information would not be penalised if the information was not 'genuinely confidential'. But the Labour government has introduced the Public Interest Disclosure Act 1998 which amends the Employment Rights Act 1996 and which will, under s 43E, at least provide some protection for the civil servant who 'whistle blows' from employment detriment.

Similarly, no general defence of prior publication is provided by the 1989 Act; the only means of putting forward such argument would arise in one of the categories in which it was necessary to prove the likelihood that harm would flow from the disclosure; the prosecution might find it hard to establish such a likelihood where there had been a great deal of prior publication because no further harm could be caused. Obviously, once again, this will depend on the level at which the harm test operates. Where it operates at its lowest level, prior publication would be irrelevant. Thus, where a member of the Security Services repeated information falling within s 1 which had been published all over the world and in the UK, a conviction could still be obtained. If such publication had occurred but the information fell within s 1(3), the test for harm might be satisfied on the basis that although no further harm could be caused by disclosure of the particular document, it nevertheless belonged to a class of documents the disclosure of which was likely to cause harm. However, where harm flowing from publication of a specific document is relied on, *Lord Advocate v Scotsman Publications Ltd* suggests that a degree of prior publication may tend to defeat the argument

---

30 For discussion of the situation of UK and USA civil servants and developments in the area see Cripps, Y [1983] *PL* 600; Zellick [1987] *PL* 311–13; Starke (1989) 63 *ALJ* 592–94.
31 HMSO Open Government 1993. See below pp 265–68 for discussion.

that further publication can still cause harm. However, this suggestion must be treated with care since the ruling was not given under the 1989 Act and the link between the Act and the civil law of confidence may not form part of its *ratio*.[32] It should also be noted that s 6 provides that information which has already been leaked abroad can still cause harm if disclosed in the UK. The only exception to this arises under s 6(3) which provides that no liability will arise if the disclosure was authorised by the state or international organisation in question.

Conclusions

The claim that the Act is an improvement on its predecessor rests partly on the substance or significance of the information it covers. Such substance is made relevant first by the use of categorisation; impliedly, trivial information relating to cups of tea or colours of carpets in government buildings is not covered (except in Security Service buildings) and secondly because even where information *does* fall within the category in question its disclosure will not incur liability unless harm will or may flow from it. Thus, on the face of it, liability will not be incurred merely because the information disclosed covers a topic of significance such as defence. In other words, it does not seem to be assumed that because there is a public interest in keeping information of the particular type secret, it inevitably relates to any particular piece of information. However, in relation to many disclosures it is in fact misleading to speak of using a second method to narrow down further the amount of information covered because, as noted above, establishing that the information falls within the category in question is in fact (or may be; no guidance is given as to when this will be the case) synonymous with establishing that harm will occur in a number of instances.

Clearly, if only to avoid bringing the criminal law into disrepute, 'harm tests' which allow the substance of the information to be taken into account are to be preferred to the width of s 2 of the 1911 Act. However, although the 1989 Act embodies and emphasises the notion of a test for harm in its reiteration of the term 'damaging', it is not necessary to show that harm has *actually occurred*. Bearing this important point in mind, it can be seen that the test for harm actually operates on four different levels:

(1) The lowest level arises in two categories, s 1(1) and s 4(3), where there is no explicit test for harm at all – impliedly, a disclosure is of its very nature harmful.

(2) In one category, s 3(1)(b), the test for harm is more apparent than real in that it may be identical to the test determining whether the information falls within the category at all.

---

32 Above note 27. Only Lord Templeman clearly adverted to such a link.

(3) In s 1(3) there is a harm test but the harm need not flow from or be likely to flow from disclosure of the specific document in question.

(4) In three categories, ss 2, 3 and 4, there is a harm test but it is only necessary to prove that harm would be *likely* to occur due to the disclosure in question whether it has occurred or not.

Even at the highest level where it is necessary to show that the actual document in question would be likely to cause harm, the task of doing so is made easy due to the width of the tests themselves. Under s 2(2) for example, a disclosure of information relating to defence will be damaging if it is likely to seriously obstruct the interests of the UK abroad. Thus the harm tests may be said to be concerned less with preventing damaging disclosures than with creating the *impression* that liability is confined to such disclosures.

These tests for harm are not made any more stringent in instances where a non-Crown servant – usually a journalist – discloses information since under s 5, if anyone discloses information which falls into one of the categories covered, the test for harm will be determined by reference to that category. The journalist who publishes information and the Crown servant who discloses it to him or her are treated differently in terms of the test for harm only where the latter is a member of the Security Services disclosing information relating to those Services.

One of the objections to the old s 2 of the 1911 Act was the failure to include a requirement to prove *mens rea*. The new Act includes such a requirement only as regards the leaking of information by non-Crown servants; in all other instances it creates a 'reversed *mens rea*': the defence can attempt to prove that the defendant did not know (or have reasonable cause to know) of the nature of the information or that its disclosure would be damaging. We will return to this defence below. However, under ss 5 and 6 the prosecution must prove *mens rea* which includes a requirement to show that the disclosure was made in the knowledge that it would be damaging. This is a step in the right direction and a clear improvement on the 1911 Act; nevertheless the burden of proof on the prosecution would be very easy to discharge where the low level harm tests of ss 1(3) and 3(1)(b) applied once it was shown that the defendant knew that the information fell within the category in question. Arguably, the Act should have afforded greater recognition to the important constitutional role of the journalist. As things stand a journalist who repeated allegations made by a future Peter Wright as to corruption or treachery in MI5 could be convicted if it could be shown first, that he or she knew that the information related to the Security Services and secondly, that disclosure of that *type* of information would be *likely* to cause damage to the work of the Security Services, regardless of whether the particular allegations would cause such damage. In the case of a journalist who repeated allegations made by a future Cathy Massiter it would only be necessary to show that the allegations related to telephone tapping and that the journalist knew that they did. Clearly, this would be a burden which would be readily discharged. Thus it may be said that this improvement is in certain respects more apparent than real.

It may be argued – bearing in mind the scarcity of prosecutions under the 1911 Act – that the Official Secrets Acts were put in place mainly in order to create a deterrent effect and as a centrepiece in the general legal scheme engendering government secrecy, rather than with a view to their invocation. The 1989 Act may be effective as a means of creating greater government credibility in relation to official secrecy than its predecessor. It allows the claim of liberalisation to be made and gives the impression that the anomalies in existence under the 1911 Act have been dealt with. It appears complex and wide ranging partly due to overlapping between and within the categories and therefore will be likely to have a chilling effect because civil servants and others will not be certain as to the information covered except in very clear cut cases. It may therefore prove more effective than the 1911 Act in deterring the press from publishing the revelations of a future Peter Wright in respect of the workings of the Security Service. Thus it may rarely need to be invoked and in fact may have much greater symbolic than practical value.

In considering the impact of the Act, it must be borne in mind that many other criminal sanctions for the unauthorised disclosure of information exist and some of these clearly overlap with its provisions. Sections 1 and 4(3) work in conjunction with the provisions of the Security Services Act 1989 to prevent almost all scrutiny of the operation of the Security Service. Even where a member of the public has a grievance concerning the operation of the Service it will probably not be possible to use a court action as a means of bringing such operations to the notice of the public: under s 5 of the Security Services Act complaint can only be made to a tribunal and under s 5(4) the decisions of the tribunal are not questionable in any court of law. In a similar manner s 4(3) of the Official Secrets Act, which prevents disclosure of information about telephone tapping, works in tandem with the Interception of Communications Act 1985. Under the 1985 Act complaints can be made only to a tribunal whose decisions are not published, with no possibility of scrutiny by a court. Moreover, around 80 other statutory provisions provide sanctions to enforce secrecy on civil servants in the particular areas they cover. For example, s 11 of the Atomic Energy Act 1946 makes it an offence to communicate to an unauthorised person information relating to atomic energy plant. Further, s 1 of the Official Secrets Act 1911 is still available to punish spies. Thus it is arguable that s 2 of the 1911 Act could merely have been repealed without being replaced.

Breach of confidence

Introduction[33]

Breach of confidence is a civil remedy affording protection against the disclosure or use of information which is not generally known and which has been entrusted in circumstances imposing an obligation not to disclose it without authorisation from the person who originally imparted it. This area of law developed as a means of protecting secret information belonging to individuals and organisations.[34] However, it can also be used by government to prevent disclosure of sensitive information and is in that sense a back-up to the other measures available, including the Official Secrets Act 1989.[35] The government has made it clear that actions for breach of confidence will be used against civil servants and others in instances falling outside the protected categories. In some respects breach of confidence actions may be more valuable than the criminal sanction provided by the 1989 Act. Their use may attract less publicity than a criminal trial, no jury will be involved and they offer the possibility of quickly obtaining an interim injunction. The latter possibility is very valuable because in many instances the other party (usually a newspaper) will not pursue the case to a trial of the permanent injunction since the secret will probably be stale news by that time.

However, where the government, as opposed to a private individual, is concerned, the courts will not merely accept that it is in the public interest that the information should be kept confidential. It will have to be shown that the public interest in keeping the information confidential due to the harm its disclosure would cause is not outweighed by the public interest in disclosure. Thus, in *AG v Jonathan Cape*[36] when the Attorney General invoked the law of confidence to try to stop publication of Richard Crossman's memoirs on the ground that they concerned Cabinet discussions, the Lord Chief Justice accepted that such public secrets could be restrained but only on the basis that the balance of the public interest came down in favour of suppression. As the discussions had taken place 10 years previously it was not possible to show that harm would flow from their disclosure; the public interest in publication therefore prevailed.

The nature of the public interest defence – the interest in disclosure – was clarified in *Lion Laboratories v Evans and Express Newspapers*.[37] The Court of

---

33 General reading: Gurry, F, *Breach of Confidence*, 1985; Bailey, Harris and Jones, pp 435–52; Robertson, G and Nichol, AGL, *Media Law*, Chap 4; Wacks, R, *Personal Information*, 1989, Chap 3; Feldman, D, *Civil Liberties*, 1993, pp 648–68.
34 See Chap 8 pp 324–31.
35 For comment on its role in this respect see Bryan, MW (1976) 92 *LQR* 180; Williams, DGT (1976) *CLJ* 1; Lowe and Willmore, 'Secrets, Media and the Law' (1985) 48 *MLR* 592.
36 [1976] QB 752.
37 [1985] QB 526; [1984] 2 All ER 417, CA.

Appeal held that the defence extended beyond situations in which there had been serious wrongdoing by the plaintiff. Even where the plaintiff was blameless publication would be excusable where it was possible to show a serious and legitimate interest in the revelation. Thus the *Daily Express* was allowed to publish information extracted from the manufacturer of the intoximeter (a method of conducting breathalyser tests) even though it did not reveal iniquity on the part of the manufacturer. It did, however, reveal a matter of genuine public interest: that wrongful convictions might have been obtained in drink driving cases due to possible deficiencies of the intoximeter.

The Spycatcher *litigation*

The leading case in this area is now the House of Lords decision in *AG v Guardian Newspapers Ltd (No 2)*[38] which confirmed that the *Lion Laboratories Ltd v Evans* approach to the public interest defence is the correct one and also clarified certain other aspects of this area of the law. In 1985 the Attorney General commenced proceedings in New South Wales[39] in an attempt (which was ultimately unsuccessful)[40] to restrain publication of *Spycatcher* by Peter Wright. The book included allegations of illegal activity engaged in by MI5. In the UK on 22 and 23 June 1986 the *Guardian* and the *Observer* published reports of the forthcoming hearing which included some *Spycatcher* material and on 27 June the Attorney General obtained temporary *ex parte* injunctions preventing them from further disclosure of such material. *Inter partes* injunctions were granted against the newspapers on 11 July 1986. On 12 July 1987 *The Sunday Times* began publishing extracts from *Spycatcher* and the Attorney General obtained an injunction restraining publication on 16 July.

On 14 July 1987 the book was published in the United states and many copies were brought into the UK. On 30 July 1987 the House of Lords decided[41] (relying on *American Cyanamid Co v Ethicon Ltd*)[42] to continue the injunctions against the newspapers on the basis that the Attorney General still had an arguable case for permanent injunctions. In making this decision the House of Lords were obviously influenced by the fact that publication of the information was an irreversible step. This is the usual approach at the interim stage: the court considers the balance of convenience between the two parties and will tend to come down on the side of the plaintiff because of the irrevocable nature of publication. However, since an interim injunction

---

38 [1990] 1 AC 109; [1990] 3 WLR 776; [1988] 3 All ER 545, HL.
39 [1987] 8 NSWLR 341.
40 HC of Australia (1988) 165 *CLR* 30; for comment see Mann, FA (1988) 104 *LQR* 497; Turnbull, M (1989) 105 *LQR* 382.
41 *AG v Guardian Newspapers Ltd* [1987] 3 All ER 316; for comment see Lee, S, 103 *LQR* 506.
42 [1975] AC 396; [1975] 1 All ER 504, HL.

represents a prior restraint and is often the most crucial and indeed sometimes the *only* stage in the whole action, it may be argued that a presumption in favour of freedom of expression should be more readily allowed to tip the balance in favour of the defendant. This may especially be argued where publication from other sources has already occurred which will be likely to increase and where the public interest in the information is very strong.

It is arguable that the House of Lords should have been able in July 1986 to break through the argument that once the confidentiality claim was set up the only possible course was to transfix matters as at that point. The argument could have been broken through in the following way: the public interest in limiting the use of prior restraints could have been weighed against the interest in ensuring that everyone who sets up a legal claim has a right to have it heard free from interference. A prior restraint might be allowed even in respect of a matter of great public concern if the interest it protected was clearly made out, it did not go beyond what was needed to provide such protection and it was foreseeable that the restraint would achieve its objective. If it seemed probable that the restraint would not achieve its objective it would cause an erosion of freedom of speech to no purpose. In the instant case, although the first of these conditions may have been satisfied the other two, it is submitted, were not; the restraint should not, therefore, have been granted. Such reasoning would bring the law of confidence closer to adopting the principles used in defamation cases as regards the grant of interim injunctions.[43]

This judgment will do nothing to curb the use of 'gagging injunctions' in actions for breach of confidence where there has not been prior publication of the material. In any such action, even if the claim is of little merit, it is at present possible to argue that its subject matter should be preserved intact until the merits of the claim can be considered. Even if the claimant then decides to drop the action before that point publication of the material in question will have been prevented for some substantial period of time. The House of Lords' decision has now been found to be in breach of Article 10 of the European Convention on Human Rights; the effect of that decision will be considered below.

In the trial of the permanent injunctions, *AG v Guardian (No 2)*,[44] the Crown argued that confidential information disclosed to third parties does not thereby lose its confidential character if the third parties know that the disclosure has been made in breach of a duty of confidence. A further reason for maintaining confidentiality in the particular instance was that the unauthorised disclosure of the information was thought likely to damage the

---

43 See *Bonnard v Perryman* [1891] 2 Ch 269; *Herbage v The Times Newspapers and Others* (1981) *The Times*, 1 May.
44 [1990] 1 AC 109; [1990] 3 WLR 776; [1988] 3 All ER 545, HL; in the Court of Appeal [1990] 1 AC 109; [1988] 3 All ER 545, 594.

trust which members of MI5 have in each other and might encourage others to follow suit. These factors, it was argued, established the public interest in keeping the information confidential.

On the other hand, it was argued on behalf of the newspapers that some of the information in *Spycatcher*, if true, disclosed that members of MI5 in their operations in England had committed serious breaches of domestic law in, for example, bugging foreign embassies or effecting unlawful entry into private premises. Most seriously, the book included the allegations that members of MI5 attempted to de-stabilise the administration of Mr Harold Wilson and that the Director General or Deputy Director General of MI5 was a spy. The defendants contended that the duty of non-disclosure to which newspapers coming into the unauthorised possession of confidential state secrets may be subject, does not extend to allegations of serious iniquity of this character.

It was determined at first instance and in the Court of Appeal that whether or not the newspapers would have had a duty to refrain from publishing *Spycatcher* material in June 1986 before its publication elsewhere, any such duty had now lapsed. The mere making of allegations of iniquity was insufficient, of itself, to justify overriding the duty of confidentiality but the articles in question published in June 1986 had not contained information going beyond what the public was reasonably entitled to know and in so far as they went beyond what had been previously published, no detriment to national security had been shown which could outweigh the public interest in free speech, given the publication of *Spycatcher* that had already taken place. Thus, balancing the public interest in freedom of speech and the right to receive information against the countervailing interest of the Crown in national security, continuation of the injunctions was not necessary. The injunctions however continued until the House of Lords rejected the Attorney General's claim (*AG v Guardian Newspapers Ltd (No 2)*)[45] on the basis that the interest in maintaining confidentiality was outweighed by the public interest in knowing of the allegations in *Spycatcher*. It was further determined that an injunction to restrain future publication of matters connected with the operations of the Security Service would amount to a comprehensive ban on publication and would undermine the operation of determining the balance of public interest in deciding whether such publication was to be prevented; accordingly, an injunction to prevent future publication which had not yet been threatened was not granted.

It appears likely that the permanent injunctions would have been granted but for the massive publication of *Spycatcher* abroad. That factor seems to have

---

45 [1990] 1 AC 109; [1990] 3 WLR 776; [1988] 3 All ER 545 at 638; for comment see Williams, DGT (1989) *CLJ* 1; Cripps, Y [1989] *PL* 13; Barendt, E (1989) *PL* 204; Michael, J (1989) 52 *MLR* 389; Narain, BJ (1988) 39 *NILQ* 73 and (1987) *NLJ* 723 and 724; Burnett, D and Thomas, R (1989) 16 *JLS* 210; Jones, G (1989) 42 *CLP* 49; Kingsford-Smith, D and Oliver, D, eds, *Economical With the Truth*, 1990, chapters by Pannick, D and Austin, R; Ewing and Gearty, *Freedom Under Thatcher*, pp 152–69; Turnbull, M, *The Spycatcher Trial*, 1988; Bailey, Harris and Jones, pp 435–50.

tipped the balance in favour of the newspapers. It is clear that the operation of the public interest defence involves a value judgment by the judge rather than application of a clear legal rule. The danger is that without a Bill of Rights to protect freedom of speech judges may be too prone to be swayed by establishment arguments. The judgment also made it clear that once the information has become available from other sources, even though the plaintiff played no part in its dissemination and indeed tried to prevent it, an injunction would be unlikely to be granted. This principle was affirmed in *Lord Advocate v Scotsman Publications Ltd*[46] which concerned the publication of extracts from *Inside Intelligence* by Antony Cavendish. The interlocutory injunction sought by the Crown was refused by the House of Lords on the ground that there had been a small amount of prior publication and the possible damage to national security was very nebulous. The decision suggests that the degree of prior publication may be weighed against the significance of the disclosures in question: if less innocuous material had been in issue an injunction might have been granted.

The *Observer* and the *Guardian* applied to the European Commission on Human Rights claiming, *inter alia*, that the grant of the temporary injunctions had breached Article 10 of the Convention, which guarantees freedom of expression. Having given its opinion that the temporary injunctions constituted such a breach, the Commission referred the case to the court. In *Observer and Guardian v UK*[47] the court found that the injunctions clearly constituted an interference with the newspapers' freedom of expression; the question was whether the interference fell within one of the exceptions provided for by para 2 Article 10. The injunctions fell within two of the para 2 exceptions: maintaining the authority of the judiciary and protecting national security. However, those exceptions could be invoked only if the injunctions were necessary in a democratic society in the sense that they corresponded to a pressing social need and were proportionate to the aims pursued.

The court considered these questions with regard first to the period from 11 July 1986 to 30 July 1987. The injunctions had the aim of preventing publication of material which, according to evidence presented by the Attorney General, might have created a risk of detriment to MI5. The nature of the risk was uncertain as the exact contents of the book were not known at that time because it was still only available in manuscript form. Further, they ensured the preservation of the Attorney General's right to be granted a permanent injunction; if *Spycatcher* material had been published before that claim could be heard the subject matter of the action would have been damaged or destroyed. In the court's view these factors established the existence of a pressing social need. Were the actual restraints imposed

---

46 [1990] 1 AC 812; [1989] 2 All ER 852, CA.
47 (1991) 14 EHRR 153; for comment see Leigh, I [1992] *PL* 200–08.

proportionate to these aims? The injunctions did not prevent the papers pursuing a campaign for an enquiry into the operation of the security services and, though preventing publication for a long time – over a year – the material in question could not be classified as urgent news. Thus it was found that the interference complained of was proportionate to the ends in view.

The court then considered the period from 30 July 1987 to 30 October 1988, after publication of *Spycatcher* had taken place in the US. That event changed the situation: in the court's view the aim of the injunctions was no longer to keep secret information secret; it was to attempt to preserve the reputation of MI5 and to deter others who might be tempted to follow Peter Wright's example. It was uncertain whether the injunctions could achieve those aims and it was not clear that the newspapers who had not been concerned with the publication of *Spycatcher* should be enjoined as an example to others. Further, after 30 July it was not possible to maintain the Attorney General's rights as a litigant because the substance of his claim had already been destroyed; had permanent injunctions been obtained against the newspapers that would not have preserved the confidentiality of the material in question. Thus the injunctions could no longer be said to be necessary either to protect national security or to maintain the authority of the judiciary. Maintenance of the injunctions after publication of the book in the US therefore constituted a violation of Article 10.

This was a cautious judgment. It suggests that had the book been published in the US after the House of Lords' decision to uphold the temporary injunctions, no breach of Article 10 would have occurred, despite the fact that publication of extracts from the book had already occurred in the US[48] and the UK. The court seems to have been readily persuaded by the Attorney General's argument that a widely framed injunction was needed in July 1986 but it is arguable that it was wider than it needed to be to prevent a risk to national security. It could have required the newspapers to refrain from publishing Wright material which had not been previously published by others until (if) the action to prevent publication of the book was lost. Such wording would have taken care of any national security interest; therefore wording going beyond that was disproportionate to that aim.

Thus, although the newspapers 'won', the judgment is unlikely to have a significant liberalising influence on the principles governing the grant of temporary injunctions on the grounds of breach of confidence. The minority judges in the court set themselves against the narrow view that the authority of the judiciary is best preserved by allowing a claim of confidentiality set up in the face of a strong competing public interest to found an infringement of freedom of speech for over a year. Judge Morenilla argued that prior restraint

---

48 The *Washington Post* published certain extracts in the US on 3 May 1987.

should be imposed in such circumstances only where disclosure would result in immediate, serious and irreparable damage to the public interest.[49] It might be said that such a test would impair the authority of the judiciary in the sense that the rights of litigants would not be sufficiently protected. However, at present the test at the interlocutory stage allows a case based on a weak argument to prevail on the basis that the court cannot weigh the evidence at that stage and must grant an injunction in order to preserve confidentiality until the case can be fully looked into. As noted above, this may mean that the other party does not pursue the case to the permanent stage and therefore freedom of speech is suppressed on very flimsy grounds. Thus a greater burden to show the well-founded nature of the claim of danger to the public interest – even if not as heavy as that under the test proposed by Judge Morenilla – should be placed on the plaintiff.

The result of the ruling in the European Court of Human Rights appears to be that where there has been an enormous amount of prior publication an interim injunction should not be granted but that it can be when there is at least some evidence of a threat to national security posed by publication coupled with a lesser degree of prior publication. Thus the action for breach of confidence is still of great value as part of the legal scheme bolstering government secrecy.

Confidence and contempt

Recent developments in common law contempt will allow breach of confidence a greater potential than it previously possessed to prevent dissemination of government information. While the temporary injunctions were in force the *Independent* and two other papers published material covered by them. It was determined in the Court of Appeal (*AG v Newspaper Publishing plc*)[50] that such publication constituted the actus reus of contempt. The decision therefore affirmed the principle that once an interlocutory injunction has been obtained restraining one organ of the media from publication of allegedly confidential material, the rest of the media may be in contempt if they publish that material even if their intention in doing so is to bring alleged iniquity to public attention. Such publication must be accompanied by an intention to prejudice the eventual trial of the permanent injunctions, although this only need be in the sense that it was foreseen that such prejudice, while undesired, was very likely to occur.

Thus the laws of confidence and contempt were allowed to operate together as a significant prior restraint on media freedom and this principle

---

49 He relied on the ruling to this effect of the US Supreme Court in *Nebraska Press Association v Stuart* 427 US 539 (1976).

50 (1990) *The Times*, 28 February (see further Chap 3 p 163).

was upheld by the House of Lords (*AG v Times Newspapers Ltd*).[51] Arguably this ruling afforded insufficient recognition to the public interest in knowing of the allegations made in *Spycatcher* which should have outweighed the possibility that publication of the allegations would constitute an interference with the administration of justice. It may be that the House of Lords did not appreciate the extent to which this decision, in combination with the possibility of obtaining a temporary injunction where an arguable case for breach of confidence had been made out, would hand government an effective and wide ranging means of silencing the media when publication of sensitive information was threatened.

However, the potential of this method should already have been apparent. In 1987 the BBC wished to broadcast a programme to be entitled *My Country Right or Wrong* which was to examine issues raised by the *Spycatcher* litigation. The Attorney General obtained an injunction preventing transmission on the ground of breach of confidence (*AG v BBC*).[52] According to the Attorney General the injunction then affected every organ of the media because of the July ruling of the Court of Appeal in *AG v Newspaper Publishing plc*[53] (this was a preliminary ruling on the *actus reus* of common law contempt which was affirmed as noted above).

It seems fairly clear that although the government eventually lost in the *Spycatcher* litigation, the decision will not have any liberalising impact as far as enhancing the ability of newspapers to publish information about government is concerned. The most pernicious aspect of breach of confidence – the ease with which interim injunctions may be obtained – remains largely unaffected by the outcome of the litigation and where such an injunction is obtained it will affect all of the media in the sense that they probably will not wish to risk criminal liability for contempt of court. Thus, these developments in the use of the common law as a means of preventing disclosure of information provide a further means of ensuring secrecy where information falls outside the categories covered by the Official Secrets Act, or where it is thought appropriate not to invoke criminal sanctions. *AG v Guardian Newspapers* has demonstrated that temporary injunctions may be obtained to prevent disclosure of official information even where prior publication has ensured that there is little confidentiality left to be protected. Once the Human Rights Act is in force it is probable that this development of common law contempt and confidence may be found to breach Article 10 and s 12 of the Act, which provides special protection for the media.

---

51 [1992] 1 AC 191; [1991] 2 All ER 398; [1991] 2 WLR 994, HL.
52 (1987) *The Times*, 18 December. For comment see 10 *OJLS* 430, 435; Thornton, P, *Decade of Decline*, 1989, pp 9–11.
53 [1988] Ch 333; [1987] 3 All ER 276; [1988] 3 WLR 942, CA.

Defence Advisory notices[54]

The government and the media may avoid the head-on confrontation which occurred in the *Spycatcher* litigation by means of a curious institution known until 1992 as the 'D' (Defence) notice system. This system, which effectively means that the media censor themselves in respect of publication of official information, may obviate the need to seek injunctions to prevent publication. The 'D' Notice Committee was set up with the object of letting the Press know which information could be printed and at what point: it was intended that if sensitive political information was covered by a 'D' notice an editor would decide against printing it. The system is entirely voluntary and in theory the fact that a 'D' notice has not been issued does not mean that a prosecution under the Official Secrets Act 1989 is precluded, although in practice it is very unlikely. Further, guidance obtained from the Secretary to the Committee does not amount to a straightforward 'clearance'. Press representatives sit on the committee as well as civil servants and officers of the armed forces.

The value and purpose of the system was called into question due to the injunction obtained against the BBC in respect of *My Country Right or Wrong* as mentioned above. The programme concerned issues raised by the *Spycatcher* litigation; the BBC consulted the 'D' Notice Committee before broadcasting and were told that the programme did not affect national security. However, the Attorney General then obtained an injunction preventing transmission on the ground of breach of confidence, thereby disregarding the 'D' Notice Committee.

Some criticism has been levelled at the system: in the Third Report from the Defence Committee[55] the 'D' notice system was examined and it was concluded that it was failing to fulfil its role. It was found that major newspapers did not consult their 'D' notices to see what was covered by them and that the wording of 'D' notices was so wide as to render them meaningless. The system conveyed an appearance of censorship which had provoked strong criticism. It was determined that the machinery for the administration of 'D' notices and the 'D' notices themselves needed revision. The review which followed this reduced the number of notices and confined them to specific areas. The system was reviewed again in 1992 (*The Defence Advisory Notices: A Review of the D Notice System*, MOD Open Government Document No 93/06) leading to a reduction in the number of notices to six. They were renamed Defence Advisory notices to reflect their voluntary nature.

---

54 On the system generally see Jaconelli, J, 'The "D" Notice System' [1982] *PL* 39; Fairley, D (1990) 10 *OJLS* 430.
55 (1979–80) HC 773, 640 i–v, *The 'D' Notice System*.

Public interest immunity

Discovery may be needed by one party to an action of documents held by the other in order to assist in the action or allow it to proceed. Where a member of the government or other state body is the party holding the documents in question it may claim that it is immune from the duty to make such disclosure, asserting public interest immunity, a privilege based on the royal prerogative.[56] The immunity is expressly preserved in the Crown Proceedings Act 1947, but this means that the courts have had to determine its scope. Section 28(1) of the 1947 Act, which provides that the court can make an order for discovery of documents against the Crown and require the Crown to answer interrogatories, is qualified by s 28(2) which preserves Crown privilege to withhold documents on the grounds of public interest in a variety of cases.

Certain decisions demonstrate the development there has been in determining the scope of this privilege. The House of Lords in *Duncan v Cammell Laird and Co*[57] held that documents otherwise relevant to judicial proceedings are not to be disclosed if the public interest requires that they be withheld. This test may be found to be satisfied either (a) by having regard to the contents of the particular document or (b) by the fact that the document belongs to a category which, on grounds of public interest, must as a class remain undisclosed.[58] Crown privilege as formulated here was an exclusionary rule of evidence based on public interest and the minister was deemed the sole judge of what that constituted. In *Ellis v HO*,[59] a prisoner on remand who was severely injured by a mentally disturbed prisoner in the prison hospital, sued the Crown for negligence. Privilege was claimed to prevent the disclosure of medical reports on his assailant and so the action had to fail. The danger clearly arose that, since the executive was the sole judge of what was in the public interest, matters embarrassing to government might be concealed. In *Conway v Rimmer*[60] the speeches in the House of Lords revealed the degree of concern which had arisen in the judiciary as to the danger of injustice created by the use of this privilege by ministers. In that case a police constable was prosecuted for theft. The charge was dismissed but he was dismissed from the police force. He brought an action for malicious prosecution against his former superintendent but the Home Office objected

---

56 See Cross and Tapper, *Cross on Evidence*, 7th edn, 1990, Chap XII; [1942] 1 All ER 587. For a discussion of the legal and historical background; Jacob, 'From Privileged Crown to Interested Public' [1993] *PL* 121; Bradley, 'Justice, Good Government and Public Interest Immunity' [1992] *PL* 514; Ganz, 'Matrix Churchill and Public Interest Immunity' (1993) 56 *MLR* 564; Allan, 'Public Interest Immunity and Ministers' Responsibility' (1993) *CLR* 661.
57 [1942] AC 624.
58 *Ibid* at 592.
59 [1953] 2 QB 135.
60 [1968] AC 910, HL.

to the disclosure of reports relevant to the case. The House of Lords, in a landmark decision, overruled the minister's claim of Crown privilege and ordered disclosure.

This decision substituted judicial discretion for executive discretion regarding disclosure of documents. However, the judges have tended to exercise this discretion cautiously. Disclosure is unlikely to be ordered unless the party seeking it can show: first, that the material is clearly relevant to a specific issue in the case; second, that it will be of significant value in the fair disposal of the case; and third, following *Air Canada v Secretary of State for Trade (No 2)*[61] that it will assist the case of that party. The main issue for determination in Air Canada concerned the conditions which have to be satisfied before a court will inspect documents for which public interest immunity is claimed. If the court does not inspect it cannot order disclosure. The court considered that the documents were relevant in the case and necessary for its fair disposal. However, this did not lead the majority to find that inspection was necessary in order to determine whether non-disclosure would prevent the court from judging the issues. Instead, the majority found that the party seeking disclosure must show that 'the documents are very likely to contain material which would give substantial support to his contention on an issue which arises in the case'.[62]

After *Air Canada*, in effect, three tests had to be satisfied before disclosure could be ordered. The documents in question must be relevant to the case; they must be assistance in disposing of it and the party seeking disclosure must show that they will assist his or her own case. As Zuckermann points out, this means that if the party seeking disclosure does not know in detail what the documents contain he or she will not be able to satisfy the third test and the court will therefore refuse to inspect the documents to see if the second test is satisfied.[63] The second test mentioned above has received an interpretation restrictive of disclosure; the need to show that the material in question will be of *substantial* assistance to the court was emphasised in *Bookbinder v Tebbit (No 2)*.[64] Even where these three tests may be satisfied discovery may be refused due to the nature or 'class' of the material in question even where it clearly falls outside the protected categories covered by the Official Secrets Act 1989. In *Halford v Sharples*[65] the applicant claimed sex discrimination in that she had not been recommended for promotion, and sought discovery of documents from *inter alia* the police authority which had failed to interview her and the Chief Constable of her own force. The Court of

---

61 *Air Canada v Secretary of State for Trade (No 2)* [1983] 1 All ER 910, 923–25 HL(E).
62 *Per* Lord Fraser [1983] 1 All ER 917.
63 Zuckerman, AAS, 'Public Interest Immunity – A Matter of Prime Judicial Responsibility' (1994) *MLR* 703.
64 [1992] 1 WLR 217.
65 [1992] 3 All ER 624, CA.

Appeal found that all documents of any type relating to internal police inquiries were protected by public interest immunity and that therefore production of the files would not be ordered. It also found that immunity from disclosure was also an immunity from use. Thus no use at all could be made of the information contained in the documents in question, regardless of the fact that both parties were aware of their contents.

The House of Lords in *Chief Constable of West Midlands Police, ex parte Wiley, Chief Constable of Nottinghamshire Police, ex parte Sunderland*[66] considered that there was insufficient evidence to support Lord Oliver's conclusion in *Neilson* as to the need for a new class claim to public interest immunity. Thus it was found that *Neilson* must be regarded as wrongly decided, but that did not mean that public interest immunity would never attach to police complaints documents: whether it did or not would depend on the particular contents of the document.[67] This decision emphasises that a clear case must be made out for use of a broad class claim to public interest immunity and as far as documents in the hands of public authorities are concerned it is preferable that each case be considered on its own facts and not on the basis of a class claim. Moreover, it is to be welcomed in the interests of justice as going some way towards ensuring that civil actions against the police are not undermined by claims that relevant information cannot be disclosed.

One of the most controversial assertions of public interest immunity occurred in the *Matrix Churchill* case,[68] as AAS Zuckermann has indicated.[69] Zuckermann observes that, after *Conway v Rimmer*, ministers were relieved of the responsibility of considering suppressing evidence by way of public interest immunity certificates on the administration of justice. On this basis, the responsibility for the suppression of evidence lies with the courts, not ministers, and therefore Zuckermann does not condemn the ministerial practices revealed in the Scott report. He ends by arguing that the courts, 'not just ministers', should be put on trial for their part in the *Matrix Churchill* affair. On this view, judicial responsibility for the suppression of evidence, claimed in *Conway*, is in a sense a double-edged sword; on the one hand it allows the judges to provide a check on the actions of the executive, but on the other it frees the executive from keeping a check on itself as regards the potential effect of a PII certificate on the administration of justice. Zuckermann assumes that the only public interest which ministers can be expected to understand and evaluate – in the light of judicial approval of 'closed' government – is the interest in secrecy. Once that interest is established they

---

66 [1995] 1 AC 274, 281, 291–306; (1995) 1 Cr App R 342, HL.
67 See *Taylor v Anderton* [1995] 2 All ER 420, CA.
68 See Leigh, *Betrayed: The Real Story of the Matrix Churchill Trial*, 1993; Tomkins, 'Public Interest Immunity after *Matrix Churchill*' [1993] *PL* 530.
69 Zuckerman, AAS, 'Public Interest Immunity – A Matter of Prime Judicial Responsibility' (1994) *MLR* 703.

can and perhaps should close their eyes to the likely consequences attendant on issuance of the certificate, such as the possibility that an innocent person might be convicted, even where such a possibility that an innocent person might be convicted, even where such a possibility is self-evident due to the nature of the material sought to be suppressed (as it seems to have been in the *Matrix Churchill* case) and despite their knowledge of judicial timidity and reluctance to resist PII claims, especially in national security cases. Possibly, Zuckermann's understandable eagerness to condemn judicial bolstering of the 'wall of silence blocking access to public documents' has led him to accept too readily ministerial claims of inability to understand or take any responsibility for the requirements of the interests of justice so long as a public interest in non-disclosure can be made out. Possibly, he also displays a readiness to accept that ministers are seeking to act in the public rather than the government interest when a claim for suppression of evidence is made. In the light of Lord Templeman's comments in *Wiley*, above, it is suggested that both ministerial and judicial responsibility for creating 'the wall of silence' should be clearly condemned.

Zuckermann's conclusions as regards the use of PII certificates generally and as regards their use in the *Matrix Churchill* case in particular, do not harmonise with those of Sir Richard Scott in the *Scott Report*.[70] Scott found that the government attitude:

> ... to disclosure of documents to the defence was consistently grudging. The approach ought to have been to consider what documents the defence might reasonably need and then to consider whether there was any good reason why the defence should not have them ... the actual approach ... seems to have been to seek some means by which refusal to disclose could be justified.[71]

The danger in the argument, reiterated by Lord Scarman in *Air Canada* (above), that judges take the responsibility for considering the effect of suppression of evidence on the administration of justice, is that both judiciary and ministers succeed in shuffling off the responsibility for such suppression: the judges accept, as ministers strongly demand they should, that matters of public safety can be judged only by the executive, while ministers hide behind the fiction that the judiciary will weigh up the interest in such matters against the interest in justice. Thus, ministers are able to adopt the convenient constitutional position of demanding on the one hand that the judiciary should not look behind PII claims based on national security interests and on the other that if judges accede to such demands they must take the responsibility for doing so. Clearly, there is a strong argument that judges should be less timid when faced with such claims but there also appears to be

---

[70] *Inquiry into Exports of Defence Equipment and Dual-Use Goods to Iraq and Related Prosecutions*, HC 115 I (1995–96).

[71] Section G of the *Scott Report*. See also the debate in Parliament on the *Scott Report*, *Hansard*, HC Deb, 26 February 1996; HC Deb, Vol 272 No 51, in particular Col 612.

merit in Scott J's argument[72] that ministers must take some responsibility for putting them forward, bearing in mind ministerial responsibility for upholding the proper administration of justice. It is suggested that the creation of a dichotomy between ministerial and judicial responsibility in this matter, in order to ensure that the latter prevails, is unnecessary and leads to situations such as the one which arose in *Matrix Churchill*. Thus, in the light of *Matrix Churchill* there is arguably a need for greater regulation of the issue of PII certificates which would be based on the acceptance of initial ministerial responsibility for their potential effects on justice, although the judiciary should remain the final arbiters in the matter.[73]

The argument, criticised by Scott J, that before signing a PII certificate ministers need to do no more than satisfy themselves that documents fall into a prescribed class may be based partly on 'entrenched conventions of public administration' including the rule that 'secrecy is in the interests of good government'. In future this argument may become less sustainable in the face of the new culture of openness depending from the 1994 Code of Practice on Access to Government Information (discussed below). Although the Code excludes many matters from its ambit, including categories of information which would be likely to be the subject of PII claims, it is based on the principle that responsibility for ensuring access to official information lies with departments, not with the judiciary, thus suggesting not only that good government requires a degree of openness but that it accepts sole responsibility for ensuring that openness is maintained. It may also be noted, in support of this point, that the duties and responsibilities of ministers set out in *Questions of Procedure for Ministers* include: '... the duty to give Parliament and the public as full information as possible about the policies, decisions and actions of the government and not to ... knowingly mislead Parliament and the public ... [and] the duty to ... uphold the administration of justice.'

The then Conservative government responded to the Scott Report by announcing that changes would be made to Public Interest Immunity certificates issued by the government.[74] The distinction between class and contents claims would be abolished and an immunity claim would be made only where a real danger to the public interest could be shown. The certificate itself would explain the harm which might be caused, unless to do so would in itself bring about the harm in question. Although these changes were expressed to apply only to government claims for immunity, it was accepted that they might apply in other instances.

---

72 See para G18.67 of the Scott Report.
73 See further Leigh, I, 'Reforming Public Interest Immunity' (1995) Webb *JCLI* (2) 49–71.
74 *HC Deb,* Vol 576 Col 1507, *HC Deb,* Vol 287 Col 949, 18 December 1996.

3 ACCESS TO INFORMATION[75]

Freedom of information abroad

All the measures discussed above may be contrasted with the position in other democracies which have introduced freedom of information legislation[76] within the last 30 years. Canada introduced its Access to Information Act in 1982 while America has had such legislation since 1967. Its Freedom of Information Act 1967 applies to all parts of the Federal government unless an exemption applies. Exempted categories include information concerning defence, law enforcement and foreign policy. The exemptions can be challenged in court and the onus of proof will be on the agency withholding the information to prove that disclosure could bring about the harm the exemption was intended to prevent. However, although the principle of freedom of information in America has attracted praise, its application in practice has often been criticised.[77] In particular, the American business community considers that the system is being abused by persons who have a particular financial interest in uncovering commercial information. A number of reforms have been suggested since 1980 and in 1986 a major FOIA reform was passed which extended the exemption available to law enforcement practices.

The Public Records Acts

The UK Public Records Act 1958, as amended by the Public Records Act 1967, provides that public records will not be transferred to the Public Records Office in order to be made available for inspection until the expiration of 30 years and longer periods can be prescribed for 'sensitive information'. Such information will include personal details about persons who are still living and papers affecting the security of the state. Some such information can be withheld for 100 years or forever and there is no means of challenging such decisions. For example, at the end of 1987 a great deal of information about the Windscale fire in 1957 was disclosed although some items are still held back. Robertson argues that information is withheld to prevent

---

[75] See generally Birkinshaw, P, *Freedom of Information*, 2nd edn, 1996; *Government and Information*, 1990; *Reforming the Secret State*, 1990; 'The White Paper on Open Government' [1993] *PL* 557.

[76] See McBride, T, 'The Official Information Act 1982' (1984) 11 *NZULR* 82; Curtis, LJ, 'Freedom of Information in Australia' (1983) 14 *Fed LR* 5; Janisch, HN, 'The Canadian Access to Information Act' [1982] *PL* 534; for America, see Supperstone, M, *Brownlie's Law of Public Order and National Security*, 1982, pp 270–87; Birkinshaw, P, *Freedom of Information*, 1996, Chap 2.

[77] For discussion of criticism in the US see Birkinshaw, *Freedom of Information*, pp 39–40.

embarrassment to bodies such as the police or civil servants rather than to descendants of persons mentioned in it; and in support of this he cites examples such as police reports on the NCCL (1935–41), flogging of vagrants (1919), decisions against prosecuting James Joyce's *Ulysses* (1924) as instances of material which in January 1989 was listed as closed for a century.[78]

However, a somewhat less restrictive approach to the release of archives became apparent in 1994. In 1992–93 a review was conducted of methods of ensuring further openness in government and its results were published in a White Paper entitled *Open Government* (Cm 2290). The White Paper stated that a Code of Practice on Access to Government Information would be adopted (the Code is discussed below) and there would be a reduction in the number of public records withheld from release beyond 30 years. A review group established by Lord Mackay in 1992 suggested that records should only be closed for more than 30 years where their disclosure would cause harm to defence, national security, international relations and economic interests of the UK; information supplied in confidence; personal information which would cause substantial distress if disclosed. Under s 3(4) of the 1958 Act records may still be retained within departments for 'administrative' reasons or for any other special reason.[79]

The Code of Practice on Access to Government Information

The attitude to secrecy exemplified by US freedom of information legislation, which is founded on the presumption that information must be disclosed unless specifically exempted, may be contrasted with that in the UK which takes the opposite stance. No general provision is made for such disclosure; the starting point is to criminalise disclosure in certain categories of information. American freedom of information provision can in particular be contrasted with provision under the UK Public Records Act 1958. Considering all the various and overlapping methods of preventing disclosure of official information in the UK and bearing in mind the contrasting attitude to this issue evinced in other democracies, it may appear that the UK was being increasingly isolated in its stance as a resister of freedom of information legislation.

There have been certain recent developments which suggest that a gradual movement towards more open government has been taking place in the UK over the last decade. The Data Protection Act 1984 allows access to personal information held on computerised files. The Campaign for Freedom of Information has, from 1985 onwards, brought about acceptance of the

---

78 See Robertson, *Media Law*, 1990, p 338.
79 The White Paper proposals in relation to public records are considered by Birkinshaw, 'I Only Ask for Information – the White Paper on Open Government' [1993] *PL* 557.

principle of access rights in some areas including local government. Disclosure of a range of information was decriminalised under the Official Secrets Act 1989. After the 1992 election the Prime Minister promised a review of secrecy in Whitehall to be conducted by William Waldegrave, the minister with responsibility for the Citizen's Charter, which would concentrate on the large number of statutory instruments which prevent public disclosure of government information in various areas, with a view to removing those which did not appear to fulfil a pressing need. It was also promised that a list of secret Cabinet committees with their terms of reference and their ministerial membership would be published. Reform of the Official Secrets Act 1989 would be undertaken so that disclosure of a specific document would be criminalised as opposed to disclosure of a document belonging to a class of documents which might cause harm. A White Paper on Open government (Cm 2290) was published in July 1993.

A new Code of Practice on Access to Government Information was introduced from April 1994 as promised in the White Paper and is now in its 2nd edition. The Code provides that certain government departments will provide information on request and will volunteer some information. The White Paper describes the role of the PCA as follows:

> The Parliamentary Commissioner for Administration (PCA), the Parliamentary Ombudsman, has agreed that complaints that departments and other bodies within his jurisdiction have failed to comply with this Code can be investigated if referred to him by a Member of Parliament. When he decides to investigate he will have access to the department's internal papers and will be able in future to report to Parliament when he finds that information has been improperly withheld. The Select Committee on the PCA will then be able to call departments and ministers to account for failure to supply information in accordance with the Code, as they can now call them to account for maladministration or injustice. The Ombudsman has the confidence of Parliament and is independent of the government. Parliamentary accountability will thus be preserved and enhanced. Ministers and departments will have a real spur to greater openness and citizens will have an independent investigator working on their behalf.

However, no legal remedies are provided for citizens if the Code is breached and a number of matters are excluded from it. The exemptions can be divided into two groups: those which are subject to a harm test and those which are not. The key exemptions within the former group cover information relating to: defence, security and international relations, internal discussion and advice, law enforcement and legal proceedings, effective management of the economy and collection of tax, effective management and operations of the public service, privacy, third parties' commercial confidence. The latter group includes information within the following categories: communications with the Royal Household, immigration and nationality information, public employment, public appointments and honours, publication and prematurity in relation to publication, information given in confidence. The harm tests are varied and some are more complex than others, but none of them seek to explain what is meant by 'harm'. Thus, in relation to defence, security and international relations part of the harm test is concerned with 'information whose disclosure would harm national security or defence'. However, the inclusion of harm tests narrows down the exemptions: clearly the Code does not simply exempt, for example, information concerning the effective management of the economy from its provisions; it does so only when disclosure of such information would 'harm the ability of the government to manage the economy or where such disclosure could prejudice the conduct of official market operations or lead to improper gain or advantage'. How far it would be possible to be sure that information which did not satisfy the harm test was not being withheld is another matter. But in theory the harm tests are a step in the direction of disclosure. This cannot be said of information falling into categories where it is not requited that harm should be shown.

One of the key criticisms of the Code relates to the extensiveness of the list of exemptions and their breadth. Compare, for example, the confidentiality provision in the Code (14a) with the equitable doctrine of confidence. The key difference is that under the latter, before the publication of the information concerned can be actionable, the plaintiff must show that disclosure would cause him some kind of detriment.[80] Additionally, the defendant may still defeat the plaintiff's claim if he can show that publication would be in the public interest, a defence which appears to have widened in scope recently,[81] thus affording more recognition to freedom of speech and of information. The Code does not require the department concerned to show that any detriment would flow from the requested disclosure, nor is there any public interest exception. This provision in the Code thus affords freedom of information less recognition than the existing law. Not only are the exemptions very broad, they are likely to give rise to grave difficulties of interpretation. If a department considers, on its interpretation of one of the exempting provisions, that the exemption applies, although the information seeker and Ombudsman disagree, the department cannot be compelled to release the information. No avenue of challenge to the exclusions from the Code is available.

Where an exemption clearly does not apply, a department cannot be forced to disclose the information. If the Ombudsman recommends that a department should reveal information and the department does not accept the recommendation, it may be called upon to justify itself before the Select Committee on the Parliamentary Commissioner for Administration (PCA).

---

80 See, for example, the well known exposition of the doctrine in *Coco v AN Clark (Engineers) Limited* [1969] RPC 41 at 47. Some doubt has been expressed as to whether detriment is a necessary ingredient of the action (*dicta* of Lord Keith in *AG v Guardian Newspapers (No 2)* [1988] 3 All ER 545 at 640) but the orthodox view remains that it is.

81 See, for example, *Lion Laboratories v Evans and Express Newspapers* [1985] QB 526; [1984] 2 All ER 852, HL and *W v Egdell* [1990] Ch 359.

However, this will not have the same impact as if the enforcement mechanism for the Code were to be legally binding since the committee cannot compel a department to release information. A survey published in March 1997[82] showed that public bodies are not meeting the standards of openness laid down in the government Code. Fifty government departments were asked for information to which the public is entitled under the Code. Eleven gave wrong or inadequate information and three refused to reply at all. Among those showing poor practice were the Legal Aid Board and the Commission for Racial Equality. The Department for Education and Employment and the Office for National Statistics were among those which refused to reply. If the Code is amended, as the Select Committee on the PCA recommends in its Second Report,[83] it may allow access to more sensitive matters. The need for an enforcement mechanism available through the courts rather than the PCA may then become more apparent.

The Code is apparently based on the presumption that all useful government information will be released unless there are pressing reasons why it is in the public interest that it should remain secret. This is the general principle on which freedom of information is based. However, in relation to major policy decisions (Part I s 3(i)) the Code only relates to information considered 'relevant' by the government. In countries which have FOI, the usefulness or relevance of documents containing information is determined by the person who seeks it rather than by government ministers or civil servants. Usefulness is not an objective quality but depends on the purposes of the seeker which only he or she can appreciate. Further, the Code promises only to afford release of information as opposed to documents. As pointed out in the memorandum submitted by the Campaign for Freedom of Information,[84] and endorsed in the Second Report from the Select Committee on the PCA, the information seeker will be unable to ensure that all significant parts of the document in question have been disclosed. Thus, both these limitations undermine the principle of 'openness' and add to the number of avenues available to a department which is subject to the Code to use in order to avoid complying with it in relation to sensitive information. The Second Report from the Select Committee on the PCA[85] and the First Special Report from the Public Service Committee recommended that the access under the Code should be to the documents themselves.[86] The then Conservative government stated that documents could already be released under the Code

---

82 The journalists' magazine UKPG published the survey on 7 March 1997, para 9.
83 *Second Report from the Select Committee on the Parliamentary Commissioner for Administration*, HC 84 (1995–96), Open Government.
84 Appendices to the Minutes of Evidence taken before the Select Committee on the PCA, session 1993–94, HC 33 (1993–94), Vol II p 258.
85 HC 84 (1995–96) Para 83.
86 *Public Service Committee First Special Report*, HC 67 (1996–97) para 32.

but considered that this would not necessarily be a helpful approach for Departments dealing with Code requests.

As the Select Committee on the PCA points out, the government has made little effort to publicise the Code and this may be one reason for the lack of interest shown in it by individual citizens (see further the Second Report of the Parliamentary Commissioner for Administration, HC 91 (1994–95), para 5). Individual citizens who are aware of its existence may be deterred from using the Code due to the charges which have been imposed for providing information, which have in some instances been excessive.[87]

Under s 5(1) of the Parliamentary Commissioner Act 1967 the Ombudsman can take up a complaint only if the citizen has suffered injustice as a result of maladministration; both maladministration and injustice must be shown and there must be a causal link between them. These requirements will be relaxed in relation to complaints relating to the Code of Practice. In relation to the Ombudsman's wider role in combatting maladministrative secrecy – where the Code makes no commitment to release particular information – these requirements must of course be met.

The Second Report from the Select Committee concludes that the Ombudsman should not be given binding powers in relation to the FOI aspects of his role but should maintain an integrated approach (para 119). The Committee notes that in New Zealand the Official Information Act is enforced by an Ombudsman but the recommendations on disclosure were made legally binding unless vetoed by an Order in Council within 21 days. This suggests that the traditional, recommendatory approach of the Ombudsman was seen as inappropriate in relation to freedom of information. The Committee rejects this model. However, it is suggested that the Committee gives insufficient consideration to the possibility of providing binding powers for the Ombudsman in relation to the Code. Its grace and favour basis is arguably inappropriate in relation to freedom of information, although the recommendatory nature of the PCA's role may be appropriate in relation to his main function.

Certain matters set out in Schedule 3 of the Parliamentary Commissioner Act 1967 are excluded from the investigation by the PCA. These include extradition and fugitive offenders, the investigation of crime by or on behalf of the Home Office, security of the state, action in matters relating to contractual or commercial activities, court proceedings and personnel matters of the armed forces, teachers, the civil service or police. The government has always resisted the extension of the Ombudsman system into these areas. The Code at present takes these exclusions into account and goes even further than they do in exempting a number of matters from the access which are within the

---

[87] See further the Citizen's Charter report on the operation of the Code, *Open Government* (1994).

jurisdiction of the PCA. Future review of the Code may consider narrowing down the exemptions from the Code but the question would remain whether the PCA's supervision should be allowed to extend into areas from which, traditionally, he has been excluded.

Criticism can also be made of the use of the MP filter in relation to Code-based complaints. Citizens who need to obtain access to the Ombudsman system may not be able to do so because having contacted an MP with a complaint, the MP may decide not to refer the complaint on to the PCA. Furthermore, MPs may appear to be hampered by their political allegiance in contrast to the Ombudsman who is independent. Although MPs may not know the political allegiance of a constituent who makes a complaint regarding a refusal of access to politically sensitive information and might in any event be uninfluenced by it, the constituent might assume that the complaint would be more forcibly pursued by an Opposition MP. In some instances MPs may have an interest in seeing that the information is withheld and therefore may face a conflict of interests. The Public Service Committee recommended that MPs should be able to make a complaint to the Ombudsman directly concerning the withholding of information by a government department without having to act through another member.[88] The then Conservative government considered that this would involve a departure from the basic principles under the Parliamentary Commissioner Act 1967 and stated that it would seek the view of the Select Committee on the PCA before responding.

It is of particular importance to note that findings and recommendations made by the PCA are not enforceable in law, so that the adverse publicity which would be generated by a refusal to comply with a recommendation is the only sanction for non-compliance. However, research indicates that the influence of the PCA is far greater in practice than his limited formal powers might suggest. Rodney Austin notes 'Whitehall's record of compliance with the non-binding recommendations of the ombudsman is actually outstanding; on only two occasions have government departments refused to accept the PCA's findings and in both cases the PCA's recommendations were [nevertheless] complied with'. However, Austin goes on to note that:

> ... compliance with the PCA's recommendations usually involves the payment of an *ex gratia* compensation or an apology or the reconsideration of a prior decision by the correct process. Rarely does it involve reversal on merits of an important policy decision. Governments will fight tenaciously to preserve secrets which matter to them ... there is little ground for optimism that in a crucial case the government would not choose to defy the PCA ...[89]

---

88 *Public Service Committee First Special Report*, HC 67 (1996–97), para 9.
89 'Freedom of Information: The Constitutional Impact', in Jowell, J and Oliver, D, eds, *The Changing Constitution*, 1994, p 443.

If the PCA's ability to underpin the Code were enhanced by making the Ombudsman's recommendations enforceable in the courts as in New Zealand, a number of problems would remain. The complainant would not be able to enforce the Code in person. Many avenues of escape from it would still exist due to the limitations of the Ombudsman's jurisdiction. The Ombudsman might eventually find that he was almost unable to cope with the volume of complaints under the Code and this situation would probably be exacerbated if he was also involved in litigation in attempting to enforce recommendations. Enhancing the role of the Ombudsman along New Zealand lines might amount merely to tinkering with the problems.

It therefore appears that the Code should be replaced by a broad statutory right of access to information, enforceable by another independant body or through the courts. The Conservative governments of 1979–97 had no plans to enact such legislation. General statutory rights of access to personal information and to health and safety information were proposed in the White Paper. The Select Committee on the PCA therefore concluded that statutory freedom of information is needed covering both these areas and those which will remain within the Ombudsman's remit with the Ombudsman as the final appeals process in relation to all areas. However, this would mean that rights of access to personal information and to health and safety information would be unenforceable. In a sense this is an argument for 'levelling down'. The fact that rights of access to information within certain areas will be made available and will apparently be enforced by mechanisms external to the Ombudsman might instead lead to the conclusion that access to information generally should be made enforceable by another independant body or through the courts ('levelling up') and this is discussed below.

Many commentators consider that one of the messages of the Scott Report published in February 1996 is that the UK needs a Freedom of Information Act. The report tellingly reveals the lack of 'openness' in government: the system appears to accept unquestioningly the need to tell Parliament and the public as little as possible about subjects which are seen as politically sensitive. It would not appear that the voluntary Code can provide a sufficient response to the concerns which the report has aroused. The *Matrix Churchill* affair which led to the Scott Inquiry would not, it seems, have come to the attention of the public but for the refusal of the judge in the *Matrix Churchill* trial to accept that the information covered by the public interest immunity certificates, relating to the change in the policy of selling arms to Iraq, could not be revealed. As the Select Committee on the PCA points out in its Second Report, a freedom of information Act would tend to change the culture of secrecy in government departments.

Statutory freedom of information

It is Labour Party policy to enact a Freedom of Information Act. In the Queen's Speech following the 1997 General Election, Labour promised to publish a White Paper on the subject, and the White Paper was published on 11 December 1997. It may therefore be assumed that legislation is imminent. It may be noted that the Second Report of the Select Committee on the PCA recommended the introduction of a Freedom of Information Act,[90] although this proposal was rejected by the then Conservative government.[91]

Once the Act is passed how far will freedom of information be assured? A significant improvement on the current arrangements will be the use of an independant Information Commissioner who will order the disclosure of official documents. However, the Commissioner's decisions will not be appeallable in the courts. It will also become a criminal offence to shred documents requested by outsiders, including the media and the public.

The experience of other countries which have Freedom of Information Acts suggests that the practical problems which already lessen the efficacy of the Code, as the Select Committee pointed out in its Second Report, will also affect the Act, and that some new problems might arise. The Act will refer to 'documents' as opposed to 'information'; this is welcome, but the ordinary citizen seeking to use it might find that he or she could not frame the request for information specifically enough in order to obtain the particular documents needed. The request might be met with the response that one million documents were available touching on the matter at issue; the citizen might lack the expert knowledge needed to identify the particular document in question. The ability of the ordinary citizen to use the Act may also be affected by the cost of searches for information and the arrangements for meeting such cost. If the citizen has to meet most of it the likelihood is that many searches will not be initiated or will not be pursued. Government departments may tend to respond to the passing of the Act by moving from formal documentation of meetings and decisions to informal meetings without minutes, thereby evading the Act. (As the Select Committee Report suggested, this may be occurring already under the voluntary Code.)

The exceptions under the future UK Freedom of Information Act, while likely to be less wide ranging than those under the current Code, may nevertheless mean that sensitive matters of great political significance could remain undisclosed, even though some harm tests are to be introduced. In particular, the breadth and uncertainty of the term 'national security' may allow matters which fall only doubtfully within it to remain secret. Had such an Act been in place at the time of the change in policy regarding arms sales to

---

90 Paragraph 126.
91 HC 75, HC 67 (1996–97).

Iraq, the subject of the Scott Report, it is likely that information relating to it would not have been disclosed since it could have fallen within the exception clauses. The whole subject of arms sales will probably fall within the national security exception and possibly within other exceptions as well.[92] There will be a number of broad exemptions from the new Act. The Security Services will be completely exempted from its provisions. Most files containing civil servants' advice to ministers will remain exempt, although most such advice, including background information, will be disclosed after ministerial decisions have been taken. Thus, while it is suggested that the Freedom of Information Act, enforceable by the Information Commissioner, will be a clear improvement on the current Code, and will represent a far more significant break with the UK tradition of government secrecy, its role in bringing about 'open government' should not be exaggerated.

---

92 See further the Minutes of Evidence before the Public Service Committee, HC 313–1, (1995–96), QQ 66 *et seq*. Under the new Act information deemed to be commercially confidential will be exempt. This exemption may cover information about government contractors, including arms companies.

CHAPTER SEVEN

FREEDOM OF ASSOCIATION AND ASSEMBLY

1 INTRODUCTION

Freedom of association and assembly are sometimes linked in human rights documents as they are in Article 20 of the Universal Declaration of Human Rights and in Article 11 of the European Convention on Human Rights. Often an individual will be claiming the right to associate with a group in order to make his or her views known publicly and obtain public support. Clearly a protest or plea for support will be more effective if carried out collectively rather than individually. All free societies recognise the need, first to allow citizens to join or support groups which express a view at variance with the government view and secondly to allow such groups to assemble in order to express their views publicly. Toleration of public protest is one of the main distinctions between totalitarian societies and democracies.

Usually, in order to make an effective public protest or demonstration a group needs to have coherence and a structure. Thus freedom of assembly would be emasculated were it not underpinned by freedom of association; only spontaneous meetings and marches would receive protection. Equally, freedom of association would almost cease to exist if citizens could join a group but could not meet regularly with it. However, the two freedoms can of course be exercised entirely separately; freedom of association includes the freedom to be a member of a group which never meets but communicates with its members by other means. Equally, it includes the freedom to choose not to join a group (see the judgment of the European Court of Human Rights in *Young, James and Webster v UK*).[1] Similarly, freedom of assembly covers the freedom to engage in an entirely spontaneous demonstration and probably also the freedom of a single individual to make a public protest.

Both freedoms partly derive their legitimacy from their close association with freedom of speech,[2] in that both protect the freedom to propagate opinions publicly, thereby fostering public debate, the search for truth and participation in the democracy. Arguably, most forms of public protest

---

1   A.44; (1981) 4 EHRR 38.
2   See Lord Denning's comments on this point in *Hubbard v Pitt* [1976] QB 142. However, in America it has been determined in the leading 'symbolic speech' case that speech and conduct can be disentangled: the one can be punished so long as the incidental restriction caused to the other goes no further than is necessary for the furtherance of the interest in question. (*United States v O'Brien* 391 US 367 (1968); for criticism see Nimmer [1973] 21 UCLA LR 38–44.) See Barendt's discussion of the relationship between freedom of speech and freedom of association: *Freedom of Speech*, 1987, pp 280–98.

involve an intertwining of speech and conduct which cannot sensibly be disentangled, whether support for a group or its views is shown through the medium of pure speech accompanied by conduct (shouting, waving placards, distributing leaflets) or through conduct amounting to symbolic speech (wearing uniforms or conducting a silent vigil).[3]

2 FREEDOM OF ASSOCIATION[4]

In general there are no restrictions under UK law on the freedom to join or form groups which do not constitute conspiracies,[5] although equally there are no legal guarantees of this freedom. However, in two areas freedom of association is subject to constraints.

Groups associated with the use of violence

A number of specific statutory provisions place limits on the freedom to join or support groups which are associated with the use of violence. The most general restriction arises under s 2 of the Public Order Act 1936 which prohibits the formation of military or quasi-military organisations. Under s 2(1)(b) a quasi-military organisation is defined as 'one organised and trained or organised and equipped either for the purpose of enabling them to be employed for the use or display of physical force in promoting any political object or in such a manner as to arouse reasonable apprehension that they are organised and either trained or equipped for that purpose'. The use of the latter words extends the ambit of this provision and means that it has the potential to catch quite a wide range of groups, assuming that they have or appear to have, a political objective. However, not many prosecutions have been brought under this provision. The last successful one was in *Jordan and Tyndall*.[6] The defendants were both members of a fascist group called *Spearhead*. They engaged in various activities which included practising foot drill and storing sodium chloride with the probable aim of using it to make bombs. It was held

---

3   The European Commission of Human Rights has left open the possibility that Article 10 may protect some forms of symbolic speech. Appl 7215/75, *X v UK* (1978) Yearbook XXI; (1978) 3 EHRR 63. The case concerned denial of a right to engage in homosexual practices thereby expressing love for other men. The Commission, having found the application admissible, decided in its report on the merits that the particular facts did not give rise to an issue covered by Article 10.

4   General reading: Bailey, Harris and Jones, pp 157–61; Feldman, D, *Civil Liberties in England and Wales*, 1993, 783–84; Walker, C, *The Prevention of Terrorism*, 1992, Chap 5.

5   For criminal or civil law purposes. See Chap 5 pp 171–72 for consideration of the wide-ranging common law offence of conspiracy to corrupt public morals. For general discussion see Hazell, R, *Conspiracy and Civil Liberties*, 1974, Chap 6.

6   [1963] *Crim LR* 124. For discussion see Williams, DGT, *Keeping the Peace*, 1967, pp 222–23; Walker, M, *The National Front*, 1977, pp 39–45.

that their activities satisfied the test under s 2(1)(b). Alternatively, under s 2(1)(a) a group organised, trained or equipped in order to allow it to usurp the function of the army or the police would fall within this prohibition against quasi-military groups, thus possibly catching vigilante groups such as the *Guardian Angels* (a group organised with the object of preventing crime on underground railways).

Certain other provisions which place limits on freedom of association are aimed at a number of specified groups. The Prevention of Terrorism (Temporary Provisions) Act (PTA) 1989[7] makes it an offence under s 2 to belong to a proscribed organisation. The organisations currently proscribed are listed in Schedule 1 to the Act; at present the IRA and INLA are proscribed and these powers are extended to Northern Ireland by virtue of s 28 of the Northern Ireland (Emergency Provisions) Act 1991.[8] 'Organisations' are widely defined as 'any association or combination of persons' (s 1(6) of the PTA). Further, an organisation need not engage in terrorism itself; it is enough if it promotes or encourages it. If an organisation was proscribed on insufficient grounds there would be little possibility of challenge to the order. There is no right of appeal against proscription and judicial review, while theoretically available, is likely to be extremely limited. In *McEldowney v Forde*[9] an order was made under statutory instrument banning republican clubs or any like organisation, thus potentially outlawing all Nationalist political parties. Nevertheless, the House of Lords preferred not to intervene, Lord Diplock stating that he would do so only if proscription were extended to bodies obviously distanced from Republican views.

Proscription may be seen as providing a legitimate means of expressing outrage at IRA activities, thereby tending to prevent illegitimate expressions of public anger. It has been argued that it may discourage supporters of terrorist organisations and may signal political strength.[10] On the other hand it has been argued that these benefits are minimal and that it is 'a cosmetic part of the PTA' which is in fact 'counter productive as it impedes criminal investigation and political discussion'.[11] Lord Jellicoe's review of the operation of the PTA doubted the value of proscription, considering that its detrimental effects in terms of constraining the free expression of views about Northern Ireland outweighed its benefits.[12] In response, a Home Office circular was issued[13] giving guidance to the police as to the proper use of ss 1

---

7 For commentary on the PTA provisions see Bonner, D [1989] *PL* 440.
8 For commentary on the predecessor to the 1991 Act see *Review of the Operation of the Northern Ireland (Emergency Provisions) Act 1978*, Cmnd 9222; Bonner, D [1984] *PL* 348.
9 [1971] AC 632.
10 Wilkinson, P, *Terrorism and the Political State*, 1986, p 170.
11 See Walker, C, *The Prevention of Terrorism in British Law*, 2nd edn, 1992, p 64.
12 Cmnd 8803, 1983; the review did not however recommend deproscription, since it would create public resentment.
13 On 9 August 1983 (Current Law Statutes 1984 note to s 1(1)).

and 2, bearing in mind the possible effect on freedom of expression. It has been argued that, *prima facie* proscription breaches Articles 9, 10 and 11 of the European Convention on Human Rights but that, apart from exceptions contained in those Articles, Article 17 might justify it since it limits Convention guarantees to activity in harmony with its aims and this could not be said of IRA methods.[14]

Restrictions on the use of badges or uniforms as signals of support for certain organisations are intended to have the dual effect of preventing communication – by those means – of the political message associated with the organisation and of tending to minimise the impression that the organisation is supported, thereby denying reassurance to the members of the organisation, lowering their morale and preventing them from arousing public support. Under s 3 of the PTA 1989 it is an offence to wear any item which arouses a reasonable apprehension that a person is a member or supporter of a proscribed organisation. Under s 1 of the Public Order Act 1936 it is an offence to wear a uniform signifying association with any political organisation or with the promotion of any political object. Section 1 was invoked in *Whelan v DPP*[15] against leaders of a Provisional Sinn Fein protest march against internment in Northern Ireland, all of whom wore black berets while some wore dark glasses, dark clothing and carried Irish flags. It was found that, first, something must be 'worn' as apparel and secondly that it must be a uniform. Something might amount to a uniform if worn by a number of persons in order to signify their association with each other or if commonly used by a certain organisation. By this means the third requirement that the uniform must signal the wearer's association with a particular political organisation could also be satisfied. Alternatively, it might be satisfied by consideration of the occasion on which the uniform was worn without the need to refer to the past history of the organisation. It was found that the items worn could amount to a uniform; this decision therefore greatly diminished the distinction between this offence and that under the PTA. The justification for retention of the PTA provisions is therefore doubtful due to the overlap between the two offences.

Trade unions

Freedom not to join a trade union

This issue was considered by the European Court of Human Rights in *Young, James and Webster v UK*.[16] In 1975, British Rail entered a closed shop

---

14 Walker, C, *The Prevention of Terrorism in British Law*, pp 49–50.
15 [1975] QB 864.
16 A.44; (1981) 4 EHRR 38; for commentary see (1982) 41 *CLJ* 256 and (1982) 15 *Cornell ILJ* 489.

agreement which made membership of a certain trade union a condition of employment. The three applicants, who were already employed by British Rail, disagreed with the political activities of trade unions; they therefore refused to join the union and were dismissed. They claimed that their dismissal on this ground constituted an infringement of Article 11 of the European Convention.

The European Court of Human Rights found that the agreement between British Rail and the unions was lawful under the Trade Union and Labour Relations Act 1974 which allowed for dismissal for refusing to join a trade union unless the refusal was on grounds of religious belief. In determining whether that provision infringed Article 11 the court considered the 'negative aspect' of freedom of association, in other words, the right not to join a group. It was found that the negative aspect was not on the same footing as the positive aspects but that when an individual's freedom of choice in association was so abridged – where there was only one ground on which it was possible to refuse to join a union – then an interference with freedom of association had occurred since it must necessarily include freedom of choice. This did not mean that all closed shop agreements would infringe Article 11; the court was careful to confine its argument to the facts of the specific case. (The drafters of the Convention were aware of closed shop agreements operating in certain of the Member States in 1949 and therefore deliberately omitted a clause protecting an individual's right not to be compelled to join an association.) The court did not find that the agreement was necessary under Article 11(2) but decided the case solely under para 1. In response, UK law was changed by means of a provision inserted into s 58 of the Employment Protection (Consolidation) Act 1978 which widened the exception on grounds of religious belief to include making a dismissal unlawful if the person objected on the grounds of a deeply held conviction to being a member of a trade union.

Freedom of choice between unions

The need to show a very clear curtailment of choice where the negative aspect of freedom of association is in question was affirmed by the decision of the European Court of Human Rights in *Sibson v UK*,[17] which concerned a choice between unions rather than a choice as to whether to join one at all. The applicant had resigned from his union, the TGWU, due to dissatisfaction with its decision in respect of a complaint he had made; he had then been ostracised by his workmates who threatened to go on strike unless he rejoined the union or was employed elsewhere. He joined another union and his employer then sought to employ him at a depot some distance away; he refused this offer, resigned and claimed constructive dismissal. When this

---

17 A.258; (1993) *Guardian*, 10 May; (1993) *The Times*, 17 May.

claim failed in the domestic courts, he applied to the European Commission on Human Rights, alleging a breach of Article 11. The court found that no breach had occurred: his treatment did not infringe the very substance of his freedom of association; he had not been subject to a closed shop agreement and had had the offer of continuing to work for the company without joining the union. Moreover, he had had no objection to union membership as such.

Possibly this decision should not be characterised as one entirely concerned with the negative aspect of freedom of association since in order to rejoin the TGWU the applicant would have had to resign from the second union. Therefore the claim could be characterised as concerning the right of an employee to choose which particular union to join free from pressure from workmates or the employer. The applicant had been faced with the choice of working elsewhere or resigning from one union and joining another. It might appear that such a situation concerns a highly significant interest: the freedom to choose between associations and that therefore this decision is unfortunate in leaving such freedom unprotected so long as the employee retains the basic freedom not to join a union. It is instructive to note that the International Covenant on Economic, Social and Cultural Rights, unlike the European Convention, includes 'the right to join the trade union of *his choice*' (emphasis added).

Freedom to join a union

During the Conservative government's period of office from 1979 to 1997 no move was made to outlaw union membership *per se*. Such a move would of course have constituted a clear breach of Article 11. However, certain measures have been taken which have curtailed choice of unions or had the effect of reducing the size of the group which retains the right to union membership. Certain bodies such as the army under the Army Act 1955, the police under s 47 of the Police Act 1964 and certain public officials have traditionally been debarred from union membership but this group was enlarged when civil servants working at Government Communications Headquarters (GCHQ) were de-unionised. Their challenge to the ban on trade unions was considered in *Council of Civil Service Unions v Minister for the Civil Service*[18] (the *GCHQ* case). The Minister for the Civil Service, the Prime Minister, Margaret Thatcher, gave an instruction issued under Article 4 of the Civil Service Order in council to vary the terms of service of the staff at GCHQ with the effect that staff would no longer be permitted to join national trade unions. Six members of staff and the union involved applied for judicial review of the minister's instruction on the ground that she had been under a duty to act fairly by consulting those concerned before issuing it. In the House of Lords it had first to be determined whether the decision was open to

---

18 [1985] AC 374; [1985] 3 WLR 1174; [1985] 3 All ER 935; for comment see [1985] *PL* 177, 186.

judicial review. In this instance the Prime Minister was exercising powers under the royal prerogative which were traditionally seen as unsusceptible to judicial review as deriving from the common law and not from statute. However, Lord Denning in *Laker Airways v Department of Trade*[19] seemed to have effected some erosion of that principle and following his lead the House of Lords determined that the mere fact of the power deriving from the prerogative as opposed to statute was not a sufficient reason why it should not be open to review.

Having made this determination the House of Lords then found that the decision-making process had in fact been conducted unfairly. Usual practice had created a legitimate expectation that there would be prior consultation before the terms of service were altered; therefore there was a legitimate expectation that that practice would be followed which had not been fulfilled. However, the Prime Minister argued that national security considerations had outweighed the duty to act fairly; had there been prior consultation this would have led to strikes which would have affected operations at GCHQ – the very reason why union membership had been withdrawn. In her assessment, the requirements of national security outweighed those of fairness. The appellants argued first that this argument was an afterthought and secondly that national security had not been and would not be affected, in part because the unions were offering a no-strike agreement. However, the House of Lords held that the Prime Minister was better placed than the courts to determine what was needed by national security, although it was held that there must be some evidence of danger to national security; a mere assertion that such danger existed would be insufficient. As some evidence of such a danger had been put forward the challenge to the union ban failed.

A group from GCHQ applied to the European Commission alleging a breach of both Article 11 and of the Article 13 provision that there must be an effective remedy for violation of a Convention right.[20] They were claiming that judicial review did not afford such a remedy. Accepting that the ban infringed the applicants' freedom of association, the government argued that it fell within Article 11(2) because it was adopted in furtherance of the interests of national security and that the margin of appreciation allowed to Member States in that respect should be wider than in respect of the other exceptions[21] since it should be assumed that only the domestic authorities were competent to make a determination as to the needs of national security. Therefore, once it had made a determination that national security would be affected by industrial disruption and that a no-strike agreement would be inadequate, its decision could not be questioned by an outside body. It

---

19 [1977] QB 643.
20 *Council of Civil Service Unions v UK* (1987) 20 DRECom HR 228; (1988) 10 EHRR 269.
21 This had been accepted in other decisions including the *Klass* case Publ ECHR, A.28; (1979) 2 EHRR 214.

followed that the blanket ban imposed was not disproportionate to the end in view which was to protect national security.

The applicants argued, on the other hand, that the exception under Article 11(2) in respect of the needs of national security could not apply because the ban was out of proportion to the aim pursued; there was no sufficiently pressing need to impose it. Only if such a need could be shown could such a grave infringement of freedom be justified. No such pressing need could be shown because there had been no recent action at GCHQ and when there had been such action the government had not reacted to it for three years, thereby suggesting that it was not over-concerned about the effect on national security. Further, the government had stated in 1981 in Parliament that action at GCHQ had not affected national security. A no-strike agreement, it was argued, would be in proportion to the requirements of national security.

The government's second argument was that the applicants fell within the second sentence of para 11(2) which allowed restrictions to be imposed on the police, armed forces or the members of the administration of the state. It was argued that 'restriction' could include a total ban. The applicants, however, argued that the sentence should be narrowly construed; the word 'lawful' should mean that it should be interpreted in accordance with Convention limits and that, accordingly, it could not authorise a complete denial of trade union membership.

The Commission found that the ban amounted to a clear *prima facie* breach of Article 11; the question was whether it could be justified. The word 'lawful' was interpreted as meaning 'in accordance with national law'. The Civil Service Order in Council which had been made fulfilled that requirement. Could the term 'restriction' mean 'destruction'? It was found that the fact that the ban was complete did not mean that it would not be proportionate to the aim pursued, which was to protect national security, one of the exceptions contained in Article 11(2). The second sentence of Article 11 was considered. It was found that it allowed for restrictions which could not be justified under the first sentence; it was also applicable to the ban. The application was found to be manifestly ill-founded as far as Article 11 was concerned. The Commission further accepted the government's argument in relation to the alleged breach of Article 13 that judicial review afforded a sufficient remedy. Thus the application was found to be inadmissible. Those who refused to give up their trade union membership were eventually sacked. The right to join a union was only reinstated at GCHQ in 1997 after the Labour government came to power.

The Conservative governments between 1979 and 1997 brought about a further curtailment of freedom of choice in union membership due to its policy of allowing non-industrial civil servants to choose only those unions which were not affiliated to the Labour Party, on the ground that to do otherwise would imperil the political neutrality of the civil service. Thus a non-industrial civil servant who wished to join an affiliated trade union could not do so, while a civil servant whose industrial grade became non-industrial might have to give up the membership of an affiliated union for that of a non-affiliated one. In pursuance of this policy the Conservative government informed Ministry of Defence regraded security guards in April 1992 that it would no longer be able to recognise the TGWU and GMB as their representatives due to the political affiliation of those unions.

A possibly related policy concerned the use of penalties against employees who refused offers to give up union membership. In *Associated British Ports v Palmer and Others*[22] the Court of Appeal found that granting pay rises only to employees who were prepared to renounce their right to union representation was in breach of s 23 of the Employment Protection (Consolidation) Act 1978 which renders unlawful action taken against an employee with the purpose of deterring him from trade union membership. The government immediately responded to this decision by introducing an amendment to the Trade Union Reform and Employment Rights Bill 1993 (then at the report stage in the House of Lords) during its third reading in the House of Lords, allowing employers to award pay rises selectively in order to encourage employees to give up Union membership.[23] On appeal the House of Lords found in *Associated British Ports* and in *Associated Newspapers*[24] that the term 'action' did not include omissions in this context, taking the legislative history of the provision into account. This decision almost completely emasculated the protection offered under the Act. It also meant that the amendment made to the Trade Union Reform and Employment Rights Act was probably unnecessary. Deakin and Morris comment on the House of Lords decision: 'It is possible to argue that in *Associated Newspapers* the courts have gone well-beyond what even the government thought desirable or at least politically expedient in this area.'[25] The House of Lords' decision is likely to be enormously influential in deterring employees from joining or remaining in trade unions. It remains to be seen whether the current Labour government will reverse it or whether reception of the European Convention on Human Rights into domestic law may encourage a challenge to the House of Lords' decision under Article 11. Although the decision does not in formal terms affect the freedom to join a union, it substantively undermines it.

---

22 (1993) *The Times*, 5 May; see also *Associated Newspapers Ltd v Wilson* (1993) reported on the same day.
23 On 24 May 1993 the House of Lords therefore adopted the unusual procedure of recommitment of a section to the Bill, followed by a report stage, followed by the third reading of the remainder of the Bill.
24 [1995] 2 All ER 100.
25 Deakin and Morris, *Labour Law*, 1995, p 643. For further discussion of this area see Chap 8 *op cit*.

3 FREEDOM OF ASSEMBLY

Introduction[26]

A tension clearly exists between the legitimate interest of the state in maintaining order on the one hand and on the other the protection of freedom of assembly. Therefore this chapter focuses on those provisions of the criminal law most applicable in the context of demonstrations, marches or meetings. These restraints are not aimed specifically at assemblies but generally at keeping the peace. However, freedom of assembly is affected by them and, as it has no special constitutional protection, it is in a very vulnerable position due to their number and width. To an extent the number of restraints available is unsurprising because the range of state interests involved is wider than any other expressive activity would warrant: they include the possibilities of disorder, of violence to citizens and damage to property. Clearly, the state has a duty to protect citizens from the attentions of the mob. The need to give weight to these interests explains the general acceptance of freedom of assembly as a non-absolute right[27] even though it may be that violent protest is most likely to bring about change.

On the other hand, as argued above, the individual right to assemble and make public protest is bolstered by the interests justifying freedom of speech – furthering the search for truth and the participation of the citizen in the democracy. The justification for expression based on the need for citizens to participate in the democracy is particularly applicable to public protest since it is probably one of the most effective means by which ordinary citizens can bring matters to the attention of others, including members of Parliament. Ordinary citizens are unlikely to be able to gain access to the media to publicise their views; they may, for example, distribute leaflets or posters without assembling in order to do so but such methods are probably less effective if they are not part of a public protest. Therefore, allowing forms of protest suggests that a society wishes to encourage participation in the

---

26 On this topic see generally Williams, DGT, *Keeping the Peace*, 1967 (excellent historical account); Brownlie, I and Supperstone, M, *Law Relating to Public Order and National Security*, 2nd edn, 1981; Marshall, G, 'Freedom of Speech and Assembly' in *Constitutional Theory*, 1971, p 154; Bevan, VT, 'Protest and Public Disorder' [1979] *PL* 163; Uglow, S, *Policing Liberal Society*, 1988; Smith, ATH, *Offences Against Public Order*, 1996; Sherr, A, *Freedom of Protest, Public Order and the Law*, 1989; Ewing and Gearty, *Freedom under Thatcher*, 1990, Chap 4; Bailey, Harris and Jones, *Civil Liberties: Cases and Materials*, 4th edn, 1995, Chap 3; Whitty, Murphy and Livingstone, *Civil Liberties Law*, 1995, Part V; Feldman, D, *Civil Liberties and Human Rights in England and Wales*, 1993, Chap 17; Waddington, PAJ, *Liberty and Order*, 1994. For discussion and criticism of the Public Order Act 1986 see Bonner, D and Stone, R, 'The Public Order Act 1986: Steps in the Wrong Direction?' [1987] *PL* 202; Card, R, *Public Order: the New Law*, 1987; Smith, ATH, 'The Public Order Act 1986 Part I' [1987] *Crim LR* 156.

27 See the leading US case, *Hague v Committee for Industrial Organisation* 307 US 496 (1938). For further discussion see Williams, DGT [1987] *Crim LR* 167.

democratic process since citizens will thereby be able to signal their response to government policies, encourage changes in policy and deter the government from repressive measures. Thus public protest provides a direct means of allowing democratic participation to occur outside election periods. On this argument the acceptance of the freedom to protest poses no threat to the established authorities but rather underpins the democratic process which placed them where they are and from which they derive their legitimacy. Even an assembly which publicised anti-democratic views would fall within the justification from the argument from truth. Thus justifications deriving from freedom of speech and from effective participation in the democracy underpin freedom of assembly and public protest.

It is clear that these justifications are not equally present in relation to all forms of what may loosely be termed protest. The argument from democracy most clearly supports peaceful assemblies or marches which use speech in some form to persuade others, including the authorities, to a particular point of view. If the group seeks not to persuade others but to bring about the object in question by direct action the democratic process may be said to have been circumvented rather than underpinned. Direct action may include, in its most extreme form, group violence intended to force others into compliance with a certain view. This would include political riots intended to overthrow the government. This would be unjustifiable in relation to a democratically elected government following the arguments above. However, some forceful action may not be intended in itself to bring about the object in question directly but may be used as a desperate expedient to draw attention to a cause where peaceful means have failed. It may be distinguished from direct action since it is still intended to bring about its object by democratic means; it may be used to draw attention to a cause and to persuade the electors and Parliament that action is necessary. Such action may be preferred to direct action due to the nature of the object in question. The history of the suffragette movement shows that after peaceful protest had failed forceful or violent protest was adopted.

Some forms of non-violent action may well be combined with attempts at verbal persuasion but may also be intended in themselves to bring about the object in question or at least to obstruct others in their attempts to bring about various objects. Such action would include industrial and other forms of picketing and protests such as those of hunt or fishing saboteurs who physically obstruct the activity in question, albeit usually by non-violent means. Does such action fall within the justifications for freedom of assembly at all? If it is non-violent it may be lawful in itself on the principle that everything which is not legally forbidden is allowed. Sleeping in a tree in order to prevent it being cut down, throwing twigs into water to disrupt angling is not intrinsically unlawful but if no rights-based justification protects such activity and if it impinges on the lawful activity of others, it may appear reasonable to proscribe it. However, such activity could be viewed as symbolic speech – message-bearing speech – and therefore as deserving of a degree of protection on that basis. It could be viewed both as obstructing the activity in question but also as calling attention to it, fuelling debate and thereby potentially activating the democratic process.

Taking the justifications underpinning public protest considered above into account and weighing them against the interest of the state and its citizens in the maintenance of public order, it is clear that some restraint on public protest is needed. The difficulty is that, in furtherance of the interest in public order (which in itself protects freedom of assembly), the constitutional need to allow freedom of assembly in a democracy may be obscured. The concern of this section is to determine how far the legal scheme governing public order manages to reconcile the two interests. The Public Order Act 1986 and the public order provisions of the Criminal Justice and Public Order Act 1994 form a very significant part of the legal framework within which freedom of assembly operates, but it is also important to take into account the part played by a number of wide-ranging and sometimes archaic powers which spring partly from a mix of other statutory provisions, partly from the common law and partly from the royal prerogative.[28]

The 1980s witnessed a series of disturbances beginning with the Brixton riots in 1981[29] and continuing with the disorder associated with the miners' strike 1984–85. Such disorder formed the background to the Public Order Act 1986 but it is unclear that further police powers to control disorder were needed. It did not appear that the police had lacked powers to deal with these disturbances; on the contrary, a number of different common law and statutory provisions were invoked, including powers to prevent breach of the peace, obstruction of a constable and watching and besetting under s 7 of the Conspiracy and Protection of Property Act 1875.[30] However, the government took the view that the available powers were confused and fragmented and that there was scope for affording the police additional powers to prevent disorder before it occurred.[31] The 1986 Act itself, however, came to be seen as inadequate as a means of controlling certain forms of protest and the Criminal Justice and Public Order Act 1994 was passed with a view to creating a further curb on the activities of certain groups such as hunt saboteurs or motorway

---

28 For discussion of the various offences see Smith, JC, *Smith and Hogan Criminal Law*, 8th edn, 1996 (standard criminal law text), Chap 21; Thornton, P, *Public Order Law*, 1987.

29 See the inquiry by Lord Scarman, *The Brixton Disorders*, 1981, Cmnd 8427.

30 See McCabe, S and Wallington, P, *The Police, Public Order and Civil Liberties: Legacies of the Miners' Strike*, 1988, esp Appendix 1; Wallington, P, 'Policing the Miners' Strike' (1985) 14 *ILJ* 145. During the miners' strike over 10,000 offences were charged; see Wallington, P (1985) 14 *ILJ* 145.

31 For the background to the 1986 Act see: House of Commons, *Fifth Report from the Home Affairs Committee*, Session 1979–80, *The Law Relating to Public Order*, HC 756–51; Lord Scarman, *The Brixton Disorders*, Cmnd 8427, Part VI; Smith, ATH, 'Public Order Law 1974–83; Developments and Proposals' [1984] *Crim LR* 643; White Paper, *Review of Public Order Law*, Cmnd 9510, 1.7.

protesters. However, since the 1994 Act did not remove any of the existing powers, there now exists a web of various overlapping offences.[32]

The offences take the form of both prior and subsequent restraints. Prior restraint on assemblies may mean that an assembly cannot take place at all or that it can take place only under various limitations. Subsequent restraints, usually arrests and prosecutions for public order offences, may be used after the assembly is in being. Although the availability of subsequent restraints may have a 'chilling' effect, they are used publicly and may receive publicity. If an assembly takes place and subsequently some of its members are prosecuted for public order offences, it will have achieved its end in gaining publicity and may in fact have gained greater publicity due to the prosecutions. If the assembly never takes place its object will probably be completely defeated.

Developments in the law during the 1980s and 90s, which have provided the police with new and extensive powers to control public protest, have been matched to an extent by developments in methods of policing disorder. Equipment has become more effective; in 1981 the Home Secretary announced that stocks of CS gas, water cannon and plastic bullets would be held in a central store available to Chief Officers of Police for use in situations of serious disorder, although only as a last resort.[33] The conditions under which these weapons may be used are not defined in any statute and it may be that their use is unreviewable by the courts. When a local police authority tried to prevent the Chief Constable applying for plastic bullets from the central store the Court of Appeal declared that the Crown had a prerogative power to keep the peace which allowed the Home Secretary to 'do all that was reasonably necessary to preserve the peace of the realm'.[34] As the power is undefined it appears to render lawful any measures taken by the Home Secretary which can be termed 'reasonably necessary' in order to keep the peace. However, CS gas has not been used to control disorder since 1981 and water cannons were withdrawn from availability in 1987.[35] The possibility that the use of forceful tactics may exacerbate public order situations has been recognised since Lord Scarman's report into the Brixton disorders in 1981. Greater sensitivity in public order policing in the 1990s may also be due to changes in the nature of public protest during that period. Large scale disorder has not occurred since

---

32 For the background to the 1994 Act, which received the Royal Assent on 3 November 1994, see the introduction in Wasik and Taylor's *Guide to the Act*, 1995, p 1. For discussion of the public order offences see Smith, ATH [1995] *Crim LR* 19.

33 *Report of HM Chief Inspector for Constabulary for 1981* (1981–82 HC 463). For discussion of police riot control techniques and equipment see Waddington, *The Strong Arm of the Law*, Chap 6.

34 *Secretary of State for the Home Dept, ex parte Northumbria Police Authority* [1989] QB 26; [1988] 2 WLR 590; [1988] 1 All ER 556, CA; for criticism see Beynon, H [1987] *PL* 146 (on the Divisional Court decision); Bradley, AW [1988] *PL* 298.

35 See Jason-Lloyd, L (1991) 141 *NLJ* 1043.

the anti-poll-tax marches of 1990–91. The 1990s has seen an enormous growth in the use of direct action by a variety of groups, usually protesting about environmental issues. These include hunt saboteurs, fishing saboteurs, motorway and by-pass protesters, veal calf protesters. Riot control techniques are usually inappropriate as methods of controlling direct action; usually methods of physically removing the protesters from particular places are necessary. Such powers are available either under the common law doctrine of breach of the peace or under the 1994 Act.

Traditional legal recognition of freedom of assembly?[36]

It is generally thought that there is a right to assemble in certain places, such as Trafalgar Square or Hyde Park, but it is a fallacy that UK law has recognised any legal right to do so.[37] Until Article 11 is enacted, UK law will continue to afford virtually no recognition to rights to meet or to march. However, there are two instances in which such recognition is given. There is a very limited right to hold meetings, applying only to Parliamentary candidates before a general election, which arises under ss 95 and 96 of the Representation of the People Act 1983. This right will normally be upheld even when it appears that it is being abused by a minority group: in *Webster v Southwark London Borough Council*[38] the Labour Council had wished to deny it to a National Front candidate but the court upheld the statutory right of the group to meet. Once an election meeting is in being the law will afford a limited protection: it is an offence under s 97 of the 1983 Act to use disorderly conduct in order to break up a lawful public election meeting and this will include meetings held on the highway.[39]

Further, s 43 of the Education (No 2) Act 1986 provides that university and college authorities are under a positive duty to 'ensure that freedom of speech within the law is secured for members, students and employees of the establishment and for visiting speakers'.[40] Although there may be an argument that this provision is to be welcomed as promoting free speech interests, it is somewhat anomalous, to say the least, that a right to meet arises in certain specified buildings but not in others, such as town halls, while it does not arise at all in public places such as town squares or parks. Thus, a very limited positive obligation is placed on the state to allow meetings to take

---

36 See Barnum, DG [1977] *PL* 310 and (1981) 29 *Am Jo of Comparative Law* 59; also Stein, LA [1971] *PL* 115 for discussion of the constitutional status of public protest.

37 In respect of Trafalgar Square see *Ex parte Lewis* (1888) 21 QBD 191. By statutory instrument an application must be made to the Department of the Environment to hold a meeting in Trafalgar Square (SI 1952/776). There is no right to hold meetings in the Royal Parks: see *Bailey v Williamson* (1873) LR 8 QB 118.

38 [1983] QB 698; [1983] 2 WLR 217.

39 *Burden v Rigler* [1911] 1 KB 337.

40 For discussion of this provision see Barendt, *Freedom of Speech*, pp 321–22.

place but apart from this provision, a group which is prevented from holding an effective meeting due to the activities of other groups has no special protection.[41] This limited provision may be compared with more general provisions from other jurisdictions making it an offence to disrupt any meeting which has not been prohibited.[42]

On the other hand, the law affords great prominence to the freedom to pass and repass along the highway. Section 37 of the Highways Act 1980 provides that a person will be guilty of an offence if he 'without lawful authority or excuse wilfully obstructs the free passage of the highway'. It might appear therefore that the negative freedom to assemble is entirely abrogated so far as the highway is concerned since almost any assembly will create some obstruction. However, according to *Hirst and Agu v Chief Constable of West Yorkshire*[43] the term 'lawful excuse' refers to activities which are lawful in themselves and which are reasonable and this was found to cover peaceful demonstrations. This decision supports the view that freedom of assembly is recognised as a common law principle which can only be abrogated by clear statutory words. Where there is leeway to do so the courts will not accept that it has been broadly abrogated. Further, s 14 of the Public Order Act 1986 impliedly recognises the freedom to meet so long as the statutory requirements are complied with, and this argument may be supported by the existence of certain specific statutory prohibitions on meetings in certain places or at certain times such as s 3 of the Seditious Meetings Act 1817 which prohibits meetings of 50 or more in the vicinity of Westminster during a Parliamentary session. Such restrictions impliedly support the existence of a general freedom to meet or march which will exist if not specifically prohibited. The decision in *Burden v Rigler*[44] that for the purposes of s 97 of the Representation of the People Act 1983 the fact that the meeting is held on the highway will not of itself render it unlawful, also supports this view.

This general freedom, however, is in a precarious, not to say anomalous position. It appears to be recognised under the criminal law, but as far as the civil law of trespass is concerned it would seem that until Article 11 is enacted assemblies (not marches) will always be unlawful since any assembly, however small, which is stationary for a more than minimal period of time, is outside the purpose for which the public is permitted to use the highway.[45]

---

41 See discussion of this point in the European Court of Human Rights in *Platform 'Ärzte für das Leben' v Austria* (1988) 13 EHRR 204; it was found that freedom of assembly could not be reduced to a mere duty on the part of the state not to interfere; it did require the state to take some positive steps to be taken although the state was not expected to guarantee that a demonstration was able to proceed.
42 See eg Articles 284 and 285 of the Austrian Criminal Code.
43 (1986) 85 Cr App R 143. See also *Nagy v Weston* [1966] 2 QB 561; [1965] 1 WLR 280; *cf Arrowsmith v Jenkins* [1963] 2 QB 561; [1963] 2 All ER 210; for comment see [1987] *PL* 495.
44 [1911] 1 KB 337.
45 See discussion of *Jones and Lloyd v DPP* [1997] 2 All ER 119, below pp 297–98.

Legal regulation of meetings and marches: the statutory framework

Advance notice of public processions

Sections 12 and 13 of the 1986 Act, which allow banning or limitation of a march, are underpinned by s 11 which provides that the organisers of a march (not a meeting) must give advance notice of it to the police in the relevant police area[46] six clear days before the date when it is intended to be held.[47] This national requirement was an entirely new measure, although in some districts a notice requirement was already imposed under local regulations. It represents the first step to involving the police so that they will have an opportunity to impose conditions. It should be remembered of course that organisers of a sizeable march would probably have to involve the police in any event as they might need traffic to be held up while crossing busy roads. As the main purpose of s 11 is to allow conditions to be imposed on marches which might disrupt the community but as those are the very marches which the police would tend to know of in any event, the need for a new provision of this nature is questionable.

However, the notice requirement does not apply under s 11(1) if it was not reasonably practicable to give any advance notice. This provision was intended to exempt spontaneous demonstrations from the notice requirement but is defective due to the use of the word 'any'. Strictly interpreted, this word would suggest that a telephone call made five minutes before the march set off would fulfil the requirements, thereby exempting very few marches. In most circumstances, even though a march sets off suddenly, it might well be reasonably practicable to make such a telephone call. However, it can be argued that the word 'any' should not be interpreted so strictly as to exclude spontaneous processions where a few minutes was available to give notice, because to do so would defeat the intention behind including the provision. If read in combination with the requirements as to giving notice by hand or in writing, it should be interpreted to mean 'any written notice'. If it were not so interpreted it might be argued that s 11 breaches the guarantee of freedom of assembly under Article 11 of the European Convention on Human Rights, since it could criminalise the organiser of a peaceful spontaneous march. Section 11 may be said to fall within the rule to be introduced under the Human Rights Act 1998[48] that 'so far as it is possible to do so' possible statutes should be interpreted so as to conform with the Convention.

---

46 Section 11(4).
47 Section 11(5) and (6).
48 Section 3(1).

Advance notice must be given if the procession is held 'to demonstrate support or opposition to the views or actions of any person or body of persons, to publicise a cause or campaign or to mark or commemorate an event'. This provision was included in order to exempt innocuous crocodiles of children from the requirement. Processions customarily held are expressly exempted.[49] The notice must specify the date, time and proposed route of the procession and give the name and address of the person proposing to organise it. Under s 11(7) the organisers may be guilty of an offence if the notice requirement has not been satisfied or if the march deviates from the date, time or route specified. If it does, an organiser may have a defence under s 11(8) or (9) that he or she either had no reason to suspect that it had occurred or that it arose due to circumstances outside his or her control.

Section 11 criminalises what may be trivial administrative errors and, although police officers may use a discretion in bringing prosecutions under it, this leaves the power open to abuse and means that potentially at least it could be more rigidly enforced against marchers espousing unpopular causes. At present prosecutions under s 11 are very rarely being brought and therefore its deterrence value to organisers may become minimal.[50] For example, the organisers of a large peace march held on the date the UN Security Council ultimatum against Iraq[51] expired, failed to comply with the notice requirements under s 11 but no prosecution was brought. However organisers of the 'veal calves' protest at Brightlingsea in April 1995 were threatened with prosecution under s 11.

Applying conditions to meetings or marches

Section 12 of the 1986 Act reproduces in part the power under s 3 of the Public Order Act 1936 allowing the Chief Officer of Police to impose conditions on a procession if he apprehended serious public disorder. However, the power to impose conditions under s 12 may be exercised in a much wider range of situations than the old power. It arises in one of four situations which may be known as 'triggers'. In making a determination as to the existence of one of these 'triggers' the senior police officer in question should 'have regard to the time or place at which and the circumstances in which, any public procession is being held or is intended to be held and to its route or proposed route'. Bearing these factors in mind, he or she must reasonably believe that 'serious public disorder, serious damage to property or serious disruption to the life of the community' may be caused by the procession (s 12(1)(a)). The third phrase used is a very wide one which clearly offers police officers some scope for

---

49 Section 11(2). Funeral processions are also covered by this exemption.
50 Waddington, PAJ, *Liberty and Order*, 1994, pp 37–40.
51 Contained in SC resolution 678, 15 January.

interpretation and may be said to render the other two 'triggers' redundant. This 'trigger' has attracted particular criticism from commentators. It has been said that 'some inconvenience is the inevitable consequence of a successful procession. 'The Act ... threatens to permit only those demonstrations that are so convenient that they become invisible.'[52] Bonner and Stone have warned of 'the dangers that lie in the vague line between serious disruption and a measure of inconvenience'.[53] Further, it has been noted that the term 'the community' is ambiguous. In the case of London it is unclear whether the term could be applied to Oxford Street or central London or the whole Metropolitan area.[54] The more narrowly the term is defined the more readily a given march could be said to cause serious disruption. Serious obstruction of traffic might arguably amount to some disruption of the life of a small area which might be said to constitute a 'community'. Imposition of conditions allows police officers to cut down the cost of the policing requirement for an assembly and therefore may encourage them to interpret 'the community' or 'disruption' in the manner most likely to bring the 'trigger' into being, since the conditions then imposed, such as requiring a limit on the numbers participating, might lead to a reduction in the number of officers who had to be present. However, in answer to some of these fears it can be noted that in *Reid*[55] it was determined that the 'triggers' should be strictly interpreted: the words used should not be diluted.

The fourth 'trigger', arising under s 12(1)(b), consists of an evaluation of the purpose of the assembly rather than an apprehension that a particular state of affairs may arise. The senior police officer must reasonably believe that the purpose of the assembly is 'the intimidation of others with a view to compelling them not to do an act they have a right to do or to do an act they have a right not to do'. This requires a police officer to make a political judgment as to the purpose of the group in question because it must be determined whether the purpose is coercive or merely persuasive. Asking police officers to make such a judgment clearly lays them open to claims of partiality in instances where they are perceived as out of sympathy with the aims of the group in question. It should be noted that the fourth 'trigger' requires a reasonable belief in the presence of two elements – intimidation and coercion. Therefore a racist march through an Asian area would probably fall outside its terms since the element of coercion would probably be absent. It might however fall within the terms of the third 'trigger'. On the other hand, a march might be coercive without being intimidatory. In *Reid* the defendants shouted, raised their arms and waved their fingers; it was determined that such behaviour might cause discomfort but not intimidation and that the two

---

52 Ewing and Gearty, *Freedom under Thatcher*, p 121.
53 'The Public Order Act 1986: Steps in the Wrong Direction?' [1987] *PL* 202 at 226.
54 Ewing and Gearty, p 121.
55 [1987] *Crim LR* 702.

concepts could not be equated. In *News Group Newspapers Ltd v SOGAT*[56] it was held that mere abuse and shouting did not amount to a threat of violence for the purposes of intimidation under s 7 of the Conspiracy and Protection of Property Act 1875. Thus behaviour of a fairly threatening nature would have to be present in order to cross the boundary between discomfort and intimidation.

The conditions that can be imposed under s 12 if one of the above 'triggers' is thought to be present are very wide in the case of processions: any condition may be imposed which appears necessary to the senior police officer in order to prevent the envisaged mischief occurring. The conditions imposed may include changes to the route of the procession or a prohibition on it entering a particular public place. If the march is already assembling the conditions may be imposed by the senior police officer present at the scene who may be a constable; if the conditions are being considered some time before this point they must be determined by the Chief Officer of Police.

Section 14 of the 1986 Act allows the police to impose conditions on assemblies.[57] It was introduced in the 1986 Act as an entirely new power. Conditions may be imposed only if one of four 'triggers' under s 14(1) – identical to those arising under s 12 – is present. However, once it is clear that one of the 'triggers' is present the conditions which may be imposed are much more limited than those which may be imposed on marches. They are confined to such 'directions ... as to the place at which the assembly may be (or continue to be) held, its maximum duration or the maximum number of persons who may constitute it' as appear to the senior police officer 'necessary to prevent the disorder, damage, disruption or intimidation'. It must be clear that the condition was communicated to the members of the march. In *Brickley and Kitson v Police*[58] anti-apartheid demonstrators outside the South African embassy were asked to move away from the front of the embassy to a nearby street, Duncannon Street. The pickets in Duncannon Street increased and four of the demonstrators moved back in front of the embassy. The Chief Officer of Police feared that further disorder might be caused and imposed a condition under s 14 requiring the pickets to stay in Duncannon Street. This was conveyed to them over a megaphone. However, it was uncertain whether this information was actually communicated to the pickets and therefore their convictions in respect of failure to abide by the condition were quashed. The defences available if there is a failure to comply with the conditions are identical to those under s 12, as is the power of arrest arising under s 14(7).

---

56 [1986] ICR 716.

57 Under s 16 an assembly consists of 20 or more people in a public place; a public place is defined as one which is wholly or partly open to the air. Section 16 defines a public procession as one in a place to which the public have access. No further guidance is given. Presumably the procession must be moving and will become an assembly if it stops and if it consists of 20 or more people, in which case different rules will apply.

58 *Legal Action,* July 1988 p 21 (Knightsbridge Crown Court).

An organiser[59] will incur liability under ss 12(4) or 14(4) if he or she knowingly fails to comply with the conditions imposed, although he or she will have a defence if it can be shown that the failure arose from circumstances beyond his or her control. Thus the *organiser* must actually breach the condition in question; he or she would not incur liability merely because some members of the march or assembly did so and therefore where a march contains an unruly element which deliberately breaches conditions imposed the persons involved will incur liability but the organiser may escape it. An organiser may also incur liability if he or she incites another knowingly to breach a condition which has been imposed (ss 12(6) and 14(6)). According to the Court of Appeal in *Hendrickson and Tichner*[60] incitement requires an element of persuasion or encouragement; moreover, following *Krause*,[61] the solicitation must actually come to the notice of the person intended to act on it. Therefore, merely assuming the position of leader of a march or assembly which is in breach of a condition would not seem to be sufficient of itself to amount to incitement. However, express or implied encouragement to bring about or continue a breach, such as leading the group in a certain forbidden direction, would amount to incitement if the leader was aware of the breach of the condition.

The scope for challenging the conditions is very limited: there is no method of appealing from them and it is only possible to have them reviewed for procedural errors or unreasonableness in the High Court. The power to impose any condition thought necessary under s 12 is so subjective that until Article 11 is enacted it leaves the courts little scope for assessing the legality of the decision made,[62] although the condition must relate to the mischief it is designed to avert. However, in dealing with police action to maintain public order, the courts have been very unwilling to find police decisions to have been unlawful.[63] Applying the rule from *Kent v Metropolitan Police Commission*[64] one can infer that a challenge to a condition would almost certainly fail, although a challenge mounted where a senior officer had evinced a belief in the existence of a 'trigger' which no reasonable officer could entertain, might succeed due to the need to show a reasonable belief in

---

59 The 1986 Act does not define the term 'organiser' and there is no post-Act case law on the issue. It is submitted that on the dictionary definition of the term, stewards and others who have some role as marshals will be organisers. This contention is supported by the ruling from *Flockhart v Robinson* [1950] 2 KB 498 that a person who indicated the route to be followed should be designated an organiser as well as the person who planned the route. Thus it appears probable that the term includes stewards as well as leaders of the assembly or march.
60 [1977] *Crim LR* 356.
61 (1902) 18 *TLR* 238.
62 See eg *Secretary of State for Education and Science v Tameside* [1977] AC 1014.
63 See eg *Secretary of State for the Home Department ex parte Northumbria Police Authority* [1989] QB 26; [1988] 2 WLR 590; [1988] 1 All ER 556, CA.
64 (1981) *The Times*, 13 May.

relation to the 'triggers'. Until Article 11 is received into UK law, it would seem that no presumption in favour of freedom of assembly would be imported.

Banning orders

Under s 13 of the 1986 Act a ban must be imposed on a march if it is thought that it may result in serious public disorder. This power arises under s 13(1) and is exercised as follows:

> If at any time the Chief Officer of Police reasonably believes that, because of particular circumstances existing in any district or part of a district, the powers under s 12 will not be sufficient to prevent the holding of public processions in that district or part from resulting in serious public disorder, he shall apply to the council of the district for an order prohibiting for such period not exceeding three months as may be specified in the application the holding of all public processions (or of any class of public procession so specified) in the district or part concerned.

In response, the council may make the order as requested or modify it with the approval of the Secretary of State. It should be noted that once the Chief Officer of Police has come to the conclusion in question he must, not may, apply for a banning order. This power is exercised in respect of London by the Commissioner of Police for the City of London or the Commissioner of Police of the Metropolis. A member of the march or a person who organises it knowing of the ban will commit an offence under s 13(7) and (8) and can be arrested under s 13(10).

This reproduces the old power under s 3 of the Public Order Act 1936. Assuming that a power was needed to ban marches expected to be violent, this power was nevertheless open to criticism in that once a banning order had been imposed it prevented all marches in the area it covered for its duration. Thus a projected march likely to be of an entirely peaceful character could be caught by a ban aimed at a violent march. The Campaign for Nuclear Disarmament attempted to challenge such a ban after it had had to cancel a number of its marches (*Kent v Metropolitan Police Commissioner*)[65] but failed due to the finding that an order quashing the ban could be made only if there were no reasons for imposing it at all. The court found that the Commissioner had considered the relevant matters and, further, that CND had a remedy under s 9(3) (now s 13(5) of the 1986 Act) as they could apply to have the order relaxed.

It is arguable that the 1986 Act should have limited the banning power to the particular marches giving rise to fear of serious public disorder but this possibility was rejected by the government on the ground that it could be subverted by organisers of marches who might attempt to march under

---

65 (1981) *The Times*, 13 May.

another name. It would therefore, it was thought, have placed too great a burden on the police who would have had to determine whether or not this had occurred. However, in making this decision it is arguable that too great a weight was given to the possible administrative burden placed on the police and too little to the need to uphold freedom of assembly. A compromise solution – banning all marches putting forward a political message similar to that of the offending march – could have been adopted. This power was being used with increased frequency up to the mid-1980s: there were 11 banning orders in the period 1970–80 and 75 in the period 1981–84[66] (39 in 1981, 13 in 1982, nine in 1983 and 11 in 1984). Interestingly, however, as Waddington has noted, there have been few bans of marches in London since the passing of the 1986 Act.[67] The power may have been used sparingly because police officers preferred to police a march known about for some time as opposed to an assembly formed hastily in response to a ban or a hostile, unpredictable and disorganised march. As Waddington has argued, such considerations may account for the police refusal to ban the third anti-poll-tax march to Trafalgar Square, although such a march had previously led to a riot and in the face of fierce pressure to ban from Westminster City Council, local MPs and the Home Secretary.[68] However, the power to ban and to impose conditions gives the police bargaining power to use in negotiating with marchers and enables them to adopt a policy of strategic under-enforcement as part of the price of avoiding trouble when a march occurs.

It might seem that the s 13 banning power would be in breach of Article 11 of the European Convention on Human Rights, in that the banning of a march expected to be peaceful would not appear to be justified under para 2 in respect of the need to prevent disorder. However, in *Christians Against Racism and Fascism v UK*,[69] the applicants' argument that a ban imposed under s 3(3) of the Public Order Act 1936 infringed *inter alia* Article 11 was rejected by the Commission as manifestly ill-founded, on the ground that the ban was justified under the exceptions to Article 11 contained in para 2 since there was a real danger of disorder which it was thought could not be 'prevented by other less stringent measures'. Thus it may be irrelevant that a particular march affected by the ban was unlikely in itself to give rise to disorder.

The 1986 Act contained no power to ban assemblies but such a power was provided by s 70 of the Criminal Justice and Public Order Act 1994 which inserts s 14A into the 1986 Act. Section 14A provides that a Chief Officer of Police may apply for a banning order if he reasonably believes that an assembly is likely to be trespassory and may result in serious disruption to the

---

66 White Paper, Cmnd 9510 para 4.7.
67 Waddington, PAJ, *Liberty and Order*, 1994, pp 58–61.
68 Waddington, *op cit*.
69 (1984) 24 *YBECHR* 178.

life of the community or damage to certain types of buildings and structures. An order under the new banning power is subject to certain limitations: it can subsist for up to four days and operate within a radius of up to five miles around the area in question. Apart from these restrictions, this is a wider power than that arising under s 13 since it is partly based on the very broad and uncertain concept of 'serious disruption to the life of the community'. Section 14A is particularly objectionable since it uses the weakest 'trigger' as the basis for using the most draconian form of prior restraint – a complete ban, albeit in restricted circumstances.

Just as s 13 catches peaceful processions, the provisions of s 14A mean that assemblies which are not likely in themselves to cause the prohibited harm under s 14A(1) or 14A(4) may nevertheless be banned. Section 14A is backed up by s 14C (inserted into the 1986 Act by s 71 of the 1994 Act). Section 14C provides a very broad power to stop persons within a radius of five miles from the assembly if a police officer reasonably believes that they were on their way to it and that it is subject to a s 14A order. If the direction is not complied with and if the person to whom it has been given is aware of it, he or she may be arrested and may be subject to a fine if convicted. Thus this power operates before any offence has been committed and hands the police a very wide discretion.

Section 14A was considered in *Jones and Lloyd v DPP*[70] The case concerned an assembly which on the route leading to Stonehenge, at a time when a s 14A order was in force. The order prohibited the holding of trespassory assemblies within a four mile radius of Stonehenge and covered the period from 29 May to 1 June 1995. The main question which arose was whether the assembly in question was subject to the s 14A order. This depended on s 14A(5) of the 1994 Act which provides that once an order is in being it operates to prohibit any assembly which is held on land to which the public has no or only a limited, right of access and which takes place without the permission of the owner of the land or exceeds the limits of the permission or of the public's right of access. In this instance, the assembly was simply present on the highway but within the relevant four mile radius. Section 14A(9) provides that 'limited' in relation to a right of access by the public to land means that their use of it is restricted to a particular purpose. Thus the key question was whether the category of legitimate purposes for which the highway might be used included use of it by peaceful assemblies. The Divisional Court found that the highway was to be used for passing and repassing only and that assembling on it was outside the purpose for which the implied licence to use it was granted. In so finding the court relied on *Hickman v Maisey*.[71] The decision concerned the defendant's use of the highway in order to gain information by

---

70 [1997] 2 All ER 119.
71 [1900] 1 QB 752, CA.

looking over the plaintiff's land. The defendant was on the highway watching the plaintiff's land. It was found that the plaintiff owned the sub-soil under the highway and that the defendant was entitled to make ordinary and reasonable use of it. Such watching was held not to be reasonable; the defendant had gone outside the accepted use and therefore had trespassed.

On behalf of the respondents it was argued that any assembly on the highway is lawful so long as it is peaceful and non-obstructive since such an assembly is making a reasonable use of the highway. The court however took the view that s 14A(5) operates to prohibit any assembly which exceeds the public's limited right of access. The right of access was found to be limited to the right to pass along the highway, not to hold a meeting or demonstration on it. Such activities might be tolerated but there could be no legal right to engage in them. Section 14A(5) was found to operate to prevent assemblies which would otherwise be permitted. Thus, since the assembly had exceeded the limited rights of access to the highway it fell within s 14A(5) and the fact that but for the s 14A order, it would probably have been permitted could not affect this argument. It was also argued on behalf of the respondents that unless there was a right to hold an assembly as opposed merely to a toleration, Article 11 of the European Convention on Human Rights would be breached. However, the court found that recourse to the Convention was unnecessary since the law in question was not ambiguous and, further, that since peaceful assemblies are normally permitted, the law was in any event in conformity with the Convention. The case was remitted to the Crown Court for a re-hearing.

John Wadham of Liberty said of this decision: 'A peaceful non-obstructive gathering is a reasonable use of a public highway. To say that it is a form of trespass seems extraordinary.'[72] Nevertheless, this decision may represent a reasonable interpretation of the very restrictive provisions of s 14A. No authority clearly suggests that there is a legal right to assemble on the highway since it is difficult to support an argument that assembling on the highway and remaining there for a substantial period of time is incidental to passage along it. Therefore if the term 'right' within s 14A(1) means 'legal right' then any activity on the highway, other than passing along it, involving twenty or more people, is illegal if a s 14A order is in force. The decision might, however, be attacked on the ground that it does not merely place assemblies in a category of tolerated activity; it makes it clear that peaceful non-obstructive assemblies are unlawful under the civil law, since any assembly, however small, which is stationary for a more than minimal period of time, is outside the purpose for which the public is permitted to use the highway. It would appear that this position is incompatible with Article 11. It may be that s 14A is an instance of a provision which is unambiguously

---

72 (1997) *The Times*, 24 January.

incompatible with the Convention. If so, test cases which challenge s 14A in future, once Article 11 is received into domestic law, may present the judiciary with a dilemma since they will be expected to construe existing law so that it complies with the Convention, 'in so far as it is possible'. One way out of the dilemma would be to find that since Article 11 imports a right to freedom of assembly, one of the legal 'rights' recognised by s 14A must be a right to assemble on the highway. Thus, an assembly which was present and stationary on the highway while a s 14A order was in force but which did not otherwise infringe s 14A, would not give rise to liability under s 14B.

Obstructing the highway and public nuisance

Section 137 of the Highways Act 1980 provides that a person will be guilty of an offence if he 'without lawful authority or excuse in any way wilfully obstructs the free passage of the highway'. The only right in using the highway is to pass and re-pass along it – to make an ordinary reasonable use of it as a highway. Since obstruction of the highway is a criminal offence it might therefore appear that all assemblies on the highway are *prima facie* unlawful since they are bound to cause some impediment to those passing by and therefore they can only take place if the police refrain from prosecuting. However, the courts seem to take the stance that not every such assembly will be unlawful; the main issue will be what was reasonable in the circumstances.

In *Arrowsmith v Jenkins*[73] it was determined that minor obstruction of traffic can lead to liability under the 1980 Act. A pacifist meeting was held in a certain street which linked up two main roads. The meeting blocked the street and the organiser co-operated with the police in unblocking it. It was completely blocked for five minutes and partly blocked for 15 minutes. The police had advance notice of the meeting and the organiser was under the impression that the proceedings were lawful especially since other meetings had been held there on a number of occasions without attracting prosecutions. Nevertheless, the organiser was convicted. This use of the Highways Act is open to criticism; it places such meetings in a very precarious position since it seems to hand a power to the police to licence them, thereby seriously undermining freedom of assembly. However, in *Nagy v Weston*[74] it was held that a reasonable user of the highway will constitute a lawful excuse and that in order to determine its reasonableness or otherwise, the length of the obstruction must be considered, its purpose, the place where it occurred and whether an actual or potential obstruction took place. The purpose of the obstruction, mentioned in *Nagy*, was given greater prominence in *Hirst and*

---

73 [1963] 2 QB 561; [1963] 2 All ER 210; for comment see [1987] *PL* 495.
74 [1966] 2 QB 561; [1965] 1 WLR 280.

Agu v Chief Constable of West Yorkshire:[75] it was said that courts should have regard to the freedom to demonstrate. This was found in relation to the behaviour of a group of animal rights supporters who had conducted a demonstration in a busy street; their actions as part of a protest on matters of public concern were found to be reasonable. On that basis the purpose of an assembly as a means of legitimate protest may suggest that it can amount to a reasonable user of the highway.

The common law offence of public nuisance will arise if something occurs which inflicts damage, injury or inconvenience on all members of a class who come within the sphere or neighbourhood of its operation.[76] Liability for committing a public nuisance may arise by blocking the highway; however, according to *Clarke (No 2)*[77] the disruption caused must amount to an unreasonable user of the highway in order to found such liability. Thus, once obstruction has been shown the question of reasonableness arises. It would appear from *News Group Newspapers Limited v SOGAT*[78] that to cause a minor disruption for a legitimate purpose such as a march does not constitute an unreasonable user of the highway and will not therefore amount to a nuisance. It might seem that an assembly could not constitute a reasonable user of the highway under the Highways Act and yet nevertheless amount to a public nuisance. However, *dicta* in *Gillingham Borough Council v Medway Dock Co*[79] suggest that this might, exceptionally, be possible.

Breach of the peace, binding over and bail conditions[80]

Justices and any court of record having criminal jurisdiction, have a power at common law[81] to bind over persons to keep the peace. Under the Justices of the Peace Act 1361 there is also a power to bind over persons to be of good behaviour. If a person refuses a binding over order he or she can be imprisoned for up to six months. These powers are of great significance in relation to direct action, demonstrations and public protest generally.

The *contra bono mores*, 'contrary to a good way of life', power under the 1361 Act allows the binding over of persons whose behaviour is deemed by a

---

75 (1986) 85 Cr App R 143.
76 See *Halsbury's Laws of England*, 4th edn, Vol 34, para 305. For discussion of the offence see Spencer, JR (1989) 48 *CLJ* 55.
77 [1964] 2 QB 315; [1963] 3 All ER 884, CA.
78 [1986] ICR 716; [1986] IRLR 337.
79 [1992] 3 All ER 931.
80 For discussion of this power see Grunis, A [1976] *PL* 16; The Law Commission Paper, 'Binding Over: The Issues' 1987 Paper 103: for comment, see [1988] *Crim LR* 355; 'The Roots and Early Development of Binding Over Powers' (1988) *CLJ* 101–28; Kerrigan, K, 'Breach of the Peace and Binding Over – Continuing Confusion' (1997) 2(1) *J Civ Lib* 30.
81 See s 1(7) of the Justices of the Peace Act 1968 and Schedule 5 of the Administration of Justice Act 1973.

bench of magistrates to be anti-social although not necessarily unlawful. This vague and broad power hands an unacceptably wide discretion to magistrates to determine the standards of good behaviour; it has been severely criticised as a grave breach of rule of law standards.[82] The power has been used in this century against those engaging in political public protest and against groups such as animal rights activists. In *Hughes v Holley*[83] the Court of Appeal confirmed the existence of the power and its availability regardless of the lawfulness of the behaviour in question. This principle has been applied in relation to hunt saboteurs. In one instance a hunt saboteur had blown a horn with the intention of disrupting a hunt. There was no threat of violence and no breach of the peace. Blowing a horn is not unlawful. However, it was probable that he would have repeated the behaviour in question which was found to be anti-social by the magistrates. He was therefore bound over to be of good behaviour and the binding over order was upheld on appeal. The case led to an application to the European Commission on Human Rights under Articles 10, 11 and 5. It was declared admissible under Articles 10 and 11.[84] Whatever the outcome of this case it would appear that the *contra bono mores* power should be reviewed once the Convention becomes part of UK law. It may well be too vague and unpredictable in its operation to satisfy the 'prescribed by law' requirement under Articles 8–11.[85] The finding of the court in *Sunday Times v UK*[86] that 'a norm cannot be regarded as a "law" unless it is formulated with sufficient precision to enable the citizen to regulate his conduct', would not appear to be satisfied.

The notion of breaching the peace is less vague and uncertain but it has quite frequently been interpreted very broadly. If a police officer suspects that a breach of the peace is likely to be committed – for example, a march is expected to be disorderly – a person or persons can be arrested without a warrant under common law powers to prevent a breach of the peace and can be bound over to keep the peace, in other words not to continue the behaviour thought likely to lead to the breach of the peace. Thus the march could be prevented from occurring. If the person refuses the binding over order he or she can be imprisoned.

The flexible common law power to prevent a breach of the peace[87] overlaps with a number of the powers arising under the 1986 Act and is in general more useful to the police than they are as its definition is so vague.

---

82 Glanville Williams (1953) 16 *MLR* 417. See also Hewitt, P, *The Abuse of Power*, p 125.
83 (1988) 86 Cr App R 130.
84 *Hashman and Harrup v UK* (1996) 22 EHRR CD 184.
85 Article 8 uses the formulation 'in accordance with the law' but it was established in *Silver v UK*, Judgment of 25 March 1983, A.61; (1983) 5 EHRR 347 that both formulations are to be read in the same way.
86 Judgment of 26 April 1979, A.30 para 49.
87 For comment see 'Breaching the Peace and Disturbing the Quiet' [1982] *PL* 212; Williams, DGT, *Keeping the Peace: The Police and Public Order*, 1967.

This vagueness means that it can be used in such a way as to undermine attempts in the statutory provisions to carve out more clearly defined areas of liability. The leading case is *Howell*[88] in which it was determined that breach of the peace will arise if an act is done or threatened to be done which either: harms a person or *in his presence* his property or is likely to cause such harm or which puts a person in fear of such harm. Under this definition, threatening words might not in themselves amount to a breach of the peace but they might lead a police officer to apprehend a breach. Another and rather different definition of the offence was offered in *Chief Constable for Devon and Cornwall ex parte CEGB*[89] by Lord Denning. His view was that violence or the threat of it, was unnecessary; he considered that 'if anyone unlawfully and physically obstructs a worker – by lying down or chaining himself to a rig or the like – he is guilty of a breach of the peace'. On this view peaceful protest could be severely curtailed. It is generally considered that the view taken in *Howell* is the correct one[90] but the fact that as eminent an authority as Lord Denning could offer such a radically different definition of the offence[91] from that put forward in *Howell* only a year earlier, epitomises the disturbingly vague parameters of breach of the peace. The *Howell* definition in itself is extremely wide, largely because it does not confine itself to violence or threats of violence. Nor does it require that the behaviour amounting to a breach of the peace or giving rise to fear of a breach of the peace, should be unlawful under civil or criminal law. Further, it has been recognised for some time by the courts that a person may be bound over for conduct which is not itself a breach of the peace and which does not suggest that the individual concerned is about to breach the peace but which may cause another to breach the peace.[92] This third possibility is arguably implicit in the *Howell* definition itself and indeed is not sufficiently distinguished, within that definition, from conduct which in itself amounts to a breach of the peace. This additional possibility is of great significance in the context of public protest since it means that in certain circumstances peaceful, lawful protest can lead to the arrest and binding over of the protesters.

The width of powers to prevent a breach of the peace means that they can be used to curtail freedom of assembly in situations in which statutory powers might be inapplicable. For example, *Piddington v Bates*[93] suggested that the courts could be, at times, very unwilling to disagree with the finding of the

---

88 [1981] 3 All ER 383.

89 [1982] QB 458.

90 See eg Thornton, P, *Public Order Law*, 1987, p 74. In *Percy v DPP* [1995] 3 All ER 124, DC, the *Howell* definition as opposed to that of Lord Denning was preferred. Lord Denning's definition was rejected as erroneous.

91 It should be noted that breach of the peace, though arrestable, is not a criminal offence.

92 *Wise v Dunning* [1902] 1 KB 167; *Lansbury v Riley* [1914] 3 KB 229.

93 [1961] 1 WLR 162.

police officer on the ground. In that case the defendant wished to join other pickets at a printer's works but was told by police officers that only two men were to be allowed to picket each of the main entrances. The defendant then tried to push 'gently' past the police officer and was arrested for obstructing a police officer in the course of his duty. On appeal it was held that the officer had reasonably apprehended that a breach of the peace might occur and the limiting of the number of the pickets was designed to prevent it; however, the main reason for fearing trouble was apparently merely that there were 18 pickets at the works. In effect, therefore, a condition was imposed on a static assembly, reducing its numbers to four. It is interesting to note that if that situation were to occur today, with the 1986 Act in force, the powers under s 14 allowing control of assemblies could not be used since less than 20 people were present and even had more than 20 pickets been there, it seems probable that none of the 'trigger' conditions would have been satisfied. The case illustrates the readiness of the common law to sanction police interference with free assembly on production of what can only be described as minimal evidence of a risk of disorder.

This power, in conjunction with the offence of obstruction of an officer in the execution of his duty, was used extensively during the miners' strike.[94] The most notorious[95] instance of its use occurred in *Moss v McLachlan*.[96] A group of striking miners were stopped by the police a few miles away from a number of collieries; the police told them that they feared a breach of the peace if the miners reached the pits and that they would arrest the miners for obstruction if they tried to continue. After some time, a group of miners tried to push past the police, were arrested and convicted of obstruction of a police officer in the course of his duty. Their appeal on the ground that the officers had not been acting in the course of their duty was dismissed. It was said that there was no need to show that individual miners would cause a breach of the peace, nor even to specify at which pit disorder was expected. A reasonable belief that there was a real risk that a breach would occur in close proximity to the point of arrest (the pits were between two and four miles away) was all that was necessary. (A case in Kent in which striking miners were held up over 200 miles away from their destination suggests that this requirement of close proximity may be becoming otiose.)[97] In assessing whether a real risk existed, news about disorder at previous pickets could be taken into account; in other words there did not appear to be a requirement that there was

---

94 March 1984 to March 1985.
95 The case has attracted widespread criticism; see Ewing and Gearty, *Freedom under Thatcher*, pp 111–12; Newbold [1985] *PL* 30.
96 [1985] IRLR 76.
97 *Foy v Chief Constable of Kent* (20 March 1984, unreported). It has also been noted by Thornton, *Public Order Law*, 1987, pp 97–98 that the Attorney General, in a written answer to a Parliamentary question tabled during the miners' strike omitted the requirement of an imminent threat to public order.

anything about these particular miners to suggest they might cause a breach of the peace.[98] Thus, a number of individuals were lawfully denied their freedom of both movement and assembly apparently on no more substantial grounds than that other striking miners had caused trouble in the past, without having themselves provided grounds on which violence could be foreseen.

These cases concerned preventive powers used against those who could be viewed as likely to breach the peace at some future point. An equally broad view has been taken by the courts of conduct which might provoke others to breach the peace. *Beatty v Gillbanks*[99] established the important principle that persons acting lawfully could not be held responsible for the actions of those who were thereby induced to act unlawfully. However, in *Duncan v Jones*[100] a speaker wishing to address a public meeting opposite a training centre for the unemployed, was told to move away to a different street because the police apprehended that her speech might cause a breach of the peace. A year previously there had been some restlessness among the unemployed following a speech by the same speaker. She refused to move away from the centre and was arrested for obstructing a police officer in the course of his duty. On appeal it was found that the police had been acting in the course of their duty because they had reasonably apprehended a breach of the peace. The case therefore clearly undermined the *Beatty v Gillbanks* principle in that the freedom of the speaker was infringed, not because of her conduct but because of police fears about the possible response of the audience. In the later case of *Jordan v Burgoyne*[101] it was found that a public speaker could be guilty of breach of the peace if he spoke words which were likely to cause disorder amongst the particular audience present, even where the audience had come with the express intention of causing trouble. In *Percy v DPP*[102] Collins J ruled:

> The conduct in question does not in itself have to be disorderly or a breach of the criminal law. It is sufficiently if its natural consequence would, if persisted in, be to provoke others to violence.[103]

This very wide finding received a more restrictive interpretation in *Nicol v DPP*[104] which concerned the behaviour of fishing protesters. During an

---

98 The miners apparently gave a hostile reception to passing NCB coaches but this it appears occurred after the police had stopped them and informed them that they could not proceed. It does not appear therefore that it could have formed part of the basis for the police decision that a breach of the peace was to be expected.
99 (1882) 9 QBD 308.
100 [1936] 1 KB 218; for comment see Daintith [1966] *PL* 248.
101 [1963] 2 QB 744; [1963] 2 All ER 225, DC. It should be noted that the case was concerned with breach of the peace under s 5 of the Public Order Act 1936.
102 [1995] 3 All ER 124, DC.
103 *Ibid* at 110.
104 (1996) 1 *J Civ Lib* 75. See, further, Steel v UK (1998) judgment of the Court of HR, available on the Internet.

angling competition the protesters blew horns, threw twigs into the water and attempted verbally to dissuade the anglers from fishing. This provoked the anglers so that they were on the verge of using force to remove the protesters. The protesters were arrested for breach of the peace. It was found that they were guilty of conduct whereby a breach of the peace was likely to be caused since their conduct although lawful was unreasonable and was likely to provoke the anglers to violence. This finding may curb the use of breach of the peace in this context since it means that behaviour which has as its natural consequence the provoking of others to violence will not amount to a breach of the peace unless it is also unreasonable. However, since the test for reasonableness indicated in the decision is wide and uncertain any such curb may be more theoretical than real. The judiciary may be disinclined to find that the behaviour of groups such as hunt saboteurs or tree protesters, while lawful, was reasonable.

In *Morpeth Ward Justices, ex parte Ward*,[105] which concerned the behaviour of protesters against pheasant shooting, Brooke J stated:

> ... provocative disorderly behaviour which is likely to have the natural consequence of causing violence, even if only to the persons of the provokers, is capable of being conduct likely to cause a breach of the peace.[106]

Thus, the reasonableness of the shooters' behaviour or potential behaviour was not called into question. The court did not lay down a test to determine the point at which a violent reaction to provoking behaviour might be termed an unnatural consequence of such behaviour. It focused simply on the question whether the natural consequence of the behaviour in question was to provoke violence, thus leaving open the possibility that an extreme reaction from those provoked, although probably unreasonable, might be termed natural. In *Nicol v DPP*, however, the reasonableness of the behaviour of those provoked was considered. Simon-Brown J found that unless their rights had been infringed, it would not be reasonable for them to react violently. This finding offers some clarification of the 'natural consequence' test although since there is no right to fish the rights referred to are unclear. The term 'liberties' rather than 'rights' would have been more appropriate. Possibly in referring to an infringement of rights Simon-Brown J was seeking to distinguish so-called direct action from other forms of protest. It is unclear at present whether the test from *Nicol* or from *ex parte Ward* will prevail. Clear adoption of the *Nicol* test would go some way towards restoration of the *Beatty v Gillbanks* principle.

Adoption of the *Nicol* test in relation to protest by speech rather than by means of direct action might allow a distinction to be drawn between forceful speech calling the attention of others to arguments, issues or events and

---

105 (1992) 95 Cr App R 215.
106 *Ibid* at 221.

speech which consists of an attack upon the hearers with the intent of causing extreme provocation. The crucial difference should be the verbal attack which renders the speaker directly responsible for awakening hatred and violence. Arguably, the first type of speech should never be restrained but it may be acceptable to restrain the second when it offers extreme provocation to its hearers.[107] Sections 4 and 5 of the Public Order Act 1986 appear to be aimed only at the latter, deliberately provocative form of speech, although they are not confined to instances of extreme provocation. However, as seen above, the power to prevent a breach of the peace fails to distinguish at present clearly between the two situations.

Binding over to keep the peace may form part of a bail condition but bail conditions may be more specific than this. A person charged with any offence may be bailed as long as they promise to fulfil certain conditions.[108] This aspect of criminal procedure can readily be used by the police against protesters or demonstrators; they can be charged with a low level public order offence or bound over to keep the peace, thus allowing the imposition of conditions which may prevent participation in future protest. If the conditions are broken the bailee can be imprisoned. The Bail Act 1976 requires that applications for bail should be individually assessed in order to determine whether conditions should be imposed, thereby reflecting concern that the bailing procedure should not result in any further deprivation of liberty than is necessary. Despite this, during the miners' strike there was evidence that conditions were being routinely imposed without regard to the threat posed by the individual applicant. The Divisional Court however found that such practices were lawful (*Mansfield Justices, ex parte Sharkey*).[109]

Criminalising public disorder

Sections 4 and 5 of the Public Order Act 1986

Section 5 is the lowest level public order offence contained in the Act and the most contentious, since it brings behaviour within the scope of the criminal law which was previously thought of as too trivial to justify the imposition of criminal liability.[110] It criminalises the person who 'uses threatening, abusive or insulting words or behaviour or disorderly behaviour' or 'displays any writing, sign or other visible representation which is threatening or abusive or insulting' which takes place within the 'hearing or sight of a person likely to

---

107 For comment on this issue see Birtles (1973) 36 *MLR* 587. For discussion in the context of race hatred see above pp 226–27.
108 See Feldman, D, *Civil Liberties in England and Wales*, pp 835–42.
109 [1985] QB 613.
110 For background to s 5 see Law Commission Report No 123, *Offences relating to Public Order*, 1983; for comment see Williams, D [1984] *PL* 12.

be caused harassment, alarm or distress thereby'. The word 'likely' imports an objective test into the section: it is necessary to show that a person was present at the scene but not that he or she actually experienced the feelings in question, although it must be shown that in all the circumstances he or she would be likely to experience such feelings. In so showing it is not necessary to call the person in question as a witness. In *Swanston v DPP*[111] it was found that if a bystander gives evidence to the effect that the 'victim' perceived the threatening, abusive or insulting words then the court can draw the inference that they were so perceived. There is no need to aim the words or behaviour at a specific individual, so long as an individual can be identified and the inference can be drawn that he or she would have perceived the words or behaviour in question. It was determined in *DPP v Orum*[112] that a police officer may be the person caused harassment, alarm or distress but in such instances Lord Justice Glidewell thought it might be held that a police officer would be less likely to experience such feelings than an ordinary person.

Whether the words used were insulting etc is a question of fact for the magistrates. The terms used must be given their ordinary meaning: *Brutus v Cozens*.[113] Following *Ambrose*[114] rude or offensive words or behaviour may not necessarily be insulting, while mere swearing may not fall within the meaning of 'abusive'. However, threatening gestures such as waving a fist might suffice. Whether or not the words are insulting is not a purely subjective test and therefore the mere fact that the recipient finds them so will not be sufficient. The House of Lords so held in *Brutus v Cozens*[115] in respect of disruption of a tennis match involving a South African player by an anti-apartheid demonstrator. Some of the crowd were provoked to violence but the conduct of the demonstrator could not be described as insulting. The conviction of the defendant under the predecessor of s 4 was therefore overturned. The test appears to be whether a reasonable person sharing the characteristics of the persons at whom the words in question are directed would find them insulting. However, whether or not the speaker knows that such persons will hear the words is immaterial as far as this ingredient of s 4 is concerned (*Jordan v Burgoyne*).[116] It was found in *DPP v Fidler*[117] that a person whose own behaviour would not satisfy the requirements of s 5 may be guilty as aiding and abetting this offence if he or she is part of a crowd who are committing it.

---

111 (1997) *The Times*, 23 January.
112 [1988] 3 All ER 449.
113 [1973] AC 854; [1972] 2 All ER 1297; [1972] 3 WLR 521, HL.
114 (1973) 57 Cr App R 538.
115 [1973] AC 854; [1972] All ER 1297; [1972] 3 WLR 521; (1973) 57 CR App R 538, HL.
116 [1963] 2 QB 744; [1963] 2 All ER 225.
117 [1992] 1 WLR 91; for comment see Smith, JC [1992] *Crim LR* 63.

Thus, taken at its lowest level, s 5 criminalises a person who displays disorderly behaviour calculated to create harassment. Section 5 was included as a measure aimed at anti-social behaviour generally but its breadth and vagueness have given rise to the criticism that the police have been handed a very broad power.[118] The criminalisation of speech which causes such low level harm as alarm or distress may be contrary to *dicta* of the European Court of Human Rights in *Müller v Switzerland*[119] to the effect that the protection of free speech extends equally to ideas which 'offend, shock or disturb'.[120] It is not alarmist to suppose that s 5, far from being confined to restraining rowdy hooligans, will be used against political speech. In the so-called *Madame M* case, four students were prosecuted for putting up a satirical poster depicting Margaret Thatcher as a 'sadistic dominatrix';[121] the students were acquitted but the fact that such a case could even be brought in a democracy is highly disturbing. This was not an isolated use of s 5 against political speech: protestors outside abortion clinics have been prosecuted[122] and in Northern Ireland, s 5 has been used against a poster depicting youths stoning a British Saracen with a caption proclaiming 'Ireland: 20 years of resistance'.[123] Similarly, as one commentator noted when the Act was passed, 'In the context of pickets shouting or gesturing at those crossing their picket lines, the elements of this offence will usually be established without difficulty'.[124]

Further, the sheer number of prosecutions being brought under s 5 conclusively demonstrates that the police are not showing restraint in using this area of the Act. The old s 5 offence under the Public Order Act 1936, an offence with a higher harm threshold,[125] accounted for the majority of the 8,194 charges brought in connection with the miners' strike of 1984. In a survey of 470 public order cases in 1988, conducted that year, in two police force areas, it was found that 56% of the sample led to charges under s 5. Research has also shown that during the period 1986–88 the number of charges brought for public order offences doubled and this is thought to be

---

118 See comment on s 5 [1987] *PL* 202.
119 (1991) 13 EHRR 212.
120 It should be noted that in *Brutus v Cozens* [1973] AC 854; [1972] 2 All ER 1297; [1972] 3 WLR 521; (1973) Cr App R 538, HL, Lord Reid said that s 5 of the previous Public Order Act 1936 was 'not designed to penalise the expressions of opinion that happen to be disagreeable, distasteful or even offensive, annoying or distressing'. The new s 5 offence precisely does cover 'distressing' speech but use could be made of Reid's *dicta* to argue that expression of opinions *per se* should not be criminalised.
121 Thornton, P, *Decade of Decline: Civil Liberties in the Thatcher Years*, 1990, p 37.
122 *DPP v Fidler* [1992] 1 WLR 91; *DPP v Clarke* [1992] *Crim LR* 60.
123 Reported in the *Independent* 12 September 1988; mentioned in Ewing and Gearty, *Freedom under Thatcher*, p 123.
124 Williams, D [1987] *Crim LR* 167.
125 It was similar to the offence which replaced it, s 4 of the 1986 Act.

due not to increased unrest but to the existence of new offences, particularly s 5 with its low level of harm.[126]

However, the *mens rea* requirements of the offence may offer a degree of protection to free expression. Under s 6(4) it is required that the defendant intended his words or behaviour or the writing etc to be threatening, abusive or insulting or was aware that they might be. Persons participating in forceful demonstrations may sometimes be able to show that behaviour which could be termed disorderly and which might be capable of causing harassment to others, was intended only to make a point and that it had not been realised that others might find it threatening, abusive or insulting. In *DPP v Clarke*[127] it was found that to establish liability, it is not sufficient to show that the defendant intended or was aware that he might cause the forbidden harm; it must be shown that he intended his conduct to be threatening, abusive or insulting or was aware that it might be. Thus, showing that the defendant was aware that he might cause distress was not found to be equivalent to showing that he was aware that his speech or behaviour might be insulting. Applying this subjective test, the magistrates acquitted the defendants and this decision was upheld on appeal. The burden imposed by the subjective test for intention or awareness is to be welcomed since it means that an offence which strikes directly at freedom of expression and can only doubtfully be justified is harder to make out.

Demonstrators shouting at passers-by to support their cause, whose behaviour could readily be termed threatening or disorderly etc and likely to cause one of the passers-by harassment, distress or alarm,[128] will have a defence under s 5(3)(c) if they can show that their behaviour was reasonable. The Act gives no guidance as to the meaning of the term but it has been determined that the defence is to be judged objectively,[129] and it will therefore depend on what a bench of magistrates considers reasonable. The behaviour described might fall within this defence on the basis that in the context of a particular demonstration which had a legitimate political aim such behaviour was acceptable and therefore reasonable. An argument for giving such a wide interpretation to the term 'reasonable' can be supported on the basis that as argued above, to criminalise such behaviour would arguably amount to a very far-reaching curb on the freedom to protest; such a curb might be found to be in breach of Article 10 or Article 11 of the European Convention once the Human Rights Act 1998 is in force, bearing in mind the need to interpret

---

126 Newburn, T *et al*, 'Policing the Streets' (1990) 29 *HORB* 10 and 'Increasing Public Order' (1991) 7 *Policing* 22; quoted in Bailey, Harris and Jones, *op cit* pp 229–30.
127 [1992] *Crim LR* 60.
128 It is not necessary to prove that anyone actually felt harassment, merely that this was likely.
129 *DPP v Clarke* above note 127. It was found that displaying pictures of an aborted foetus during an anti-abortion demonstration was unreasonable conduct.

statutory provisions in conformity with the Convention.[130] Whether a forceful demonstration which included some disorderly behaviour could fall within Article 11, which extends only to peaceful protest is debatable but there is at least room to argue that liability would not be incurred under s 5 in the circumstances described.

Section 154 of the Criminal Justice and Public Order Act 1994 inserts s 4A into the 1986 Act, thereby providing a new and wide area of liability which to some extent overlaps with s 5. The *actus reus* under s 4A is the same as that under s 5 with the proviso that the harm in question must actually be caused as opposed to being likely to be caused. The *mens rea* differs somewhat from that under s 5 since the defendant must intend the person in question to suffer harassment, alarm or distress. Section 4A provides another possible level of liability with the result that using offensive words is now imprisonable, without any requirement (as under s 4, below) to show that violence was intended or likely to be caused. It may therefore offend against the protection for freedom of speech under Article 10 of the European Convention on Human Rights which, as pointed out above, clearly includes protection for forms of forceful or offensive speech.

Section 4 of the Act covers somewhat more serious behaviour than s 5. It is couched in the same terms except for the omission of 'disorderly behaviour' but instead of showing that a person present was likely to be caused harassment etc it is necessary to show 'intent to cause that person to believe that immediate unlawful violence will be used against him or another by any person or to provoke the immediate use of unlawful violence by that person or another or whereby that person is likely to believe that such violence will be used or it is likely that such violence will be provoked'. One or more of these four possibilities must be present. The behaviour in question must be specifically directed towards another person. If the defendant does not directly approach the person being threatened he or she might be unlikely to apprehend immediate violence. However, there might remain the possibility that the defendant intended his or her words to provoke others to violence against the victim.

It was found in *Horseferry Road Metropolitan Stipendiary Magistrate, ex parte Siadatan*[131] that 'violence' in this context must mean immediate and unlawful violence. The case arose from publication and distribution of *The Satanic Verses* by Salman Rushdie. The applicants alleged that the book contained abusive and insulting writing whereby it was likely that unlawful violence would be provoked contrary to s 4. On appeal from the decision of the magistrates not to issue a summons against the distributors of the books, Penguin Books, Watkins LJ found:

---

130 Section 3(1). See Chap 3 pp 127–35.
131 [1991] 1 QB 260; [1991] 1 All ER 324; [1990] 3 WLR 1006.

We find it most unlikely that Parliament could have intended to include among sections which undoubtedly deal with conduct having an immediate impact on bystanders, a section creating an offence for conduct which is likely to lead to violence at some unspecified time in the future.

The finding that the violence provoked must be immediate, although not necessarily instantaneous, led to dismissal of the appeal. This strict interpretation was confirmed in *Winn v DPP*[132] and it was made plain that the prosecution must ensure that all the ingredients of the particular form of the offence charged under s 4 are present. The appellant threatened and abused a Mr Duncan who was attempting to serve a summons on him. On appeal the ingredients of the s 4 offence were considered. It was clear from the provision of s 7(2) of the Act that s 4 creates only one offence; however, it is clear that the offence can be committed in one of four ways. Common to all four are the requirements first, that the accused must intend or be aware that his words or behaviour are or may be threatening, abusive or insulting (s 6(3) which governs the *mens rea* requirement) and secondly, that they must be directed to another person. The offence charged included a statement of the required intention and was based on the fourth way it could be committed: that he used threatening and abusive words and behaviour whereby it was likely that violence would be provoked. The charge therefore required proof of a likelihood that Mr Duncan would be provoked to immediate unlawful violence and as there was no evidence to that effect the direction to the justices was that the charge under s 4 should have been dismissed. Had the charge related to the first form of the offence – 'intent to cause that person to believe that immediate unlawful violence will be used against him' – it might have succeeded. It should be noted that such intent must be shown in addition to the *mens rea* under s 6(3).

Riot, violent disorder and affray

Section 9 of the Public Order Act 1986 abolishes the common law offences of riot, unlawful assembly and affray and replaces them with similar statutory offences of riot (s 1), violent disorder (s 2) and affray (s 3).[133] Each of these offences may be committed in a public or a private place and it is not necessary that any person should actually have feared unlawful violence. Violent disorder would be most commonly used against unruly demonstrations since it can be committed by words alone.

In order to establish an affray it must first be shown that the defendant used or threatened unlawful violence towards another, secondly that his conduct was such as would cause a person of reasonable firmness present at the scene to fear for his personal safety and thirdly, under s 6(2), that he

---

132 (1992) 142 *NLJ* 527.
133 For comment on the new offences see 'Public Order Act Offences' (1989) December LAG.

intended to use or threaten violence or was aware that his conduct might be violent or threaten violence. Under s 3(3) a threat cannot be made by the use of words alone. A demonstration in which threatening gestures were used might fulfil the first limb of s 3(1) but a strong argument can be advanced that it does not fulfil the second. If the gestures are part of a demonstration, it is probable that a person of reasonable firmness would not fear unlawful violence even though such a person might feel somewhat distressed. In *Taylor v DPP*[134] Lord Hailsham, speaking of the common law offence, said 'the degree of violence ... must be such as to be calculated to terrify a person of reasonably firm character'. The Act of course refers to 'fear' as opposed to terror but this ruling suggests that 'fear' should be interpreted restrictively.

Violent disorder is a completely new offence which was aimed in part at curtailing the activities of violent pickets. It is couched in the same terms as affray but requires that three or more persons are involved. In order to establish violent disorder it must first be shown that the defendant was one of three or more persons who used or threatened unlawful violence; secondly, that his conduct was such as would cause a person of reasonable firmness present at the scene to fear for his personal safety and thirdly, that the defendant himself actually used or threatened violence. The mental element under s 6(2) is the same as for affray. It may be argued that in the context of a demonstration, threatening gestures would not be termed a threat of violence. 'Violence' is a strong term which should not be watered down. In one respect, however, violent disorder is wider than affray since it may be committed by the use of words alone. If no threats are used by a defendant he could not incur liability under s 2 even if it was found that he encouraged violence by others.[135]

Riot is the highest level public order offence created by the Act and is similar to the offence of violent disorder. However, it is narrower in that it requires that 12 or more persons who are present together use or threaten unlawful violence for a common purpose and that the defendant must actually use violence intending to do so or being aware that his conduct may be violent. The requirement that the conduct of them (taken together) is such as would cause a person reasonable firmness present at the scene to fear for his personal safety is common to all three offences.

Criminal trespass[136]

Simple trespass – walking onto someone's land without permission or refusing to leave when asked to do so – has never been a crime under UK law.

---

134 [1973] AC 964.
135 *McGuigan and Cameron* [1991] *Crim LR* 719; *Fleming and Robinson* [1989] *Crim LR* 658; *cf Caird* (1970) 54 Cr App R 499.
136 For comment on this offence see Vincent-Jones, P (1986) 13 *JLS* 343; *Stonehenge* (1986) NCCL; Ewing and Gearty, *Freedom under Thatcher*, pp 125–28.

However, the 1986 Act created a special form of criminal trespass under s 39 which involved the application of a two-limb test. Under the first limb (s 39(1)) it had to be shown that two or more persons had come onto the land as trespassers with the common purpose of residing there for some period of time and that reasonable steps had been taken to ask them to leave on behalf of the occupier. Further, they must have brought 12 or more vehicles onto the land or threatened or abused the occupier or his agents or family or damaged property on the land. If the senior police officer believed that these conditions were satisfied he could direct the persons to leave. Under the second limb (s 39(2)) if they then failed to comply with the direction or came back onto the land within three months they committed a criminal offence punishable with three months imprisonment. Section 39 was aimed at certain forms of assemblies, including animal rights activists and the 'Peace Convoys' which gather for the summer solstice festival at Stonehenge. As a number of commentators pointed out it was probably unnecessary to enact this offence given the availability of civil remedies and the possibility of using powers to prevent a breach of the peace against mass trespassers or of charging them with low level public order offences.[137] It has also been suggested that the provision failed to confine itself to preventing the mischief it was created to prevent.[138] It could also be criticised as adding to the number of offences which can occur due to disobedience to police orders; it has been argued that a person should be obliged to take orders from the police only in the narrowest of circumstances.[139]

Section 39 was repealed by the Criminal Justice and Public Order Act 1994 and its provisions replaced by s 61. Section 61, however, closely resembles s 39 and the changes it makes tend to have the effect of widening the offence. Under s 61 the persons in question need not have entered the land originally as trespassers; the question is whether they are trespassing whether or not they originally entered the land as trespassers. If they did not enter as trespassers the power to eject them only arises if there is a reasonable belief that the other conditions under s 61(1) are satisfied. The conditions under s 61(1) are similar to those under s 39(1) but the number of vehicles has been reduced from 12 to six and damage to the land itself has been included as well as damage to property on the land.

The Criminal Justice and Public Order Act 1994 also created the new offence of aggravated trespass under s 68 which is aimed at certain groups such as hunt saboteurs or motorway protesters.[140] Section 68 creates a two-stage test; first it must be shown that the defendant trespassed on land in the open air and secondly in relation to lawful activity which persons are

---

137 Smith, ATH, *Offences Against Public Order*, 1987, para 14–18.
138 Card, R, *Public Order: the New Law*, 1987, takes this view: see pp 146–48.
139 See [1987] *PL* at p 211.
140 See *Hansard*, Commons, 11 January 1994, Col 29.

engaging in or are about to engage in that he did there anything intended by him to have the effect of either intimidating those persons so as to deter them from the activity or of obstructing or disrupting that activity. No defence is provided and it is not necessary to show that the activity was actually affected. This is a broadly worded provision; its impact in practice will depend on the meaning attached to 'disrupt' and 'obstruct'. A great many peaceful but vociferous demonstrations may have some impact of an obstructive nature on lawful activities. It is however limited in that it does not apply to demonstrations on a metalled highway, although it does include public paths such as bridleways and excludes most but not all buildings.[141] Section 68 has been used against hunt saboteurs and others on a number of occasions and some of the decisions on the section have had the effect of widening the area of liability created still further. In *Winder v DPP*,[142] for example, the appellants had been running after the hunt. It was accepted that they did not intend disrupt it by running but it was found that the running was more than a preparatory act and that it was close enough to the contemplated action to incur liability. Thus the offence under s 68 could be established if the appellants were trespassing on land in open air with the general intention of disrupting the hunt and were intending when in range to commit the acts in question with the required intention. This decision comes very close to punishing persons for their thoughts rather than for their actions. Possibly an attempt to commit the offence under s 68 should have been charged, rather than the full offence.

New provisions under s 69 underpin s 68. Section 69 provides, *inter alia*, that if the senior officer present at the scene reasonably believes that a person is committing, has committed or intends to commit the offence under s 68 he can direct them to leave the land. Under s 69(3) if the person in question, knowing that the s 69 direction has been given, fails to leave the land or re-enters it within three months he or she commits an imprisonable offence. It is a defence for the person to show that he or she was not trespassing on the land or that he or she had a reasonable excuse for failing to leave the land or for returning as a trespasser. Although s 68 may not lead to the criminalisation of persons who simply walk on to land as trespassers, s 69 appears to have the potential to do so, depending on the interpretation given by the courts to the 'reasonable excuse' defence. For example, where a person is in receipt of the direction under s 69, even though it was erroneously given (since in fact, although she was trespassing, she did not have the purpose of committing the s 68 offence), she may still commit an offence if thereafter she re-enters the land in question during the specified time. The fact that on the second

---

141 'Land' is defined in s 61(9); it does not include metalled highway or buildings apart from certain agricultural buildings and scheduled monuments; common land and non-metalled roads are included.

142 (1996) *The Times*, 14 August.

occasion she was merely walking peacefully on to land in order to engage in a non-obstructive public protest would be irrelevant unless she could also produce an excuse which could be termed reasonable. Whether the erroneousness of the senior police officer's original 'reasonable belief' would amount to a reasonable excuse is left unclear.

Wasik and Taylor note that 'The creeping criminalisation of various forms of trespass in the 1994 Act ... has been vigorously opposed by those who fear that it will provide an inappropriate disincentive to group protest'.[143] As argued in the introduction to this section, forms of direct action are less justifiable under rights-based arguments than other forms of protest. But the concern generated by ss 61, 68 and 69 is that over-reaction to the activities of hunt saboteurs has led to an unnecessary distortion of this area of the criminal law, to the detriment of freedom of protest.

Power to enter meetings on private premises

So far the emphasis has largely been on meetings in public places. The provisions of ss 11, 12, 13 and 14 of Part II of the Public Order Act 1986 do not cover private meetings although the general public order offences of Part I do. Any meeting held in wholly enclosed premises will be a private meeting (s 16), including a meeting held in a town hall, although the town hall is owned by a public body. The control of indoor meetings is, generally speaking, the responsibility of the persons holding the meeting and to that end a reasonable number of stewards should be appointed (s 2(6) of the Public Order Act 1936) who may use reasonable force to control disorder and to eject members of the public whose behaviour does not constitute reasonable participation in the meeting.

The power of the police to enter indoor meetings is uncertain. It was generally thought that the police had no power to enter unless they were invited in. However, such a power may derive from the decision in *Thomas v Sawkins*.[144] A meeting was held in a hall to protest regarding the provisions of the Incitement to Disaffection Bill which was then before Parliament. The police entered the meeting and its leader, who considered that they were trespassing, removed one of the officers who resisted the ejectment. In response the leader brought a private prosecution in which he sought to show that the officers were trespassers and that therefore he had a right to eject them, in which case their resistance would amount to assault and battery. The court found that the officers had not been trespassing. Although the meeting had not constituted or given rise to a breach of the peace the officers had reasonably apprehended a breach because seditious speeches and incitement

---

143 The Criminal Justice and Public Order Act 1994, p 81.
144 [1935] 2 KB 249.

to violence might have occurred. The police had therefore been entitled to enter the premises. This decision has been much criticised.[145] Nevertheless, it does not hand the police *carte blanche* to enter private meetings; it should mean that the police can enter the meeting only if there is a clear possibility that a breach of the peace may occur.

A more narrow right to enter premises which might be applicable in respect of some meetings arises under s 17(1)(c) of the Police and Criminal Evidence Act 1984. A police officer has the right to enter and search premises with a view to arresting a person for the offence arising under s 1 of the Public Order Act 1936 of wearing a uniform in connection with a political object. Furthermore, the police can enter premises in order to arrest a person for an offence under s 4 of the Public Order Act 1986. It should be noted that the offence under s 4 (discussed above) can be committed in a private or public place although not in a dwelling. Presumably it could therefore be committed in a town hall. Thus a meeting during which violence might be threatened to persons present would give police officers the right to enter if they had reasonable suspicion that such could be the case. If it was thought that one of the serious public order offences under ss 1, 2 or 3 of the 1986 Act was occurring or about to occur the police could arrest under the general arrest power of s 24 of the Police and Criminal Evidence Act 1984. We will return to this arrest power and police powers of entry to premises in Chapter 9 below.

Private law remedies

Apart from control by the police, meetings and demonstrations can be prevented or curbed by private persons who seek injunctions to that end.[146] An interim injunction may be obtained very quickly in a hearing in which the other party is not represented. Even if a permanent injunction is not eventually granted the aim of the demonstration may well have been destroyed by that time. In *Hubbard v Pitt*[147] the defendants mounted a demonstration outside an estate agent in order to protest at what was seen as the ousting of working class tenants in order to make way for higher income buyers, thereby effecting a change in the character of the area. They therefore picketed the estate agents. The plaintiffs sought an injunction to prevent this on various grounds including that of nuisance. At first instance it was held that a stationary meeting would not constitute a reasonable user of the Highway and the grant of the interim injunction was upheld by the Court of Appeal, Lord Denning dissenting on the ground that the right to demonstrate is so closely analogous to freedom of speech that it should be protected.

---

145 See Goodhart, AL (1936–38) *CLJ* 22.
146 For discussion of such use of injunctions see Wallington, P, 'Injunctions and the right to demonstrate' (1976) 35 *Camb LJ* 82. For discussion of their use in the context of labour disputes see (1973) 2 *ILJ* 213; Miller, *Contempt of Court*, 1989, pp 412–22.
147 [1976] QB 142.

PART THREE

THE PROTECTION OF PRIVACY[1]

Privacy is not only accepted as part of the domestic law of a number of countries[2] and of international human rights instruments,[3] it is also firmly embedded in the popular consciousness. Most people probably feel intuitively that they know what privacy is and consider that it should be defended. However, despite this general acceptance, privacy seems to have become a complex and perhaps almost unworkably broad concept due to the variety of claims or interests which have been thought to fall within it.[4] The European Court of Human Rights has accommodated many disparate issues within the concept of privacy arising under Article 8 of the European Convention on Human Rights: they range from the right to engage in homosexual practices[5] to the right to receive information about oneself.[6] The Convention does not attempt to define privacy[7] but various definitions have been put forward which tend to be very broad; it has been termed 'a circle around every individual human being which no government ... ought to be permitted to overstep' and 'some space in human existence thus entrenched around and sacred from authoritative intrusion'.[8] Such phrases suggest that some aspects of an individual's life which can be identified as private aspects are of particular value and therefore warrant special protection. At an intuitive level the notion that boundaries can and should be placed around such aspects of an individual's life seems to be accepted as the basis of the idea of privacy[9] and seems to underlie decisions under Article 8.

---

1   See generally Wacks, R, *The Protection of Privacy*, 1980; Westin, AF, *Privacy and Freedom*, 1970; Bailey, Harris and Jones, *Civil Liberties: Cases and Materials*, 4th edn, 1995, Chap 8; Eady, D, 'A Statutory Right to Privacy' (1996) 3 *EHRLR* 243; Winfield, P (1981) 47 *LQR* 23; Yang, TL (1966) 15 *ICLQ* 175; Wacks, R, 'The Poverty of Privacy' (1980) 96 *LQR* 73; Seipp, D, 'English Judicial Recognition of the Right to Privacy' (1983) 3 *Ox JLS* 325.

2   For example, the US Privacy Act 1974 and the tort or torts of invasion of privacy, the Canadian Protection of Privacy Act 1974, Article 1382 of the French Civil Code; German courts can protect privacy under 823(1) of the Civil Code and a right to privacy arises under the German Basic Law Article 10 (albeit limited to posts and telecommunications).

3   It appears in the European Convention on Human Rights Article 8 and the International Covenant on Civil and Political Rights Article 17.

4   See Wacks, *The Protection of Privacy*, Chap 1, pp 10–21.

5   *Dudgeon* (1981) 4 EHRR 149.

6   *Gaskin* (1990) 12 EHRR 36.

7   See further p 61 above.

8   Mill, JS, *Principles of Political Economy*, p 306 (Winch, D, ed, 1970).

9   See Seipp, p 333.

Privacy seems to derive its value partly from its close association with personal autonomy in the sense that freedom from interference by the authorities will foster the conditions under which autonomy can be exercised. Thus some authoritative invasions of privacy may be said to lead to interference with individual autonomy. The exercise of autonomy may not be entirely dependent on establishing a state of privacy but may at least be fostered thereby. However, privacy may also be associated with self-fulfilment in the sense that protection for the private life of the individual may provide the best conditions under which he or she may flourish. In other words, self-fulfilment may be fostered if the individual is able to enjoy the benefits of the private: the dropping of the public mask, the communion of intimates, the expression of the deepest emotions.

Since considerations of this nature involve an implied contrast between the public and the private it may be helpful at this point to consider the division between the two spheres in order to come closer to examining what may be encompassed by the notion of privacy. A variety of referents may be used. The private might be viewed as a sphere which should be almost entirely unregulated by the public (law) although also delineated by it. This division, however, poses problems. It will be argued below that unless the private sphere is regulated by law the benefits it offers may be diminished. Instead a broader social division between the public and the private may be suggested: arguably, the public includes state activity, aspects of the world of work, the pursuit of public interests, while the private includes the home, the family, the expression of sexuality and of the deepest feelings and emotions. Postulating such a division need not obscure the fact that these spheres are not entirely distinct but must interact. The pursuit of the public interest will often affect and even determine some aspects of the private life of the family and the individual in terms, for example, of housing and welfare policy, while at the same time, the need to afford respect to the private will help to shape such policies.

The values of personal autonomy and of self-fulfilment appear broadly to underpin two key privacy interests: the interest in enabling the individual to maintain control over information pertaining to him or herself and over his or her personal life, and this division will be used in this chapter as one possible convenient means of approaching the complexities of the concept of privacy. In considering each interest it will be argued that they involve not only requiring guarantees against arbitrary authoritative intrusion on personal aspects of the individual's life, but that they may also, more controversially, impose positive obligations on others to act in order to enable the individual to retain the power of choice in relation to those aspects.

The right to respect for privacy, in common with the guarantees under Articles 9–11 of the European Convention on Human Rights, is not treated as an absolute right; under Article 8 it competes not only with a number of public interests, such as the prevention of crime, but also with other individual rights such as freedom of expression. Moreover, it is clear that although various interest may be treated as falling, roughly speaking, within the area of privacy considered above, their claims will vary greatly in strength when measured against competing interests. 'Control over personal life' will be treated as covering areas as disparate as allowing a homosexual to choose to express his or her sexuality free from state interference, and enabling an individual to enjoy his or her property free from the attentions of reporters. On the one hand the individual's privacy is invaded through the criminalisation of certain activities, while on the other he is complaining that the criminal law does not prevent an invasion of privacy. In the former case if the homosexual were to be prevented from expressing his sexual preference the government would be using its coercive powers to give effect to the moral conviction that the homosexual's way of life is contemptible. Thus it would clearly be failing in its duty to treat its citizens with equal respect; to prevent this, under the liberal analysis of rights, the homosexual should be given a 'strong' right to sexual autonomy which would overcome any competing claims of society.

By contrast, the state in failing to control the activities of the reporter, is not thereby giving expression to feelings of contempt for the individual's way of life; rather, it is arguably erring on the side of free expression as it collides with the interest of the individual in securing her privacy. Thus in this case the individual's claim is weaker in itself and, further, has to compete with a strong claim to free expression which the interest in moral autonomy does not face. Moreover, in the case of public figures claiming privacy rights against the press, the argument that views free speech as essential in order to ensure meaningful participation in a democracy has particular strength. In practical terms this would lead one to suggest that in the case of public figures the claims of free expression should override privacy unless the person whose privacy is invaded could demonstrate that the information gained was in no way related to their fitness to carry out their public functions. In the case of a purely private figure, freedom of expression would still compete with the claim of privacy; however, two of the important justifications for free speech – the arguments from truth and from political participation – would be largely irrelevant so that the strength of the free expression claim would be appreciably diminished.

Privacy also comes into conflict with both competing individual and societal claims since it may allow restriction not only of activities of the state detrimental to individuals, but also of beneficial activity. Once a 'circle' has been drawn round the home or the family, privacy interests can be invoked to prevent action to benefit the weaker members within it.[10] Once the state has relinquished responsibility for the regime inside the circle it will be regulated informally in a manner which may work unfairness for the weaker members

---

10 For full discussion of this issue see Donovan, K, *Sexual Divisions in Law*, 1985, Chap 5.

within it. This statement from the Association of Chief Police Officers on domestic violence illustrates the danger: '... we are ... dealing with persons bound in marriage and it is important for a host of reasons to maintain the unity of the spouses.'[11] A similar view was expressed by the Home Office in 1975: '... the point at which the state should intervene in family violence should be higher than that which is expected in the case of violence between strangers.'[12] Such views are less often expressed at the present time although the recent debate on marital rape[13] produced some of a similar nature; it was suggested by one commentator that marital rape should be equated with a trivial crime such as assault partly on the basis that otherwise the marriage might not survive. The danger may be summed up as a desire on the part of the state to devote its energies to keeping the circle intact rather than trying to regulate what occurs within it.[14] Such informal withdrawal of regulation might be bolstered by the guarantee of privacy under Article 8. Of course, the danger of an assertion of individualism at the expense of social responsibility is not confined to feminist concerns. Socialist and Marxist theorists have argued that delineation of an area as private hampers state organisation of society for the benefit of weaker groups because intervention in housing or education policy in order to ensure equality can be met by a claim of privacy.[15]

However there are signs that such abuse of privacy will be rejected; it may be argued that Article 8 jurisprudence recognises this danger and has rejected the notion that respect for family life and perhaps for privacy generally entails failure to interfere in the family when other rights or freedoms are in danger of abuse. In *Marckx v Belgium*[16] the applicant complained under Article 8 in conjunction with Article 14 that an illegitimate child was not recognised as the child of his or her mother until the latter had formally recognised the child as such. Also, the child was treated under Belgium law as in principle a stranger to the parents' families. In finding that the state was under an obligation to ensure the child's integration in the family and therefore that Article 8 applied, the court impliedly rejected the view put forward by the UK judge, Sir Gerald Fitzmaurice:

> It is abundantly clear ... that the main if not indeed the sole object and intended sphere of application of Article 8 was that of what I will call the

---

11 HC, *Select Committee on Violence in Marriage Report*, 1975 p 366.
12 *Op cit* note 98 p 418.
13 See Chap 14 p 613.
14 This argument is complicated, it has been suggested, by the 'male oriented' nature of the law; in other words looking to the state for an objective source of control of the private sphere may be misguided (see MacKinnon, C, 'Feminism, Marxism, Method and the State' (1982) 7 *Signs* 515.
15 See Unger, R, *Law in Modern Society*, 1976; Kamenka, E, 'Public/Private in Marxist Theory and Marxist Practice' in Benn and Gaus, eds, *Public and Private in Social Life*, 1983.
16 (1979) 2 EHRR 330.

'domiciliary protection' of the individual. He (*sic*) and his family were no longer to be subjected to ... domestic intrusions ... Such and not the internal regulation of family relationships was the object of Article 8 ...

There may therefore be some grounds for arguing that the dangers outlined above in respect of the 'circle' of privacy will not be realised when Article 8 protection becomes available in domestic law.

It may be concluded that privacy is in a weak position in so far as its ability to overcome public interests or other individual rights is concerned. It is only, it is suggested, where preservation of privacy may lead to upholding an individual's moral autonomy, that privacy should be treated as a strong individual right able to overcome various public interests and compete on equal terms with other rights-based interests.

Traditionally, UK law has recognised no general right to respect for privacy, although there is some evidence, as will be seen, that judges consider this to be an evil which should be remedied. It has been argued that various areas of tort or equity such as trespass, breach of confidence, copyright and defamation are instances of a general right to privacy,[17] but it is reasonably clear from judicial pronouncements that these areas and others must be treated as covering specific and distinct interests which may only incidentally offer protection to privacy[18] – despite the fact that the term 'privacy' is used in a number of rulings.[19] In such instances it will be found that a recognised interest such as property actually formed the basis of the ruling. Thus it will be found that UK law offers only piecemeal protection to privacy and therefore a number of privacy interests are largely unprotected. In so far as protection for privacy has been broadened recently, the initiative has largely come not from the courts or the government but from Europe – either from European Community directives or from claims under the European Convention on Human Rights. When Article 8 of the Convention is received into domestic law under the Human Rights Act 1998 UK citizens will, for the first time, have a guarantee of a right to respect for their privacy. It will be enforceable against public authorities, such as the BBC, but not against private bodies including the press. Citizens may sue public authorities in respect of breaches of Article 8, relying on existing causes of action, unless no cause of action covers the situation in question. In that case a tort of invasion of privacy would have to be developed which would be applicable only against public authorities. Private bodies would be immune from the new tortious liability,

---

17 See Warren and Brandeis, 'The Right to Privacy' (1890) 4 *Harv L Rev* 193.

18 See for example the comments of Lord Justice Glidewell in *Kaye v Robertson* [1991] FSR 62 CA: 'It is well known that in English law there is no right to privacy ... in the absence of such a right the plaintiff's advisers have sought to base their claim on other well-established rights of action.'

19 For example, *Prince Albert v Strange* (1849) 2 De Gex & Sm 652; *Clowser v Chaplin* (1981) 72 Cr App R 342.

but existing causes of action could be invoked which would be interpreted in the light of the Convention guarantees and common law principle. The need to broaden existing means of protecting privacy, such as the doctrine of confidence, by these means will become more pressing after the Convention is received into domestic law since it would seem unacceptable and anomalous for a private body to be able to invade privacy with impunity where liability would arise if a public body was involved. The current methods of protecting privacy discussed below will therefore remain highly significant.

CHAPTER EIGHT

PERSONAL INFORMATION[20]

1 MEDIA INTRUSION

At present no tort of invasion of privacy exists in the UK as in the US[21] to control the activity of the media in obtaining information regarding an individual's private life and then publishing the details perhaps in exaggerated, lurid terms. However, certain legal controls do exist, although they are not aimed directly at the invasion of privacy, and they can be used against the media and others when private information is published. These controls affect both the publication of the information and the *methods* used to obtain it. When information such as a photograph is obtained, there may often be some kind of intrusion on property, albeit of a nebulous kind, such as long range surveillance. Legal controls relevant to the *publication* of information will be considered first, followed by the legal control of intrusions.

Breach of confidence[22]

The common law doctrine of breach of confidence will protect some confidential communications and its breadth has supported the view that it could provide a general means of protecting personal information. The Younger Committee, which was convened to report on privacy,[23] considered that confidence was the area of the law which offered most effective protection of privacy for the privacy of personal information. However, less emphasis has been placed on the ability of the doctrine to protect privacy in

---

20 See: Wacks, R, *Personal Information Privacy and the Law*, 1993; Wacks, R, *Privacy and Press Freedom*, 1996; Younger Committee, *Report of the Committee on Privacy*, Cmnd 5012, 1972 (criticised: MacCormick, DN, 'A Note on Privacy' (1973) 84 *LQR* 23); *Report of the Committee on Privacy and Related Matters*, Chairman David Calcutt QC (Calcutt Report) Cmnd 1102, 1990; Calcutt, Sir D, *Review of Press Self-regulation*, Cm 2135, 1993; National Heritage Select Committee, 'Privacy and Media Intrusion' Fourth Report, HC 291–91, 1993; Lord Chancellor's Green Paper, *Infringement of Privacy*, 30 July 1993, CHAN J060915NJ.7/93; *Privacy and Media Intrusion*, White Paper (1995) Cm 2918; Eady, D, 'A Statutory Right to Privacy' (1996) *EHRLR* 243; Markesinis, B, 'The Right to be Let Alone versus Freedom of Speech' [1986] *PL* 67; Wilson, W, 'Privacy, Confidence and Press Freedom' (1990) *MLR* 43.

21 US Restatement 2d Torts (1977) No 652A.

22 See generally Dworkin, G, *Confidence in the Law*, 1971; Gurry, F, *Breach of Confidence*, 1991; Jones, G (1970) 86 *LQR* 463.

23 See *Report of the Committee on Privacy*, Cmnd 5012, 1972.

some recent discussions of both privacy and confidence.[24] This area of law developed largely as a means of protecting commercial secrets.

The House of Lords in *AG v Guardian Newspapers (No 2)*[25] found that the ruling in *Coco v AN Clark (Engineers) Limited*[26] conveniently summarised the three traditionally accepted key elements of the law of confidence:

> First the information itself ... must have the necessary quality of confidence about it. Secondly, that information must have been imparted in circumstances importing an obligation of confidence. Thirdly, there must be an unauthorised use of that information to the detriment of the party communicating it.

Development of the doctrine[27]

Under the doctrine as traditionally conceived information would have a confidential quality if three ingredients were present: the material must not be in the public domain; it must be capable of amounting to 'information' for the purposes of the doctrine, and a public interest must be served by protecting it. The last of these ingredients has become difficult to distinguish from the circumstances needed to impose the duty of confidence and therefore it will be considered in that context, below. In *AG v Guardian Newspapers (No 2)*[28] Lord Keith indicated that whether information is in the public domain will often be a matter of degree and therefore prior disclosure to a limited group of people might not rob the information of its confidentiality. His Lordship was referring to the possibility of publication abroad, but the principle behind his comments – that the true test is whether further and more serious damage will flow from the fresh disclosure contemplated[29] – could apply in a case in which the relevant information had been previously disclosed in this country but in such a manner or at such a distance in the past that the information could not fairly be characterised as being currently in the public domain. Probably it has also been the case that confidence would not cover instances where the information was initially obtained through observation in a public place. However, the decision in *HRH Princess of Wales v MGN Newspapers Limited and Others*[30] casts some doubt on this contention, since the information

---

24 See the Calcutt Committee on *Privacy and Related Matters* (para 32, Cmnd 1102, 1990) and Wacks, *Privacy and Press Freedom*, 1995, p 56); compare the earlier view of the Younger Committee (*Report of the Committee on Privacy*, Cmnd 5012, 1972, p 26).

25 [1990] 1 AC 109.

26 [1969] RPC 41 at 47.

27 This section is largely drawn from Fenwick, H and Phillipson, G, 'Confidence and Privacy: A Re-examination' (1996) 55(3) *CLJ* 447.

28 [1990] 1 AC 109 at 260.

29 Note the similar findings in the privacy context on this point in *Broadcasting Complaints Commission, ex parte Granada TV Limited* (1993) *The Times*, 31 May (affirmed (1994) *The Times*, 16 December, CA).

30 Transcript, Association of Official Shorthandwriters Limited, 8 November 1993. Discussed below.

in question was obtained in a gymnasium attended by other club members and therefore, clearly, it had been disseminated to an extent, albeit in a manner limited enough to prevent it from being viewed as in the public domain. An interim injunction to protect the information was nevertheless granted. Thus information obtained by means of observation in similar semi-public places, such as small restaurants, might now be found to retain the necessary quality of confidence. 'Public domain' has apparently become a rather more flexible – and imprecise – concept.

What is 'information' for the purposes of the law of confidence? It is suggested that both substance and form will be in question. The traditional view was that equity would not intervene to protect trivial information. However, there are signs that the categories of information capable of being accounted sufficiently substantial are widening: information concerning an individual's sexual orientation (*Stephens v Avery*)[31] and physical appearance (*HRH Princess of Wales*) has been found to merit protection.

Recent decisions suggest that the courts will also adopt a flexible approach to the form of the information. In *HRH Princess of Wales*, Drake J had no hesitation in granting interim injunctions to prevent the *Daily Mirror* and others from publishing photographs of the Princess exercising in a gymnasium, taken by the gymnasium owner without her knowledge or consent. The plaintiff's case was based both on breach of contract and on confidence, but Drake J appeared to take the view that although the contractual claim was more clearly made out, either limb of the claim would have justified the injunction.[32] Similarly, in *Shelley Films Limited v Rex Features Limited*[33] the defendant was restrained by injunction from publishing photographs which had been taken without permission on the set of the film *Frankenstein*. The possibility that the taking of photographs can amount to the acquiring of confidential information was also expressly accepted by Mr Justice Laws in *Hellewell v Chief Constable of Derbyshire*.[34] These three decisions go much further, it is suggested, than simply affirming that photographs can carry information for the purposes of the law of confidence.[35] A photograph is merely a record and as such may be treated as any other means of recording information. However, in these instances the 'information' had not been captured and contained in any particular form until the defendant brought that about. It would seem to follow that had the gymnasium owner in the *HRH Princess of Wales* case merely observed Princess Diana's appearance in the gymnasium without recording it, he would have been in possession of 'information', and an interim injunction to restrain publication of the

---

[31] [1988] Ch 449.
[32] *Ibid* at pp 4–5.
[33] 10 December 1993, transcript from LEXIS.
[34] [1995] 1 WLR 804, at 807.
[35] As earlier indicated by *Pollard v Photographic Company* (1888) Ch 345.

observations would have been available. Thus it appears, it is submitted, that a record (using that term in its widest possible sense to include human memories) of any matter of substance not already in the public domain may amount to confidential information for the purposes of the doctrine of confidence.

Since *Stephens v Avery* the basic principle on which the doctrine of confidence has been based appears to be that confidentiality will be enforced if the information was received 'on the basis that it is confidential'.[36] This will depend on all the circumstances of the case, and the imposition of confidence is not limited (as had previously been thought) to instances in which there was a pre-existing relationship between the parties:

> The basis of equitable intervention to protect confidentiality is that it is unconscionable for a person who has received information on the basis that it is confidential, subsequently to reveal that information ... The relationship between the parties is not the determining factor.[37]

It is suggested that this explanation of the basis of the doctrine weakens the requirement to identify the public interest, such as the interest in preserving the stability of the family,[38] which would be served by protecting the information in question.

The fact that the information is given in confidence may be expressly communicated to the defendant (as in *Stephens v Avery*), but can be implied from the circumstances surrounding the communication. In *Fairnie (Dec'd) and Others v Reed and Another*[39] the confidential information (the format of a board game which the plaintiff wished to market) was mentioned by him incidentally during conversation with a virtual stranger about another matter; it was therefore transmitted only in passing, and the recipient was not told that it was given in confidence. The Court of Appeal found that there was an arguable case that the information had been transmitted in confidence relying primarily on the fact that the information was of clear commercial value.[40]

---

36 [1988] Ch 449, at 482.
37 *Ibid*.
38 As in *Duchess of Argyll v Duke of Argyll* [1967] 1 Ch 302.
39 20 May 1994 CA, transcript from LEXIS.
40 '[Plaintiff's counsel] submits that in the context [the plaintiff] disclosed to [the defendant] a confidential idea which he believed could be commercially successful, particularly with his indorsement. In my judgment, that is an arguable inference ... It all depends precisely on the language used, and the circumstances in which the conversation took place ... [defendant's counsel] points out that ... if the plaintiff simply blurted out or casually referred to the number one game ... then the defendant could not be taken as understanding that he was being given that information in confidence. That may be so, but in my judgment it is not possible to say ... precisely what inference should be drawn by the reasonable man who was the bystander and observer of the conversation', *per* Stuart Smith LJ, at pp 7–8. The hearing was an appeal upon an application to strikeout, so the court did not have to decide whether an obligation of confidence was in fact imposed.

It appears that an obligation of confidence may be imposed even where the information was not intentionally communicated to the defendant by the plaintiff. In *AG v Guardian Newspapers (No 2)*[41] Lord Goff suggested *obiter* that the nature of the information and the fact that it was not intended that the defendant should acquire it[42] could in itself impose the duty, using the example of '... an obviously confidential document ... dropped in a public place and then picked up by a passer-by ...'. *Francome v Mirror Group Newspapers* (1984),[43] in which the information was obtained by means of a telephone tap, suggests that a duty of confidence may arise on the basis of such factors,[44] as does *Shelley Films Limited v Rex Features Limited*.[45] These findings further confirm that the duty can still be imposed (or perhaps imposed *a fortiori*) where the defendant sets out deliberately to acquire the information without the plaintiff's knowledge, as opposed to stumbling across it inadvertently.[46] Presumably this would also be the case where the defendant acquired the information with the awareness but without the consent of the plaintiff and where, as in *Hellewell v Chief Constable of Derbyshire*,[47] the defendant was acting under a legal power in acquiring the information for one specific purpose but wished to use it for another.[48] The decisions in *Rex Features*, *HRH Princess of Wales* and *Hellewell* also indicate that there need be nothing recognisable as a 'communication' from the plaintiff to any other person for the duty to arise,[49] although presumably the information concerned must in some sense emanate from the plaintiff.

---

41 [1990] 1 AC 109, at 281.

42 *Fairnie* suggests that it will not always be essential to show that this element is present.

43 [1984] 1 WLR 892.

44 *Cf* the *obiter* remarks in *Malone v Commissioner of Police of the Metropolis (No 2)* [1979] Ch 344, at 376 to the effect that those who spoke of confidential matters in situations in which it was foreseeable that they could be overheard (eg on the telephone) could not claim that any eavesdroppers were bound by a duty of confidentiality. However, in *Malone v UK* (1984) 7 EHRR 14 the European Court of Human Rights reaffirmed (at p 38) the place of telephone conversations within Article 8 and therefore must be taken to have rejected the notion that citizens assume a lack of confidentiality in communication by telephone.

45 *Ibid* at p 13 *per* Mr Mann QC (sitting as a deputy judge): '... [the photographer] was not an invitee and assuming that he saw the signs [forbidding photography] ... (I am not convinced that it would be fatal to Shelley's case if he did not) ... it is impossible ... not to conclude that what he saw and understood from his location might not have fully and sufficiently fixed him with knowledge [that the plaintiff wished to keep the appearance of 'the Creature' and its costume secret] according to any of the relevant standards ...' The Australian case of *Franklin v Giddins* [1978] 1 QdR 72 was relied upon as persuasive authority.

46 For the contrary view that a duty will only be imposed where there is unlawful action by the taker of information see Wei, G, 'Surreptitious takings of confidential information' (1992) LS 302. For critical discussion of Wei's view, see the articles cited by him at p 309.

47 The case concerned the taking of photographs under Code of Practice D (para 4) made under the Police and Criminal Evidence Act 1984 of a suspect in police custody. The police wished to allow a 'shop watch' scheme to use the photographs. An injunction was refused on the basis that the public interest was clearly served by the disclosure in question.

48 See also *Marcell and Others v Commissioner of Police of the Metropolis* [1992] Ch 224, esp at 236–37.

49 See Thompson, *Confidentiality and the Law*, 1990, p 73.

It would appear, therefore, that the obligation of confidence can now be imposed unilaterally; it is not founded on the express or implied agreement of the parties that the communication would be confidential.[50] In *Maudsley v Palumbo and Others*[51] Knox J said (*obiter*) that while the absence of actual belief on the part of the defendants that they were being given confidential information was 'quite capable of being significant', he '[did] not accept that ... a person who forms no belief on the question is thereby absolved from being found to have received information in confidence'. The test appears to be wholly objective.[52] What factors would lead a reasonable person to realise that the information is confidential? The authorities suggest that they would include the following: where it has clear commercial value, as in *Fairnie* and *Rex Features*, and where it is obvious that the plaintiff did not wish the information to be obtained (as in *HRH Princess of Wales* and *Rex Features*). Conversely, where the plaintiff deliberately refrains from mentioning confidentiality to the defendant this may prevent the imposition of the duty, as in *Palumbo*.

Care must be taken in extrapolating general principles from some of the decisions discussed here since a number of them concerned interim injunctions only[53] and therefore it was only necessary for the plaintiff to make out an arguable case. Others concerned appeals from applications to strike out[54] in which, as Stuart Smith LJ emphasised in *Fairnie*, the plaintiff must succeed unless his case is 'unarguable'.[55] Nevertheless, it is suggested that the courts are inclining towards a position regarding imposition of the duty to maintain confidence which may be summarised as follows. It is not necessary to establish a pre-existing relationship, an express imposition of the duty, an agreement between the parties or anything resembling a communication of the information by the plaintiff to the defendant or anyone else.[56] It seems that there is only one ingredient which is essential: it must be shown that a reasonable person who acquired the information would have realised that it was confidential.

---

50 An approach indicated earlier in *Coco v AN Clark (Engineers) Ltd* [1969] RPC 41, at 48.
51 (1995) *The Times*, 19 December, transcript from LEXIS; the case concerned an application for an injunction to restrain the defendants from making use of an idea for a dance club disclosed to them by the plaintiff.
52 In *Li Yau-wai v Genesis Films Limited* [1987] HKLR 711, a Hong Kong decision, an 'officious bystander' test was used to impose the duty of confidence (*per* Rhind J at p 719). An objective test was also employed in *Lam v Koo and Chiu* [1992] Civil Transcript No 116, see esp p 30 (Hong Kong Court of Appeal). See Wacks, *Privacy and Press Freedom*, above note 1, pp 62–63; Loh, E, 'Intellectual Property: Breach of Confidence?' (1995) 17 *EIPR* 405–07.
53 *Rex Features*; *HRH Princess of Wales*; *Francome v Mirror Group Newspapers Ltd*.
54 *Fairnie*; *Stephens v Avery* [1988] Ch 449.
55 *Ibid* p 1.
56 Following *AG v Guardian Newspapers (No 2)* [1990] 1AC 109; [1990] 3 WLR 776; [1988] 3 All ER 545, HL, the defendant need not be the person to whom the information was originally 'communicated'.

The third element identified as essential in *Coco v AN Clark (Engineers) Ltd* appears to require two ingredients – unauthorised use of the information and detriment arising from such use. This point was addressed by the House of Lords in *AG v Guardian Newspapers (No 2)*, but the Law Lords were divided as to the need to show detriment where a private individual was claiming a breach of confidence. Lord Griffiths considered that detriment had to be shown even in such a case;[57] Lords Brightman and Jauncey were silent as to the issue, while Lord Goff considered that the question should be left open.[58] Lord Keith, however, was of the view that in this respect a private individual should not be treated in the same way as a state body:

> The right to personal privacy is clearly one which the law should in this field seek to protect ... I would think it is sufficient detriment to the confider that information given in confidence is to be disclosed to persons who he would prefer not to know of it even though the disclosure would not be harmful to him in any positive way.[59]

Obiter dicta in *Shelley Films Limited v Rex Features Limited* appear to favour the position taken by Lord Goff,[60] while Lord Keith's view receives some support from the finding in *HRH Princess of Wales v MGN Limited and Others*[61] which suggests that in relation to private individuals, the courts may be prepared to assume the presence of detriment. The point remains unclear.

It used to be thought that confidence was of limited value in protecting privacy, since it only covered those specific instances in which information was communicated in confidence. Thus, for example, it was not thought to cover situations where reporters took unauthorised photographs by means of telephoto lenses or surreptitiously recorded conversations with a view to publication. However, the developments described above significantly widen the circumstances in which the duty of confidence will be imposed, with the result, it is suggested, that many of the activities of reporters engaged in uncovering private facts may now be caught by the law of confidence. As Laws J remarked *obiter* in *Hellewell*:

> If someone with a telephoto lens were to take ... a photograph of another engaged in some private act, his subsequent disclosure of the photograph would in my judgment ... amount to a breach of confidence ... In such a case the law would protect what might reasonably be called a right of privacy, although the name accorded to the cause of action would be breach of confidence.[62]

---

57 [1990] 1 AC 109 at 269–70.
58 *Ibid* pp 281–82.
59 *Ibid* pp 255–63.
60 10 December 1993, transcript from LEXIS at p 16.
61 Transcript, Association of Official Shorthandwriters Limited, 8 November 1993.
62 [1995] 1 WLR 804, at 807.

Clearly, the doctrine will not always provide a remedy when agents of the media invade privacy.[63] For example, it cannot affect instances where a physical intrusion takes place but usable information is not acquired, subsequently disclosed or otherwise used. Further, as Wacks observes, the plaintiff may be denied a remedy if he has made a prior disclosure himself 'which is of a greater order of impropriety than the revelation of which he now complains' due to the operation of the 'clean hands' doctrine.[64] More significantly the doctrine remains subject to the public interest defence, thereby affording some recognition to media freedom.

The public interest defence

Confidential information will not be protected if the public interest served by disclosing the information in question outweighs the interest in preserving confidentiality. This aspect of the doctrine is often termed the 'public interest' defence. In *Woodward v Hutchings*[65] intimate facts about Tom Jones and another pop star were revealed to the *Daily Mirror* by a former agent who had been their confidante. The plaintiffs sought an injunction on the ground of breach of confidence. There had been a confidential relationship and they claimed that the agent should not be able to take unfair advantage of that confidentiality. The Court of Appeal failed to uphold the claim on the basis that the plaintiffs had sought to publicise themselves in order to present a certain 'image' and therefore could not complain if the truth were later revealed. This decision has been criticised on the basis that a need to reveal the truth about the plaintiffs was irrelevant to the breach of confidence on the part of the agent,[66] but it has not been overruled. The public interest in knowing the truth about the plaintiffs seemed to rest on a refusal to use the law to protect their attempt to mislead the public.

It is sometimes said that there is no confidence in iniquity: the plaintiff cannot use the law of confidence to cover up his or her own wrong-doing and therefore the public interest in disclosure will prevail. However it is uncertain whether the 'public interest defence' is limited to cases of iniquity. The House of Lords found *obiter* in *British Steel Corporation v Granada Television*[67] that publication of confidential information could legitimately be undertaken only where there was misconduct,[68] but in *Lion Laboratories v Evans*[69] Lord Justice

---

63 See further Wacks, *Privacy and Press Freedom*, 1996, at pp 55–59.

64 Wacks, *op cit* p 56. Note, however, that since the 'clean hands' doctrine is a creature of equity, it follows that if confidence develops into a common law tort, this limitation would presumably no longer apply, at least in its present form.

65 [1977] 1 WLR 760, CA.

66 Wacks, *The Protection of Privacy*, p 85.

67 [1981] AC 1096; [1981] 1 All ER 417, HL.

68 See Cripps, Y (1984) *OJLS* 184 on the public interest defence.

69 [1985] QB 526 at 537.

Stephenson said that he would reject the 'no iniquity, no public interest rule' agreeing with Lord Denning's statement in *Fraser v Evans*[70] to the effect that 'some things are required to be disclosed in the public interest in which case no confidence can be prayed in aid to keep them secret and [iniquity] is merely an instance of just cause and excuse for breaking confidence'. These rulings concerned confidential information held by private companies and seem to leave open the possibility of a broad public interest defence which, it seems from *Woodward*, may also sometimes apply in the case of public figures. Where personal information relating to a private individual is in issue, the ruling in *X v Y*[71] suggests that the public interest defence is confined to cases of iniquity. On the other hand, *Lion Laboratories v Evans and Express Newspapers*,[72] *W v Egdell*[73] and *Hellewell* suggest that the defence has broadened its focus of concern with the result that the strength of the public interest in question rather than the individual wrongdoing of the plaintiff may now tend to be the determining factor. In *W v Egdell* no such wrongdoing was relied upon in finding that the medical report relating to the plaintiff's condition should be placed before the appropriate authorities where it was in the public interest to do so. It should be noted that this decision may place some limitation on the ability of the public interest defence to afford protection to press freedom: it may sometimes be appropriate to pass information to a particular body rather than disclosing it to the public at large. On the other hand, where the public itself had previously been misled by the plaintiff, it is suggested that wide disclosure might be warranted.

The above discussion should not be taken as assuming that the public interest will always require disclosure of information and will therefore invariably be in competition with the interest of the plaintiff in suppressing it. Clearly, there is a general public interest in allowing the transmission of information from one person to another without interference, and in certain circumstances such as those which arose in *X v Y* there may be a further specific public interest in maintaining confidentiality. A newspaper wished to publish information deriving from confidential hospital records which showed that certain practising doctors were suffering from the AIDS virus. In granting an injunction preventing publication Rose J took into account the public interest in disclosure, but weighed it against the private interest in confidentiality and the public interest in encouraging AIDS patients to seek help from hospitals, which would not be served if it was thought that confidentiality might not be maintained.

---

70 [1969] 1 QB 349, 362.
71 [1988] 2 All ER 648.
72 [1985] QB 526; [1984] 2 All ER 417, CA.
73 [1990] Ch 359; see also *X v Y* [1988] 2 All ER 658 and *dicta* of Lord Goff in *AG v Guardian Newspapers (No 2)* at p 659.

Defamation and malicious falsehood

The law of defamation may offer some protection to an individual who has suffered from the unauthorised disclosure of private matters, but the interest protected by defamation – the interest of the individual in preserving his or her reputation – is not synonymous with the interest in preserving privacy. A reputation may not suffer but the fact that personal information is spread abroad may nevertheless be hurtful in itself for the individual affected. Thus, no remedy was available in *Corelli v Wall*[74] which arose from publication by the defendants, without the plaintiff's permission, of postcards depicting imaginary events in her life. Such publication was not found to be libellous, and no remedy lay in copyright as the copyright was in the creator of the cards. The ruling in *Kaye v Robertson and Another*,[75] may be said to have made clear the inadequacy of defamation as a remedy for invasions of privacy. Mr Kaye, a well-known actor, was involved in a car accident and suffered severe injuries to his head and brain. While he was lying in hospital two journalists from the *Sunday Sport*, acting on Mr Robertson's orders, got into his room, photographed him and interviewed him. Due to his injuries, he did not object to their presence and shortly after the incident had no recollection of it. The resultant article gave the impression that Mr Kaye had consented to the interview. His advisers sought and obtained an injunction restraining the defendants from publishing the photographs and the interview. On appeal by the defendants the Court of Appeal ruled that the plaintiff's claim could not be based on a right to privacy as such a right is unknown to English law. His true grievance lay in the 'monstrous invasion of privacy' which he had suffered but he would have to look to other rights of action in order to obtain a remedy, namely libel and malicious falsehood. The basis of the defamation claim was that the article's implication that Mr Kaye had consented to a first 'exclusive' interview for a 'lurid and sensational' newspaper such as the *Sunday Sport* would lower him in the esteem of right thinking people. The Court of Appeal held that this claim might well succeed but that as such a conclusion was not inevitable it could not warrant grant of an interim injunction, basing this ruling on *Herbage v Times Newspapers and Others*.[76]

The court then considered malicious falsehood. First it had to be shown that the defendant had published about the plaintiff words which were false. Their Lordships considered that any reasonable jury would find that the implication contained in the words of the article was false. As the case was, on that basis, clear cut, an interim injunction could in principle be granted. Secondly, it had to be shown that the words were published maliciously.

---

74 (1906) 22 *TLR* 532 (Ch).
75 [1991] FSR 62; (1991) *The Times*, 21 March; for comment see Prescott, P (1991) 54 *MLR* 451; Bedingfield, D (1992) 55 *MLR* 111; Markesinis, BS (1992) 55 *MLR* 118.
76 (1981) *The Times*, 1 May.

Malice would be inferred if it was proved that the words were calculated to produce damage and that the defendant knew them to be false. The reporters clearly realised that Mr Kaye was unable to give them any informed consent. Any subsequent publication of the falsehood would therefore be malicious. Thirdly, damage must have followed as a direct result of the publication of the falsehood. The words had produced damage in that they had diminished the value of Mr Kaye's right to sell the story of his accident at some later date. That ground of action was therefore made out. Therefore, an injunction restraining the defendants until trial from publishing anything which suggested that the plaintiff had given an informed consent to the interview or the taking of the photographs was substituted for the original order. However, this was a limited injunction which allowed publication of the story with certain of the photographs provided it was not claimed that the plaintiff had given consent. Thus it seemed that no effective remedy was available for the plaintiff. Legatt LJ concluded his ruling by saying: 'We do not need a First Amendment to preserve the freedom of the Press, but the abuse of that freedom can be ensured only by the enforcement of a right to privacy.'[77]

Power of court to protect minors

The privacy of children receives some protection from the courts' inherent jurisdiction to protect the privacy of minors. This was confirmed in *Central Independent Television*.[78] A programme was made depicting the work of the police which included an investigation into a man subsequently convicted of offences of indecency. The plaintiff recognised him as her husband in a trailer shown of the programme. She did not wish her daughter, aged five, who knew nothing of his convictions, to know what had occurred and therefore sought to have the programme altered so that it would not be possible to recognise her husband. The Court of Appeal refused the injunction despite accepting that it had an inherent jurisdiction to protect the privacy of minors. It found that the protection for the privacy of children would not extend to covering publication of facts relating to those who were not carers of the child in question and which occurred before the child was born.

Media self-regulation

Successive governments, including the current one, have considered that the press should regulate itself as regards protection of privacy rather than using civil or criminal sanctions. Self-discipline was preferred to court regulation in order to preserve press freedom, and to this end the Press Council was created

---

77 [1991] FSR 621 at p 104.
78 [1994] Fam 192.

in 1953. It was supposed to regulate the press and therefore issued guidelines on privacy and adjudicated on complaints. It could censure a newspaper and require its adjudication to be published. In practice, however, a number of deficiencies became apparent; the Council did not issue clear enough guidelines, its decisions were seen as inconsistent and in any event ineffective: it had no power to fine or to award an injunction. Moreover, it was seen as too lenient; it would not interfere if the disclosure in question could be said to be in the public interest, and what was meant by the public interest was uncertain. Its inefficacy led the Younger Committee, convened in 1972, to recommend a number of proposals offering greater protection from intrusion by the press.[79] These proposals were not implemented but recently a perception again began to arise, partly influenced by *Kaye*, that further measures might be needed to control the press, although at the same time there was concern that they should not prevent legitimate investigative journalism. This perceived need led eventually to the formation of the Committee on Privacy and Related Matters chaired by Sir David Calcutt (hereafter 'Calcutt I') in 1990[80] which considered a number of measures, some relevant to actual publication and some to the means of gathering information. The Committee decided that improved self-regulation should be given one final chance and recommended the creation of the Press Complaints Commission which was set up in 1991.

The Commission agreed a Code of Practice which the newspapers accepted. It can receive and pronounce on complaints of violation of the Code and can demand an apology for inaccuracy, or that there should be an opportunity for reply. Intrusion into private life is allowed under the Code only if it is in the public interest; this is defined as including 'detecting or exposing seriously anti-social conduct' or 'preventing the public being misled by some statement or action of that individual'. Harassment is not allowed. The Code makes special mention of hospitals and requires that the press must obtain permission in order to interview patients. The Commission does not require the complainant to waive any legal right of action as the Press Council was criticised for doing. However, it has the same limited sanctions as the Press Council. The Broadcasting Complaints Commission (BCC) has a similar role in adjudicating on complaints of infringement of privacy 'in or in connection with the obtaining of materials included in BBC or independent licensed television or sound broadcasts'.[81] The term 'privacy' will receive

---

79 The Committee considered the need for legal curbs on the press; it recommended the introduction of a tort of disclosure of information unlawfully acquired and a tort and crime of unlawful surveillance by means of a technical device. See Younger Committee (Cmnd 5012, 1972); criticised: MacCormick, DN 'A Note on Privacy' (1973) 84 *LQ Rev* 23.

80 *Report of the Committee on Privacy and Related Matters*, Cm 1102, 1990 (Calcutt Report); for comment see Munro, C, 'Press Freedom – How the Beast was Tamed' (1991) 54 *MLR* 104.

81 Section 142 of the Broadcasting Act 1990.

quite a wide interpretation according to the ruling in *Broadcasting Complaints Commission, ex parte Granada Television Limited*.[82] Granada television challenged a finding of the BCC that matters already in the public domain could, if republished, constitute an invasion of privacy. In judicial review proceedings it was found that privacy differed from confidentiality and went well-beyond it because it was not confined to secrets; the significant issue was not whether material was or was not in the public domain but whether, by being published it caused hurt and anguish. There were grounds on which it could be considered that publication of the matters in question had caused distress, and therefore the BCC had not acted unreasonably in the Wednesbury sense in taking the view that an infringement of privacy had occurred. However, the alleged infringement of privacy can be found to have occurred only when the broadcast is over and not earlier.[83] It should be noted that the function of the Broadcasting Complaints Commission will be undertaken in future by the Broadcasting Standards Commission (BSC) set up under s 106 of the Broadcasting Act 1996. The BSC is charged with the duty of drawing up a Code in respect of programme standards under s 107 which is based on s 152 of the 1990 Act, but for the first time the Code must also cover matters of fairness and privacy.

After self-regulation under the new Code of Practice had been in place for a year, Sir David Calcutt (hereafter 'Calcutt II') reviewed its success[84] and determined that the Press Complaints Commission 'does not hold the balance fairly between the press and the individual ... it is in essence a body set up by the industry ... dominated by the industry'. He therefore proposed the introduction of a statutory tribunal which would draw up a code of practice for the press and would rule on alleged breaches of the code; its sanctions would include those already possessed by the Press Complaints Commission and in addition the imposition of fines and the award of compensation. When the matter was considered by the National Heritage Select Committee[85] in 1993 it rejected the proposal of a statutory tribunal in favour of the creation of another self-regulatory body to be known as the Press Commission, which would monitor a Press Code and which would have powers to fine and to award compensation. At the time of writing, however, the government has made no move to appoint a new self-regulatory body or to give the Press Complaints Commission new powers. The Commission itself, however, decided in January 1994 to appoint a Privacy Commissioner with the power to recommend that newspaper editors should be disciplined for breaching the Press Code, and in 1997 the Code was made more restrictive.

---

82 (1993) *The Times*, 31 May (affirmed (1994) *The Times*, 16 December, CA).
83 *Broadcasting Complaints Commission, ex parte Barclay and Another* (1996) *The Times*, 11 October.
84 *Review of Press Self-regulation*, Cm 2135.
85 Fourth Report of the Committee 294–91, *Privacy and Media Intrusion Fourth Report*, HC 291–1 (1993).

A tort of invasion of privacy?

Legatt LJ asserted confidently in *Kaye* that a right to privacy exists in the US which will be enforced and suggested that such a right should be imported into UK law, but this proposition has come under attack,[86] on the basis that the scope of US privacy rights is limited by a general defence of 'newsworthiness'[87] which allows many stories disclosing embarrassing and painful personal facts to be published. This perhaps suggests that there is little value in looking to the US for a model if a UK right to privacy is to have any efficacy.

Proposals for enactment of such a tort in the UK have centred around the protection of personal information. As was noted above, *Stephens v Avery* may herald the development of the existing doctrine of breach of confidence with the result that greatly increased protection for control of personal information is effected. However, such development is not certain and in any event it may be preferable that protection should be achieved by a statutory tort balanced by wide ranging and carefully drawn specific public interest defences, rather than through the development of the common law of confidence with its far vaguer public interest defence. Support for a statutory tort has, however, been far from unanimous in the relevant committees. Thus, while the Younger Committee recommended the introduction of a tort of disclosure of information unlawfully acquired, Calcutt I decided against recommending a new statutory tort of invasion of privacy relating to publication of personal information, although the Committee considered that it would be possible to define such a tort with sufficient precision. Calcutt II recommended only that the government should give further consideration to the introduction of such a tort but the National Heritage Select Committee recommended its introduction as did the later Lord Chancellor's consultation paper, the Green Paper.[88] These proposals were abandoned in July 1995,[89] although it is possible that they may be revived in some form as part of the new data protection provision which will be introduced in 1998.[90] It may be noted that under the Lord Chancellor's paper there was no proposal to extend legal aid to those seeking redress under the proposed new civil privacy liability. If in future a new tort is created without the provision of legal aid it might merely be used – as arguably defamation has been – by powerful figures to protect

---

86 Bedingfield, D (1992) 55 *MLR* 111.
87 Bedingfield cites the example of *Kelley v Post Publishing Co* Mass [1951] 98 NE 2d 286. A father was unable to restrain publication of the severely injured body of his daughter due to the finding that the accident was newsworthy.
88 The paper was released on 30 July 1993 – CHAN J060915NJ.7/93. See 143 *NLJ* 1182 for discussion of these proposals.
89 The White Paper, *Privacy and Media Intrusion: the Government's Response* (Cmnd 2918, July 1995), found against creation of a statutory tort.
90 See below pp 338–39.

their activities from scrutiny while the ordinary citizen might be unable in practice to obtain redress for invasions of privacy.

The possible definition of the proposed tort put forward by Calcutt I was designed to relate only to personal information which was published without authorisation. Such information was defined as those aspects of an individual's personal life which a reasonable person would assume should remain private. The main concern of the Committee was that true information which would not cause lasting harm, was already known to some, and was obtained reputably might be caught by its provisions. The Lord Chancellor's proposals were wider: there should be a new cause of action for 'infringement of privacy causing substantial distress' (para 5.22). No definition of privacy was offered, although it was stated to include matters relating to health, personal relationships and communications, and freedom from harassment.

The Calcutt Committee did not consider that liability should be subject to a general defence of public interest, although it did favour a tightly drawn defence of justified disclosure. Under Calcutt II (para 12.23) it would be a defence to show that the defendant had reasonable grounds for believing that publication of the personal information would contribute to preventing, detecting or exposing the commission of a crime or other seriously anti-social conduct; or to preventing the public from being misled by some public statement or action of the individual concerned; or that the defendant had reasonable grounds for believing that publication would be necessary for the protection of public health or safety. The Green Paper invited comments on these defences and in particular on the question whether the public interest defence should be defined in general terms or whether it should be more specific (para 5.62–5.67). The Green Paper proposed (para 5.45) that there should be a defence that the defendant had acted under any lawful authority. *Prima facie*, these defences seem to range widely enough to prevent public figures from being able to use the tort to stifle legitimate investigative journalism. The defence of seeking to prevent the public from being misled by some public statement or action of the individual concerned is, it is submitted, essential to draw a clear distinction between the private citizen and the public figure, and to ensure the accountability of the latter.

When Article 8 of the Convention is received into domestic law under the Human Rights Act 1998 UK citizens will be able to sue public authorities in respect of breaches of Article 8.[91] The press and all non-public parts of the media will be immune from any new Convention based liability. Article 8 will not provide a remedy in the *Kaye* type of situation. It is arguable that this is unsatisfactory, bearing in mind the protection for media freedom which should follow from the enactment of Article 10. Possibly, rather than risk subjecting the media to the uncertainties of Article 8, which provides no

---

91 Section 6 of the Human Rights Act; see below, p 630.

specific defence that the matter published concerned anti-social behaviour (other than that which might follow from the 'rights of others' exception) it might be preferable to enact a tort of invasion of privacy along the lines of that proposed by Calcutt II. It may also be desirable once freedom of information and speech receive further protection to enact certain very specific and narrowly defined areas of liability, relating to particularly intrusive invasions of privacy including harassment.[92] In so doing the main aims of the defences should be to differentiate between the lives of ordinary citizens who happen to come into the public eye, and the lives of public figures, and between matters of genuine public interest and matters in which the public is interested.

Data protection

The Queen's Speech following the 1997 General Election mentioned the introduction of a new Data Protection Bill which will be based on an EU Data Protection Directive to be implemented throughout the EU in 1998. In the words of the directive, personal data must be collected 'fairly'. The Data Protection Act 1998 received the Royal Assent in July 1998. This may lead to curbs on certain techniques used by journalists to obtain information. The Deputy Data Protection Registrar has stated that he would be reluctant to intervene where information was collected about public figures, but that where such figures were not involved he would want powers to demand access to files and would want individuals to have the right to sue newspapers for compensation where unfair techniques had been used. The reception of the European Convention on Human Rights into UK law will mean that the fairness provisions will have to be interpreted in accordance with Article 8, and that where those provisions were inapplicable Article 8 could be invoked against the PCC.

In their application against the media the new provisions would represent a serious threat to freedom of speech if unbalanced by any free speech or freedom of information measure. However, the reception of the European Convention on Human Rights will allow Article 10 to be taken into account when individuals sought to sue newspapers or broadcasters in respect of the unfair collection of information or, in the case of public bodies such as the BBC and PCC, under Article 8 itself. However, the Press Complaints Commission is arguing for exemption for the media from Article 8. Such exemption was not proposed by the government which intends to rely instead on a public

---

92 Sections 1 and 2 of the Protection from Harassment Act 1997 make it an offence to pursue a course of conduct which amounts to harassment of another where the harasser knows or ought to know that this will be its effect. This offence is not aimed at reporters or photographers and is not dependent on acquiring or attempting to acquire information, but it might be applicable where individual reporters had pursued a particular individual on a number of occasions.

interest defence, now s 12 of the Human Rights Act. Although the new provisions are under the supervision of the Data Protection Registrar rather than the courts,[93] decisions of the Registrar, as a body established under statute, would be expected to be open to judicial review. Thus, the new Data Protection provisions may allow the judiciary to balance media freedom against individual privacy when considering provisions relating to the various means of collecting information.

The application of a fairness clause in instances such as these would be by no means an easy task. In an instance such as the one which arose in $X v Y$[94] a judge would have to balance the individual's strong interest in privacy against the general public interest in the potential danger to health. The difficulty of assessing the extent to which each interest was at stake suggests that Parliament should legislate on this matter, possibly along the lines proposed by Calcutt I.

The 'unfair collection of information' may be undertaken by other groups such as state agents, private detectives or even prying neighbours. The Calcutt I and II recommendations were aimed specifically at reporters, but the new Data Protection provisions are framed to apply to persons generally. They could cover the placing of surveillance devices on private property and the taking of photographs or recording the voice of a person on private property without their consent by the use of long and short range surveillance devices with the intention of publishing the information gained. It is not, however, proposed that the new provisions should also place a duty on state bodies to collect information relating to individuals fairly. Even if they were to do so, the existing mechanisms for ensuring respect for privacy under the Interception of Communications Act 1985 and the Security Services Act 1989 (see below) might be thought by the government to be adequate to the task.

Criminal and civil liability for intrusions

It has been suggested[95] that there are sufficient remedies in the common law of trespass to cover at least the kind of situation which arose in *Kaye v Robertson*.[96] The physical intrusion into the hospital involved trespass on to property (because the reporters, given their purpose, could have no implied licence to be there). Kaye could obviously not bring an action on his own account as his property had not been trespassed upon but the solution would

---

93 It may be noted that under s 13 of the Data Protection Act 1984 there is a right of appeal to a tribunal against certain decisions of the Registrar. At present it is unclear whether the jurisdiction of the tribunal under s 6 of the Act will extend to the new duties of the Registrar in relation to the 'unfair' collection of information by the media and others.
94 [1988] 2 All ER 648; see above p 331.
95 Prescott, 54 *MLR* 451.
96 [1991] FSR 62; (1991) *The Times*, 21 March; for comment see Prescott, P (1991) 54 *MLR* 451; Bedingfield, D (1992) 55 *MLR* 111; Markesinis, BS (1992) 55 *MLR* 118.

be to join the hospital as co-plaintiff in the action. Once trespass had been established the court could exercise its equitable jurisdiction to grant an injunction to prevent the defendants from profiting from their own wrong by publishing the material obtained by the trespass for gain. The case of *Chappell & Co Limited v Columbia Gramophone Co*[97] is cited as support for this course of action. In that case the defendants had wrongfully used the plaintiff's sheet music to make gramophone records. Although the making of the records themselves was not a violation of the plaintiff's legal rights, the court ordered their destruction on the grounds that the defendants should not be allowed to 'reap all the proceeds of their wrongdoing'. However, it is clear that there is no guarantee that possible co-plaintiffs (such as hotel owners) would agree to join in such actions.

Thus, the remedy available even in a case of physical intrusion onto private land would not be certain. Further, an action in trespass would be of limited application in relation to the interviewing of disaster or accident victims and their relatives generally: a person might be interviewed at or near the scene of a disaster in a public place or alternatively, some hospitalised victims of a disaster might consent to be interviewed while others did not. It would not appear that interviewing of the latter group could found a cause of action. Further, it should be noted that if detailed information regarding Mr Kaye's condition had been obtained without physically entering the hospital – perhaps by interviewing him over the telephone – an action in trespass would not be possible. Specific remedies for invasion of privacy would be more appropriate, subject to a broad public interest defence.

The Protection from Harassment Act 1997 might offer a remedy in respect of some forms of repeated media intrusions on privacy, although it was not aimed at reporters or photographers, but at 'stalkers'. Sections 1 and 2 make it an offence to pursue a course of conduct which amounts to harassment of another where the harasser knows or ought to know that this will be its effect. Apart from creating criminal liability for stalking, the Act also provides a civil remedy in s 3 in the form of damages or a restraining order.

Given the inadequacy of the remedies presently available in this area, it is not surprising that a consensus appears to have emerged that increased protection is needed. The Younger Committee proposed the introduction of a tort and crime of unlawful surveillance by means of a technical device, and both Calcutt Committees[98] recommended the creation of a specific criminal offence providing more extensive protection – a recommendation which was backed by the National Heritage Select Committee when it considered the matter.

---

97 [1914] 2 Ch 745, 752, 754, 756, CA.
98 See above pp 334–35.

The clause creating the offence under Calcutt II also offered the individual whose privacy has been invaded the possibility of obtaining injunctions in the High Court to prevent publication of material gained in contravention of the clause provisions; damages would also be available to hold newspapers to account for any profits gained through publication of such material. Criminal liability under the clause would be made out if the defendant did any of the following with intent to obtain personal information or photographs, in either case with a view to their publication: entering or remaining on private property without the consent of the lawful occupant; placing a surveillance device on private property without such consent; using a surveillance device *whether on private property or elsewhere* in relation to an individual who is on private property without his or her consent; taking a photograph or recording the voice of an individual who is on private property without his or her consent and with intent that the individual should be identifiable. This clause seemed to specify the forbidden acts fairly clearly and to be aimed at preventing what would generally be accepted to be on the face of it undesirable invasions of privacy; it is worth noting that France, Germany, Denmark and the Netherlands all have similar offences on the statute books. (It should be noted that the offence would *not* cover persistent telephoning;[99] or photographing, interviewing or recording the voice of a vulnerable individual such as a disaster victim or a bereaved relative in a *public* place).

Calcutt I and the Green Paper[100] proposed defences to the proposed criminal offences which were wider than the defences suggested in relation to a tort of invasion of privacy. Calcutt I proposed (para 6.35) that it would be a defence to any of the actions above to show that the act was done:

(a) for the purpose of preventing, detecting or exposing the commission of a crime or other seriously anti-social conduct; or

(b) for the purpose of preventing the public from being misled by some public statement or action of the individual concerned; or

(c) for the purpose of informing the public about matters directly affecting the discharge of any public function of the individual concerned; or

(d) for the protection of public health or safety; or

(e) under any lawful authority.

Calcutt I, II and the Green Paper were silent as to the mental element required with respect to the defences. There appear to be three possibilities here which for the purposes of exposition will be examined using the example of a claim of defence (a). First, the defence would succeed only if it was shown that the forbidden act *actually could have led* to the exposure of crime, so that if it turned out that in fact no criminal activity had been present – though perhaps a

---

99 The decision in *Khorasandjian v Bush* [1993] 3 All ER 669 might offer some protection in this area (see below p 364).

100 See above p 336.

reasonable person would have thought that it was – the defence would fail. Secondly, the defence would succeed if the defendant could show that she honestly and reasonably believed that she was acting with the purpose of exposing crime. Thirdly, it would succeed if the defendant could show that she honestly believed that she was acting with this purpose. It is submitted that the first possibility would be undesirable for three reasons: first, it could lead to serious injustice where a reporter had a reasonable suspicion which turned out later to be untrue; secondly it would offend against the principle of criminal law formulated in *DPP v Morgan*[101] that the defendant should be judged on the facts as she believed them to be, and thirdly, it could act as a serious deterrent to investigative journalism. The second possibility is an improvement, but it again falls foul of the Morgan principle; moreover there would be a risk that judges might demand quite a high standard of reasonable belief so that journalists would have to produce substantial evidence justifying their suspicions in order to make out the defence – a burden which would again exercise a deterrent effect. It is suggested that the third possibility is to be preferred; a journalist who honestly believes that she is acting in the public interest (within the terms of one of the defences) should not be criminalised. It may be feared that such a fully subjective test would always provide an escape from liability and thus render the offence useless. However, a journalist who merely asserted that she thought she was acting within the terms of one of the specific public interests, but was unable to adduce any grounds at all for her belief, would probably not be believed by the court. The other advantage of adopting this third possibility would be that it could come into play while the journalistic investigation was still at an inchoate stage so long as some evidence could be adduced supporting the necessary belief. On this basis the proposed offence would provide a remedy against some unjustifiable invasions of privacy but would be unlikely to deter serious journalism. However, the Lord Chancellor's consultation paper favoured narrowing the defences by omitting the words 'seriously anti-social conduct' from defence (a) and curtailing defences (b) and (c). If this occurred, the public lives of public figures such as ministers would be protected from scrutiny, an instance of curtailment of freedom of speech which would clearly prevent the full participation of the citizen in the democratic process. These issues will become significant if the Data Protection provisions regarding the unfair collection of information, to be introduced in 1998, cover the methods of information gathering considered here.

---

101 [1976] AC 182.

2 STATE SURVEILLANCE[102]

Introduction

Agents of the state may often invade privacy with the aim of promoting internal security or preventing and detecting crime. Such aims are clearly legitimate; the question is whether the safeguards against unreasonable or arbitrary intrusion are adequate. Such safeguards should include a clear remedy for the citizen who has been the subject of unauthorised surveillance or other intrusion, and strict control over the power to effect such intrusion or issue authorisation for it. The latter safeguard is particularly crucial since the citizen may not even be aware that intrusion is taking place. This is particularly true of telephone tapping and the use of surveillance devices. Moreover, general public awareness of the use of such devices is severely curtailed by the operation of the Official Secrets Act 1989, the Interception of Communications Act 1985 and the Security Services Act 1989.

State surveillance through the interception of communications has been a feature of state activity for centuries.[103] However, the methods of intercepting communications have become increasingly sophisticated. Telephonic interception has been possible for much of the 20th century, but bugging equipment has become much more sophisticated in the last 10 years, with the result that it is now very powerful, readily concealable and relatively cheap.[104] Use of such equipment is valuable both to the police and to the Security Services.[105] However, not only have legal developments failed to keep pace with technological ones, the principles which in a liberal democracy should inform the law governing the interception of communications have largely failed to find expression in it. The relevant regulatory law fails to go much further than simply reflecting an acceptance of the propriety of placing interception on a proper legal basis. The value of privacy finds little place in it.

Telephone and mail intercepts

Prior to 1985 there was no requirement to follow a particular legal procedure when authorising the tapping of telephones or the interception of mail. No special authorisation was needed to allow the tapping of telephones since so doing was neither a civil wrong[106] or a criminal offence. Interference with

---

102 For discussion see Leigh, 'The Security Service, the Press and the Courts' [1987] *PL* 12–21.
103 Foucault, *Discipline and Punishment*, 1977.
104 See Taylor, N and Walker, C, 'Bugs in the System' (1966) *J Civ Lib* Vol 1 105.
105 See Manwaring-White, S, *The Policing Revolution*, 1983; Report of the Commissioner for 1993, Cm 2522; *Security Services Work Against Organised Crime*, Cm 3065, 1996.
106 *Malone v MPC (No 2)* [1979] Ch 344.

mail was a criminal offence under s 58 of the Post Office Act 1953, but under s 58(1) such interference would not be criminal if authorised by a warrant issued by the Secretary of State. The conditions for issuing warrants for interception of postal or telephonic communications were laid down in administrative rules which had no legal force.[107] Under these rules, the interception could be authorised in order to assist in a criminal investigation, only if the crime was really serious, normal methods had been tried and had failed, and there was good reason for believing that the evidence gained by the interception would lead to a conviction. If the interception related to security matters it could be authorised only in respect of major subversion, terrorism or espionage and the matters obtained had to be directly useful to the security service in compiling information allowing it to carry out its function of protecting state security.

The use of telephone and mail intercepts is subject to certain controls arising partly under the Interception of Communications Act 1985, which was introduced partly as a direct result of the ruling in the European Court of Human Rights in *Malone v UK*[108] that the existing British warrant procedure violated the Article 8 guarantee of privacy. In 1979 Mr James Malone was on trial for receiving stolen goods. During his trial, evidence that his phone had been tapped was revealed in court when a police witness read extracts from his notebook of an intercept which had been authorised by the Home Secretary on Malone's phone. Malone sought a declaration in the High Court that it was unlawful for anyone to intercept another's telephone conversations without consent (*Malone v MPC (No 2)*).[109] This line of argument failed as did the argument, based on Article 8 of the European Convention, that there was a right to privacy which had been violated by the tapping. The judge, Sir Robert Megarry, concluded that the Convention did not give rise to any enforceable rights under English law and that therefore there was no direct right of privacy. However, he commented:

> I ... find it impossible to see how English law could be said to satisfy the requirements of the Convention ... This is not a subject on which it is possible to feel any pride in English law ... telephone tapping is a subject which cries out for legislation.[110]

Malone took his case to the European Commission on Human Rights arguing that Article 8 had been violated. Article 8(2) reads: 'There shall be no interference by a public authority with the exercise of this right *except such as is in accordance with the law*' (emphasis added). The court held that UK domestic law did not regulate the circumstances in which telephone tapping could be carried out sufficiently clearly or provide any remedy against abuse of the

---

107 See *Report of the Committee of Privy Councillors*, Cmnd 283, 1957.
108 (1985) 7 EHRR 14; for comment see (1986) 49 *MLR* 86.
109 [1979] Ch 344.
110 [1979] Ch 344 at p 380.

power. This meant that it did not meet the requirement of being 'in accordance with the law'. However, the decision only required the UK government to introduce legislation to regulate the circumstances in which the power to tap could be used, rather than giving guidance as to what would be acceptable limits on the individual's privacy. In *Klass v Federal Republic of Germany*[111] the European Court of Human Rights had found that the German telephone tapping procedures were in conformity with Article 8. They provided for compensation in proceedings in the ordinary courts for persons whose phones had been tapped, where appropriate; they were subject to the oversight of a Parliamentary board and the individual warrants had to be reviewed by a Commission headed by a person qualified for judicial office. The court did not, however, state that these were the minimal safeguards necessary.

Before the Interception of Communications Act came into force, CND brought a High Court action challenging the decision to tap the phones of certain of its members (*Secretary of State for Home Affairs, ex parte Ruddock*)[112] on the ground that the government had aroused a legitimate expectation through published statements that it would not use tapping for party political purposes. The action failed but did establish the principle that the courts were entitled to review unfair actions by government arising from the failure to live up to legitimate expectations created in this way. The judge, Mr Justice Taylor, also stated that the jurisdiction of the court to look into such a complaint against a minister should not be totally ousted. It had been argued on behalf of the Crown that the court should not entertain the action because to do so would be detrimental to national security. Mr Justice Taylor, however, ruled that such ousting of the courts' jurisdiction in a field where the citizen could have no right to be consulted would be a 'dangerous and draconian step indeed'. That decision was the last time such statements would be heard in court in respect of telephone tapping: s 7(8) of the 1985 Act then (probably) precluded the possibility of their repetition and brought about the very danger Mr Justice Taylor wanted to avert.

The response of the UK government to *Malone* in the Interception of Communications Act 1985 was to provide very wide grounds under s 2(2) on which warrants for the purposes of interception could be authorised by the Home Secretary. They include warrants necessary 'in the interests of national security'; 'for the purpose of preventing or detecting serious crime'; *or* 'for the purpose of safeguarding the economic well-being of the UK'. These seemed to be significantly wider than the old Home Office guidelines previously relied on in respect of the authorising of warrants. Under s 4(1) the warrants must be personally signed by the Home Secretary or in urgent cases by a Home Office

---

111 (1979) 2 EHRR 214. See above p 62.
112 [1987] 1 WLR 1482; [1987] 2 All ER 518.

official with express authorisation from the Home Secretary. Under s 4(5) and (6) the warrants are issued for an initial period of two months and may be renewed for one month in the case of the police and for six months in the case of the Security Services. However, there is no overall limit on renewals and some warrants are undoubtedly very long-standing. Under s 3 the warrants are supposed to be *precise*; they must specify a person and an address. However, it appears that 'a person' can equal an organisation. Once a warrant is obtained *all* communications to or from the property (or properties) specified *must* be intercepted; telephone tapping and mail interceptions are conducted by Post Office employees at the request of the police and security service members. At the end of 1989 315 warrants were in force and 522 were issued during the year.[113] By 1993 a clear upward trend in the numbers of warrants issued was evident: in 1993 1,005 warrants for telephone tapping and 115 for mail interceptions were issued; 409 warrants were in force at the end of the year.[114]

Under s 7 the Act establishes a tribunal to consider complaints from people who believe that their telephone may have been tapped or their mail intercepted. The tribunal has a duty to investigate whether a warrant has been issued and if so, whether it was properly issued – whether there were adequate grounds for issuing the warrant and whether statutory procedures were complied with. The tribunal can order quashing of the warrant and payment of compensation to the victim, but, in fact, none of the complaints to the tribunal have been upheld. In addition to the tribunal (which consists of five senior lawyers) there is a commissioner – a senior judge appointed by the Prime Minister on a part-time basis to assist the tribunal and generally monitor the warrant procedure. He has two specific duties: to notify the Prime Minister of any breach of the rules and to publish an annual report. The report must be presented to Parliament and published as a Command Paper. The Prime Minister may censor the report under s 8 of the Act if it appears to him that it contains matter 'prejudicial to national security, to the prevention and detection of serious crime or to the economic well-being of the UK'. In his annual reports the commissioner has found a few unauthorised taps which occurred as a result of clerical errors, but no instances in which a warrant was issued unjustifiably.

The tribunal has no power to deal with the problem of tapping without a warrant, in other words, unauthorised tapping. Section 1 of the 1985 Act deals with unauthorised interceptions and makes it a criminal offence to intentionally intercept a postal communication or telecommunication without authorisation. This applies to persons in the public or private sectors and would therefore catch, for example, newspaper reporters. Aspects of the

---

113 *Report of the Commissioner for 1989*, Cm 1063 p 2. Similar figures are available for other years; see reports for 1986 (Cm 108) and for 1987 (Cm 351).
114 See *Report of the Commissioner for 1993*, Cm 2522.

inadequacy of this monitoring system were illustrated in 1990 when Robin Cook complained about a tap which had been placed on the phone of one of his constituents.[115] His complaint, in essence, concerned the lack of information available to individuals who suspect that their phones have been tapped. His constituent, a telephone engineer, discovered that his phone had been tapped. As Robin Cook pointed out, it was inconceivable within the terms of the Act that a warrant authorising the tap could properly have been issued. However, it was impossible to discover whether the phone had been tapped without authorisation. As Robin Cook put it: '... the problem ... is that the police cannot investigate tapping if it was authorised and the tribunal cannot investigate it if it was not.'[116] He was informed by the Secretary of State that the police 'cannot ... investigate ... any interception which may have been authorised'. Had the tribunal investigated an unauthorised tap it would simply have found that no contravention of s 5(2) of the Act had occurred, since it has no jurisdiction to investigate unauthorised taps. Robin Cook thus raised the matter in Parliament but received only a general reply describing the function of the tribunal from Lord James Douglas-Hamilton who spoke on behalf of the government.

Further secrecy regarding interceptions is introduced by s 9 of the 1985 Act which provides that in tribunal or court proceedings no questions may be asked and no evidence adduced which suggests that an intercept warrant has been issued or that an unauthorised intercept has occurred. This appears to mean that if an intercept is used, whether unauthorised or not, the information gained will be inadmissible in evidence. However, in *Effick*[117] the defendants were prosecuted for conspiracy to supply controlled drugs and police officers obtained part of the evidence against them by means of intercepting and taping their telephone calls. The offence under s 1 had not been committed since the calls taped were made on a cordless telephone which was not found to be part of 'a public telecommunications system' as required under s 1. The appellants were convicted and appealed on the ground that the intercepted telephone calls should have been ruled inadmissible under s 9 of the Interception of Communications Act 1985, or under s 78 of the Police and Criminal Evidence Act 1984 (PACE) since they were made without a warrant for interception. It was determined that argument under s 9 failed because its provisions are aimed at preventing disclosure of information which tends to suggest that the offence of unauthorised interception (under s 1(1) of the 1985 Act) has been committed by specified persons, or that a warrant has been or is to be issued to such persons: they were not intended to render inadmissible all evidence obtained

---

115 24 May 1990, *HC Deb*, Vol 173 Cols 443–50.
116 24 May 1990, *HC Deb*, Vol 173 Col 449.
117 [1994] 3 WLR 583; (1994) 99 Cr App R 312, HL; (1992) 95 Cr App R 427, CA. For criticism of the Court of Appeal decision see Leigh (1992) 142 *NLJ* 944–45, 976–77; Smith [1992] *Crim LR* 580.

as a result of an interception. Clear statutory language would have been needed to oust the principle that all logically probative evidence should be admitted. As this was not the case, and as the instance in question did not appear to fall within s 9, the evidence was admissible. The submission in respect of s 78 of PACE failed because it was not suggested that the police officers had deliberately contravened the 1985 Act. It was found that no unfairness to the defendants had occurred due to the admission of the evidence, but this begs the question whether the very fact that the evidence was obtained by means of a criminal act could lead to unfairness at the trial.[118] The view taken of s 9 of the 1985 Act was rejected by the House of Lords in *Preston*[119] in a decision which accepted somewhat reluctantly that the Act created a scheme designed to elevate the interests of secrecy above individual rights to privacy or to a fair trial. It was found that since on the proper interpretation of s 2(2) read in conjunction with s 6(3) destruction of material gained by the intercepts must be undertaken once the criminal investigation (not the prosecution) is complete, such material would not be admissible in any event; s 9 could therefore relate only to the manner of authorising the intercept or to the source of information behind the decision to use an intercept.

The result of this decision is that although telephone tapping may be used as an investigative tool in the criminal process, evidence deriving directly from an intercept will not be admissible and the defence will not be allowed to ask any questions designed to discover whether an intercept was used. Thus, the prosecution may sometimes be disadvantaged since some probative evidence will not be admissible, but the other side of the coin is that material deriving from the intercept cannot be disclosed to the defence even if (as the defence alleged in *Preston*) it might show the innocence of the defendant. One exception, favourable to the prosecution, to the rule deriving from s 9, as interpreted in *Preston*, was allowed in *Rasool* and *Choudhary*.[120] It was determined that where intercepts record consensual evidence it will be admissible. The rule in s 9(1)(a) was not found to be sufficient to make consensual material inadmissible; it was found to be irrelevant to the question of admissibility that an offence had been committed in obtaining the evidence. Choudhary's appeal was dismissed while Rasool's was allowed on that ground.

The checks on the arbitrary use of executive power provided by this scheme are clearly very meagre. There is no judicial scrutiny of the warrant procedure prior to authorisation of the intercept at any stage and only very limited judicial and Parliamentary scrutiny after the event. The tribunal does not have to give any reasons for its decisions and they cannot be questioned in

---

118 See further Chap 11 pp 495–98.
119 [1993] 4 All ER 638; (1994) 98 Cr App R 405, HL. For discussion see Tomkin (1994) 57 *MLR* 941.
120 (1997) *The Times*, 17 February.

court. Tribunal decisions on individual cases are not published and, although the commissioner's annual report giving some information on the number of intercept warrants issued must be made available, it may, as noted above, be censored by the Prime Minister before publication. Further, since the tribunal does not deal with unauthorised intercepts the police are expected to investigate themselves in this respect. The result may be that use of such intercepts will remain unchecked. The absence or inadequacy of the controls under the 1985 Act has attracted a great deal of criticism,[121] although they may be in conformity with Article 8; the European Commission on Human Rights has found that the 1985 Act complies with the Convention.[122] In *Halford v UK*,[123] which concerned the tapping of the applicant's private telephone conversation by the police at a time when she was bringing a claim of sex discrimination against the police authority in question, the court found a breach of Article 8. The government's argument that in using the private system the applicant could not expect to retain her privacy was rejected. *Halford v UK* may lead to an amendment to the 1985 Act so that it applies to private telephone systems. Although this judgment is to be welcomed, it is suggested that extension of the ambit of the Act is of little value until its defects are addressed. At present, commentators tend to agree that the intervention of the court in *Malone v UK* has led to no substantive improvement in the protection for individual privacy.[124]

Bugging devices

Surveillance techniques offer an important weapon to the police and security services in the maintenance of law and order and the protection of national security. However, the Supreme Court of Canada has said of them: '... one can scarcely imagine a state activity more dangerous to individual privacy than electronic surveillance.'[125] This was also the view of the Younger Committee which listed the range of devices then in use.[126] Nevertheless, despite the development of such devices and the increased use of them by the police and the security services, they have continued to operate outside the control of the courts. Their use by the police was until recently authorised only under administrative guidelines[127] and therefore violated the principle from *Entinck*

---

121 See Lloyd (1986) 49 *MLR* 86; Leigh [1986] *PL* 8; Fitzgerald and Leopold, *The Secret History of Phone Tapping*, 1987.
122 *Christie v UK* (1994) 78A DRECom HR 119.
123 App No 20605/92, Judgment of the Court: [1997] IRLR 471; (1997) *The Times*, 3 July.
124 See Robertson, *Freedom the Individual and the Law*, 1993, p 139.
125 *Duarte* (1990) 65 DLR (4th) 240.
126 *Report of the Committee on Privacy*, Cmnd 5012, 1972.
127 *Guidelines on the Use of Equipment in Police Surveillance Operations*, House of Commons Library, 19 December 1984.

v Carrington[128] that executive power may not be exercised save where there is a legal basis for it. Following *Malone v UK*, the guidelines almost certainly did not fulfil the 'prescribed by law' requirement under Article 8. Their position therefore mirrored that of telephone tapping and mail intercepts before 1985. Under the guidelines, the use of the bugging device could be authorised (by the Chief Constable) in order to assist in a criminal investigation, if the following conditions were satisfied: the crime was really serious, normal methods had been tried and had failed, and there was good reason for believing that the use of such equipment would lead to a conviction. Also the authorising officer had to weigh the seriousness of the offence against the degree of intrusion necessary. Thus, the guidelines gave some weight, at least in theory, to the value of individual privacy. However, they failed to provide the element of independent scrutiny or supervision which should be available, especially when criminal investigations as opposed to investigations relating to national security, are in question.

The use of surveillance devices by the police has been in question in a number of cases which have recently come before the courts,[129] of which the most significant was *Khan (Sultan)*.[130] A bugging device had been secretly installed on the outside of a house which Khan was visiting. Khan was suspected of involvement in the importation of prohibited drugs, and the tape-recording obtained from the listening device clearly showed that he was so involved. The case against him rested mainly on the tape-recording. The defence argued, *inter alia*, that the recording was inadmissible as evidence because the police had no statutory authority to place listening devices on private property and that therefore such placement was a trespass, and, further, that admission of the recording would breach Article 8 of the European Convention on Human Rights. It was accepted in the Court of Appeal that trespass to the building had occurred as well as some damage to it and that there had been an invasion of privacy. However, the Court of Appeal found,[131] supporting the trial judge, that these factors were of slight significance and therefore were readily outweighed by the fact that the police had largely complied with the Home Office guidelines and that the offences involved were serious. The court found that since the Convention was not part of UK law it was of only persuasive assistance. The House of Lords upheld the Court of Appeal; the Lords relied on the decision in *Sang*[132] to the effect that improperly obtained evidence other than 'involuntary' confessions is admissible in a criminal trial. The House of Lords found that the *Sang* principle should be followed despite the fact that no statutory regime

---

128 (1765) 19 St Tr 1030.
129 *Chief Constable of West Yorkshire Police, ex parte Govell* (1994) LEXIS transcript.
130 [1996] 3 All ER 289; (1996) 146 *NLJ* 1024, HL; [1995] QB 27, CA.
131 *Khan* [1995] QB 27, CA.
132 [1980] AC 402; [1979] 2 All ER 1222, HL.

governing the use of bugging devices was in place, and that had the evidence been obtained by phone tapping it could not have been admitted under s 9 of the 1985 Act.

This decision clearly does not mean that even where there is no statutory authority allowing them to do so the police have a right to commit forms of trespass, including entering property without the consent of the owner. In such instances, as in the instant case, a civil action for trespass would arise. (No action for breach of privacy would arise in circumstances similar to those in the instant case since there is no such tort, although an action for breach of confidence might possibly arise.[133] Such an action would, however, almost certainly fail due to the operation of the public interest defence.) Thus this decision does not in itself violate the principle from *Entinck v Carrington*.[134] Nevertheless, it obviously offers some encouragement to the police to continue to breach the law of trespass when it appears to them to be expedient to do so. No caveat was entered in the Lords to the effect that a very clear and serious breach of the civil law would or might render evidence thereby obtained inadmissible. The decision confirms that, apart from admissions falling within s 76 of PACE (which has partly replaced the common law concept of involuntariness), improperly obtained evidence is admissible in criminal trials subject to a discretion under s 78 to exclude it. The House of Lords recommended legislation, taking into account the fact that the regime governing the use of bugging devices was not on a statutory basis and therefore might not comply with the 'prescribed by law' requirement under the Convention.

The Police Bill 1997 was put forward by Michael Howard, the then Home Secretary, early in 1997. The intention was to afford the police statutory authority to interfere with property and to plant bugs. The Police Act 1997 places current practice under the Home Office guidelines on a statutory basis. It is largely modelled on the Interception of Communications Act and therefore contains similar objectionable features. The basis for allowing the use of bugging is very broad. An authorisation may be issued if the action is expected to be of substantial value in the prevention and detection of serious crime and the objective cannot reasonably be achieved by other means (s 93(2)). Serious crime is defined to include crimes of violence, those involving financial gain and those involving a large number of people in pursuit of a common purpose; or the crime is one for which a person of 21 or over with no previous convictions could reasonably be expected to receive a prison sentence of three or more years. These definitions appear to be significantly wider than those under the old guidelines. The last possibility could allow bugging to be used against, for example, members of CND or anti-road protesters, if it was expected, *inter alia*, that their activities might

---

133 See *Hellewell* [1995] 1 WLR 804.
134 (1765) 19 St Tr 1030.

infringe ss 70 or 68 of the Criminal Justice and Public Order Act 1994.[135] Various groups and bodies put forward pleas for exemption from the provisions of the Bill. These included Catholic priests who were afraid that the confessional would be bugged, doctors and solicitors. No exemptions were, however, included. This means, for example, that once a solicitor's office has been bugged all conversations between solicitors and clients would be recorded.

As initially drafted, the Bill made no provision for any prior independent scrutiny of the bugging warrants at all. The warrants were to be issued by the Chief Constable of the force in question. Michael Howard considered that exclusion of an independent authorising body was necessary since the police must be able to react instantly to prevent crime. This proposal was severely criticised on civil libertarian grounds by Liberty and by some sections of the press, including sections of the tabloid press. It was argued that other countries accept prior judicial authorisation for bugging warrants and the UK accepts judicial involvement in other aspects of the policing process such as the authorisation of search warrants. In response to such representations Labour put forward a proposal that an information commissioner appointed from the judiciary should be involved in checking the warrants, while the Liberal Democrats proposed that a judge acting in his or her capacity as a judge should undertake this role. The House of Lords accepted both amendments and Michael Howard then reached an agreement with Jack Straw, then the Shadow Home Secretary, that an information commissioner appointed from the judiciary should be involved in checking warrants if certain categories of crime were in question.

Under s 93(5) the authorisation may be issued by the Chief Officer of Police or, if that is not practicable, by an officer of the rank of assistant Chief Constable of the force in question (s 94). The authorisation will be given in writing, except in cases of emergency when it may be given orally by the Chief Officer in person (s 95(1)). A written authorisation will last for three months, an oral one for 72 hours. Both forms may be renewed in writing for a further three months. The commissioners appointed under s 91(1) must be notified of authorisations as soon as they are made (s 96) but this does not prevent the police acting on the authorisation. If the commissioner subsequently quashes the authorisation, destruction of the records of information obtained from the search may be ordered unless they are required for pending criminal or civil proceedings. Since the records may often be so required, the intervention of the commissioner may have little impact. In certain circumstances commissioners must give prior approval to the authorisation (s 97). Such approval is needed where the specified property is believed to be a dwelling, a bedroom in a hotel or office premises. It is also needed where the authorising officer believes that the action authorised is

---

135 See above pp 296–98 and 313–15.

likely to result in any person acquiring knowledge of confidential personal information, confidential journalistic material or matters subject to legal privilege.

The involvement of special commissioners, even such a limited involvement, may provide a degree of independent oversight and scrutiny although it is important not to over-estimate the value of judicial authorisation; the commissioners will probably tend to accept and agree with police representations. Nevertheless, apart from other considerations, the involvement of commissioners will mean that internal procedures may be tightened up before representations are made. No provision is made under the Act for independent review of the authorisation of bugging in the ordinary courts. Nevertheless, under the Labour amendment scrutiny of police bugging practices will be more effective than scrutiny of security service bugging, not weaker, as Howard originally proposed. Clearly, this is a more satisfactory situation since the arguments for excluding the judiciary from the process are weaker when matters pertaining to national security are not in question.

The use of technical surveillance devices by the Security Services is governed by the Security Services Act 1989. The perception that some control on the security services was needed arose partly due to the fear aroused by the *Spycatcher* case[136] that the Security Services were insufficiently accountable and should be subject to controls in respect of their intrusions on private individuals, but was probably also influenced by the challenge to the legality of the tapping of the phones of CND members already mentioned in *Secretary of State for Home Affairs, ex parte Ruddock* which proved embarrassing to the government although it failed. However, introduction of the 1989 Act was finally forced upon the government as a response to the finding of the European Commission of Human Rights that a complaint against MI5 was admissible (*Harman and Hewitt v UK*).[137] The case was brought by two former NCCL officers, Patricia Hewitt and Harriet Harman, who were complaining of their classification as 'subversive' by MI5 which had placed them under surveillance. Part of their complaint concerned a breach of Article 13 of the European Convention on Human Rights on the basis that no effective remedy for complainants existed. In response the Security Services Act 1989 placed MI5 on a statutory basis but prevented almost all effective scrutiny of its operation.

If a member of the public has a grievance concerning the operation of MI5, complaint to a court is not possible. Under s 5 it can only be made to a tribunal and under s 5(4) the decisions of the tribunal are not questionable in any court of law. The volume of complaint will be inherently limited: citizens may often

---

136 *AG v Guardian Newspaper* [1987] 1 WLR 1248
137 Appl 121175/86; (1989) 14 EHRR 657.

be unaware that surveillance is taking place, while service personnel who feel that they have been required to act improperly in bugging or searching a person's property are not permitted to complain to the tribunal. Furthermore, the Act provides for no real form of Parliamentary oversight of the Security Service.[138] The provision of s 5(4) was criticised in 1992 by Mr Justice Kennedy in refusing an application for review of the Security Services tribunal's decision not to investigate allegations that MI5 is still holding files on Harriet Harman, the then Shadow Health Minister;[139] he considered that in some circumstances the courts certainly would have jurisdiction to intervene.

Given the width of the powers conferred on members of the Security Services under this legislation this lack of accountability is disturbing. Any private individual can have surveillance devices placed on his or her premises or can be subject to a search of the premises even though engaged in lawful political activity which is not intended to serve any foreign interest. An amendment to the Security Services Bill was put forward which would have exempted such a person from the operation of the legislation, but it was rejected by the government. If Security Services members wish to enter property the Home Secretary can issue a warrant authorising the 'taking of any such action as is specified in the warrant in respect of any property so specified'. In other words, members of MI5 can interfere in any way with property so long as it appears that they are doing so in order to discharge any of their functions. These functions are set out in s 1 of the Act and include 'the protection of national security and, in particular, its protection from ... actions intended to overthrow or undermine Parliamentary democracy by political, industrial or violent means'. It is apparent that such wording covers a very wide range of circumstances. The ease with which warrants may be obtained, and the concomitant disregard for individual privacy may be contrasted with the position in Canada regarding the powers of the Canadian Security Intelligence Service, which can only be granted warrants on the authorisation of a judge, thus ensuring a measure of independent oversight. Moreover, the warrant will not be issued unless the facts relied on to justify the belief that a warrant is necessary to investigate a threat to national security are set out in a sworn statement. Clearly, the Canadian system places greater emphasis on the privacy of the citizen and therefore appears to strike a fairer balance between privacy on the one hand and the security of the state on the other.

As mentioned in Chapter 6 these provisions will work in tandem with the s 1 of the Official Secrets Act 1989 which prevents members or former members of the Security Services disclosing anything at all about the operation of those services. All such members come under a lifelong duty to

---

138 See further Leigh, I and Lustgarten, L, 'The Security Services Act 1989' (1989) *MLR* 801.
139 *Security Services Tribunal, ex parte Hewitt* (1992) unreported; see (1992) *Guardian*, 15 February.

keep silent even though their information might reveal a serious abuse of power by the Security Services.[140] These provisions also apply to anyone who is notified that he or she is subject to the provisions of the section. Similarly, s 4(3) of the Act prohibits disclosure of information obtained by, or relating to, the issue of a warrant under the Interception of Communications Act 1985 or the Security Services Act 1989.

This Act provided a model for the Intelligence Services Act 1994 which placed MI6 and GCHQ on a statutory basis. Under s 5 it provides that a warrant will be issued by a minister if the action it covers 'would be of substantial value in assisting the Services to carry out their functions'. The 1994 Act set up, under s 10, a Parliamentary Committee, the Intelligence and Security Committee, to oversee the administration and policy of MI5, MI6 and GCHQ. However, since the Committee is not a Select Committee, its powers are limited. Therefore, although this was a welcome move, the oversight provided may have, in practice, little impact on the work of the Security Services.

The Security Services Act 1989 and the Intelligence Services Act 1994 were amended by ss 1 and 2 of the Security Services Act 1996 respectively. Section 1 adds to the two existing functions of the Security Services a third function – to act in support of the prevention and detection of serious crime. Section 2 enables the Secretary of State to issue warrants to the Security Service entitling it to interfere with or enter property or interfere with wireless telegraphy in the UK if the action relates to conduct within new s 3B. Section 3B applies if the conduct appears to constitute one or more offences and either involves the use of violence, results in substantial gain or is conduct by a large number of persons in pursuit of a common purpose or is an offence for which a person of 21 or over with no previous convictions could be expected to receive a sentence of imprisonment of three years or more.

This Act allows a barely accountable service to exercise wide powers of interference with individual privacy on the basis of executive authorisation alone. It therefore reverses the fundamental principle established in *Entinck v Carrington*[141] that interference with private property must be authorised by law. The purpose of the legislation was to allow the Security Services to aid the police in preventing and detecting serious crime, by which the government stated that it meant organised crime. However, the terms of the Act do not limit its application to serious or organised crime. It could be used, for example, against persons engaging in public protest who might well (given the breadth and vagueness of some public order law), commit an offence, such as obstruction of the highway, and who can be said to be acting in pursuit of a common purpose. The statute is very short; it creates a bare

---

140 See Chap 6 p 237.
141 (1765) 19 St Tr 1030.

bones scheme which leaves the detail to be filled in by administrative action, without any provision for Parliamentary or judicial scrutiny. In criticising the Act, Peter Duffy and Murray Hunt of the legal department of Liberty have argued that it breaches Article 8 of the European Convention on Human Rights[142] since it probably does not pass the Convention requirement that an interference with private life should comply with rule of law principles. Executive discretion is so unfettered under the Act that any interference may not be 'in accordance with the law' as interpreted in *Huvig v France*[143] and *Kruslin v France*.[144]

The wide grounds on which intrusion may be authorised, the secrecy surrounding the issuing of intercept and burgling warrants and the lack of an effective complaints procedure suggest that the balance has tipped too far away from concern for the privacy of the individual. It does not appear that the Security Services Act 1989, the Interception of Communications Act 1985, the Intelligence Services Act 1994, or the Police Act 1997 will open up the workings of internal security to greater scrutiny. In particular, the ousting of the jurisdiction of the courts under s 7 of the Interception of Communications Act 1985 and s 5 of the Security Services Act 1989 requires review given the doubts expressed by many commentators as to the ability of the tribunals in question to ensure fairness to complainants. The nature of these statutes reflects a perception that no breach of the Convention will occur so long as a mechanism is in place which is able to consider the claims of aggrieved citizens, however ineffective that mechanism might be.[145]

3   ACCESS TO PERSONAL INFORMATION

Introduction

In the UK there is no statute equivalent to the USA Privacy Act 1974 which enables persons to obtain access to information held on them in government files. In the UK certain categories of information covered by the Official Secrets Act 1989 cannot be disclosed but if personal information falls outside those categories there is no general right of access to it. The government holds a vast amount of personal information in files controlled by bodies including the DSS and NHS. The police use a national computer which stores an immense amount of personal information, as does the Inland Revenue. Until

---

142 See (1997) 1 EHRR 11.

143 (1990) 12 EHRR 547.

144 (1990) 12 EHRR 528.

145 The European Court of Human Rights has not yet ruled on the compatibility of the 1989 Act with Article 8. As considered above, the 1989 Act might be challenged under Article 8 in conjunction with Article 13 on the ground that the procedures available for the seeking of redress are ineffective.

recently the citizen had no means of knowing what information was held on him or her, and no control over the nature or use of such information. However, an inroad into the principle of secrecy was made in 1984 by the Data Protection Act[146] which was adopted in response to a European Community directive. Once access to certain computerised files became possible, access rights to some manual files began to follow, although no general statutory right of access to personal information was created, and therefore much personal information still remains inaccessible. Such a right was proposed in the 1993 White Paper on freedom of information and open government,[147] but at present the measures to be discussed below must be seen as exceptions to the general denial of access.

Information held on computer[148]

In response to the steady computerisation of information, the government decided in 1975 that those who use computers to handle personal information cannot remain the sole judges of the extent to which their own systems adequately safeguard privacy. The Committee on Data Protection was therefore set up, but the final impetus came from the Council of Europe which promulgated the Convention on Data Protection in 1981.[149] In response the Data Protection Act 1984 applying to personal information in both the public and private sectors was passed.[150] It was seen as a measure to protect privacy and a first step towards freedom of information. However, it must be questioned whether it was clear that there was a pressing need to allow access to electronically held information as opposed to a need for access to all personal information.

It may be argued that the electronic storage of information presents a particular threat to privacy because computers exacerbate problems which also exist with respect to manual files. For example, an error may creep into information held on manual files, but where information is collated from a

---

146 The provisions of the 1984 Act were extended by the Data Protection (Subject Access Modifications) Health Order SI 1987/1903.

147 Cm 2290. For further discussion of the Code of Practice on Access to government Information which was introduced in 1994 as promised in the White Paper, see pp 265–72, above. Access might be afforded to personal information falling within the categories covered by the Code, but the Code is not designed to deal with personal information, which is to be dealt with in a separate statute under the White Paper proposals.

148 General reading: see Lloyd, *Information Technology and the Law*, 2nd edn, 1997; Reed, C, ed, *Computer Law*, 1990, Chap 9; Sieghart, P, *Privacy and Computers*, 1977; Tapper, C, *Computer Law*, 4th edn, 1989; Hewitt, P, ed, *Computers, Records and the Right to Privacy*, 1979; Wacks, *Personal Information*, Chap 6.

149 Convention for the Protection of Individuals with regard to the Automatic Processing of Personal Data, 17 September 1980.

150 For commentary see 'Confidential: Computers, Records and the Right to Privacy' (NCCL); Savage, N and Edwards, C, *A Guide to the Data Protection Act*, 1985.

large number of sources, as may be more likely in respect of computerised files, an error may be more likely to occur. Moreover, once it does occur the speed with which information can be retrieved and disseminated means that an error can reach far more persons and may do more damage than a record on a manual file. It is possible to transmit data from one data bank to another much more easily than can be done using manual files. Personal information gathered for a purpose acceptable to its subject may be transferred to another data bank without the subject's knowledge or consent. It may also be linked up with other information, thus creating what may be a distorted picture.

There is a danger that the confidentiality of information may be placed at risk. Information may be given to an employer by an employee on the understanding that because there is a confidential relationship between the parties it will go no further. If it is then stored in a data bank there is a danger that the confidentiality will be lost. An action for breach of confidence could lie but the individual affected would have to be aware of the breach. The retention of data may also create disadvantages. Although a person's circumstances or behaviour may change, old data may not be up-dated but may follow him or her around with the result that (for example) he or she is refused credit. Manually held information is less likely to follow an individual so effectively.

It may therefore be said that no difference in principle between problems associated with the storage of manually held and computerised information can be discerned, but that there is a difference of degree. The 1984 Act attempts to address these problems by placing certain obligations on persons storing personal data. Any person using a computerised system in order to store data relating to people is designated the 'data user', while the person who is the subject of the data is the 'data subject'. Any data relating to a living person is termed 'personal data'.[151] The data user must register with the Data Protection Registrar. Under s 5 the data user must not use the data for any purpose other than the one it was collected for and under Schedule 1 it must be kept up-to-date. Also it must be adequately protected; appropriate security measures must be taken. Under ss 10 and 11 if the Data Registrar is satisfied that the data user is not complying with the Act he can serve an enforcement notice, and if this measure is not adequate he can serve a de-registration notice. It is a criminal offence for an unregistered person or body to store personal data.

Section 21 provides that if the data user is asked by the data subject whether personal data is held on her or him, that information must be given and the data subject must be allowed access to such data. Schedule 1 also provides that if the data is found to be inaccurate, the data subject can have it

---

151 These definitions are found in ss 4 and 5 of the Act.

corrected or erased. If the data user does not comply the subject can apply to court under s 24 for an order erasing or rectifying the data. Under s 22 compensation can be awarded if loss or damage has resulted from inaccurate data. However, compensation is available only if the data user compiled the inaccurate information, not if the data user compiled inaccurate material supplied by a malicious or careless third party. No compensation is available for circulating the inaccurate data; nor may the data subject know the third party's name.

Certain aspects of the Act have attracted criticism, especially the wide subject access exemptions which include information relating to crime, national security, and a person's physical or mental health. A broad interpretation tends to be given to these exemptions; thus the difficulties mentioned earlier may still operate in those categories. Moreover, there is still the possibility of transferring data to manual files and as provisions relating to manual files are narrow in scope, especially those under the Access to Personal Files Act 1987, it may well be that the manual file will not fall within any provisions affording access. The transfer of data from a registered data user such as the Department of Employment to an unregistered user such as the Security Services will remain secret, and national security is exempt from the principle that data users cannot allow data to be used for a purpose other than the original one.

Further, the budgetary restraint on the Data Protection Registry makes it impossible to keep a check on all data users. In any event it is considered relatively straightforward to devise an information retrieval system which only provides an incomplete copy of an individual's record; it is probable that no action for breach of the Act would follow due to the inability of the Data Registrar Officer to check up. It would take a specialist a long time to work out what had happened, and given the constraints on the Data Registrar that time is unlikely to be available. Thus it may be said that the Act is certainly a step in the direction of control over personal information but it does contain many loop-holes.

Unauthorised access to information electronically held falls within the Computer Misuse Act 1990[152] which criminalises such conduct whether or not the 'hacker' has a sinister purpose. It may be wondered why it should be an offence to access files held on an office computer, but not files held in the filing cabinet. One answer is that hacking seems to present a more widespread and pernicious danger: it is possible to access the files from a different part of the country – there is no need for the would-be hacker to break into the office as in the case of the unauthorised seeker of information in manual files. Thus the possibility that persons may gain unauthorised access to personal

---

152 For comment see 'The Computer Misuse Act 1990' (1990) *NLJ* 1117.

information should now be diminished. Together, the 1984 and 1990 Acts form a code which provides relatively comprehensive protection for privacy in relation to computerised files when compared with that available in respect of manually held files.

Manually held files

In the wake of the 1984 Act access rights to manual files were gradually extended under the influence of the Campaign for Freedom of Information, although without government support. The Access to Personal Files Bill was put forward as a Private Members' Bill and would have allowed access to a wide range of personal information. However, the government forced its proponents to accept an eviscerated Bill covering only housing and social security files. Thus, the Bill was restricted to local government because central government was resistant to any measure allowing individuals access to personal files. The Bill became the Access to Personal Files Act 1987. It allowed access to 'accessible information' and therefore provided for the rectification of errors. However, it was acknowledged in the passage of the Bill that there was nothing to prevent the keeping of a secret file behind the accessible file. Moreover, the Act does not have retrospective effect; thus it does not apply to information collected before it came into effect.

The findings of the European Court of Human Rights in the *Gaskin* case[153] illustrated the inadequacy of the available measures. Graham Gaskin wanted to gain access to the personal files on his childhood in care kept by Liverpool City Council because he wanted to sue the Council in negligence. However, the files did not fall under the Data Protection Act as they were manually held; nor did they fall within the Access to Personal Files Act 1987 because they were collected before it came into force. Thus Gaskin wished to invoke Article 8 which protects the right to privacy, and also Article 10. The first question to be determined under Article 8 was whether it could apply to such a situation since it was considered that the essential object of Article 8 is to protect the individual from arbitrary interference by the authorities. However, the court found that there could also be a positive obligation on the authorities to act in certain situations. Here the information consisted of the only coherent record of the whole of Gaskin's early childhood. It was therefore found that *prima facie* an obligation to protect privacy arose because individuals should not be obstructed by the authorities from obtaining information so closely bound up with their identity as human beings. Thus a positive obligation could arise although Article 8 would not normally import such an obligation.

---

153 *Gaskin v UK* (1990) 12 EHRR 36.

The court then considered whether the exception under Article 8(2) in respect of the rights of others could apply. On the one hand there was the need to demonstrate respect for Gaskin's privacy; on the other the contributors of the information wanted it kept confidential. It was found that the two interests should be weighed against each other by invoking the principle of proportionality. However, the local authority had not put in place any means of independently weighing the two values; thus the preference would automatically be given to the interest in maintaining confidence. Therefore the principle of proportionality was offended and a breach of Article 8 was found. Gaskin was awarded damages on the basis of the distress he had suffered. No breach of Article 10 was found. It was determined that the right to receive information protected by Article 10 meant that the government should not interfere if a willing speaker wished to impart information, but that there was no positive obligation on the government to impart it.

The government complied with this ruling by introducing the Access to Personal Files (Social Services) Regulations 1989[154] which provides that social services departments must give personal information to individuals unless the contributor of the information can be identified and he or she does not consent to the access. Certain personal health information is also exempted. Thus local authorities will now have to weigh against each other the two values considered by the Court of Human Rights. One further possible result of the *Gaskin* case may be that test cases will be encouraged in relation to *central* government files although this may become unnecessary under the new data protection measures to be introduced in 1998 (see below).

A method of obtaining access to medical information relating to oneself arises under the Medical Reports Act 1988 which also started life as a Private Members' Bill. It provides for limited circumstances in which a person can obtain access to personal medical information: if an insurance company or prospective insurer asks for a medical report for employment purposes the individual in question can see it beforehand to read it and check it for errors. An example was given in Parliamentary debate on the Bill of a woman who had had mistakenly included in her medical record a sheet from another record indicating that she was dying of cancer. She was refused insurance and would never have been able to obtain insurance since she had no chance of putting the mistake right. Similarly a mis-diagnosis might remain on a medical record and never be corrected. These possibilities are of particular significance because a medical record contains information on a person's sexual habits and family circumstances; it does not merely contain purely medical information.

The Act however creates only a limited right of access; it does not mean that a person has a general right of access to all his or her medical files. Some

---

[154] SI 1989/206.

members of the medical profession argue, paternalistically, that patients who do not have medical knowledge will not be able to place medical notes in their context, and moreover that knowing of certain conditions may exacerbate their illness as they may worry and therefore come under greater stress. Some doctors also consider that a general right of access might increase the likelihood of a negligence action; clearly such an action might fail but they do not welcome the waste of time and energy which fighting an action, even successfully, would entail. The darker side to this argument is of course, that lack of access rights might preclude a legitimate negligence action: in some instances a patient might never realise that a mistake had been made.

The Access to Health Record Act 1990, which came into force on 1 November 1991, took the principle of access in this area much further.[155] Since the introduction of the Data Protection Act 1984, patients had been entitled to have access to their computerised health records but the 1990 Act was intended to provide an equivalent right of access to information recorded in manually held health records. Access to health records will allow people to examine exactly what has been recorded about them – thus satisfying personal curiosity – but, more importantly, it will allow for mistakes to be noted and rectified. The emphasis of the Act is on an individual's *control* of personal and private information. However, several exceptions curb the actual scope of the access. First, as in the Access to Personal Files Act, no pre-commencement material must be shown, unless it is necessary for a full understanding of something which has been shown. It is clear that no right of access to pre-commencement material arises at common law.[156] Secondly, if the holder of the information – the doctor – considers that disclosure of information would result in serious physical or mental harm to the patient, access can be denied. Thirdly, patients need not be told when information is being withheld. Although the 1990 Act is a move in the direction of enabling individuals to enjoy a degree of control over personal medical information and should ensure higher standards of accuracy and objectivity on the part of doctors and other record holders, it remains the case that patients whose documents are held as computerised records enjoy greater legal protection.

In general the anomalous situation whereby an individual has greater access to and control over his or her personal information held in computerised as opposed to manual files may change once the Data Protection Act 1998 is introduced. The Bill, promised in the Queen's Speech following the 1997 General Election, will extend the individual's right of access to personal files held on him or her by government agencies, including central government bodies, health authorities and private institutions such as building societies. Certain government bodies will, however, be exempted from the new provisions, including the police and the Security Services.

---

155 See 'Access to Health Records' (1990) 140 *NLJ* 1382.
156 *Mid-Glamorgan Family Health Services and Another, ex parte Martin* (1993) *The Times*, 2 June.

CHAPTER NINE

RESPECT FOR THE HOME: FREEDOM FROM ARBITRARY ENTRIES, SEARCHES AND SEIZURES

1 INTRODUCTION

Under Article 8 of the European Convention on Human Rights the right to respect for the home includes, as a central aspect, freedom from intrusion by the authorities of the state unless intrusion can be justified under the Article 8(2) exceptions as in the public interest. The police have rights of entry to the home under UK law which would in most instances be viewed as justified under Article 8(2) as being for the prevention of disorder or crime. Private persons, including reporters, might wish to intrude on the home and a duty may be placed on the state to prevent or regulate such intrusion under Article 8, either as an aspect of private life or to protect the home.[1]

Legal remedies

Under UK law, remedies for intrusion on property are found in the torts of trespass and nuisance. Trespass is defined as entering on to land in the possession of another without lawful justification. It is confined to instances in which there is some physical entry; prying with binoculars is not covered and obviously nor is electronic eavesdropping. The limitations of the law have been determined in certain decisions. In *Hickman v Maisey*[2] the defendant, who was on the highway, was watching the plaintiff's land. It was found that the plaintiff owned the land under the highway and that the defendant was entitled to make ordinary and reasonable use of it. Such watching was held not to be reasonable; the defendant had gone outside the accepted use and therefore had trespassed. Thus it was made clear that intention in such instances is all important but that unless behaviour could be linked to some kind of physical presence on land trespass would not provide a remedy. This decision can be contrasted with that in *Bernstein v Skyviews & General Ltd*[3] in order to determine the limits of trespass. The defendants flew over the plaintiff's land in an aircraft in order to take photographs of it and the question arose whether the plaintiff had a right in trespass to prevent such intrusion. It was held that either he had no rights of ownership over the air space to that height or, alternatively, if he did have such rights, s 40 of the

---

1 See *Arrondelle v UK*, 26 D and R 5 (1982), *McLeod v UK* (1998), unreported.
2 [1900] 1 QB 752, CA.
3 [1978] QB 479; [1977] 2 All ER 902.

Civil Aviation Act 1942 exempted reasonable flights from liability. The court was not prepared to find that the taking of one photograph was unreasonable and a remedy could not be based solely on invasion of privacy as of course there is no such tort. The distinction between this decision and *Hickman* arises partly because the plaintiff could not show that he had an interest in what was violated – the air space – and so he fell outside the ambit of trespass.

How far can the tort of nuisance provide a means of protecting privacy? Liability for nuisance will arise if a person is disturbed in the enjoyment of his or her land to an extent that the law regards as unreasonable. There is a dearth of authority on the issue of straight-forward surveillance but in an Australian case, *Victoria Park Racing Company v Taylor*,[4] where a platform was erected in order to gain a view of a racecourse which diminished the value of the plaintiff's business, no remedy in nuisance was available. The activity was held not to affect the use and enjoyment of the land but *dicta* in the case suggested that there would in general be no remedy in nuisance for looking over another's premises.

However, *dicta* in *Bernstein* favoured the possibility that grossly invasive embarrassing surveillance would amount to a nuisance and that possibility was followed up (though not explicitly) in somewhat different circumstances in *Khorasandijan v Bush*.[5] An injunction was granted against the defendant restraining him from using violence to or harassing, pestering or communicating with the plaintiff, the child of the owner of the property in question. The defendant argued that apart from the restraint as to violence the judge had had no jurisdiction to grant the injunction as the other words used did not reflect any tort known to the law. The Court of Appeal noted the decision of the Alberta Supreme Court in *Motherwell v Motherwell*[6] that the legal owner of property could obtain an injunction to restrain persistent harassment by unwanted telephone calls to his home and that the partner of the owner also had such a right. It considered that it would be anomalous if such harassment was only actionable in the civil courts if the recipient of the calls happened to be the owner of the property and that there was no reason why a child of the house should not have the same right as the owner's partner. Thus the injunction granted was in principle justified. The court did not make it clear whether harassment as an area of tortious liability should be seen as a head of private nuisance or as a distinct tort but in any event it seems clear that some forms of grossly invasive activity falling short of physical intrusion will be actionable. Nevertheless, it is still fair to conclude that trespass and nuisance offer only limited protection in this area from the crudest and most obvious forms of invasions of privacy.

---

4 (1937) 58 CLR 479.
5 [1993] 3 All ER 669. For discussion of this decision see 143 *NLJ* 926 and 143 *NLJ* 1685.
6 (1976) 73 DLR (3rd) 62.

Respect for the Home: Freedom from Arbitrary Entries, Searches and Seizures

The situation which arose in *Khorasandijan* would now probably fall within the Protection from Harassment Act 1997 which creates both civil and criminal liability in respect of harassment.[7] It should further be noted that various statutes afford piecemeal protection from certain specified types of intrusion. Intrusion by creditors is regulated under s 40 of the Administration of Justice Act 1970 and by landlords under s 30 of the Rent Act 1965. Obscene phone calls are prohibited under s 66 of the Post Office Act 1953 as are unsolicited obscene publications under s 4 of the Unsolicited Goods and Services Act 1971. Section 1 of the Crime and Disorder Act 1998 provides for 'neighbour nuisance' sanctions and injunctions, but since it provides criminal penalties for civil actions it may be open to challenge under Article 6(1) of the ECHR.

2 POLICE POWERS OF ENTRY AND SEARCH[8]

In America the Fourth Amendment to the Constitution guarantees freedom from unreasonable search and seizure by the police, thus recognising the invasion of privacy which a search of premises represents. A search without a warrant will normally[9] be unreasonable; therefore an independent check is usually available on the search power.[10] In contrast, the common law in Britain, despite some rulings asserting the importance of protecting the citizen from the invasion of private property[11] allowed search and seizure on wide grounds, going beyond those authorised by statute.[12] Thus the common law did not provide full protection for the citizen and the Police and Criminal Evidence Act 1984 (PACE) goes some way to remedy this by placing powers of entry, search and seizure on a clearer basis and ensuring that the person whose premises are searched understands the basis of the search and can complain as to its conduct if necessary. Whether the new procedures actually do provide sufficient protection for the interests of the subject of the search is the question to be examined by this section.

---

7   See above p 340.
8   See generally Feldman, D, *The Law Relating to Entry, Search and Seizure*, 1986; Stone, RTH, *Entry, Search and Seizure*, 1989; Lidstone, K and Bevan, V, *Search and Seizure under the Police and Criminal Evidence Act 1984*, 1992.
9   *Coolidge v New Hampshire* 403 US 443 (1973): exception accepted where evidence might otherwise be destroyed.
10 For comment on the efficacy of this check see Lafave, W, *Search and Seizure*, 1978.
11 See eg rulings in *Entinck v Carrington* (1765) 19 St Tr 1029; *Morris v Beardmore* [1981] AC 446; [1980] 2 All ER 753.
12 The ruling in *Ghani v Jones* [1970] 1 QB 693 authorised seizure of a wide range of material once officers were lawfully on premises. *Thomas v Sawkins* [1935] 2 KB 249 allowed a wide power to enter premises to prevent crime (see below p 369).

Entry without warrant

PACE

The power to enter premises conferred by ss 17 and 18 of PACE is balanced in a manner similar to the method employed in respect of stop and search. The power can be exercised under s 17 where: an officer wants to arrest a person suspected of an arrestable offence; in order to arrest for certain offences under the Public Order Act 1936 or the Criminal Law Act 1977; to recapture someone unlawfully at large such as an escapee from a prison, court or mental hospital; to save life or limb or prevent serious damage to property or to execute a warrant of arrest arising out of criminal proceedings. This last provision allows an entry to be made to search for someone wanted under a warrant for non payment of a fine.

A further power of entry arises under s 18 if a person has been arrested for an arrestable offence and the intention is to search the person's premises immediately after arrest:

> ... a constable may enter and search any premises occupied or controlled by a person who is under arrest for an arrestable offence, if he has reasonable grounds for suspecting that there is on the premises evidence, other than items subject to legal privilege, that relates:
>
> (a) to that offence; or
>
> (b) to some other arrestable offence which is connected with or similar to that offence.

Thus the power is subject to some significant limitations; it does not arise in respect of an arrest under s 25. If a search was considered necessary in respect of a s 25 arrest a search warrant would have to be obtained unless the provisions of s 32 applied. Section 32 allows a search of premises after arrest for any offence if the arrestee was arrested on those premises or was on them immediately before the arrest.

The Prevention of Terrorism (Temporary Provisions) Act 1989

The provisions for warrantless search of premises under PACE after arrest are wide enough to cover many circumstances in which police officers might wish to search for items relating to a terrorist investigation. Where they are not they are supplemented by special powers under warrant which are discussed below and also, in an emergency, by a power arising under Schedule 7, para 7(1) of the Prevention of Terrorism (Temporary Provisions) Act (PTA) 1989 which allows a police officer of at least the rank of superintendent to authorise a search by written order if there are 'reasonable grounds for believing that the case is one of great emergency and that in the interests of the state immediate action is necessary'. There is evidence that the use of special search powers without the need to rely on reasonable suspicion or on a warrant have some value in terrorist investigations.[13] Nevertheless, the use of such powers represents an invasion of liberty which requires a strong and clear justification rather than a reliance on an uncertain phrase such as 'the interests of the state'.

A further power of search arises under s 16C and para 7 of Schedule 6A which were added to the PTA by the Criminal Justice and Public Order Act 1994. Section 16C allow police officers of at least the rank of superintendent, engaged in a terrorism investigation, to establish in certain circumstances a police cordon around an area. Once the cordon is in place para 7 of Schedule 6A gives a power of search. It must be authorised in writing by an officer of at least the rank of superintendent who must have reasonable grounds for believing that material which would be of substantial value to the investigation, and which is not excluded or special material or material covered by legal privilege, is on specified premises within the cordon. The power is exercised by a constable who may enter and search premises and may seize items not protected by legal privilege if he has reasonable grounds for believing that they will be of substantial value to the investigation.

The Police Act 1997

As discussed in Chapter 8, this Act places police powers of surveillance on a statutory basis. It also provides powers of entry, search and seizure. An authorisation may be issued if the search is believed to be necessary because it will be of substantial value in the prevention and detection of serious crime[14] and the objective cannot reasonably be achieved by other means (s 93(2)). As explained in Chapter 8[15] the main check on these extensive powers is provided by the special commissioners who are to be appointed from the senior judiciary (s 91(1)). Where the entry and search contemplated is of a dwelling house, prior approval by the commissioner is necessary, but this requirement is waived where the authorising officer believes that the search is urgent. Since the belief does not need to be based on reasonable grounds such a safeguard may have little impact in practice. These controversial extensions of the police powers of entry are therefore subject to very limited independent oversight and, unlike the s 18 power, they may be divorced from the needs of an immediate criminal investigation.

---

13 See Walker, C, *The Prevention of Terrorism*, p 195.
14 For the definition of serious crime see above p 351.
15 See above pp 352–53.

Search warrants

Searching of premises other than under ss 17 and 18 can also occur if a search warrant is issued under s 8 of PACE by a magistrate. There are also special provisions arising, *inter alia*, under s 27 of the Drug Trafficking Act 1994, s 2(4) of the Criminal Justice Act 1987 (in relation to serious fraud) and, as discussed in Chapter 8, in relation to the Security Service under the Security Service Act 1989.

PACE

A warrant under s 8 will only be issued if there are reasonable grounds for believing that a serious arrestable offence has been committed and where the material is likely to be of substantial value to the investigation of the offence. Further safeguards are set out in ss 15 and 16. The warrant must be produced to the occupier (although it seems that this need not be at the time of entry if impracticable in the circumstances)[16] and must identify the articles to be sought, although once the officer is on the premises other articles may be seized under s 19 if they appear to relate to any other offence. Further, the warrant authorises entry to premises on one occasion only. These provisions provide a scheme which is reasonably sound in theory but which is dependent on magistrates observing its requirements. Research suggests that in practice some magistrates make little or no attempt to ascertain whether the information a warrant contains may be relied upon, while it seems possible that magistrates who do take a rigorous approach to the procedure and refuse to grant warrants are not approached again.[17] A warrant authorising the police to search premises does not of itself authorise officers to search persons on the premises. The Home Office circular on PACE stated that such persons could be searched only if a specific power to do so arose under the warrant (eg warrants issued under s 23 of the Misuse of Drugs Act 1971).

The Prevention of Terrorism (Temporary Provisions) Act 1989

A wide power to search premises arises under Schedule 7, para 2 of the PTA[18] which, in contrast to the warrant power under PACE, is not dependent on the need to allege a specific offence and may therefore take place at a very early stage in the investigation. A justice of the peace must be satisfied that a terrorist investigation is being carried out and that there are reasonable grounds for believing that there is material which is likely to be of substantial value to the investigation. Also it must appear that it is impracticable to gain

---

16 *Longman* [1988] 1 WLR 619, CA; for comment see Stevens, R, *Justice of the Peace*, 1988, p 551.
17 This point is made by Dixon (1991) 141 *NLJ* 1586.
18 See Walker, pp 185–97.

Respect for the Home: Freedom from Arbitrary Entries, Searches and Seizures

entry to the premises with consent and that immediate entry to the premises is necessary. A warrant may also be issued under s 15(1) of the PTA in order to allow entry to premises to effect an arrest under s 14(1)(b). This power was thought necessary since the general PACE powers would not be applicable due to the broad nature of s 14(1)(b).[19]

Power to enter premises at common law

At common law a power to enter premises in order to prevent crime arises from the much criticised case of *Thomas v Sawkins*.[20] Lord Hewart CJ contemplated that a police officer would have the right to enter private premises when 'he has reasonable grounds for believing that an offence is imminent or is likely to be committed'. This judgment may receive some endorsement from s 17(5) and (6) which provide that all common law powers on entry are abolished except to deal with or prevent a breach of the peace. However, this narrows down the power of entry as it does not arise in respect of any offence. *Thomas v Sawkins* arose in the context of a public meeting held on private premises but common law powers do not seem to be confined to such circumstances; in *McGowan v Chief Constable of Kingston on Hull*[21] it was found that police officers were entitled to enter and remain on private premises when they feared a breach of the peace arising from a private quarrel.

Voluntary searches

Code B which governs powers of entry, search and seizure makes special provision for voluntary searches. Paragraph 4 of Code B as originally drafted provided that a search of premises could take place with the consent of the occupier and provided under para 4(2) that he must be informed that he need not consent to the search; in requiring that the consent should be in writing it recognised that there might sometimes be a doubt as to the reality of such consent and went some way towards resolving that doubt. After revision para 4 went further in that direction. Under sub-para 4.1 the officer concerned must ensure that the consent is being sought from the correct person, whereas previously this problem was only addressed in a Note for Guidance (4A) and then only in respect of lodgings. Sub-para 4.3 provides that the search must cease if the consent is withdrawn during it and also contains an express provision against using duress to obtain consent.[22] However, it has been

---

19 See below p 413.
20 [1935] 2 KB 249; for criticism see Goodhart 6 *Camb LJ* 222; see further Chap 7 p 265.
21 [1968] *Crim LR* 34. But see the ruling in *McLeod v UK* (1998), unreported.
22 For criticism of these provisions see Bevan and Lidstone, *The Investigation of Crime*, pp 117–21.

doubted whether these provisions have had much effect on ensuring that use of consensual search is not abused because it is not always made clear to occupiers that they can withhold consent.[23]

Power of seizure

At common law prior to PACE a wide power of seizure had developed where a search was not under warrant. Articles could be seized so long as they either implicated the owner or occupier in any offence or implicated third parties in the offence for which the search was conducted.[24] However, the power of seizure under PACE is even wider than this. Under s 8(2) a constable may seize and retain anything for which a search has been authorised. The power of seizure without warrant is governed by s 18(2) which provides that: 'A constable may seize and retain anything for which he may search under subsection (1) above.' This power is greatly widened, however, by the further power of seizure arising under s 19:

> The constable may seize anything which is on the premises if he has reasonable grounds for believing:
> (a) that it has been obtained in consequence of the commission of an offence; and
> (b) that it is necessary to seize it in order to prevent it being concealed, lost, damaged, altered or destroyed.
>
> The constable may seize anything which is on the premises if he has reasonable grounds for believing:
> (a) that it is evidence in relation to an offence which he is investigating or any other offence; and
> (b) that it is necessary to seize it in order to prevent the evidence being concealed, lost, altered or destroyed.

Under s 22(1) anything which has been so seized may be retained 'so long as is necessary in all the circumstances'. It was made clear in *Chief Constable of Lancashire, ex parte Parker and McGrath*[25] that the above provisions assume that the search itself is lawful; in other words, material seized during an unlawful search cannot be retained and if it is an action for trespass to goods may arise. It was accepted in this instance that the search was unlawful (see below) but the Chief Constable contended that the material seized could nevertheless be retained. This argument was put forward under the provision of s 22(2)(a) which allows the retention of 'anything seized for the purposes of a criminal investigation'. The Chief Constable maintained that these words would be

---

23 See further Dixon, D, 'Consent and the Legal Regulation of Policing' (1990) 17 *JLS* 345–62.
24 *Ghani v Jones* [1970] 1 QB 693; *Garfinkel v MPC* [1972] *Crim LR* 44.
25 [1993] 2 WLR 428; [1993] 1 All ER 56; (1992) 142 NLJ 635.

superfluous unless denoting a general power to retain unlawfully seized material. However, it was held that the subsection could not bear the weight sought to be placed upon it: it was merely intended to give examples of matters falling within the general provision of s 22(1). Therefore the police were not entitled to retain the material seized.

Excluded or special procedure material or material covered by legal privilege

Under s 9 excluded or special procedure material or material covered by legal privilege cannot be seized during a search not under warrant and it is exempt from the s 8 search warrant procedure under s 8(1). However, the police may gain access to excluded or special procedure material by making an application to a circuit judge in accordance with Schedule 1 or, in the case of special procedure material only, to a magistrate for a search warrant. Access to excluded material may only be granted where it could have been obtained under the previous law relating to such material. Excluded material is defined under s 11 to consist of material held on a confidential basis, personal records[26] samples of human tissue or tissue fluid held in confidence and journalistic material held in confidence. Personal records include records held by schools, universities, probation officers and social workers. 'Special procedure material' defined under s 14 operates as a catch-all category which is, it seems, frequently used[27] to cover confidential material which does not qualify as personal records or journalistic material.[28] A production order will not be made unless there is reasonable suspicion that a serious arrestable offence has been committed, the material is likely to be of substantial value to the investigation and admissible at trial. It should be noted that when enquiries relating to terrorist offences are made Schedule 7 para 3 of the Prevention of Terrorism Act 1989 allows access to both special procedure and excluded material. The judge only needs to be satisfied that there is a terrorist investigation in being, that the material would substantially assist it and that it is in the public interest that it should be produced. It may well be that once the first two requirements are satisfied it will be rare to find that the third is not.

The ruling in *Guildhall Magistrates' Court, ex parte Primlacks Holdings Co (Panama) Limited*[29] made it clear that a magistrate must satisfy him or herself that there were reasonable grounds for believing that the items covered by the warrant did not include material subject to the special protection. The magistrates had issued search warrants authorising the search of two solicitors' firms. Judicial review of the magistrates' decision to issue a warrant was successfully sought; it was found that the magistrate had merely accepted

---

26 Defined in s 12.
27 See Lidstone, K (1989) *NILQ* 333, at p 342.
28 For comment on these provisions see Stone, R [1988] *Crim LR* 498.
29 [1989] 2 WLR 841.

the police officer's view that s 8(1) was satisfied rather than independently considering the matter.

The strongest protection extends to items subject to legal privilege since they cannot be searched for or seized by police officers and therefore the meaning of 'legal privilege' is crucial. Under s 10 it will cover communications between client and solicitor connected with giving advice or with legal proceedings. However, if items are held with the intention of furthering a criminal purpose they will not, under s 10(2), attract legal privilege. It seems that this will include the situation where the solicitor unknowingly furthers the criminal purpose of the client or a third party.[30] This interpretation of s 10(2) was adopted on the basis that otherwise the efforts of the police in detecting crime might be hampered but it may be argued that it gives insufficient weight to the need to protect the special relationship between solicitor and client.

3   SAFEGUARDS

Code of Practice B

The power to search and seize is balanced by the need to convey certain information to the subject of the search in question, thereby rendering officers (at least theoretically) accountable for searches carried out. However, it is arguable that the provisions are largely of a presentational nature: they ensure that a large amount of information is conveyed to the occupier and make an attempt to ensure that community relations are not adversely affected by the operation of the search power[31] but have little to say about the way the search should be conducted. For example, provision for discouraging searching at night is contained only in a Note for Guidance – 5A – and does not contain a clear prohibition on such searches subject to clearly drawn exceptions. No provision is made for giving warning to the occupier that the search is imminent so that he or she can seek legal advice if desired. Such a provision would no doubt have to be subject to exceptions in order to allow urgent

---

30   In *Crown Court at Snaresbrook, ex parte DPP* [1988] QB 532; [1988] 1 All ER 315 it was found that only the solicitor's intentions regarding the criminal purpose were relevant but the House of Lords in *Central Criminal Court, ex parte Francis and Francis* [1989] AC 346; [1988] 3 All ER 375 rejected this interpretation in finding that material which figures in the criminal intentions of persons other than solicitor or client will not be privileged. For comment see Stevenson, P (1989) *LS Gaz* 1 February 26. A judge must give full consideration to the question whether particular documents have lost legal privilege: *Southampton Crown Court, ex parte J and P* [1993] Crim LR 962.

31   There is provision under para 2.5 for informing the local police community relations officer before a search of premises takes place if it is thought that it might adversely affect the relationship between the police and the community, subject to the proviso that in cases of urgency it can be performed after the search has taken place.

searching but might well be indicated in some instances. The provision that an occupier may ask a friend or neighbour to witness the search unless there are reasonable grounds for believing 'that this would seriously hinder the investigation' would usually be inadequate to allow the occupier to obtain legal advice or the presence of a solicitor.[32]

All searches: information to be conveyed

As revised in 1991, Code B provides for an increase in the amount of information to be conveyed to owners of property to be searched by use of a standard form, the Notice of Powers and Rights (para 5.7). It covers certain information including specification of the type of search in question, a summary of the powers of search and seizure arising under PACE and the rights of the subjects of searches. This notice must normally be given to the subject of the search before it begins but under para 5.8 need not be if to do so would lead to frustration of the object of the search or danger to the police officers concerned or to others. These exceptions also apply under para 5.8 to leaving a copy of the warrant where the search is made under warrant. As explained above s 18(4) provides that premises occupied or controlled by a person arrested for an arrestable offence may be searched after the arrest if an officer of the rank of inspector or above gives authority in writing. Under para 3.3 the authority should normally be given on the Notice of Powers and Rights. This clears up previous confusion[33] as to the form the authority should take.

Under original paras 4 and 5 the amount of information to be conveyed to the subject of a search depended on its status. Before any non-consensual search an officer had to convey certain information orally to its subject: his identity, the purpose of the search and the grounds for undertaking it. In the case of a consensual search it was only necessary to inform its subject of its purpose. Thus the subject of an apparently consensual search dissatisfied with its conduct or intimidated by the officers concerned would have found it more difficult to make a complaint than would the subject of a non-consensual search. Under current paras 4 and 5 as revised, the subjects of all searches, regardless of the status of the search, must receive a copy of the Notice of Powers and Rights and, under paragraph 5.8 where a consensual search has taken place but the occupier is absent, the Notice should be endorsed with the name, number and station of the officer concerned. Oddly enough, it is not stated expressly that this information must be added to the Notice where the subject of a consensual search is *present*. Sub-paragraph 5.5 provides that officers must identify themselves except in the case of enquiries linked to

---

32 Paragraph 5.11.
33 In *Badham* [1987] *Crim LR* 202 it was held that merely writing down confirmation of an oral authorisation was insufficient.

terrorism but this provision appears to apply only to non-consensual searches due to the heading of that section. It might be thought that a person who voluntarily allows police officers to come onto his or her premises does not need the information mentioned but this is to ignore the possibility that such a person might wish to withdraw consent during the search but might feel too intimidated to do so.

Providing a copy of the warrant

Under s 16 if a search is under warrant a copy of the warrant must be issued to the subject of the search. The warrant will identify the articles or persons sought and the offence suspected but need not specify the grounds on which it was issued or give the name of the constable conducting the search. A warrant, like the Notice of Powers and Rights, therefore provides the occupier with limited information. Moreover, as noted above, it need not be produced to the occupier before the search begins if the purpose of the search might be frustrated by such production.[34] However, within these limitations the courts seem prepared to take a strict view of the importance of complying with this safeguard. In *Chief Constable of Lancashire, ex parte Parker and McGrath*[35] police officers conducted a search of the applicant's premises in the execution of a search warrant issued under s 8 of PACE. However, after the warrant had been signed by the judge the police detached part of it and reattached it to the other original documents. In purported compliance with s 16 of PACE the police produced all these documents to the applicants. Thus the police did not produce the whole of the original warrant and moreover did not supply one of the documents constituting the warrant. The applicants applied for judicial review of both the issue and the execution of the warrants. It was determined that s 16(5)(b) of PACE had been breached in that the warrant produced to the applicants was not the original warrant as seen and approved by the judge and a declaration was granted to that effect. The police had admitted that there was a breach of the requirement under s 16(5)(c) that a copy of the warrant should be supplied to the occupier of the premises.

Police accountability

The PACE search and seizure provisions are clearly intended to make lawful actions which would otherwise amount to trespass to property and to goods only in very specific circumstances and only where a certain procedure has been followed. Invasion of a person's home has traditionally been viewed as an infringement of liberty which should be allowed only under tightly

---

34 *Longman* [1988] 1 WLR 619, CA.
35 (1992) 142 *NLJ* 635.

controlled conditions and in the exercise of a specific legal power. However, as already mentioned, breach of Code B will not attract tortious liability and unlike Codes C, D and E exclusion of evidence will rarely operate as a form of redress because the courts are very reluctant to exclude physical evidence[36] and therefore it can have little impact on Code B provisions. Such reluctance may be justifiable since the significance of Codes A and B can be attributed to their regulation of invasive procedures rather than to their concern to ensure the integrity of the evidence thereby obtained. Codes C, D and E on the other hand are arguably concerned more with outcome than with rights (with the exception of access to legal advice) which are fundamental in themselves. This difference is due partly to the nature of the rights involved: privacy of the home or of the person represents an important value in itself unlike a person's right to the contemporaneous recording of an interview. However, this does leave something of a gap as far as a means of redress for breaches of Codes A and B is concerned in comparison with the other three Codes since the only means available will normally be by way of a complaint.

The PACE provisions suggest some determination to strike a reasonable balance between the perceived need to confer on the police a general power to search property and the need to protect the citizen. If the powers are exceeded an action for trespass will lie. However, it may be argued that the provisions governing seizure come too close to allowing a general ransacking of the premises once a lawful entry has been effected. Moreover, the regulation of the search power under Code B emphasises the provision of information to the owner of premises so that officers can be rendered accountable for searches made, rather than regulating circumstances relating to the nature of the search itself in order to minimise the invasion of privacy represented by such searches. In contrast, searches made in order to gain evidence relating to civil proceedings, under orders known as *Anton Piller* orders,[37] must observe a number of safeguards: they must be organised on weekdays in office hours so that legal advice can be obtained before the search begins; the defendant must be allowed to check the list of items to be seized before items can be removed and in some circumstances an independent solicitor experienced in the execution of such orders must be present, instructed and paid for by the plaintiff.[38] It may be argued that there is a greater public interest in the prevention of crime than in ensuring that evidence is obtained by a party to civil proceedings and therefore the police need at times to make an immediate search of premises but the power to do so without judicial intervention should, it is submitted, be narrowed down to instances where the urgency of

---

36 See below pp 495–98.
37 From *Anton Piller KG v Manufacturing Processes Ltd* [1976] Ch 55; [1976] 1 All ER 779, CA.
38 These conditions, and others, were laid down in *Universal Thermosensors Ltd v Hibben* (1992) *NLJ* 195. For discussion of the concern created by such orders prior to this decision see (1990) 106 *LQR* 601.

the search was demonstrable, while Code B should contain clearer safeguards applicable to all searches, allowing, for instance, for a legal advisor to be present during a non-urgent search and including a clear prohibition on non-urgent searches at night. At present searches should be conducted at 'a reasonable hour'[39] and under Note for Guidance 5A this is explained to mean at a time when the occupier or others are unlikely to be asleep. But, as discussed elsewhere,[40] the Notes for Guidance are not part of the Codes and are of very uncertain legal status: a prohibition on the non-urgent entry and search of property at night by state agents – perhaps one of the most unpleasant invasions of privacy possible – requires a more certain basis.

39 Code B para 5.2.
40 See Chap 11 pp 395–96.

CHAPTER TEN

BODILY INTEGRITY AND AUTONOMY; SEXUAL EXPRESSION AND IDENTITY; FAMILY LIFE

1 BODILY INTEGRITY AND AUTONOMY

Introduction

Under Article 8 bodily privacy has a number of aspects. The European Court of Human Rights adopted a broad definition of privacy in *X and Y v Netherlands*:[1]

> ... [the concept of] private life ... covers the physical integrity ... of the person ... Article 8 does not merely compel the state to abstain from ... interference [with the individual]: in addition to this primarily negative undertaking, there may be positive obligations inherent in effective respect for private ... life.[2]

Thus Article 8 recognises that individuals have an interest in preventing or controlling physical intrusions on the body and they may therefore lay claim to a negative right to be 'left alone' in a physical sense. Such a right might also encompass positive claims on the state to ensure that bodily integrity is not infringed. Thus the state may fail to respect privacy if it fails to prevent infringement of it by others or if in itself it allows such infringement. The European Court of Human Rights has also recognised that private life covers individual, personal choices: *Dudgeon v UK*.[3] Thus, the interest of individuals in exercising freedom of choice in decisions as to the disposal of or control over the body may be protected. Usually the individual is, in effect, asking the state to leave him or her alone to make such decisions in order to preserve autonomy. In some instances however, the individual will be requiring the assistance of the authorities in ensuring that he or she is able to exercise autonomy. It is unclear at present that the European Court would characterise a claim that the state was under an obligation to provide such assistance as necessary in order to demonstrate respect for private life.

Bodily integrity

Interference with bodily integrity may breach the guarantee of freedom from degrading punishment under Article 3 of the European Convention on Human Rights and the guarantee of respect for privacy under Article 8. In

---

1 (1986) 8 EHRR 235.
2 *Ibid*, paras 22 and 23.
3 (1981) 4 EHRR 149.

general, any compulsory physical treatment of an individual will constitute an interference with private life.[4] Thus, certain forms of physical punishment may be seen as an unjustified intrusion onto bodily integrity. Corporal punishment was outlawed in UK state schools[5] after the decision of the European Court of Human Rights in *Campbell and Cosans v UK*[6] which was determined not on the basis of Articles 3 or 8 but under Article 2 of the First Protocol which protects the right of parents to have their children educated according to their own philosophical convictions. However, corporal punishment in private schools was not outlawed and in *Costello-Roberts v UK*[7] the European Court of Human Rights found that the UK had a responsibility to ensure that school discipline was compatible with the Convention even though the treatment in question was administered in an institution independent of the state. However, although the court considered that there might be circumstances in which Article 8 could be regarded as affording protection to physical integrity which would be broader than that afforded by Article 3, in the particular circumstances the adverse effect on the complainant was insufficient to amount to an invasion of privacy. The court took into account the 'public' context in which the punishment had occurred and its relatively trivial nature.

Under Article 8(2) physical intrusions on the bodily integrity of individuals by state agents may be allowed if they fall within one of the exception clauses or if in the particular circumstances no infringement of private life has occurred. UK law also recognises a need to create a balance between the interest of the state in allowing physical interference with individuals for various purposes, including the prevention of crime and the interest of the individual in preserving his or her bodily integrity. UK law determines that in certain circumstances bodily privacy may give way to other interests. For example, s 55 of the Police and Criminal Evidence Act 1984 allows intimate strip searches but recognises that the violation they represent may occur only in well-defined circumstances. Examination may occur only if there is reasonable suspicion that drugs or implements which might be used to harm others may be found. The examination may only be carried out by a nurse (or a medical practitioner in respect of drugs or a weapon) or if that is not practicable it can be carried out by a police officer who must be of the same sex as the person to be searched.

The question as to how far clothing could properly be removed for other purposes in police custody was considered in *Lindley v Rutter*[8] and a general order to remove the bras of all female detainees in the police station was

---

4   *X v Austria*, 18 D and R 154 (1979).
5   Under the Education (No 2) Act 1986.
6   (1982) 2 EHRR 293.
7   Judgment of 25 March 1993, A.247-C; (1993) *The Times*, 26 March.
8   [1980] 3 WLR 661.

challenged. Justification was put forward for the order on the grounds that the detainees might otherwise injure themselves. However, it was found that such treatment constituted an affront to human dignity and therefore needed a clearer justification which could be derived only from the specific circumstances of the arrestee: something particular about the individual in question would be needed to support a suspicion that she might do herself an injury. It was found that in removing a detainee's bra where such specific justification did not exist the police officer in question had acted outside her duty. Thus the court evinced a reluctance to accept a generalised basis for invasion of privacy.

Bodily autonomy

Personal autonomy has been recognised for some time in the USA as strongly linked to privacy. In *Doe v Bolton*[9] Douglas J said that 'the right to privacy means freedom of choice in the basic decisions of one's life respecting marriage, divorce, procreation, contraception, education and upbringing of children'. Personal autonomy connotes an interest not only in preventing physical intrusion by others but also with the extent to which the law allows an individual a degree of control over his or her own body. Recognition of the need to allow individual bodily self-determination has arguably become more prominent this century. Thus abortion and suicide are no longer crimes under the Abortion Act 1967 and the Suicide Act 1961. However, limits as to self-determination are represented by the Prohibition of Female Circumcision Act 1985 and the Surrogacy Act 1985 (although it should be noted that surrogacy is only curbed by the Act, not outlawed: it only prevents commercial surrogacy arrangements). We will return below to the question as to the level of consensual bodily harm which will be forbidden.

The notion of personal autonomy has arisen frequently in the context of allegedly negligent medical treatment but the law has not so far made much progress in the direction of granting it recognition.[10] It was argued in *Sidaway v Board of Governors of the Bethlem Royal Hospital*[11] that a patient who was not fully informed as to the risks associated with the operation she was to undergo should be able to succeed against the doctor in negligence when one of those risks did materialise. However, it was found that so long as the doctor had acted in accordance with practice accepted as proper by a body of medical practitioners (the test deriving from *Bolam v Friern HMC*)[12] with regard to disclosure of risks the action must fail. It may be argued that this stance fails to

---

9 410 US 179 (1973); [1973] 35 L E 2d 201.
10 See Teff, H, 'Consent to Medical Procedure: Paternalism, Self-Determination or Therapeutic Alliance?' (1985) 101 *LQR* 432.
11 [1985] AC 871; [1985] 2 WLR 480, HL.
12 [1957] 2 All ER 118.

accord sufficient weight to the personal autonomy of the patient. Where a number of choices of treatment lie before a patient how far might it be expected that he or she should participate in the decision-making process? For example, if a patient had a serious cancerous condition there might be two main options: radical treatment which would be disfiguring but might prolong life or conservative treatment which would not prolong life but would not disfigure. Length of life would have to be weighed against quality of life. It might appear that only the patient who knows intimately which of the options fits with his or her own aspirations and lifestyle and who must live for the rest of his or her life with the decision taken, should make it and therefore all the risks and benefits of both courses of action should be disclosed.

Furthermore, it might be argued that the degree of self-determination allowable should be greater depending on the type of operation in question. For this purpose treatment could be divided into three categories: it might be termed elective (sterilisation, cosmetic surgery), semi-elective (this would be a large category which would include on the one hand pain relieving operations and on the other operations in the face of life-threatening conditions such as cancer) and non-elective (emergency operations where the patient due either to unconsciousness or extreme pain was unable to make a choice). It might be argued that self-determination should be complete in respect of purely elective operations and should be a highly significant factor in respect of semi-elective ones. In other words, the law should not impose or allow any further constraint on the patient's exercise of self-determination than is inherent in the situation already.

The law has not however recognised these distinctions or indeed any general right to bodily privacy in terms of disclosure of risks. The *Sidaway* case concerned an operation which might be termed semi-elective in that it was aimed at pain relief but where a purely elective operation was in question in *Gold v Haringey Health Authority*[13] the same principles applied. Clearly, in order that a patient can exercise self-determination he or she must know of the options for treatment and of the likely outcome in each instance. The patient can then give or withhold consent to the proposed course of treatment and, further, can question it. However, the test to be applied as to whether a doctor has been negligent in failing to inform the patient of certain possibilities – the *Bolam* test – does not lay a heavy burden upon doctors in terms of the amount of information which must be given. This test may be acceptable in respect of decisions as to diagnosis and treatment (although it may be argued that it puts the plaintiff in medical negligence cases in an extremely difficult position) but arguably it is unacceptable in respect of the duty to disclose information so that the patient can give an informed consent to the treatment proposed. It appears that judges have put their fear of defensive medicine and a flood of

---

13 [1987] 2 All ER 888.

medical litigation before the need to uphold the right of the patient to control over his or her own body.

2 SEXUAL EXPRESSION AND IDENTITY

Introduction

In the UK individuals enjoy a limited power of choice as to the expression of sexuality. At present sexual freedom is restricted by the criminal law which prohibits certain acts.[14] The rationale for such prohibition seems to depend partly on use of the criminal law as the means of affirming and upholding a certain moral standard and partly on the need to prevent certain specific harms. The debate as to whether or not the proper function of the criminal law is to interfere in the private lives of citizens in order to enforce a particular pattern of behaviour where no clear harm will arise from the prohibited behaviour remains unresolved.[15] However, the view put forward in the *Wolfenden Report* 1957[16] to the effect that the criminal law should confine itself to prohibiting specific harms has received widespread support.

Incest

Incest is punishable with a maximum sentence of seven years or life if with a girl under 13 years of age.[17] One justification for prohibiting incest is that the genetic risks associated with it appear to be high but this argument could equally be extended to anyone affected by a hereditary disease who would then also be prohibited from intercourse. Moreover, the risk of producing children with genetic defects can provide only a partial rationale for the existence of the offence since it may arise whether or not the man is sterile or the woman past child-bearing age or otherwise unable to have children.[18] On the other hand, the erosion of freedom created by this offence is limited, since it only prohibits acts with a certain group of persons. Following the principles put forward in the *Wolfenden Report* 1957 this offence should be abolished, although a more limited offence would have to be replace it in order to protect younger members of families from the attentions of adult members.

---

14 For consideration of such offences see Smith and Hogan, *Criminal Law*, 8th edn, 1996, Chap 14; Honore, T, *Sex Law*, 1978.
15 For discussion of the relationship between privacy and morality see Leander, S, 'The Right to Privacy, the Enforcement of Morals and the Judicial Function: An Argument' (1990) *Current Legal Problems* 115.
16 Cmnd 247. This view was challenged by Lord Devlin, *The Enforcement of Morals*, 1965.
17 Sections 10 and 11 of the Sexual Offences Act 1956.
18 It may be noted that s 44 of the 1956 Act defines sexual intercourse as penetration without the need to show emission of seed.

Buggery

The offence of buggery consisted at common law of intercourse *per anum* by a man with a man or woman and intercourse *per anum* or *vaginum* with an animal and it could be committed by a husband with his wife.[19] The common law was enacted in s 12(1) of the Sexual Offences Act 1956. An exception was provided to the common law position by s 1 of the Sexual Offences Act 1967 which permitted consensual buggery between two males both of whom were 21 or over (the highest age of consent for homosexual intercourse in the European Community until 1994), done in private.

Under s 12(1) of the 1956 Act a homosexual act done in 'public' will be an offence and this will include any place where anyone apart from the two parties is present. Thus a homosexual act occurring in a house owned by one of the parties (known either as the 'agent' or the 'patient') would be criminalised if another person was in the same room although unaware of what was occurring. If there is uncertainty as to whether a place is private or public it must be resolved by reference to all the facts including the likelihood of a third person coming on the scene.[20] It is an offence under s 4 of the 1967 Act to procure another man to commit with a third man an act of buggery, while any agreement between two or more persons to facilitate homosexual activity may be caught by the common law offence of conspiracy to corrupt public morals. The existence of this offence was affirmed in *Knuller Ltd v DPP*[21] in which Lord Reid made clear the policy of the law regarding homosexual acts:

> I read the [1967] Act as saying that, even though [buggery] may be corrupting, if people choose to corrupt themselves in this way that is their affair and the law will not interfere. But no licence is given to others to encourage the practice.

He went on to equate homosexual connection with prostitution as an activity which was not in itself unlawful but which was not 'lawful in the full sense'. Thus it is fair to say that the legalisation of homosexual acts was effected in almost the narrowest conceivable manner and suggested a bare toleration of them.[22]

Dudgeon v UK[23] concerned the law in Northern Ireland (Offences Against the Person Act) 1861 which made buggery between consenting males of any age a crime. Dudgeon, who was suspected of homosexual activities, was arrested on that basis and questioned but the police decided not to prosecute.

---

19 *Jellyman* (1838) 8 C & P 604.
20 *Reakes* [1974] *Crim LR* 615.
21 [1973] AC 435; [1972] 3 WLR 143; (1972) 56 Cr App R 633, HL.
22 For discussion see Michael, J, 'Homosexuals and Privacy' (1988) 138 *NLJ* 831.
23 (1981) 4 EHRR 149.

He applied to the European Commission on the grounds of a breach of the right to privacy under Article 8. The European Court of Human Rights held that the legislation in question constituted a continuing interference with his private life which included his sexual life. He was forced either to abstain from sexual relations completely or to commit a crime. However, the court considered that some regulation of homosexual activity was acceptable; the question was what was necessary in a democratic society. The court took into account the doctrine of the margin of appreciation (the discretion of the Member State authorities as to what is necessary) as considered in the *Handyside* case[24] where it was held that state authorities were in the best position to judge the requirements of morals. However, the court found that the instant case concerned a very intimate aspect of private life. A restriction on a Convention right cannot be regarded as necessary unless it is proportionate to the aim pursued. In the instant case there was a grave detrimental interference with the applicant's private life and on the other hand there was little evidence of much damage to morals. The law had not been enforced and no evidence had been adduced to show that this had been harmful to moral standards. So the aim of the restriction was not proportional to the damage done to the applicant's privacy and therefore the invasion of privacy went beyond what was needed. In response to this ruling Northern Irish law was changed under the Homosexual Offences (NI) Order 1982. *Dudgeon* demonstrates that the European Court of Human Rights is prepared to uphold the right of the individual to choose to indulge in homosexual practices[25] and suggests that the term 'private life' in Article 8 may be used to cover a wide range of situations where bodily or sexual privacy is in question.

In the European Community, Irish criminal law was until recently the most hostile to homosexuals; sexual acts between members of the same sex were outlawed in the Republic until June 1993 when the Irish government introduced reform by lowering the age of consent for homosexual acts to 17, thus bringing it into line with the more progressive European countries. It was argued in *Dudgeon* that the age of consent should be lowered in order to ensure respect for the private life of homosexuals but the European Court accepted that it was within the Member States' margin of appreciation to fix the age of consent at a level which would seem to protect the rights of others. It was recommended in 1984 by the Criminal Law Revision Committee that the age of consent should be lowered to 18 but this recommendation was not implemented. However, Parliament decided to include in the Criminal Justice and Public Order Bill 1994 a clause lowering the age of consent for male homosexuals to 18. Adoption of 16 as the age of consent was debated but rejected.

---

24 (1976) 1 EHRR 737.
25 *Cf* the stance of the US Supreme Court in *Bowers v Hardwick* 478 US 186 (1986); for comment see (1988) 138 *NLJ* 831.

The position is now governed by s 143 of the Criminal Justice and Public Order Act 1994 which amended s 12(1) of the Sexual Offences Act 1956. Section 12(1)(1A) now lowers the age of consent for male homosexual intercourse to 18. The act must still take place in private and s 12(1)(1B) provides that the act will not be in private if it takes place when two or more persons take part or are present or it takes place in a public lavatory. Heterosexual buggery is decriminalised by s 143 so long as both parties are over 18. Despite these changes it cannot be said with certainty that the current law governing the sexual freedom of homosexuals is in accord with Article 8 of the European Convention on Human Rights. The UK government has taken the view, which it put forward in *Dudgeon*, that female homosexual activity does not present as great a danger to society and particularly to young persons, as male homosexual activity. This may explain why the age of consent for lesbian acts remains the same as for heterosexual intercourse. That 16 is the age of consent is apparent on the basis that although such acts may be capable of being indecent assaults[26] they will normally be consented to and so will not be assaults. However, a girl under 16 cannot give the relevant consent and so any homosexual act done to or with a girl beneath that age would be unlawful as would a heterosexual act. The reason given in *Dudgeon* for this apparent liberalism on behalf of the UK has been attacked as misleading; Edwards argues that its true basis lies in a traditional belief in the sexual passivity of females.[27] It may be noted that in its impact this differentiation between male and female homosexuals is an instance of straightforward sexual discrimination working to the disadvantage of men. Section 143 of the 1994 Act has been successfully challenged under Article 8 in conjunction with Article 14 on the basis that it allows discrimination between male and female homosexuals, since the age of consent for female homosexual intercourse is 16 under the criminal law as it stands at present.[28] The Labour government intends to allow a free vote on lowering the age of consent to 16.

The differential ages of consent under s 143 also of course allow discrimination between homosexuals and heterosexuals. When this issue returns to the European Court of Human Rights it might be prepared to reconsider its remarks on the point in *Dudgeon* but it tends to take the view that in sensitive matters of this nature it should hold back until a clear European standard seems to be emerging; at the stage when a trend is clear but no such standard has emerged it will tend to invoke the margin of appreciation.[29]

---

26 Under s 14 of the Sexual Offences Act 1956.
27 Edwards, *Female Sexuality and the Law*, 1981, p 42.
28 *Sutherland v UK* (1996) 22 EHRR CD 182. The application was declared admissible by the Commission which gave its opinion on 7 October 1997 that the age of consent should be reduced to 16 in accordance with Article 8.
29 See discussion on this point in relation to transsexuals, below p 388.

Sado-masochism[30]

Most sado-masochistic acts are currently unlawful in the UK regardless of the participants' consent to them. Following *Donovan*[31] a person can consent to the infliction of minor or trivial injury but not to 'any hurt or injury calculated to interfere with health or comfort ... it need not be permanent but must be more than merely transient or trifling'. *Donovan* appears to be incompatible with *Aitken*[32] in which it was found, in effect, that a person can consent to the risk of serious injury. However, in the leading case of *Brown*[33] the House of Lords followed *Donovan* in finding that a person cannot consent to the infliction of harm amounting to actual bodily harm. However, consent to such harm may negate liability if there is good reason for the harm to be caused. There are a number of activities involving the causing of or the risk of consensual harm which have been found to be justified as in the public interest. These include rough horseplay,[34] organised games and some informal friendly athletic contests (although not prize fights).[35]

In *Brown*[36] a group of sado-masochistic homosexuals had regularly over a period of 10 years willingly participated in acts of violence against each other for the sexual pleasure engendered in the giving and receiving of pain. They were charged with causing actual bodily harm contrary to s 47 and with wounding contrary to s 20 of the Offences Against the Person Act 1861 and were convicted. The convictions were upheld by the Court of Appeal which certified the following point of law of general public importance: 'Where A wounds or assaults B occasioning him actual bodily harm in the course of a sado-masochistic encounter, does the prosecution have to prove lack of consent on the part of B before they can establish A's guilt under s 20 and s 47 of the Offences Against the Person Act 1861.' The House of Lords by a majority of three to two answered this question in the negative, finding therefore that consent could operate only as a defence and would be allowed so to operate only where the public interest would thereby be served. It was found that in a sado-masochistic context the inflicting of injuries amounting to actual bodily harm could not fall within the category of 'good reason' and therefore, despite the consent of all the participants, the convictions of the defendants were upheld.

---

30 For discussion see Leigh, LH (1976) 39 *MLR* 130.
31 [1934] 2 KB 498.
32 [1992] 1 WLR 1006.
33 [1993] 2 WLR 556; [1993] 2 All ER 75; for comment see (1993) 109 *LQR* 540; (1994) 20(3) *JLS* 356.
34 *Jones* (1986) 83 Cr App R 375.
35 *Coney* (1882) 8 QBD 534.
36 [1993] 2 WLR 556; [1993] 2 All ER 75, HL.

The judgments of the majority in the House of Lords are couched in terms which suggest that distaste for the activities in question was a significant influencing factor. Lord Mustill, in the minority in the House of Lords, considered each of the grounds considered by the majority to be in favour of criminalising the activities in question and discounted each of them. These included fear of the spread of AIDS and the possibility that things might get out of hand if activities such as these were allowed. AIDS, as Lord Mustill pointed out, may be spread by consensual buggery, which is legal, rather than by the activities in question. If a person consents to a lesser harm than that which is actually inflicted, the existing law could be used to punish the perpetrator.

It is unclear that any public interest was served by bringing the prosecution: the activities in question were carried on privately and there was no suggestion that any of the 'victims' were coerced into consenting to them: all had apparently chosen freely to participate. No hospital treatment was needed and the police only discovered what had been occurring by chance. Thus, this decision may be criticised for its subjectivity; it is unclear why it is acceptable that boxing contests may be carried out which can result in serious permanent injury or even death, while activities such as those in *Brown* are criminalised although they may result in a lesser degree of harm.[37] Similarly, it is difficult to reconcile *Brown* with *Aitken*[38] and with *Wilson*.[39] In *Aitken* a group of RAF officers, including G, at a party set fire to G's fire resistant suit, as a practical joke. G attempted to resist them but was badly burned. The convictions of the officers for causing grievous bodily harm contrary to s 20 of the Offences Against the Person Act 1861 were quashed on appeal on the ground that the officers honestly believed that G had consented to their actions. In other words it was found that G could consent to the risk of serious injury, injury of a more serious nature than that inflicted in *Brown*. In *Wilson*[40] a husband branded his wife's buttocks with a hot knife at her request. The Court of Appeal found that consensual activity between husband and wife in the privacy of the matrimonial home was not a proper matter for criminal prosecution. An inference which may be drawn from the contradictory nature of decisions in this area is that while boxing, rough horseplay or private heterosexual activities are regarded by some members of the judiciary as acceptable and perhaps 'manly', they have little or no sympathy with or understanding of the value of some aspects of sexual expression, especially the sexual expression of homosexuals. The majority in the House of Lords did

---

37 See further on this point P Roberts's discussion of the Law Commission Consultative Paper *Consent in the Criminal Law* (No 139 HMSO 1995) (1997) 17(3) *OJLS* 389.
38 [1992] 1 WLR 1006.
39 [1996] 3 WLR 125.
40 [1996] 3 WLR 125.

not appear to regard the decision as allowing an interference with private sexual activity between adults but rather as an application of the criminal law to offences of violence which had a sexual motive.

Three of the men who were convicted in *Brown* applied to the European Commission on Human Rights, arguing that their convictions were in breach of Article 8 of the Convention,[41] since they constituted an interference with their private life. The Commission found that no violation of Article 8 had occurred and referred the case to the Court, which came to the same conclusion: *Laskey, Jaggard and Brown v UK*.[42] The Court considered that the activities in question could be seen as occurring outside the private sphere: many persons were involved and videos had been taken. However, as the issue of privacy was not in dispute the Court accepted that an interference with the applicants' private life had occurred. The question was whether the interference was necessary in a democratic society. The harm was serious since it concerned genital torture. The state is entitled to regulate the infliction of physical harm and the level of harm to be tolerated by the state where the victim consents is in the first instance a matter for the state concerned. The activities had the potential to cause harm in the sense that if encouraged, harm, including the spread of AIDS, might occur in future. Was the interference proportionate to the aim pursued? Numerous charges could have been preferred but only a few were selected. The level of sentencing reflected the perception that the activities were rendered less serious by the consent of the 'victims'. The Court therefore found that the state had not overstepped its margin of appreciation, taking the need for regulation of such harm into account and the proportionate response of the authorities into account. Thus no violation of Article 8 was found. The partly dissenting judgment of Judge Pettiti is of interest. He reasoned that the case did not fall within Article 8 at all since Article 8 provides protection for persons' intimacy and dignity, not for a person's baseness or criminal immorality. The wording of this judgment echoes the wording of parts of the majority judgments of the House of Lords in allowing distaste and lack of sympathy for the activities in question to have some bearing.

The judgment of the Court reflects, it is suggested, the tendency of the operation of the margin of appreciation to dilute the Convention standards. As suggested elsewhere in this book[43] a strong justification for trusting human rights and freedoms to the judicial as opposed to the democratic process is that the interests of minorities (including sexual minorities) may thereby be safeguarded, whereas if they were at the mercy of majoritarianism

---

41 *Laskey, Jaggard and Brown v UK* (Appl No 21974/93). The case of *V, W, X, Y and Z v UK* (Appl No 21627/93) raises the same issues.
42 (1997) 24 EHRR 39.
43 See Chap 1 pp 5–6.

they might be at risk. This judgment lends credibility to the arguments of those who view the Convention as ineffective as a protector of such rights and freedoms.

Sexual identity

UK law does not at present give full expression to the fundamental interest of individuals in determining their own identity. This significant aspect of private life has arisen in two cases brought under the European Convention on Human Rights against the UK by transsexuals. In *Rees v UK*[44] the applicant, who was born a woman but had had a gender re-assignment operation, complained that he could not have his birth certificate altered to record his new sex, thereby causing him difficulty in applying for employment. However, the court refused to find a breach of Article 8 because it was reluctant to accept the claim that the UK was under a positive obligation to change its procedures in order to recognise the applicant's identity for social purposes. It followed a similar route in *Cossey v UK*[45] although it did consider whether it should depart from its judgment in *Rees* in order to ensure that the Convention might reflect societal changes. However, it decided not to do so because developments in this area in the Member States were not consistent and still reflected a diversity of practices. In *B v France*[46] it was found that although there had been development in the area no broad consensus among Member States had emerged. Nevertheless, the civil position of the applicant in terms of her sexual identity was worse than that of transsexuals in the UK and on that basis a breach of Article 8 could be found. These decisions accept that sexual identity is an aspect of private life, although they do not afford full recognition to a right of individuals to determine both their own identity and the public expression of it.

3   FAMILY LIFE

This concept under Article 8 may encompass many types of 'family' – formal or informal – but if the 'family' in question might not fall within the term as, for example, a foster parent might not do, there might still be an interference with private life. Generally a close relationship falling within the term will be presumed where close ties such as those between parent and child exist; for other relations the presumption will be the other way.

---

44   (1987) 9 EHRR 56.
45   European Court of Human Rights, A.184; (1990) 13 EHRR 622.
46   (1992) 13 HRLJ 358; for comment see [1992] *PL* 559.

Bodily Integrity and Autonomy; Sexual Expression and Identity; Family Life

Various aspects of family life have been in issue in cases brought against the UK. *W, B and UK*[47] concerned a claim that access should be allowed to children in the care of the local authority. The court noted that Article 8 does not contain any explicit procedural requirements but found that in itself that fact could not be conclusive. When the local authority made decisions on children in its care the views and interests of parents should be taken into account and the decision-making process should allow for this. If parents' views were not taken into account then family life was not being respected. Therefore a breach of Article 8 was found on the basis that there was insufficient involvement of the applicants in the process. This decision thus avoided a judgment on the substantive merits of denying parents a right of access to children in care. Had the parents been involved in the decision-making process which had then led to the same conclusion, it would seem that no breach of Article 8 would have occurred.

Although the term 'family' may receive a broad interpretation, this has not consistently been the case with respect to the requirements arising from the need to respect family life. In *X v UK*[48] which was found inadmissible by the Commission, it was determined that 'family life' cannot be interpreted so broadly as to encompass a father's right to be consulted in respect of an abortion. The Commission could have rested the decision on para 2 – the 'rights of others' exception – by taking the rights of the woman in question into account but it preferred to interpret the primary right restrictively. Had it not adopted such an interpretation 'family life' might have come into conflict with 'private life' since pregnancy and its management has been accepted as an aspect of a mother's private life, although not to be divorced entirely from consideration of the life of the foetus.[49] Family life has also received a narrow interpretation in immigration cases in respect of a right to enter a country. In *Abdulaziz, Cabales and Balkandali v UK*[50] it was found that:

> The duty imposed by Article 8 cannot be considered as extending to a general obligation ... to respect the choice by married couples of the country of their matrimonial residence and to accept the non-national spouses for settlement in that country.

However, where an alien is in contrast faced with expulsion from a country in which he or she has lived for some time and where members of the family are

---

47 Judgment of 8 July 1987, A.121; (1987) 10 EHRR 29.
48 Appl 8416/79, D and R 19 (1980) p 244.
49 *Brüggemann and Scheuten v Federal Republic of Germany* (6959/75) 10 D and R 100 (1975), Eur Comm HR, Report of 12 July 1977. See above p 35 for possible conflict between Article 8 and Article 2 in respect of abortions. See Chap 8 p 272 for further discussion of the possible conflict between family life and private life.
50 Judgment of 28 May 1985, A.94, 1985; (1985) 7 EHRR 471. A breach of the Convention was found when Article 8 was read in conjunction with Article 14 (see above pp 77–78).

389

established, the Court has recently shown itself willing to uphold the right to maintain family ties if satisfied that the ties are clearly in existence.[51]

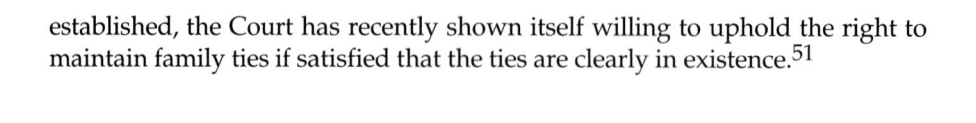

[51] See *Moustaquim v Belgium*, A.193, 1991; (1991) 13 EHRR 802 and *Djeroud v France*, A.191-B, 1991; for comment see (1991) *Yearbook of European Law* pp 554–56.

PART FOUR

PERSONAL LIBERTY

Part IV considers the extent to which agents of the state have the power to interfere with individual freedom of movement. Such interference occurs in the name of the prevention of crime, national security or, in the case of immigration controls, in the interests of the economic well-being of the country. This Part will consider whether the curtailment of liberty represented by such interference is justified by the nature of the public interest in question, whether adequate safeguards against abuse of the powers are provided and how far they are in harmony with the European Convention on Human Rights and other international human rights instruments.

In conjunction with these matters, this Part also considers the due process aspects of decisions to infringe freedom of movement. For example, how far, under UK law, must due process infuse decisions to exclude or deport individuals? How far does due process influence criminal investigations, bearing in mind the ultimate possibility of loss of liberty which may flow from them? Such questions will take into account the social cost of due process in terms of the public interest in crime control and in the economic aspects of controlling entry to the country but it will be argued that these are complex matters: for example, more due process does not inevitably mean less crime control. Further, in a civilised, democratic society one would not expect the question of, for example, the treatment of asylum seekers to be resolved only on economic grounds.

CHAPTER ELEVEN

FREEDOM FROM ARBITRARY SEARCH, ARREST AND DETENTION: SUSPECTS' RIGHTS IN CRIMINAL INVESTIGATIONS

1 INTRODUCTION[1]

The exercise of police powers such as arrest and detention represents an invasion of personal liberty which is tolerated in the interests of the prevention and detection of crime. However, the interest in personal liberty requires that such powers should be strictly regulated. Thus the rules governing the exercise of police powers are of crucial importance as providing safeguards for civil liberties. At present these rules are largely contained in the scheme created under the Police and Criminal Evidence Act 1984 (PACE), which is made up of rules deriving from the Act itself, from the Codes of Practice made under it and the Notes for Guidance contained in the Codes. It is also influenced by Home Office circulars. The difference in status between these four levels and the significance of adopting this four tiered approach is considered below. It will be found that one group of suspects – those suspected of crimes under the Prevention of Terrorism Act 1989 are covered by this scheme but that at many points they receive less protection than other suspects because they are perceived as representing a more serious danger.

Before the inception of PACE the police had no general and clear powers of arrest, stop and search or entry to premises. They wanted such powers put on a clear statutory basis so that they could exercise them where they felt it was their duty to do so without laying themselves open to the possibility of a civil action. Thus PACE was introduced in order to provide clear and general police powers but these were supposed to be balanced by greater safeguards for suspects which took into account the need to ensure that miscarriages of justice such as that which occurred in the *Confait* case,[2] would not recur. The Royal Commission on Criminal Procedure,[3] whose report influenced PACE,

---

1 For background reading see: Hewitt, P, *The Abuse of Power*, 1982, Chap 3; Lustgarten, *The Governance of Police*, 1986; Leigh, *Police Power*, 2nd edn, 1985; Robilliard, J and McEwan, J, *Police Powers and the Individual*, 1986; Benyon and Bourn, *The Police: Powers, Procedures and Proprieties*, 1986; Newburn, T, *Crime and Criminal Justice Policy*, 1995, Chap 3; Leishman, F, Loveday, B and Savage, S, eds, *Core Issues in Policing*, 1996; Morgan, R and Newburn, T, *The Future of Policing*, 1997. For early comment on the Police and Criminal Evidence Act see [1985] *PL* 388; [1985] *Crim LR* 535. For current comment on the 1984 Act and on the relevant provisions under the Criminal Justice and Public Order Act 1994 see: Feldman, D, *Civil Liberties and Human Rights in England and Wales*, 1993, Chaps 5 and 9; Sanders and Young, *Criminal Justice*, 1994; Levenson and Fairweather, *Police Powers*, 1990; Bailey, Harris and Jones, *Civil Liberties: Cases and Materials*, 4th edn, 1995, Chap 2; Zander, M, *The Police and Criminal Evidence Act 1984*, 3rd edn, 1995; Lidstone, K and Palmer, C, *The Investigation of Crime*, 2nd edn, 1996.
2 See *Report of the Inquiry* by the Hon Sir Henry Fisher HC 90 of 1977–78.
3 *Royal Commission on Criminal Procedure Report*, Cmnd 8092, 1981 (RCCP Report).

was set up largely in response to the inadequacies of safeguards for suspects which were exposed in the *Confait* report.[4] Ironically, a further spate of miscarriages of justice, some post-dating the introduction of PACE,[5] led in 1992 to the setting up of another Royal Commission in order to consider further measures which could be introduced to address the problem.[6]

However, the report of that Commission did not suggest any significant safeguards for suspects which could be introduced in order to balance increases in police powers. Since the Commission reported, the Major government has passed legislation, most notably the Criminal Justice and Public Order Act 1994, which increases police powers significantly while removing a number of safeguards for suspects. In particular, the 1994 Act curtailed the right of silence, although the Runciman Royal Commission had recommended that the right should be retained since its curtailment might lead to further miscarriages of justice. Thus, there have been significant developments in police powers during the Major years and the balance PACE was supposed to strike between such powers and due process has, it will be argued, been undermined.

In this chapter the powers of the police and the safeguards which affect the use of their powers are considered first and this is followed by a consideration of the means of redress available if the police fail to comply with the rules.

2 THE SOURCES OF THE RULES

PACE and the Codes

There are at present five Codes of Practice: Code A covering stop and search procedures, Code B covering searching of premises, Code C covering interviewing and conditions of detention, Code D covering identification methods and Code E covering tape-recording. Thus each covers a particular area of PACE although not all areas are covered: arrest, for example, is governed only by statutory provisions.[7] It may be asked why all of the stop

---

4   *Report of an Inquiry* by Sir Henry Fisher, *ibid.*
5   Including the *Cardiff Three* case (*Paris* (1993) 97 Cr App R 99, CA; [1994] *Crim LR* 361) and the *Silcott* case (1991) *The Times*, 8 December. For comment provoked by these cases see Dennis, I [1993] *PL* 291; Greer, S (1994) *MLR* 58.
6   The Royal Commission on Criminal Procedure chaired by Lord Runciman; it was announced by the Home Secretary on 14 March 1991, *HC Deb*, Vol 187 Col 1109. It reported on 6 July 1993, Cm 2263, 1993; see 143 *NLJ* 933–96 for a summary of its recommendations in respect of police investigations, safeguards for suspects, the right to silence and confession evidence. For commentary on the proposals see (1994) *MLR* 75; [1993] *Crim LR* 808 as regards safeguards for suspects; [1993] *Crim LR* 817 for the evidence recommendations.
7   However the Code A provisions relating to the concept of reasonable suspicion may be of relevance. See below p 398.

and search rules, for example, were not merely made part of the Act. The answer may partly lie in the need for some flexibility in making changes: the Codes are quicker and less cumbersome to amend than statutory provisions. However, it is also possible that the government did not want to create rules which might give rise to liability on the part of the police if they were broken; rules which could operate at a lower level of visibility than statutory ones may have appeared more attractive.

Section 67(10) of PACE makes clear the intended distinction between Act and Codes in providing that no civil or criminal liability will arise from a breach of the Codes. This distinction is of significance in relation to the stop and search, arrest and detention provisions of Parts I to IV of PACE.[8] However, it does not seem to have any significance as far as the interviewing provisions of Part V are concerned. The most important statutory safeguard for interviewing, the entitlement to legal advice, has not been affected by the availability of tortious remedies.[9] Thus statutory *and* Code provisions concerned with safeguards for suspects are in an equally weak position in the sense that a clear remedy is not available if they are breached. The context in which breaches of the interviewing provisions have been considered is that of exclusion of evidence.[10] In that context the courts have not drawn a distinction between provisions of Act or Codes except to require that breach of a Code provision should be of a substantial and significant nature[11] if exclusion of evidence is to be considered.

Notes for Guidance

The Notes for Guidance are contained in the Codes but are not part of them.[12] They were apparently intended, as their name suggests, to be used merely as interpretative provisions. However as will be seen they contain some very significant provisions although it is unclear what the consequences of breach of a Note are. Evidence tainted by breach of a Note for Guidance is unlikely to

---

8   In that respect such claims are becoming very significant; in 1991 the Metropolitan Police faced an increase in claims of 40% over 1990. See *HC Deb*, Vol 193 Col 370w. For discussion of the use of tortious claims in this context see below pp 500–03.

9   The question whether an unlawful denial of access to legal advice amounts to a breach of statutory duty has been considered in an unreported case, 26 October 1985, QB, Mr Justice Rose, which is cited by Clayton and Tomlinson in *Civil Actions Against the Police* (1992) at p 359. It was held that the application would be refused even if jurisdiction to make the order sought existed as it would 'cause hindrance to police enquiries'.

10 In over 150 reported decisions breach of a code provision has been taken into account in determining whether or not a confession should be excluded, usually under s 78 of PACE. Breach of a code provision will not lead to automatic exclusion of an interview obtained thereby but a substantial and significant breach may be the first step on the way to its exclusion (see *Walsh* [1989] *Crim LR* 822, CA, transcript from LEXIS).

11 *Keenan* [1989] 3 All ER 598, CA.

12 This is provided for in the first paragraph of each Code; see eg Code C para 1.3.

be excluded since, unlike Code provisions, s 67(11) of PACE does not require a court to take the Notes into account in determining any question.[13] However, in *DPP v Blake*[14] the Divisional Court impliedly accepted that a Note for Guidance will be considered in relation to exclusion of evidence if it can be argued that it merely amplifies a particular Code provision and can therefore be of assistance in determining whether breach of such a provision has occurred. Moreover, certain Notes need not merely be considered in conjunction with the paragraph they derive from; the ruling in *DPP v Rouse* and *DPP v Davis*[15] that they can sometimes be used as an aid to the interpretation of Code C as a whole extended their potential impact. Thus it may be said that the Notes are of a very uncertain status but that their importance is beginning to be recognised in decisions as to admission of evidence.

Home Office circulars

There are a large number of such circulars dealing with disparate subjects relevant to the use of police powers; some of them are intended to work in tandem with a part of PACE as amplifying provisions and some operate in an area uncovered by the other provisions. They are in an even more equivocal legal position than the Notes. Their legal significance derives from their relevance to the obligations arising from the relationship between police forces and the Home Office and it is likely to be in that context rather than in relation to questions of admissibility that they will be considered.[16] Clearly, argument that a court may be disinclined to consider a Note for Guidance applies *a fortiori* to the circulars.[17] It also seems clear that a decision taken in breach of a circular will not be susceptible to judicial review.[18]

---

13 Section 67(11) of PACE provides: 'In all criminal and civil proceedings any such code shall be admissible in evidence; and if any provision of such a code appears to the court or tribunal conducting the proceedings to be relevant to any question arising in the proceedings it shall be taken into account in determining that question.'

14 [1989] 1 WLR 432, CA.

15 (1992) Cr App R 185.

16 See *Home Secretary, ex parte Westminster Press Ltd* (1991) *Guardian*, 12 February; *Secretary of State for the Home Dept, ex parte Lancashire Police Authority* (1992) *The Times*, 26 May. They may also be relevant to issues arising under s 51 of the Police Act 1964. In *Collins and Wilcock* [1984] 3 All ER 374; [1984] 1 WLR 1172. Home Office circular 109/59 was wrongly interpreted by a police officer; her actions in reliance on the incorrect interpretation were held to be outside the execution of her duty. However, the question whether breach of provisions contained in a circular could lead to exclusion of evidence has not yet been determined.

17 This point was made in 'The Questioning Code Revamped' [1991] *Crim LR* 232 by Wolehover, D and Heaton-Armstrong, A, with reference to the revision of Code C.

18 See *Gillick v West Norfolk and Wisbeach Area Health Authority* [1986] AC 112, HL (non-statutory administrative guidance by government departments to subordinate authorities is not as a general rule subject to judicial review). Applicability of this rule to circulars directed to the police was confirmed in *Home Secretary, ex parte Westminster Press Ltd*, note 16 above.

3 STOP AND SEARCH POWERS

Current statutory stop and search powers are meant to maintain a balance between the interest of society, as represented by the police, in crime control and national security, and the interest of the citizen in personal liberty. The use of such powers is probably a necessary part of effective policing and represents less of an infringement of liberty than an arrest but on the other hand their exercise may create a sense of grievance and of violation of personal privacy. Such feelings may contribute to the alienation of the police from the community, leading to a breakdown in law and order expressed in its most extreme form in rioting[19] and otherwise in a general lack of co-operation with the police. Thus, the extensiveness of stop and search powers may tell us something about the extent to which UK society values individual liberty but it is also clear that this is a complex issue: too great an infringement of liberty may be as likely to result ultimately in less effective crime control as too great a restriction of police powers.

The PACE stop and search power

There was no general power at common law to detain without the subject's consent in the absence of specific statutory authority.[20] Instead there was a miscellany of such powers, the majority of which have been superseded. Under s 1 of PACE for the first time a general power to stop[21] and search persons or vehicles[22] is conferred on police constables if reasonable suspicion arises that stolen goods, offensive weapons or other prohibited articles may be found.[23] It may be that the suspect appears to be in innocent possession of the goods or articles; this will not affect the power to stop although it would affect the power to arrest and in this sense the power to stop is broader than the arrest power. Under s 1(6) if an article is found which appears to be stolen or

---

19 See on this point Lord Scarman, *The Brixton Disorders*, Cmnd 8427, 1981; McConville, M, 'Search of Persons and Premises' [1983] *Crim LR* 604–14.

20 For a full list of the powers arising from 16 statutes see *RCCP Report* 1981.

21 It should be noted that the police do not need to search the suspect once he or she has been stopped; they may decide not to. Nevertheless reasonable suspicion that stolen goods or articles are being carried must arise before the stop can be made.

22 A power to stop vehicles which is not dependent on reasonable suspicion arises under s 163 of the Road Traffic Act 1988. Section 4 of PACE regulates it when it is used as the basis for a general road check.

23 Under s 1(7) the articles are those '(i) made or adapted for use in the course of or in connection with an offence to which this sub-paragraph applies; or (ii) intended by the person having it with him for such use by him or by some other person'. Under s 1(8) the offences to which s 1(7)(b)(i) above applies are – (a) burglary; (b) theft; (c) offences under s 12 of the Theft Act 1968; (d) offences under s 15 of that Act. Section 1(8A) applies to (any article which falls within) s 139 of the Criminal Justice Act 1988.

prohibited the officer can seize it. The power may be exercised in any public place, in any place to which the public or a section of it, have access or in any other place 'to which people have ready access at the time when [the constable] proposes to exercise the power but which is not a dwelling'. The power to enter a dwelling arises under ss 17 and 18 but an officer can search a person outside a dwelling (assuming of course that the provisions of s 1 as to reasonable suspicion are fulfilled) if it appears that he or she does not have the permission of the owner to be there (s 1(4)). This general power to stop, search and seize is balanced in two ways. First, the concept of reasonable suspicion allows it to be exercised only when quite a high level of suspicion exists. Secondly, under s 2 the police officer must provide the person to be searched with certain information.

The concept of reasonable suspicion as the basis for the exercise of stop and search powers is set out briefly in Code of Practice A on Stop and Search paras 1.6 and 1.7 as revised in 1995 and 1997. It is not enough for a police officer to have a hunch that a person has committed or is about to commit an offence; there must be a concrete basis for this suspicion which relates to the particular person in question and could be evaluated by an objective observer. When Code A was revised in 1997 (SI 1997/1159) some departure from this stance was effected. Paragraph 1.6A allows an officer to take into account information that members of a particular gang habitually carry knives, other weapons or have drugs in their possession. Paragraph 1.7AA provides that if a person wears an item of clothing or other insignia suggesting that he belongs to such a gang he may be stopped and searched. Paragraphs 1.6 and 1.7 explain the objective nature of reasonable suspicion and forbid stereotyping in arriving at such suspicion:

1.6 An officer will need to consider the nature of the article suspected of being carried in the context of other factors such as the time and the place and the behaviour of the person concerned or those with him. Reasonable suspicion may exist, for example, where information has been received such as a description of an article being carried or of a suspected offender; a person is seen acting covertly or warily or attempting to hide something; or a person is carrying a certain type of article at an unusual time or in a place where a number of burglaries or thefts are known to have taken place recently. But the decision to stop and search must be based on all the facts which bear on the likelihood that an article of a certain kind will be found.

1.7 ... a person's colour, age, hairstyle or manner of dress or the fact that he is known to have a previous conviction for possession of an unlawful article, cannot be used alone or in combination with each other as the sole basis on which to search that person. Nor may it be founded on the basis of stereotyped images of certain persons or groups as more likely to be committing offences.

The most significant change brought about when Code A was revised in 1991 was the omission of the requirement that the suspicion should be of the same level as that necessary to effect an arrest.[24] The original intention behind including this provision was to stress the high level of suspicion required before a stop and search could take place; this change therefore tends to remove some of that emphasis and could be taken to imply that there are two levels of suspicion, the level required under Code A being the lower. However, although this omission may convey such a message to police officers it may not make much difference to the way the police actually operate stop and search powers in practice; research in the area suggests that there is already a tendency to view reasonable suspicion as a flexible concept which may denote quite a low level of suspicion.[25]

Misuse of drugs

Section 23 of the Misuse of Drugs Act 1971 provides a stop and search power which is frequently invoked. Under s 23 a constable may stop and search a person whom the constable has reasonable grounds to suspect is in possession of a controlled drug. This power may be exercised anywhere, unlike the power under s 1 of PACE; thus, persons on private premises may be searched once police officers are lawfully on the premises. The provisions as to reasonable suspicion will be interpreted in accordance with Code A. Code A and ss 2 and 3 of PACE apply to this as they do to other statutory stop and search powers unless specific exceptions are made (see below).

Prevention of terrorism and anticipated local violence

The Prevention of Terrorism Act (PTA) 1989 provides a power to stop and search under s 15(3) which does not depend on the need to show reasonable suspicion that the suspect is carrying the items which may be searched for. However, the officer must have reasonable grounds for suspecting that the suspect is liable to arrest under s 14 of the 1989 Act. Section 14(1)(b) provides a power of arrest if involvement in terrorism is suspected on reasonable grounds which does not depend on suspicion relating to any specific offence. The s 15(3) power arises in addition to the general PACE power to stop and search in connection with all offences including, of course, those under the PTA. Code A applies to the use of this power. There is a further power to search a person who has arrived in or is seeking to leave Britain or Northern

---

24 Previously contained in Annex B para 4 of Code A.
25 See Dixon, D (1989) 17 *Int J Soc Law* pp 185–206. However, in *Black v DPP*, 11 May 1995 (unreported), the fact of visiting a well-known drug dealer was found to be insufficient as a basis for reasonable suspicion.

Ireland under para 4(2) of Schedule 5 to the 1989 Act and again this power is not dependent on showing reasonable suspicion in relation to particular articles. Note 1C of Code A provides that this power is not a power of stop and search as defined in para 1.3 and so is not covered by the Code but searches carried out under para 4(2) should follow the procedures laid down in the Code as far as practicable. Thus, one of the main safeguards arising in respect of general stop and search powers – reasonable suspicion – is removed, while the other – Code A procedures – is eroded.[26]

The 1989 Act was amended by s 81(1) of the Criminal Justice and Public Order Act 1994 to provide a new power to stop and search vehicles and their occupants in localities specified by officers of or above the rank of commander (for the Metropolitan or City of London police) or of or above the rank of Assistant Chief Constable for other areas. The authorisation may be made where it appears to the officer in question that 'it is expedient to do so in order to prevent acts of terrorism'. The 1989 Act was also amended by the Prevention of Terrorism (Additional Powers) Act 1996 to include a number of new stop and search powers. These include a power to stop and search citizens in designated areas without reasonable suspicion under s 1 which inserts s 13B into the PTA. The authorisation to search persons in a designated area may be given on the same grounds as that under s 13A. A designation, once in force, will subsist for 28 days and can be renewed. The use of the word 'expedient' in ss 13A and B appears to signal something much more uncertain than reasonable suspicion and its was questioned in debate in Parliament on that ground.

Section 60 of the Criminal Justice and Public Order Act 1994 also provides police officers with a stop and search power which does not depend on showing reasonable suspicion of particular wrong-doing on the part of an individual. Section 60 provides a power to stop and search persons and vehicles in localities specified by an officer of or above the rank of superintendent. The authorisation may be made if the officer in question reasonably believes that 'incidents involving serious violence may take place in an locality in his area and it is expedient to [give the authorisation in order] to prevent their occurrence'. An authorisation, once in force, will subsist for 24 hours and can be renewed for a further six hours. It confers on police constables a power to stop persons, vehicles and their occupants and search for offensive weapons or dangerous instruments whether or not there any grounds for suspecting that such articles are being carried.

It is notable that no judicial body is involved in the supervision of the powers under ss 60, 13A or B. All of them are subject to supervision by the

---

[26] For discussion see Walker, C, *The Prevention of Terrorism in British Law*, 2nd edn, 1992, pp 191–97.

police themselves, except the s 13B power which is subject to supervision by the Home Secretary. The then Conservative government considered that introduction of the powers under the 1996 Act, including in particular that under s 13B, was necessary due to the threat of IRA activity on the British mainland in Spring 1996. However, s 13B may be criticised on the basis that it hands the police a power which is clearly open to abuse since a decision to undertake a stop and search can be taken on very flimsy grounds. It is, however, unclear that s 13A or s 13B will be effective in preventing terrorist activity. In debate on the Prevention of Terrorism (Additional Powers) Bill Michael Howard was asked how many arrests and convictions had followed use of the existing s 13A power to stop and search. In reply he said that there had been 1,746 stops, 1,695 searches of vehicles and 2,373 searches of persons as occupants of vehicles in the five Metropolitan police areas and 8,142 stops and 6,854 searches of vehicles and 40 searches of persons as occupants of vehicles within the Heathrow perimeter. These had together led to two arrests under the PTA and to 66 other arrests.[27] The point was made that this does not represent the whole picture since would-be terrorists may be diverted from their activity and weapons may be found. This point was not backed up by any specific evidence.

These figures suggest that stopping and searching without reasonable suspicion leads to an extremely low level of arrests and therefore may not be the most effective use of police resources. They also suggest that use of such powers leads to a low level of apprehension of persons engaged in non-terrorist offences. This very low level of arrests may be compared with the general level of arrests flowing from stop and search with reasonable suspicion, which is around 13%. This figure itself is low (and may not be reliable) but nevertheless suggests that stop and search with reasonable suspicion (even though that concept may be interpreted very flexibly) is more productive on the face of it in crime control terms than stop and search without it.

Research into past use of blanket police powers suggests that they may tend to arouse resentment rather than lead to a clear reduction in crime. Since the powers under s 60 of the 1994 Act and ss 13A and B of the 1989 Act on their face allow for stop and search on subjective grounds, they may tend to be used disproportionately against the black community. In 1995 of 160,000 people stopped under PACE in London 60% were black. The justification given by the police was that the number of arrests which followed use of this power against black people was the same as the proportion arrested from other stops of whites. In 1995 Note 1A of Code A was revised to add the requirement that the selection of those questioned or searched is based upon objective factors and not upon personal prejudice'. Thus, this requirement

---

27   *HC Deb*, 2 April 1996, 211.

contained in a non-legal provision is the only 'safeguard' against a racially stereotyped use of these powers.

The ss 60, 13A and 13B powers are (or in the case of s 13B, will soon be) subject to the same procedural requirements under Code A as those relating to the powers under s 1 of PACE, apart from the Code A provisions relating to reasonable suspicion (Code A, para 1.5(b)). At present Code A does not apply to the amendments made by the 1996 Act. However, in debate on the Bill Mr Howard said that Code A will be applied to it and that until the new provisions are brought formally within the scope of Code A the police will apply the Code A provisions voluntarily. Under s 2(1) of PACE the procedural safeguards it sets out, together with those under s 3, apply to the PACE power and to powers under any other statutory provisions.

Procedural requirements

The procedural requirements of ss 2 and 3 and Code A must be met. Under s 2 and Code A para 2.4, the constable must give the suspect certain information before the search begins including 'his name and the name of the police station to which he is attached; the object of the proposed search; the constable's grounds for proposing to make it'. Under s 3 the constable must make a record of the search either on the spot if that is practicable or as soon as it is practicable.[28] The subject of the search can obtain a copy of the search record later on from the police station. Such record keeping may ensure that some officers do not over-use the stop and search power, partly because it means that the citizen can make a complaint and partly because the police station will have a record of the number of stops being carried out. The guidance as to the conduct of the search contained in Code A para 3 is fairly general; it requires the officer to complete the search speedily, to minimise embarrassment and to seek co-operation.

Voluntary searches

Code A does not in general affect ordinary consensual contact between police officer and citizen; officers can ask members of the public to stop and can ask them to consent to a search and, at least theoretically, the citizen can refuse. However, voluntary contacts can have a sinister side: some people might 'consent' to a search in the sense of offering no resistance to it due to uncertainty as to the basis or extent of the police power in question.[29] The search could then be classified as voluntary and subsequently it would be

---

28 This provision is explained and amplified in Code A para 4.
29 For further discussion of this point see Dixon, D, 'Consent and the Legal Regulation of Policing' (1990) 17 *JLS* pp 245–362.

difficult if not impossible to determine whether such classification was justifiable. Once a search is so classified none of the statutory or Code A safeguards need be observed. Original Code A failed to recognise this problem although a Home Office circular issued in December 1985[30] did make an effort to address it in para 1:

> ... The co-operation of the citizen should not be taken as implying consent ... Whilst it is legitimate to invite co-operation from the public in circumstances where there is no power to require it, the subject of a voluntary search should not be left under the impression that a power is being exercised. Voluntary search must not be used as a device for circumventing the safeguards established in Part I of the Act.

When the Codes were revised in 1991 the concerns articulated in the circular were given expression in new Notes for Guidance 1D(b) and 1E which created certain restrictions on voluntary searches. Under Note 1E persons belonging to three of the vulnerable groups recognised throughout the Codes as requiring special treatment – juveniles, the mentally handicapped or mentally disordered – may not be subject to a voluntary search at all. The prohibition also applies to a range of other persons who do not appear capable of giving an informed consent to a search. This group may well include the hearing impaired or persons not proficient in English who are also recognised in the Codes as belonging to vulnerable groups,[31] but perhaps they should have been expressly included. Persons who do not fall within the above groups may be subject to a voluntary search under Note 1D(b) as revised in 1995 but the officer should 'always make it clear that he is seeking the consent of the person concerned to the search being carried out by telling the person that he need not consent and that without his consent he will not be searched'.

These provisions represent a welcome move towards dealing with this problem but it may be argued that they are deficient in a number of respects.[32] No specific form of words need be used under Note 1D(b). A requirement that an officer issue a caution in similar terms to that used in Code B para 4.2 in respect of searching of premises might have clarified matters, eg 'You do not have to consent to this search but anything that is found may be used in evidence against you'. Further, under the 1995 revision these important provisions continued to appear as Notes for Guidance only, when it might have been expected that due to their specific wording and prescriptive nature they would have become part of Code A.

---

30 Circular No 88/1985.
31 See in particular Code C para 3(b), Detained Persons: Special Groups.
32 See Fenwick, H, 'Searching People and Places under the Revised PACE Codes' (1992) *Criminal Lawyer*, p 1.

Breaches of the stop and search rules

If a search is conducted unlawfully the citizen is entitled to resist and to sue for assault. However, there is no provision under either PACE or Code A to the effect that if the procedural requirements are not complied with the search will be unlawful. It has been held that a failure to make a written record of the search will not render it unlawful,[33] whereas a failure to give the grounds for it will do so: *Fennelley*.[34]

A breach of the Code A rules will not give rise to civil or criminal liability. Thus it may be necessary to seek the limited form of redress represented by exclusion of evidence which has been obtained as a result of a breach of PACE or Code A. A stop and search is most likely to produce physical evidence such as drugs or perhaps a weapon, but the courts are very reluctant to exclude such evidence unless there has been deliberate illegality because it is less likely to be unreliable than confession or identification evidence.[35] Thus the mechanism of exclusion of evidence as a form of redress for breach of a Code provision which has operated to underpin Codes C and D, is not as appropriate in relation to Code A (or Code B, see below) although an effective sanction is clearly needed.

This weakness is further exacerbated in relation to voluntary searches because provisions relevant to such searches are contained in Notes for Guidance rather than Code A itself and since the Notes do not have the same legal status as Code provisions they may be more likely to be ignored. If the intention was that these provisions should have some impact they should have been made part of Code A. The fact that provision for voluntary searches now appears in the Notes as opposed to the Circular but not in the Code itself suggests that while the need for an important change has been recognised there has been a failure to carry it through fully. What would be the position if, for example, a police officer persuaded a mentally handicapped person to consent to a voluntary search in breach of Note for Guidance 1E? A judge might well be minded to view breach of a Note for Guidance as of insufficient significance to lead to exclusion of the products of the search even if prepared to depart from the general presumption that physical evidence, however obtained, is admissible.

Disciplinary action, the other form of redress for breach of a Code provision, may be even less effective in relation to Code A than Codes C, D and E which largely govern interrogation and identification, because stop and search powers are exercised away from the police station, at a low level of visibility. Moreover, if a police officer decides that a search can be called

---

33 *Basher v DPP* 2 March 1993 (unreported).
34 [1989] *Crim LR* 142.
35 See the pre-PACE ruling of the House of Lords in *Fox* [1986] AC 281; also *Thomas* [1990] *Crim LR* 269 and *Effick* (1992) 95 Cr App R 427; (1992) 142 *NLJ* 492, CA; cf *Edward Fennelly* [1989] *Crim LR* 142.

Freedom from Arbitrary Search, Arrest and Detention

voluntary he need not give his name or number and therefore it will be almost impossible to bring a complaint against him. Thus it is fair to say that in so far as the balance between police powers and individual rights is supposed to be maintained by the Code A provisions, it is largely dependent on voluntary adherence to them.

4 POWERS OF ARREST AND DETENTION

Arrest may often be the first formal stage in the criminal process. It does not need to be; the process could begin with a consensual interview with the suspect, perhaps in his or her own home, followed by a summons to appear at the magistrates' court. It appears that arrests are sometimes effected unnecessarily; this contention is supported by the pre-PACE variation in practice regarding arrest between police areas[36] which does not seem to be explicable on the ground of necessity but seems to be attributable to different policies in the different areas.

Any arrest represents a serious curtailment of liberty; therefore use of the arrest power requires careful regulation. An arrest, in common with the exercise of other police powers, is seen as *prima facie* illegal necessitating justification under a specific legal power. If an arrest is effected where no arrest power arises a civil action for false imprisonment may lie. Despite the need for clarity and precision such powers were until relatively recently granted piecemeal with the result that prior to PACE they were contained in a mass of common law and statutory provisions. No consistent rationale could be discerned and there were a number of gaps and anomalies. For example, the Criminal Law Act 1967 gave a power of arrest without warrant where the offence in question arose under statute and carried a sentence of five years. Thus no power of arrest arose in respect of common law offences carrying such a sentence. This situation was detrimental to civil liberties due to the uncertainty of the powers but it may also have been detrimental in crime control terms since officers may have been deterred from effecting an arrest where one was necessary. The powers are now contained largely in PACE but common law powers remain, while some statutes create a specific power of arrest which may overlap with the PACE powers.

---

36 For example, in 1976 in Cleveland 1% of persons were summonsed for an indictable offence, whereas in Derbyshire 76% of suspects were as were 40% of suspects in West Yorkshire and North Wales. Royal Commission Report 1981, Cmnd 8092 para 3.72. See further Bailey, SH and Gunn, MJ, *Smith and Bailey on the Modern English Legal System*, 2nd edn, 1991, pp 630–32.

At common law – power to arrest for breach of peace

PACE has not affected the power to arrest which arises at common law for breach of the peace. Factors present in a situation in which breach of the peace occurs may also give rise to arrest powers under PACE but may extend further than they do due to the wide definition of breach of the peace. The leading case is *Howell*[37] in which it was found that breach of the peace will arise if violence to persons or property either actual or apprehended occurs. Threatening words are not in themselves a breach of the peace but they may lead a police officer to apprehend that a breach will arise. A police officer or any other person may arrest if a breach of the peace is in being or apprehended but not when it has been terminated unless there is reason to believe that it may be renewed.[38]

Under PACE: power of arrest without warrant

PACE contains two separate powers of arrest without warrant, one arising under s 24 and the other under s 25. In very broad terms s 24 provides a power of arrest in respect of more serious offences while s 25 covers *all* offences however trivial (including, for example, dropping litter) *if* – and this is the important point – certain conditions are satisfied *apart from* suspicion that the offence in question has been committed. Thus s 25 operates to cover persons suspected of offences falling outside s 24. The difference between ss 24 and 25 is quite significant because once a person has been arrested under s 24 he or she is said to have been arrested for 'an arrestable offence' and this may have an effect on his or her treatment later on. An 'arrestable offence' is therefore one for which a person can be arrested if the necessary reasonable suspicion is present without the need to demonstrate that any other ingredients were present in the situation at the time of arrest.

Arrest under s 24

Section 24 applies:
- (1) (a) to offences for which the sentence is fixed by law;
    - (b) to offences for which a person of 21 years of age or over (not previously convicted) may be sentenced to imprisonment for a term of

---

37 [1982] QB 416; [1981] 3 All ER 383, CA; for comment see Glanville Williams (1982) 146 *JPN* 199–200, 217–19.

38 For commentary on this point and on breach of the peace generally see Glanville Williams [1954] *Crim LR* 578. The view that there is no power to arrest once a breach of the peace is over was put forward in the Commentary on *Podger* [1979] *Crim LR* 524 and endorsed *obiter* in *Howell* note 37 above. See Chap 7 pp 300–06 for full discussion of the use of breach of the peace.

five years (or might be so sentenced but for the restrictions imposed by s 33 of the Magistrates' Courts Act 1980); and

(c) to the offences to which s 24(2) applies and in this Act 'arrestable offence' means any such offence.[39]

A police officer can arrest for one of the offences covered by s 24 if he or she has reasonable grounds to suspect that the offence is about to be, is being or has been committed. An ordinary citizen can arrest under s 24 in the same way with the omission of the possibility of arresting where the offence is about to be committed. Offences for which a person can be arrested under s 24 may also be classified as 'serious arrestable offences' under s 116. This does not affect the power of arrest but it does affect various safeguards and powers which may be exercised during detention. The s 24 offences which may also fall into this category fall into two groups as defined under s 116 – first, those which are so serious (such as murder, manslaughter, indecent assault which amounts to gross indecency) that they will always be serious arrestable offences and secondly, those which will be so classified only if their commission has led to certain specified consequences, namely, serious harm to the security of the state or public order, serious interference with the administration of justice or investigation of offences, death or serious injury, substantial financial gain or serious financial loss. This last possibility may considerably widen the category of serious arrestable offences in that whether or not a loss may be serious may need to be judged in relation to the financial consequences to the person suffering it: a loss of a small amount of money might be serious to a poor person; someone arrested on suspicion of its theft could therefore be classified as in detention for a serious arrestable offence.

Arrest under s 25

The police acquired the general power of arrest under s 25 which they had lacked previously. However, as mentioned above, this power does not merely allow an officer to arrest for *any* offence so long as reasonable suspicion can be shown. Such a power would have been viewed as too draconian. It is balanced by what are known as the 'general arrest conditions' which must also be fulfilled. Therefore in order to arrest under s 25 two steps must be taken: first, there must be reasonable suspicion relating to the offence in question; second, there must be reasonable grounds for thinking that one of the arrest conditions is satisfied. The need for the officer to have reasonable suspicion relating to the offence in question and to the general arrest conditions was emphasised on appeal in *Edwards v DPP*.[40]

---

39 Section 24(2) covers a miscellany of offences including offences under the Official Secrets Act 1989 and under the Theft Act 1968. It amends s 2 of the Criminal Law Act 1967 and contains the powers of arrest which already existed.
40 (1993) 97 Cr App R 301; (1993) *The Times*, 29 March.

A police constable (but not an ordinary citizen) can arrest if he or she has reasonable grounds to suspect the person of having committed or having attempted to commit the offence or of being in the course of committing or attempting to commit it. The general arrest conditions are:

(a) that the name of the relevant person is unknown to and cannot be readily ascertained by, the constable;

(b) that the constable has reasonable grounds for doubting whether a name furnished by the relevant person as his name is his real name;

(c) that:
  (i) the relevant person has failed to furnish a satisfactory address for service; or
  (ii) the constable has reasonable grounds for doubting whether an address furnished by the relevant person is a satisfactory address for service;

(d) that the constable has reasonable grounds for believing that arrest is necessary to prevent the relevant person:
  (i) causing physical injury to himself or any other person;
  (ii) suffering physical injury;
  (iii) causing loss of or damage to property;
  (iv) committing an offence against public decency; or
  (v) causing an unlawful obstruction of the highway;

(e) that the constable has reasonable grounds for believing that arrest is necessary to protect a child or other vulnerable person from the relevant person.

It can be seen that these conditions divide into two groups: those in which there is or appears to be a failure to furnish a satisfactory name or address so that the service of a summons later on would be impracticable and those which concern the immediate need to remove the suspect from the street which would make it inappropriate to serve a summons later. The inclusion of these provisions implies that the infringement of civil liberties represented by an arrest should be resorted to only where no other alternative exists. In practice, however, arrest under s 25 may be resorted to quite readily; whether this will occur will depend on the interpretation given to 'reasonable grounds'. The phrase suggests that a clear, objective basis for forming the view in question should exist. However, in *G v DPP*[41] a belief that an address was false based on a general assumption that people who commit offences give false details was accepted as based on reasonable grounds. On this interpretation the general arrest conditions would be unlikely to act as a limiting requirement: once an offence was suspected, it would seem that one of them would be almost automatically fulfilled. However, the decision in *Edwards v DPP*[42] suggests that the courts appreciate the constitutional

---

41 [1989] *Crim LR* 150. For comment see [1993] *Crim LR* 567.
42 Above note 40.

significance of upholding the requirements under the general arrest conditions. In *Edwards* an officer arrested the appellant in the course of a struggle, stating that the arrest was 'for obstruction'. Since no power of arrest arises in respect of obstruction[43] the arrest must have been under s 25. However, it was found to be necessary to demonstrate that the officer had the general arrest conditions in mind when arresting. This might have been inferred but the express reference to obstruction was thought to preclude an inference that he had other matters in mind.

'Reasonable suspicion'

Sections 24 and 25 both depend on this concept; the idea behind it is that an arrest should take place at quite a late stage in the investigation; this limits the number of arrests and makes it less likely that a person will be wrongfully arrested. It seems likely that it will be interpreted in accordance with the provisions as to reasonable suspicion under Code A although as will be discussed below the courts have not relied on Code A in ruling on the lawfulness of arrests. However, Annex B para 4 of original Code A stated that the level of suspicion for a stop would be 'no less' than that needed for arrest. Although this provision is omitted from the revised Code A, it would seem that in principle the Code A provisions should be relevant to arrests if the Codes and statute are to be treated as a harmonious whole.[44] Moreover, it would appear strange if a more rigorous test could be applied to the reasonable suspicion necessary to effect a stop than that necessary to effect an arrest. If this is correct it would seem that certain matters, such as an individual's racial group could *never* be factors which could support a finding of reasonable suspicion. It would seem that a future revision of the Codes might usefully state that the concept of reasonable suspicion in Code A applies to arrest as well; if so, it would at least outlaw the use of such factors as the basis of reasonable suspicion.

The objective nature of suspicion required under Code A is echoed in various decisions on the suspicion needed for an arrest.[45] In *Dallison v Caffrey*[46] Lord Diplock said the test was whether 'a reasonable man assumed to know the law and possessed of the information which in fact was possessed by the defendant would believe there were [reasonable grounds]'. Thus it is not enough for a police officer to have a hunch that a person has committed or is about to commit an offence; there must be a clear basis for this suspicion

---

43 An offence under s 51(3) of the Police Act 1964.
44 This general principle was made explicit in relation to the aim of coherent and harmonious interpretation of provisions within the Codes in *DPP v Rouse* and *DPP v Davis* (1992) 94 Cr App R 185.
45 For example, *Nakkuda Ali v Jayaratne* [1951] AC 66, at 77; *Allen v Wright* (1835) 8 C & P 522.
46 [1965] 1 QB 348 at 371.

which relates to the particular person in question and which would also be apparent to an objective observer. If an officer only has a hunch – mere suspicion as opposed to reasonable suspicion – he or she might continue to observe the person in question but could not arrest until the suspicion had increased and could be termed 'reasonable suspicion'.

However, this still leaves a great deal of leeway to officers to arrest where suspicion relating to the particular person is at a low level but they want to further the investigation by gathering information. At present the courts seem prepared to allow police officers such leeway and it should be noted that PACE endorses a reasonably low level of suspicion due to the distinction it maintains between belief and suspicion, suspicion probably being the lower standard.[47] The decision in *Ward v Chief Constable of Somerset and Avon Constabulary*[48] suggests that a high level of suspicion is not required and this might also be said of *Castorina v Chief Constable of Surrey*.[49] Detectives were investigating a burglary of a company's premises and on reasonable grounds came to the conclusion that it was an 'inside job'. The managing director told them that a certain employee had recently been dismissed and that the documents taken would be useful to someone with a grudge. However, she also said that she would not have expected the particular employee to commit a burglary. The detectives then arrested the employee, having found that she had no previous criminal record. She was detained for nearly four hours and then released without charge. She claimed damages for false imprisonment and was awarded £4,500. The judge considered that it was necessary to find that the detectives had had 'an honest belief founded on a reasonable suspicion leading an ordinary cautious man to the conclusion that the person arrested was guilty of the offence'. However, the Court of Appeal overturned the award on the basis that the test applied by the judge had been too severe. It was held that the question of honest belief was irrelevant; the issue of reasonable suspicion had nothing to do with the officer's subjective state of mind. The question was whether there was reasonable cause to suspect the plaintiff of burglary. Given that certain factors could be identified, including inside knowledge of the company's affairs and the motive of the plaintiff, it appeared that there was sufficient basis for the detectives to have reasonable grounds for suspicion.

---

47 Section 17(2)(a) requires belief, not suspicion, that a suspect whom an officer is seeking is on premises; similarly, powers of seizure under s 19(2) depend on belief in certain matters. The difference between belief and suspicion and the lesser force of the word 'suspect' was accepted as an important distinction by the House of Lords in *Wills v Bowley* [1983] 1 AC 57 at 103, HL. See also *Johnson v Whitehouse* [1984] RTR 38 which was to the same effect.

48 (1986) *The Times*, 26 June; cf *Monaghan v Corbett* (1983) 147 JP 545, DC (however, although this demonstrated a different approach the restriction it imposed may not be warranted: see *DPP v Wilson* [1991] *Crim LR* 441, DC).

49 *NLJ* 180, transcript from LEXIS.

Purchas LJ also ruled that once reasonable suspicion arises officers have discretion as to whether to arrest or do something else, such as making further enquiries but that this discretion can be attacked on *Wednesbury* principles.[50] In making this ruling Purchas J relied on the ruling of the House of Lords in *Holgate-Mohammed v Duke*.[51] The House of Lords had confirmed that in addition to showing that the relevant statutory conditions are satisfied, the exercise of statutory powers by officers must not offend against Wednesbury principles; officers must not take irrelevant factors into account or fail to have regard to relevant ones; an exercise of discretion must not be so unreasonable that no reasonable officer could have exercised it in the manner in question. Thus, an arrest will be found to be unlawful if no reasonable person looking at the circumstances could have considered that an arrest should be effected, if the decision is based on irrelevant considerations and if it is not made in good faith and for a proper purpose.[52] It was found in *Castorina* that no breach of these principles had occurred and as reasonable grounds for making the arrest were found the first instance judge had erred in ruling that further enquiries should have been made before arresting. In applying these principles the civil liberties dimension of police decisions to arrest, etc will be relevant in determining when an officer has acted unreasonably, following the decision in *Secretary of State for Defence, ex parte Smith and Others*.[53] The Court of Appeal affirmed that the court could not interfere with the exercise of an administrative discretion on substantive grounds save where it was satisfied that the decision was unreasonable in the sense that it was beyond the range of responses open to a reasonable decision maker but that in judging whether the decision-maker had exceeded that margin of appreciation the human rights context was important; the more substantial the interference with human rights, the more the court would require by way of justification before it was satisfied that the decision was reasonable.

Thus, the need to make further enquiries would be relevant to the first stage – arriving at reasonable suspicion – but not to the second – determining whether to make an arrest. That it must be relevant to the first is axiomatic: an investigation passes through many stages, from the first in which a vague suspicion relating to a particular person arises, up until the point when that person's guilt is established beyond reasonable doubt. At some point in that process reasonable suspicion giving rise to a discretion as to whether to effect an arrest arises; thus there must be a point in the early stages at which it is possible to say that more enquiries should have been made, more evidence gathered, before the arrest could lawfully take place. As the courts appear

---

50 *Associated Provincial Picture Houses Ltd v Wednesbury Corpn* [1948] 1 KB 223; [1948] 2 All ER 680, CA.
51 [1984] 1 AC 437; [1984] 1 All ER 1054, HL.
52 For discussion of police discretion in this respect see [1986] *PL* 285.
53 [1996] All ER 257; [1996] ICR 740.

prepared to accept that arrest at quite an early stage in this process may be said to be based on reasonable grounds and that the application of *Wednesbury* principle leaves little leeway for challenge to the decision to arrest, it may be said that the interest of the citizen in his or her personal liberty is not being accorded sufficient weight under the current tests.[54] As Sanders and Young observe, commenting on *Castorina*, 'The decision gives the police considerable freedom to follow crime control norms, in that it allows them to arrest on little hard evidence'.[55]

Under s 24(4), (5) and (7) it is not *always* necessary to show that reasonable suspicion exists. If an arrestable offence is *in fact* being committed or has been committed or is about to be committed, a constable can arrest even if he or she is just acting on a hunch which luckily turns out to be justified. Of course if an officer arrests without reasonable suspicion he or she is taking a risk. These provisions were included because it might seem strange if a person could found an action for false imprisonment on the basis that although he was committing an offence he should not have been arrested for it. However, if it cannot be established that the offence was committed or was about to be committed it is not enough to show that reasonable grounds for suspicion did in fact exist although the officer did not know of them. In *Siddiqui v Swain*[56] the Divisional Court held that the words 'reasonable grounds to suspect' used in s 8(5) of the Road Traffic Act 1972 include the requirement that the officer should actually suspect. This approach was also adopted in *Chapman v DPP*.[57] In *O'Hara v Chief Constable of the RUC*,[58] a decision on s 12(1) of the Prevention of Terrorism Act 1989, the House of Lords found that a constable could form a suspicion based on what he had been informed of previously as part of a briefing by a superior officer, or otherwise. The question to be asked was whether a reasonable man would personally have formed the suspicion after receiving the relevant information. It was not enough for the arresting officer to have been instructed by a superior officer to arrest; his own personal knowledge must provide him with the necessary reasonable suspicion. In the instant case the arresting officer had sufficient personal knowledge of matters, which it was found provided a basis for reasonable suspicion. The House of Lords stated that these findings applied to arrest powers other than the one arising under s 12.

---

54 See further as to reasonable grounds for suspicion Clayton and Tomlinson (1988) *LS Gaz* 7 September, p 22; Dixon, D, Bottomley, K and Coleman, C, 'Reality and Rules in the Construction and Regulation of Police Suspicion' (1989) 17 *Int J Soc Law* 185–206; Sanders and Young, *Criminal Justice*, 1994, pp 85–98.
55 Sanders and Young, *Criminal Justice*, 1994, p 86.
56 [1979] RTR 454.
57 (1988) Cr App R 190; [1988] *Crim LR* 843.
58 [1997] WLR 1; [1997] 1 All ER 129.

Power of arrest with warrant

This power does not arise under PACE. There are a large number of statutory provisions allowing an arrest warrant to be issued of which the most significant is that arising under s 1 of the Magistrates' Courts Act 1980.[59] Under this power a warrant may be issued if a person aged at least 17 is suspected of an offence which is indictable or punishable with imprisonment or of any other offence and no satisfactory address is known allowing a summons to be served. This provision therefore limits the circumstances under which a warrant can be sought as an alternative to using the non-warrant powers under PACE and as the police now have such broad powers of arrest under ss 24 and 25 arrest in reliance on a warrant is used even less under PACE than it was previously. The result is that judicial supervision of arrests is minimised.[60] This tendency leaves the operation of the arrest power to the discretion of the police and is part of a general move away from the judicial supervision of police powers.

Arrest under the Prevention of Terrorism (Temporary Provisions) Act 1989

Almost all the indictable offences under the Prevention of Terrorism (Temporary Provisions) Act 1989 (PTA) carry a penalty of at least five years' imprisonment and are therefore arrestable offences under s 24 of PACE. There is also a power of arrest under s 14 of the PTA itself. This power has two limbs. The first, s 14(1)(a), empowers a constable to arrest for certain specified offences under the PTA. As these offences are arrestable offences in any event this power overlaps with that under s 24. However, if an arrest is effected under s 14 of the PTA as opposed to s 24 of PACE this has an effect on the length of detention as will be seen below. The second limb of s 14, s 14(1)(b), provides a completely separate power from the PACE power; it allows arrest without needing to show suspicion relating to a particular offence. Instead the constable needs to have reasonable grounds for suspecting that a person is concerned in the preparation or instigation of acts of terrorism connected with the affairs of Northern Ireland or 'any other act of terrorism except those connected solely with the affairs of the UK or a part of the UK'. This arrest is not for an offence but in practice for investigation, questioning and general intelligence gathering which may be conducted, it has been said, for the purpose of 'isolating and identifying the urban guerrillas and then detaching them from the supportive or ambivalent community'.[61] Thus the inclusion of this power may be criticised as representing a clear departure from the

---

59 See [1962] *Crim LR* 520, 597 for comment on these powers.
60 See *Criminal Statistics*, Cm 2680, 1993 (HMSO) Table 8.2 p 191.
61 Lowry, DR (1976–77) 8–9 *Col Human Rights LR* 185, 210.

principle that liberty should be curtailed only on clear and concrete grounds which connect the actions of the suspect to a specific criminal offence. [62]

Other statutory powers of arrest

If a statute creates an offence which is a serious offence falling within s 24 then obviously the arrest power under s 24 is applicable. If a statute creates a more minor offence then equally the arrest power under s 25 is applicable so long as one or more of the general arrest conditions are satisfied. Section 11 of the Public Order Act 1986 and s 51 of the Police Act 1964 provide examples of such offences. However, certain statutes expressly create specific powers of arrest which are *not* dependent on ss 24 or 25 such as ss 12 and 14 of the Public Order Act. In such cases the procedure under s 28 of PACE (which is discussed below) will still apply.

Procedural elements of a valid arrest[63]

For an arrest to be made validly, not only must the power of arrest exist, whatever its source but the procedural elements must be complied with. The fact that a power of arrest arises will not alone make the arrest lawful. These elements are of crucial importance due to the consequences which may flow from a lawful arrest which will not flow from an unlawful one.[64] Such consequences include the right of the officer to use force in making the arrest if necessary and the loss of liberty inherent in an arrest. If an arrest has not occurred the citizen is free to go wherever she will and any attempt to prevent her doing so will be unlawful.[65] It is therefore important to convey the fact of the arrest to the arrestee and to mark the point at which the arrest comes into being and general liberty ceases. At common law there had to be a physical detention or a touching of the arrestee to convey the fact of detention, unless he or she made this unnecessary by submitting to it;[66] the fact of arrest had to be made clear[67] and the reason for it had to be made known.[68]

---

62 For discussion of this arrest power under the PTA 1984 see Walker, C (1984) 47 *MLR* 704–08; Bonner, D, *Emergency Powers in Peace Time*, 1985, pp 170–81.

63 The term 'valid arrest' is open to attack on the ground that there can be no such thing as an invalid arrest. However, a valid arrest may be contrasted with a purported arrest and this is the sense in which it is used in this section.

64 The question as to the difference between a valid and invalid arrest has been much debated; see Lidstone, KW [1978] *Crim LR* 332; Clark, D and Feldman, D [1979] *Crim LR* 702; Zander, M (1977) *NLJ* 352; Smith, JC [1977] *Crim LR* 293.

65 *Rice v Connolly* [1966] 2 QB 414; *Kenlin v Gardner* [1967] 2 QB 510 (see below pp 419–21 in relation to obstruction of or assault on a police officer in the course of his duty).

66 *Hart v Chief Constable of Kent* [1983] RTR 484.

67 *Alderson v Booth* [1969] 3 QB 216.

68 *Christie v Leachinsky* [1947] AC 573; [1947] 1 All ER 567, HL.

Freedom from Arbitrary Search, Arrest and Detention

The common law safeguards have been modified and strengthened by s 28 of PACE which provides that both the fact of and the reason for the arrest must be made known at the time or as soon as practicable afterwards. However, an ordinary citizen is not under this duty if the fact of the arrest and the reason for it are obvious. Conveying the fact of the arrest does not involve using a particular form of words[69] but it may be that reasonable detail must be given so that the arrestee will be in a position to give a convincing denial and therefore be more speedily released from detention.[70] Given the infringement of liberty represented by an arrest and the need therefore to restore liberty as soon as possible, consistent with the needs of the investigation, it is unfortunate that s 28 did not make it clear that a reasonable degree of detail should be given.

However, the reason for the arrest need only be made known as soon as practicable. The meaning and implications of this provision were considered in *DPP v Hawkins*.[71] A police officer took hold of the defendant to arrest him but did not give the reason. The youth struggled and was therefore later charged with assaulting an officer in the execution of his duty. The question which arose was whether the officer was in the execution of his duty since he had failed to give the reason for the arrest. If the arrest was thereby rendered invalid he could not be in the execution of his duty since it could not include effecting an unlawful arrest. It was determined in the Court of Appeal that the arrest became unlawful when the time came at which it was practicable to inform the defendant of the reason but he was not so informed. This occurred at the police station or perhaps in the police car but did not occur earlier due to the defendant's behaviour. However, the arrest did not become retrospectively unlawful and therefore did not affect acts done before its unlawfulness came into being, which thus remained acts done in the execution of duty.

Thus the police have a certain leeway as to informing the arrestee; the arrest will not be affected and nor will other acts arising from it, until the time when it would be practicable to inform of the reason for it has come and gone. However, if there was nothing in the behaviour of the arrestee to make informing him or her impracticable then the arrest will be unlawful from its inception. Following the decision in *Hawkins* what can be said as to the status of the suspect before the time came and passed at which the requisite words should have been spoken? Was he or was he or not under arrest at that time?

---

69 The Court of Appeal confirmed this in *Brosch* [1988] *Crim LR* 743. In *Abassey and Others v Metropolitan Police Commissioner* [1990] 1 WLR 385 it was found that there was no need for precise or technical language in conveying the reason for the arrest; the question whether the reason had been given was a matter for the jury. See also *Nicholas v Parsonage* [1987] RTR 199.

70 *Murphy v Oxford*, 15 February 1985, unreported, CA. This is out of line with the CA decision in *Abassey* above note 69 in which *Murphy* unfortunately was not considered.

71 [1988] 1 WLR 1166; [1988] 3 All ER 673, DC; see also *Brosch* [1988] *Crim LR* 743, CA.

In *Murray v Ministry of Defence*[72] soldiers occupied a woman's house, thus clearly taking her into detention but did not inform her of the fact of arrest for half an hour. The question arose whether she was falsely imprisoned during that half hour. The House of Lords found that delay in giving the requisite information was acceptable due to the alarm which the fact of arrest, if known, might have aroused in the particular circumstances – the unsettled situation in Northern Ireland. Members of Mrs Murray's family applied to the European Commission on Human Rights, alleging a breach of Article 5 which guarantees liberty and security of the person and of Article 8 which protects the right to privacy. In *Murray v UK*[73] the court found no breach was of Article 5(2), which provides that a person must be informed promptly of the reason for arrest. Mrs Murray was eventually informed during interrogation of the reason for the arrest and in the circumstances it was acceptable to allow an interval of a few hours between the arrest and informing her of the reason for it. The violation of privacy fell within the exception under Article 8(2) in respect of the prevention of crime and was found to be necessary and proportionate to the aims of that exception. No violation of the Convention was therefore found. Thus it seems that where special circumstances may be said to obtain, an arrest which does not comply with all the procedural requirements will still be an arrest, for a period of time, as far as all the consequences arising from it are concerned, under Article 5. This would be acceptable in an emergency situation which informing of an arrest might exacerbate but it would not appear on the facts of *Murray* that giving such information would raise alarm which had not already been raised when the soldiers entered the house. Therefore, on somewhat doubtful grounds, the Convention has allowed some departure from the principle that there should be a clear demarcation between the point at which the citizen is at liberty and the point at which her liberty is restrained. Sanders and Young observe, commenting on the House of Lords decision in *Murray*, 'Even where the legislature, as in s 28 of PACE, appears to be creating strong inhibitory rules, the judiciary still manages to draw their due process sting by rendering them largely presentational' and this might also be said of the decision of the European Court.[74]

Where the procedural elements are not complied with but no good reason for such failure arises (or if no power to arrest arose in the first place) the arrestee will have grounds for bringing an action for false imprisonment. Moreover, if a false arrest occurs and subsequently physical evidence is discovered or the defendant makes a confession, the defence may argue that the evidence should be excluded due to the false arrest. This is considered below.[75]

---

[72] [1988] All ER 521, HL; for comment see Williams (1991) 54 *MLR* 408.
[73] (1994) EHRR 193.
[74] Sanders and Young, *Criminal Justice*, 1994, p 103.
[75] At p 481.

Consensual detainment

Apart from situations in which reasonable suspicion relating to an offence arises there is nothing to prevent a police officer asking any person to come to the police station to answer questions. There is no legal power to do so but equally there is no power to prevent such a request being made. The citizen is entitled to ask whether he or she is being arrested and if not to refuse. However, if he or she consents, no action for false imprisonment can arise. This creates something of a grey area since the citizen may not realise that he or she does not need to comply with the request.[76] The government refused to include a provision in PACE requiring the police to inform citizens of the fact that they are not under arrest. However, certain provisions were included in Code of Practice C (see below) intended to ensure that volunteers were not disadvantaged in comparison with arrestees.[77] Of course such provisions do not affect the fact that some 'volunteers' might not have gone to the police station at all had they realised at the outset that they had a choice.

Use of force[78]

The police may use reasonable force so long as they are within one of the powers allowed under the PACE scheme. This is provided for under s 3 of the Criminal Law Act 1967 and s 117 of PACE 1984. Section 3 is in one sense wider than s 117 since it authorises the use of force by any person although only in relation to making an arrest or preventing crime. The prevention of crime would include resistance to an unlawful arrest. Section 117 only applies to police officers and then only in relation to provisions under PACE which do not provide that the consent of someone other than a constable is required. Force may include as a last resort the use of firearms; such use is governed by Home Office guidelines[79] which provide that firearms should be issued only where there is reason to suppose that a person to be apprehended is so dangerous that he could not be safely restrained otherwise. An oral warning should normally be given unless impracticable before using a firearm.[80] Under the 1967 Act, the force can only be used if it is 'necessary' and the amount of force used must be 'reasonable'. 'Reasonable' is taken to mean

---

76 See McKenzie, I, Morgan, R and Reiner, R, 'Helping the Police with their Enquiries' [1990] *Crim LR* 22.
77 In particular Code C paras 3.15 and 3.16. See pp 437–38 below for further discussion of the position of volunteers.
78 For consideration of the use of force see [1982] *Crim LR* 475; *Report of Commissioner of Police of the Metropolis for 1983*, Cmnd 9268; Waddington, PAJ, *The Strong Arm of the Law*, 1991.
79 The guidelines were reviewed in 1987 and reissued: see 109 *HC Deb*, 3 February 1987 Cols 562–63; (1987) 151 *JPN* 146.
80 For comment on the use of firearms see [1990] *Crim LR* 695.

'reasonable in the circumstances'[81] and therefore allows extreme force if the suspect is also using or appears to be about to use extreme force. It may be argued that further guidance as to the meaning of 'reasonable' should be provided in PACE. Section 117 provides that, 'the officer may use reasonable force, if necessary, in the exercise of the [PACE] power'. This could be taken to mean that any force used which was not, objectively speaking, absolutely necessary will be unreasonable or it might suggest that any force used which appeared necessary at the time will be reasonable, but it is likely that the courts will adopt the latter view. Article 2 of the European Convention allows the use of force which is 'absolutely necessary' in order to arrest; therefore UK law may not be in harmony with the Convention since a reasonableness test is used. The Convention requirements refer to the amount of force to be used, not to the question whether to use any force at all. But the Convention jurisprudence suggests that in terms of planning operations[82] and executing them in the immediate situation[83] the reasonableness standard and the 'absolutely necessary' standard may diverge.[84]

5   ASSAULT ON OR OBSTRUCTION OF A POLICE CONSTABLE IN THE EXECUTION OF HIS DUTY

Obstruction of a constable

The offence of obstruction of a constable which arises under s 89(2) of the Police Act 1996 (and formerly under s 51(3) of the Police Act 1964) creates an area of liability independent of any other substantive offence. In other words, it may criminalise activity which is otherwise lawful. Of course, this statement may appear superfluous: *all* offences criminalise otherwise lawful activity. However, criminal law largely concerns behaviour which has some general anti-social impact. In contrast this offence criminalises behaviour in relation to police officers which would not give rise to criminal liability if directed at any other group of persons. Thus some contacts between police officer and citizen may result in the creation of liability where otherwise none would have existed.[85]

Of course, society considers it desirable that the police should be able to make contact with citizens in order to make general enquiries without invoking any specific powers; on the other hand citizens do not need to reply to such enquiries. A police officer can ask a citizen to refrain from doing

---

81 See the ruling in *Farrell v Secretary of State for Defence* [1980] 1 All ER 1667, HL.
82 *McCann, Farrell and Savage v UK* (1995) 21 EHRR 97, A.324, Council of Europe Report. For further discussion of this issue see above pp 38–39.
83 *Andronicus and Constantinou v Cyprus* (1996) 22 EHRR CD 18.
84 See above pp 38–39.
85 See further on this point [1983] *Crim LR* 21, 36.

something but in general the citizen may refuse if the action is not in itself unlawful. If this was not the case there would be little need for other specific powers; an officer could, for example, merely ask a person to submit to a search and if he refused warn him that he could be charged with obstruction. However, some otherwise lawful behaviour, including failure to obey a police officer, may bring a citizen within the ambit of this offence and therefore the way it has been interpreted determines the borderline between legitimate and illegitimate disobedience to police instructions or requests.[86]

Following *Rice v Connolly*[87] three tests must be satisfied if liability for this offence is to be made out. First it must be shown that the constable was in the execution of his or her duty. Actions outside an officer's duty would seem to include any action which is unlawful or contrary to Home Office circulars[88] or the Codes of Practice. However, some actions which may be termed unlawful may be found too trivial to take the officer outside the execution of his or her duty. In *Bentley v Brudzinski*[89] an officer laid a hand on the shoulder of the defendant in order to detain him so as to ask further questions. The court found that in trying to prevent the defendant from returning home the officer was acting outside the execution of his duty but considered that not all instances in which an officer used some physical restraint would be treated in the same way. Reference was made to *Donelly v Jackman*[90] in which on very similar facts it was found that an officer was not outside the execution of his duty. All that can be said then is that all the circumstances of the case must be considered in determining whether an officer is within the execution of his duty and that the more significant the restraint used, the more likely it is that the officer will be outside it. Does it follow that any action of an officer which is not unlawful or contrary to official guidance will be *within* the execution of duty? It was found in *Coffin v Smith*[91] that any action within the officer's duty as a 'keeper of the peace' would be within his or her duty. Thus an officer does not need to point to a specific requirement to perform a particular duty imposed by superiors but equally some actions which are not unlawful would seem to fall outside his duty.

Secondly it must be shown that the defendant did an act which made it more difficult for the officer to carry out her or his duty. Physically attempting to prevent an arrest as in *Hills v Ellis*[92] will satisfy this test. This is not to imply

---

86 For discussion of the development of this offence see [1982] *PL* 558; (1983) *MLR* 662; [1983] *Crim LR* 29; [1983] *Crim LR* 21.
87 [1966] 2 QB 414; [1966] All ER 649; [1966] 3 WLR 17, DC.
88 In *Collins v Wilcock* [1984] 3 All ER 374; [1984] 1 WLR 1172 a police officer wrongly interpreted a Home Office circular; her actions in reliance on the incorrect interpretation were held to be outside the execution of her duty.
89 [1982] *Crim LR* 825; (1982) *The Times*, 3 and 11 March.
90 (1970) Cr App R 229; [1970] 1 WLR 562.
91 (1980) Cr App R 221.
92 [1983] QB 680; [1983] 1 All ER 667.

that a physical act must occur but that the police must actually be impeded in some way. In *Lewis v Cox*[93] a persistent enquiry as to where an arrested friend was being taken was held to amount to obstruction. The defendant opened the door of the police van, clearly preventing it from driving off, in order to make the enquiry after being told to desist. The ruling in *Ricketts v Cox*[94] that a refusal to answer questions accompanied by abuse was obstruction may delineate the lowest level of behaviour which may be termed obstructive. According to *Rice v Connolly* a refusal to answer questions does not amount to obstruction; therefore the abuse alone must have constituted the obstruction. This decision, which has been widely criticised,[95] is perhaps hard to reconcile with *Bentley v Brudzinski* and possibly interpreted the meaning of obstruction too widely.

It must finally be shown, following *Lewis v Cox*, that the defendant behaved wilfully in the sense that he acted deliberately with the knowledge and intention that he would obstruct the police officer. A defendant may be 'wilful' even though his purpose is to pursue some private objective of his own rather than to obstruct the officer, so long as his act is deliberate and he realises that it will in fact impede the officer. This will be the case, according to *Hills v Ellis*, even if the purpose of the defendant is to help the officer.[96]

Assault on a constable

This offence now arises under s 89(1) of the Police Act 1996 and may be fulfilled even though the defendant is unaware that the person he is assaulting is a police officer.[97] This is strange since the only justification for creating an area of liability in addition to common law assault and battery would seem to be that there is greater culpability in striking an officer rather than any other individual due to the officer's special position as keeper of the peace. However, if the defendant believes that unlawful force is being used against him he can avail himself of the defence of self-defence, although according to *Albert v Lavin*,[98] the belief in the need to act in self-defence must be based on reasonable grounds. This limitation was not accepted by the Court of Appeal in *Gladstone Williams*:[99] it was found that an honest belief would be sufficient.

---

93 (1985) Cr App R 1.
94 (1981) Cr App R 298; see commentary by Birch, D [1982] *Crim LR* 184; Smith and Hogan, *Criminal Law*, 6th edn, 1988, p 394; Lidstone, K [1983] *Crim LR* 29 pp 33–35.
95 See Glanville Williams, *Textbook of Criminal Law*, 1983, p 204; Lidstone, K [1983] *Crim LR* 29 pp 33–35.
96 *Cf Wilmott v Atack* [1977] QB 498; [1976] 3 All ER 794.
97 *Forbes* (1865) 10 Cox CC 362; for criticism see Glanville Williams p 200.
98 [1982] AC 546; [1981] 3 All ER 878, HL. See (1972) 88 *LQR* 246 on the use of self-defence in these circumstances.
99 (1983) Cr App R 276; see commentary [1984] *Crim LR* at 164.

However, it appears that if the honest belief is arrived at due to intoxication the facts will be considered as an objective observer would have perceived them.[100] Apart from the assault the other elements will be interpreted as for obstruction.

6 DETENTION IN POLICE CUSTODY

Time limits on detention after arrest

The position under the law prior to the 1984 Act with regard to detention before charge and committal before a magistrate was very vague. It was governed by s 43 of the Magistrates' Courts Act 1980 which allowed the police to detain a person in custody until such time as it was 'practicable' to bring him before a magistrate, in the case of a 'serious' offence. Since a person would be charged before being brought before the magistrate this meant that the police had to move expeditiously in converting suspicion into evidence justifying a charge.[101] However, the common law had developed to the point when it could be said that detention for the purpose of questioning was recognised.[102] Thus, prior to PACE the police had no clearly defined power to hold a person for questioning. The detention scheme governed by Part IV of PACE put such a power on a more certain basis and it was made clear under s 37(2) that the purpose of the detention is to obtain a confession.

Under s 41 the detention can be for up to 24 hours but in the case of a person in police custody for a serious arrestable offence (defined in s 116) it can extend to 96 hours. Part IV does not apply to detention under s 14 and Schedules 2 or 5 of the Prevention of Terrorism Act (see below) or to detention by immigration officers.[103] Under s 42(1) a police officer of the rank of superintendent or above can sanction detention up to 36 hours if three conditions apply: he or she has reasonable grounds for believing that either the detention is necessary to secure or preserve evidence relating to an offence for which the detainee is under arrest or to obtain such evidence by questioning him; an offence for which the detainee is under arrest is a serious arrestable offence; and the investigation is being conducted diligently and expeditiously. After 36 hours detention can no longer be authorised by the police alone. Under s 43(1) the application for authorisation must be supported by information and brought before a magistrates' court who can authorise detention under s 44 for up to 96 hours if the conditions are met as

---

100 See *O'Connor* [1991] *Crim LR* 135.
101 See *Holmes* [1981] 2 All ER 612; [1981] *Crim LR* 802.
102 *Holgate-Mohammed v Duke* [1984] AC 437; [1984] 1 All ER 1054, HL.
103 Section 51 of PACE.

set out above. Detention must be reviewed periodically[104] and the detainee or his solicitor (if available) has the right to make written or oral representations.[105] However, research suggests that these reviews are not treated as genuine investigations into the grounds for continuing the detention but merely as formal procedures which must be gone through.[106]

These are very significant powers which are however intended to embody the principle that a detained person should normally be charged within 24 hours and then either released or brought before a magistrate. They are supposed to be balanced by all the safeguards created by Part V of PACE and Codes of Practice C and E. It may be noted that a person unlawfully detained can apply for a writ of *habeas corpus* in order to secure release from detention and this remedy is preserved in s 51(d). Its usefulness in practice is, however, very limited since the courts have developed a practice of adjourning applications for 24 hours in order to allow the police to present their case. Thus detention can continue for that time allowing the police to carry out questioning or other procedures in the meantime.

Detention under the Prevention of Terrorism (Temporary Provisions) Act 1989

If a person is arrested under s 14 of the PTA as opposed to s 24 of PACE, whether the arrest is for an offence or otherwise (see discussion above),[107] the detention provisions under PACE do not apply. The arrestee may be detained for up to 48 hours following arrest (s 14(4) of the PTA) but this period can be extended by the Secretary of State by further periods not exceeding five days in all (s 14(5) of the PTA). Thus the whole detention can be for seven days and, in contrast to the general PACE provision, the courts are not involved in the authorising process; it occurs at a low level of visibility as an administrative decision. The similar provision under PTA was found to be in breach of the European Convention Article 5(3) in *Brogan v UK*[108] on the ground that holding a person for longer than four days without judicial authorisation was a violation of the requirement that persons should be brought promptly before a judicial officer. The government made no move to comply with this requirement; instead it entered a derogation under Article 15 to Article 5(3)

---

104 Section 40(1)(b).
105 Section 40(12) and (13).
106 Dixon, D et al, 'Safeguarding the Rights of Suspects in Police Custody' (1990) 1 *Policing and Society* 130–31.
107 At p 413.
108 Judgment of 29 November 1988; (1989) 11 EHRR 117; A.145, 1989.

which was challenged unsuccessfully as broader than it needed to be.[109] The European Court of Human Rights found that the derogation was justified since the state of public emergency in Northern Ireland warranted exceptional measures. As a result, at present, periods of up to six days' detention will not breach Article 5. This might appear an unfortunate decision because the derogation was entered *after* the *Brogan* decision. On the other hand states should not be encouraged to enter derogations too readily on 'insurance' grounds in order to pre-empt claims; it might be said that although there was a state of emergency in 1989 the UK had *chosen* not to enter a derogation even though one would have been warranted. Whatever the merits of this argument in the particular situation, it is questionable whether the exigencies of the situation do require detentions of six days without recourse to independent review. It might be possible to arrange for such review without prejudicing the legitimate purpose of the investigation.

Schedule 5 of the PTA allows a person to be detained for 12 hours before examination at ports of entry into Britain or Northern Ireland but the period may be extended to 24 hours if the person is suspected of involvement in the commission, preparation or instigation of acts of terrorism. This 24 hour period seems to create a largely illusory restriction since it is subject to the provisions of Schedule 5 para 6 which allow further detention on three different grounds. These are: 'pending conclusion of his examination'; pending consideration of the Secretary of State whether to make an exclusion order or pending the decision of the Attorney General whether to institute proceedings against the detainee. Such detention may be for 48 hours on the authority of the examining officer and for a further period, up to a maximum of seven days on the authority of the Secretary of State. If exclusion of the detainee is to take place he or she may be further detained pending removal (Schedule 2 para 7(1)); there is no statutory limit on such detention.

At no stage during this detention scheme is there need for recourse to a court; the introduction under Schedule 3 of the PTA of the need for periodic review of detention placed such review in the hands of police officers. If the review officer does refuse to grant a further extension of detention the Secretary of State may still grant it under Schedule 3 para 3(1)(b).[110]

Searches of detained persons

Detained persons may not automatically be searched but the power to search under s 32 is quite wide. It arises under s 32(1) if an officer has reasonable

---

109 *Brannigan and McBride v UK*, Appls 14553/89 and 14554/89. The ruling of the European Court of Human Rights was given on 26 May 1993: *Brannigan and McBride v UK* (1993) *The Times,* 28 May.

110 See (1989) 40 *NILQ* 250 for criticism of the review procedure.

grounds to suspect that a detained person has anything on him which might be evidence relating to an offence or might be used to help him escape from custody or that he may present a danger to himself or others. The much wider power arises under s 32(2) and allows search, again on reasonable grounds, for anything which might be evidence of an offence or could help to effect an escape from lawful custody. The nature of the search must relate to the article it is suspected may be found; if it is a large item the search may not involve more than removal of a coat. Such searching may occur routinely but it must be possible to point to objectively justified grounds in each case which must not go beyond those specified.[111] A power of search also arises under s 54 as amended allowing search to ascertain property the detainee has with him or her, which will apply if someone has been arrested at the police station or brought there after being arrested elsewhere. The custody officer must determine whether it is necessary to conduct a search for this purpose.

7 QUESTIONING AND TREATMENT OF SUSPECTS INSIDE AND OUTSIDE THE POLICE STATION

This section does not concentrate only on treatment of suspects *inside* the police station because contact between police and suspect takes place a long time before the police station is reached and this has been recognised in the provisions of Part V of PACE and Code of Practice C which govern treatment of suspects and interviewing but have some application outside as well as inside the police station. It should be noted that many of the key provisions relating to treatment and interviewing are contained in Code C rather than in PACE itself. The most crucial event during a person's contact with police will probably be the interview and therefore this section will concentrate on the safeguards available which are intended to ensure that interviews are fairly conducted and are properly recorded wherever they take place. This section, however, begins by a brief consideration of some general features of the treatment of the suspect once he or she has arrived at the police station. It will then go on to examine the key aspects of the interviewing scheme in the following manner:

(1) identification of the points at which the various safeguards must be in place;

(2) value and efficacy of the legal advice scheme;

(3) the conduct of the interview and the means of recording it;

(4) the right to silence.

---

111 *Eet* [1983] *Crim LR* 806.

It should be noted that if police officers detain a person under the provisions of PTA 1989, Code C will govern his or her treatment although at certain points there are differences in the treatment of such a detainee and an ordinary detainee. However, if the detention under PTA is by examining officers who are not police officers Code C will not apply; the officers need only 'have regard' to its provisions (s 67(9) of PACE).

General treatment inside the police station[112]

Custody officers

The general use of custody officers provided for under s 36 is a key feature of the Part IV scheme. The custody officer's role is to underpin the other safeguards by ensuring that the suspect is treated in accordance with PACE and the Codes and by generally overseeing all aspects of his or her treatment. Use of custody officers was intended to ensure that somebody independent of the investigating officer could keep a check on what was occurring. The scheme was not a new idea; in certain police stations an officer was already fulfilling this role but PACE clarifies the duties of custody officers and ensures that most stations have one. Thus best practice is now placed on a statutory basis.

However, the efficacy of the custody officer scheme may be called into question on two grounds. First, it may not always be in operation: in non-designated police stations there must simply be someone who can act as custody officer if the need arises and in designated police stations there need not always be a custody officer on duty. The ruling in *Vince and Another v Chief Constable of Dorset*[113] made it clear that s 36 does not require that a custody officer must always be present. The plaintiffs (acting for members of the joint branch board of the Police Federation of England and Wales of the Dorset Police) sought a declaration that by virtue of s 36(1) of PACE a custody officer should normally be available in a police station. However, it was found that s 36(1) clearly provided that the Chief Constable had a duty to appoint one custody officer for each designated police station and a power to appoint more in his discretion which had to be reasonably exercised. It was found that there had been no breach by the Chief Constable, implying that a decision that a custody officer need not always be on duty is a reasonable one. It may be argued that this case exposes a weakness in one of the central safeguards provided under PACE. This was referred to by Lord Justice Steyn who

---

112 For discussion of judicial interpretation of the PACE provisions see Feldman, D [1990] *Crim LR* 452.
113 (1992) *The Times*, 7 September.

commented that the Royal Commission on Criminal Procedure[114] might wish to consider this loophole in the PACE provisions.

Secondly, the custody officer may not always be able to take a stance independent of that of the investigating officer. This weakness in the scheme arises from the lowly rank of the custody officer; under s 38(3) the officer need only be of the rank of sergeant and may therefore be of a lower rank than the investigating officer, making it very difficult to take an independent line on the treatment of the suspect. If the two disagree the custody officer must refer up the line of authority (s 39(6)); there is no provision allowing the custody officer to overrule the investigating officer. Thus there is a danger that the custody officer will merely rubber-stamp the decisions of the investigating officer; whether this occurs in practice may largely depend on the attitude of the superior officers in a particular force to the provisions of the PACE scheme.

Caution and notification of rights

When the detainee arrives at the police station he or she will be 'booked in'. The crucial nature of this stage in the proceedings is made clear below in relation to the discussion of the legal advice provisions. Under para 3 of Code C a person must be informed orally and by written notice of four rights on arrival at the police station after arrest: the right to have someone informed of his detention;[115] the right to consult a solicitor and the fact that independent legal advice is available free of charge; the right to consult Code C and the other Codes of Practice and the right to silence as embodied in the caution. The caution is in the following terms: 'You do not have to say anything. But it may harm your defence if you do not mention when questioned something which you late rely on in court. Anything you do say may be given in evidence.'[116] Minor deviations do not constitute a breach of this requirement provided that the sense of the caution is preserved. The caution must be repeated during the interview if there is any doubt as to whether the detainee realises that it still applies. If a juvenile or a person who is mentally disordered or mentally handicapped is cautioned in the absence of the appropriate adult, the caution must be repeated in the adult's presence.[117] The change to the caution which occurred when s 34 of the Criminal Justice and Public Order Act 1994 came into force means that the suspect is warned that refusing to answer questions may lead to the drawing of adverse inferences in court.

---

114 Set up in 1992 after the miscarriage of justice which occurred in the case of the Birmingham Six. See p 394, note 6 above.

115 Under para 5.1 if the person cannot be contacted the person in charge of detention or of the investigation has discretion to allow further attempts until the information has been conveyed (see Notes 5C and 5D).

116 Para 10.4. Modification to the caution occurred in order to reflect s 34 of the Criminal Justice and Public Order Act 1994. See further below pp 458–62.

117 Para 10.6.

Vulnerable groups

Throughout Code C recognition is given to the special needs of certain vulnerable groups: juveniles, the mentally disordered or handicapped, those not proficient in English, the hearing impaired or the visually handicapped. Juveniles and the mentally handicapped or disordered should be attended by an 'appropriate adult'. Under para 1 the 'appropriate' adult in the case of a juvenile will be the parent or guardian, a social worker or another adult who is not a police officer. The suspect should be informed by the custody officer that the appropriate adult is there to assist and advise him and can be consulted with privately (para 3.12). However, research suggests that this requirement is not always observed and that in any event appropriate adults often seem unclear as to the role they are supposed to play.[118] Under the revision of Code C in 1991 and 1995 the estranged parent of a juvenile can no longer be the appropriate adult,[119] if the juvenile expressly and specifically objects to his presence'. Previously this was possible and in such instances the parent was likely to collude with the police or generally show hostility to the juvenile rather than look after his or her interests.[120] This change was probably prompted by the decision in *DPP v Blake*[121] that a confession obtained from a juvenile in the presence of an estranged parent acting as the appropriate adult may be excluded from evidence. Compliance with the original Note 13C (now sub-para 11.16), which indicated the respects in which the appropriate adult should look after the interests of the juvenile, could not be ensured if an estranged parent was present; now Note 1C may go some way towards ensuring that sub-para 11.16 can be given full effect. Under Note 1F the solicitor should not be the appropriate adult; this provision was included in response to some evidence that the police had been treating the solicitor as the appropriate adult, thereby producing a conflict of interests.[122] It was thought that the roles of legal adviser and appropriate adult differed; the same person could not therefore fulfil both. It should be noted that the juvenile can be interviewed without the presence of an appropriate adult if an officer of the rank of superintendent or above considers that delay will involve an immediate risk of harm to persons or serious loss of or serious damage to property.[123] At various points to be discussed the particular vulnerability of juveniles is recognised but although this is to be welcomed research suggests

---

118 Brown, D, Ellis, T and Larcombe, JK, *Home Office Research Study No 129*, HMSO.
119 Note 1C.
120 See Softley, P, 'Police Interrogation: An Observational Study in Four Police Stations' (1985) *Policing Today* pp 115–30, 119.
121 [1989] 1 WLR 432, CA; this problem also arose recently at first instance in *Morse* [1991] Crim LR 195.
122 *LAG Bulletin*, November 1989.
123 See Annex C: urgent interviews.

that the treatment of juveniles, particularly during interviews, is still at times unsatisfactory.[124]

In the case of a mentally disordered or handicapped detainee the appropriate adult under para 1 will be a relative, guardian, other person responsible for his or her welfare or an adult who is not a police officer.[125] The custody officer must as soon as practicable inform the appropriate adult of the grounds for the person's detention and ask the adult to come to the police station to see him or her. If a person appears mentally ill the custody officer must immediately call the police surgeon or, in urgent cases, send the person to hospital or call the nearest available medical practitioner.[126] The notification of rights must be given in the presence of the adult[127] which may mean repeating the notification but if the suspect wants legal advice this should not be delayed until the adult arrives.[128] The appropriate adult who is present at an interview, should be informed that he or she is not expected to act simply as an observer; and also that the purposes of being present are, first, to advise the person being interviewed and to observe whether or not the interview is being conducted properly and fairly and, secondly, to facilitate communication with the person being interviewed.[129] The Runciman Royal Commission Report 1993 recommended review of the role of appropriate adults with a view to considering their training and availability and the criteria employed by the police in order to determine when an adult was needed.[130] In response, the Home Office set up a review group which in June 1995 made a number of recommendations. They included entitling appropriate adults to a confidential interview with the suspect, defining the role of appropriate adults in Code C, providing guidance for professionals and others likely to act in this role and setting up local appropriate adult panels.[131]

It will be found in discussion below of unreliable confessions that mentally handicapped or disordered persons are very likely to make an untrue or exaggerated confession and therefore it is particularly important that all the safeguards available should be in place when such a person is interviewed. However, there is provision for urgent interviewing of such persons without the appropriate adult if an officer of the rank of superintendent or above

---

124 Evans, R, 'The Conduct of Police Interviews with Juveniles' (1993) *Home Office Research Study No 8*. On the treatment of juveniles generally see Dixon, D, 'Juvenile Suspects and PACE' in Freestone, D, ed, *Children and the Law*, 1990, pp 107–29.

125 Paragraph 1.7(b).

126 Paragraph 9.2.

127 Paragraph 3.11.

128 Note 3G and Annex E Note E2.

129 See para 11.16.

130 Proposal 72. For further discussion see Hodgson J [1997] *Crim LR* 785.

131 The Report is available from the Chairman of the Review Group: Mr Stephen Wells, F2 Division, Home Office.

considers that delay will involve an immediate risk of harm to persons or serious loss of or serious damage to, property.[132] The main defect in the provisions relating to the mentally handicapped or disordered is that they rely on the ability of officers who will have had little no or training in the field to make the judgment that a person is mentally disordered.[133] It would seem essential that custody officers at least should have special training in this regard.

Various provisions are available for the protection of members of the other vulnerable groups mentioned. A blind or visually handicapped person must have independent help in reading documentation.[134] A deaf or speech handicapped person or someone who has difficulty understanding English must only be interviewed in the presence of an interpreter,[135] but this may be waived in the case of urgent interviewing under Annex C.

Physical treatment

Physical treatment of detainees is governed by para 8 of Code C and it is intended that they should be provided with basic physical care. Paragraph 8 embodies the principle that the detainee's physical safety should be ensured and his physical needs met. It does however allow more than one detainee to be placed in the same cell if it is impracticable to do otherwise and although a juvenile must not be placed in a cell with an adult, does not make clear provision for frequent checks on juveniles in police cells. It provides that cells should be adequately heated, cleaned, lit and ventilated and that three meals should be offered in any 24 hour period. A juvenile will only be placed in a police cell if no other secure accommodation is available and the custody officer considers that it is not practicable to supervise him if he is not placed in a cell. Persons detained should be visited every hour but where possible juveniles should be visited 'more frequently';[136] those who are drunk should be visited every half hour. No additional restraints should be used within a locked cell unless absolutely necessary and then only suitable handcuffs. Reasonable force may be used if necessary (para 8.9) but only to secure compliance with reasonable instructions and to prevent escape, injury, damage to property or the destruction of evidence. Under para 9 if a person appears mentally or physically ill or injured or does not respond normally to questions or conversation (other than through drunkenness alone) or

---

132 See para 11.14 and Annex C.

133 Annex E para 1 provides that if an officer 'has any suspicion or is told in good faith that a person of any age, whether or not in custody, may be suffering from medical disorder or mentally handicapped or cannot understand the significance of questions put to him or his replies, then he shall be treated as a mentally disordered or mentally handicapped person'.

134 Paragraph 3.14.

135 Paragraph 13.

136 Note 8A.

otherwise appears to need medical attention, the custody officer must immediately call the police surgeon (or, in urgent cases, send the person to hospital or call the nearest available medical practitioner).

Intimate searches

Under s 55 an intimate search can only be ordered if an officer of the rank of superintendent or above has reasonable grounds for believing that an article which could cause physical injury to a detained person or others at the police station has been concealed or that the person has concealed a Class A drug which he intends to supply to another or to export. Even if such suspicion arises the search should not be carried out unless there is no other means of removing the object. Before it can be carried out the reasons for undertaking it must be explained to the suspect and a reminder given of the entitlement to legal advice.[137]

An intimate search at a police station may only be carried out by a registered medical practitioner or registered nurse unless the authorising officer considers, in the case of a concealed object which could cause injury, that it is not practicable to wait, in which case a police officer of the same sex as the suspect can carry it out. An intimate search at a police station of a juvenile or a mentally disordered or mentally handicapped person must take place only in the presence of the appropriate adult of the same sex unless the suspect requests otherwise.[138]

The interviewing scheme: bringing the safeguards into play

Under the pre-PACE rules safeguards for the interview were governed largely by the Judges' Rules and Administrative Directions to the Police[139] and s 62 of the Criminal Law Act 1977. The latter provided for access to a solicitor (though it was frequently ignored). The former provided *inter alia* for the issuing of cautions when a person was charged (not necessarily when he was arrested) and for the exclusion in evidence of statements and confessions which were not 'voluntary' (see below). Under PACE those rules were replaced by new rules contained either in the Act itself or in Codes of Practice C or E. The interviewing rules form the most detailed and complex part of the whole scheme.

It might be expected that the distribution of the provisions governing the interviewing scheme would give some recognition to theoretical differences in

---

137 See Code C para 4.1 and Annex A.
138 Under Annex A para 5 in the case of a juvenile, the search may take place in the absence of the appropriate adult only if the juvenile signifies in the presence of the appropriate adult that he prefers the search to be done in his absence and the appropriate adult agrees.
139 For example, Home Office circular 89/1978 Appendices A and B.

status between PACE, the Codes, the Notes for Guidance and Home Office circulars, the most fundamental provisions being contained in the Act and so on. In fact, this is not the case: although the Act contains the right to legal advice, the other important features of the interviewing scheme, including the right to silence,[140] are governed by non-statutory provisions. Just as it cannot be assumed that Code provisions are less weighty than statutory ones, equally the Notes for Guidance and even the circulars,[141] do not invariably contain less crucial provisions than the Codes. In other words, the distribution of provisions between the four tiers does not follow a consistent pattern: the source of a provision may possibly have an effect on the likelihood that it will be complied with but does not necessarily say much about its significance.

The most significant safeguards available for interviews include contemporaneous noting down of the interview or tape-recording, the ability to verify and sign the notes of the interview as a correct record, the legal advice provisions and, where appropriate, the presence of an adult. One of the most important issues in relation to these safeguards and reflected in the 1991 (and, to an extent, the 1995) revision of Code C, is the question when they come into play. There may be a number of stages in a particular investigation beginning with first contact between police and suspect and perhaps ending with the charge. At various points the safeguards mentioned have to come into play and two factors can be identified which decide which safeguards should be in place at a particular time. First, it must be asked whether an exchange between police and suspect can be termed an interview and secondly whether it took place inside the police station or was lawfully conducted outside it.

Interviews and non-interviews

The correct interpretation of the term 'interview' under the original Code C scheme was highly significant because the relevant safeguards were unavailable unless an exchange[142] between police officer and suspect was designated an interview. The term therefore tended to be given a wide interpretation[143] and eventually the definition given to it by the Court of

---

140 As contained in the caution: Code C para 10.4.
141 For example, a provision in the 1991 circular required that where a suspect had changed his mind after requesting legal advice a note should be made in the custody record of the reason for the change. The provision was presumably included with a view to discouraging police officers from providing misleading information which might induce the suspect to forego legal advice.
142 'Exchange' will be used throughout this section to denote any verbal interaction between suspect and police officer including unsolicited admissions.
143 The Court of Appeal in *Absolam* (1989) 88 Cr App R 332 defined it as 'a series of questions directed by the police to a suspect with a view to obtaining admissions'. This definition was quite wide in that it obviously included informal questioning.

Appeal in *Matthews*[144] – 'any discussion or talk between suspect and police officer' – brought within its ambit many exchanges far removed from formal interviews. It also covered many interviewees as it spoke in terms of 'suspects' not arrestees. However, it was qualified by the ruling in *Scott*[145] that unsolicited admissions cannot amount to 'interviews' and by the ruling in *Marsh*[146] to the same effect as regards 'genuine requests' from the police for information. In *Marsh* police officers investigating a burglary suddenly came across wraps of papers and asked the appellant about them; the questions and answers were admissible although no caution had been given because until that point the officers had had no reason to suspect her of any drug related offence. The ruling in *Marsh* bears some resemblance to that in *Maguire*[147] which pre-dated *Matthews*. It was determined that questioning an arrestee near the scene of the crime apparently in order to elicit an innocent explanation did not constitute an interview. Thus the original interpretation of an interview created some leeway – but not much – for gathering (or apparently gathering) admissions in informal situations before any safeguards were in place.

In one respect distinguishing between interviews and non-interviews will not be as crucial under the current scheme as it was previously: under para 11.13 as revised *any* comments relevant to the offence made by a suspected person outside the context of an interview must be accurately recorded[148] and then verified and signed by the suspect. However, making such a distinction will still be highly significant because it remains the first step towards bringing the other safeguards into play.

A definition of the term 'interview' is now contained in para 11.1A which reads:

> An interview is the questioning of a person regarding his involvement or suspected involvement in a criminal offence or offences which by virtue of Para 10.1 of Code C is required to be carried out under caution.

Paragraph 10.1 reads:

> A person whom there are grounds to suspect of an offence must be cautioned before any questions about it (or further questions if it is his answers to previous questions which provide the grounds for suspicion) are put to him regarding his involvement or suspected involvement in that offence if his answers or his silence (ie failure or refusal to answer a question or to answer

---

144 (1990) Cr App R 43; [1990] *Crim LR* 190, CA, transcript from LEXIS.
145 [1991] *Crim LR* 56, CA. See also *Younis* [1990] *Crim LR* 425, CA.
146 [1991] *Crim LR* 455.
147 (1989) Cr App R 115; [1989] *Crim LR* 815, CA.
148 It may be noted that the weight actually given to this provision may depend on the question whether its breach may be described as substantial and significant (see below pp 482–83); in this respect it is disturbing to note a first instance decision in which it was found that it should not be so described: *Oransaye* [1993] *Crim LR* 772.

satisfactorily) may be given in evidence to a court in a prosecution. He therefore need not be cautioned if questions are put to him for other purposes, for example, solely to establish his identity or his ownership of any vehicle or to obtain any information in accordance with any relevant statutory requirement ... or in furtherance of the proper and effective conduct of a search.

It may be noted that the list of examples of instances under para 10.1 in which no caution would be necessary is not exhaustive. No such definition appeared in the original Code but Note 12A read: 'The purpose of any interview is to obtain from the person concerned his explanation of the facts and not necessarily to obtain an admission.' The new definition obviously differs from this considerably and differs even more from the definition of an interview contained in *Matthews*.[149] It echoes the rulings of the Court of Appeal in *Maguire*[150] and *Marsh*[151] in attempting to draw a distinction between questioning a person regarding suspected involvement in an offence and questioning for other purposes. It appears that cautioning would not be required if the information obtained is *in fact* relevant to the offence but the questioning was not directed towards uncovering such information. Such an interpretation would be in conformity with the ruling in *Marsh* that the level of suspicion excited in police officers present at the scene determines when an exchange becomes an interview. This approach is readily justifiable. However, para 11.1A combined with para 10.1 does not make it sufficiently clear that where an explanation of the facts does relate to suspected involvement in an offence *and* is either perceived to do so by the officer concerned or would be by the ordinary reasonable officer,[152] an interview will take place.

Thus, para 11.1A might on occasion act as an invitation to police officers to play down the level of suspicion excited by the circumstances in order to demonstrate that no interview took place. Such tactics might amount to a self-fulfilling prophecy in the sense that the officer concerned would have an interest in viewing the exchange as a non-interview requiring only accurate rather than contemporaneous recording; such recording would create more scope for giving the exchanges the character of a non-interview and it would therefore appear for future purposes that a non-interview did indeed take place. The only person able to impede this process would be the suspect who must be asked to verify and sign the record of the exchanges; it is unlikely, however, that he would appreciate the implications of what had occurred.

---

[149] [1990] *Crim LR* 190.
[150] (1989) 90 Cr App R 115; [1989] *Crim LR* 815.
[151] [1991] *Crim LR* 455.
[152] This qualification must be introduced to take account of the situation which arose in *Sparks* [1991] *Crim LR* 128; the officer who questioned the appellant apparently did not recognise the significance of the admissions made and therefore did not consider it necessary to caution him.

The para 11.1A test must be qualified by the ruling of the Court of Appeal in *Weekes*.[153] Once an exchange becomes an interview that fact will have a retrospective effect on earlier exchanges; if safeguards applicable to an interview were not available in respect of such exchanges they will be excluded from evidence. It will not be possible to sever them from the 'interview'. This ruling seems to be in conflict with *Marsh*. However, as the *Weekes* ruling concerned a juvenile it may be confined to such instances.

Where the level of suspicion clearly falls within para 10.1 as, of course, it will do after arrest, the use of the term 'questioning' in para 11.1A nevertheless impliedly excludes instances where nothing definable as questioning has taken place. This is the correct interpretation where the police have apparently merely recorded what was said, according to the Court of Appeal in *R v Menard*.[154] Paragraph 11.1A may also exclude chats or discussions between suspect and police officer or statements or commands which happen to elicit an incriminating response.[155] This interpretation seems to lead to a conflict between para 11.1A and the ruling from *Matthews*[156] which could be resolved by arguing that rulings of the Court of Appeal will prevail over a provision contained only in a Code provision.[157] This would be the more satisfactory result as more likely to curtail opportunities for 'verballing' (concocting admissions). However, a possible response might be that the definition from *Matthews* is now enshrined in para 11.13 and is not therefore inconsistent with para 11.1A. In other words, the *Matthews* definition applies to most exchanges between suspect and police officer but para 11.1A applies to certain particularly important ones labelled 'interviews'. This interpretation is to an extent supported by the wording of para 11.13: 'a written record shall also be made of any comments made by a suspected person, including unsolicited comments which are outside the context of an interview but which might be relevant to the offence ...', thus implying that comments relevant to the offence other than unsolicited comments will not invariably be part of an interview. It also receives some support from the ruling in *Williams*[158] which seems to have accepted impliedly that 'social visits' by police to suspects in the cells involving conversation relevant to the offence in question do not constitute interviews although they are to be

---

153 [1993] *Crim LR* 222; (1992) *The Times*, 15 May, CA.
154 (1995) Cr App R 306.
155 See *Absolam* (1989) 88 Cr App R 332.
156 If statements or commands eliciting a response from the suspect could be said to fall outside the *Matthews* (above note 144) definition of an interview, which is unlikely, they could still constitute an interview according to the ruling in *Absolam* (above note 155).
157 The Codes of Practice brought in by a resolution of both Houses of Parliament do not have statutory authority. It has, however been held by the Court of Appeal that they can prevail over rules derived from case law (*McCay* [1990] *Crim LR* 338) although commentators have thought that the Court of Appeal was mistaken in this view (Birch, D [1990] *Crim LR* 340).
158 (1992) *The Times*, 6 February, CA.

discouraged. This interpretation would mean that a number of exchanges which would previously have been interviews will no longer be so labelled and this is especially of concern due to the evidence that police officers tend to favour the informal chat in the police station.[159]

The improvement in the position of some suspects should not be allowed to obscure the fact that certain safeguards may now be triggered off only in a confined group of situations. Whether this will be the effect of para 11.1A is still unclear but in *Cox*[160] the Court of Appeal adopted what might be termed a 'purposive approach' to Note 11A (which previously contained the definition of an interview, under the 1991 revision) in finding that the intention of the 1991 revision was to *increase* rather than decrease protection for suspects and therefore Note 11A should be interpreted in the light of previous decisions such as *Matthews* which *broadened* the definition of an interview. This was followed in *Oransaye*[161] which suggested that the emphasis should not be placed on the *form* of the exchange – ie on whether or not questions were asked – but on whether what was said went to 'the heart of the matter'. If so the exchange should be termed an interview.[162]

Interviews inside and outside the police station

Once an exchange could be called an interview the safeguards applying to it under the original provisions differed quite markedly depending on where it took place. Those available *inside* the police station included contemporaneous recording[163] or tape-recording,[164] the ability to read over, verify and sign the notes of the interview as a correct record,[165] notification of legal advice,[166] the right to have advice before questioning[167] and, where appropriate, the presence of an adult.[168] If the interview took place on 'other premises' the

---

159 See Holdaway, S, *Inside the British Police*, 1985; Sanders, A [1990] *Crim LR* 494, referring to his research on access to legal advice in police stations (research undertaken by Sanders, A, Bridges, L, Mulvaney, A and Crozier, G, entitled *Advice and Assistance at Police Stations*, November 1989) found that such practices were still continuing post-PACE.
160 [1993] *Crim LR* 382; see also *Goddard* [1994] *Crim LR* 46.
161 [1993] *Crim LR* 772.
162 For discussion of the meaning of 'interview' see Field, S, 13 (2) *LS* 254.
163 Original para 11.3 provided that if the interview took place in the police station or at other premises 'the record must be made during the course of the interview unless in the investigating officer's view this would not be practicable or would interfere with the conduct of the interview'.
164 Under original para 11.3.
165 Under Code E para 3.
166 Under original para 12.12.
167 Under para 3.1.
168 The Court of Appeal in *Absolam* (above note 155) determined that no questioning could take place inside the police station before the suspect had been notified of the right to legal advice; answers allegedly made to questions put before such notification were thereby rendered inadmissible.

same safeguards would apply apart from the requirements to *inform*[169] of the right to legal advice and to allow the suspect to verify and sign the record of the interview.

In the street, however, it was only necessary to ensure that an accurate record of the interview was made,[170] and where appropriate an adult was present.[171] Thus originally a minimum level of protection only was available creating scope for impropriety, including fabrication of confessions. In particular, it meant that only the experienced suspect interviewed outside the police station would be aware of the right to legal advice. Thus, however widely the term 'interview' was interpreted, it was of little use to suspects who made (or allegedly made) admissions outside the police station.

The 1991 revision reduced the significance of this factor to some extent. Provision for giving the suspect the record of the interview to verify and sign was moved out of para 12 applying only to interviews in the police station and into para 11[172] which is headed 'Interviews general',[173] although this change was made less significant by the provisions of para 11.13. The verifying and signing rules were supplemented in 1995 by the requirement, imposed, however, only in a Note for Guidance, Note 11D, that the suspect should declare in his or her own hand on the interview record that it is correct. Such a provision clearly has more value than the requirement only to obtain a signature. Under para 11.5 the interview must be recorded contemporaneously wherever it takes place unless this would not be practicable.

However, the unseasoned suspect interviewed outside the police station will still be unaware of the right to legal advice[174] and it is also at present unlikely that the interview would be tape-recorded: Code E does not envisage tape-recording taking place anywhere but inside the police station.[175] In some

---

169 Under original para 13.
170 Section 58 governing the right of access to legal advice is expressed to apply to persons in police detention but para 3.1 governing the right to be notified of the s 58 entitlement was (and is) expressed to apply only to those in the police station. However, volunteers under caution in the police station or on other premises had the right to be informed of the entitlement to legal advice under original para 10.2.
171 Original para 13 did not state expressly that an adult must be present during any interview whether conducted in or out of the police station when a juvenile was interviewed. However this could be implied; the ruling in *Fogah* [1989] *Crim LR* 141 confirmed that this was the correct interpretation.
172 Para 11.10.
173 The Court of Appeal determined in *Brezenau and Francis* [1989] *Crim LR* 650 that these provisions could only apply inside the police station; departure from the clear words of para 12 was not warranted.
174 This is governed by para 3.1 which is expressed to apply only to persons in the police station.
175 Code E para 3.1 states: '... tape-recording shall be used at police stations for any interview ...' Some police forces have experimented with hand held tape recorders used outside the police station but at present this is by no means common practice.

circumstances suspects will not, however, be disadvantaged by these differences due to the provisions of para 11.1, introduced by the 1991 revision, which reads:

> Following a decision to arrest a suspect he must not be interviewed about the relevant offence except at a police station [except in certain instances specified in 11.1(a), (b) and (c) which call for urgent interviewing]. For the definition of an interview see Note 11A.

Paragraph 11.1 could merely have read: 'A suspect must not be interviewed about the relevant offence except at a police station ...' Clearly it was designed to allow *some* interviewing outside the police station due to its requirement of a higher level of suspicion than that denoted by para 11.1A and para 10.1. It implies that a police officer should categorise someone either as possibly involved in an offence or as on the verge of arrest; so long as the first category is applicable questioning can continue. This category was presumably intended to include persons under caution because a caution must be given 'when there are grounds to suspect (him) of an offence'.[176] Obviously these categories will tend to merge into each other. However, it will be difficult to be certain in retrospect as to which applied although the police may find it difficult where there are very strong grounds for suspicion to support a claim that interviewing could continue because the decision to arrest had not been taken. It is clear that the problems associated with exchanges between suspect and officer still remain and it is evident that a significant number of suspects are still interviewed outside the police station.[177] The Runciman Royal Commission proposed that admissions made outside the police station should be seen as needing some form of corroboration such as their acceptance by the suspect on tape at the police station,[178] and this was implemented under the 1995 revision in para 11.2A. However, crucially, para 11.2A does not provide that admissions or silences made outside the police station will be inadmissible if *not* accepted on tape by the suspect at the police station. Therefore, presumably, if no breaches of Code C have occurred, they would be admissible even though uncorroborated.

Original para 10.2 provided that a volunteer who was questioned under caution on 'other premises' had to be told of his right to legal advice. This placed such persons in a better position than arrestees and therefore tended to be evaded by bringing forward the moment of arrest. Current para 10.2 removes the special requirement for volunteers. However, in removing one loophole another has been created: volunteers under caution outside the police station are disadvantaged because they can be questioned without

---

[176] Para 10.1.

[177] Brown, D, Ellis, T and Larcombe, JK, *Home Office Research Study No 129*, HMSO. The study showed that questioning and/or unsolicited comments occurred in 24% of cases. Questioning occurred in 10% of cases.

[178] *Royal Commission Report 1993*, Proposal 40.

notification of the right to legal advice, whereas once the decision to arrest has been made a suspect should not normally be questioned before arrival at the police station, where he will be informed of the right. In other words, in the context of the current provision under para 11.1, the old requirement under para 10.2 would have had some value; had it been retained and extended to all volunteers under caution it would have removed some of the incentive which now exists to delay or apparently delay, the decision to arrest in order to interview outside the police station. Clearly this would have been a radical move but it might have been welcome as harmonising the position of such suspects with that of arrestees.

Where the level of suspicion would obviously justify an arrest a police officer who is eager to keep a suspect out of the police station for the time being might be able to invoke one of the more broadly worded exceptions allowing urgent interviewing in order to avert certain specified risks. The first exception under para 11.1(a), allowing interviewing to take place at once where delay might lead to interference with evidence could be interpreted very broadly and could apply whenever there was some likelihood that evidence connected with any offence but not immediately obtainable was in existence. Even if there were no others involved in the offence who had not been apprehended it could be argued that the evidence was at risk from the moment of arrest because news of the arrest might become known to persons with a motive for concealing it. This argument could also apply to the exception under (c) with the proviso that it will apply to a narrower range of offences.

Once the suspect is inside the police station under arrest or under caution,[179] any interview[180] (using this term to connote an exchange which falls within para 11.1A) should be tape-recorded unless he or she is suspected of involvement in terrorism or of espionage under s 1 of the Official Secrets Act 1989. This provision under Code E para 3.2 is clarified under Note for Guidance 3G of Code E; interviews with those suspected of terrorism solely connected with the affairs of the UK or any part of the UK other than Northern Ireland should be tape-recorded. A written contemporaneous record will still be made of interviews which fall within Code E para 3.2. This exemption was included because it was feared that the contents of tapes might become available to terrorist organisations. At present the Home Office has it under review,[181] and it is suggested that two issues in particular deserve attention. First, what is the likelihood that tape-recording an interview or part of an interview, possibly with editing of the tape, would create more of a

---

179 Under para 3.4 of Code E once a volunteer becomes a suspect (ie at the point when he should be cautioned) the rest of the interview should be tape-recorded.
180 Under para 3.1(a) an interview with a person suspected of an offence triable only summarily need not be taped.
181 House of Commons, *Hansard*, Vol 168 Col 273, 1 March 1990.

threat to national security than making contemporaneous notes available to the defence? The difficulty of editing the tape as compared to editing notes should be weighed against the advantages of tape-recording which seem to be generally recognised.[182] Second, bearing in mind that persons apparently connected with the relevant terrorist offences may vary enormously in terms of their experience and ability to withstand pressure from the police, it must be questioned whether the imposition of a blanket ban on tape-recording of all such interviews can be justified. At the least it is arguable that interviews with mentally disordered or handicapped terrorist suspects (such as Judith Ward)[183] might reasonably be exempted from the para 3.2 provision. It should be recognised that tape-recording is to an extent irrelevant as a safeguard against miscarriages of justice while this exemption exists, especially as terrorist cases may be most likely to miscarry.[184]

Varying levels of protection for exchanges

It is now possible to identify the points at which the safeguards will be brought to bear and it is apparent that there are four levels of protection available:

(1) Inside or outside the police station, if the exchange cannot be labelled an interview even though it may be relevant to the offence, it seems that the level of protection provided by para 11.13 only will apply. This will be the case even where the suspect is an arrestee or a volunteer under caution.

(2) If an interview takes place outside the police station but falls outside the para 11.1 prohibition the verifying and recording provisions under paras 11.10 and 11.5 will apply with the proviso that contemporaneous recording may be impracticable.[185] What is impracticable does not connote something that is extremely difficult but must involve more than mere inconvenience.[186] Where appropriate an adult must be present.[187]

---

182 See Wills, C, Mcleod, J and Nash, P, *The Tape-recording of Police Interviews with Suspects*, 2nd Interim Report, Home Office Research Study No 97, 1988. The study found that police officers and prosecutors generally welcomed taping. There were fewer allegations of 'verballing'.

183 See *Ward* [1993] 1 WLR 619; [1993] 2 All ER 577.

184 Out of the six recent miscarriage of justice cases all but two (the *Silcott* and *Kiszco* cases) have concerned convictions for offences connected with terrorism: the *Birmingham Six*, the *Guildford Four*, the *Maguire Seven* and the *Judith Ward* case.

185 The mere fact that an interview is conducted in the street may not be enough to support an assertion that it could not be contemporaneously recorded. This seems to follow from the decision in *Fogah* [1989] *Crim LR* 141.

186 *Parchment* [1989] *Crim LR* 290. Note-taking while the suspect was dressing and showing the officers round his flat was held to be impracticable.

187 Paragraph 11.14.

(3) Inside the police station, if the person in question is an arrestee or a volunteer under caution[188] and the exchange is an interview, all the available safeguards including tape-recording will apply.[189]
(4) If the conditions under (3) are satisfied but the person is suspected of involvement in terrorism under para 3.2 (or falls within one of the other exemptions from tape-recording)[190] all the available safeguards except tape-recording will apply.

Thus, wide but uncertain scope still remains for interviewing outside the police station and for gathering admissions outside the context of an interview. The main objection to this scheme, apart from its complexity,[191] is that the degree of protection available is too dependent on factors irrelevant to the level of suspicion in question. It may be pure chance or something more sinister, which dictates whether a volunteer under caution is interviewed inside or outside the police station or whether or not an exchange with an arrestee can successfully be characterised or disguised as a non-interview. Bearing in mind that unreliable confessions may be most likely to emerge from informal exchanges, it is argued that the mechanisms triggering off the main safeguards – para 11.1A and para 11.1 – are deficient both in creating large areas of uncertainty as to the level of protection called for at various points and in allowing the minimal level of protection under para 11.13 to operate in too many contexts.

The legal advice scheme

The provision of legal advice in police custody is or course, merely a part of the general interviewing scheme but due to its enormous significance as a safeguard for the suspect it will also be considered here as a separate topic. Before the Police and Criminal Evidence Act 1984 was passed the right to legal advice when in police custody was more honoured in the breach than in the

---

188 Under new para 3.15, which largely reproduces original para 3.9 volunteers under caution have the right to be told that they may obtain legal advice. The other important Code C safeguards are contained in paras 11 and 12 and apply to arrestees and volunteers under caution. Under Code E tape recording must be used for interviews with persons under caution in the police station (E 3.1(a)).

189 Unless under Code E para 3.3 it would not be reasonably practicable to tape the interview due to failure of the recording equipment or non-availability of an interview room or recorder. Note 3K of Code E provides that if necessary an officer must be able to justify the decision not to delay the interview.

190 Above note 189.

191 The need to adopt a common sense approach to the rules was expressed in *Marsh* [1991] *Crim LR* 455 by Bingham LJ in relation to the original scheme. However, the current scheme does not lend itself readily to a simple interpretation. See especially the comments of McCullough J in *Cox* [1993] *Crim LR* 382 regarding Note 11A.

observance.[192] With a view to ensuring that suspects actually receive legal advice, the Act entitles a person to consult a solicitor privately[193] and provides for duty solicitors to attend suspects.[194] A detainee is to be informed of this right,[195] given if necessary, the name of the duty solicitor[196] and permitted to have the solicitor present during questioning.[197] In cases involving 'serious arrestable offences' however, there are certain saving provisions[198] allowing an officer of at least the rank of superintendent to authorise delay and a further power to delay access arises under Code C.[199] Thus Parliament drew back from making this right absolute; nevertheless the exceptions are narrowly drawn and so should not significantly undermine it. However, the factor which previously motivated the police to delay (or refuse) access to legal advice remains unchanged: the suspect still has the right to remain silent and the legal adviser may advise him or her to exercise it in the particular circumstances of the case, despite the risk that adverse inferences may be drawn later at court. Even if the solicitor does not advise silence the police may think that they are more likely to obtain incriminating admissions from detainees in the absence of a solicitor and therefore at times may deny the access to one envisaged by s 58. A number of formal and informal methods of evading the scheme are available and five such methods are identified below.

---

192 Section 62 of the Criminal Law Act 1977 declared a narrow entitlement to have one reasonably named person informed of the arrest. It did not provide that the arrestee must be informed of this right nor did it provide any sanction for non-compliance by a police officer. That statutory form of this right gave it no greater force than the non-statutory Judges' Rules (rules of practice for the guidance of the police. See Practice Note [1984] 1 All ER 237; 1 WLR 152). The Judges' Rules upheld the right of the suspect/arrestee in the police station to communicate with/consult a solicitor but permitted the withholding of such access 'lest unreasonable delay or hindrance is caused to the process of investigation or the administration of justice.' Any officer, in relation to a person detained for any offence could deny access to legal advice on these broad grounds. See *Lemsateff* [1977] 1 WLR 812; [1977] 2 All ER 835.
193 Section 58(1): 'A person who is in police detention shall be entitled, if he so requests, to consult a solicitor privately at any time.'
194 Section 59: 'In s 1 of the Legal Aid Act 1982 (duty solicitors) ... (c) the following subsection shall be inserted ... (1A) A scheme under s 15 of the Principal Act ... may provide that arrangements ... be ... framed so as to preclude solicitors from providing such advice and representation if they do not also provide advice and assistance ... for persons ... held in custody.'
195 Code C para 3.1(ii).
196 Code C Note 6B.
197 Code C para 6.5.
198 Section 58(8): 'An officer may only authorise delay where he has reasonable grounds for believing that the exercise of the right ...

   (a) will lead to interference with or harm to evidence connected with a serious arrestable offence or interference with or physical injury to other persons; or

   (b) will lead to the alerting of other persons suspected of having committed such an offence but not yet arrested for it; or

   (c) will hinder the recovery of any property obtained as a result of such an offence.'
199 Code C para 6.3(b)(ii). Where a solicitor has agreed to attend, awaiting his arrival would cause unreasonable delay to the process of the investigation. See also Annex B.

(i) Denying access

The most direct method of denying legal advice involves invoking one of the three s 58(8) exceptions. The exceptions come into operation if the suspect is in police detention for a serious arrestable offence[200] and the decision to invoke them must be taken by an officer of at least the rank of superintendent. If both these conditions are fulfilled, access, if requested, can be denied if the officer believes on reasonable grounds that exercise of the right at the time when the person in police detention desires to exercise it *will* lead to the solicitor acting as a channel of communication between the detainee and others – alerting them or hindering the recovery of stolen property.

The leading case determining the scope of the s 58 exceptions is *Samuel*.[201] The appellant was arrested on suspicion of armed robbery and, after questioning at the police station, asked to see a solicitor. The request was refused, apparently on the grounds that other suspects might be warned[202] and that recovery of the outstanding stolen money might thereby be hindered.[203] The appellant subsequently confessed to the robbery and was later convicted. On appeal the defence argued that the refusal of access was not justifiable under s 58(8) and that therefore the confession obtained should not have been admitted into evidence as it had been obtained due to impropriety. The Court of Appeal considered the use of the word 'will' in s 58(8) which suggests that the police officer must be virtually certain that a solicitor if contacted will thereafter either commit a criminal offence or unwittingly pass on a coded message to criminals. It must be asked first whether he did believe this and secondly whether he believed it on reasonable grounds. The court considered that only in the remote contingency that evidence could be produced as to the corruption of a particular solicitor would a police officer be able to assert a reasonable belief that a solicitor would commit a criminal offence. They went on to hold that showing a reasonable belief that a solicitor would inadvertently alert other criminals would also be a formidable task; such a belief could only reasonably be held if the suspect in question was a particularly resourceful and sophisticated criminal or if there was evidence that the solicitor sought to be consulted was particularly inexperienced or naive. It was found that as no evidence as to the naivety or corruption of the solicitor in question had been advanced it could not be accepted that the necessary reasonable belief had existed. The police had made no attempt to consider the real likelihood that the solicitor in question would be utilised in this way; in fact it was apparent that the true

---

[200] Defined in s 116. Section 99 of the Criminal Justice Act 1988 extends these exceptions to drug trafficking offences.
[201] [1988] QB 615; [1988] 2 All ER 135; [1988] 2 WLR 920, CA.
[202] Section 58(8)(b).
[203] Section 58(8)(c).

motive behind the denial of access was a desire to gain a further opportunity to break down the detainee's silence. It should be noted that Code C[204] expressly disallows denial of access to a solicitor on the ground that he or she will advise the suspect to remain silent.[205]

This interpretation of s 58(8) has greatly narrowed its scope since it means that the police will not be able to make a general, unsubstantiated assertion that it was thought that others might be alerted if a solicitor was contacted. The authorising officer will have to show, on very specific grounds, why this was thought to be the case (the question of exclusion of the confession due to this impropriety is considered below).[206] This decision may have prevented mere refusals to allow access to advice in some instances. However, there are a number of loopholes in the legal advice scheme which may allow for less formal methods of evading its provisions and it may be that the suspects who are thereby most disadvantaged are those most in need of legal advice.

(ii) Subverting notification

Notification of the right to advice under para 3.1 of Code C is still reserved for arrival at the police station, thus disadvantaging certain suspects not already aware of it at the point when admissions may be made.[207] It is probably fair to assume, first, that many suspects, including those who are criminally experienced,[208] are aware of the right to legal advice and, secondly, that the group who are not so aware would tend to include some of the more vulnerable members of society. It has already been noted above that there is leeway in the interviewing scheme to allow admissions to be made before notification of advice during 'booking in' at the police station.

At the point of notification the suspect not already aware of the right to advice is in a very vulnerable position since he is dependent for information on the very persons who have an interest in withholding it or misleading him. Research conducted by Sanders[209] has demonstrated that notification can be subverted by various methods, most commonly by ensuring that suspects

---

204 In *Delaney* (1989) 88 Cr App R 338; (1988) *The Times*, 20 August, CA, the status of the Codes was considered. It was held that the mere fact that there had been a breach of the Codes of Practice did not of itself mean that evidence had to be rejected. Section 67(11) of the Act provides that '... if any provision of such Code appears to the court ... to be relevant to any question arising in the proceedings it shall be taken into account in determining that question'.

205 Annex B, para 2.

206 At p 484.

207 Softley's research into the issue indicated that when suspects were informed of this right requests for advice were three times as high as when they were not so informed (Softley, *Police Interrogations* (1980)).

208 The Sanders research, above note 159, supports this suggestion; out of 60 suspects who knew that they had a right to legal advice, only 23.3% did not know this before informed of it by the police, *op cit* p 46.

209 Above note 159.

never really take in what is on offer.[210] When Code C was revised in 1991 and in 1995 this problem was recognised and an attempt was made to address it. The requirement of notification under para 3.1 was backed up by new para 6.3, requiring that police stations display a prominent poster (under new Note 6H with ethnic translations if appropriate) advertising the right to have advice. However, it must be questioned whether the provision of posters will make much difference. The 'booking in' stage is likely to be one of the more traumatic points in the process especially for the suspect who is inexperienced or in some way vulnerable. Whether he is likely to notice and take in a message conveyed in this way which is not specifically directed at him is open to question. If he remains silent in the face of a rapid notification, his silence can be taken as a waiver of advice when in actuality it merely denotes incomprehension. The requirement introduced in 1995 under para 6.5 that the suspect should be asked his reason for declining legal advice and that this should be noted on the custody record, may go some way towards ensuring that suspects understand what is on offer and may curb 'ploys' (see below), as may the requirement to point out that the suspect may speak on the telephone with a solicitor. Nevertheless, the possibility of manipulation of the custody record remains since the whole process of making the record remains in the hands of the custody officer.[211] Research conducted after the 1991 revision of Code C found that a higher proportion of suspects were being informed of the right to legal advice[212] but that the information was given in a quarter of cases in an unclear or unduly rapid fashion.

(iii) Encouragement to defer the decision

If the suspect does take in what is being offered he may be encouraged not to exercise the right straight away. In fact, the Sanders research suggested that encouraging a suspect to defer the decision to have advice was quite popular.[213] The 1991 revision of Code C did address this problem. Paragraph 3.1 now provides that it is a 'continuing right which may be exercised at any

---

210 Sanders found that the most popular ploy (used in 42.9% of the instances observed) was to read the rights too quickly or incomprehensibly or incompletely, *op cit* p 59.

211 It has been suggested (by Wolchover, D and Heaton-Armstrong, A (1990) *NLJ* at pp 320–21) that a requirement of an own hand declaration of waiver of advice would have represented an effective means of addressing the problem because it would have forced the custody officer to ensure that the suspect understood what was being offered and would require positive action on the suspect's part to refuse it.

212 Brown, D, Ellis, T and Lancombe, K, *Changing the Code: Police Detention under the revised PACE Codes of Practice* (research conducted for the Royal Commission on Criminal Procedure), 1993, Home Office Research Study 129. It found that 73% of suspects as opposed to 66% prior to April 1991 received notification.

213 This 'ploy' was used in 8.2% of the cases observed. In a further 1.8% of cases it was suggested that the suspect waited until after his transfer to another station before having advice and in a further 2.7% of cases that he waited until he got out of the police station, *op cit* p 59.

stage' and under para 11.2 a suspect must now be reminded of the right before each interview in the police station. Although this change is to be welcomed it should not obscure the value of having advice before any interviewing at all takes place.[214] It is therefore unfortunate that para 3.1 does not make this clear and could even be said to encourage the suspect to defer the decision. However, Note 3G seems designed to dissuade some suspects from deferring it by providing that a request for advice from a mentally disordered or handicapped person or a juvenile should be pursued straight away without waiting for the appropriate adult to arrive. It appears intended to prevent police officers playing off adult against suspect by telling the suspect to defer making a decision about advice until the adult arrives,[215] and then giving the adult the impression that the juvenile has waived advice or does not need it.[216] It appears that this provision has not had much impact,[217] which might be because it is contained in a Note and not in the Code itself. Provision aimed at preventing this ploy could have been taken further by including a requirement that even where a suspect had waived advice, suspect and adult should be left alone together for a few minutes after re-notification of the right.

(iv) Encouragement to forego advice

Suspects who are thinking of asking for legal advice straight away may still be persuaded out of doing so by various methods and the Sanders research found that such methods – termed 'ploys' – were most successful against least experienced suspects.[218] However, there has been some attempt to combat the use of such ploys. For example, suspects were supposed to be given a leaflet under original Note 3E explaining the arrangements for obtaining advice, including the fact that it was free but in practice a number of suspects did not receive it or did not understand it, thereby enabling police officers to mislead them.[219] Under para 3.1(ii) the suspect must now be informed that advice is free[220] (although the posters need not carry this

---

214 Sanders found that suspects had often made admissions in the absence of the solicitor and that therefore 'the potential impact of the solicitor was neutralised in advance by the police', *op cit* p 143. This finding arose in the context of informal questioning but could be equally applicable to instances where the suspect defers the decision to have advice.

215 This ploy was used in 5.4% of instances observed, *op cit* p 59.

216 This ploy was used in 2.4% of instances observed, *op cit* p 59.

217 Brown, D *et al*, 'Changing the Code' above note 212; apart from this propensity, particular problems were found with the notification of this right to juveniles with a wide variation in the number of juveniles requesting advice in the different stations: 7% to 58%.

218 The take-up rate for advice among suspects with no previous convictions 'declined sharply as more ploys were used.' This was contrasted with the smaller correlation between the use of ploys and take up rate among all suspects, *op cit* pp 57 and 61.

219 This ploy was used in less than 1.5% of the instances observed, *op cit* p 59.

220 The research by Brown, D *et al*, shows a dramatic improvement in the number of suspects informed that advice is free after the revision of the Codes: 73% compared with 5%.

information). Further, general discouragement of ploys is articulated in new para 6.4 which provides that no attempt should be made to dissuade the suspect from having advice.

The detainee who has decided to have advice can nevertheless change his or her mind; this is provided for by sub-para 6.3(d), if the consent is given in writing or on tape. However, there is some leeway allowing police officers to engineer a change of heart. No limitations were placed on the reasons for giving such consent, thus creating a serious flaw in the legal advice provisions. In particular, if the consent is based on a police misrepresentation ought it to be treated as genuine? This question arises in part due to the lack of certainty as to the relationship between sub-para 6.3(d) and (c). Sub-para 6.3(c) provides that the detainee can be interviewed without legal advice if the nominated solicitor is unavailable and notification of the duty solicitor scheme is given but the duty solicitor is unavailable or not required. The provisions under sub-paras 6.3(c) and (d) appear to be expressed as alternatives but the draughtsman's intention must surely be that the police cannot obtain the detainee's consent to be interviewed merely by failing to inform him or her of the scheme.

The first instance decision in *Vernon*[221] suggested that the consent must be genuine; in other words it must not be based on misleading information given by the police. The defendant consented to be interviewed under the misapprehension that if her own solicitor was unavailable there was no alternative means of obtaining advice; the confession so obtained was excluded. Andrew J held that as her consent to the interview was given under the misapprehension that otherwise the interview would be delayed till the morning this could not be termed true consent: had she known of the availability of the duty solicitor she would have withheld her consent. Thus, the exception under sub-para 6.3(d) was not fulfilled: para 6.3 had been breached. This ruling suggests that although the exceptions under sub-paras 6.3(c) and (d) are expressed disjunctively they should be read together; if a detainee has fallen within sub-para 6.3(c) by nominating a solicitor and being disappointed, he or she should then be informed of the alternative. It would not seem to accord with the draughtsman's intention to treat the consent of such a person in the same way as that of a detainee who has decided against having a solicitor at all.

The ruling of the Court of Appeal in *Hughes*,[222] however, suggested that if the police misled the suspect without bad faith a resultant consent would be treated as genuine. The appellant, disappointed of obtaining advice from his own solicitor, enquired about the duty solicitor scheme but was informed,

---

221 [1988] *Crim LR* 445.
222 [1988] *Crim LR* 519, CA, transcript from LEXIS.

erroneously, (but in good faith) that no solicitor was available. Under this misapprehension he gave consent to be interviewed and the Court of Appeal took the view that his consent was not thereby vitiated. Sub-paragraphs 6.3(c) and (d) were to be treated as alternatives and the fact that the detainee was within (c) did not vitiate his consent under (d). Thus, no breach had occurred.

The court did not advert to the difficulty that there can be no difference in principle between failing to inform a detainee of the scheme and informing him or her of it but stating wrongly that no solicitor is available. This ruling opens the possibility that the consent given in *Vernon* will in future be treated as true consent. The only distinction between the cases is that in *Hughes* the misrepresentation was apparently made innocently, while in *Vernon* the failure to give the information was deliberate: *Vernon* demonstrates a willingness to interpret Code C restrictively against the police if bad faith is demonstrated. The view was taken in *Hughes* that if the misrepresentation had been made negligently or deliberately a different conclusion would have been reached. This seems to confuse the para 6.3(d) issue and the issue of fairness under s 78 (which will be considered fully below);[223] the judgment would have been clearer if the court had considered first whether a breach of para 6.3 had occurred and, second, whether the breach in the circumstances would have an adverse effect on the fairness of the trial. Innocence or bad faith on the part of the police has been determined to be relevant when considering s 78[224] but there is nothing in Code C to suggest that these matters are relevant in relation to the narrow question of failure to fulfil a Code provision. Generally, consent to forego a right should be treated with caution when the parties are on an unequal footing; and the possible unfairness is exacerbated when the party who will obtain an advantage from the consent gives false information in obtaining it. Had the Court of Appeal found itself able to hold that such consent is not true consent the onus would have been placed on the police to ensure that administrative practice in relation to the duty solicitor scheme was tightened up. As it is, moves towards obtaining consent in similar circumstances may become more marked and it is likely to be the more suggestible detainee who suffers.

Under the 1991 revision, once the suspect has changed his mind about having advice, the interview can proceed subject to the need to obtain the permission of an officer of the rank of inspector or above. This is the main change from the original Code and is obviously not a full safeguard against the possibility of pressure from the police considered above. Inclusion of a provision that a consent based on erroneous information given by the police could not be treated as true consent might have encouraged the police to tighten up administrative practices and perhaps avoided a recurrence of the

---

223 At pp 483–89.
224 See *Alladice* (1988) 87 Cr App R 380, CA; [1988] *Crim LR* 608. See below pp 489–90.

Hughes type of situation. A provision included in the 1991 Home Office circular[225] requiring a note to be made in the custody record of the reason for the suspect's change of heart, may allow a court to determine whether the consent *was* based on misleading information. This circular provision, in the form of a requirement to record the reason for the change of mind and repeat it on tape, became part of para 6.5 under the 1995 revision to Code C. This provision may allow a court to determine whether the consent was based on misleading information but it leaves open the possibility of treating the consent as valid so long as such information was apparently given in good faith.

(v) Debarring solicitors' clerks

As already noted, s 58(1) entitles the detainee to consult a solicitor at any time. This provision does not extend to solicitors' clerks but, under Code C para 6.9, if the solicitor who has been contacted decides to send a clerk, he or she should be admitted to the police station. After the decision in *Samuel*[226] access to a solicitor can be delayed only in very specific circumstances. These exceptions do not apply to clerks but, since the decision of the Court of Appeal in *Chief Constable of Avon, ex parte Robinson*,[227] access to a clerk can be denied in a much wider range of circumstances. The Chief Constable had issued instructions that the character and antecedents of certain unqualified clerks employed by the applicant – a solicitor – were such as to make their presence at police interviews with suspects undesirable. The Chief Constable left the final decision on access to the officer in question but gave his opinion that it would only rarely be appropriate to allow these particular clerks access to a suspect. The applicant sought judicial review of the instructions, contending that they were in breach of para 6.9.

The Court of Appeal considered the scope of the express exception to para 6.9: '... the clerk shall be admitted unless an officer of the rank of inspector or above considers that such a visit will hinder the investigation of crime.' It was held that the investigating officers had been entitled in each instance to invoke the exception because they had known of the criminal activities of the clerks. They had been informed of such activities by the Chief Constable but he had not imposed a blanket ban on the clerks; the discretion to debar the clerks had been left with the officers concerned. Accordingly, there had been no breach of para 6.9 and the application would therefore be refused. May LJ, in a lengthy *dictum*, also considered that there was an implied requirement under para 6.9 that a clerk be capable of giving advice on behalf of the solicitor and therefore a police officer would be entitled to exclude a clerk if he appeared

---

225 When the revised PACE Codes came into force in April 1991 a Home Office circular was issued in conjunction with them by F2 Division, Home Office.
226 [1988] QB 615; [1988] 2 All ER 135; [1988] 2 WLR 920, CA.
227 [1989] All ER 15; [1989] 1 WLR 793.

incapable of giving advice due to his age, appearance, mental capacity or known background.

The concern as to the possible effects of employing these untrained clerks is understandable but the result of this decision is to confer a very wide power on the police to exclude clerks which may have unfortunate consequences. If, in future, a detainee asks for legal advice and a clerk arrives but is not admitted to the police station on one of the grounds considered above or if he or she is not allowed to remain in the interview, the police under Code C para 6.14 must give the original solicitor the opportunity of making other arrangements. The Code is silent as to what should happen if the solicitor is unable to do so, although under para 6.10 if a *solicitor* is excluded from the station the police must give the suspect an opportunity to consult another solicitor. Paragraph 6.12 provides that para 6.10 applies to clerks and therefore in the circumstances described the police as a last resort presumably ought to inform the detainee of the duty solicitor scheme.

It is probably regrettable that the Court of Appeal suggested such wide grounds on which to exclude clerks. If the police take advantage of their width to exclude clerks rather too readily, some detainees may be likely to experience substantial delay in obtaining advice. There is always the danger when advice is delayed that a detainee will succumb to pressure to get the interview over with quickly and will consent to be interviewed without advice. The 1995 revision addressed this possibility to some extent: para 6.12 restricts the grounds for exclusion as far as clerks or other accredited representatives of solicitors are concerned since it defines such persons as 'solicitors'. This means that the trainee, clerk or legal executive is 'accredited in accordance with the Law Society's scheme for accreditation'. Therefore the more restrictive provisions relating to exclusion from the interview of solicitors, paras 6.9, 6.10 and 6.11, will apply. Under para 6.9 the solicitor may be excluded from the interview if his or her conduct is such that the investigating officer is unable properly to question the suspect. Under para 6.12 a non-accredited or probationary representative may be excluded from the police station if an officer of the rank of inspector or above considers that the visit would hinder the investigation of crime and directs otherwise. The factors influencing the discretion to exclude such advisers from the police station are set out in paras 6.12 and 6.13 and include taking account of 'any matters set out in any written letter of authorisation provided by the solicitor'. It is unclear that this discretion is markedly narrower than that indicated in *Robinson* and therefore it will be hard ever to challenge a decision to exclude such persons, leaving open the possibility that officers may at times exercise this power rather too readily. Once advice is delayed a detainee may succumb to pressure to forego it in order to speed matters up. The real answer to this difficulty seems to be that *solicitors* should provide advice; this is discussed below in relation to the *quality* of advice given.

Value of legal advice and relationship with the right to silence

It is generally thought that the provision of legal advice to the suspect in police custody is one of the most fundamental rights provided by PACE and this is partly due to the relationship between access to legal advice and the right to silence. This is a complex relationship[228] but the available research seems to lend some support to the following propositions. The suspect will probably be aware that he can keep silent and that this may be a risky course of action, if he has had advice especially if the legal adviser attends the interview. The legal adviser may sometimes advise silence and may help the suspect to maintain silence[229] where advice alone might not be enough.[230] It should be recognised, however, that the key question is not whether the presence of a legal adviser means that the detainee remains silent but whether it means that he is unlikely to make an unreliable confession. Further, assuming for the moment an inverse correlation between a legal adviser's presence and an unreliable confession, what contribution to it, if any, is made by the right to silence in its current modified form? Obviously the detainee will not make such a confession if he remains silent but this is a rather crude and in any event ineffective[231] way of tackling the risk of such confessions; the real concern here is with the question whether the legal adviser will enable the detainee to maintain a selective silence or refuse to depart from his version of events at key points in the interview.

Clearly, the recent curtailment of the right to silence discussed below may tend to affect the nature of custodial legal advice. It may change the role of the legal advisor in the police station; that role is already, it seems, interpreted in a variety of ways by advisors but in circumstances where silence would previously have been advised by most of them it seems possible that in future it may not be. Possibly the difficulty of advising the client as to when to remain silent and when not to take the risk of so doing may mean that some advisors tend to adopt the role of referee or counsellor rather than that of legal

---

228 The relationship is a matter of some controversy; the Home Office Working Group on the Right to Silence (C Division, Home Office, London, 13 July 1989; see [1989] *Crim LR* 855 for comment) considered that there was a causal relationship between legal advice and silence but this finding has been doubted by Dixon, D: see 'Solicitors, Suspects, Runners, Police'; findings reported at [1991] *PL* 233 at p 251. However, the Sanders research (above note 159) found that suspects confess less often when they have advice: 35.8% of those whose solicitor was present at the interrogation confessed as opposed to 59.6% of those who did not receive advice (*op cit* p 136).

229 See the research undertaken by Sanders, A et al, 'Advice and Assistance at Police Stations' (November 1989) at p 129 which found that out of 24 suspects only two were advised to remain silent. Dixon, D, above note 228 *op cit* p 243, found to the same effect.

230 The Sanders research found that telephone advice had little impact on suspects: 50% of those who received telephone advice made admissions as opposed to 59.6% of those who received no advice.

231 The Sanders research, above note 159, found that only 2.4% of suspects exercised their right to silence as against 54.1% who made admissions (the others denied the offence) (*op cit* p 136).

advisor. More experienced advisors will, however, be of great value to the client since they will be able to advise on the risks of staying in silent which may be much greater in response to certain questions than to others.[232]

The main studies in this area[233] recognised that interviews may be a means of *constructing* or creating truth rather than discovering it but their concern was more with the causal relationship between the presence of a legal adviser and exercise of the right to silence than with the relationship between such presence and the making of an unreliable confession. This issue was touched on in the study by Dixon[234] which found that legal advisers were more likely to advise silence at least temporarily if the client was in a confused or emotional state[235] or had been bullied or deceived.[236] A further study, conducted for the Royal Commission on Criminal Justice[237] found, not surprisingly, that the relationship between legal advice and the right to silence was affected by the quality of the advice given. The research found that many 'legal advisers' are clerks, secretaries and former police officers with no legal education or training in the provision of custodial legal advice. Such persons, it was found, often had little or no grasp of the case in question and little apparent understanding of the need, at times, for the client to maintain a selective silence. According to the research, 78% of the advisers counselled the client to co-operate with the police.

Thus, despite the general perception that legal advice reduces the likelihood that unreliable confessions will be made, the available empirical evidence relating specifically to the issue allows only the tentative suggestion that the adviser may ensure that the client is aware of the right to silence and may sometimes advise that he exercises it, despite the risks, especially where the client does not seem able to cope with the interview.[238] In this context it is worth bearing in mind that it tends to be a feature of cases in which a miscarriage of justice has occurred that the confessions were uttered in the absence of a legal adviser.[239] This has not invariably been the case; the

---

232 For further discussion see Fenwick, H [1995] *Crim LR* 132; Jackson, D [1995] *Crim LR* 587.
233 The Sanders research above note 159, the Home Office Study above note 228 and the study by Brown *et al* above note 212.
234 Above note 228.
235 *Op cit* p 244.
236 *Op cit* pp 246 and 247.
237 The study by Hodgson, J and McConville, M, took place over an eight month period during which the researchers followed suspects and advisers into 180 interrogations; see 143 *NLJ* 659.
238 It is worth noting that the Court of Appeal has accepted as a general rule that most suspects unless clearly experienced and independently minded are less likely to make any confession in the presence of a solicitor (*Samuel* [1988] 1 QB 615; [1988] 2 All ER 135; [1988] 2 WLR 920, CA; *Dunford* (1990) 140 *NLJ* 517, CA).
239 For example, the *Confait* case, see the Report of an Enquiry by the Hon Sir Henry Fisher (1977) *HC* 90; the case of the *Birmingham Six* (1991) *The Times*, 28 March; *Silcott* (1991) *The Times*, 8 December.

confessions gained by oppression in the case of the Cardiff Three were obtained in the presence of a solicitor.[240] Of course, if an unreliable confession is made in the presence of a legal adviser this may say much more about the quality of the advice given than it does about the principle of having legal advice.

The presence of a solicitor can affect the reliability of the confession in other ways. The suspect may feel generally reassured due to the presence of a person independent of the police who is undaunted by the interview process. Moreover, his or her presence may sometimes be a potent factor discouraging use of improper tactics,[241] and may help to alter the balance of power between interviewer and interviewee, thus tending to create a climate in which an unreliable confession is less likely to be uttered. Reassurance deriving from the presence of a solicitor is not merely valuable in terms of the reliability of the confession; it may serve to make the whole experience of police detention less traumatic and daunting. In theory the solicitor will intervene if the interview is conducted in an intimidatory fashion or if other improper tactics are used. However, the availability of legal advice may not always have such effects. Sanders criticised the great variation in practice between solicitors and considered that too many gave telephone advice only, thereby depriving the client of most of the benefits of legal advice.[242] As noted above, other recent research echoed these findings as to the quality of advice and suggested that solicitors were adopting a passive stance in interviews, failing to intervene where intervention was clearly called for.[243] Professor McConville found that the presence of some legal advisers in interviews may have had a *detrimental* impact on suspects: 'Lacking any clear understanding of their role in the process, some advisers simply become part of the machine which confronts the suspect.'[244] In other words, the mere fact

---

240 *Paris* (1993) 97 Cr App R 99; [1994] *Crim LR* 361, CA. This also occurred in *Heron* below note 332; the judge, Mr Justice Mitchell, drew attention to the fact that only a legal executive was present during oppressive questioning and said that this was unacceptable.

241 One of the conclusions of the Sanders research (above note 159) *op cit* p 150 was that suspects who did not receive advice or whose solicitors did not attend the interrogation would have been greatly assisted had the solicitor been present. Two examples are given at pp 138 and 139 of forceful or threatening questioning which produced a possibly unreliable confession from an easily intimidated suspect in the absence of a solicitor. This finding received some support from Dixon's study (above note 228).

242 The Sanders research found that only 50% of solicitors attended the police station: 25% gave advice over the telephone and 25% gave no advice. Even attendances at the police station were not always followed by attendance at the interview. A few solicitors merely put the police case to the suspect (*op cit* p 150). Anecdotal evidence uncovered by the author suggests that some solicitors who do attend the interview actually disadvantage the client by seeming to give their imprimatur to improper police behaviour.

243 *The Role of Legal Representatives at Police Stations*, 1992, HMSO Research Study No 3, summarised at [1993] *Crim LR* 161. For criticism of the approach of the research see Roberts, D [1993] *Crim LR* 368 with reply by Baldwin at p 371.

244 McConville, M and Hodgson, J, *Custodial Legal Advice and the Right to Silence*, Royal Commission Study No 13.

that a person labelled a 'legal adviser' turns up at the police station and may be present in the interview may have little impact in terms of evening up the balance of power between suspect and police officer. Indeed, the presence of such a person may be to the disadvantage of the suspect as it may offer a reassurance which it does not warrant.

Improving the legal advice scheme

There seem to be two main weaknesses in the scheme as it stands – the ease of evading its provisions and the quality of advice given – which may mean that the right to legal advice is little more valuable to the suspect than it was prior to PACE. If so, the balance between suspects' rights and police powers is not being maintained.

The main 'sanction' for breach of the legal advice provisions is exclusion of evidence. However, most of the methods of evading the legal advice provisions considered here tended to consist of rule evasion as opposed to rule breaking. court s tend to prefer the defence to point to a specific breach of a Code provision before deciding whether to invoke s 78 to exclude admissions.[245] However, the disapproval of persuading an inexperienced suspect to forego advice expressed in *Beycan*[246] suggests that there may be a growing willingness on the part of the judiciary to consider rule evasion in this context. Where it seems that such evasion has occurred it could be characterised as general subversion of the legal advice scheme or perhaps as a breach of the para 6.4 provision that no attempt must be made to persuade the suspect to waive advice. There would be scope for such argument where, for example, a suspect who made admissions in an interview after he had waived his entitlement to advice stated that something an officer said (such as an over-statement of the time needed to contact a solicitor) or failed to say to him, persuaded him to that decision. Although para 6.4 seems to be aimed at preventing such improper persuasion at the 'booking in' stage it might also apply if it appeared that police officers had pressurised or misled a suspect into reversing the decision to have advice. For example, an untrue representation (even though made in good faith) that the duty solicitor was unavailable which had the *effect* of persuading the detainee to reverse the decision to have advice might be brought within para 6.4. If no reason for such a reversal was recorded as required by the 1991 Home Office circular, that might lend weight to the argument that the suspect was improperly persuaded to forego advice. It is clear that although para 6.4 has not so far received much attention it does open up a number of possibilities. This point will be returned to below when exclusion of evidence as a form of redress for a breach of PACE is considered. However, it should be noted here that even if

---

245 See, for example, *Keenan* [1989] 3 WLR 1193.
246 [1990] *Crim LR* 185.

methods of evading the legal advice scheme could be given the character of a breach of PACE, exclusion of evidence would not inevitably follow. Thus this 'sanction' remains extremely weak and is, of course, inapplicable to a suspect who is improperly denied advice or encouraged to forego it but later pleads guilty.

Various suggestions for reform of the legal advice scheme have already been made above which could bring about significant improvement without necessitating a radical change. There are other possibilities: ploys could be discouraged and untrue allegations by suspects of lack of notification of advice precluded if the booking in stage were video or audio taped.[247] Such an innovation could be used in conjunction with the para 6.4 prohibition of attempts to dissuade the suspect to forego advice. Inadequate notification of advice could be characterised as an attempt at persuasion to forego it on the ground that it was intended to and did have that effect. Finally and very importantly, notification of legal advice could take place on arrest or even on caution, thereby harmonising the position of all suspects. Clearly, such changes would not ensure that all suspects who needed it received advice; the process of affording access to advice would still remain in the hands of a body which has an interest in withholding it, while many suspects would continue to need disinterested advice regarding the decision whether to have advice.[248]

Improvement in the quality of advice can be brought about only by an increase in funding for the scheme. It may be argued that only specially trained solicitors should offer advice but until better funding is available solicitors will delegate this function. The Royal Commission in its 1993 report proposed that the performance of solicitors should be monitored and that the police should receive training in the role solicitors are expected to play (Proposals 64–69). However, it may be that more radical action is necessary to address this problem. There are various possibilities; for example, legal advisers (who might be trainee solicitors and should at least have some legal education) could be employed on a temporary basis to attend all interviews in police stations except where the suspect requested his own solicitor or a duty solicitor or specifically required that a legal adviser should not be present. Such advisers could receive some special training concerned specifically with advising the suspect in the police station.[249] Apart from such advisers,

---

247 The suggestion of video taping was made by Judge Jeremy Fordham (1991) *NLJ* 677. He suggested that it could take place by means of a fixed camera focused on the 'booking in' desk. The Royal Commission Report 1993 also proposed (Proposal 57) that a waiver of advice at this point should be video-taped.

248 The Sanders research found that suspects quite often asked officers whether or not they should have advice: *op cit* p 65.

249 For example, the College of Law course: 'Advising the suspect at the police station'. It may be noted that in response to the McConville study reported at 143 *NLJ* 659, the Law Society and Legal Aid Board have announced that from October 1993 legal aid will not be available for police station work unless advisers have been through a training course and passed a Law Society test.

persons other than solicitors should not attend the suspect during interviews. Such a scheme would not only address most of the difficulties outlined here but also the problems caused by the reluctance of solicitors to attend the police station[250] and the variation in the quality of the response of solicitors to the request for advice.[251]

Interviewing techniques and recording methods

The recording of police interviews must be one of the most rapidly developing areas of policing. The recent introduction of tape-recording[252] replacing contemporaneous note taking[253] may eventually be overtaken by video-taping;[254] if so the process will have gone as far as technology will presently allow it to go. There seems to be general agreement that the use of tape-recording is to be welcomed as reflecting a truer picture of an interview than note-taking,[255] and due to recent developments the jury are in one sense even *better* placed than they would have been had they been present at the interview because they may be allowed to take the tape-recordings into the jury room[256] to replay as necessary.[257] Video-taping of police interviews is currently at the experimental stage but the Home Office has signalled that it

---

250 The Sanders research found that 25.6% of solicitors gave telephone advice only, which was less valuable for the suspect: *op cit* p 104.
251 The Sanders research found an enormous variation in the quality of service offered in this context, *op cit* pp 112–17.
252 Governed by Code of Practice E which came into force on 29 July 1988.
253 Originally governed by Code C para 11.3 and under revised Code C by para 11.5. Tape-recording has not entirely replaced contemporaneous note-taking, first because it does not apply to all interviews: see Code E para 3 and secondly because contemporaneous note-taking applies to interviews outside the police station where practicable, whereas tape-recording is at present only required inside it: Code E para 3.1.
254 Video-taping of interviews as opposed to audio taping was one of the possibilities considered by the Royal Commission on Criminal Procedure chaired by Lord Runciman. See (1991) *NLJ* 1512 for a brief interim report by John Baldwin of a study of video-taping experiments currently taking place in four police stations. At present the police can video-tape a confession if they first obtain the consent of the accused: *Li Shu-Ling* [1989] *Crim LR* 58 PC. The Royal Commission proposed that further research into the use of video-taping for interviews should be carried out (Proposal 70). However, the Home Office issued a circular on video-recording of interviews which advised against moving quickly to introduce video-recording due to the cost of so doing (Circular 6/1993).
255 See the *Home Office Research Study No 97* 1988: 'The Tape-Recording of Police Interviews with Suspects: A Second Interim Report.' It found that police officers and prosecutors generally welcomed taping. However, research conducted by J Baldwin and J Bedward of the Institute of Judicial Administration, University of Birmingham, on summaries made of tape recorded interviews found that the summaries were often of a very poor quality and presented a distorted picture of what occurred during the interview. However, they also found that the police were aware of this problem and were beginning to address it. See [1991] *Crim LR* 671.
256 *Emmerson* [1991] *Crim LR* 194. In *Riaz and Burke* [1991] *Crim LR* 366 the Court of Appeal held (in instances where the jury had not already heard the tapes) that better practice would be to reassemble the court and play the tapes in open court.
257 This permission was expressed to extend only to those parts of the tapes which had been heard in open court; other material would have to be edited out.

gives some support to its introduction[258] as a step in the direction of preventing miscarriages of justice. Commentators have given video-taped interviews a cautious welcome;[259] criticism has largely been directed towards the difficulty of ensuring that they are not subverted by 'informal' contacts between police and suspect,[260] rather than at the quality of the recordings.[261] Arguably such difficulties are endemic in the interviewing scheme as currently conceived regardless of the recording technique used.

There seems to be a tendency in some quarters to see developments in recording techniques as going a long way towards solving the problem of unreliable confessions.[262] However, there is a danger that other relevant issues will be obscured. It is important not to over-emphasise the value of recording techniques at the expense of provisions which may have a more direct effect on their reliability. This danger was perhaps most readily apparent in the juxtaposition in the remit of the Royal Commission on Criminal Procedure of the possibility of introducing video-taping with that of abolishing the right to silence.[263] In this connection it is instructive to compare the enthusiasm for video-taping of interviews[264] with the decision to abolish the right to silence.[265] Probably video-taping is to be welcomed but arguably

---

258 In response to a request from Sir John Farr MP for video-taping of all police interviews in order to prevent miscarriages of justice, John Patten then Minister at the Home Office indicated that this course would be considered after the results of a pilot project conducted for the Association of Chief Police Officers in conjunction with the Home Office were known. *HC Deb,* Vol 200 Col 391, 5 December 1991.

259 See eg Barnes, M, 'One Experience of Video-Recorded Interviews' [1993] *Crim LR,* p 444.

260 See McConville, M, 'Video-taping interrogations: police behaviour on and off camera' [1992] *Crim LR* 532.

261 However, quality has been questioned: see John Baldwin's interim report of experiments with video-taping of interviews which found that there were fairly serious or very serious problems with video-taping in over 20% of the recordings. These included poor picture or sound quality or camera malfunction. Above note 254.

262 When Kenneth Baker, the then Home Secretary, announced the inception of the Royal Commission on Criminal Procedure he suggested that recent improvements in the provision for recording of police interviews would prevent miscarriages of justice in future. *HC Deb,* Vol 187 Col 1109, 14 March 1991.

263 In announcing the Royal Commission (above note 262) the Home Secretary stated that part of its remit was to consider 'the extent to which the courts might draw proper inferences from any failure (on the part of the suspect) to take advantage of opportunities to state his position', at Col 1115. On 5 December 1991 Mr John Patten, Secretary of State for the Home Office, made it clear that the Royal Commission would be considering video-taping of police interviews: above note 258.

264 Above note 258; see also Campbell, D, 'Videos of Interviews "would help police"', *Guardian,* 9 December 1991.

265 The Home Office set up a working group in 1989 to consider the right to silence: above note 228 after the right had already been modified in Northern Ireland by the Criminal Evidence (Northern Ireland) Order 1988. The group's recommendations assumed that abolition was necessary. For criticism see Greer, S, 53 *MLR* 709 and Zuckerman, A [1989] *Crim LR* 855. Kenneth Baker signalled that interest in this possibility was still very much alive when announcing the remit of the Royal Commission on Criminal Procedure: above note 262. The Home Secretary announced in October 1993 that the right to silence would be abolished and this was brought about under ss 34, 36 and 37 of the Criminal Justice and Public Order Act 1994.

its value should not be over-stressed. Video-taping might faithfully reflect the interview during which a confession was made,[266] but fail to affect the pressure likely to make it unreliable flowing from the suspect's perception that he must speak. The fact that it was video-taped might give the confession a spurious credibility. This is not an argument against video-taping in general but against its use as part of the justification for failing to reverse the modification of the right to silence. It might be argued that unreliable confessions would be almost eliminated by the use of such advanced recording techniques, thereby providing a justification for increasing the pressure on the suspect to speak.

Improvement in the recording provisions is not aimed directly at promoting the reliability of a confession but at allowing a court to consider an accurate record of it and to assess what occurred when it was made. In contrast to the success of the scheme in this direction there has been little development in the area of provisions able to *affect* what occurred; PACE does not attempt to regulate the conduct of the interview except in so far as such regulation can be implied from the provision of s 76 that confessions obtained by oppression[267] or in circumstances likely to render them unreliable will be inadmissible. Obviously the provisions governing detention and the physical comfort of the detainee[268] have relevance in this context; they provide the setting for the interrogation and remove from the situation some of the reasons why a suspect might make an unreliable confession. But once their limits have been set they cannot influence what occurs next and it seems that use of intimidation, haranguing, use of indirect threats is still quite common, especially in interviews with juveniles.[269] The Runciman Royal Commission which reported on 6 June 1993, proposed that the role of the appropriate adult should be reviewed[270] and that officers should receive training in the role a solicitor would be expected to play[271] but did not make general proposals as to outlawing or regulating use of certain interviewing techniques.[272] Such proposals would be particularly relevant after the evidence of use of bullying techniques in interrogations which arose from the post-PACE case of *Miller*

---

266 But see John Baldwin's findings above note 254.
267 Misleading statements made during an interview distorting the state of the evidence against the defendant or hectoring and bullying may well lead to exclusion of any confession obtained under either s 76 or s 78. See *Mason* [1987] *Crim LR* 119; [1987] 3 All ER 481, CA; *Beales* [1991] *Crim LR* 118; *Blake* [1991] *Crim LR* 119; *Heron* (1993) (unreported).
268 Paras 8 and 9 of Code C; para 12.4 regulates the physical conditions in the interviewing room.
269 See Evans, R, *The Conduct of Police Interviews with Juveniles*, Home Office Research Study No 8, 1993. See 144 *NLJ* 120 and 144 *NLJ* 203 for criticism of a variety of interview techniques.
270 Proposal 72.
271 Proposal 64.
272 See Baldwin, J (1993) 143 *NLJ* 1194 for criticism of the failure of the Royal Commission in this respect. See also Reiner, R [1993] *Crim LR* 808.

(the *Cardiff Three*).[273] In fact, such techniques may be in the process of being replaced by a more subtle 'investigative approach'[274] but this is no substitute for guidance under Code C as to improper techniques.

The right to silence

It might appear that the right to silence would have a significant impact on the conduct of the interview and would ensure that a suspect had a bulwark against giving in to pressure to speak. In fact few suspects refuse to answer questions[275] and as discussed above silence is not routinely advised by solicitors. The main reason for reinstating the right to silence is that the suspect may be under stress and unable to assess the situation clearly; he or she may have a number of reasons for reluctance to speak, including fear of incriminating another and uncertainty as to the legal significance of various facts. It may also be argued that the right should be reinstated in order to guard against the possibility that the suspect will concoct a confession in order to escape the pressure of the interrogation. A juvenile suspect in the *Silcott* case,[276] questioned about the murder of police officer Blakelock by a riotous mob, made up a detailed confession based on suggestions put to him by police officers, although it was later found that he could not have been present at the scene. This suspect made the confession despite his right to exercise silence, suggesting that the right to silence alone will not benefit such suggestible detainees. However, as argued above, the right to silence *in conjunction with* advice from an experienced solicitor would seem to provide a surer safeguard against false confessions than either silence or legal advice alone.

It is generally thought that pressure on the suspect in police interviews is already high and is not compensated for by other factors such as tape-recording and access to legal advice; thus the large body of writing on the right to silence generally comes down on the side of its retention.[277] The Runciman Royal Commission favoured retention[278] but considered that once the prosecution case was fully disclosed defendants should be required to

---

273 (1991) *The Times*, 18 December. See (1993) 97 Cr App R 99.
274 Baldwin, J, notes (143 *NLJ* at pp 1195 and 1197) that 1993 training manuals for police interviewers advocate this approach. It is advocated in the Interviewers Rule Book.
275 See Leng, R, *The Right to Silence in Police Interrogation*, Home Office Research Study No 10, 1993. Only 4.5% of suspects exercised their right to silence.
276 (1991) *The Times*, 8 December.
277 See *Report of the Home Office Working Group on the Right to Silence* 1989 (in favour of modification of the right). For criticism of the report see Zuckermann [1989] *Crim LR* 855. For review of the debate see Greer, S (1990) 53 *MLR* 709; Coldrey, J (1991) 20 *Anglo-Amer LR* 27. In favour of modification of the right see Glanville Williams 137 *NLJ* 1107; editorial (1988) *Police Review* 29 April.
278 Cm 2263, Proposal 82.

Freedom from Arbitrary Search, Arrest and Detention

offer an answer to the charges made against them at the risk of adverse comment at trial on any new defence they then disclosed. This proposal would have dealt with the 'ambush defence', often put forward as one of the reasons for abolishing the right to silence while leaving the right itself intact in the investigation as a safeguard against undue police pressure to speak. However, in October 1993 the Home Secretary announced that the recommendation of the Royal Commission as to retention of the right to silence would be rejected.

Sections 34, 36 and 37 of the Criminal Justice and Public Order Act 1994 brought about curtailment of the right to silence, in the sense of the privilege against self-incrimination, in the police interview. Curtailment of the right to silence rather than abolition is referred to since it is suggested that the common law right of silence which received recognition in Code C para 10.4 has only been curtailed by the provisions of ss 34–37 and that in so far as it has not been expressly abolished it will continue to exist.[279] The general caution under para 10.4 of revised Code C, which answers to the provisions of s 34 of the 1994 Act, provides in essence that a person may remain silent but if he or she holds back matters which are later relied on in court his or her defence may be harmed. Further special cautions have been adopted under para 10.5A(a) and (b) of revised Code C which answer to the provisions of ss 36 and 37 of the 1994 Act. Paragraph 10.5A provides that adverse inferences may be drawn from a failure to account for possession of substances or objects or presence at a particular place.

The Runciman Royal Commission considered that abolition of the right to silence might create the risk that wrongful convictions would be obtained. Some suspects, in particular vulnerable and suggestible persons interviewed outside the police station, may be confused by the caution (usually the para 10.4 caution since it can be used before arrest) and without the benefit of legal advice may be pressurised into making inaccurate and ill-considered admissions. Persons interviewed outside the police station who remain silent in the face of the caution, perhaps confused by its contradictory message – you need not speak but on the other hand it may be dangerous not to – may find that adverse inferences are drawn at court although had they had legal advice they might not have made admissions. This may also be true of those who do not have legal advice in the police station, either because they choose not to or because they were encouraged to forego it. However, in such circumstances the defence might be able to put forward a sound argument that it would not be proper for a court to draw adverse inferences from silence. In this context the ruling of the European Court of Human Rights in *Murray (John)*[280] may be

---

[279] For further discussion of the changes and their implications see Zander, *The Police and Criminal Evidence Act 1984*, 1995, pp 303–23; Fenwick, H [1995] *Crim LR* 132–36; Jackson, D [1995] *Crim LR* 587–601; Pattenden, R [1995] *Crim LR* 602–11; Morgan, D, and Stephenson, G, *Suspicion and Silence*, 1994; Williams, J (1997) 141(23) Sol Jo 566.

[280] (1996) EHRR 29.

relevant, particularly bearing in mind the imminent reception into UK law of Article 6 of the Convention. The court found that *Murray* should have been allowed access to legal advice since his right to silence had been curtailed. Advice was essential since he was in a position where adverse inferences could be drawn from his silence. These findings may be relevant where silences prior to the point at which legal advice is available are put forward in court by the prosecution in order to invite the drawing of adverse inferences. It is suggested that this unsatisfactory situation is not cured, for the purposes of an argument based on *Murray*, by the provision of para 11.2A Code C to the effect that any significant silence outside the police station should be put to the suspect at the beginning of an interview at the police station.

Inferences may only be drawn from silence if a sound explanation for silence is not put forward. In other words, it cannot be inferred that the reason for silence was the need to concoct a defence or a false explanation of incriminating factors if the real and innocent reason for silence is put forward. It might be argued that the defendant interviewed without legal advice (perhaps in breach of the legal advice scheme or in the street) had needed the presence of a legal advisor partly in order to provide support and partly to advise on his or her response to the new-style caution. The defendant might argue that lacking such support and advice he or she had stayed silent, uncertain under pressure what to say. Alternatively, a defendant might argue that he had stayed silent until aware of the prosecution case, a judge might accept that in the circumstances that was reasonable (since the question of what is reasonable in the circumstances can properly be taken into account under s 34) and would not allow the drawing of adverse inferences.

The courts are at present coming to grips with ss 34, 36 and 37 of the 1994 Act. The decision in *Cowan*[281] on s 35 suggested that, although these provisions are at variance with established principle, the courts will not be prepared to radically marginalise and reduce them although a restrictive approach may be taken. Other early decisions on the new scheme reflect the same spirit. In *Condron and Another*[282] the appellants were to be questioned by police at the police station on suspicion of being involved in the supply and possession of heroin. Their solicitor considered that they were unfit to be interviewed since they were suffering withdrawal symptoms and so advised them not to answer any questions. They relied on that advice during the interview. At trial the prosecution argued that they could reasonably have been expected to mention at interview the facts they now relied on in their defence. They were cross-examined on their failure to mention such facts. In summing up the judge directed the jury that they must determine whether any adverse inferences should be drawn from the failure of the appellants to

---

281 [1995] All ER 939. See also *Friend* [1997] 2 All ER 1012, on s 35.
282 (1997) 1 Cr App R 185; (1997) 161 JP 1; (1996) *The Times*, 4 November, CA. For comment see Tregilgas-Davey, M (1997) 161(22) JP 525.

mention the facts in question during the police interview. The appellants were convicted and appealed, arguing that the jury should not have been directed that they could draw adverse inferences from the failure to answer questions if they considered it appropriate to do so. The Court of Appeal found that if an accused gives as the reason for not answering questions in a police interview that he has been advised not to do so this assertion without more will not amount to a sufficient reason for not mentioning relevant matters which may later be relied on in defence. The jury may draw an adverse inference from the failure unless the accused gives the reason for the advice being given. The reason for the advice is legally privileged since it is part of a communication between solicitor and client but once the client has disclosed the reason this will probably amount to a waiver of privilege so that the solicitor and/or client can then be asked about the reasons for the advice in court. Thus that ground of appeal failed. Had this decision been to the contrary effect, legal privilege would have been protected and the provisions of ss 34, 36 and 37 of the Criminal Justice and Public Order Act 1994 would have been greatly undermined. The effect of this decision is that legal privilege surrounding custodial legal advice will often be rendered valueless since the client is caught in a cleft stick. He can either refuse to waive legal privilege and accept that adverse inferences will be drawn from silence or he can waive it and hope that the reasons given for the advice will be accepted in order to discourage the drawing of adverse inferences. This decision will not encourage legal advisers to advise silence even where there seem to be good reasons for doing so.

Condron also gave guidance as to the circumstances in which adverse inferences may be drawn. The principles enunciated in *Cowan* were applied to police questioning. The principles were as follows:

(1) A jury cannot infer guilt from silence alone (s 38(3)) so that the jury should only consider drawing inferences if there is a *prima facie* case to answer made out by the prosecution. Also, the burden of proof remains throughout on the prosecution to prove its case; in effect a silence will be only one factor which can be used to make out the case.

(2) Inferences can only be drawn if the only sensible explanation of silence is that the suspect had no defence or none that would stand up to cross-examination. The use of the word 'only' suggests that if there were two equally plausible explanations for the silence – one innocent, one incriminating – then in those circumstances the jury would not be entitled to draw inferences. Thus, the Court of Appeal interpreted the requirements quite strictly.

In *Argent*[283] the Court of Appeal gave further guidance as to the circumstances in which adverse inferences could be drawn from silence under

---

283 (1996) *The Times*, 19 December.

s 34 of the 1994 Act. The conditions to be met were indicated in quite specific form by Lord Bingham. They are summarised here:

(1) The failure to answer questions must occur during questioning under caution and before charge.
(2) The questioning has to be directed towards trying to discover whether or by whom the alleged offence has been committed.
(3) There must be a fact relied upon by the defendant in his defence which he failed to mention when being questioned; whether such a fact can be identified is a matter for the jury as the tribunal of fact.
(4) The fact has to be one which in the circumstances existing at the time the defendant could reasonably have been expected to mention. In considering the relevant circumstances, the court should not take a restrictive approach but should take into account matters such as the defendant's age, health, experience, mental capacity, sobriety, tiredness, personality and legal advice (s 34(1)). The ruling emphasises that this is a subjective test. It is a matter for the jury to resolve whether, bearing these matters in mind, the defendant could have been expected to mention the fact in question, although the judge may give them guidance. Once these conditions are met the jury can draw such inferences as appear to it proper. In the instant case, bearing the inference-drawing role of the jury in mind, it was found that the conviction for manslaughter was not unsafe.

This scheme is at an early stage but the *Argent* conditions are likely to play a significant part in it for some time. In affording the jury a major role in the scheme they tend, it is suggested, to underpin its crime control stance. The guidance given does not include the need for a warning from the judge that in certain circumstances the jury should be directed to draw no inferences. For example, no inference should be drawn, it is suggested, from the response of a defendant during questioning on the street prior to arrest and without either legal advice or the knowledge that it is available. As pointed out above, there is leeway in the PACE scheme for this to occur without any breach of the rules. Arguably, it is also unreasonable in many circumstances to expect a person to answer questions as to his or her defence before knowing what offence might be charged. This could have been made clear in *Argent*. Further, the guidance could have included a warning that although inferences might be drawn once certain conditions are met, the inference to be drawn might be an innocent one. It should be clearly pointed out to juries that inference-drawing does not necessarily mean that an adverse inference need be drawn. The *Argent* conditions, it is suggested, leave open too much scope for prejudice to the defendant due to the possibility that the jury will assume that silence, even occurring in adverse circumstances, probably equals guilt. However, if the *Condron* principles are applied, the scope for drawing inferences will be narrowed.

Freedom from Arbitrary Search, Arrest and Detention

The modification of the right to silence was foreshadowed in Northern Ireland by the Criminal Evidence (Northern Ireland) Order 1988. Also, in England and Wales in one group of cases – those involving serious fraud – the right to silence has been quietly eroded and has now reached the point where it may be said to have virtually disappeared.[284] If, for example, enquiries are made into a failed business its owner may receive a 's 2 notice' from the Serious Fraud Office issued under the Criminal Justice Act 1987 which means that a criminal offence will be committed if he or she does not attend for interview and answer questions. Also if the company is being investigated he or she may have to answer questions under s 432(2) of the Companies Act 1985 and it seems that a refusal to do so will also attract criminal liability.

In *Director of the Serious Fraud Office, ex parte Smith*,[285] after Mr Smith had been charged with an offence under s 458 of the Companies Act 1985, the director of the Serious Fraud Office (SFO) decided to investigate him and served a notice on him under s 2(2) of the Criminal Justice Act 1987 requiring him to attend for an interview. He was informed that he would not be cautioned but would be obliged to answer questions truthfully and that his replies could be used in evidence against him if anything he said at his trial was inconsistent with them. He applied for judicial review. The question to be determined was whether the 1987 Act had effected an erosion of the right to silence which had been preserved by Code of Practice C in the caution. If a person fell within s 2(2) of the 1987 Act would he lose the protection conferred by Code C? The answer given by the Divisional Court was that some such erosion had taken place but not to the extent claimed by the SFO: the 1987 Act could override the right to silence as enshrined in the caution given on arrest but could not do so once the suspect had been charged. Only the clearest language used in s 2(2) would have supported the latter claim but the language used could not do so. Section 2(13) allows a person to escape a penalty for failing to comply with s 2(2) if a 'reasonable excuse' can be established; the right to silence would furnish such an excuse. Thus Mr Smith could not be compelled to answer questions about the offence with which he had already been charged. The House of Lords, however, took a completely different approach in finding that the powers under s 2 operated *even after* charge on the basis that Parliament had clearly intended to institute an inquisitorial regime. Thus even though the prosecutor must have thought that there might well already be sufficient evidence to convict, questioning could continue. Did this mean it could continue up to and even during the court hearing? The House of Lords thought not but nevertheless it was clear that it could do so up until some point at which the trial was obviously imminent. Obviously the answers

---

284 See *Re London United Investments* [1992] 2 All ER 842; *Ex parte Nadir* (1990) *The Times*, 5 November; *Bishopsgate Investment Management Ltd v Maxwell* [1992] 2 All ER 856, CA.

285 [1993] AC 1; [1992] 3 WLR 66; see also *AT&T Istel Ltd v Tulley* [1992] 3 All ER 523, HL.

given would be used at trial. Thus this decision eroded the right to silence not only in the police interview but to an extent also at trial.[286]

Saunders[287] also concerned the existence of the right to silence in serious fraud investigations. Inspectors of the Department of Trade and Industry interviewed Saunders regarding allegations of fraud. They acted under s 437 of the Companies Act 1985 which provides for a sanction against the person being investigated if he refuses to answer questions. Thus Saunders lost his privilege against self-incrimination, which he argued was unfair and amounted to an abuse of process. He further argued that the transcript of the answers given should have been found inadmissible under s 78 of the Police and Criminal Evidence Act 1984. It was found that Parliament had eroded the privilege against self-incrimination in relation to DTI interviews and that therefore that ground alone could not provide a basis for finding that an abuse of process had occurred. In relation to exclusion of the interviews the House of Lords considered the relevance of Article 6 of the European Convention on Human Rights which provides *inter alia* that the presumption of innocence must not be eroded. However, it was found that domestic law was unambiguous and therefore must be applied regardless of Article 6. In exercising discretion under s 78 the judge could take into account the question whether the statutory regime in question had created unfairness but in the particular circumstances it was found that admission of the evidence did not render the trial unfair. The appeal was therefore dismissed. This decision will clearly have no impact in terms of curbing the erosion of the privilege against self-incrimination which has been brought about under the particular statutory regime in question. That regime is to an extent in accord with the general regime now in place under ss 34, 36 and 37 of the Criminal Justice and Public Order Act 1994, although it is clearly of a harsher nature.

It is possible that curtailment of the right to silence under ss 34, 36 and 37 of the 1994 Act may breach Article 6 of the ECHR on the basis that it infringes the presumption of innocence under Article 6(2) and/or on the basis that it infringes the right to freedom from self-incrimination which the court has found to be covered by the right to a fair hearing under Article 6(1) (*Funke v France*).[288] In *Murray (John) v UK*[289] however, the Commission did not find that Article 6(1) had been breached where inferences had been drawn at trial from the applicant's refusal to give evidence. The court found no breach of Article 6 in the particular circumstances of the case, taking into account the

---

[286] The Royal Commission considered that this erosion of the right to silence should continue (Proposal 84). It may be noted that in *Martinez-Tobon* (1993) *The Times*, 1 December, the Court of Appeal found that certain adverse comments on a defendant's silence were acceptable. *Cf* the decision in *United Norwest Co-operative Ltd v Johnstone* (1994) *The Times*, 24 February.

[287] (1995) *The Times*, 28 November.

[288] (1993) EHRR 297.

[289] (1996) *The Times*, 9 February; for comment see Munday, R [1986] *Crim LR* 370.

fact that 'the right to silence' could not be treated as absolute, the degree of compulsion exerted on the applicant and the weight of the evidence against him. When Saunders applied to the Commission, alleging a breach of Article 6 (*Saunders v UK*)[290] the Commission found that the applicant's right to freedom from self-incrimination had been infringed in that he had been forced to answer questions put to him by inspectors investigating a company takeover or risk the imposition of a criminal sanction. The ruling of the court was to the same effect.[291] Its finding that the regime in question was in breach of Article 6 might possibly call into question the provisions affecting the right to silence under the Criminal Justice and Public Order Act 1994. However, it is probable, taking the *Murray* decision into account, that these provisions are in accord with Article 6 since they are less coercive than those in issue in *Saunders*. Therefore the government response to the ruling could be confined only to the powers of DTI inspectors and could leave the general regime curtailing the right to silence intact.

8 IDENTIFICATION OF SUSPECTS

The identification procedure is largely governed by the provisions of Code D which has as its overall aim the creation of safeguards against wrongful identification, bearing in mind that mistaken identification can be a very significant cause of wrongful convictions.[292] It also contains provisions which are intended to safeguard vulnerable groups and to ensure that the invasion of privacy represented by some methods of identification is kept to a minimum consistent with the Code's overall aim. Many of the procedures will only take place with the suspect's consent although if consent is not forthcoming, this may be used in evidence against him or her. In the case of a mentally handicapped or disordered person consent given out of the presence of the 'appropriate adult' will not be treated as true consent while the consent of a juvenile alone will not be treated as valid if the adult does not also consent.[293] Identification can take place by various means which include by witness, by fingerprints and by the taking of samples from the body of the suspect.[294] It should be noted that, apart from the provisions relating to identification by fingerprints and by bodily samples, terrorist suspects detained under s 14 or Schedule 5 of the Prevention of Terrorism Act 1989, are not covered by the provisions of Code D (Code D paras 1.15 and 1.16).

---

290 No 19187/91 Com Re, paras 69–75.
291 *Saunders v UK* (1997) 23 EHRR 313.
292 The Criminal Law Revision Committee 1972 considered that wrongful identification was the greatest cause of wrongful convictions (para 196).
293 Paragraph 1.11.
294 Identification can also be by photographs under Code D Annex D.

Witness identification

Methods

If identification is to be by witness Code D para 2.1 provides that the following methods may be used: a parade, a group identification, a video film or a confrontation. A group identification consists of allowing the witness an opportunity of seeing the suspect in a group of people and it should, if practicable, be held in a place other than a police station (for example, in an underground station or shopping centre). The suspect will be asked to consent to a group identification but where consent is refused the identification officer has the discretion to proceed with a group identification if practicable. Under para 2.13 if neither a parade nor a video identification nor a group identification procedure is arranged, the suspect may be confronted by the witness and such a confrontation does not require the suspect's consent but it may not take place if any of the other procedures are practicable.

Practicability

A parade must be used if the defendant requests it and it is practicable. A parade may also be held if the officer in charge of the investigation considers that it would be useful and the suspect consents. The aim is to use the best means of identification available; therefore if it is impracticable to use a parade the police may move on to a group identification; they cannot merely move straight to the last possible method – a confrontation.[295] However, there is uncertainty as to when it could legitimately be said to be impracticable to hold an identification parade. In *Ladlow, Moss, Green and Jackson*[296] 20 suspects had been arrested and the confrontation method of identification was used, as otherwise it would allegedly have been necessary to hold 221 separate parades. Despite this it was ruled that evidence derived from the parades would be excluded. However, in *Penny*[297] the police wrongly thought it impracticable to hold a parade but the trial judge admitted the evidence and the Court of Appeal refused to interfere with the decision. It is unfortunate that the opportunity of clarifying the position was not taken when Code D was revised in 1991 especially as the uncertainty also affects the term 'practicable' used in para 2 with respect to video and group identification. However, where it is genuinely hard to assemble sufficient persons resembling the defendant to take part in the parade, due perhaps to alienation

---

295 *Ladlow, Moss, Green and Jackson* [1989] *Crim LR* 219.
296 Above note 295.
297 (1991) *The Times*, 17 October.

of the particular group from the police,[298] video identification may provide a means of obtaining acceptable evidence. If group identification takes place in the street, the area in question may be relevant; if the defendant is of a certain race a mixed race area should be chosen in order to increase the chances that someone of the same race might pass by.[299]

Safeguards

The officer in charge of the identification ('the identification officer') must not be below the rank of inspector and must not be involved with the investigation. No officer involved with the investigation of the case against the suspect may take any part in the procedures.[300] It is also important that witnesses should not be able to confer before the identification; if they do so confer the identification may be excluded from evidence.[301]

When Code D was revised various new safeguards for witness identification were introduced: under new para 2.15 the suspect must be reminded that free legal advice is available before taking part in the identification procedure and under new para 2.16 the identification procedure and the consequences, if consent to taking part is not forthcoming, must be explained in a written notice which the suspect must be given reasonable time to read.

Under para 2.15 before the means of identification is arranged, the identification officer must explain a number of matters to the suspect orally and in writing: the fact that he is entitled to free legal advice and can have the adviser present; the fact that he does not have to take part in a parade or co-operate in a group identification or with the making of a video film and, if it is proposed to hold a group identification or video identification, his entitlement to a parade if this can practicably be arranged. However, he must also be told that if he does not consent to take part in a parade or co-operate in a group identification or with the making of a video film his refusal may be given in evidence in any subsequent trial and police may proceed covertly without his consent or make other arrangements to determine whether a witness identifies him.

---

298 See *Campbell and Another* [1993] *Crim LR* 47, CA; the police had arranged a confrontation because they had not found sufficient Rastafarians to take part in a parade. Lack of co-operation between the police and the Rastafarian community was condemned by the Court of Appeal.
299 *Jamel* [1993] *Crim LR* 52.
300 *Gall* (1990) 90 Cr App R 64; *Jones* [1992] *Crim LR* 365.
301 *Finley* [1993] *Crim LR* 50, CA.

Identification by fingerprints or bodily samples

Under para 3 of Code D a person over the age of 10 may be identified by fingerprints if he or she consents or without consent under ss 27 and 61 of PACE which also allow the use of force. A person may also be identified by bodily samples, swabs and impressions but only if the offence is a serious arrestable offence, the officer has reasonable grounds to believe that such an impression or sample will tend to confirm or disprove the suspect's involvement in the offence and with the suspect's written consent.[302] However, the Royal Commission has proposed that these provisions should also apply in the case of all offences.[303] A juvenile has the right to have the appropriate adult present unless he or she requests otherwise in the presence of the adult.[304]

However, the suspect will be warned that a refusal may be treated, in any proceedings against him, as corroborating relevant prosecution evidence. He must also be reminded of his entitlement to have free legal advice and the reminder must be noted in the custody record. Intimate samples[305] can only be taken by a registered medical or dental practitioner whereas non-intimate samples[306] may be taken by a police officer. They may be taken without consent if an officer of the rank of superintendent or above has reasonable grounds for suspecting that the offence in connection with which the suspect is detained is a serious arrestable offence and for believing that the sample will tend to confirm or disprove his involvement in it.

9 REDRESS FOR POLICE IMPROPRIETY

Introduction

This chapter has been concerned so far with the question of the balance to be struck between the exercise of powers by the police in conducting an investigation on the one hand and safeguards for the suspect against abuse of power on the other. As we have seen, PACE sets out to maintain this balance by declaring certain standards for the conduct of criminal investigations. However, it may be that an investigation does not, at certain points, reach those standards. The police may sometimes feel hampered by all the PACE and Code provisions; they may feel, for example, that they are close to

---

302 Under para 5.
303 Proposal 19.
304 Paragraph 5.12.
305 'Blood, semen or any other tissue fluid, urine, saliva or pubic hair or a swab taken from a person's body orifice' (s 65 of PACE).
306 Including hair other than pubic hair or a sample taken from a nail or from under a nail (s 65 of PACE).

obtaining a confession from a detainee but that in order to obtain it they need to bend the interviewing rules a little. Similarly, police officers may purport to act within a power such as the power to arrest or search premises where no power to do so arises. In such circumstances two remedies may be available: a civil action leading to an award of damages, if successful or a complaint leading to disciplinary action against the officers involved, if upheld. However, as already noted, civil actions are not available for breach of the Codes and will be inapplicable to some breaches of PACE itself such as improper denial of access to legal advice. Police disciplinary action is applicable to breaches of both PACE itself and the Codes but, as will be argued below, it does not represent a very effective remedy. Apart from these two remedies a further means of redress exists represented by the use of exclusion of evidence and it is in this context that many breaches of PACE and the Codes have in fact been considered.

Exclusion of evidence

An example may illustrate the effect of exclusion of evidence. Assume that the police have arrested a man on suspicion of theft. They are pretty certain that he is guilty and think that they have a good chance of getting him to confess. However, he asks for legal advice. The police think that a solicitor may advise him not to answer some questions or may at least help him to withstand certain questioning techniques and so they tell him (untruthfully) that the duty solicitor is unavailable and that they might as well get on with the interview rather than prolong the process. They then question him for four hours without a break. Eventually, he succumbs to the pressure and makes a full confession to theft.

The police have breached PACE and Code C (s 58, paras 6.6 and 12.7) and the suspect does have a means of redress. He can make a complaint but whether he pursues this remedy or not the flawed interrogation may continue to produce consequences for him: it may lead to a trial, a conviction and possibly imprisonment. He may, of course, decide to plead guilty. But if he pleads not guilty his counsel may ask the judge at the trial not to admit the confession in evidence on the basis that the interrogation which produced it was conducted unfairly. The trial judge could then ensure that the original abuse of power on the part of the police produced no more consequences for the detainee. It may not lead to a conviction and imprisonment if the judge refuses to admit the confession in evidence (depending on any other evidence against the defendant). The judge can hold a *voir dire* (a trial within a trial) by sending out the jury and then hearing defence and prosecution submissions on admitting the confession. If it is not admitted the jury will never know of its existence and will determine the case on the basis of any other available evidence. The judge is in a difficult position. On the one hand it is apparent that the police have abused their powers; the judge does not want to condone such behaviour by admitting evidence gained thereby. On the other, the prosecution case may collapse and a possibly guilty man walk free from the court if the confession is excluded.

If the defendant did commit the theft it might be said that the end in view – the conviction – justifies the means used to obtain it but should the judge ignore the fact that the confession might not be before the court at all had the police complied with Code C? Should the judge merely consider the fate of one defendant in isolation? If the confession is admitted the judge is in effect making a public declaration that the courts will not use their powers to uphold standards for police investigations. The result may be that in future that PACE standards are not adhered to and that, occasionally, an innocent citizen is convicted after a false confession has been coerced from him. The multiplicity of issues raised by examples of this nature have provoked a long-running debate among academics and lawyers as to the purpose of excluding evidence which has been obtained improperly and three main schools of thought have arisen advocating different principles on which evidence should be excluded.

The crime control position is that evidence should be excluded only if it appears to be unreliable, ie, in the case of a confession, false or inaccurately recorded.[307] Taken to its logical conclusion this would mean that if a true confession has been extracted by torture it should nevertheless be admitted. This is argued on the basis that the function of a criminal court is to determine the truth of the charges against the accused not to enquire into alleged improprieties on the part of the police. It is not equipped to conduct such an enquiry; therefore if evidence is excluded on the basis that impropriety occurred in the investigation, the reputation of the police officer in question will be damaged after a less than full investigation into his conduct. Also, even if impropriety did occur in the investigation, this should not allow an obviously guilty defendant to walk freely from the court. On this argument, the court in admitting evidence obtained by improper methods is not condoning them. It is acknowledging that it is not within its function to enquire into them.

From a due process stance, it has been argued[308] that a court cannot merely inquire into the truth of the charges against a particular defendant: it must also play a part in maintaining standards in criminal investigations. The court has one particular part to play in the processing of the defendant through the criminal justice system: it should not play its brief part and ignore what has gone before. If the courts are prepared to accept evidence obtained by improper methods the police may be encouraged to abuse their powers to the detriment of the citizen. The disciplinary principle may encompass either a

---

307 See Wigmore, *Treatise on Evidence*, 3rd edn, 1940, and Andrews [1963] *Crim LR* 15, 77.
308 eg Cross, *Cross on Evidence*, 5th edn, 1979, pp 318–28.

deterrent or a punitive role for exclusion of evidence, although it is recognised that no clear-cut relationship between police behaviour and rejection of evidence should be envisaged.[309]

The use of exclusion of evidence to punish the police has therefore come to be viewed by most commentators as a clumsy and possibly ineffective means of protecting due process and this has led Ashworth to suggest a somewhat different principle, which he terms protective.[310] He contends that once a legal system has declared a certain standard for the conduct of investigations the citizen obtains corresponding rights to be treated in a certain manner. If such rights are denied and evidence gained as a result the court can wipe out the disadvantage to the defendant flowing from the denial by rejecting the evidence in question. If, for example, it appears that the defendant made the confession because the police failed to caution him or her, the judge could recreate the situation for the jury's benefit as it would have been had the caution been given, by excluding the confession. In the eyes of the jury the position would be as if the right had never been denied; the judge would therefore have succeeded in protecting the defendant's right to silence in the interrogation. (It may be noted that this argument will be greatly weakened if the caution becomes a warning that silence may be commented on adversely in court. If the new style caution is not given it might be argued that such a failure could not be related to the confession since the defendant would have confessed in any event. This point will be returned to below.)

The US Supreme Court has taken the disciplinary and protective principles into account in determining that evidence obtained by improper methods should be excluded. For example, in *Mapp v Ohio*[311] the police conducted an illegal search of Mrs Mapp's boarding house and seized certain obscene materials. The Supreme Court held that the evidence obtained in the course of the illegal search was inadmissible. The majority opinion gave two main reasons for reaching this conclusion: first, that the police should be discouraged from conducting illegal searches; and, secondly, that the defendant's entitlement to freedom from such search and seizure should be recognised by excluding the evidence obtained thereby. The *Mapp* rule on searches was mirrored by the *Miranda* rule that improperly obtained confessions would be inadmissible in evidence.[312] However, there has been some retreat recently from *Mapp* and *Miranda* seen in decisions such as that in *Moran v Burbine*[313] which have brought America closer to the position adopted under UK common law.[314]

---

309 See Cross p 328.
310 See Ashworth [1979] *Crim LR* 723.
311 367 US 643 (1961).
312 Deriving from *Miranda v Arizona* 384 US 436 (1966).
313 475 US 412 (1986).
314 See Stuntz, W, 'The American Exclusionary Rule and Defendants' Changing Rights' [1989] *Crim LR* 117.

The common law pre-PACE went some way towards endorsing the crime control 'reliability' principle. Illegally obtained evidence other than 'involuntary' confessions was admissible in a criminal trial. Involuntary confessions were inadmissible on the ground that if a defendant was in some way induced to confess during a police interrogation his confession might be unreliable. A confession would be involuntary if it was obtained by oppression[315] or 'by fear of prejudice or hope of advantage exercised or held out by a person in authority'.[316] According to the Court of Appeal in *Isequilla*[317] 'oppression' denoted some impropriety on the part of the police but the House of Lords in *Ping Lin*[318] doubted whether such impropriety was necessary if the real issue was the reliability of the confession. Uncertainty as to the need for impropriety on the part of the police and as to the kind of impropriety which could amount to oppression, allowed cases such as the *Confait* case[319] to slip through the net. In that case, three young boys, one of them mentally handicapped, confessed to involvement in a murder they could not have committed after they had been denied both legal advice and the presence of an adult during the police interrogation. The confessions were admitted in evidence and led to the conviction of all three. They were finally exonerated seven years later.

The concept of fear of prejudice or hope of advantage was at one time interpreted strictly against the police and very mild inducements were held to render a confession involuntary. In *Zaveckas*,[320] for example, the Court of Appeal held that a confession had been rendered involuntary because the defendant had asked the police officer whether he could have bail if he made a statement. However, in the case of *Rennie*[321] Lord Lane held that a confession need not be excluded simply because it had been prompted in part by some hope of advantage. This case paved the way for the relaxation of this rule which can be found in the PACE scheme on exclusion of evidence.

Physical evidence discovered as a result of an inadmissible confession was admissible;[322] the police witness would have to state at the trial that after interviewing the defendant the evidence in question was discovered – in the hope that the jury would see the connection. Illegally or improperly obtained non-confession evidence, such as fingerprints, was admissible at common law unless the evidence had been tricked out of the detainee[323] in which case

---

315 *Prager* [1972] 1 All ER 1114, CA.
316 *Ibrahim* [1914] AC 599.
317 [1975] All ER 77.
318 [1976] AC 574.
319 See Price, C, *The* Confait *Confessions*, 1976; Report of the Inquiry by the Hon Sir Henry Fisher HC 90 of 1977–79.
320 (1969) Cr App R 202.
321 [1982] All ER 385.
322 *Sang* [1980] AC 402; [1979] 2 All ER 1222, HL.
323 *Callis v Gunn* [1964] 1 QB 495.

there would be a discretion to exclude it. However, the House of Lords in *Sang*[324] re-affirmed the rule that non-confession evidence, however obtained, is admissible and there is no general discretion to exclude it.

Exclusion of evidence was largely placed on a statutory basis under PACE.[325] PACE contains four separate tests which can be applied to a confession to determine whether it is admissible in evidence. In theory, all four tests could be applied to a particular confession, although in practice it may not be necessary to consider all of them. The four are the 'oppression' test under s 76(2)(a), the 'reliability' test under s 76(2)(b), the 'fairness' test under s 78 and the residual common law discretion to exclude evidence, preserved by s 82(3). It will become apparent that there is a large area of overlap between all four tests. Section 78 could cover unreliable evidence and also evidence obtained by the use of improper methods whether amounting to oppression or not. Equally, certain types of improper behaviour could be termed oppressive, thus falling within s 76(2)(a) but they could also be viewed as circumstances likely to render a confession unreliable, falling therefore within s 76(2)(b). The courts have gone some of the way towards creating a distinct role for each test but not all the way.[326] In some circumstances a confession will obviously fail one of the tests under s 76 and there will be no need to consider the other three. In other circumstances it may be worth considering all four tests. The scheme in respect of non-confession evidence is less complex: only ss 78 and 82(3) are applicable. Physical evidence which is discovered as a result of an inadmissible confession will be admissible under s 76(4)(a).

Section 76(2)(a): the 'oppression' test

Section 76(2)(a) provides that where:

> ... it is represented to the court that the confession was or may have been obtained by oppression of the person who made it ... the court shall not allow the confession to be given in evidence against him except in so far as the prosecution proves to the court beyond reasonable doubt that the confession (notwithstanding that it may be true) was not obtained as aforesaid.

This test derives from the rule as it was at common law: if the prosecution cannot prove beyond reasonable doubt that the police did not behave oppressively the confession produced is inadmissible. The judge has no discretion in the matter. The idea behind this is that threats of violence or other oppressive behaviour are so abhorrent that no further question as to the reliability of a confession obtained by such methods should be asked. This rule appears to have the dual function of removing any incentive to the police

---

324 [1980] AC 402; [1979] 2 All ER 1222, HL.
325 For general commentary see Birch, D [1989] *Crim LR* 95; Feldman, D [1990] *Crim LR* 452.
326 See Birch, D, 'Confessions and Confusions under the 1984 Act' [1989] *Crim LR* 95.

to behave improperly and of protecting the detainee from the consequences of impropriety if it has occurred. Under this head, once the defence has advanced a reasonable argument (*Liverpool Juvenile Court, ex parte R*)[327] that the confession was obtained by oppression it will not be admitted in evidence unless the prosecution can prove that it was not so obtained. The reliability of a confession obtained by oppression is irrelevant: it matters not whether the effect of the oppression is to frighten the detainee into telling the truth or alternatively into lying in order to get out of the situation.

The only evidence given in the Act as to the meaning of oppression is the non-exhaustive definition contained in s 76(8): 'In this section "oppression" includes torture, inhuman or degrading treatment and the use or threat of violence (whether or not amounting to torture).' The word 'includes' ought to be given its literal meaning according to the Court of Appeal in *Fulling*.[328] Therefore the concept of oppression may be fairly wide: the question is whether it encompasses the old common law rulings on its width. In Fulling the Court of Appeal held that PACE is a codifying Act and that therefore a court should examine the statutory language uninfluenced by pre-Act decisions. The court then proffered its own definition of oppression: '... the exercise of authority or power in a burdensome, harsh or wrongful manner; unjust or cruel treatment of subjects, inferiors, etc; the imposition of unreasonable or unjust burdens.' It thought that oppression would almost invariably entail impropriety on the part of the interrogator. However, the terms 'wrongful' and 'improper' used in this test could cover any unlawful action on the part of the police. This would mean that any breach of the Act or Codes could constitute oppression. This wide possibility has been pursued at first instance[329] but the Court of Appeal in *Hughes*[330] held that a denial of legal advice due not to bad faith on the part of the police but to a misunderstanding could not amount to oppression. In *Alladice*[331] the Court of Appeal also took this view in suggesting, *obiter*, that an improper denial of legal advice, if accompanied by bad faith on the part of the police would certainly amount to 'unfairness' under s 78 and probably also to oppression. In *Beales*[332] rather heavy-handed questioning accompanied by misleading suggestions, although not on the face of it a very serious impropriety, was termed oppressive because it was obviously employed as a deliberate tactic. In *Paris*,[333] the case of the *Cardiff Three*, confessions made by one of the

---

327 [1987] All ER 688.
328 [1987] QB 426; [1987] 2 All ER 65, CA.
329 In *Davison* [1988] *Crim LR* 442.
330 Above note 222.
331 (1988) 87 Cr App R 380, CA.
332 [1991] *Crim LR* 118. See to the same effect *Heron* (1993) (unreported); forceful questioning was accompanied by lies as to the identification evidence.
333 (1993) 97 Cr App R 99; [1994] *Crim LR* 361, CA.

defendants after some 13 hours of highly pressured and hostile questioning were excluded on the ground of oppression. He was a man of limited intelligence but the Court of Appeal thought that the questioning would have been oppressive even with a suspect of normal intelligence.

This emphasis on bad faith may be criticised because from the point of view of the detainee it matters little if mistreatment occurs because of an administrative mix-up, an innocent misconstruction of powers or malice. Looking to the state of mind of the victim rather than that of the oppressor would enable account to be taken of the very great difference in impact of certain conduct on a young, inexperienced suspect and on a hardened, sophisticated criminal. However, at present the courts have not shown much desire to import a subjective assessment of oppression into s 76(2)(a) although at common law such an assessment would have been warranted.[334]

On the other hand, it cannot be said that the Court of Appeal has consistently invoked s 76(2)(a) rather than s 78 when the police *have* deliberately misused their powers in obtaining a confession; in *Mason*,[335] for example, a trick played deliberately on the appellant's solicitor led to exclusion of the confession under s 78. In *Blake*[336] misleading statements made to the detainee, presumably in bad faith, led to exclusion of the confession under s 76(2)(b) or s 78. Thus, apart from the requirement of bad faith, it also seems necessary to show that the improper behaviour has reached a certain level of seriousness in order to show oppression.[337] However, the case law does not yet clearly indicate the level of seriousness needed. All that can be said with some certainty is that bad faith appears to be a necessary but not sufficient condition for the operation of s 76(2)(a), whereas it will probably automatically render a confession inadmissible under s 78.[338]

Improper treatment falling outside s 76(8) and unaccompanied by bad faith could fall within s 76(2)(b) if the confession was likely to have been rendered unreliable thereby. The emphasis on bad faith at least gives an indication as to when improper behaviour on the part of the police will lead to automatic exclusion of the confession under s 76(2)(a) and when it will merely suggest the likelihood of unreliability under s 76(2)(b).

---

334 *Priestley* (1965) 51 Cr App R 1.
335 [1987] *Crim LR* 119; [1987] 3 All ER 481, CA.
336 [1991] All ER 481, CA.
337 See L [1994] *Crim LR* 839.
338 For discussion of the effect of bad faith under s 78 see pp 489–90 below.

Section 76(2)(b): the 'reliability' test

Section 76(2)(b) provides that where a confession was or may have been obtained:

> ... in consequence of anything said or done which was likely in the circumstances existing at the time, to render unreliable any confession which might be made by him in consequence thereof, the court shall not allow the confession to be given in evidence against him except in so far as the prosecution proves to the court beyond reasonable doubt that the confession (notwithstanding that it may be true) was not obtained as aforesaid.

The 'reliability' test derives from the rule as stated in *Ibrahim*[339] on inducements to confess. However, as will be seen below, it represents a relaxation of that rule as it was applied in *Ibrahim*. It also works certain changes in the emphasis of the test. The test does not reflect the full rigour of the reliability principle which requires that a confession extracted by torture but determined to be true should be admitted in evidence.[340] Instead it is concerned with objective reliability: the judge must consider the situation at the time the confession was made and ask whether the confession would be *likely* to be unreliable, not whether it is unreliable.

It must be borne in mind that if an offer of some kind is made to the detainee in response to an enquiry from him this will not render the subsequent confession unreliable,[341] thus explicitly rejecting the *Zaveckas* approach. It is not necessary, under this section, to show that there has been any misconduct on the part of the police. In *Harvey*[342] a mentally ill woman of low intelligence may have been induced to confess to murder by hearing her lover's confession. Her confession was excluded as being likely to be unreliable. In *Harvey* the 'something said or done' (the first limb of the test under s 76(2)(a)) was the confession of the lover while the 'circumstances' (the second limb) were the defendant's emotional state, low intelligence and mental illness. The 'something said or done' cannot consist of the defendant's own mental or physical state according to *Goldberg*.[343] In that case the defendant was a heroin addict who confessed because he was desperate to leave the police station and obtain a 'fix'. The contention of the defence counsel that the defendant's decision to confess prompted by his addiction amounted to 'something said or done' was not accepted by the court.

In many instances the 'something said or done' will consist of some impropriety on the part of the police and in such instances a court will go on

---

339 [1914] AC 599; see p 472 note 316 above.
340 As advocated by Andrews [1963] *Crim LR* 15, 77; see p 470 above.
341 Code C para 11.3.
342 [1988] *Crim LR* 241.
343 [1988] *Crim LR* 678.

to consider whether any circumstances existed which rendered the impropriety particularly significant. The 'circumstances' could include the particularly vulnerable state of the detainee. In *Mathias*[344] the defendant was particularly vulnerable because he had not been afforded legal advice although an offer of immunity from prosecution had been made to him. The Court of Appeal held that the offer had placed him in great difficulty and that this was a situation in which the police should have ensured that he had legal advice. From the judgment it appears that if an inducement to confess is offered to the detainee the police should ensure that he or she can discuss it with a solicitor, even if the police are entitled to deny access to legal advice, on the ground that the detainee falls within s 58(8) (see above). Thus the 'circumstances' will be the lack of legal advice and the 'something said or done', the inducement.

The vulnerability may relate to a physical or mental state. In *Trussler*[345] the defendant, who was a drug addict, had been in custody 18 hours, had been denied legal advice and had not been afforded the rest period guaranteed by Code C para 12. His confession was excluded as likely to be unreliable. In *Delaney*[346] the defendant was 17, had an IQ of 80 and, according to an educational psychologist, was subject to emotional arousal which would lead him to wish to bring a police interview to an end as quickly as possible. These were circumstances in which it was important to ensure that the interrogation was conducted with all propriety. In fact, the officers offered some inducement to the defendant to confess by playing down the gravity of the offence and by suggesting that if he confessed he would get the psychiatric help he needed. They also failed to make an accurate, contemporaneous record of the interview in breach of Code C para 11.3. Failing to make the proper record was of indirect relevance to the question of reliability since it meant that the court could not assess the full extent of the suggestions held out to the defendant. Thus, in the circumstances existing at the time (the mental state of the defendant), the police impropriety did have the special significance necessary under s 76(2)(b). The decision in *Marshall*[347] was to similar effect although it did not identify a specific breach of Code C: the defendant was on the borderline of sub-normality and therefore after an interview accompanied by his solicitor he should not have been re-interviewed unaccompanied about the same matters.

From the above it appears that the 'circumstances existing at the time' may be circumstances created by the police (as in *Mathias*) or may be inherent in the defendant (as in *Delaney*). Impropriety on the part of the police can go to either limb of the test but a state inherent in the detainee (such as mental

---

344 (1989) *The Times*, 24 August.
345 [1988] *Crim LR* 446.
346 (1989) 88 Cr App R 338; (1988) *The Times*, 20 August, CA.
347 (1992) *The Times*, 28 December.

illness) can go only to the 'circumstances' limb. Thus a single breach of the interviewing rules such as a denial of legal advice in ordinary circumstances would not appear, as far as the current interpretation of s 76(2)(b) is concerned, to satisfy both limbs of the test. On the other hand, a doubtful breach or perhaps no breach but rather, behaviour of doubtful propriety, such as misleading the suspect as to the need to have legal advice, might satisfy the 'something said or done' test where special circumstances were also present.

So far, the courts have considered instances where something is said or done, in particularly significant circumstances, which increases the likelihood that a confession will be unreliable. However, it is arguable that s 76 might exceptionally be applicable where something is said or done which might affect a subsequent confession but the circumstances are normal. The example was given above of a detainee who was deprived of sleep as a result of an administrative mix-up. Deprivation of sleep would be likely to render a confession unreliable but which 'circumstances' could be pointed to as existing at the time – the second limb of s 76(2)(b)? The answer would probably be that the ordinary police methods of interrogation, applied to a detainee who had been deprived of sleep, would amount to 'circumstances' falling within s 76(2)(b). Thus this would be an impropriety which could go to both limbs of the test. Such instances of breaches of Code C could also fall within s 78 as will be seen below. However, defence counsel would always argue the point first under s 76(2)(b) as the prosecution would then have the onus of proving beyond reasonable doubt that the deprivation of sleep did not take place.

It must now be apparent that s 76(2)(b) could be used to exclude all confessions obtained by oppression. It may then be wondered why s 76(2)(a) exists at all. The principle lying behind the two heads of s 76 appears to be that some types of impropriety on the part of the police are so unacceptable that it would be abhorrent in a court to go on to consider the reliability of a confession gained by such methods. In other words, s 76(2)(a) speeds up a process which could be carried out under s 76(2)(b).

Causation and the two heads of s 76

The words of s 76(2): ' [if] it is represented to the court that the confession was or may have been obtained' (by oppression or something conducive to unreliability) appear to import a causal link between the police behaviour (the 'something said or done' or the oppression) and the confession. Thus, if the police threaten the suspect with violence *after* he has confessed this will clearly be irrelevant to admission of the confession. However, it is possible that under s 76(2)(a) the causal link will not be much scrutinised so long as the oppression precedes the confession. This receives some support from *dicta* in

Alladice;[348] the Court of Appeal determined that the improper denial of legal advice had not caused the detainee to confess but still found that, had it been accompanied by bad faith, exclusion of the confession under s 76 might have been undertaken. The general rule appears then to be that where the causal link in question clearly does not exist s 76(2)(a) cannot be invoked but in all other instances the fact that the confession was made subsequent to the oppression may be sufficient.

The question of causation under s 76(2)(b) appears, on the face of it, complex. From the wording of the sub-section it appears to be necessary to adopt a two-stage test, asking first whether something was said or done, likely in the circumstances to render any confession made unreliable, an objective test and secondly, whether that something caused the detainee to confess, a subjective test.

Relationship between ss 76 and 78

In general, the s 76 tests for admissibility of confessions could work to the detriment of inexperienced and more vulnerable detainees. In *Canale*[349] the police breached the recording provisions and allegedly played a trick on the appellant in order to obtain the confession. Ruling that the confession should have been excluded under s 78 the Court of Appeal took into account the fact that the appellant could not be said to be weak minded; it was therefore thought inappropriate to invoke s 76(2)(b).[350] Thus, the need to identify special factors in the situation in order to invoke either head of s 76 means that breaches of the interviewing rules unaccompanied by any such factor are usually considered under s 78. Furthermore, allegedly fabricated confessions cannot fall within s 76(2) due to its requirement that something has happened to the defendant which caused *him* to confess; its terms are not therefore fulfilled if the defence alleges that no confession made by the defendant exists. Thus s 78 operates as a catch-all section, bringing within its boundaries many confessions which pass the tests contained in either head of s 76. Section 78 is also likely to be invoked where police questioning meets with a no-comment response from a defendant. Such an interview could not be considered within s 76 due to the use of the word 'confession' within that section. It would seem to be straining statutory language too greatly to use the term 'confession' to

---

348 (1988) 87 Cr App R 380, CA.
349 [1990] All ER 187, CA.
350 Section 76(2)(a) was not invoked although apparently the police *deliberately* breached the recording provisions. Presumably breaches of the interviewing rules were not seen as behaviour serious enough to be termed 'oppression'. However, if the defence makes a – contested – allegation that the police made threats or deliberately tricked the detainee into confessing the prosecution might not be able to prove beyond reasonable doubt that the police had in fact behaved properly due to the breach of the recording provisions. This alternative line of argument could have been considered in *Canale* [1990] All ER 187, CA.

cover a silence. If a silence is excluded from evidence under s 78 adverse inferences cannot be drawn from it (unless the jury or magistrate becomes aware of it in the course of hearing other evidence) and therefore argument on this issue is likely to arise in future.

Section 78: the 'fairness' test[351]

Section 78 provides:
> In any proceedings the court may refuse to allow evidence on which the prosecution proposes to rely to be given if it appears to the court that, having regard to all the circumstances, including the circumstances in which the evidence was obtained, the admission of the evidence would have such an adverse effect on the fairness of the proceedings that the court ought not to admit it.

Section 78 confers an exclusionary *discretion* on a judge and appears to have been conceived to cover the very narrow function of the old common law discretion[352] to exclude improperly obtained non-confession evidence. Until the ruling in *Mason*[353] it was uncertain whether s 78 also covered confessions. Section 78 can be used to exclude evidence if admitting it would render the trial unfair. In adopting this formula it was clear that the government did not wish to import into this country a USA-type exclusionary rule. The Home Secretary informed the House of Commons[354] that the function of exclusion of evidence after police misconduct must not be disciplinary but must be to safeguard the fairness of the trial. The idea behind this was that non-confession evidence obtained by improper means could still be admitted on the basis that police misconduct could be dealt with by internal disciplinary procedures. Similarly, confessions obtained improperly in circumstances falling outside s 76 could nevertheless be admissible in evidence with the proviso that the trial should not thereby be rendered unfair. In fact, as will be seen, the courts have managed to create a role for s 78 which, as far as confessions are concerned, is probably rather far removed from the government's original intention. The approach adopted to confessions tends to reflect the protective principle.

---

351 For discussion of the operation of s 78 see Allen, CJW (1990) *CLJ* 80; Gelowitz, M, 106 *LQR* 327; May, R [1988] *Crim LR* 722.
352 See *Sang* [1980] AC 402; (1979) 2 All ER 1222, HL.
353 [1987] Crim LR 119; [1987] All ER 481, CA.
354 1983/4 *HC Deb*, 29 October 1984, Col 1012.

Confessions obtained in breach of the PACE scheme

The courts have been very reluctant to lay down general rules for the application of s 78[355] but the attempt will be made here, albeit tentatively, to identify some of the factors which tend to be taken into account. It may be noted that s 78 is not explicit as to who bears the burden of proof where a breach of the rules is alleged but in *Vel v Owen*[356] the Divisional Court ruled that the defence should make good its objection. In *Anderson*,[357] however, the court said that it was not entirely clear where the burden of proof lay. If it is found that admission of an interview would render the trial unfair then not only the interview affected but possibly any interviews subsequent to that one,[358] may be excluded from evidence under s 78.

The PACE interviewing scheme may be infringed or undermined in a variety of ways. In the paradigm case there may be a clear failure to put in place one of the safeguards such as access to legal advice or tape-recording. However, it is not always possible to identify such a clear breach of the rules. The failure to do so may have contributed to the decision in *Hughes*:[359] the misrepresentation as regards unavailability of legal advice made to the appellant did not involve breach of a specific Code provision and therefore may have led to reluctance to exclude the confession. Similarly, in *Khan*[360] it was found that while s 30(1) of PACE allowed officers to keep a suspect out of the police station for a time in order to make investigations, including a search, questioning during that time should be limited since otherwise the provisions of the interviewing scheme would be subverted. Some of the questions which had in fact been asked went beyond what was needed for the search; however, they should not have been excluded as the matter was 'a question of degree' although officers did not have carte blanche to interview suspects in such circumstances.

In contrast to this approach, there has been some willingness at first instance to consider situations where the PACE scheme seemed to have been infringed although it was impossible to point to a clear breach.[361] The interviewing scheme lends itself to many methods of infringement, some of which may occur at a low level of visibility but which may nevertheless be of

---

355 See the comments of Auld J in *Katz* (1990) 90 Cr App R 456, CA.
356 (1987) JP 510.
357 [1993] *Crim LR* 447.
358 *Ismail* [1990] *Crim LR* 109, CA; cf *Gillard and Barrett* (1991) 155 JP Rep 352 and *Y v DPP* [1991] *Crim LR* 917. Later interviews may be found to have been contaminated by earlier breaches if those breaches are of a fundamental and continuing character and the accused has not had sufficient opportunity of retracting what was said earlier: *Neill* [1994] *Crim LR* 441, CA.
359 Above note 222. See associated text for discussion of the decision.
360 [1993] *Crim LR* 55, CA.
361 See eg *Vernon* [1988] *Crim LR* 445; *Woodall and Others* [1989] *Crim LR* 288.

significance. For example, there may be breach of a rule contained in an instrument other than PACE itself or Code C;[362] there may be evasion or bending of a rule as opposed to breaking it and instances where the interviewing scheme itself leaves it unclear whether or not a particular safeguard should have been in place at a given stage in the process.[363] Of course, a court may never have an opportunity to hear such argument. Infringement of this type is difficult to detect; for example, a suspect who is persuaded to forego legal advice at the 'booking in' stage may be unaware that something has occurred to his disadvantage, unlike the suspect who has been straightforwardly refused advice. Even assuming that the suspect pleads not guilty, defence counsel may be reluctant to argue for exclusion of a confession if unable to point to a clear breach of the rules.

In *Keenan*[364] the Court of Appeal ruled that once a breach of the rules can be identified it will be asked whether it is substantial or significant. It found that a combination of breaches of the recording provisions satisfied this test. In contrast, a breach of para 10.2 requiring a police officer to inform a suspect that he is not under arrest, is free to go and may obtain legal advice has been held to be insubstantial.[365] This view of para 10.2 also seems to have been implicit in the ruling of the Court of Appeal in *Joseph*,[366] although a breach of para 10.5 in contrast was clearly found to be substantial and significant in order to merit exclusion of the confession. In *Walsh*[367] the Court of Appeal held that what was significant and substantial would be determined by reference to the nature of the breach except in instances where the police had acted in bad faith: '... although bad faith may make substantial or significant that which might not otherwise be so, the contrary does not follow. Breaches which are themselves significant and substantial are not rendered otherwise by the good faith of the officers concerned.'

This test has so far been applied only to Code provisions. It seems likely that breach of rules contained in Notes for Guidance or Home Office circulars might fail it – assuming that a court was prepared to consider such breaches at all – but this hypothesis has not yet been tested because the courts have been reluctant to take such rules into account in the context of exclusion of evidence

---

362 The Notes for Guidance, which are not part of the Codes (see Code C para 1.3 and the provision to the same effect is the first para of each Code) and therefore may in effect be said to form part of a separate instrument; Home Office circulars; Force Standing Orders.

363 This may be said in particular of Code C para 11.1 and Note 11A which determine when the safeguards surrounding interviews should be in place. See above pp 356–63 (discussed in Fenwick, H, 'Confessions, Recording Rules and Miscarriages of Justice' [1993] *Crim LR* 174).

364 [1989] 3 WLR 1193; [1989] All ER 598, CA.

365 *Rajakuruna* [1991] *Crim LR* 458.

366 [1993] *Crim LR* 206, CA.

367 [1989] *Crim LR* 822; (1989) 19 Cr App R 161.

or, as far as the Notes are concerned, in any other context. This was the approach taken in *DPP v Billington*;[368] the Court of Appeal preferred not to consider Note 6C of Code C despite its relevance to the question before it. However, there are some signs that the judiciary are beginning to react to the Notes differently, perhaps due to a perception that their legitimacy derives from their nature as opposed to their source. In *DPP v Blake*[369] the Divisional Court impliedly accepted that a Note for Guidance will be considered if it can be argued that it amplifies a particular Code provision and can therefore be of assistance in determining whether breach of such a provision has occurred. The question arose whether an estranged parent could be the appropriate adult at the interview of a juvenile under Code C para 13.1;[370] that provision was interpreted in accordance with Note 13C which describes the adult's expected role,[371] and it was then found that para 13.1 had been breached.[372] A variation on this view of the Notes which nevertheless supports the argument that they are unlikely to be considered in their own right has been expressed recently by the Court of Appeal in relation to one of the most significant Notes, Note 11A. It was taken into account on the basis that it could be seen as part of para 11.1 and could thereby acquire the status of a paragraph.[373]

Once a court has identified a significant and substantial breach of the interviewing rules it may then take some account of the function of the rule in question. Rules governing access to legal advice and the right to silence provide rights which are valuable in themselves since they tend to place the suspect on a more even footing with police officers during the interview. An innocent detainee who is confused and upset by the interrogation may be less likely to make false admissions if a legal adviser is present at the interview.[374] In contrast, the verifying and recording rules may be said to be concerned

---

368 (1988) Cr App R 68; [1988] 1 All ER 435. The court had to consider whether a desire to consult a solicitor first could properly found a refusal to furnish a specimen of breath under s 8(7) of the Road Traffic Act 1972. Para 6 of Code C provides that a person who has requested legal advice may not be interviewed until he has received it. Note 6C provides that the s 8 procedure does not constitute an interview but Lloyd LJ preferred not to take it into account while reaching a conclusion which was nevertheless in accordance with it. Thus the issue which fell to be determined did not concern the question of exclusion of evidence but has a bearing upon the general question whether courts are prepared to place any reliance upon the Notes.
369 [1989] 1 WLR 432, CA.
370 Now para 11.14 under the revised Code.
371 This role is now described in new para 11.16; this provision has therefore been elevated in status, indicating its importance. The decision in *DPP v Blake* has found recognition in new Note for Guidance 1C.
372 This decision was followed in the first instance decision of *Morse* [1991] *Crim LR* 195; see also *DPP v Rouse* and *DPP v Davis* (1992) 94 Cr App R 185.
373 *Cox* (1993) 96 Cr App R 464; [1993] *Crim LR* 382; (1992) *The Times*, 2 December.
374 As pointed out at a number of points in this chapter, the evidence as to the advantage to the detainee of having the advisor present at the interview is of a rather mixed nature; see eg comment on the solicitor's role at [1993] *Crim LR* 368.

mainly with the evidential integrity of the evidence rather than with providing rights valuable in themselves. Categorising the interviewing rules in this way – by means of their dominant function – may be useful as a means of determining the type of unfairness which may flow from their breach. However, occasionally, what may be termed the *subordinate* function of a rule may be relevant to the question of fairness with the result that, for example, breach of a recording rule could be treated in the same way as breach of the legal advice provisions.

In *Samuel*[375] the Court of Appeal found that the confession should have been excluded under s 78 because it was causally linked to the police impropriety – a failure to allow the appellant access to legal advice. In order to establish this point the solicitor in question gave evidence that had he been present he would have advised his client to remain silent in the last interview, whereas in fact Samuel made damaging admissions in that interview which formed the basis of the case against him. It could not be said with certainty that he would have confessed in any event: he was not, it was determined, a sophisticated criminal who was capable of judging for himself when to speak and when to remain silent. Thus – although this was not made explicit – the Court of Appeal was prepared to make the judgment that a trial *would* be rendered unfair if a court associated itself with a breach of the PACE interrogation procedure. The Court of Appeal in *Alladice*,[376] also faced with a breach of s 58, accepted that the key factor in exercising discretion under s 78 after a breach of the interrogation procedure was the causal relationship between breach and confession, (and, by implication, between breach and fairness at the trial). On the basis of this factor it was determined that the confession had been rightly admitted despite the breach of s 58 because no causal relationship between the two could be established. This finding was based partly on the defendant's evaluation of the situation (that he only wanted the solicitor to see fair play and did not require legal advice) and partly on the fact that he had exercised his right to silence at certain points. Therefore, it was determined that he would have made the incriminating admissions in any event – even with the benefit of legal advice. Possibly this was surprising in view of the fact that the appellant, as the court itself accepted, was an unsophisticated criminal who did in fact make admissions in the absence of a solicitor which formed the basis of the case against him.[377]

---

375 [1988] QB 615; [1988] 2 All ER 315; [1988] 2 WLR 920, CA.

376 (1988) 87 Cr App R 380. The Court of Appeal appeared to have a similar test in mind in relation to a failure to caution in *Weerdesteyn* (1995) 1 Cr App R 405; [1995] *Crim LR* 239, CA.

377 See also *Dunford* (1990) 91 Cr App R 150; (1990) 140 *NLJ* 517, CA: the Court of Appeal determined that the criminally experienced appellant had made his own assessment of the situation in deciding to make certain admissions and legal advice would not have affected his decision; the failure to allow legal advice was not therefore causally linked to the confession.

At times there has been a tendency for judges to move rather rapidly from a finding that the police have breached Code C to a determination that s 78 should be invoked without explicitly considering whether a causal relationship between the breach and the confession exists.[378] Such a tendency can be discerned in the case of *Absolam*[379] in which the Court of Appeal in finding that 'the prosecution would not have been in receipt of these admissions if the appropriate procedures had been followed' seemed to assume that the causal relationship between the impropriety[380] and the admissions did exist. The chain of causation would have been fairly long – had the detainee been informed of his right to legal advice he would have exercised it; had he exercised it he would not have made the incriminating admissions – but the Court of Appeal did not make much attempt to scrutinise its links.[381] However, in *Walsh*[382] the Court of Appeal reaffirmed the need to identify the causal relationship between the breach in question and the confession.

Deciding that an impropriety is causally linked to the confession does not of itself explain why admission of the confession will render the trial unfair, although it is perhaps reasonable to conclude that admission of a confession which is not so linked will *not* render the trial unfair. The necessary unfairness must arise due to admission of the confession, in other words *after* its admission; the unfairness in the interrogation cannot therefore without more satisfy this requirement; instead, the unfairly-obtained confession must be the agent which somehow creates unfairness at the trial. It has to be said that at present the courts have not addressed this question. In *Samuel*, for example, the Court of Appeal merely stated:

> ... the appellant was denied improperly one of the most important and fundamental rights of the citizen ... if [the trial judge] had found a breach of s 58 he would have determined that admission of evidence as to the final interview would have 'such an adverse effect on the fairness of the proceedings' that he ought not to admit it.[383]

Broadly speaking, it could be argued that if the court refuses to take the opportunity afforded by s 78 to put right what has occurred earlier in the process this will give an appearance of unfairness to the trial. This argument is

---

378 See *Williams* [1989] *Crim LR* 66 and *Mary Quayson* [1989] *Crim LR* 218.
379 (1989) Cr App R 332.
380 A failure to inform Absolam of his right to legal advice in breach of Code C para 3.1(ii).
381 Possibly this may have arisen because the defendant had denied making the admissions in question; the court was therefore placed in the position of accepting the word of the police officer against that of the defendant – precisely the problem which Code C was designed to prevent. The Court of Appeal, while speaking in the language of causation, may simply have had a doubt as to whether the admissions were made at all.
382 [1989] *Crim LR* 822.
383 [1988] 2 WLR 920 at p 934.

based on the 'protective principle':[384] if admissions gained in consequence of denial of a right (in the broad sense of an entitlement) are excluded the particular right is being protected in the sense that the defendant is being placed at trial – as far as the jury is concerned – in the position he or she would have been in had the right not been denied. If s 78 is, at least in part, concerned with ensuring fairness to the defence it is arguable that the court should take the opportunity offered to it of upholding the standards of fairness declared by PACE. However, if the police unfairness has had no consequences for the defendant the court need not exclude the confession since to do so would place him in a *more* favourable position than he would have been in had the proper standard of fairness been observed.

An alternative but allied argument may be termed the 'reputation' principle. It can be argued that admitting the confession causes the trial to appear unfair because the court thereby appears to condone or lend itself to the original unfairness. The imprimatur of the court is necessary in order to allow the impropriety to bear fruit. If the trial is viewed, not as a separate entity but as the culmination of a process in which the court and the police both play their part as emanations of the state, it can be argued that the court should refuse to lend itself to the unfairness which has gone before in order to ensure that the state does not profit from its own wrong. It cannot wipe out the unfairness but it can wipe out its consequences, thereby ensuring that the reputation of the criminal justice system is not tarnished. But it need concern itself with the police unfairness only if that unfairness did have consequences. If it concerned itself with an inconsequential breach the reputation of the criminal justice system would also suffer since the detriment caused to society in allowing someone who has perpetrated a serious crime to walk free from the court would be perceived as entirely outweighing the detriment to the defendant caused by the breach.

Admittedly, both these arguments assume that the court will appear to be associating itself unfairly with the prosecution, rather than dealing even-handedly, if it admits the evidence in question and that therefore the court should refuse to do so. They therefore seem to beg the very question to which s 78 demands an answer. If admitting the confession despite the breach *could* be seen as fair the court would not be associating itself with unfairness and could not be seen as lacking even-handedness. But bearing in mind the balance PACE is supposed to create between increased police powers and safeguards for suspects it can perhaps be argued that to accept evidence deriving from an interview in which the police were able to use their powers to the full but the defendant was unable to take advantage of an important safeguard, would not be perceived by most reasonable people as fair.

---

384 See Ashworth, AJ [1977] *Crim LR* 723.

In this context the curtailment of the right to silence is particularly significant. One result of its curtailment may be that it becomes harder to establish that an improper denial of access to legal advice should lead to exclusion of evidence under s 78. This is because the main basis for excluding confessions gained after denial of legal advice may disappear. The courts are excluding them mainly on the ground that had the legal adviser been present he or she would probably have advised the client to remain silent but if this cannot be contended the causal relationship between breach and confession is destroyed. Whether this will happen depends, of course, on the general readiness of legal advisers to advise their clients to remain silent in the face of the knowledge that such silence may be commented on in court. At present this must be a matter of conjecture but if legal advisers become less disposed than they are at present to advise silence, a number of consequences may follow. The police may perhaps be encouraged to afford access to a legal adviser but, on the other hand, any disincentive to deny access – the result of such decisions as *Samuel* and *Absolam* – may be removed. The balance may still come down in favour of discouraging or denying access. If, on a *voir dire*, a court has to consider such a denial it may be harder to contend confidently that the legal adviser would have advised the client to remain silent, with the result that in future the courts will find themselves less able to uphold this particular safeguard for the suspect. Of course it might be said, in the light of recent research,[385] that it is *already* becoming difficult to contend confidently that a legal adviser would have advised silence, except perhaps in cases where the client was under very obvious pressure.[386] However, that problem could be addressed by means of better training in the provision of custodial legal advice. The effect of curtailment of the right to silence, however, will probably be in the long run to undermine the main prop holding up the legal advice scheme.

Breach of rules aimed at ensuring that the record of an interview can be relied on at trial need not be considered under s 78 in terms of their impact on the defendant. Once such a breach, of a substantial nature, has been identified, a court will be likely to react by excluding the confession on the basis that it is impossible to be sure of its reliability[387] and therefore its prejudicial quality may outweigh its probative value. In other words, a jury may place reliance on an inaccurate record or believe a fabricated confession which clearly has no evidential value at all. An obvious example of such a breach is a failure to make contemporaneous notes of the interview in breach of Code C para 11.5,

---

385 McConville, M and Hodgson, J, *Custodial Legal Advice and the Right to Silence*, 1993, Royal Commission Study No 16.
386 See Dixon's findings in this respect: [1991] *PL* 233, at p 244: '... silence may be advised ... when the suspect is confused or highly emotional ... several solicitors stressed that their clients are under great pressure.'
387 See eg *Keenan* [1989] 3 WLR 1193; [1989] 3 All ER 598, CA.

allowing a challenge to the interview record by the defence on the basis that the police have fabricated all or part of it. The court then has no means of knowing which version of what was said is true, precisely the situation which Code C was designed to prevent. In such a situation a judge may well exclude the interview record on the basis that it would be unfair to allow evidence of doubtful reliability to go before the jury. If, however, as in *Dunn*[388] the defence has an independent witness to what occurred – usually a solicitor or solicitor's clerk – the judge may admit the confession as the defence now has a proper basis from which to challenge the police evidence.

It is fairly clear that allowing a confession which may have been fabricated to go before the jury may render a trial unfair: on the one hand the jury may rely on a confession which may be entirely untrue, while on the other, if the defendant alleges that the police fabricated the confession the prosecution can then put his character in issue and the jury may hear of his previous convictions. The jury may then tend to rely on his convictions in deciding that his guilt is established on this occasion. In both circumstances the defendant is placed at a clear disadvantage.

When a breach of Code C has occurred which casts doubt on the accuracy of the interview record the defence may not necessarily submit that the police have fabricated admissions; the judge may merely have to determine whether the trial will be rendered unfair if a possibly inaccurate record of an interview is admitted in evidence. There is authority to suggest that a judge in such circumstances will exclude the record[389] presumably due to the chance of a risk that the jury will rely on fabricated admissions.

As noted above, identifying the dominant function of the interviewing rule in question need not circumscribe the enquiry into the unfairness caused by its breach. Although identifying the dominant function of a rule may simplify this task in most circumstances, it is suggested that a court may sometimes focus on its subordinate function. For example, a breach of the recording provisions would be directly relevant to placing the suspect in a disadvantageous position at interview where there was no dispute between defence and prosecution as to the admissions made (although the defence may be alleging that they are untrue) but there was an allegation that the breach had allowed some impropriety to occur which had pressurised the suspect into making admissions. It may now be impossible to determine whether the defence or prosecution version of events during the interview is correct due to the defective record. Equally, access to legal advice can affect the evidential integrity of a confession: the legal adviser can give evidence in court as to what occurred during the interview and if the interview record is defective can support the defendant's version of what was said, thus lending

---

[388] (1990) 91 Cr App R 237; [1990] *Crim LR* 572, CA.
[389] *Foster* [1987] *Crim LR* 821; *Keenan* [1989] 3 All ER 598.

support to the argument that the interview should be admitted. Conversely, if in such circumstances legal advice had been improperly denied but the defendant was able to cope without advice, the unfairness would arise due to the inability of the defence to challenge the detective interview record rather than to the adverse effect of lack of advice.[390] In such instances the subordinate function of the rule should determine the test to be applied. Thus, in the first example given, the only question would be whether the causal relationship between impropriety and confession could be established, assuming that it was impossible to determine the truth or otherwise of the allegation of impropriety.

In the cases considered above it was not clear that the police had *deliberately* failed to comply with the rules; the failures in question may have arisen due to a mistake as to the application of PACE or because of an administrative error. It seems that if the police have acted deliberately the exercise under s 78 will be far less complex. Lord Lane CJ in *Alladice*[391] stated that he would not have hesitated to hold that the confession should have been excluded had it been demonstrated that the police had acted in bad faith in breaching s 58. The lack of emphasis he thought should in general be placed on the causal relationship in question if bad faith on the part of the police could be demonstrated was the most striking feature of this decision. His approach appears to involve asking only whether a breach was accompanied by bad faith. If so, that would appear to be the end of the matter: exclusion of the confession would follow almost automatically. If the breach occurred in good faith, however, a close scrutiny of the causal relationship should follow.

Using the questions of bad faith and causation as alternatives to keep a check on a too ready exclusion of confessions can be criticised because it is hard to see why an instance of bad faith on the part of the police which is not causally linked to the confession should be considered in relation to its admissibility. Deliberate denial of rights certainly gives a greater appearance of unfairness to the interrogation than an innocent denial but if the detainee is unaffected by it why should it affect the trial? It cannot be said that the court is associating itself with or condoning the bad faith displayed by the police in the interrogation because the link between the two – the admissions arising from the denial of rights – is missing. If in future the situation which arose in *Alladice* recurs but with the added ingredient of bad faith it is hard to see why the consequences for the future defendant should differ so greatly. The only justification appears to be that the police are 'punished' for their deliberate impropriety but the disciplinary approach has been explicitly repudiated (in

---

390 This occurred in *Dunn* (1990) 91 Cr App R 237; [1990] *Crim LR* 572, CA. Ironically, the confession was admitted into evidence due to the fact that the defendant's legal adviser had been present and could support his assertion that it had been fabricated; the jury presumably disbelieved her and convicted on that basis.

391 (1988) 87 Cr App R 380.

Delaney)[392] on the basis that it is not part of the proper purpose of a criminal trial to enquire into wrongdoing on the part of the police. Nevertheless, at present, deliberate breaches of Code C will almost certainly lead to exclusion of evidence under s 78 whether the breaches were linked to the confession or not. The Court of Appeal in *Walsh*[393] confirmed that this was the correct approach and suggested that it would be followed even if the breach was of a trivial nature. In fact the dearth of cases on this point suggests that courts are reluctant to accept that a breach of PACE may have been perpetrated deliberately.

It may be noted that a judge may exceptionally admit the confession after deciding to exclude it because some particular feature of the trial proceedings makes it necessary to do so in order to maintain the balance of fairness between prosecution and defence.[394] In other words, if it was clear that in some way the prosecution is at a disadvantage which could be seen as equal to that experienced by the defendant, the judge might allow the confession to be admitted. This flows from the concern of s 78 with the fairness of the proceedings rather than simply fairness to the defence. Reconsidering the decision to *admit* the confession could not occur under s 78 since it only operates *before* evidence is admitted (although s 82(3) might be invoked – see below).

Evidence obtained by tricks, secret recording and undercover work[395]

Sang[396] stated the general rule that improperly obtained evidence other than 'involuntary' confessions is admissible in a criminal trial subject to a very narrow discretion to exclude it. The fact that the police have acted as *agents provocateurs*, entrapping the defendant into a crime he would not otherwise have committed, was not found in *Sang* to mean that the evidence gained thereby should be excluded. The current position as regards tricks or undercover work by police was stated by the Court of Appeal in *Smurthwaite*.[397] The mere fact that the evidence has been obtained by entrapment or by an *agent provocateur* does not of itself require a judge to

---

392 (1989) 88 Cr App R 339; (1988) *The Times*, 20 August, CA.
393 [1989] *Crim LR* 822.
394 See *Allen* [1992] *Crim LR* 297: having decided to exclude a conversation between police officers and the defendant due to breaches of the recording provisions the judge reconsidered when the nature of the defence case became apparent; it placed prosecution witnesses at an unfair disadvantage if they were unable to refer to the excluded conversation. Thus it appears that in such circumstances the original unfairness caused to the defendant may be outweighed by unfairness to the prosecution if the confession is not admitted.
395 For discussion see Sharpe, S [1994] *Crim LR* 793; Robertson, G, *Crim LR* 805; Heydon, JD [1980] *Crim LR* 129; Birch, D (1994) *Current Legal Problems* 73.
396 [1980] AC 402; [1979] All ER 1222, HL.
397 [1994] All ER 898; (1994) 98 Cr App R 437, CA.

exclude it. Everything will depend on the particular circumstances in question. For example, how active or passive was the officer's role in obtaining the evidence? What is the nature of the evidence and is it unassailable? *Smurthwaite* indicates that the discretion to exclude 'unfair' evidence is of a wider scope than that indicated in *Sang*. This is of course in accord with the stance taken under s 78 where there has been a breach of PACE: the discretion exercised to exclude evidence is of a much wider scope than that recognised in *Sang*. However, in the majority of cases evidence obtained by a deception has been admitted[398] but where the deception 'creates' the evidence and it is not possible to say that the defendant has applied himself to the ruse the courts will tend to exclude it.[399]

In *Mason*[400] the defendant had been tricked into confessing to damaging his neighbour's car by the police who had falsely informed him and his solicitor that his fingerprints had been found on incriminating evidence. The Court of Appeal held that the confession should have been excluded under s 78: the trial judge had erred in omitting to take into account the deception practised on D's solicitor. The court appeared to view the deliberate deception practised by the police as the most significant factor without making it clear why the trial would be rendered unfair by admission of the confession gained thereby. It might have been better to have shown explicitly that the confession should be excluded on the basis that the police had acted improperly in deceiving the solicitor; the deception of the solicitor had resulted in receipt of the confession and the failure to exclude it meant that the court of first instance had, in effect, condoned the impropriety involved.

However, although deliberate impropriety may lead to the exclusion of admissions, it must, of course, be determined whether certain techniques will be designated improper. This issue has arisen particularly in the context of undercover police operations and secretly taped conversations. In *Bailey*[401] investigating officers and the custody officer put on a charade intended to convince the suspects who had been charged that they did not wish to place them both in the same cell which was bugged. This fooled the suspects who made incriminating admissions. It was submitted that the admissions should not have been admissible as undermining the spirit of Code C and especially the right to silence, since the men could not have been questioned by police at that point. However, the Court of Appeal rejected this argument on the basis

---

398 See, for example, *Maclean and Kosten* [1993] *Crim LR* 687; *Gill and Ranuana* [1991] *Crim LR* 358; *Edwards* [1991] *Crim LR* 45, CA.
399 See *Colin Stagg* (1994) unreported but see national newspapers 15 September 1994; *H* [1987] *Crim LR* 47.
400 [1987] *Crim LR* 119; [1987] 3 All ER 481, CA; see also *Woodall and Others* [1989] *Crim LR* 288 in which the 'trick' consisted of allowing the detainee to think that an off-the-record interview could take place in the police station.
401 (1993) *The Times*, 22 March; [1993] 3 All ER 513.

that the evidence was reliable and that the conversation between the suspects could not be equated with a police interview.

In *Christou*[402] undercover police set up a jeweller's shop purporting to be willing to deal in stolen property and transactions with customers were recorded by means of recording equipment hidden in the shop. The police officers engaged in conversation with the defendants who came to sell recently stolen jewellery and asked them questions. They also asked the defendants to sign receipts for the jewellery. The defendants were convicted of handling stolen goods and appealed on the basis that all the evidence against them gained through the undercover operation should have been excluded either at common law under the principles enunciated in *Sang*[403] or under s 78 as obtained by deception: they would not have entered the shop had they known its true nature. This submission was rejected on the basis that the appellants had not been tricked but had 'voluntarily applied themselves to the trick'; although specific deception had occurred such as the request to sign the receipts that was to be treated as part of the general deceit concerning the dishonest jeweller's shop. Therefore the trick had not resulted in unfairness. The test for unfairness was the same at common law and under s 78.

It was also submitted that the conversations were an interview within the purview of Code of Practice C; the provisions applying to interviews should therefore have been followed. This submission was rejected on the basis that the Code provisions were intended to apply only where police officer and suspect were on an unequal footing because the officer was perceived to be in a position of authority. However, this was not to be taken as encouragement to officers to use undercover operations as a method of circumventing the Code provisions. In saying this the court clearly recognised the danger that this ruling might encourage plain clothes police officers to operate secretly using hidden tape-recorders to tape admissions, in preference to arresting openly and administering a caution. However, their remarks left open the possibility that such action if cleverly enough disguised as a genuinely necessary undercover operation could lead to circumvention of Code C and consequent erosion of the privilege against self-incrimination.

In *Bryce*[404] the Court of Appeal were clearly fully alive to this danger. An undercover police officer posed as the buyer of a stolen car and in conversation with the appellant asked him questions designed to show that the car in question was stolen. The appellant allegedly gave incriminating replies. He was then arrested, refused to comment during the tape-recorded interview but allegedly made further admissions after the tape-recorder had

---

402 [1992] QB 979; [1992] 4 All ER 559, CA. See also *Williams and O'Hare v DPP* [1993] *Crim LR* 775; *Smurthwaite* [1994] 1 All ER 898, CA.
403 [1980] AC 402; [1979] 2 All ER 1222, HL.
404 [1992] 4 All ER 567; (1992) Cr App R 320; (1992) *NLJ* 1161, CA.

been turned off. He appealed against conviction on the ground that the evidence of the conversations and the interview was inadmissible under s 78. On the issue as to the admissibility of the conversation with the undercover officer, it was determined that the case differed from that of *Christou* on the following grounds: first, the questions asked went directly to the issue of dishonesty and were not necessary to the undercover operation; second, the possibility of concoction arose whereas in *Christou* the conversations were taped. As to the unrecorded interview, the possibility of concoction clearly arose due to the suspicious willingness of the appellant to make admissions after refusing to do so during the recorded interview. Therefore the judge at trial should have exercised discretion to exclude both the conversation and the unrecorded interview. Difficulty will arise after these two cases where it appears possible that a purported undercover operation has been used to circumvent the provisions of Code C especially the need to caution but the possibility of concoction does not arise due to the use of a hidden tape-recorder. A court may have to draw a very fine line between questions asked going directly to the issue of guilt and those touching obliquely on it.

The common theme running through the cases considered is the use of a deception of one sort or another. The courts have had to draw fine lines between degrees of deception in determining whether or not admission of the evidence obtained would render the trial unfair. A rather different stance is taken towards instances of secret recording in which no positive deception occurs, those in which it may be said that the role of the police is confined only to recording a conversation which would have taken place in any event. In such instances it cannot be said that the police deception is instrumental in obtaining the evidence except in the hypothetical sense: had the defendant applied his mind to the possibility of secret recording he might not have made the admissions in question. Passive secret recording may thus be contrasted with instances in which the police or someone acting on their behalf, have created a situation which makes it likely that admissions will be made where otherwise they would not have been. This distinction may have led the courts to accept evidence derived from secret recordings[405] (except in the case of telephone tapping where special rules apply)[406] more readily than evidence deriving from a 'positive' deception, since in comparison with other forms of deception secret recording seems to be at the lower end of the scale. Moreover, although evidence obtained from secret recordings may have the same inculpatory effect as a confession made in police custody, the courts seem to view the two methods of obtaining admissions differently. The tendency,

---

[405] See eg *Shaukat Ali* (1991) *The Times*, 19 February; *Chief Constable of West Yorkshire Police ex parte Govell* (1994) transcript from LEXIS; *Effick* (1992) 95 Cr App R 427, CA; [1994] 3 All ER 458, HL; *Roberts* (1997) 1 Cr App R 217.
[406] *Preston* [1993] 4 All ER 638; (1994) 98 Cr App R 405, HL.

which reflects the reliability principle, is to view secretly recorded evidence as unaffected by the manner of its acquisition, unlike admissions made to the police in an interview conducted in breach of PACE. However, although secret recording may be regarded as less improper than the use of a positive deception, it may involve other forms of impropriety. Thus, in focusing only or mainly on the reliability of evidence obtained, the courts have demonstrated a clear preference for crime control over due process.

Most secret recording by police is now regulated under the Police Act 1997.[407] The position as regards unlawfully obtained evidence, which reflects a crime control stance, is as stated by the House of Lords in *Khan (Sultan)*.[408] A bugging device had been secretly installed on the outside of a house which Khan was visiting. Khan was suspected of involvement in the importation of prohibited drugs and the tape-recording obtained from the listening device clearly showed that he was so involved. The case against him rested wholly on the tape-recording. The defence argued first that the recording was inadmissible as evidence because the police had no statutory authority to place listening devices on private property and that therefore such placement was a trespass and, further, that admission of the recording would breach Article 8 of the European Convention on Human Rights which protects the right to privacy. Secondly it was argued that even if the recording was admissible it should be excluded from evidence under s 78 due to the breach of Article 8 which would occur if it was not so excluded. It was accepted in the Court of Appeal that trespass to the building had occurred as well as some damage to it and that there had been an invasion of privacy. However, the Court of Appeal found,[409] supporting the trial judge, that these factors were of slight significance and therefore were readily outweighed by the fact that the police had largely complied with the Home Office guidelines and that the offences involved were serious. The court found that since the Convention is not part of UK law it was of only persuasive assistance.

The House of Lords upheld the Court of Appeal. The Lords relied on the decision in *Sang*[410] to the effect that improperly obtained evidence other than 'involuntary' confessions is admissible in a criminal trial. Involuntary confessions were inadmissible on the ground that if a defendant was in some way induced to confess during a police interrogation his confession might be unreliable. It was argued for the appellant that the recording fell within the category of involuntary confessions and therefore was outside the rule from *Sang*. The House of Lords disagreed and went on to find that *Sang* would be inapplicable only if there were a right to privacy in UK law and breach of such

---

407 See above pp 352–53.
408 [1996] All ER 289; (1996) 146 NLJ 1024. For comment see Carter, PB (1997) 113 *LQR* 468.
409 *Khan* [1996] 3 All ER 289; (1996) 146 *NLJ* 1024, HL; [1995] QB 27, CA.
410 [1980] AC 402; [1979] 2 All ER 1222.

a right could be treated as a form of impropriety different in kind from that covered by *Sang* and so serious that it would render evidence thereby obtained inadmissible. Neither of these two new principles was accepted; therefore the recording was admissible.

Should the recording have been excluded under s 78, taking Article 8 into account? The House of Lords found that although a judge in exercising discretion under s 78 might take Article 8 into account; or any relevant foreign law, an apparent breach of Article 8 would not necessarily lead him or her to conclude that the evidence in question should be excluded. The key question would be the effect of the breach upon the fairness of the proceedings. The House of Lords concluded that the circumstances in which the evidence was obtained, even if they involved a breach of Article 8, were not such as to require exclusion of the evidence.

This decision confirms that, apart from admissions falling within s 76 of PACE (which has partly replaced the common law concept of involuntariness), improperly obtained evidence is admissible in criminal trials subject to a discretion to exclude it. Thus it fails to take a stance which protects due process. However, the decision lays down a role for the European Convention on Human Rights within s 78, albeit a narrow one. The House of Lords was only prepared to find that the Convention would be 'relevant' to the exercise of discretion under s 78 and further found that where a breach of the Convention was found this would not necessarily lead a judge to conclude that evidence should be excluded. In future the judicial discretion conferred by s 78 should be exercised in accordance with the Convention. The question will be whether Article 8 has been breached. The principles which would be used by the European Court of Human Rights, including the principle of proportionality, in making such a determination will then determine the result in the instant case. The discretion under s 78 will be structured by reference to the Convention and to Convention jurisprudence whenever an issue bearing on admissibility of evidence arises within the areas governed by the Convention. The reception of Article 6 of the Convention into UK law may clarify this situation.

Exclusion of non-confession evidence[411]

The arguments above have concentrated on exclusion of admissions but it must be borne in mind that non-confession evidence can also be excluded under s 78 (or s 82(3)) although not under s 76. Where non-confession

---

[411] For discussion see Gelowitz, M, 106 *LQR* 327; Choo, AL-T (1989) 9 *LS* No 3 261; Allen, CJW (1990) 49 *Camb LJ* 80; Choo, AL-T (1993) *Journal of Crim Law* 195.

evidence is concerned the courts have taken a mixed stance which reflects the attitude they tend to display towards admissions obtained by secret recording on the one hand and those obtained in police interviews which breach PACE on the other. The general stance taken is that improperly obtained evidence is admissible in a criminal trial subject to a discretion to exclude it and the discretion tends to be wide or narrow depending on the type of evidence in question and the effect which the manner of its acquisition may have had on it. Thus, *identification* evidence is seen as particularly vulnerable and may therefore be treated in the same way as a confession obtained in breach of PACE. If some doubt is raised as to the reliability of the identification due to delay[412] or to a failure to hold an identification parade where one was practicable,[413] the identification evidence is likely to be excluded. Although there is as yet less case law on the point than in relation to confessions it would be possible to divide the rules relating to identification according to function as has been done above in relation to confessions. For example, if no reminder as to the availability of legal advice were given before an identification was arranged it could be argued that the form of the identification used prejudiced the position of the defendant who would have asked for a different form had he had advice. It could be argued that no identification would have been made had the other form been used and that therefore the failure to remind of the right to advice was causally linked to the identification evidence obtained.

If bad faith is shown in conducting the identification procedure it seems that the courts will react to it as they would in relation to confessions.[414] It will mean that no causal relationship between the breach and the evidence obtained need be shown and, presumably, that the breach need not be substantial and significant. It may be argued that there is a stronger case than that considered above in relation to confessions for treating bad faith shown during the identification process with particular stringency due to the appearance of unfairness created to the defendant who may think that there has been collusion between witnesses and the police.

On due process grounds the above argument as to the causal relationship between an impropriety and a confession (where bad faith is not shown) should be applied to *physical* evidence, such as a weapon or drugs found on the suspect or his premises due to an improper or unlawful search. However, where physical evidence is in question the discretion under s 78 is applied narrowly. The first instance decision in *Edward Fennelly*[415] in which a failure to give the reason for a stop and search led to exclusion of the heroin found is out of line with most of the other decisions. Indeed, even if the principles

---

412 *Quinn* [1990] *Crim LR* 581, CA; (1990) *The Times*, 31 March.
413 *Ladlow* [1989] *Crim LR* 219.
414 *Finley* [1993] *Crim LR* 50, CA.
415 [1989] *Crim LR* 142.

developed under s 78 with respect to confession evidence were generally applied to other evidence, *Edward Fennelly* would still be a doubtful decision since on the facts no causal relationship could exist between the impropriety in question and the evidence obtained. According to *Thomas*[416] and *Quinn*[417] physical evidence will be excluded only if obtained with deliberate illegality; the pre-PACE ruling of the House of Lords in *Fox*[418] would also lend support to this contention. In *Fox* the police made a *bona fide* mistake as to their powers in effecting an unlawful arrest and the House of Lords, in determining that the physical evidence obtained was admissible, considered that the unlawful arrest was merely part of the history of the case and not the concern of the court. This stance is in accord with that taken in *Sang*[419] and confirmed as correct in *Khan (Sultan)*. It appears to be in accord with the general PACE scheme since evidence obtained as a result of an inadmissible confession will be admissible under s 76(4).

On the other hand, as Zander points out,[420] citing, *inter alia*, *Sharpe v DPP*,[421] the courts have rejected the 'real' evidence of intoxication in certain drink-driving cases under s 78 due to the way in which the evidence was obtained, even where bad faith may not have been present. Zander views the Divisional Court decision in *Sharpe*, along with the decisions in cases such as *Samuel* and *Gall*[422] (on identification evidence) as affirming an abandonment of 'the amoral common law tradition of receiving non-confession evidence regardless of how it was obtained'.[423] However, no post-PACE decision of the Court of Appeal is available in which it has been found that physical evidence should have been excluded due to police impropriety in obtaining it. Further, the House of Lords decision in *Khan*, now the leading case on s 78, suggests that a narrow exclusionary discretion only is available under s 78, save where a confession may be said to be involuntary (in which case it would be excluded under s 76). The impact of *Khan* on evidence obtained in breach of the interviewing or identification rules is uncertain and, as suggested above, there are grounds on which such breaches might be distinguished from the impropriety which occurred in *Khan*. However, as far as secretly recorded and, almost certainly, physical evidence, is concerned *Khan* appears to herald a return to 'the amoral common law tradition'. Thus it seems that improperly obtained physical evidence will generally be admissible subject to a very

---

416 [1990] *Crim LR* 269. See to the same effect *Wright* [1994] *Crim LR* 55.
417 [1990] *Crim LR* 581, CA.
418 [1991] AC 281; see to the same effect *DPP v Wilson* [1991] *Crim LR* 441. On similar facts, in *Matto v Wolverhampton Crown Court* [1987] RTR 337 physical evidence was excluded since the police had acted with *mala fides*.
419 [1980] AC 402; [1979] 2 All ER 1222, HL.
420 Zander, 1995, pp 236–37.
421 (1993) JP 595.
422 (1988) 390 Cr App R 64.
423 Zander, *The Police and Criminal Evidence Act 1984*, 1995, p 236.

narrow discretion to exclude it. This stance seems to afford encouragement to police officers to disregard suspects' rights in the pursuit of such evidence and amounts to a declaration by the courts that a conviction may be based on evidence which would not be before a court had police officers not acted unlawfully. In due process terms, a principled justification for creating a distinction between improperly obtained but probably reliable confession evidence and improperly obtained physical evidence is not apparent.

Section 82(3): the common law discretion

Section 82(3) provides:

> Nothing in this part of the Act shall prejudice any power of a court to exclude evidence (whether by preventing questions from being put or otherwise) at its discretion.

This presumably preserves the whole of the common law discretion to exclude evidence due to inclusion in it of the words 'or otherwise'. In practice its role as regards exclusion of evidence is likely to be insignificant due to the width of s 78. However, a distinct function for s 82(3) was suggested in *Sat-Bhambra*;[424] it was held that ss 76 and 78 only operate before the evidence is led before the jury but that s 82(3) can be invoked after that point. Similarly, Zander[425] argues that the common law discretion to exclude evidence is covered by both s 78 and s 82(3). Thus at present s 82(3) may have a significant role to play only in preserving the judicial function of the judge in protecting witnesses or asking the jury to disregard evidence. The judge can at any point direct the jury to disregard evidence which has already been admitted and which may be unreliable.

In *O'Leary*[426] May CJ expressed the view that s 82(3) rather than s 78 preserves the common law discretion to exclude unreliable evidence (presumably in circumstances falling outside s 76(2)(b)). However, it is hard to see how to separate the questions of the admissibility of unreliable evidence and of unfairness at the trial. Admission of unreliable evidence will always affect the trial. In *Parris*[427] evidence which may have been fabricated by the police was excluded under s 78, not s 82(3). It appears likely that s 78 will continue to be used as a means of excluding unreliable evidence if s 76(2)(b) cannot be invoked.

---

424 (1988) JP Rep 365; (1988) Cr App R 55.
425 *The Police and Criminal Evidence Act 1984*, 2nd edn, 1990, p 210. Case law has not identified a distinction between the functions of the two sections (see eg *Christou* [1992] 4 All ER 559).
426 [1988] *Crim LR* 827, CA.
427 (1989) 9 Cr App R 68, CA.

Mentally handicapped or ill defendants: special rules

As noted above, the confession of a suspect who is mentally disordered or of low intelligence may be rendered inadmissible under s 76(2)(b) if the interrogation is not conducted with particular propriety.[428] However, special rules will apply in the case of some mentally disordered defendants. The confession of a mentally retarded defendant must be treated with particular caution. Under s 77 in such an instance if the confession was not made in the presence of an independent person and if the case depends largely on the confession, the jury must be warned to exercise particular caution before convicting. (This does not apply to the mentally ill although the Royal Commission has recommended that it should be extended to cover all categories of mentally disordered suspects.)[429]

In some such instances s 77 need not be invoked because the judge should withdraw the case from the jury. In *McKenzie*[430] the appellant, who was of subnormal intelligence and had sexual problems, was arrested and questioned about arson offences and about the killing of two elderly women. He made detailed admissions as to the arson offences and the two killings in a series of interviews. He also admitted to 10 other killings which he had not committed. He appealed against his conviction for manslaughter and arson and it was held on appeal that where the prosecution case depends wholly on confession evidence, the defendant is significantly mentally handicapped and the confessions are unconvincing, the judge should withdraw the case from the jury. When these three tests were applied in the instant case in respect of the confessions to the killings, it was found that they were satisfied, the third largely due to the doubt cast on the appellant's credibility due to his confessions to killings he could not have committed. However, the first test was not satisfied in respect of the convictions for arson. Those convictions could therefore stand but those for manslaughter were quashed. These rules are clearly of value as a means of affording protection to a group of persons who are least able to withstand pressure from the police and most likely to make a false confession. However, it is suggested that the second test could usefully be broadened so that it includes all those suffering from significant mental impairment at the time when the offences took place.

---

428 See above pp 476–77.
429 Report Proposal 85.
430 [1993] 1 WLR 453; (1992) 142 *NLJ* 1162, CA.

Tortious remedies[431]

Tort damages will be available in respect of some breaches of PACE. For example, if a police officer arrests a citizen where no reasonable suspicion arises under ss 24 or 25 of PACE, an action for false imprisonment will be available. Equally, such a remedy would be available if the Part IV provisions governing time limits on detention were breached.[432] Trespass to land or to goods will occur if the statutory provisions governing search of premises or seizure of goods are not followed. Malicious prosecution will be available where police have abused their powers in recommending prosecution to the Crown Prosecution Service. Also, one of the ancient 'malicious process torts' may be available where a malicious search or arrest has occurred, although in fact these actions are extremely rare and their continued existence is in doubt.[433] Such actions may not be brought because a claim of false imprisonment is preferred but there is a distinction between malicious process torts and false imprisonment in that in the former case but not the latter, all the proper procedural formalities will have been carried out. Actions for malicious prosecution are quite common but the plaintiff carries quite a heavy burden in the need to prove that there was no reasonable or probable cause for the prosecution.[434] It may be that if the prosecution is brought on competent legal advice this action will fail but this is unclear.[435]

Almost the whole of the interviewing scheme which is contained mainly in Codes C and E rather than in PACE itself is unaffected by tortious remedies. Section 67(10) of PACE provides that no civil or criminal liability arises from breaches of the codes of practice. This lack of a remedy also extends to some statutory provisions, in particular the most significant statutory interviewing provision, the entitlement to legal advice. There is no tort of denial of access to legal advice; the only possible tortious action would be for breach of statutory duty. It has been thought that an action for false imprisonment might lie; argument could be advanced that where gross breaches of the questioning provisions had taken place, such as interviewing a person unlawfully held incommunicado, a detention in itself lawful might thereby be rendered unlawful. However, although the ruling in *Middleweek v Chief Constable of Merseyside*[436] gave some encouragement to such argument, it

---

431 See Clayton and Tomlinson, *Civil Actions Against the Police*, 2nd edn, 1992; for a list of examples of recent damages awards see *op cit* pp 411–31.
432 For example, *Edwards v Chief Constable of Avon and Somerset*, 9 March 1992 (unreported); the plaintiff was detained for eight hours 47 minutes following a lawful arrest. The detention was wrongful because it was 'unnecessary'; compensation awarded.
433 See Clayton and Tomlinson, p 284. For discussion see Winfield, *History of Conspiracy and Abuse of Legal Process*, 1921.
434 See *Glinskie v McIver* [1962] AC 726.
435 *Abbott v Refuge Assurance Co Ltd* [1962] 1 QB 632.
436 [1992] AC 179; [1990] 3 WLR 481.

now seems to be ruled out due to the decision in *Weldon v Home Office* [437] in the context of lawful detention in a prison. It seems likely therefore that access to legal advice, like the rest of the safeguards for interviewing, will continue to be unaffected by the availability of tortious remedies.

Where actions in tort *are* available against the police they may be of particular value due to the willingness of the courts to accept that exemplary or punitive damages may sometimes be appropriate. Such damages are awarded to punish the defendant and will be available only in two instances:[438] where there has been 'oppressive, arbitrary or unconstitutional behaviour by the servants of the government' or where the profit accruing to the defendant due to his conduct may be greater than the compensation awarded to the plaintiff. Only the first of these two categories will be relevant in actions against the police and in order that such damages should be available the term 'servant of the government' has been broadly interpreted to include police officers.[439]

If a civil action is brought against an officer on the basis that he or she has acted *ultra vires* and the officer shows that the statutory conditions for the exercise of power were present, the onus lies on the plaintiff to establish relevant facts (*Greene v Home Secretary*).[440] In *Holgate-Mohammed v Duke* (1984)[441] the House of Lords confirmed that, in addition to showing that the relevant statutory conditions are satisfied, the exercise of statutory powers by officers must not offend against *Wednesbury* principles; officers must not take irrelevant factors into account or fail to have regard to relevant ones; an exercise of discretion must not be so unreasonable that no reasonable officer could have exercised it in the manner in question. In *Ministry of Defence, ex parte Smith and Others*,[442] the Court of Appeal affirmed that in judging whether the decision-maker had decided unreasonably, the human rights context was important; the more substantial the interference with human rights, the more the court would require by way of justification before it was satisfied that the decision was reasonable.

Such civil actions often attract high levels of damages. One of the highest awards was made in *White v Metropolitan Police Commissioner*.[443] Police officers unlawfully entered a house and, it was alleged, attacked one of the

---

437 [1991] WLR 340, CA.

438 This limitation was imposed by the House of Lords in *Rookes v Barnard* [1964] AC 1129 at 1226. Note that the *Law Commission Consultation Paper on Punitive Damages* (Paper No 132, 1993) advocates in its provisional conclusion retention of such damages but that they should be placed on a more principled basis.

439 *Broome v Cassell and Co* [1972] AC 1027 at 1088.

440 [1942] AC 284, HL.

441 [1984] AC 437; [1984] 1 All ER 1054, HL.

442 [1996] 1 All ER 257; [1996] ICR 740.

443 (1982) *The Times*, 24 April.

plaintiffs, an elderly man. The police then charged both plaintiffs with various offences in order to cover up their own conduct. The plaintiffs were awarded £20,000 exemplary damages each plus, respectively £6,500 and £4,500 aggravated damages. One of the highest recent awards was made in *Treadaway v Chief Constable of West Midlands*:[444] £50,000, which included £40,000 exemplary damages, was awarded in respect of a serious assault perpetrated in order to obtain a confession. In 1996 a number of very high awards were made against the Metropolitan Police. In *Goswell v Commissioner of Metropolitan Police*[445] the plaintiff was awarded £120,000 damages for assault, £12,000 for false imprisonment and £170,000 exemplary damages for arbitrary and oppressive behaviour. Mr Goswell, who is black, was waiting in his car when a police officer approached. Goswell complained about the lack of police activity over an arson attack on his home. He was handcuffed to and then struck by the officer; the blow required stitches and left a permanent scar. Goswell was then arrested for assault and threatening behaviour. He was cleared of these charges and then brought the successful civil action. In *Hsu v Commission of Metropolitan Police*[446] the plaintiff won £220,000 damages for assault and wrongful arrest at his home. In *Kownacki v Commissioner of Metropolitan Police*[447] actions for false imprisonment and malicious prosecution against the Metropolitan Police were successful; 200 police invaded the plaintiff's pub and charged him with supplying cannabis and allowing the premises to be used for drug dealing. When the case came to trial the prosecution offered no evidence and he was acquitted. As a result he suffered depression and paranoia which affected his work. The jury found that the officers had failed to prove that they had seen cannabis being openly smoked and sold on the premises during the surveillance operation; £108,750, including £45,000 of punitive damages, were awarded to reflect the jury's disapproval. The question of the appropriate level of damages was addressed by the Court of Appeal in *Thompson v Commissioner of Police for the Metropolis*.[448] The court laid down guidelines for the award of damages which took as a starting point a basic award of £500 for the first hour of unlawful detention, with decreasing amounts for subsequent hours. Aggravated damages could be awarded where there were special features of the case such as oppressive or humiliating conduct at the time of arrest. Such damages would start at around £1,000 but would not normally be more than twice the level of the basis damages. Exemplary damages should only be awarded where aggravated and basic damages together would not appear to provide a sufficient punishment. Exemplary damages would be not less than £5,000 but

---

[444] (1994) *The Times*, 25 October.
[445] (1996) *Guardian*, 27 April.
[446] (1996) unreported.
[447] (1996) *Guardian*, 30 April.
[448] [1997] 2 All ER 762.

the total figure awarded as exemplary damages would not be expected to amount to more than the basic damages multiplied by three. The overall award should not exceed £50,000. In accordance with these guidelines, the award made in *Hsu* was reduced to £50,000.

The value of civil actions against the police in terms of ensuring police accountability is limited. If a civil action against a police officer is successful, he or she will not be personally liable. Section 48 of the Police Act 1964 provides that a chief constable will be vicariously liable in respect of torts committed by constables under his direction or control in the performance or purported performance of their functions. The cost factor will deter most potential plaintiffs from suing the police, especially now that legal aid is unavailable for an increasing section of the population. Even where a civil action is successful, disciplinary charges are unlikely to be brought against the officers concerned. This is justified by the police on the basis of the differing standards of proof: civil claims need only be proved on the balance of probabilities while disciplinary charges at present must be proved beyond reasonable doubt. The high jury awards of damages in 1996 may reflect a growing public perception that the police are insufficiently accountable. If nothing else, a continuing propensity to make such awards might have helped to draw public and Parliamentary attention to an unsatisfactory situation. However, the decision of the Court of Appeal in *Thompson* will make this less likely.

Police complaints[449]

Commentators tend to view the police complaints mechanism as ineffective as a means of redress.[450] The fundamental defect they find in the complaints system, despite the involvement (albeit limited) of the Police Complaints Authority (PCA), is that it is administered by the police themselves. Under s 67 of the Police Act 1996 a complaint will go in the first instance to the Chief Officer of Police of the force in question who must determine by reference to the section whether or not he is the appropriate person to deal with it. A complaint must be referred to the PCA if it concerns serious misconduct[451] and in addition there is a discretionary power to refer complaints to the PCA. It does not carry out the investigation itself in such cases but supervises it and

---

449 See Maguire, M, 'Complaints Against the Police: the British Experience' in Goldsmith, A, ed, *Complaints Against the Police: A Comparative Study*, 1990; Greaves, A [1985] *Crim LR*; Khan, A, 129 *SJ* 455; *Williams* [1985] *Crim LR* 115; Lustgarten (1986), pp 139–40. The Runciman Commission considered that the existing arrangements probably do not command public confidence: Cm 2263, p 46; Harrison, J, *Police Misconduct: Legal Remedies*, 1987; *Triennial Review of the PCA 1991–94*, HC 396 (1994–95); *Fourth Report of the Home Affairs Committee*, HC 179 (1991–92); Sanders and Young, *Criminal Justice*, 1994, pp 400–15.

450 See eg comment from Harrison, J and Cragg, S (1993) 143 *NLJ* 591.

451 Section 70 of the Police Act 1996, formerly s 87(4) of PACE.

receives a report at the end of it. Thus its role in relation to complaints is limited.

The system does not allow for compensation to the victim or for the victim to attend any disciplinary proceedings. The disciplinary hearing itself may be perceived as unduly favourable to the officer in question due to the current burden of proof – the criminal standard – and the low success rate.[452] In fact very few complaints even lead to a hearing[453] as many as 30% of complaints are dealt with by informal resolution[454] and commentators have suggested that unreasonable pressure may be put on complainants to adopt the informal resolution process. Clayton and Tomlinson note that the 16,712 complaints dealt with in 1990 led to 305 criminal or disciplinary charges and advice or admonishment in 573 cases;[455] thus less than 2% of complaints led to any disciplinary action. Maguire and Corbett conducted a review of the operation of the complaints system from 1968–68[456] which found that the majority of complainants were dissatisfied and that the public did not have confidence in the system.

The PCA report of 1995 stated that, out of 245 complaints of serious assault by police officers, eight led to disciplinary charges; none led to dismissal of an officer from the service. Out of 6,318 complaints of assaults, in only 64 cases were disciplinary charges preferred: none led to dismissal of the officer concerned. The experience in *Goswell v Commissioner of Metropolitan Police*[457] may have been typical. The plaintiff also made a complaint prior to bringing the civil action. The complaint led to the sacking of the officer concerned in the assault but he appealed against his dismissal and was reinstated by the then Home Secretary, Michael Howard.

Bringing a complaint may affect any civil action available detrimentally since, until the *Wiley* decision discussed below, statements made in relation to the complaint could not be disclosed in civil proceedings,[458] while by bringing it the plaintiff has to disclose part of his or her case to the police.[459] The position of the plaintiff and defendant in relation to disclosure of material relating to a complaint have been placed on a more equal basis as a result of *Chief Constable of West Midlands Police, ex parte Wiley, Chief Constable of*

---

452 This is around 2%; *Annual Report of PCA for 1990*, HC 351 (1991). See Clayton and Tomlinson, pp 12–13.

453 Clayton and Tomlinson note (p 13) that the 16,712 complaints dealt with in 1990 led to 305 criminal or disciplinary charges and advice or admonishment in 573 cases; thus less than 2% of complaints led to any disciplinary action.

454 *PCA Triennial Review 1985–88*, HC 466, para 1.14, p 8.

455 *Civil Actions Against the Police*, 1992, p 13.

456 *A Study of the Police Complaints System*, HMSO, 1991.

457 (1996) *Guardian*, 27 April.

458 *Neilson v Laugharne* [1981] 1 QB 736, CA; *cf Bearmans v Metropolitan Police Receiver* [1961] 1 WLR 634.

459 See Clayton and Tomlinson, pp 61–63.

Nottinghamshire Police, ex parte Sunderland.[460] All the parties concerned argued that public interest immunity did not attach to documents coming into existence during a police complaints investigation. The House of Lords had to consider whether *Neilson v Laugharne*[461] and the decisions following it were wrongly decided. In *Neilson* Lord Oliver had determined that a class immunity should attach to police complaints documents on the basis that the police complaints procedure would be placed in jeopardy if that was not the case. However, the House of Lords considered that there was insufficient evidence to support Lord Oliver's conclusion as to the need for a new class claim to public interest immunity. Thus it was found that *Neilson* must be regarded as wrongly decided but that did not mean that public interest immunity would never attach to police complaints documents: whether it did or not would depend on the nature of the particular document or documents in question. This decision may be welcomed as emphasising that a clear case must be made out for use of a broad class claim to public interest immunity. It is in the interests of justice since it goes some way towards ensuring that, in civil actions against the police, plaintiff and defendant have access to the same information. However, it left open the possibility of a contents claim or of a class claim in relation to specific groups of documents, although a strong justification would be required to establish such a claim. In *Taylor v Anderton*[462] the Court of Appeal found that the reports prepared by investigating officers were entitled to class immunity but that a litigant might nevertheless obtain disclosure of part or all of a report if the judge could be persuaded that the public interest in disclosure outweighed the interest in immunity.

The severe criticism which has been directed against the whole police disciplinary process including the hearings,[463] led the Runciman Royal Commission to propose that the burden of proof in such hearings should no longer be the criminal standard.[464] The government issued a consultation paper in April 1993 which included various proposals, including abolition of the criminal standard of proof in discipline cases and the double jeopardy rule, which means that criminal proceedings against officers are not followed by disciplinary proceedings.[465] This rule was abolished under s 37(f) of the Police and Magistrates' Courts Act 1994, as part of an overhaul of the police disciplinary process. It is intended that the civil standard of proof will apply

---

460 [1995] AC 274; [1994] 3 All ER 420; (1995) 1 Cr App R 342, HL.
461 [1981] QB 736.
462 [1995] All ER 420, CA. See also *Kelly v Commissioner of Police of the Metropolis* (1997) *The Times*, August 20 in which it was found that PII attaches to certain of the new forms which are sent to the CPS by police forces.
463 Cm 2263, p 46.
464 Cm 2263, proposal 77.
465 See 143 *NLJ* 591; in its *Triennial Review 1988–91*, HC 352, 1991 the PCA also made this proposal.

in formal disciplinary procedures, although that change has not yet been implemented. Changes in the system are part of the Labour Government's overhaul of the police service generally which will occur partly in response to the Runciman Royal Commission report and partly in response to the Report of the Select Committee on Home Affairs (HC 258/I 1997–98). The Labour Government's proposals (HC 683 1997–98) mirror those of the 1993 Consultation Paper and also address the tendency of police officers who are facing disciplinary charges to take extended sick leave and/or early retirement, thereby evading the disciplinary process. Legislation is not expected until 2001 or later.

An independent complaints system is not proposed. In its briefing guide in 1984 the Home Office stated that an independent system would be ineffective as it would probably be unable to obtain the confidence of police officers; friction might develop and thus public confidence in the system would be lost. The *PCA Triennial Review 1991–94* was opposed to the establishment of a body staffed by independent investigators, considering that it would require a very substantial allocation of resources which, on the evidence available, would not be justifiable and that it might fail to wind the co-operation of the police. Maguire and Corbett commented in their 1991 review that an independent system might lead to an improvement in public confidence in the system, although they expressed doubts about its effectiveness in other respects. The current overhaul of the complaints procedure has not included introduction of a new, independent element into the process. The Police and Magistrates' Courts Act 1994, which was then consolidated in the Police Act 1996, made only limited changes to the functions and powers of the PCA. Part IV of the Police Act 1996, which now governs complaints and discipline, was merely a consolidating, not a reforming, measure. At present, radical change in the complaints procedure, as opposed to the police disciplinary process, is not proposed.

However, the argument for an entirely independent system seems to be gaining strength and it would seem that the present system cannot be sustained for much longer. A clear remedy for many breaches of PACE, especially those arising in the interviewing scheme, is obviously needed. As this chapter has shown, exclusion of evidence under s 78 has been used, in effect, as a partial means of filling the gap. However, as has also been argued, it will often be unavailable since most defendants plead guilty and it may be inappropriate where a breach has had no consequences in evidential terms. Until a proper remedy is available, the rights of the suspect as enshrined in PACE will remain in a vulnerable position.

10   CONCLUSIONS

A recurring theme throughout this chapter has concerned the extent to which a 'balance' is struck between suspects' rights and police powers. It may be said that on the face of it the balance struck is fairly acceptable, at least in relation to the non-terrorist suspect, despite the increased powers of arrest and stop and search which PACE confers. Concern may be expressed as to the uncertainty of the concept of reasonable suspicion on which these powers depend but, nevertheless, taking PACE and the Codes at face value, a concern to protect the rights of suspects appears to be evident.

The problem is, and again this has been a recurring theme, that no sufficient sanction is available if the police do not abide by the rules laid down to protect suspects' rights. This is particularly true of Code C; it creates a scheme which seems to make every effort to ensure fair treatment in custody and in the interview but which operates outside the realm of general legal sanctions since breaches may be remedied (in the accepted sense of that word) only in internal disciplinary proceedings and only very rarely then. The right to legal advice, although on a statutory basis, is an equally weak position. The Notes for Guidance which occupy key points in the scheme appear intended to have no legal status at all. Since no other effective means is available of ensuring that the rules are adhered to, the courts have stepped into the breach and have developed complex rules for the exclusion of confessions obtained in breach of the interviewing rules. Thus, in effect, exclusion of evidence has become the main method of upholding the rights of the suspect while in custody and in the interview. (This may partly explain the very stark distinction drawn by the courts between exclusion of confession and physical evidence: tort remedies may well be available when the latter is improperly obtained.)

The use of exclusion of evidence as a means of redress leads to very uncertain protection for suspects' rights since it can only operate where the case comes to court and the suspect pleads not guilty. Thus the police may still be inclined to break the rules in the hope of obtaining a guilty plea and therefore many interviews may be conducted which fall below the PACE standard. If, in particular instances, this does not come to light in court a false confession may be accepted leading to a miscarriage of justice, while on the other hand general failure to observe proper standards in the interview may sometimes mean that reliable confession evidence cannot be accepted in court, although it would have been had the rules been observed. If confession evidence would not have been available but for oppressive questioning it is suggested that the energies of the police should have been devoted to uncovering other evidence. The complexity of the interviewing rules seems to be related to these twin problems; arguably it represents an attempt to give an appearance of credibility to the scheme in order to deal with the latter problem while refusing steadfastly to provide a proper sanction for breaches of it which would tend to deal with both. Curtailment of the right to silence has merely exacerbated the situation since it is likely in itself to increase the pressure on the suspect to speak and it may also undermine the safeguard which it is suggested has most real value in the interview: the provision of legal advice from an experienced solicitor. It is therefore suggested that urgent and radical reform of the criminal investigation system should be undertaken which would first sweep away these complex levels of quasi-legislation based on no proper sanctions and secondly place the rights of suspects on a clear legal basis, with accompanying remedies. The reception of Article 6 of the European Convention on Human Rights into UK law under the Human Rights Act 1998 may lead to some changes in the criminal process. Their effect may be to infuse greater fairness into pre-trial procedure. But the application of Article 6 is unlikely to bring about the radical overhaul of the system which, it is argued, is needed.

CHAPTER TWELVE

FREEDOM OF MOVEMENT

1 INTRODUCTION

There is no general enforceable right to enter, remain in or move freely about in the UK or travel abroad and therefore this freedom is in a vulnerable position, although in practice the government has not generally tended to interfere with it as far as British citizens are concerned. However, non-British citizens born in or resident in the UK, may not be allowed to remain, enter or re-enter or may be separated from families because the families cannot obtain entry. Persons who have a claim to enter the UK may not find that the claim receives full consideration, while persons may be expelled from the UK who have a claim to remain. Obviously such expulsion represents one of the clearest possible infringements of freedom of movement and although it must be weighed against the right of every nation to place limits on those who can enter or remain within its boundaries,[1] the mechanism for balancing the two interests should in principle allow them to be fully and fairly weighed against each other.

A person who had not studied immigration law might think that a clear distinction could be drawn between the two groups mentioned: aliens without freedom to enter or remain in the UK and British citizens possessing such freedom. In fact, the status of a person as a British citizen whose freedom of movement will probably remain untrammelled or as a non-British citizen who will enjoy no such immunity is not always readily ascertainable; there may be at any one time a group of persons whose status is indeterminate. Thus the mechanisms for making such a determination, which may allow a number of restraints on freedom of movement to be imposed, are of crucial significance. Moreover, persons may visit the UK temporarily for work or to visit relatives and while here have a claim not to be expelled before their stay is over unless it can be determined that the freedom to remain no longer applies. The extent to which UK law allows such determinations to be fairly and clearly made is the main issue addressed by this chapter although it should be pointed out that full and detailed consideration of the lengthy and complex provisions in question is outside the scope of this book.

It may be noted that freedom of movement is in an even more precarious position than most freedoms in the UK since the obvious routes allowing recourse to the European Court of Human Rights are unavailable; the UK has

---

1   Recognised by the European Court of Human Rights; see the *East African Asians* cases (1981) 3 EHRR 76.

failed to ratify Protocol 4[2] of the European Convention on Human Rights which under Article 2 protects freedom of movement within a state's boundaries and the freedom to leave the state. Article 3 of Protocol 4, which contains no exceptions, guarantees the right of persons not to be expelled from the state of which they are nationals and to enter that state, while Article 4 prohibits the collective expulsion of aliens. The UK has also failed to ratify Protocol 7[3] which goes much further than Article 4 of Protocol 4 since it prohibits the expulsion of an alien unless he or she has been given an opportunity to submit reasons against expulsion and have the case reviewed by the 'competent authority'. The authority need not be a judicial body which complies with Article 6 of the Convention and compliance with Article 4 of the Protocol would be achieved if that authority merely reconsidered the matter. Thus, this guarantee is of a limited and circumspect nature. It should be noted that domestic incorporation of the Convention will not affect the availability of these guarantees to UK citizens since these later Protocols will not initially be received with the rest of the Convention into domestic law. Argument that separation from family or from a particular community amounts to a violation of the Article 8 guarantee of privacy, remains a possibility. In *Beldjoudi v France*[4] the European Court of Human Rights found that the right to family life under Article 8 encompasses the right of an alien to remain in a Convention state if it has been demonstrated that he or she has a long established and settled family life there.[5] However, EU nationals have the right to freedom of movement subject to limited exceptions under the Treaty of Rome 1957 and the Treaty of European Union which will be interpreted in accordance with Protocol 4, while Article 1 of Protocol 7 may come to have more influence on EU policy in future and may therefore have an influence on the UK through the back door. Article 12 of the International Covenant on Civil and Political Rights 1976 provides protection for freedom of movement but the UK entered a number of important reservations to this right on ratification. In any event, unlike the Convention, it is not enforceable as far as the UK is concerned by means of individual petition.

2 FREEDOM TO TRAVEL ABROAD[6]

UK law has traditionally presumed that UK citizens would be free to travel abroad but this freedom is in practice dependent on the possession of a valid

---

2 The Protocol came into force on 2 May 1968.
3 It came into force in November 1988.
4 A.234-A (1992); (1992) 14 EHRR 801.
5 See also the opinion of the European Commission of Human Rights in *Uppal v UK (No 2)* (1981) 3 EHRR 399.
6 For comment see Williams, DW, 'British Passports and the Right to Travel' (1974) *ICLQ* 642; Jaconelli (1975) 38 *MLR* 314.

passport although in law it is possible to enter or leave Britain without one. A passport was defined in *Brailsford*[7] as a 'document issued in the name of the Sovereign ... to a named individual ... to be used for that individual's protection as a British subject in foreign countries'. As this definition suggests, passports grew up not as a restriction on freedom of movement but as an affirmation of it but the position today hardly reflects such an affirmation. Passports are issued by the Passport Office, a department of the Home Office, under the royal prerogative. Thus the Home Secretary can exercise a discretion to withhold a passport where a person wishes to travel abroad to engage in activities which are politically deplored although legal. Because these powers arise under the royal prerogative it was thought that they would not be open to review until the ruling in *Council for Civil Service Unions v the Minister for the Civil Service* (the *GCHQ* case)[8] in which the House of Lords determined that the mere fact of the power deriving from the prerogative as opposed to statute was not a sufficient reason why it should not be open to review. Lord Roskill said that the executive may act under statute which has, by necessary implication, replaced a former prerogative power or may act under the prerogative alone but that in either case it would be an archaism to talk of the act of the executive as the act of the sovereign. This decision was applied in *Secretary of State for Foreign and Commonwealth Affairs, ex parte Everett*,[9] the Court of Appeal holding that review was available of a refusal to issue a passport to a British citizen living in Spain. Thus refusal or withdrawals of passports must be made fairly and reasonably although the merits of such decisions cannot be considered.

3 EXCLUSION ORDERS

There are no general powers to exclude British citizens from the country except in one instance. Exclusion orders can be made under s 5 of the Prevention of Terrorism (Temporary Provisions) Act (PTA) 1989 in respect of a British citizen (as defined under the British Nationality Act 1981 below) who has been ordinarily resident in Britain for three years or less, although he or she cannot be excluded from Britain altogether, only moved from one part of it to another. It is irrelevant whether the person excluded to Northern Ireland was born in Britain and has family there so long as he or she has only been ordinarily resident in Britain for three years or less.[10] The order prevents the citizen being in or entering Britain; an order under s 6 prevents the citizen being in or entering Northern Ireland. A s 7 order excludes a non-British

---

7   [1905] 2 KB 730, 745.
8   [1985] AC 374; [1985] 3 WLR 1174; [1984] 3 All ER 935, HL.
9   [1989] QB 891; [1989] 1 All ER 655, CA.
10 This occurred in the *Mathews* case, 7 July 1993, unreported.

citizen from either Britain or Northern Ireland. In effect these powers mean that Northern Irish citizens can be forced to go back to Northern Ireland; there is little reciprocity in terms of excluding Irish citizens to Britain.[11]

Influence on terrorism[12]

An order may be made if the person is suspected of involvement in acts of terrorism or is attempting or may attempt to enter Britain with a view to being concerned in such an offence. The Home Secretary must be 'satisfied' that the person in question is so involved. If an order is served on a person he or she has the right within seven or 14 days to make written representations to the Secretary of State and to have a personal interview with an adviser nominated by the Secretary (Schedule 2 para 4 of the PTA). There is no requirement for the Secretary of State to give reasons for making an order. Once the order is made, the exclude cannot re-enter the forbidden territory at all until it is revoked; there is no power to suspend the order for a short period of time in order to allow the exclude to attend family occasions such as funerals. Exclusion orders expire in three years and this means that the case will be reviewed every three years but a fresh order can be issued before the end of the three year period.

These provisions were reviewed by Lord Jellicoe in 1983;[13] he concluded that they have value in curbing terrorism but accepted that dumping the problem in Northern Ireland as opposed to Britain was merely transferring it from one area to another. He also accepted that by this means the whole problem of political terrorism might be exacerbated due to the alienation the suspected terrorist would feel in being up-rooted. In accordance with his Report the period of ordinary residence for s 5(4) purposes was reduced to three years from 20 with a view to bringing within the net only those who might well have come to Britain specifically with the idea of perpetrating terrorist offences. The Report concluded that the exclusion power should be allowed to lapse as soon as circumstances suggested that it was not strictly necessary.[14]

---

11 Walker, *The Prevention of Terrorism*, 2nd edn, 1992, pp 84–85; only four persons have been excluded to Britain.

12 Reading: for background Laquer, *The Age of Terrorism*, 2nd edn, 1987; Wilkinson, *Terrorism and the Liberal State*, 2nd edn, 1986; Gearty, *Terror*, 1991; in relation to Ireland: Townshend, *Political Violence in Ireland*, 1983; on exclusion orders specifically: Walker, C, *The Prevention of Terrorism in British Law*, 2nd edn, 1992, Chap 6; Bonner, D, *Emergency Powers in Peacetime*, 1985, Chap 4; Ewing and Gearty, *Freedom under Thatcher*, Chap 7, pp 217–21; Bonner, D [1989] *PL* 452–56; on application of exclusion orders to MPs see Walker, C [1983] *PL* 537.

13 *Report on the Operation of the Prevention of Terrorism (Temporary Provisions) Act 1978.*

14 Jellicoe (1983): para 200; however the review by Lord Colville recommended on this basis that power to make exclusion orders should be repealed (*Report on the Operation in 1990 of the Prevention of Terrorism Act 1989*).

There may be some value in exclusion orders; they may have the effect of disrupting lines of communication and breaking up terrorist units. Also they can prevent terrorists travelling freely between Britain and Ireland. Obviously, imprisonment would be a more effective way of achieving these objects but if evidence had to be produced in court it might endanger informers and witnesses. Also such orders allow preventive action before a group can become established in the UK; they may also be useful where a terrorist is currently imprisoned but it is clear that he or she will return to terrorism on release. They can even be used where a person has been *acquitted* of terrorist offences,[15] where the evidence, while failing to connect the defendant beyond reasonable doubt to particular offences, does suggest that there may be some involvement in terrorism. This has also occurred where a person has been arrested but not charged.[16]

Justifications and safeguards

However, it is unclear that the serious infringement of civil liberties which these orders represent can be justified by reference to their value. The power to exclude a person from a particular place where he or she may be surrounded by friends and family to a place where he or she may be a target for terrorists on grounds which may have not been fully tested represents a gross infringement of personal liberty which requires a very strong justification and should be balanced by effective safeguards. Such justification would be shown if exclusion orders had a clear effect on terrorism and the individuals affected were unlikely to engage in terrorist activities in the place to which they were excluded. However, it is not possible to be sure that these conditions are met, especially as by its nature the exclusion process allows persons to be excluded of whom it cannot be said that they are clearly implicated in terrorism. The decision to exclude takes place secretly and may be based on material of doubtful worth.[17] The safeguards available are of limited scope: the individual concerned can write to the Home Secretary requesting an interview, the interview will be with an adviser appointed by the Home Secretary and accountable to him. It hardly amounts, therefore, to an independent review of the decision. Moreover there is no need for the Home Secretary to give reasons for the order and therefore the individual concerned cannot challenge it effectively. Detention may be based on an exclusion order even where the grounds for the order are flimsy or non-

---

15 The cases of *McBrearty* (1990) *The Times,* 9 January, p 2 and *Ellis* (1991) *The Times*, 31 October, p 3.
16 For example, *Hagan* (1987) *The Times*, 20 May.
17 Lord Shackleton in his review of the PTA warned that some of the material had no evidential value and had to be treated with great caution (para 41 of the review). See also Ewing and Gearty, *Freedom under Thatcher*, p 218.

existent. In *Breen v Chief Constable for Dumfries and Galloway*,[18] police detained Breen while an exclusion order was being made. When the detention was challenged it was found that the police can detain on this basis so long as they are unaware that there may be no grounds for the order. Thus police accountability for such detention is extremely limited.

Decisions to exclude appear to be subject to extremely limited judicial review. In *Secretary of State for Home Affairs, ex parte Stitt*,[19] it was found that considerations of national security and confidentiality meant that the Secretary of State need not give any reasons at all for the decision to exclude. However, it seems to follow from *dicta* in *Secretary of State for Home Affairs, ex parte Cheblak*[20] that although the decision to exclude is effectively excluded from review there may be some review of preconditions and procedures.[21] The case concerned a deportation as opposed to an exclusion order[22] but the relevant principles would seem to be applicable in both circumstances. The deportation notice informed the applicant that he could make representations to an independent panel who would advise the Secretary of State. Lord Donaldson MR said, in relation to this panel, 'I have no doubt that the advisory panel is susceptible of judicial review if, for example, it could be shown to have acted unfairly within its terms of reference'.[23] These comments would be applicable to an interview with an adviser where exclusion had been ordered. However, so long as a fair procedure seems to have been followed, bearing in mind the constraints on the disclosure of the case against him to the applicant, it seems that no redress will be available if the Secretary of State decides to ignore the advice of the adviser or if the grounds for exclusion are flimsy or based on error. This is because the courts view decisions taken on national security grounds as purely a matter for the executive despite their impact on civil liberties.[24]

Some progress was made towards less restricted review in *Secretary of State for Home Affairs, ex parte McQuillan*.[25] The applicant applied for judicial review of the Home Secretary's decision to exclude him from Great Britain and the subsequent refusal to reconsider that decision in spite of the changed circumstances of the applicant. Evidence was adduced by the applicant to show that he had not at any time been involved in any terrorist activity and also that his life would continue to be endangered if he was forced to remain in Northern Ireland. It was found that the case raised human rights issues and

---

18 (1997) *The Times*, 24 April.
19 (1987) *The Times*, 3 February.
20 [1991] 1 WLR 890; [1991] 2 All ER 319, CA. For comment see [1991] *PL* 331.
21 See Walker, pp 90–92.
22 See p 541 below.
23 [1991] 1 WLR 890 at 907.
24 *Council of Civil Service Unions v Minister for the Civil Service* [1985] AC 374 at 412.
25 [1995] 3 All ER 400; (1994) *Independent*, 23 September.

that therefore the order required close scrutiny. However, it was found that on national security grounds the Home Secretary's decision must stand: he could not be required to give any reasons for it and thus the court was unable to assess its rationality. The argument that the human rights context requires close scrutiny of a decision was confirmed as correct in *Secretary of State for Defence, ex parte Smith and Others*.[26] The Court of Appeal found that: '... the more substantial the interference with human rights, the more the court will require by way of justification before it [will be] satisfied that the decision was reasonable.'[27] However, the national security justification which will be put forward in exclusion cases will probably always satisfy even this more stringent requirement of reasonableness.

It should be noted, however, that it is a fundamental principle of English law that the courts always have a duty to ensure that a body exercising power does so within the parameters set for it by the primary legislation. In *Anisminic*[28] it was held that this power of the court to keep the deciding body within the remit defined in the Act which gave it its powers could not be excluded, despite clear words in a statute to the contrary. To allow the court's supervisory jurisdiction to be ousted would be to accede to the proposition that the body in question had arbitrary powers and the courts are not prepared to believe that such powers are ever granted, since the grant of them would undermine the basic principle of the rule of law. However, in the area of exclusion orders, since the courts have decided that the minister is not obliged to give them reasons for his decisions, they have made it effectively impossible for them to determine whether the minister has acted within his powers. In practice, therefore, though not in theory, review by the courts will be limited to cases in which the order given is bad on its face, because, for example, it purports to exclude a suspect for more than three years contrary to Schedule 2, para 2. To assert that the courts would not have the power to quash such an order through the writ of *certiorari* would be tantamount to asserting that the minister has been endowed with an unlimited and arbitrary power in which case, by definition, the power would not be a legal one. It is submitted therefore that the courts retain the power of supervisory review of exclusion orders but that in practice review will be impossible except in the improbable case of an order which palpably purported to exceed the powers given to the minister under the Act.

A challenge by way of the European Convention might be a possibility although the UK has not ratified the Fourth Protocol which would be the most

---

26 [1996] 1 All ER 257; [1996] ICR 740; (1995) *The Times*, 6 November. See also *Cambridge Health Authority, ex parte B* [1995] *TLR* 159, CA; [1995] 1 WLR 898 pp 904–05; *Secretary of State for Home Affairs, ex parte McQuillan* [1995] 3 All ER 400; (1994) *Independant*, 23 September, in which Laws J's approach was expressly followed. Sedley J was unable to find for the applicant due to the particular statutory framework in question.

27 *Ibid* p 263.

28 [1969] 2 AC 147, HL.

obvious route. A challenge could be brought under Article 8 in the UK courts, once the Human Rights Act is fully in force, due to the impact of exclusion on family life[29] or even purely private life, but the judiciary might apply a form of margin of appreciation due to the national security considerations. At the present time, however, under the Labour Government, exclusion orders are not being used.

4 THE RIGHT OF ABODE[30]

Prior to 1962, all UK and Commonwealth subjects had the same freedom of movement in terms of entering and remaining in the UK. Immigration control under the Immigration Act 1962 extended control beyond aliens for the first time.[31] The 1962 Act was intended to impose control on the numbers of entrants except for those possessing personal or ancestral connections with the UK itself. It therefore marked the development of a policy allowing persons from the mainly white Old Commonwealth to enter while restricting entrants from the mainly black New Commonwealth, which was to continue in subsequent enactments.

However, the 1962 Act did not cover many would-be entrants. In particular, many Asians in Kenya chose, when Kenya became independent in 1963, to opt for retaining their citizenship of the UK and Colonies rather than becoming Kenyan citizens. They would therefore have been able to enter the UK under the terms of the 1962 Act and to curb this the Commonwealth Immigrants Act 1968 was passed. It imposed controls to cover holders of UK passports issued outside the UK, unless such persons could show parental or

---

29 In *Moustaquim, A.*193; (1991) 13 EHRR 802 it was found that deporting the applicant to Morocco from Belgium where his family lived would entail a breach of Article 8; this claim outweighed the claim of the Belgium state that expelling Moustaquim was necessary for the 'prevention of disorder and crime'. Of course, had his expulsion been characterised as necessary on grounds of national security the outcome would probably have been different. The European Court of HR tends to show timidity in the area of national security on the ground that the Member State is best placed to determine its needs (see *Leander v Sweden* (1987) 9 EHRR 443) and see further Chap 2 pp 82–85.

30 General reading see: Evans, JM, *Immigration Law*, 2nd edn, 1983; Grant, L and Martin, I, *Immigration Law and Practice*, 1982 and supplements; MacDonald, I and Blake, N, *Immigration Law and Practice*, 4th edn, 1995; Supperstone, M, *Immigration Law*, 2nd edn, 1988; Dummett, A and Nichol, A, *Subjects, Citizens, Aliens and Others – Nationality and Immigration Law*, 1990; Supperstone, M and Cavanagh, J, *Immigration*, 1992. See also Harlow, C and Rawlings, R, *Law and Administration*, 1984, Chap 16 and 17; the *Reports of the Commission for Racial Equality, Immigration Control and Procedures: Report of a Formal Investigation*, 1985 and the Select Committee on Home Affairs: *Immigration from the Indian Subcontinent* (1981–82, HC 90–1); Papademetriou, G, *The European Union's Struggle with Immigration and Asylum*, 1996, International Migration Policy Programme, Carnegie Endowment for International Peace.

31 For background to this Act and the 1968 Act which followed it see Steel, D, *No Entry*, 1969; Bevan, V, *The Development of British Immigration Law*, 1986; Drummett, A and Nichol, A, *Subjects, Citizens, Aliens and Others*, 1990.

grandparental links with the UK itself (patriality). This test appeared neutral on its face but in fact discriminated against black Commonwealth citizens in favour of white ones. It also meant that some citizens who now lost UK entry and settlement rights had no such rights in the countries from which they sought entry and so found themselves unable to enter either country.

The 1968 Act thus avoided making an overt affirmation that the UK was prepared to operate arbitrary distinctions between would-be entrants but in fact created hardship for particular groups. Eventually it was condemned as racially motivated by the European Commission of Human Rights in the *East African Asians* cases[32] on the basis that it had subjected then to racial discrimination which in the circumstances of the case could be termed 'degrading treatment' within Article 3. However, well before that ruling the concept of patriality had become the basis of the main immigration measure, the Immigration Act 1971, which, as amended, is the current governing legislation replacing the Commonwealth Immigrants Acts. It was amended by the British Nationality Act 1981 which attempted to simplify matters by defining the categories of citizens who would be subject to controls and those who would not. 'British citizens', as defined under the Act, are immune from controls while all others are subject to control including those within the new categories of 'British Dependent Territories Citizens' and 'British Overseas Citizens', a category covering UK and colonies citizens resident in independent Commonwealth countries without citizenship of those countries. The first category includes residents of Hong Kong. However, these new categories cannot be relied on without reference to the 1971 Act in order to determine whether a person is immune from immigration controls because the concept of British citizen is itself defined to include all those who had such immunity when the 1981 Act came into force in 1983.

Thus the 1971 Act creates two groups of people: those who have the 'right of abode' and those who do not and are therefore subject to controls. The latter group may be able to enter the UK and remain, if various conditions are fulfilled or if already in the UK may remain there. Members of this group may move into the former group by acquiring the right of abode. Thus the meaning of 'right of abode' is crucial; whether a person falls within the group possessing the right will determine the extent of his or her freedom of movement because once the right of abode is established, s 1 of the 1971 Act provides that a citizen may remain in, leave or return to the UK without hindrance except such as may be imposed on any citizen. This would include exclusion under the Prevention of Terrorism Act 1989.[33] As the right of abode is the main mechanism determining whether restriction on freedom of movement may operate, it is unfortunate that the concept is not free from uncertainty.

---

32 (1973) 3 EHRR 76.
33 See above pp 512–15.

The right of abode is governed by s 2 of the 1971 Act as amended which provides:

(1) A person is under this Act to have the right of abode in the United Kingdom if:
   (a) he is a British citizen; or
   (b) he is a Commonwealth citizen who–
      (i) immediately before the commencement of the British Nationality Act 1981 was a Commonwealth citizen having the right of abode in the United Kingdom by virtue of s 2(1)(d) or s 2(2) of this Act as then in force; and
      (ii) has not ceased to be a Commonwealth citizen in the meanwhile.

(2) In relation to Commonwealth citizens who have the right of abode in the United Kingdom by virtue of subsection (1)(b) above, this Act, except this section and s 5(2), shall apply as if they were British citizens; and in this Act (except as aforesaid) 'British citizen' shall be construed accordingly.

In general terms the Act largely placed Commonwealth citizens in the same position as aliens in respect of the right of abode, apart from EEA citizens who have special rights of entry (see below). Therefore two categories of citizens had the right of abode: those who had acquired rights before commencement of the Act and those who were British citizens.

Acquired rights

Section 1(2) of the 1971 Act protects those who had acquired rights to remain in the UK due to having been settled there for some time before 1973 when the 1971 Act came into force: '... indefinite leave to enter or remain in the United Kingdom shall by virtue of this provision, be treated as having been given under this Act to those in the United Kingdom at its coming into force, if they are then settled there.' In other words, persons settled in the UK in 1973 could be treated as though they had the right of abode as far as leave to remain was concerned. Section 1(2) does not, however, confer an automatic right of re-entry. The provision was also limited in scope due to requirements connoted by the term 'settled'. In *Secretary of State for Home Department, ex parte Mughal*[34] it was found that it meant 'being ordinarily resident ... without being subject under the immigration laws to any restriction on the period for which he may remain'. Moreover, it was found that the immigrant must have been present in the UK when the 1971 Act came into force. However, in *Shah v Barnet London Borough Council*[35] the House of Lords considered that a person whose permanent home remained elsewhere and who might intend in future to

---

34 [1974] QB 313.
35 [1983] 2 AC 309.

leave the UK would nevertheless be 'ordinarily resident' in the UK if he normally resided there from choice and for a settled purpose during the time in question.

British citizens

Obviously only the category of British citizens is ongoing; therefore it is important to consider the mechanisms by which a person can become a British citizen. Citizenship can be acquired by birth, although not by birth alone, adoption, descent, registration and naturalisation. In practice the relevant group will largely consist of Commonwealth immigrants who were born in the UK, have a UK-born parent or in some cases, grandparent or have been settled in the UK for some time.

After 1983, merely being born in the UK was not enough to acquire British citizenship of the United Kingdom and Colonies; the further requirement was imposed that the child's father or mother be, at that time, either a British citizen or 'settled' in the UK.[36] The meaning of 'settled' is considered above. If the child was illegitimate, however, the question of settlement would only be relevant in relation to the *mother*.[37] This discriminates against the father and although the Family Law Reform Act 1987 has equated the positions of legitimate and illegitimate children in a number of respects it has not done so in this one despite a recommendation to do so by the Law Commission.[38] If a child is born outside the UK after 1983 and either parent is a British citizen the child will acquire citizenship[39] but again the father is discriminated against if the child is illegitimate since he will not be able to pass on his right to British citizenship.

One fundamental problem arising from the provisions relating to those born in the UK after 1983 is that it may not be clear whether the parent is 'ordinarily resident' (settled). Much will depend on the residence intentions of the parents at the time of the birth. A person's citizenship entitlement may therefore remain uncertain for a substantial period. However, if the parent is not a British citizen or settled at the time of the birth but becomes so before the child is 18 he or she can still become a British citizen. Alternatively he or she can become a British citizen if until the age of 10, in any one year for all those 10 years, the number of days on which he or she was absent from the UK did not exceed 90.[40] The Home Secretary has a discretion to register even where the 90 day period has been exceeded in any or all of those first 10 years under s 1(7).

---

36 Section 1(1) of the 1981 Act.
37 See s 50(9)(b).
38 Law Comm No 118 para 11.20.
39 Section 2 of the 1981 Act.
40 Sections 1(3) and (4).

Various other persons have the right to be registered as British citizens including certain former citizens of the UK and colonies who did not become British citizens under the 1981 Act and have remained in the UK for five years without breach of the immigration laws and have been accepted for settlement.[41] The Home Secretary can also register certain persons such as minors as citizens at his discretion.[42]

Naturalisation is at the discretion of the Home Secretary under s 6 of the 1981 Act. The Home Secretary may 'if he thinks fit' grant a certificate of naturalisation to a person who appears to him to satisfy the requirements of Schedule 1 of the Act. These requirements relate to past residence in the UK, intention to remain there, good character and knowledge of the language.

Before 1981 wives of citizens of the UK and Colonies acquired on marriage the right to obtain citizenship by registration. In contrast, husbands of citizens of the UK and Colonies could only apply for naturalisation. This distinction was, however, removed by the 1981 Act which took away the registration rights of wives and made the grant of citizenship discretionary in both cases. The Immigration Act 1988 placed a further restriction on wives who could acquire the right of abode. A polygamous wife used to be able to claim the right under s 2(2) of the 1971 Act (before amendment) but it is now provided that the first polygamous wife to exercise such right, by entry or by obtaining a certificate of entitlement shall, by so doing, exclude the rights of others.

Citizenship can be acquired by naturalisation but in contrast to the right of certain persons considered above to citizenship by registration, citizenship by naturalisation is only at the discretion of the Home Secretary. In exercising this discretion he will take into account the requirements of Schedule 1.[43] The requirements include past residence in the UK, good character, knowledge of language and intention to remain; they may not be so stringently applied where the applicant is married to a British citizen.

Proving the right of abode

It may be that a person who is not in the UK has a claim to right of abode. However, this does not mean that such a person may enter the UK and then seek to prove the claim. Under s 3(9) of the 1971 Act, he or she must prove that right of abode by means of a certificate of entitlement. The certificate must be obtained in the country of origin which means that a person who has the right of abode may nevertheless be unable to enter the UK until the certificate is

---

41   Section 4(2) of the 1981 Act.
42   See s 3(1) of the 1981 Act – power to register any minor; and under ss 1(7), 3(4) and (5), 7(6) and (8): persons who have not fulfilled certain requirements which if fulfilled would have placed the Home Secretary under a duty to register them.
43   Section 6 of the 1981 Act.

granted. This severe restriction on freedom of movement has been somewhat alleviated by cutting down waiting time for such certificates but there is still likely to be delay.[44] British citizens, on the other hand, may enter the UK merely by producing a passport showing them to be such[45] since this is the most ready method of proving their status.

The position of EU and EEA nationals[46]

EU nationals have enforceable rights to freedom of movement under the Treaty of Rome[47] and these were extended to nationals of Austria, Finland, Iceland, Norway and Sweden under the Immigration (European Economic Area) Order 1994 (SI 1994/1895). Prior to 1994 the Immigration Rules could only affect EU nationals to the extent permitted by Community law.[48] It was clear that any conflict between the Rules and EU provisions had to be resolved in favour of the latter.[49] The position of EU nationals was strengthened when s 7(1) of the Immigration Act 1988 was brought into force in July 1994: 'A person shall not ... require leave to enter or remain ... in any case in which he is entitled to do so by virtue of an enforceable Community Right ...' Thus EEA nationals must be viewed as entering as of right rather than falling into categories of persons who need administrative permission to enter. This does not mean that EEA nationals may not be subject to border controls. In *Secretary of State for Home Affairs, ex parte Flynn*[50] the applicant sought judicial review of the decision of the Home Secretary to maintain border controls affecting the free movement of persons between Member States of the EU. He relied on Article 7(a) of the EC Treaty (inserted by Article 13 of the Single European Act 1986 and renumbered by Article G(9) of the Treaty on European Union 1992) which provides that the Community shall adopt measures with 'the aim of progressively establishing the internal market over a period expiring on December 1992 ... The internal market shall establish an area without internal frontiers in which the free movement of goods, persons ... is ensured'. The appellant argued that Article 7(a) required the abolition of

---

44 See further Shah, R, 'Proving the Right of Abode and Racial Discrimination' (1992) *SJ* 16 October 1023.
45 Theoretically a British citizen could enter without a passport; see above p 511.
46 See generally Evans, AC (1982) 45 *MLR* 97; (1984) *American Journal of Comparative Law* 679; Steiner, J, *Textbook of EC Law*, 1990, Chap 18 for further reading in respect of the EU relevant provisions.
47 See Rules 68–70; acceptability of discrimination between EU nationals and non-EU nationals reiterated in *Immigration Appeal Tribunal ex parte Al-Sabah* [1992] Imm AR 223, CA.
48 Council Regulations 1612/68 EEC, 1251/70 EEC; Council Directives 64/221 EEC, 68/360 EEC, 72/194 EEC, 73/148 EEC, 75/34 EEC, 75/35 EEC; Council Declaration 1451/68 EEC.
49 See *Giangregorio v Secretary of State for Home Affairs* [1983] 3 CMLR 472; *Monteil v Secretary of State for Home Affairs* [1974] 1 CMLR 265; *Rubruck v Secretary of State for Home Affairs* [1984] 2 CMLR 499.
50 (1995) *The Times*, 20 July.

border controls by that date and that he had been detrimentally affected since he had been subjected to such controls. In Case 44/84 *Hurd v Jones*[51] the ECJ had found that a provision produces direct effects between the Member States and their subjects only if it is clear and unconditional and not contingent upon any discretionary implementing measure. Article 7(a) did not satisfy those requirements since no clear and precise obligation was imposed by Article 7(a): the establishment of the internal market was not an obligation but an aim. Article 7(a) was therefore not of direct effect so that individuals could invoke it.

Article 48 is the principal provision governing the free movement of workers and it is supplemented by implementing secondary legislation. The fact of employment brings the provisions into play as regards the worker and his or her family and this has been interpreted, at least in the English courts, to mean that a person divorced from a worker is no longer entitled to remain in the UK.[52] The free movement to work may include the right to seek work,[53] although it may be necessary to show that the person has a genuine chance of obtaining work,[54] while the term 'worker' includes persons working to fulfil some economic purpose even though the work is part time and the worker must partly rely on public funds for support.[55]

These rights do not extend to those wishing to enter and remain to exercise civil or political rights.[56] Moreover, they are not absolute; EU law permits a Member State to refuse a Community national permission to enter and remain on various grounds. States can deny these rights to workers on the grounds of 'public policy, public security and public health' (Article 48(3)).[57] This principle has been enshrined in Directive 64/221. Public policy is the most uncertain term and potentially very wide; however it has been held by the European Court of Justice (ECJ) in *Van Duyn v Home Office (No 2)*[58] that Member States are not free to interpret it unilaterally, although it has been accepted that the concept of public policy will vary from state to state and so states will have an area of discretion within the limits defined by the Treaty. In *Rutili v Ministre de l'Interieur*[59] the ECJ found that restrictions on the free

---

51 [1986] ECR 29.
52 *Secretary of State for Home Affairs ex parte Sandhu* [1983] 3 CMLR 131.
53 *Hoth v Secretary of State for Home Affairs* [1985] Imm AR 20; *Bouanimba v Secretary of State for Home Affairs* [1986] Imm AR 343, IAT (Articles 48–51).
54 *Immigration Appeal Tribunal ex parte Antonissen* [1992] Imm AR 196: appeal against a deportation order failed as the applicant who had served a prison sentence for a serious crime was thought to have no chance of finding employment.
55 *Kempf v Staatssecretaris van Justitie* [1987] 1 CMLR 764.
56 See *Levin v Secretary of State for Justice* [1982] ECR 1035; and *Re a Belgian prostitute* [1976] 2 CMLR 527.
57 For consideration of Article 48 see O'Keeffe, D [1982] 19 CMLR 35.
58 [1974] ECR 1337.
59 [1975] ECR 1219; [1976] 1 CMLR 140.

movement of EU nationals could be imposed only where an individual's presence constituted a 'genuine and sufficiently serious threat to public policy'. The court considered that this principle embodied the principle applied to the restrictions on the rights under the European Convention that restrictions should be accepted only when necessary. Thus the test of proportionality must be applied to restrictions on movement on grounds of public policy. In *Bouchereau*[60] the concept of public policy was further narrowed, the ECJ holding that it connoted a threat 'affecting one of the fundamental interests of society'.

Under Article 3(1) of the directive, moreover, the power to restrict movement by deportation or otherwise may only be exercised on grounds of personal unacceptability.[61] Thus if the *sole* reason relied upon to justify exclusion or deportation is past membership of an undesirable organisation the exclusion or deportation will not be lawful. It is necessary to show that there is something substantively undesirable about the specific individual in question. Reliance on the commission of a criminal offence *simpliciter* to justify exclusion or deportation would be contrary to the directive. Thus the EU national would retain his or her rights to enter and stay if re-offending was not anticipated or the crimes committed were fairly trivial, because the 'public policy' condition would not be satisfied.[62] The ruling in *Bouchereau* gave some guidance as to the factors to be taken into account in making a determination as to the relevance of criminal activity; the relevant factors included the type of offence, the defendant's assumed propensity to re-offend and the seriousness of the offence if recommitted.[63] In *Escuriaza*[64] the Court of Appeal considered that these tests are the same as those which will generally be applied in order to deport an alien but it is suggested that cases may arise of a less clear cut nature than *Escuriaza* in which it will be important to apply the more stringent Community test.

5 CLAIMS TO ENTER OF THOSE WITHOUT RIGHTS OF ENTRY

This chapter has considered the right of abode and the rights of EU and EEA nationals. It now moves on to consider the treatment of those who do not have such rights but may have a claim to enter this country or remain in it. In

---

60 [1977] ECR 1999.
61 *Van Duyn v Home Office (No 2)* [1974] ECR 1337.
62 See *Bonsignore v Oberstadtdirektor of the City of Cologne* [1975] ECR 297.
63 See also *Puttick v Secretary of State for Home Affairs* [1984] Imm AR 118; *Immigration Appeal Tribunal ex parte Tamdjid-Nezhad* [1986] Imm AR 396.
64 [1989] 3 CMLR 281. For further discussion of deportation of EU nationals see Vincenzi, C [1994] *Crim LR* 163.

contrast to the provisions governing the right of abode which arise under statute and are reasonably precise, the administration of immigration controls is mainly dependent on the Immigration Rules which are rules of guidance issued by the Home Secretary under the 1971 Act. Section 3(2) of the 1971 Act provides:

> The Secretary of State shall from time to time ... lay before Parliament statements of the rules, laid down by him as to the practice to be followed ... in this Act for regulating the entry into and stay in the United Kingdom of persons required by this Act to have leave to enter, including any rules as to the period for which leave is to be given and the conditions to be attached in different circumstances ...

The immigration rules provide an example of quasi-legislation which, like the Codes of Practice under the Police and Criminal Evidence Act 1984 (PACE),[65] are informed by other levels of quasi-legislation – unpublished Home Office guidelines or policy documents deployed in the Department of Employment. Like the PACE Codes they do not acquire the legal status of delegated legislation.[66] However, the Rules have a higher legal status than the Codes, which apart from their evidential value can be considered only in internal police disciplinary provisions.[67] Section 19 of the 1971 Act provides that an appeal against a decision of an immigration officer will succeed if it appears that it was not taken in accordance with any immigration rules applicable to the case. Thus, unlike the PACE Codes which seem to have a lower status than PACE itself, the Rules have the same legal status as the 1971 Act in immigration tribunal cases.

Although where the rules are misapplied there may be redress, they employ a discretionary wording which makes them harder to challenge. In other words, they do not straightforwardly provide that a person may enter once certain conditions are satisfied; on the contrary, they provide expressly that merely because a person seeking entry or leave to remain satisfies the formal requirements of the Rules this will not mean that such entry or leave will be automatically granted.[68] All the relevant circumstances of the case will be considered and this will include matters not referred to in a particular Rule. Thus it will be hard for the would-be entrant to predict what the outcome of a decision will be.

---

65 For discussion of the legal status of the PACE Codes see Chap 11 pp 395–96.
66 See *Secretary of State for Home Affairs ex parte Hosenball* [1977] 1 WLR 766; [1977] 3 All ER 452, CA; *Pearson v Immigration Appeal Tribunal* [1978] Imm AR 212; Cf *Chief Immigration Officer, Heathrow Airport ex parte Salamat Bibi* [1976] 1 WLR 979.
67 Section 67 of PACE.
68 See Rules 78 and 99–102.

Temporary entrants and entrants intending to remain

Visitors will be allowed to enter for six months and will not usually be allowed to take employment. They are only given leave to enter the country temporarily; in contrast persons coming in for employment, marriage or as a person of independent means will initially come in temporarily but such entry can eventually give rise to a claim to remain indefinitely. Where persons are coming in with a view to marriage a number of conditions must be met under Rule 290 of the Immigration Rules 1994. It must be clear that the parties will not need to rely on public funds either before or after the marriage. Also, it must appear that the marriage is genuine – 'It is not the primary purpose of the intended marriage to obtain admission to the United Kingdom' – and the parties intend to live together permanently as husband and wife.[69] Rule 290 indirectly discriminates against arranged marriages since they would, it seems, fall foul of the requirement that the parties to the proposed marriage must show that they have met.[70] However, where an arranged marriage does not involve a 'passionate relationship' this will not in itself suggest that its primary purpose is to allow entry to the UK.[71] It also directly discriminates on the grounds of sexual orientation as it gives no recognition to homosexual couples.

The main objection to the 'primary purpose' rule, which applies to spouses as well (see below), arises because persons may be turned away despite the fact that the intention to marry is genuine, because they have not had a full chance to prove this. There is an opportunity to appeal but the person refused entry will not be able to enter the UK in order to present the appeal in person. If a person is allowed to enter under this rule he or she can apply for an extension of stay after the six months have expired; if this is allowed a prohibition on employment will be imposed under Rule 48.

The provisions under Rule 281 of the 1994 Rules relating to spouses wishing to enter the UK are similar to those under Rule 190 in relation to the requirement that the couple should not be a charge on the public funds. Before 1985 a woman living in the UK had greater difficulty in getting her husband into the country than did a man bringing in his wife. However, such sexual discrimination was the subject of a successful application under Article 8 in conjunction with Article 14 in the European Court of Human Rights in *Abdulaziz, Cabales and Bankandali v UK*.[72] The UK argued that the discrimination was justified as a reasonable measure to protect the local workforce on the basis that 'men were more prone to take employment than

---

69 See for discussion Sachdera, *The Primary Purpose Rule in British Immigration Law*, 1993.
70 However, such marriages will not automatically fall foul of the primary purpose rule: *Immigration Appeal Tribunal ex parte Hoque* [1988] Imm AR 216, CA.
71 *Immigration Appeal Tribunal ex parte Iqbal* (1992) *The Times*, 24 December.
72 (1985) 7 EHRR 471.

women,' but this was not accepted. Following this decision the Rules were revised in 1985 in order to secure equality but it was achieved not by improving the rights of women to be joined by their partners but by restricting the rights of men. Since 1985 the former rules about fiancées and wives have been made applicable to both sexes. It follows that the 'genuine marriage-primary purpose' rule is now applied to all such admissions, not just those of men. Rule 281 appears to relate only to *two* parties to a marriage and is therefore indirectly discriminatory in that it would have a disproportionately adverse effect on any members of a race which practices polygamy or polyandry. It may be noted that soon after its election in April 1997 the present government announced its intention to abolish the primary purpose rule. Ironically, protest against its abolition has come from Asian women who have used the rule as a protection against the entry of unwanted husbands and would-be husbands.[73]

Under Rule 284 a person holding an entry clearance will initially be admitted for up to 12 months. The applicant must satisfy the officer of the following: the marriage satisfies the requirements that its main purpose is not simply to settle in the UK; the parties intend to live permanently together as man and wife. Establishing the above will often prove a heavy burden to discharge; in *Immigration Appeal Tribunal ex parte Hoque*[74] Slade LJ explained that the fact that parties do intend to live permanently together as man and wife might nevertheless be compatible with a finding that the primary purpose was to obtain admission.

Under Rules 297–303 children may be admitted if they hold an entry clearance (which will be refused if they may be a burden on public funds) and if both parents are settled or on the same occasion admitted for settlement in the UK. Children of single parent families can be admitted only if the other parent is dead or, it seems, deserted the family at the child's birth and the remaining parent is settled or on the same occasion is admitted for settlement.[75] If children are refused entry because their relationship with their sponsors is doubted, subsequent proof supporting the relationship claimed (such as DNA tests) will not be admissible as fresh evidence; if it was, the earlier decisions to refuse clearance could be quashed.[76]

Parents and grandparents of persons settled in the UK may also be admitted[77] but under stringently regulated circumstances: entrants must be at least mainly dependent upon children in the UK and must have no close relatives in their own country to whom they could instead turn. Widowed

---

73 Methods of using the rule as such a protection included using self-injury as a silent means of drawing the attention of Immigration Tribunals to their wish to avoid the marriage.
74 [1988] Imm AR 216, CA.
75 Rule 298 of the 1994 Rules.
76 *Uddin, Rahim, Ejaz Sattar v Secretary of State for Home Affairs* [1991] Imm AR 587, CA.
77 Rule 317.

fathers, mothers or grandparents must be over 65 before they may be granted settlement unless exceptional compassionate circumstances apply and they are mainly dependent on relatives in the UK.[78] The necessary dependency need not relate only to a home and financial support[79] according to *Immigration Appeal Tribunal, ex parte Singh*;[80] it was also recognised that there were other needs arising out of loneliness and isolation.[81]

A person coming in for employment must generally have a work permit under Rule 128 but an exception to this rule is created by Rule 186: if a person has an ancestral connection with the UK (a grandparent born there) he or she will be permitted to enter without any particular job to go to. This rule will tend to favour entrants from the 'old commonwealth countries': in other words, white entrants. Work permits are issued by the Department of Employment and the rules for their issue are laid down in internal policy documents. They will be issued to people with particular qualifications or skills and in relation to a particular job where there is no one suitable for it in the UK or EC countries. Thus the operation of Rule 128 is carried on at a low level of visibility, especially as there is no right of appeal in relation to work permits. Under Rules 194–99 of the 1994 Rules the spouse and dependents of someone coming in under Rules 128–93 can also be admitted so long as they will not be a charge on public funds. A further category of persons who enter temporarily but may be permitted to remain permanently in the UK encompasses those who have not less than £200,000 which they intend to invest in a business in the UK,[82] and those who have not less than £1 million of which they intend to invest not less than £750,000 in the UK.[83]

Under s 13 of the 1971 Act as amended by the Immigration Act 1988, appeals against refusals of entry, refusals of certificates of entitlement and entry clearances are possible to an adjudicator.[84] The right of appeal was, however, removed from short term students and visitors by the Asylum and Immigration Appeals Act 1993 which inserted s 13(3A) into the 1971 Act. Subsection 3B removed rights of appeal from those bound to be refused entry clearance. This means that where the basis on which such refusal would have

---

78 Rule 317(e).
79 This limited the ambit of *Immigration Appeal Tribunal ex parte Bastiampillai* [1983] 2 All ER 844.
80 [1973] 3 All ER 690.
81 Examples given in *Singh* include 'the need for some close relative to turn to and who will be willing and able to cope, in the event of accident or sudden emergency to the elderly parent; it is difficult to imagine anything more worrying to a loving child settled here than the fear of an accident to a parent thousands of miles away with no-one to cope'.
82 Rule 201.
83 Rule 224.
84 For criticism of this procedure see Harlow, C and Rawlings, R, *Law and Administration*, 1984, Chaps 16 and 17; Feldman, *Civil Liberties*, pp 337–39. For criticism of the limitations on the right of appeal see Juss, S, 'What is happening to the right of appeal in immigration law?' (1992) 12 *LS* 304.

been given is not factually established, although an entry clearance officer mistakenly forms the contrary view, no right of appeal is available. Any decision of an adjudicator or the IAT is challengeable in the High Court by way of judicial review if it is not in accordance with the Immigration Rules or was arrived at on the basis of an incorrect interpretation of the Rules.[85] However, in deciding whether or not to grant leave to apply for judicial review the High Court will take account of the availability to the applicant of 'alternative remedies', such as a right of appeal. The exercise of the right of appeal will normally be dependent on leaving the UK. This means that the applicant may be caught in a hopeless situation; if he does not exercise the right of appeal because he does not want to leave the UK but instead applies for judicial review, he may be refused leave due to the existence of a right which is valueless to him due to the constraint attached.[86] However, in *Chief Immigration Officer, Gatwick Airport ex parte Kharrazi*[87] it was accepted that where the right of appeal was rendered pointless by the conditions attached to it by the state in which it would have to be heard, judicial review would be available.

Asylum[88]

The UK accepts certain international treaty obligations in respect of asylum seekers under the United Nations Convention Relating to the Status of Refugees 1951, as amended by the 1967 Protocol relating to the Status of Refugees. These are reflected in the 1994 Immigration Rules (Rules 327–52) and given statutory force under s 1 of the Asylum and Immigration Appeals Act 1993, as regards appeals, although neither the Treaty nor the Protocol have been enacted directly into UK law. Under the Convention Article 1A(2) asylum should not be refused if the only country to which the person could be removed is one to which he is unwilling to go owing to a well-founded fear of being persecuted for reasons of race, religion, nationality, membership of a particular social group or political opinion. A duty to grant asylum is not directly imposed but if no safe alternative destination can be found for the asylum seeker the country in question will have to grant asylum. The grant of

---

85 See *Chief Immigration Officer, Gatwick Airport ex parte Kharrazi* [1980] 3 All ER 373; [1980] 1 WLR 1396, CA.
86 See eg *Secretary of State for Home Affairs ex parte Swati* [1986] 1 All ER 717, CA.
87 [1980] 3 All ER 373; [1980] 1 WLR 1396, CA.
88 See generally Burgess, D (1991) 141 *NLJ* 50; Bhaba, J, 'Deterring Refugees' (1992) *Imm and Nat LP* 133; Stanley, A, 'The legal status of international zones: the British experience with particular reference to asylum seekers' (1992) *Imm and Nat LP* 126; with reference to EU migration control: Grant, S, 143 *NLJ* 608; Bernstein, M, 'Political asylum' 142 *NLJ* 1097; on the 1993 Act Munir, E, 143 *NLJ* 1149 and Chowdhury, 144 *NLJ* 207; *The Detention and Imprisonment of Asylum Seekers in the UK*, Amnesty International British Section, 1996; Goodwin-Gill, GS, 'Who to Protect ... How and the Future' (1997) *Int Journal of Refugee Law* 9(1) 1.

asylum is governed by Rule 334 of the Immigration Rules 1994 which provides that asylum will be granted if the Secretary of State is satisfied that: the applicant is in the UK; he is a refugee as defined in the Convention; 'refusing his application would result in his being required to go in breach of the Convention and Protocol to a country in which his life or freedom would be threatened on account of his race, religion, nationality, political opinion or membership of a particular social group'. It would appear that Rule 334 goes further than the Convention in requiring a threat to life or freedom. These appear to be more stringent requirements than those denoted by a well-founded fear of persecution due to membership of a particular social group.

The Treaty and Protocol are concerned only with *political* asylum seekers and this is reflected in the ambit of Rule 334, so that those fleeing from natural disasters or economic crises are not covered. Sometimes it may be hard to make this distinction when persons leave a country which is in the middle of a civil war. The applicant must belong to a group which is likely to be persecuted and this will include a 'social group'. The meaning of this term of Rule 75 (now Rule 334) was considered in *Secretary of State for Home Affairs, ex parte Binbasi*:[89] it was held to mean that a group of persons could be identified as sharing fundamental unchangeable characteristics or as sharing characteristics to which they had an overriding moral commitment on religious or other grounds.[90]

An asylum seeker may well enter the country without a valid passport or without other documents establishing his or her identity or nationality. However, the House of Lords has ruled that such a person cannot be treated as an illegal entrant under the 1971 Act.[91] If a person seeks asylum the case must be referred by the immigration officer to the Home Office for decision even though it appears that the claim is unjustified. The Home Office will consider the case in accordance with the provisions of the Convention and Protocol relating to the Status of Refugees and the claimant will not be removed until such consideration is completed. However, it will be irrelevant that an applicant may have a genuine case for refugee status if the 'third country' rule applies. This rule is now enshrined in Rule 354 of the 1994 Rules. If an applicant has had an opportunity to seek asylum in a safe third country en route to the UK he or she will be sent back to that country to seek asylum there. If this appears to be the case the Secretary of State need not give substantive consideration to the claim and need not contact the authorities in the third country in order to make a judgment as to the likely response to the asylum seeker's application. This can mean that where a plane has simply touched down briefly in a third country the asylum seeker will be returned to

---

89 [1989] Imm AR 595.
90 For discussion of the meaning of this term as applied to homosexuals see Bamforth, N [1995] *PL* 382.
91 *Nailie and Kanesarajah* [1993] AC 674; [1993] 2 WLR 927, HL.

that country. It may also mean that he or she may be returned to a country which can only doubtfully be regarded as safe and which may return the asylum seeker to the original country, as occurred in *Bugdaycay*, below.[92]

In making a decision the Home Secretary may take into account guidance given by the advisory Executive Committee to the High Commissioner for Refugees as to the interpretation of the Treaty and Protocol.[93] If an interpretation of the Immigration Rules is adopted which does not conform with the Convention the decision may be quashed for 'illegality' or 'irrationality' as occurred in *Bugdaycay v Secretary of State for Home Affairs*.[94] The applicant was a Ugandan refugee whose father and cousins had been killed by the secret police and who therefore feared for his life if he should return to Uganda. He had lived in Kenya and the Home Secretary in rejecting his claim for asylum determined to deport him there regardless of the fact that Kenya had been known to return such refugees to Uganda. The House of Lords found that when the Immigration Rules were interpreted in accordance with Article 33 of the Convention it was found that the decision to deport him would contravene it because although deportation to Kenya would not directly threaten his life, it might lead to such a threat due to the probability that Kenya would deport him. However, the Court of Appeal in *Munongo v Secretary of State for Home Affairs*[95] confirmed that the courts would not interfere with the Home Secretary's decision as long as he had followed the correct procedure and his decision was not *Wednesbury* unreasonable – tainted by illegality or irrationality. They would not therefore question the basic credibility of the Home Secretary's decision as long as there was some evidence to support his findings. The arbitrariness of an executive decision in respect of asylum seekers will be irrelevant to its reasonableness according to the High Court in *Special Adjudicator ex parte Kandasamy*.[96] The applicant, a Tamil, left Sri Lanka, travelled to Sweden and from there to the UK with the intention of claiming asylum in Canada. He and another person in the same circumstances, S, were detained in the UK and then claimed political asylum. Substantive consideration of their applications was refused but then S's application was substantively considered. The applicant sought judicial review of the decision of the Special Adjudicator to refuse substantive consideration of his application on the ground that the adjudicator's findings were perverse in failing to acknowledge the fact that the situations of S and the applicant were identical or flawed in failing to make plain the respects in

---

92 See also *Secretary of State for Home Affairs ex parte Mehari* [1994] 2 WLR 349.
93 See *Miller v Immigration Appeal Tribunal* [1988] Imm AR 358, CA; *Bugdaycay v Secretary of State for Home Affairs* [1987] AC 514, HL; *Immigration Appeal Tribunal ex parte Yassine* [1990] Imm AR 354, QBD.
94 [1987] AC 514; [1987] 1 All ER 940.
95 [1991] Imm Ar 616, CA.
96 (1994) *The Times*, 11 March.

which they differed. The fact that an applicant had been treated differently from another in very similar circumstances was not found to provide a ground for review. Public law acknowledged no general principle of consistency. The application therefore failed.

If an asylum seeker applies for leave to move for judicial review of the decision not to grant asylum it would be expected that he or she would not be removed from the UK pending the further hearing. If he or she is so removed an injunction may be issued ordering the minister in question to return him or her to the jurisdiction of the court. If that injunction is breached the minister may be in contempt of court. The House of Lords so held in *M v Home Office*;[97] the case concerned defiance of a court order by the then Home Secretary, Kenneth Baker. Immigration officials had placed a refugee from torture in Zaire back on a plane to that country despite the order prohibiting this. In making the finding of contempt the House of Lords affirmed the fundamental constitutional principle of obedience of the executive to the law. This contempt conviction of a Cabinet minister persuaded the government to enshrine in law the principle that refugee claimants have a right to remain in the country until a decision is made on their claim (s 6 of the 1993 Act).

The term 'persecution' has been interpreted fairly restrictively as meaning 'to oppress for holding a heretical opinion or belief;[98] under this strict interpretation 'harassment' will not always be sufficient.[99] The House of Lords in *Secretary of State for Home Affairs ex parte Sivakumaran*[100] laid down the test for determining whether the fear of persecution is well-founded. Once it appears that the applicant genuinely fears persecution, the Secretary of State is required to ask himself on the basis of all the available information whether there has been demonstrated a 'real likelihood' or 'reasonable chance' of persecution.[101] The applicant has the burden of proving that there are grounds for thinking that persecution may occur. However, information may be taken into account of which he or she is unaware. Thus the fear must be based on reasonable grounds, objectively assessed. It therefore appears that the question is not whether a person in possession of the information known to the applicant would have feared persecution but whether such fear would have been felt by an objective observer in possession of *all the available information*.

The emphasis of this test differs from that put forward by the High Commissioner which involves asking whether, subjectively, a real fear of

---

97 (1993) 143 NLJ 1099; [1993] 3 All ER 537, HL; [1992] 1 All ER 75, CA; for comment on this decision see [1993] *PL* 586.
98 See *per* Nolan J in *Immigration Appeal Tribunal ex parte Jonah* [1985] Imm AR 7.
99 *Secretary of State for Home Affairs ex parte Yurekli* [1990] Imm AR 334, QBD.
100 [1988] AC 958; [1988] 1 All ER 193.
101 See Lord Diplock's judgment in *Fernandez v Government of Singapore* [1971] 2 All ER 691 at 697.

persecution is present and then considering whether it is a fear no one would reasonably hold. The test put forward by the House of Lords therefore provides less protection for refugees and moreover, the imprecise nature of expressions such as 'real likelihood' leaves considerable latitude for differences of opinion as to the severity of the risk of persecution. The House of Lords' decision in *Ex parte Sivakumaran* to uphold the Secretary of State in refusing asylum applications of the six applicant Tamils from Sri Lanka differed from that of the adjudicator who later heard the appeals of the Tamils from abroad and found that there was a sufficient risk of persecution based upon race, religion and political opinion.[102] The fact that all the available information must be considered may also of course work to the advantage of the applicant since it will mean that a court cannot disregard any piece of information: this will include what has happened in the past which should be related to any current events,[103] although the mere fact that an asylum seeker has been persecuted in the past will not raise a presumption in his favour that he is a refugee.[104] However in determining the well-foundedness of the fear, the fact that the applicant has not been singled out for persecution will not be conclusive of the issue.[105]

It may be noted that gender is not included expressly in the Convention but that women may in certain circumstances form a persecuted group. There seems to be an increasing possibility that women who are subject to barbaric practices and grossly unequal treatment due to their gender in certain countries (such as be-heading on suspicion of adultery in some Islamic countries, denial of freedom of movement or education under some fundamentalist regimes, genital mutilation in India) may be able to seek asylum on those grounds.[106] The rights of women and girls may be recognised and declared through the medium of asylum seeking in a manner which, it is suggested, gives the lie to cultural relativism. Such asylum seeking may lead to a greater recognition in the West that unequal practices in some cultures cannot be defended from a human rights perspective as forming part of a strong cultural tradition, since they merely reflect long-standing male dominance in the particular culture.

If the test as to persecution is satisfied and if, as in *Bugdaycay*, the refugee cannot be returned to another safe country, he or she can settle in the UK but the United Nations Convention requires under Article 2 that measures

---

102 *Immigration Appeal Tribunal, ex parte Secretary of State for Home Affairs* [1990] 3 All ER 652, CA; for comment see Blake, N (1989) *Imm and Nat LP* Vol 4 No 1, p 7; Burgess, D (1991) 141 NJL 50.
103 *Secretary of State for Home Affairs, ex parte P* [1992] COD 295.
104 *Secretary of State for Home Affairs, ex parte Direk* [1992] Imm AR 330.
105 *Secretary of State for Home Affairs, ex parte Gulbache* [1991] Imm AR 526.
106 See, for example, *IAT, ex parte Shah* (1996) *The Times*, 12 November.

relating to public order must be observed. If they are not observed the refugee can be removed but not back to the country he or she originally fled from or any other where persecution would be likely to arise.[107]

If leave to enter was refused to a claimant to refugee status he used to be in the same position as other persons seeking entry: under s 13 of the 1971 Act he had no right of appeal while in the UK. The Asylum and Immigration Appeals Act 1993, however, provides for the first time a statutory right of appeal in limited circumstances to a Special Adjudicator under s 8. This is balanced, however, by a short cut procedure for claims for asylum which the Home Secretary considers to be without foundation. Under the fast track procedure many asylum applicants have to submit their appeal against refusal of refugee status within 48 hours and it will be heard and decided within seven days. Those who arrive from countries officially designated as ones from which asylum applications will be presumed to be unfounded (countries on the official so-called 'white list')[108] will also be dealt with by this procedure, which may mean that their personal circumstances, which do place them in danger, are not considered. The Asylum and Immigration Act 1996 extends the fast track method; the procedure to be followed is laid down in the Asylum Appeals Procedure Rules 1996.[109] Sections 2 and 3 of the 1996 Act remove the 'in country' right of appeal in third country cases. Section 1(2) places the notion of the white list on a statutory basis, although the designated countries are set out in the Asylum (Designated Countries of Destination and Designated Safe Countries) Order 1996.[110]

In determining that a country may be seen as safe the courts may allow the Home Secretary a wide discretion. In *Secretary of State for Home Affairs, ex parte Canbolat*[111] it was found that the Home Secretary was entitled to decide that France was a safe third country, despite evidence to the contrary. The Special Adjudicator had considered that France was not a safe country. However, it was found that the Home Secretary was entitled to form a contrary opinion which could not be challenged on its merits. In *Secretary of State for Home Affairs ex parte Abdi; Secretary of State for Home Affairs, ex parte Gawe*[112] the applicants appealed to the Special Adjudicator regarding certificates issued by the Home Secretary to the effect that their claim to asylum was without foundation. The applicants, Somalian nationals, had flown to Spain; they had not claimed asylum there but had claimed it in the UK. The Home Secretary considered that there was no reason to believe that Spain would not comply

---

107 Immigration Rule 173.
108 For the countries designated by Michael Howard, the then Home Secretary, as safe for white list purposes see *Hansard,* HC, Vol 268 Col 703.
109 SI 1996/2070.
110 SI 1996/2671.
111 (1997) *The Times,* 24 February.
112 (1996) *The Times,* 17 February.

with its obligations under the Convention. It was found that the Home Secretary was not obliged to reveal all the material on which he had based the 'without foundation' certificates. Further, the Home Secretary's letters of decision alone were sufficient as a basis on which the Adjudicator could uphold the decision. This decision in particular affords judicial review a very narrow role in rendering the Home Secretary accountable for decisions regarding the safety of third countries. Similar leeway was also allowed to the Home Secretary in *Secretary of State for Home Affairs, ex parte Chahal*.[113]

Commentators tend to agree that the Conservative governments of 1989 to 1997, especially the Major government, demonstrated an illiberal and mean-minded attitude towards asylum seekers.[114] The lengths to which the government was prepared to go were demonstrated in 1996. The Social Security (Persons from Abroad) Miscellaneous Amendment Regulations 1996 SI 1996/30 removed all entitlement to income-related benefit from asylum-seekers who failed to claim asylum immediately upon arrival in the UK and from those who were pursuing appeals. Thus some genuine asylum seekers were faced with the choice of staying in the UK awaiting determination of their claims while homeless and destitute or abandoning their claims and returning to face persecution. In *Secretary of State for Social Security, ex parte Joint Council for the Welfare of Immigrants; Secretary of State for Social Security, ex parte B*[115] the applicants sought judicial review of the regulations on the ground that they were *ultra vires* the Asylum and Immigration Appeals Act 1993, the enabling Act, since, *inter alia*, they created interference with the exercise of rights under the Act. The Court of Appeal found that the *Leech* principle was of assistance to the applicants. *Secretary of State for Home Affairs, ex parte Leech (No 2)*[116] concerned the right of prison governors to open and read letters to a solicitor and a right exercisable on grounds of prolixity or objectionability to stop them (Rule 33(3)) unless a writ had already been issued. The opening and reading of such letters was challenged by way of judicial review. The Court of Appeal found that it was a principle of great importance that every citizen had an unimpeded right of access to a court and that this was buttressed by the principle of legal professional privilege. A common law privilege of this nature could openly be taken away by subordinate legislation only where that was expressly authorised by the enabling legislation (s 47 of the Prison Act 1952). Section 47 might authorise some screening of correspondence but it must be strictly construed in accordance with the presumption against statutory interference with common law rights. The court found that the instant case involved taking the *Leech*

---

113 (1993) *The Times*, 12 March.
114 See, for example Robertson, G, *Freedom, the Individual and the Law*, 1993, at p 407.
115 [1996] 4 All ER 385; (1996) 146 *NLJ* 985. For comment see Harvey, CJ [1997] *PL* 394. See also *The Royal Borough of Kensington and Chelsea, ex parte Kihara* (1996) *The Times*, 10 July.
116 [1993] 4 All ER 539.

principle a step further. *Leech* had concerned a direct interference with basic rights. The instant case concerned an indirect interference with such rights. However, the Court of Appeal considered that the step in question should be taken. Simon-Brown LJ found that the rights conferred on asylum-seekers under the 1993 Act would be rendered nugatory for some of them due to the impact of the 1996 Regulations. The only alternative would be for them to experience a destitution which no civilised nation could tolerate. Lord Justice Simon-Brown said: 'Parliament cannot have intended a significant number of genuine asylum seekers to be impaled on the horns of so intolerable a dilemma: the need either to abandon their claims to refugee status or to maintain them as best they can but in a state of utter destitution.' On these grounds the 'uncompromisingly draconian' regulations were held to be *ultra vires*.

The Social Security Secretary Peter Lilley then decided to reverse the decision of the Court of Appeal by means of primary legislation. An amendment to the Asylum and Immigration Bill 1996 was therefore rushed through Parliament. When the 1996 Act came into force many asylum seekers were placed in the situation described by Simon-Brown LJ as one which 'no civilised nation can tolerate' (under s 11 and Schedule 1 of the 1996 Act). The asylum seekers in question were helped by voluntary and church groups but such groups were placed under a great strain as a direct result of the government policy. It became hard, if not impossible, for many asylum seekers to pursue the legal right to claim asylum. However, the asylum seekers' lawyers discovered that the National Assistance Act 1948 obliges local authorities to provide temporary accommodation for those in need. Obviously the doctrine of implied repeal would have been expected to mean that the 1948 Act was repealed to the extent of its inconsistency with the 1996 Act. It was very difficult to argue with credibility that the Conservative dominated Parliament had not intended that asylum seekers should be rendered destitute under the terms of the 1996 Act since that was clearly what it had intended. Nevertheless, when the issue was considered in the High Court (*Hammersmith and Fulham LBC, ex parte M*),[117] Mr Justice Collins found 'it was impossible to believe that an asylum seeker who was lawfully here and could not lawfully be removed from the country should be left destitute, starving and at grave risk of illness and even death'. This judgment was upheld on appeal in February 1997 by a court headed by the Master of the Rolls, Lord Woolf.[118] Thus at present withdrawal of accommodation is no longer used to deter asylum seekers and encourage them to abandon their claims.

---

117 (1996) *The Times*, 10 October.
118 *Hammersmith and Fulham LBC, ex parte M* (1997) *The Times*, 19 February.

Nevertheless, the system is still very heavily weighted against a successful claim by means of the application of the third country rule, the use of the white list, the conditions and length of detention awaiting resolution of the claim[119] and the limitations placed on rights of appeal. Amnesty International estimates that only about six in every 100 applications to the UK are successful. The current Labour government has said that it will uphold Britain's obligations under international law and will make a fresh start with asylum policy. It remains to be seen how far it will be prepared to dismantle some of the more draconian asylum rules. In 1995 Jack Straw called the introduction of the white list 'the most crude playing of the race card I have ever seen and we are going to resist it. We will have no truck with the crude racist legislation which Mr Howard is proposing'.[120]

The Labour government will in any event need to reconsider the rules relating to non-substantive consideration of the asylum seekers' case after the ruling of the European Court of Human Rights in *Chahal v UK* (below). If it fails to implement that ruling asylum seekers will inevitably challenge the Rules in question in the UK courts after incorporation of the Convention. Reform may also be imposed upon the UK due to changes in EU policy on asylum seekers. In June 1997 a proposed revision to the Treaty of Rome was considered at the Amsterdam summit meeting and included in the Treaty of Amsterdam. It would allow the European Commission to make proposals for harmonisation of asylum policy which would require only qualified majority voting rather than unanimity. The revision is intended to address the lack of uniformity in EU policy on asylum. Some areas are governed by EU standards but others are the preserve of the individual states. This leaves some areas uncoordinated, including the length of time an asylum seeker might wait in order to hear whether a third country – the one in which he or she should have claimed asylum – will take him or her back. Minimum standards for the reception of asylum seekers are also left to be determined by the individual countries as are the procedures for dealing with the applications. Harmonisation of policy in the EU may lead to improved standards in relation to some aspects of asylum seeking, although previous harmonisation has probably lead to a general lowering of standards. For example, the British rule that asylum must be sought in the first 'safe' country of arrival is now part of EU policy. It may be noted that as part of the proposed reforms Spain wishes to amend the EU Treaty so that nationals from one EU country cannot seek asylum in another EU country. However, such an amendment would override the 1951 Convention and would fail to take account of possible future human rights abuses in EU countries.

---

119 See *The Detention and Imprisonment of Asylum Seekers in the UK*, Amnesty International British Section, 1996.
120 BBC Radio 4 Today programme, 26 October 1995.

6 ILLEGAL ENTRANTS

An illegal entrant can be detained and removed under the powers contained in s 4(2) and Schedule 2 paras 9 and 16(2) of the 1971 Act. Such persons may also be arrested without warrant under the 1971 Act, Schedule 2 para 17 by immigration officers and constables and constables may obtain a search warrant to search named premises on reasonable suspicion of finding such persons. A person will be an illegal entrant if he has entered in breach of a deportation order or the immigration laws. Under ss 13(3) and 15(4) of the 1971 Act a person who is removed under these provisions can only appeal first to the adjudicator and then to the Immigration tribunal after he or she has been removed from the country. Thus a person removed as an illegal entrant is in a much worse position than one who is under threat of deportation due to overstaying or failure to observe conditions as to remaining, who need not leave before appealing.

A person who has entered by deception will be termed an illegal entrant and deception has been interpreted very widely by the Home Office to include anyone who has failed to disclose a material fact even where the person did not realise that non-disclosure was material, if a reasonable person would have realised its materiality.[121] The courts have upheld a positive duty to disclose information known to be material to the immigration officer's decision but have been less ready to extend this principle to entrants who failed to disclose material information but who did not appreciate that the information was material to the entry decision.[122] This would have placed a very burdensome duty of disclosure on the entrant but since the ruling in *Secretary of State for Home Affairs, ex parte Khera; ex parte Khawaja*[123] it seems that the duty only extends to the making of statements known or thought to be false. The failure to make statements will not constitute deception unless non-disclosure will render misleading that which has been disclosed. Thus the duty of disclosure has been curtailed; where it exists as a positive duty aside from the duty to answer questions it is clear from the rulings in *Ex parte Khawaja* that it will be necessary for the entrant to appreciate the materiality of the disclosure.

It does not matter that the entrant may not have realised the significance of the deception[124] which in fact enabled his entry. Further, once the deception is established it is immaterial that the entrant might in fact have been able to gain entry had he told the truth and applied for entry under another

---

121 See Evans, JM, *Immigration Law*, 2nd edn, 1983, at p 323 at note 37.
122 *Zamir* [1980] AC 930 at 940.
123 [1984] AC 74; [1983] 1 All ER 765; [1983] 2 WLR 321; [1982] Imm AR 139, HL.
124 *Secretary of State for Home Affairs, ex parte Adesina* [1988] Imm AR 288, QBD.

ground.[125] Even if an entrant did not realise that the deception which took place would assist him in securing entry he might still be found to be an illegal entrant.

The grounds of appeal against removal are extremely limited: so long as the power to remove the entrant exists the exercise of discretion in enforcing it cannot be challenged. It was noted in *Secretary of State for Home Affairs, ex parte Khawaja* that only one appeal against removal under s 16 of the 1971 Act had ever succeeded. The only method of proceeding which may be of real value to the applicant may be by way of judicial review which since the decision in *Khawaja* can include consideration whether on the balance of probabilities (albeit probability of a high degree) fraud has been made out.[126] Before that ruling, since the decision in *Zamir*, the authorities would only review a decision of an immigration officer that a person should be removed as an illegal entrant on the ground that no evidence at all existed on which that conclusion could be based. In *Khawaja* Lord Bridge, in a robust and determined condemnation of the claim that the citizen could be imprisoned without trial prior to removal from the country, ruled that only where an immigration officer could prove on the balance of probabilities that a person had practised fraud in order to enter the country could such detention and expulsion be justified. If such proof was not forthcoming the decision could be quashed since the person could not be termed 'an illegal entrant' and therefore no power to remove him or her could exist. This interpretation of the term represented a very significant departure from the previous meaning and arose from his determination to construe the 1971 Act strictly against the government where the rights of the citizen were in question. The decision joins a number of decisions taken in judicial review proceedings including some on prisoners' rights[127] which have acted as a substitute (although necessarily an inadequate one) for safeguards under a Bill of Rights.

7 DEPORTATION

Deportation represents the clearest infringement of freedom of movement and therefore should be used only where there is clear justification and where there are mechanisms allowing careful scrutiny of the decision to deport.[128] Broadly speaking, a person who is not a British citizen is liable to deportation under s 3(5) of the 1971 Act as amended, on three grounds: he does not

---

125 See *Secretary of State for Home Affairs, ex parte Bugdaycay* [1986] 1 All ER 458 at 464–65, CA; *Secretary of State for Home Affairs, ex parte Snichon Chomsuk* [1991] Imm AR 29, 32, QBD.
126 See *Ali v Secretary of State for Home Affairs* [1984] 1 All ER 1009.
127 For example, *Leech v Deputy Governor of Parkhurst Prison* [1988] AC 533, HL.
128 For criticism of the procedure see Zellick, G [1973] *Crim LR* 612; Robertson, G, *Freedom, the Individual and the Law*, pp 322–28.

observe a condition attached to a limited leave to enter or remain or stays beyond the time limited by the leave; the Secretary of State deems his deportation to be conducive to the public good; or a court recommends deportation after his conviction for a criminal offence. A person may also be deported on other than personal grounds if he or she belongs to a family of which the wife or husband is deported. This rule arises under s 5(4) and is overtly discriminatory in that a wife will normally be deported with her husband whereas a husband may remain when his wife is deported. The wife will not be automatically deported with the husband: Rules 365 and 367 of the 1994 Rules provide that various circumstances should be taken into account including her own wishes and her ability to maintain herself, without charge on the public funds for the foreseeable future. A wife will not normally be deported with the husband under Rule 365 of the 1994 Rules where she qualifies for settlement in her own right or where she is living apart from the husband. However, the bland assumption that all husbands, whatever their actual circumstances, should be treated differently from all wives is unjustifiable.

In considering the merits of the decision to deport, Rule 364 provides guidance as to the factors to be taken into account:

> ... the public interest will be balanced against any compassionate circumstances of the case. While each case will be considered in the light of the particular circumstances, the aim is an exercise of the power of deportation which is consistent and fair as between one person and another, although one case will rarely be identical with another in all material respects ...

Deportation after conviction

Deportation due to conviction of a criminal offence is fairly readily resorted to but as the Court of Appeal held in *Nazari*,[129] it should not be undertaken without full inquiry into all the circumstances. It should not be done, as has sometimes happened in the past, '... as if by an afterthought at the end of observations about any sentence of imprisonment'. A number of factors were identified which a court might bear in mind when considering deportation: the long criminal record of the accused; the seriousness of the offence bearing in mind the circumstances surrounding it, not merely its nature;[130] the effect that an order recommending deportation will have on others who are not before the court and who are innocent persons, in terms of hardship and breaking up of families. The court should not however take into account the nature of the regime to which the deportee will return.

---

129 [1980] 3 All ER 880, CA.
130 See Sachs LJ in *Caird* (1970) 54 Cr App R 499 at 510.

An important circumstance will be the likelihood of the repetition of the offence; where this factor is present it may aggravate an otherwise trivial offence; where it is absent it may have a mitigating effect on a serious offence.[131] This seems to have been accepted in *Serry*:[132] one offence of shoplifting did not support deportation, presumably because there were no particular aggravating circumstances.

Deportation for the public good

This head of deportation, which is probably the most contentious in civil liberties terms, can cover a number of factors but it seems reasonably clear that the decision to deport should be based on all the circumstances relevant to the particular evil in question and the consequences flowing from the deportation. Thus in *Immigration Appeal Tribunal, ex parte (Mahmud) Khan*[133] the applicant successfully challenged the IAT's dismissal of his appeal against deportation, on the ground that the tribunal's reasons for its decision – that he had entered into a marriage of convenience – failed to show that it had properly considered whether the couple did intend to live as man and wife. In other words, grounds which might raise an inference that the marriage was merely one of convenience were not examined to see whether this was actually the case.[134] Similarly, it is not enough to show that a person has behaved in an anti-social manner in the past; it must be considered whether future-wrong doing is likely.[135] In considering circumstances flowing from the deportation it would appear that detriment flowing from it to the public or part of the public as well as good may be considered: the two may be balanced against each other. Thus in *Singh v Immigration Appeal Tribunal*[136] the House of Lords held that the immigration adjudicatory authorities ought to have taken into account the detrimental effect on the Sikh community in the UK which deportation of the applicant would have. The applicant was a valued member of that community by virtue of his religious, charitable and cultural activities.

The 'conducive to public good' ground for deportation can be used where a person is convicted of an offence but the court does not recommend deportation and also, most controversially, against individuals who have engaged in some form of undesirable political activity.[137] The use of this

---

131 See *Tshuma* (1981) 3 Cr App R (S) 97.
132 (1980) 2 Cr App R (S) 336.
133 [1983] QB 790.
134 The ruling in *Immigration Appeal Tribunal, ex parte Ghazi Zubalir Ali Khan* [1983] Imm AR 32 was reached on similar grounds.
135 *Malik v Secretary of State for Home Affairs* [1981] Imm AR 134; *Immigration Appeal Tribunal, ex parte Ullah* (1983) *The Times*, 14 January.
136 [1986] 2 All ER 721, HL.
137 See *Martinez-Tobon v Immigration Appeal Tribunal* [1988] Imm AR 319, CA.

power to exclude people on political rather than criminal grounds has attracted most criticism. For example, the student activist Rudi Deutschke was deported back to West Germany in 1969, on the basis that he might 'become a focus for student unrest'.[138] Similarly the journalists, Agee and Hosenball, were deported on national security grounds, Agee presumably due to the damage he might have done to the CIA in writing books exposing certain of their activities.[139] It was unclear, however, that damage to the public good would be averted by the deportation. Similarly, rather flimsy grounds were relied on in deciding to deport a number of Iraqi or Kuwaiti residents during the Gulf War 1991. For example, a Lebanese citizen, Cheblak, a known pacifist who had lived and worked as an academic in the UK for 15 years, had two children who were British Citizens and who had campaigned for an Iraqi withdrawal from Kuwait, was ordered to be deported on national security grounds. Cheblak sought leave to apply for judicial review of the Home Secretary's decision, partly on the basis that it was irrational or that all relevant circumstances had not been taken into account. The Court of Appeal, however, preferred not to make any inquiry into these possibilities on the basis that national security matters are the sole preserve of the executive.[140] Ultimately Cheblak was not deported after his case was considered by the advisory panel set up to replace a statutory right of appeal. However, 14 persons were deported and of these it is not known whether the panel advised revocation of the order or whether the grounds on which it was ordered were as doubtful on the face of it as those which applied in *Cheblak's* case.

The purpose of deportation on this ground should be clear: that removal of the deportee is necessary for the public good and that even if this is not the only purpose it should be the dominant one.[141] However, in a number of rulings courts have not applied a 'dominant purpose' test in considering the relevance of other purposes which may have influenced the Secretary of State's decision to deport. In *Brixton Prison Governor ex parte Soblen*,[142] a deportation order was challenged on the grounds that the Secretary of State had allegedly acted for an improper purpose – in order to comply with a request from the United States for S's return made in order to circumvent the non-availability of extradition proceedings which were not possible due to the nature of S's offences. The Court of Appeal upheld the deportation order on the basis that the Secretary of State could act for a plurality of purposes. The fact that this might be termed extradition by the back door did not affect the validity of the order. The court considered that the need to serve the public

---

138 For discussion see Hepple, B (1971) 45 *MLR* 501.
139 See *Secretary of State for Home Affairs, ex parte Hosenball* [1977] 1 WLR 766; [1977] 3 All ER 452, CA.
140 *Secretary of State for Home Affairs, ex parte Cheblak* [1991] 1 WLR 890. See below p 543. For discussion see [1991] *PL* 333.
141 See in another context *Westminster Corporation v London and North Western Rly Co* [1905] AC 426.
142 [1963] 2 QB 243.

good by the removal of S need not be the dominant motive in making the order although the minister must have a genuine belief that removal was necessary on that basis. It did not matter if the minister's main motive for acting might have been to comply with the request from the USA.

The danger in this approach is clearly that the individual circumstances of the person in question may become much less significant than the political expediency of falling in with the wishes of particular governments. However, there are signs that this approach may not be sustained. In subsequent cases it has been accepted that there may be a 'plurality of purposes' but that it should be shown that the same decision would have been reached even in the absence of consideration of the 'improper' purpose.[143]

If the decision to deport has been taken for reasons of 'public good', on grounds of 'national security', 'diplomatic relations' or for 'reasons of a political nature' the ordinary right of appeal is excluded unless the deportee is an asylum seeker, in which case Schedule 2 para 2(a) of the Asylum and Immigration Appeals appears to afford him or her the right to appeal to a special adjudicator. Similarly, a person refused entry on grounds of public good (without anything more specific as to reason) has no right of appeal (ss 15(3)(4)(5), 14(3)). In such cases, as mentioned above, there is a right to an *ex gratia* hearing before the Three Advisers. The procedure was described by the then Home Secretary as follows:

> The person concerned ... will be given ... such particulars of allegations as will not entail disclosure of sources of evidence. He will be notified that he can make representations to the three advisers ... The advisers will ... allow him to appear before them, if he wishes ... As well as speaking for himself he may arrange for a third party to testify on his behalf. Neither the sources of evidence nor evidence that might lead to disclosure of sources can be revealed to the person concerned but the advisers will ensure that the person is able to make his points effectively ... Since the evidence against a person necessarily has to be received in his absence, the advisers in assessing the case will bear in mind that it has not been tested by cross-examination and that the person has not had the opportunity to rebut it ... On receiving the advice of the advisers the Secretary of State will reconsider his original decision but the advice given to him will not be revealed.[144]

Thus a person may be deported after a hearing in which he is unable to challenge the case against him, in which evidence which he is unable to contest is given in his absence and in which he cannot call witnesses or have legal representation. He will not be informed of the decision taken by the Advisers, will not know whether it was complied with or why it was not complied with and cannot appeal from it. Mark Hosenball challenged this

---

143 See *Inner London Education Authority, ex parte Westminster City Council* [1986] 1 All ER 19; *Broadcasting Complaints Commission, ex parte Owen* [1985] QB 1153; and *Lewisham London Borough Council, ex parte Shell UK Ltd* [1988] 1 All ER 938.

144 819 *HC Deb*, Written Answer, 15 June 1971, Col 376.

procedure in respect of the decision to deport him on grounds of national security (see *Secretary of State for Home Affairs, ex parte Hosenball* above) on the basis that it did not comply with the principles of natural justice since he had not been given adequate particulars of the allegations against him. The Court of Appeal, while acknowledging that the principles of natural justice would normally require that such particulars would be given, said that in cases where national security is involved, 'the rights of the individual (including his entitlement to natural justice) must be subordinated to the protection of the realm' (*per* Geoffrey Lane LJ). Lord Denning considered that in such cases it was not the proper role of the courts to attempt to determine the proper balance between the requirements of national security and the claims of the individual; this role fell correctly within the ambit of the Home Secretary's responsibilities. Similarly, in *Ex parte Cheblak*[145] the applicant complained that the reasons given for the decision that his deportation would be for the public good were wholly insufficient to enable him to challenge the order. Lord Donaldson MR referred to Geoffrey Lane LJ's comments in *Secretary of State for Home Affairs, ex parte Hosenball* and said:

> In accepting, as we must, that to some extent the needs of national security must displace civil liberties ... it is not irrelevant to remember that the maintenance of national security underpins and is the foundation of all our civil liberties.[146]

He used the analogy of a person who is detained pending trial and then found innocent. However, he did not address the flaw in the analogy: there must be reasonable suspicion that the person remanded in custody has committed the offence, whereas in the case of the deportee there may be a very insufficient objective basis for determining that deportation is in the public good. Nevertheless, no check exists which can prevent the deportation if the Home Secretary's personal decision is that it should be carried out. Thus, civil liberties may be severely infringed in a manner arguably unwarranted by the needs of national security.

This was eventually found to be the case by the European Court of Human Rights in *Chahal v UK*.[147] Originally an illegal immigrant, Mr Chahal obtained leave to remain in Britain indefinitely in 1974. In 1984 he visited the Punjab for a family wedding and met the chief advocate of creating an independent Sikh state to be carved out of India. Later he was arrested by the Indian police and allegedly tortured. He escaped from India and became the founder of the International Sikh Youth Federation in the UK. After a fight at a Sikh temple he was arrested and convicted of assault and affray but his conviction was overturned by the Court of Appeal. In 1990 he was arrested after a meeting at

---

[145] [1991] 1 WLR 890; [1991] 2 All ER, CA. See also *Secretary of State for Home Affairs, ex parte Chahal* (1993) *The Times*, 12 March.
[146] [1991] WLR 890 at p 907.
[147] (1997) 23 EHRR 413.

a Southall temple. The Home Office accused him of involvement in Sikh terrorism; the Secretary of State made a determination that deportation of the applicant would be conducive to the public good and therefore he was liable to be deported under s 3(5)(b) of the Immigration Act 1971. However the applicant claimed asylum in the UK on the basis that he was a refugee within the meaning of the Convention relating to the Status of Refugees 1951 as recognised in the Immigration Rules 1990 Rule 173. He claimed that he would be tortured if sent back to India. The Secretary of State maintained that the question whether he was a refugee was irrelevant once the decision to deport had been made. The applicant sought judicial review of the decision to deport him on the basis that his status as a refugee should have been taken into account.[148]

The main question at issue was whether a balancing exercise between the threat to the security of the UK posed by the applicant and the threat to the life or freedom of the applicant if deported to the country in question (India) should have been carried out. It was found that the combined effect of the Convention and the 1990 Rules required that it should have been. However, although the Secretary of State had not deemed such an exercise necessary, there was no evidence that it had not been carried out. The court was not able to determine whether, after carrying out such an exercise, the Secretary of State's decision could be called irrational, since while there was a great deal of evidence as to the risk to the applicant there was none as to the risk to national security in the UK which he posed. However, the court could consider whether the Secretary of State had been correct in his assessment of the risk to the applicant if returned to India. The Secretary of State had observed that under the Indian Constitution the applicant could come to harm only if convicted of a crime by due process and in accordance with the law. That still left open the possibility of informal ill treatment; nevertheless there were not considered to be sufficient grounds for finding that the Secretary of State had made an irrational or perverse decision in determining that the applicant's claim for asylum status was not made out. The application therefore failed.

Mr Chahal was then imprisoned while he pursued an application to the European Commission of Human Rights, alleging a breach of Article 3, which guarantees protection from torture and from inhuman and degrading treatment and of Article 5 which guarantees judicial control over loss of liberty. The European Court of Human Rights noted that the protection of Article 3 of the Convention is absolute (no derogations are provided or allowed) and found that there were strong grounds for believing that Mr Chahal would indeed have been tortured had he been returned to India. Thus had the order to deport been implemented a breach of Article 3 would have occurred. Article 5(1) not only provides that deprivation of liberty is only

---

148 *Secretary of State for Home Affairs, ex parte Chahal* (1993) *The Times*, 12 March.

permitted within the specified exceptions, it also requires that it should be 'in accordance with a procedure prescribed by law'. In *Winterwerp v Netherlands*[149] the court found that this meant that the procedure in question must be in accordance with national and Convention law and it must not be arbitrary. In the instant case the applicant complained, *inter alia*, that he had been detained although there had been no court hearing. The court found that a breach of Article 5 had occurred since his detention should have been subject to scrutiny in court. It had been considered by an advisory panel but that did not provide sufficient procedural safeguards to qualify as a court. Further, a breach of Article 5 read in conjunction with Article 13 had occurred since effective remedies did not exist before the courts in England.

It may be noted that other applications are following this one on the Article 3 issue. In *MAR v UK*,[150] for example, the applicant is arguing that if deported to Iran he will be likely to meet with Article 3 treatment due to his drug convictions. The application has been declared admissible. *D v UK*[151] also concerns the risk of Article 3 treatment on deportation. The European Court of Human Rights found that removing a drug courier in an advanced stage of AIDS to his country of origin, St Kitts, would expose him to Article 3 treatment there. In St Kitts much less effective treatment for AIDS is available; he would have no accommodation and no means of support. The intention had been to expel him after he had served his sentence for carrying drugs.

The judgment in *Chahal v UK* now stands in stark contrast to the executive-minded judgments in *Secretary of State for Home Affairs ex parte Hosenball*. This decision will force the government to change the procedure it applies to those seeking asylum due to fear of torture. The courts will have to be allowed to test the claims in question. As regards decisions to detain persons who are alleged to pose a risk to national security, it would appear that methods of disclosing to a court some of the material on which that claim is based will have to be put in place. Both aspects of this decision are to be welcomed as enhancing the role of the judiciary in relation to persons who are often in an extremely vulnerable position. At the same time it should be borne in mind that Mr Chahal was detained for six years in breach of Article 5 of the Convention. Thus his fundamental rights were violated for all that period of time. This decision is encouraging in view of the imminent reception of the Convention into domestic law, assuming that the English judiciary can be trusted to behave with the same independence as the Strasbourg judges. The remarks noted above in *Hosenball* do not lend much credence to such an assumption but some may be found in the much more activist stance of the judiciary in the 1990s as seen in the asylum seekers' cases considered above.

---

149 A.33; (1979) 2 EHRR 387.
150 Unreported.
151 (1997) *The Times*, 12 May.

PART FIVE

EQUALITY AND THE THEORY OF ANTI-DISCRIMINATION LAWS

One of the main themes in human rights jurisprudence concerns the duty of states to treat citizens with equal concern and respect. This does not mean that no differentiation between citizens may occur but that inequality of treatment should not be based on factors which do not justify it. Thus, discrimination may be defined as morally unjustifiable as opposed to justifiable differentiation.[1] It may be said that the latter occurs when a difference in treatment is accorded due to behaviour which is the result of voluntary choice, the former when it is based on an attribute over which the individual has no control such as sex or skin colour. Thus, in a society which allows or imposes discrimination in this sense the groups affected will be entirely frustrated in pursuing their objectives in all areas of life because the disadvantage they are under cannot be removed. These statements alone, however, are inadequate as failing to deal with behaviour which may in a sense be the result of voluntary choice but might also be said to be determined by social conditioning. Further, they do not explain whether differentiation would be justified if based on behaviour to which a person is morally committed due to her membership of a certain group. Thus it should also be argued that morally unjustifiable differentiation would also occur, at least presumptively, if different treatment was based on behaviour over which the individual had little real choice. Finally, this argument should encompass the notion that the physical attribute or behaviour in question may, exceptionally, be objectively relevant to the differential treatment and thereby could justify it.

Once factors which do not justify differentiation are identified (they would include at the 'core' gender or skin colour) the state can be said to be under a duty to ensure that unequal treatment on the basis of such factors does not occur, at least in spheres under its control. However, at different times and according to different schools of thought the *scope* of the duty varies. Under early classic liberal rights theory the state came under a duty to ensure that no formal discriminatory mechanisms were in place but once that was done it was thought that individuals would have equal freedom to exercise their talents.[2] However, this theory came to encompass the notion of state intervention in order to ensure that some individuals did not prevent others from exercising their talents. This is the dominant theory underpinning the UK legislative policy on equality: it assumes that once people have equal freedoms they will have equal opportunities and thus all that is needed is to

---

1 See Wallman, S, 'Difference, differentiation, discrimination', 5 *New Community* 1.
2 See Mill, JS, *The Subjection of Women*, 1869.

ensure such freedoms. Some egalitarians would go further, insisting that persons should be placed in a similar position, even if in order to do so they are treated unequally. Some forms of liberal thought[3] would now also support treating persons unequally in order to ensure equality of opportunity. However, broadly speaking, liberals view equality as formal, while egalitarians, including socialists or communitarians, view it as substantive. Formal equality[4] (or treating like as like) is the limitation placed upon equality legislation by liberalism; its drawback is that it puts the protection of such legislation beyond the reach of those who are differently situated.[5] If women's domestic and parental roles[6] tend to differ from those of men and those roles interfere with women's role as (cost efficient) workers, in a formal equality model which takes the male as the norm and assumes that a woman is like a man, the employer may justifiably treat women differently. If some persons from minority groups are educationally or socially disadvantaged their difference of situation cannot be addressed by means of legislation based on a formal equality model.

This argument does not imply that the imposition of formal equality has *no* impact on the distribution of social benefits. In particular, formal equality affects the market by inducing it not to act in an arbitrary and ultimately inefficient fashion. Formal equality, if fully established, disallows the individual biases of employers to feed into the market,[7] and may therefore promote genuine competition based on individual merit, thereby preventing the unwarranted under – or over – advantaging of certain groups. Perpetuation of an unequal pay policy may not seem to lead clearly and immediately to an inefficient operation of the market. If a certain group can be treated disadvantageously in terms of pay this may appear in some respects to benefit the market since the availability of cheap labour may lead to increased productivity and market expansion. Nevertheless, unequal pay may eventually distort the operation of market forces creating dysfunction in the market since certain professions and certain specialities within professions

---

3   See Raz, J, *The Morality of Freedom*, 1986; Dworkin, R, *Taking Rights Seriously*, 1976, p 272.
4   Under classic liberalism as expressed by Mill, JS, *On the Subjection of Women*, 1929.
5   Several feminist writers have pointed out that the principal limitation of the formal equality principle is that it assumes that the male is the norm. MacKinnon puts it particularly aptly, 'Why should you have to be the same as a man to get what a man gets simply because he is one?'. See MacKinnon, 'Difference and Dominance: On Sex Discrimination' in Bartlett and Kennedy, *Feminist Legal Theory*, 1991; see also MacKinnon, 'Reflections on Sex Equality Under Law' (1991) 100 *Yale Law Journal*, 1281–1328, at 1286–93.
6   Matters belonging to the 'private' sphere, in a liberal conception. Mill's view, as expressed in *On the Subjection of Women*, 1929, was that formal equality operates in certain 'public' spheres, such as franchise, employment and education.
7   This argument is put forward by Weiler in 'The Wages of Sex: The Uses and Limits of Comparable Worth' (1986) 99 *Harv L Rev* 1728, at 1762: '... real world labour markets leave a good deal of leeway for countless managerial judgments about how to classify, value and pay certain jobs in comparison to others.'

may be shunned by advantaged groups due to the low pay they offer with the result once again that genuine competition is not fostered within them.

Thus it may be argued that formal equality 'perfects' the market: rather than allowing bias to benefit certain individuals at the expense of others, it forces the market to treat every employee or would-be employee as an autonomous individual having made a free choice as regards position in the market. Further, it can force the market to treat each individual as an equivalent 'unit of production'.[8] Beyond that it will not go and therefore it is not ultimately gravely disruptive of market forces. Once a formal equality regime is established and internalised by the market, market forces can have free rein.

Substantive equality, on the other hand, demands not merely that persons should be judged on individual merit but that the real situation of many women and/or members of minority groups which may tend to place them in a weaker position in the market should be addressed by a variety of means including anti-discrimination legislation. Proponents of this argument recognise that the achievement of substantive equality involves more than a few discrimination claims. Such claims can only have limited impact in bringing about social change; far-reaching structural changes can be achieved only as a result of government policy and changed social expectations. Nevertheless, under a substantive equality model equality legislation would attempt to reflect and further the societal movement towards equality which is taking place in the Member States of the EU.

Phases in the movement towards equality

Over the last 100 years in Western democracies it has been possible to discern a pattern in the movement towards acceptance of equal treatment of persons based on a right to equal freedoms and away from the acceptance of unjustifiable differentiation, which reflects to an extent the different theories considered above. In the first phase such differentiation expressly enshrined in the law is gradually removed; in the second there may be a hiatus during which the law is neutral and there is freedom to discriminate and in the third the law may be used to try expressly to prevent discrimination or at least certain aspects of it. In this phase the law may also *permit* discrimination – termed positive or affirmative action – on the ground that it is morally justified as a temporary measure intended to combat the effects of previous discrimination. However, although this general pattern can usually be identified, it may well be that particular aspects of the first phase which for

---

8   In other words, formal equality requires in general that one employee should not be perceived as more expensive than another and therefore the market need not accommodate the cost of individuals who are given unnecessary special protection such as, for example, barring women from night work during pregnancy.

various reasons are especially resistant to change, are still in existence during the third phase. Such aspects will still tend to follow the general trend but more slowly and will themselves almost certainly move eventually from one phase to another.[9] In other words, some specific inequalities may still be enshrined in law in the third phase. Moreover, *within* each phase there may be movement; in the first legislation may enshrine gross and absolute inequality which gradually gives place to a lesser and more pragmatic inequality. An example is afforded by the legal regulation of sexual acts between consenting males: until 1967 these were merely forbidden, on the ground that sexual satisfaction gained in this manner was inimical to the moral basis of society. The removal of this barrier but the fixing of the age of consent for male homosexuals at 21 and then at 18 suggested a retreat from an absolutist position but a disinclination to carry through such a retreat fully.

Since slavery was abolished at the beginning of the 19th century, generalised racial inequality has never been enshrined in law in the UK as sexual inequality has been until relatively recently. People from certain ethnic backgrounds have not been prevented from voting, from holding civic office, from owning property or from forming contracts. The legal scheme which until quite recently governed sexual inequality in the UK would probably find parallels in terms of racial inequality only under regimes such as that in South Africa during the apartheid years.

The movement towards equality on the grounds of sexual orientation is still poised between the first and second phases. In the UK there is no clear sign at present that its entry into the third is imminent but it seems inevitable that it will do so sometime within the next 10 years. The signs that this is likely to occur are already in place: the existence of pressure groups operating within the UK and abroad; official recognition afforded to such groups in some other Western democracies coupled with instances in which their policies have been afforded a degree of legal recognition.[10] Moreover, instruments which are capable of affecting law and policy in the UK already enshrine guarantees of freedom from discrimination on this ground, including the European Convention on Human Rights and the International Convention on Civil and Political Rights. Arguments in favour of discrimination on the ground of sexual preference in various spheres such as employment seem to be rooted, it is submitted, only in prejudice: the social need to retain such

---

9   An example is afforded by the exclusion of women from the Anglican priesthood, an instance of 'first phase' discrimination which survived until 1994. 'First phase' discrimination in this context, although almost squeezed out of existence, will subsist: under the current arrangements women priests cannot become bishops.

10 For example, the armed forces in Belgium, Denmark, the Netherlands, Spain are all open to homosexuals. See further *Homosexuality: A Community Issue* (1993), a report compiled by the European Human Rights Foundation.

discrimination is unclear.[11] At present such prejudice is allowed free rein and therefore can affect every area of life from employment to expressions of sexuality and since the UK does not in general recognise same-sex partners they suffer in comparison with heterosexual couples in relation to immigration,[12] pensions and inheritance rights.

Anti-assimilationism

Although this chapter concentrates on the extent to which the law has influenced equality of opportunity, it does not imply that all members of the groups in question will necessarily *want* the opportunity to adopt the way of life of the dominant group. Some women and some members of ethnic minorities believe that true equality means accepting and respecting different values rather than trying to extinguish them.[13] The notion of 'assimilationism' has come particularly under attack[14] in various writings on feminist legal theory which have advocated the 'feminism of difference' and rejected the rights analysis of the liberal feminist.[15] Of course, there is a crucial difference here between the assertion of the values of groups of persons belonging to ethnic minorities and those of women, in that women will be committed to an enormous and disparate range of values and will therefore behave as differently from each other as men do.[16] However, assuming for the purposes of the argument that a body of values of a more nurturing, caring, conscience-based kind can be associated with women, just as certain values and beliefs

---

11 Some Conservative opinion takes the view that homosexuality is a form of immorality which should be suppressed in order to uphold the moral bonds which keep society together. This view may derive from that expressed by Lord Devlin (The Maccabaean Lecture, *The Enforcement of Morals*, 1959, reprinted in 1965). It seems likely that this body of opinion would not support legislation aimed at preventing discrimination in, for example, employment on grounds of sexual orientation. For discussion of Lord Devlin's view see Chap 5 p 182.

12 See Chap 11 p 461–62.

13 eg MacKinnon, C, 'Toward Feminist Jurisprudence', 34 *Stanford Law Review*; Littleton, CA, 'Reconstructing Sexual Equality' in Bartlett, K and Kennedy, R, eds, *Feminist Legal Theory*, 1991.

14 See Gilligan, C, *In A Different Voice: Psychological Theory and Women's Development*, 1982. It should be noted that the 'feminism of difference' has itself come under attack from postmodern feminists as impoverished and limited in its assumption that there is essential commonality between all women. See Cain, P, 'Feminist Jurisprudence: Grounding the Theories' in Bartlett, K and Kennedy, R, eds, *Feminist Legal Theory*, 1991, pp 265–68.

15 'Feminist rights analysis generally pretends that there are no differences between men and women and attempts to advance women by giving them the rights men have': Olsen, F, 'Statutory Rape: A Feminist Critique of Rights Analysis' in Bartlett, K and Kennedy, R, eds, *Feminist Legal Theory*, 1991, p 312.

16 The argument that women can and should be viewed as an homogeneous group has been put by Martha Minow: 'cognitively we need simplifying categories and the unifying category of "woman" helps to organise experience even at the cost of denying some of it' (Minow, M, 'Feminist Reason: Getting It and Losing It', 38 *J Legal Educ* pp 47, 51).

can be associated with groups such as Sikhs or Muslims, it could be argued that such values are not necessarily opposed in their entirety to those of the dominant group and in any event need not be rejected in seeking to overcome disadvantage. In suggesting this the danger should be borne in mind that extreme forms of 'celebration of difference' may be merely another route to economic and political subjugation; history does not afford many examples of groups who overcame disadvantage by rejoicing in their rejection of the whole body of values which originally placed them in that position. In any event, despite a difference of emphasis, there is a measure of harmony between moderate anti-assimilationist theory and liberal rights theory as regards the need to protect people from discrimination on unjustifiable grounds by outlawing sex and race based disadvantages, so that women or members of ethnic minorities can choose whether or how far to accept – while perhaps working to modify – the lifestyle associated with the dominant group.

Discrimination and the law

This Part begins by considering the legislation aimed specifically at preventing discrimination based on race or sex. Broadly speaking, the legislation embodies two methods of challenging direct discrimination and discriminatory practices: under the first, the 'individual' method, the responsibility lies mainly with the victim of discrimination to bring an action against the discriminator, while under the second, termed the 'general' method, an institution or body uses various methods of seeking to ensure that discrimination is prevented. The main emphasis of this chapter will be on the means of distinguishing between relevant and irrelevant factors founding differentiation, since only the former provide a morally justifiable basis for different treatment. The legal means of ensuring that such distinctions can be made may then be contrasted in Chapter 14 with the failure to ensure that homosexuality *per se* is not regarded by the law as an irrelevant factor on which to base differentiation in such spheres as employment, housing and education

Anti-discrimination discourse tends to focus on the specific areas covered by the relevant legislation. However, discrimination affects all areas of life and some areas of law may embody and reinforce it; therefore Chapter 14 goes on to consider the effect in this area of criminal law and the criminal process as positively or negatively influencing equality. The analysis of civil anti-discrimination legislation undertaken in Chapter 13 will focus on its efficacy in identifying, compensating for or preventing unjustifiable differentiation and this will also be the case in relation to the criminal law and the criminal justice system: consideration will be given to the role of the criminal law in preventing certain expressions of discrimination which are unaffected by the civil anti-discrimination legislation but which have a severe impact on the lives of certain groups, while the extent to which the criminal justice system positively seeks to eliminate discriminatory behaviour by those who administer it will be explored. However, the criminal law and the criminal justice system will also be considered in another light; it will be considered how far they may be said to contain provisions which themselves discriminate on the basis of morally irrelevant factors. Such provisions may be particularly significant since they may amount to a denial of moral autonomy and may also be said to signal the acceptance of some forms of discrimination as part of British culture.

CHAPTER THIRTEEN

ANTI-DISCRIMINATION LEGISLATION

1 INTRODUCTION[17]

Discrimination on grounds of gender[18]

At common law and under statute women were historically subject to a number of legal disabilities but the end of the 19th and the beginning of the 20th century saw the gradual removal of such disabilities by statute. Women were given the right to sign contracts, to own property irrespective of their marital status, to vote and to stand for Parliament. The Sex Disqualification (Removal) Act 1919 removed any disqualification by way of sex or marriage for those who wished to exercise a public function, hold a civil or judicial office, enter any civil profession or vocation or be admitted to any incorporated society. However, the marriage bar continued to operate in many jobs until the Second World War.[19] Once these disabilities had been removed there was opposition to further legislation.[20] It was thought that the barriers preventing women entering public life were down and therefore further measures were unnecessary. However, the fact that women were for the first time able to enter the public domain did not mean that they were accepted there. Theoretically women had the same opportunities as men but

---

17 General reading on race and sex discrimination, see: Hepple, B and Szyszczak, E, eds, *Discrimination and the Limits of the Law*, 1992; Deakin, S and Morris, G, *Labour Law*, 1995, Chap 6; Feldman, D, *Civil Liberties*, 1993, Chap 18; Dine, J and Watt, B, eds, *Discrimination Law*, 1996; Palmer, C, *Discrimination at Work*, 3rd edn, 1996; von Prondzynski, F and Richards, W, 'Tackling Indirect Discrimination' [1995] *PL* 117; Gardner, J, 'Discrimination as Injustice' (1996) 16(3) *OJLS* 353; Gregory, J, *Sex, Race and the Law: Legislating for Equality*, 1987.

18 General reading: Atkins and Hoggett, *Women and the Law*, 1984, pp 1–63 for background; Pannick, D, *Sex Discrimination Law*, 1985; Bourne, C and Whitmore, J, *Anti-discrimination Law in Britain*, 1996; Townshend-Smith, R, *Sex Discrimination in Employment*, 1989; Honeyball, S, *Sex, Employment and the Law*, 1991; McCrudden, C, ed, *Anti-discrimination Law*, 1991; Rhode, D, *Justice and Gender: Sex Discrimination and the Law*, 1989; Fenwick, H and Hervey, T, 'Sex Equality in the Single Market: New Directions for the European Court of Justice' [1995] 32 *CMLR* 443–70; Hervey, T, *Justifications for Sex Discrimination in Employment*, 1993; Ellis, E, 'The Definition of Discrimination in EC Sex Equality Law' 19 *EL Rev* 563; Millar and Phillips, 'Evaluating Anti-discrimination Legislation in the UK: Some Issues and Approaches' (1983) 11 *Int J Soc Law* 417; McGinley 'Judicial Approaches to Sex Discrimination in US and UK – a comparative study' (1986) *MLR* 415; on pregnancy see Conaghan, J (1993) *JLS* 71.

19 The 1919 Act was found to mean only that the employers must lift restrictions on women; it did not prevent particular employers imposing restrictions on women and it gave rise to no right of litigation: see *Price v Rhondda Urban Council* [1923] 2 Ch 372.

20 Atkins and Hoggett note the lack of Parliamentary concern about women at work and failure to debate the problem: *ibid* at p 19.

555

in practice since there were no formal barriers to discrimination by employers and others these practices continued. It may be assumed that this was due in part to prejudice and in part to the operation of the market which had no interest in ensuring better treatment for a group of employees who could traditionally be treated badly. Employers openly paid the 'women's' rate for the job,[21] a lower rate than that for men and openly refused to appoint women above a certain level or to do certain jobs.[22] Under the common law it was immaterial that the grounds for such decisions might be capricious or reprehensible.

The view taken in the 1974 White Paper on Sex Discrimination preceding the 1975 Act was that women were being held back in employment and other fields because they were not being judged on their individual merits but on the basis of a general presumption of inferiority. It was apparent that the common law was not going to bring about change, partly because the judiciary saw the creation of a comprehensive anti-discrimination code as the province of Parliament but also because, even in the 1970s, sympathy with discriminatory practices was evident among certain judges. In *Morris v Duke-Cohen*[23] for example, a judge was prepared to find a solicitor negligent for taking advice from a wife when a husband was available, on the basis that a sensible wife would expect her husband to make the major decisions.

The legislation affords recognition to two competing views as to the most effective means of securing equality: the so-called formal equality approach and the pluralist approach.[24] The former, which as mentioned above is based on classic liberalism and is the dominant approach, assumes that in a just society the sex of a person would carry no expectations with it; it would be as irrelevant as their eye colour. It takes the view that women and men are equally able to take advantage of opportunities and that therefore if a man would have been expected to satisfy the same conditions as the woman no discrimination has occurred. Thus once specific instances of differential treatment based on sex are prevented or addressed women will no longer be placed at a disadvantage. The pluralist approach, on the other hand, which was imported from the US,[25] takes a number of factors such as past discrimination or social conditioning into account and asks whether policies and practices which are neutral on their face actually have an adverse impact on women due to factors which particularly affect them. It accepts that there

---

21 In 1970 women's average pay was 63.1% that of men (EOC 1988b p 45).
22 The study by National Segregation 1979 showed that by 1971 over half of all men were in occupations where they outnumbered women by at least 9 to 1 and 77% worked in occupations which were at least 70% male.
23 (1975) *Sol Jo* 826.
24 See Gardner (1989) 9 *OJLS* 1 and Brest (1976) 90 *Harvard LR* 1 on the different philosophies apparent in the legislation.
25 For a comparative discussion of the approaches to UK and US discrimination see McGinley (1986) 49 *MLR* 413.

may be differences between the situation of men and women but holds that penalties should not inevitably attach to the recognition of those differences. This approach derives from the Supreme Court decision in *Griggs v Duke Power Company*;[26] when the defendant company administered an aptitude test to all job applicants it was shown that significantly fewer blacks than whites passed the test and that the skills examined by the test were not particularly relevant to the jobs applied for. In these circumstances, it was held that the test was discriminatory.[27]

The two methods of securing equality embodied in the legislation – the individual approach and the general administrative approach – need not entirely be considered in isolation from each other. The weakness of the first is that specific instances of discrimination may be addressed if the individual concerned is prepared to take on the burden of a legal action. Such an approach is clearly only capable of bringing about slow and piecemeal change, especially as the two parties concerned – usually the woman and her employer – are clearly not confronting each other on equal terms; the lack of legal aid exacerbates this situation. However, apart from bringing about general change by addressing itself to institutionalised discrimination, the administrative body created by the legislation can aid the individual and can undertake the investigation triggered off by an individual action.

Sex discrimination law in the UK cannot be studied without taking into account European Community law which has been a highly significant influence (race discrimination provisions have also been influenced indirectly). Article 119 of the Treaty of Rome, which was signed by Britain in 1973, governs the principle of equal pay for equal work. This is amplified by the Equal Pay Directive 75/117, while the Equal Treatment Directive 76/207 and the Pregnancy Directive 92/85 govern other aspects of sexual discrimination. These provisions are far more valuable than the guarantee of freedom from discrimination under Article 14 of the European Convention, partly because they may override domestic statutory provisions in domestic courts,[28] and partly because Article 14 only covers areas falling within the scope of the other Articles.[29] This does not mean, however that Article 14 is of *no* value in this area.[30]

---

26 401 US 424 (1971).

27 For further discussion in the US context see Wilborn, S, 'The Disparate Impact model of Discrimination: Theory and Limits' (1985) 34 *American University Law Review* 799.

28 In general, EU directives are enforceable in national courts only against the state or against bodies under the control of the state (*Foster v British Gas plc* [1990] 3 All ER 897) but not against private bodies. However, it was found in *Francovich v Italy* [1992] 21 IRLR 84; [1991] ECR I-5357; [1995] ICR 722 that an individual who suffers loss at the hands of a private body due to the state's failure to undertake full implementation of a directive may have a claim against the state. See further Ellis, E, *European Community Sex Equality Law*, 1991, Chap 4. For discussion of the influence of EU equality laws see McCrudden, C, (1993) 13 *OJLS* 320; Ellis, E [1994] 31 CMLR 43.

29 See Chap 2 pp 76–77.

30 See *Schuler-Zgraggen v Switzerland* (1993) *The Times*, 21 October.

The Sex Discrimination Act 1975 only covers the non-contractual aspects of employment – the contractual aspects fall within the Equal Pay Act 1970. As will be seen this separation has created difficulties although the two statutes are intended to work together as a complete code. The Act does not make sexual discrimination generally illegal; it only outlaws it in the contexts in which it operates: employment (s 6), education (s 22) and the provision of goods and services (s 29). Thus a two-stage approach has been created; first discrimination must be shown and then that it falls within one of the contexts covered by the Act.

Section 3, which covers discrimination on the grounds of marital status, follows the same pattern but in this instance the comparison is between a single person and a married person of the same sex. The provision against marital discrimination is more circumscribed: it is confined to the employment field only and discrimination on the grounds of divorce or of being unmarried is not covered.

Discrimination on grounds of race[31]

It was apparent that the common law would not provide a sufficient remedy for racial discrimination. For example, in *Constantine v Imperial Hotels*[32] only nominal damages were awarded in respect of clear racial discrimination although the applicant had attempted to claim exemplary damages. However, the discriminatory effect of a contract or covenant could be taken into account by a court as a matter of public policy in reaching a decision,[33] while discriminatory words contained in a trust might, under certain circumstances, be struck out although the courts have tended to be reluctant to do this.[34] The discriminatory nature of foreign legislation might also be considered in determining its impact,[35] and this possibility still exists although it is not of great significance. There seemed to be a clear need for further measures and therefore the first Race Relations Act was passed in 1965 although it was soon

---

31   General reading see: Bailey, Harris and Jones, *Civil Liberties: Cases and Materials*, 1991, Chap 10; Lustgarten, L, *The Legal Control of Racial Discrimination*, 1980; Gregory, J, *Sex, Race and the Law*, 1987; Bourne, C and Whitmore, J, *Race and Sex Discrimination*, 1993; Feldman, D, *Civil Liberties in England and Wales*, 1993, pp 874–79; Lustgarten, L, 'Racial Inequality and the Limits of Law' (1986) *MLR* pp 68–85; Bindman, G, 'Reforming the Race Relations Act' (1985) *NLJ* 1136–38 and 1167–69.

32   [1944] KB 693.

33   On public policy at common law see Cretney (1968) 118 *NLJ* 1094; Garner (1972) 35 *MLR* 478.

34   *Re Lysaght* [1966] Ch 191 (in order to qualify for a scholarship under the trust a student had to be male, British and could not be Catholic or Jewish; this was not found contrary to public policy but as the College which was to be a trustee refused to discriminate on religious grounds, those words were struck out); for comment see (1966) 82 *LQR* 10.

35   See *Oppenheimer v Cattermole* [1975] 2 WLR 347.

superseded by the 1968 Act and then by the 1976 Act. The 1976 Act is much more far-reaching than its predecessors; under the 1968 Act an individual had to complain to the Race Relations Board rather than take the complaint to court. The 1976 Act was modelled on the Sex Discrimination Act; it makes discrimination a statutory tort, follows the same pattern as regards direct and indirect discrimination and sets up the commission for racial equality with a similar role to the Equal Opportunities Commission[36] set up under the 1975 Act. It also operates in the same contexts and uses the same terms; therefore decisions under one of the two statutes affect the other. The Act provides a remedy for direct or indirect discrimination on the grounds of colour, race, nationality or ethnic or national origins but the discrimination must occur within the areas covered by the Act: employment, education, housing or the provision of goods and services.

However, there are some important differences between the two statutory schemes. The provisions under the Race Relations Act outlawing discrimination in private clubs of 25 members or more, segregation and 'transferred discrimination' – discrimination on the grounds of another's race – have no counterparts under the Sex Discrimination Act. Employment covers 'pay', thus ensuring a less complex scheme than that applying in respect of sex discrimination claims. The influence of the EU is less important, although rulings of the European Court of Justice and of the domestic courts taking EU provisions into account may well affect concepts under the Race Relations Act. It should be noted that the EU has not ignored race discrimination and has passed a number of resolutions and declarations giving guidance to Member States[37] but its influence in this area, although beginning to develop, is at a much earlier stage than its influence on sex discrimination. Aside from EU provisions the UK is a party to a number of international declarations on race discrimination and xenophobia which, although not part of UK law, may influence it.[38]

---

36 See below pp 595–97 for consideration of the role of both bodies.

37 See Resolutions, Reports and Declarations of the Council of the EC: Resolution of 16 July 1985 (OJ C186 26.7.85 p 3); Declaration of 11 June 1986 (OJ C158 25.6.86 p 1); Resolution of 24 May 1988 (OJ C177 6.7.88 p 5); Council Decision 88/348/EEC (OJ L158 25.6.88); Eurigenis Report 1991. For criticism of the EU stance on racism see Bindman, G (1994) 144 NLJ 352.

38 Articles 3 and 14 of the European Convention on Human Rights; International Labour Organisation; International Covenant on Civil and Political Rights; para 2 of the International Covenant on Economic, Social and Cultural Rights; International Convention on the Elimination of All Forms of Racial Discrimination.

2 DIRECT DISCRIMINATION ON GROUNDS OF SEX OR RACE

Sex

The concept of direct discrimination on grounds of sex governed by s 1(1)(a) embodies the formal equality approach. It involves showing that the applicant has been less favourably treated than a comparable man has been or would be treated. There is little guidance in the Act as to what is meant by a comparable man; s 5(3) merely provides that there must be no material difference between the situations of the man and the woman. It should be noted that it is possible for the applicant to compare herself with a hypothetical man; the issue is not whether a man or a woman receives a benefit but whether the woman would have been better treated if she had been a man. The test can be broken down into three stages. First, the woman must show that there has been differentiation in the treatment afforded to herself and a man (or a hypothetical man). Motive is irrelevant; the question at this stage is merely whether a woman has been treated one way and a man another. Secondly, she must show that her treatment has been less favourable and thirdly, following the ruling of the House of Lords in *James v Eastleigh Borough Council*,[39] that there is a causal relationship between her sex and the treatment; in other words that but for her sex she would have been treated as favourably as a man was or would have been. Following *Birmingham County Council ex parte EOC*[40] it is not necessary to show that the less favourable treatment is accorded due to an intention to discriminate: motive is irrelevant.

The plaintiff bears the burden of showing that the differential treatment was on grounds of sex and not for some neutral reason. She is always likely to find difficulty in discharging this burden of proof as the ruling in *Saunders v Richmond-upon-Thames LBC*[41] suggests. The applicant applied for a job as a golf professional and was asked questions at the interview which were *prima facie* discriminatory. She was asked, for example, whether she thought she would be able to control unruly male players and whether she considered the job unglamorous. She was not appointed although she was somewhat better qualified than the man who was. The Employment Appeal Tribunal (EAT) held that had her qualifications been substantially better than those of the appointee that would have raised a *prima facie* inference of discrimination which the employer would have had to rebut by giving a satisfactory explanation. It was found that the nature of the questions, taking all the circumstances into account, did not of themselves raise a sufficient inference.

---

39 [1990] AC 751; [1990] 2 All ER 607; [1989] IRLR 318; [1989] 3 WLR 122; the 'but for' test applied in *James* was put forward by Lord Goff in the House of Lords in *Birmingham City Council, ex parte EOC* [1989] 18 ILJ 247; for comment see Ellis (1989) 52 *MLR* 710.
40 [1989] AC 1155; [1989] 1 All ER 769.
41 [1978] IRLR 362.

In *Khanna v MOD*[42] it was found that the evidential burden would shift only when the evidence was all on one side but this was clarified by the finding in *Dornan v Belfast County Council*[43] that once the woman has raised a *prima facie* inference of discrimination, the burden will shift to the employer to show that the differentiation occurred on non-discriminatory grounds. In other words, although the plaintiff begins the case bearing the burden of proof it may shift to the defendant once a certain stage is reached. Thus the formal burden of proof remains on the plaintiff but once it appears that a minimum threshold of proof of discrimination is established the burden shifts to the defendant. This middle ground is arguably fairer than merely leaving the full burden with the employee or, alternatively, shifting it entirely to the employer.[44]

Dismissals and other detrimental action on the ground of pregnancy might appear to be discriminatory but the wording of s 1(1) may not allow such action to fall readily within the scope of direct discrimination because in making the comparison between a woman and a man it is required under s 5(3) that 'the relevant circumstances in the one case are the same or not materially different, in the other'. Dismissal on grounds of pregnancy was regulated from October 1994 by ss 23–25 and Schedules 2 and 3 of the Trade Union Reform and Employment Rights Act (TURERA) 1993.[45] Under the Act, such dismissal will be unfair from the date on which employment begins. At present under s 60 of the Employment Protection (Consolidation) Act 1978 if a woman is dismissed because she is pregnant then the dismissal is automatically unfair but in order to rely on this an employee must have been employed for two years; where this is not the case the employee must seek to show that the 1975 Act applies.

This was the situation which arose in *Turley v Allders*[46] because the applicant did not have the requisite period of continuous employment. The Employment Appeal Tribunal held that there was no male equivalent to a pregnant woman and therefore as no comparison could be made the action must fail. However, a method of making the comparison was found in a later EAT decision, *Hayes v Malleable WMC*;[47] it was found that it could be made between a pregnant woman and a man with a long-term health problem. Thus it would be direct discrimination if a woman was dismissed on grounds of pregnancy where a man needing the same period of absence due to illness

---

42 [1981] ICR 653, EAT.
43 [1990] IRLR 179.
44 See further [1990] IRLR 161.
45 The TURERA sections mentioned implement the EC Pregnancy Directive 92/85.
46 [1980] ICR 66.
47 [1985] ICR 703. See also *Brown v Rentokil Ltd* [1992] IRLR 302; *Shomer v B and R Residential Lettings Ltd* [1992] IRLR 317. It may be noted that dismissal on grounds of pregnancy seems to be increasing. The EOC cited a number of such instances in its 1991 report.

would not have been dismissed. This analogy has not been well received;[48] it has been pointed out that pregnancy is a healthy, normal state, not an illness;[49] moreover, it may be planned unlike an unexpected illness and in any event there will normally be far more notice before the absence takes place than there would be in a case of illness. Commentators have found the comparison between a pregnant woman and a diseased man inherently distasteful. It is also highly disadvantageous to women, a very high percentage of whom may become pregnant at some time during their working life and in particular between the ages of 20 and 35 (the time when women are most likely to become pregnant), while the percentage of men likely to take around two or more months off work during those years due to an illness or accident is likely to be far lower.

The *Hayes* approach will no longer be followed after certain decisions of the European Court of Justice. In *Dekker v VJV Centrum*[50] the court found that a woman who was not appointed to a post because she was pregnant at the time of the interview, although she was considered to be the best candidate, was the victim of direct discrimination. *Webb v Emo Air Cargo (UK) Ltd*[51] concerned the dismissal of the claimant after it was found that she was pregnant. She had been recruited to replace an employee going on maternity leave but had then discovered herself to be pregnant and therefore (it seemed) unavailable for duties in the period required. The question was whether her dismissal constituted direct discrimination within the terms of s 1(1)(a) of the Sex Discrimination Act 1975, in the light of Community law. The Court of Appeal continued the *Hayes* approach in determining that if a man with a medical condition as nearly comparable as possible (with the same practical effect upon availability to do the job) with pregnancy would also have been dismissed then the dismissal of the woman was not sex discrimination. Thus, the plaintiff who was, due to pregnancy, unavailable for duties in the period required, could be dismissed without infringing the Sex Discrimination Act because a diseased man who was similarly unavailable at the relevant time would also have been dismissed. The argument was therefore rejected that since only a woman can be pregnant, it followed that a woman who is dismissed for any reason related to her pregnancy is dismissed due to her sex and thus discriminated against. The House of Lords favoured the approach of the Court of Appeal but since it considered that the relevant rulings of the European Court of Justice did not indicate clearly whether the dismissal would be regarded as based on pregnancy or on unavailability at the relevant time, it referred the following question to the court:

---

48   See *Proposals of the Equal Opportunities Commission: Equal Treatment for Men and Women* (1988) Chap 2.
49   Lacey (1987) 14 *JLS* 411, 417.
50   [1991] IRLR 27; [1990] ECR I-3941.
51   [1993] 1 WLR 49, HL; [1992] 1 CMLR 793, CA.

Is it discrimination on grounds of sex contrary to the Equal Treatment Directive for an employer to dismiss a female employee:

(a) whom it engaged for the specific purpose of replacing another female employee during the latter's forthcoming maternity leave,

(b) when very shortly after appointment the employer discovers that the appellant herself will be absent on maternity leave during the maternity period of the other employee and the employer dismisses her because it needs the jobholder to be at work during that period, and

(c) had the employer known of the pregnancy of the appellant at the date of appointment she would not have been appointed, and

(d) the employer would similarly have dismissed a male employee engaged for this purpose who required leave of absence at the relevant time for medical or other reasons?

The European Court of Justice found that the plaintiff should not be compared with a man unavailable for work for medical or other reasons since pregnancy is not in any way comparable with pathological conditions. The court then found that, since the plaintiff had been employed permanently, her dismissal could not be justified on the ground of inability to fulfil a fundamental condition of her employment contract because her inability to perform the work was purely temporary. In other words, it could not be said that she had been taken on solely to cover a maternity leave. The court further found that the protection of Community law for pregnant women could not be dependent on the question whether the woman's presence at work during the maternity leave period is essential to the undertaking in which she is employed. Thus dismissal of the plaintiff clearly constituted sex discrimination, contrary to the Equal Treatment Directive. (When the House of Lords reconsidered the case in the light of these findings it allowed the appeal and remitted the case to the IT to consider the award of compensation to the applicant (*Webb (No 2)*.)[52]

In a similar decision, *Habermann-Beltermann*,[53] rather than relying directly upon unavailability, the employer sought to rely upon the statutory exclusion (with criminal sanctions)[54] of pregnant women from night work, which 'caused' Habermann-Beltermann's temporary unavailability for work. The court's decision that the statute could not justify Habermann-Beltermann's dismissal or the termination of her contract, reflects a refusal to focus upon a male norm or to pander to the argument that the continuation of the employment relationship in such circumstances produces undue financial burdens upon the employer.[55] However, in both *Habermann-Beltermann* and

---

52 [1995] 1 WLR 1454.
53 [1994] ECR I-1657.
54 The German *Mütterschutzgesetz* (MSchG), para 8(1), which prohibits the employment of pregnant or breast-feeding women on night work.
55 See the Opinion of the Advocate General, para 16.

Webb, the court refuses to confront clearly the question whether any adverse treatment of women connected with pregnancy amounts to sex discrimination. In both judgments, the crucial fact upon which the court relied was that the employment contracts in question were of a permanent and not fixed term nature. The decision of the court in both cases was based upon the mismatch between the period for which the employee would be unavailable and the period for which she had been employed (indefinitely). This is a very significant development from the stark statement of principle in *Dekker*. The court's conclusion that the termination of Habermann-Beltermann's contract was not 'on the ground of pregnancy' but by reason of the statutory provision in the MSchG, opens the door to a narrower interpretation of the *Dekker* ruling than that ruling seemed at first to promise.[56] The result was that the court, unlike the Advocate General,[57] was able to avoid making explicit the point that a justification based on availability, with reference to market cost to the employer, would be by definition excluded in a case of *direct* discrimination on grounds of pregnancy, thereby, by implication, leaving it open in future cases.

Likewise, the ruling in *Webb* is not ultimately fully supportive of substantive equality since it leaves open the possibility of an apparently neutral explanation for pregnancy dismissals: that a pregnant woman recruited on a temporary basis may justifiably be dismissed if unable due to unavailability to fulfil the purpose for which she was recruited. The argument is therefore left open that if a temporarily employed man or hypothetical man, would have been dismissed, if unable due to unavailability to satisfy a purpose for which he was employed, a woman so unavailable due to pregnancy, who has been dismissed, has not been discriminated against. Therefore by the recruitment of temporary staff, the employer can safeguard its market position. Elements of the ruling, however, suggest a desire to go further and it is in this sense internally inconsistent: it asserts that in general to dismiss a pregnant woman due to unavailability at a time when she is essential to a purpose of the undertaking can never be justifiable but it leaves open the possibility that the employer can do just that so long as she was recruited on a temporary basis specifically for that purpose.

Thus both judgments impliedly accept that adverse treatment flowing from pregnancy is susceptible to justification. Therefore an employer may be able to contend successfully that not only market costs associated with unavailability but also *other* costs arising from pregnancy,[58] not the pregnancy

---

56 This part of *Habermann-Beltermann* is similar to the court's ruling in *Hertz* that dismissal due to absences caused by illness, where those absences arise outside the protected period of maternity leave, is permissible, even where the illness is pregnancy related. See Shaw, 'Pregnancy Discrimination in Sex Discrimination' (1991) 16 *EL Rev*, pp 313–20.

57 Opinion of the Advocate General, para 16.

58 For example, adjustment of working conditions, time off for above-natal examinations, removal of hazardous substances from the working environment or other measures of special protection for pregnant workers required, for example by the Pregnancy and Maternity Directive, Council Directive 92/85/EEC.

itself, were the 'cause' of the dismissal of a pregnant woman. It is even possible that such an argument could be used in relation to a *permanently* employed woman, since the court's mismatch argument is not so readily applicable to a justification based on the *other* costs associated with pregnancy. This is not to contend that the court would necessarily accept such assertions by employers, merely to note that, in principle, the judgments leave open these possibilities. The effect of the judgments may be to doubly disadvantage women: they may have to take the risk that they will have no remedy if employed on a temporary basis but dismissed due to reasons connected with pregnancy,[59] and they may tend to find that they are more likely to be offered temporary contracts, thereby undermining their bargaining power in the market still further.

In both judgments, the court could have rejected a formal equality interpretation of the legislation, in favour of completely excluding the use of unavailability due to pregnancy or the cost of pregnancy as a justification,[60] thereby affording recognition to the real situation of women. In support of this, it should be pointed out that the real situation of women which may mean that they are unavailable for work for a period is only biologically determined in so far as the bearing of children is concerned; in terms of caring for children it is legally and socially determined. The legal and social factors in question which found the perception that pregnancy, maternity leave and child care are to be viewed as one single indivisible burden to be shouldered by women alone, arise, it is submitted, from a sexually stereotyped view of the child care responsibilities of males and females. Thus, unavailability for work arising or apparently arising[61] from pregnancy, maternity leave and child care, is not a sex neutral justification for adverse treatment.

At the least the court could have achieved a compromise somewhat more satisfactory in terms of promotion of substantive equality than the one it does achieve, by framing its judgment in terms of the *proportion* of the period for which the woman was employed during which she would be unavailable. Thus, a woman employed, for example, on a temporary three year contract in order to fulfil a particular purpose who would be unavailable for three months on maternity leave and therefore unable to fulfil it would be said

---

59 So long as the context allows the dismissal to be characterisable as due to unavailability and therefore inability to satisfy a particular purpose.

60 The argument for so doing was put succinctly by Stevens J in a dissenting US judgment: commenting on a rule allowing adverse treatment of women for reasons connected with pregnancy, he said: 'By definition such a rule discriminates on grounds of sex, for it is the capacity to become pregnant which primarily differentiates the female from the male.' *General Electric Co v Gilbert* 429 US 126 (1976) at 161–62.

61 It appeared that no attempt was made to ascertain the period for which the plaintiff would actually be unavailable. See *Webb v EMO Air Cargo* [1992] 4 All ER 929, HL, at 932, *per* Lord Keith. It is not mandatory that employees should be absent from work for the whole period of maternity leave or that, during maternity leave, they should be out of communication with the work place.

nevertheless to be available for a substantial part of the period. Instead, the court chose to confine its ruling to those employed for an indefinite period.

Under ss 23–25 and Schedules 2 and 3 of the Trade Union Reform and Employment Rights Act 1993 a woman is protected from dismissal on grounds of pregnancy and has an automatic right to 14 weeks' maternity leave. If she has two years continuous service she has a right to return to work within 29 weeks of the birth under s 39(1)(b) of the Employment Protection Consolidation Act 1978. Thus, *Webb* will still be relevant in relation to dismissal due to pregnancy where a woman has less than two years service.[62] Moreover, detrimental action on grounds of pregnancy other than dismissal (such as demotion or failure to appoint) will fall within the *Webb* approach and it is therefore unfortunate that the European Court of Justice failed to rule clearly that such action would be direct sex discrimination. A possible approach would be to treat detrimental action on grounds of pregnancy as indirect rather than direct discrimination on the ground that a condition is being applied to all employees not to need certain periods of time off work. As argued above this is very likely to have an adverse impact on women and arguably cannot be justified using the current tests for justification (see below).

Race

Direct discrimination arises under s 1(1)(a) of the Race Relations Act and the test to be applied mirrors that under the Sex Discrimination Act except that the unfavourable treatment in question must be on 'racial grounds'. This means that discrimination on the grounds of someone else's race is covered (transferred discrimination).[63] For example, if a waitress disobeyed an instruction to serve whites only and was dismissed for serving black customers that would be discrimination on racial grounds.[64] A decision made on racial grounds means that the alleged discriminator made a decision influenced by racial prejudice but according to the ruling in *CRE ex parte Westminster Council*[65] this does not mean that the discriminator must have a racial motive. The council wanted to employ a black man as a refuse collector but withdrew the offer after pressure from the all-white work force. The CRE (Commission for Racial Equality) initiated a formal investigation and served a non-discrimination notice on the council. The council challenged the service of

---

62 *Webb* was applied in *O'Neill* (1996) *The Times*, 7 June in relation to a pregnancy dismissal. Following *Webb* the dismissal was found to be unlawful.
63 It was confirmed in *Showboat Entertainment Centre v Owens* [1984] 1 WLR 384 that dismissal for refusal to obey an unlawful discriminatory instruction would fall within s 1(1)(a). See to the same effect *Zarczynska v Levy* [1979] 1 WLR 125.
64 See *Zarczynska v Levy* [1979] 1 WLR 125.
65 [1984] IRLR 230, QBD.

the notice by means of judicial review and sought *certiorari* on the basis that the CRE's findings were perverse – a finding that the CRE could not reasonably make. However, it was held that the decision was made on racial grounds although it was found that the employer was not motivated by racial prejudice but by the desire to avoid industrial unrest. Nevertheless, that was irrelevant; the decision was influenced by racial prejudice although it was not the prejudice of the respondent.

Often the hardest task in a direct discrimination case will be proving that unfavourable treatment was on grounds of race. However, the decision in *Dornan*[66] will apply in race discrimination cases and will mean that once an inference has been raised that discrimination has occurred, the burden of proof will shift to the employer to prove that the decision in question was made on other grounds. Raising such an inference may involve obtaining statistical material from the employer. In *West Midlands Passenger Transport Executive v Jaquant Singh*[67] the applicant who believed that he had been racially discriminated against in being refused promotion, wanted an order of discovery in respect of specific material held by his employers indicating the number of whites and non-whites appointed to senior posts. He claimed that if he was able to obtain access to the material he would be able to invite an inference of direct racial discrimination. The employers resisted discovery. The Court of Appeal held that discovery would be ordered only where it could be termed necessary but that it could be so termed since the employee had to establish a discernible pattern of treatment towards his racial group and there was no other way of raising the necessary inference.

Under s 1(2) of the Act it will be direct discrimination to maintain separate facilities for members of different races, even though they are equal in quality. However, if segregation grows up due to practices in the work force the employer will not come under an obligation to prevent it according to the ruling in *Pel Ltd v Modgill*[68] although this seems to be in conflict with s 32 of the Act which provides that an employer will be liable for acts done by employees in the course of employment unless he or she has taken reasonable steps to prevent such acts. It would seem that the employer should come under some obligation to prevent segregation even if he or she did not instigate it. Moreover, even if segregation in itself is not unlawful it may be that once a black/white divide in the work force is established a practice of treating the black group differently may develop which will raise an irresistible inference of direct discrimination even though such treatment might not raise such an inference if applied to an individual black worker.[69]

---

66 [1990] IRLR 179. See above p 561.
67 [1988] WLR 730.
68 [1980] IRLR 142.
69 See *John Haggas plc* (1993) *Guardian*, 29 May: different, less favourable treatment of the black group was found to be direct discrimination.

Harassment[70]

It has become clear that if the employer subjects the applicant to employment detriment arising from harassment, such as a transfer from one establishment to another, this will be direct discrimination.[71] Moreover, sexual or racial harassment appears to be a detriment in itself[72] under s 6(6)(b) Sex Discrimination Act or s 4 Race Relations Act which speak of 'or subjecting [the employee] to any other detriment' even though it does not lead to other unfavourable action so long as some employment disadvantage arises. In *De Souza v Automobile Association*[73] the Court of Appeal found that racial abuse in itself is not enough to cause an employee detriment within the meaning of s 4 Race Relations Act. The court must find that by reason of the act complained of a reasonable worker would or might take the view that he had thereby been disadvantaged in the circumstances in which he had thereafter to work. Such disadvantage may be interpreted quite broadly. In *Hereford and Worcester CC v Clayton*[74] fire-fighters were informed of the 'bad news: the new fire-fighter is a woman'. This was found to be a sexist insult capable of detrimental consequences. It sent the wrong signal to the fire-fighters and might have been likely to cause victimisation. This was less favourable treatment on the grounds of sex and amounted to unlawful sex discrimination.

There seems to be some uncertainty as to whether 'detriment' should be interpreted subjectively or objectively and a tendency to adopt the latter approach where the applicant is perceived as particularly sensitive[75] and the former where he or she is thought to be more robust.[76] This mixed approach may render the test for harassment under-inclusive and it is therefore suggested that an objective test should be used involving asking only whether the offending behaviour had reached a level at which reasonable people would term it humiliating.

Section 41(1) of the 1975 Act states that an act done by an employee in the course of employment shall be treated as done by the employer as well as by him or her, whether or not it was done with the employer's knowledge or approval. Thus a sexual or racial harassment claim may be brought where the employer had made little or no effort to curb the harassment.[77] In *Tower Boot*

---

70 See generally Hadjifotiou, N, *Women and Harassment at Work*, 1983; MacKinnon, C, *Sexual Harassment of Working Women*, 1979.
71 *Porcelli v Strathclyde Regional Council* [1986] ICR 564.
72 Although see (1985) 101 *LQR* 471 on this point.
73 [1986] ICR 514.
74 (1996) *The Times*, 8 October.
75 *Wileman v Minilec Engineering Ltd* [1988] ICR 318; for criticism see Gay (1990) 19 *ILJ* 35, who considered this ruling to be an 'example of judicial insensitivity'.
76 *Snowball v Gardner Merchant* [1987] ICR 719.
77 See *Enterprise Glass Co Ltd v Miles* [1990] *Ind Relations Review and Report* 412–15C.

Co v Jones[78] the Court of Appeal adopted a purposive approach to the legislation in finding that employers must take steps to make themselves aware of harassment in the workplace and must take further steps to prevent it. It was not sufficient for employers simply to argue that the harassment did not take place in the course of employment:[79] this would create an obvious anomaly since gross harassment (which occurred in *Jones*) could never be said to take place in the course of employment. The decision reaffirmed a broad liability of employers for racial abuse and in *Burton and Another v De Vere Hotels*[80] it was found that the employer will be liable if it allows employees to be subject to racial abuse where it could have been prevented. On this principle an action might be brought successfully where the employer did not know of the harassment but should have known, thus placing a duty upon employers to be aware of what is occurring in the work place.[81] These decisions were made in the employment field but would be applicable to the fields of education and housing. For example, under s 17 of the Race Relations Act, which provides that discrimination by bodies in charge of educational establishments may occur if a person is subjected 'to any other detriment', an action might be successful against school administrators who failed to prevent racial harassment of a pupil.

The European Commission has defined sexual harassment as 'conduct of a sexual nature or other conduct based on sex affecting the dignity of men and women at work'.[82] This clearly covers verbal or physical conduct. The Commission has published a Code of Practice[83] on sexual harassment based on the definition above, which has been supported by the Council of Ministers,[84] giving guidance to employees and employers and stating that harassment 'pollutes the working environment and can have a devastating effect upon the health, confidence, morale and performance of those affected by it'.[85] The Commission has recommended that the Code should be adopted by Member States[86] which should also take other action to address this

---

78 [1997] ICR 254; [1997] IRLR 168.
79 This had been accepted by the EAT: see [1995] IRLR 529.
80 (1996) *The Times*, 3 October.
81 This has been accepted in the US: *Continental Can Co v Minn* 297 NW 2d 241.
82 *Official Journal* C 157/2. See *Employment Law Review* for 1992. Below note 83.
83 Commission Recommendation of 27 November 1991 on the Protection of the Dignity of Men and Women at Work *OJ* L 49 3, 1992. This followed a report by Rubinstein, M, *The Dignity of Women at Work: a report on the problem of sexual harassment in the Member States of the European Communities*, 1987. See note 82 above. For criticism of the Code see 143 *NLJ* 1473.
84 In a Declaration (see (1992) 217 *European Industrial Relations Review* 21; see also Rubenstein (1992) 21 *ILJ* 70).
85 See *Official Journal of the European Communities*, 4 February 1992.
86 Commission Recommendation of 27 November 1991.

problem but the UK government has not yet shown any inclination to respond. However, Industrial Tribunals faced with an allegation of sexual harassment as a form of direct discrimination should have regard to the guidance offered by the Code.[87]

3 INDIRECT DISCRIMINATION ON GROUNDS OF SEX OR RACE[88]

Sex

This concept was imported into the Act under s 1(1)(b) with a view to outlawing practices which while neutral on their face as between men and women have a disproportionately adverse impact on women. It was intended to outlaw not only isolated acts of discrimination but also institutionalised discrimination. This reflects the pluralist approach; it takes account for example of past discrimination against women. In asking not whether a woman can in theory comply with a condition but whether she can do so in practice, it broadens the area of morally unjustifiable differentiation.

There are four stages in operating this concept. First, it must be shown that a condition has been applied to the applicant. It might be to be of a certain seniority, height or type of experience. Secondly, it must be shown that the condition is one which will have a disproportionate impact on women; in other words considerably less women than men will be able to comply with it. For example, less women than men might have a certain type of experience due to a now outlawed system of keeping women at a certain level and thereby preventing them gaining the experience in question. Thirdly, once the claimant has proved these two requirements the burden of proof shifts to the employer to show that the condition is justifiable regardless of sex. For example, there are less women engineering graduates than men; therefore a requirement that applicants have a degree in engineering hits disproportionately at women. However, the employer will normally be able to show that a degree in engineering is genuinely needed for the job. Fourthly, if the employer cannot show that the requirement is genuinely needed for the job the woman must show that it is to her detriment because she cannot comply with it. This requirement was included because it was thought necessary that the woman should be the victim rather than allowing anyone to bring a claim in respect of a discriminatory practice operating at her place of employment.

---

87 *Wadman v Carpenter Farrer Partnership* (1993) *The Times*, 31 May, EAT.
88 See Byre, A, *Indirect Discrimination*, 1987; McGinley 49 *MLR* 413 pp 427–35. Hunter, R, *Indirect Discrimination in the Workplace*, 1992; von Prondzynski, F and Richards, W, 'Tackling Indirect Discrimination' [1995] *PL* 117; Gardner, J, 'Discrimination as Injustice' (1996) 16(3) *OJLS* 353.

Two early decisions made clear the grounds for including this second type of discrimination in the Act and demonstrated the way in which it would operate. The case of *Steel v The Post Office*,[89] which concerned the allocation of postal walks to postmen or women, illustrated the operation of the four stages. Certain walks were more in demand than others and the walks were allocated on the basis of the seniority of the employee. Ms Steel made a bid for a walk but lost it to a younger man. She had worked for the Post Office much longer than he had but she had only been accepted into the permanent grade in 1975 when the Sex Discrimination Act came into force. Before 1975 the Post Office had directly discriminated against women by refusing to allow them to enter the permanent grade. Ms Steel's seniority had been calculated from that point. The practice in question was interpreted as a 'requirement' thereby widening the meaning of the term. It had a disparate impact on women because less of them could comply with it than men due to the past discrimination and the requirement as to seniority could not otherwise be justified. 'Justified' was strictly interpreted as meaning 'necessary'. Finally the requirement was clearly to her detriment as she could not comply with it.

The application of the phrase 'can comply' was considered in *Price v Civil Service Commission*.[90] The Civil Service had a rule that applicants had to be under 28. Mrs Price, who was 35, applied but was rejected and claimed sex discrimination. It was found that due to the prevailing social conditions more men than women could comply with the requirement because at the time there was a general expectation that women would rear a family and so would be less likely to be available in the job market at that age than men. However, women could theoretically comply with a requirement to be 28 and available in the job market; they could choose not to have children. The words 'can comply' were interpreted to mean that in practice less women could comply with the condition. The court also considered the means of identifying a group of men and women to be looked at in order to see whether less women could comply with the condition. It found that the group to be considered would be the pool of men and women with the relevant qualifications; it would not include the whole population.[91] The applicant's case therefore passed all four tests and succeeded, with the result that the Civil Service altered the age bar.

The main difficulties in the operation of indirect discrimination have arisen in three areas: the finding of a disparate impact, the meaning of justifiability and the determination as to the meaning of 'a requirement or

---

[89] [1977] IRLR 288.
[90] [1978] WLR 1417.
[91] See *Jones v University of Manchester* (1993) *The Times*, 12 January, which reaffirmed this approach to the 'pool', holding that the applicant could not redefine its parameters which would be fixed by the relevant advertisement.

condition'. The current position as regards disparate impact may be summed up in the following manner, which is based on the ruling of Mustill LJ in *Jones v Chief Adjudication Officer*:[92]

(a) Identify the criterion for selection (the condition);
(b) Identify the relevant population, comprising all those who satisfy the other criteria for selection and ignoring the allegedly discriminatory condition;
(c) Divide the relevant population into groups representing first those who satisfy the allegedly discriminatory criterion and secondly those who do not;
(d) Ascertain what are the actual male/female balances in the two groups;
(e) If women are found to be under-represented in the first group, it is proved that the criterion creates disparate impact.

The meaning of 'justifiable' has undergone considerable change since the ruling in *Ojutiku v Manpower Services Commission*[93] in which, departing from the Steel interpretation, it was held to mean 'reasons which would appear sound to right thinking people'. This obviously widened its meaning and would have allowed a great many practices to be justified, greatly undermining s 1(1)(b). However in *Clarke v Eley IMI Kynoch Ltd*[94] its meaning was somewhat narrowed. The company had a policy of always selecting part time workers for redundancy first regardless of their length of service, although for full time workers a 'last in, first out' system was in operation. Therefore the requirement to work full time so as not to be made redundant hit disproportionately at women as more women than men worked part time. The employer argued that the practice could be justified because it was long-standing and the work force liked it but it was found that this was not sufficient to render it 'justifiable' and the claimant therefore succeeded. This was clearly in accord with the policy of including indirect discrimination in the statutory scheme in order to outlaw long-standing discriminatory practices.

The test for the meaning of justifiable[95] was more precisely defined by the European Court in *Bilka-kaufhaus GmbH v Weber von Hartz*.[96] Under this test, conditions creating disparate impact will be justifiable if they amount to a means chosen for achieving an objective which correspond to a real need on the part of the undertaking, are appropriate to that end and necessary to that end. So this test would be fulfilled if, for example, an undertaking had a real need to increase its scientific expertise in a certain area. The means used to do

---

92 (1990) EOR 1991.
93 [1982] ICR 661; [1982] IRLR 418.
94 [1983] ICR 703.
95 For discussion of the test see Leigh (1986) 49 *MLR* 235.
96 [1986] IRLR 317; [1986] CMLR 701; see also *Rinner-Kuhn v FWW Spezial-Gebaudereinigung* [1989] IRLR 493.

so would have to be appropriate, such as asking that applicants have a degree in a certain science. If other means of increasing its expertise were not available it would be seen as necessary to impose the condition that applicants have a science degree. This approach was taken in *Hampson v Department of Education and Science*[97] and means that s 1(1)(b) has been brought into line with the 'material difference' defence under s 1(3) of the Equal Pay Act 1970 (see below).

The *Bilka* decision has narrowed the defence available to employers but *Perera v Civil Service Commission*[98] (a race discrimination case) has meant that a number of requirements or conditions creating disparate impact will fall outside the Act and will not require application of the *Bilka* test because they will not support an indirect discrimination claim at all. It was held in *Perera* that a condition must amount to an absolute bar in order to be termed a requirement or condition. If the employer has only taken the factor into account as one among others it will not fall within s 1(1)(b). This is very restrictive as non-absolute criteria could clearly be used and could have an adverse impact on an applicant. For example, an unjustifiable height bar might normally be operated but the employer might be prepared on occasion to consider people under it. Nevertheless, the bar could have a significantly adverse effect on women. Thus the development of indirect discrimination has been constrained and the EOC has therefore argued for reform of the meaning of the term 'condition'.[99] The decision in *Perera* may be out of accord with the ruling of the European Court of Justice in *Enderby v Frenchay*[100] which is discussed below. However, *Enderby* was an equal pay case and therefore is perhaps of limited application to an indirect discrimination claim.

Race

The tests to be applied to establish indirect discrimination under s 1(1)(b) of the 1976 Act are identical to those arising under the Sex Discrimination Act, apart from the need to show that the requirement or condition which has been applied adversely affects persons of a particular racial group. Thus the first step in a case of indirect discrimination on racial grounds is for the applicant to define which racial group he or she belongs to. For example, an individual could be defined as non-British, non-white, Asian or a sub-group of Asian. The choice of group is important since discrimination affects racial groups

---

97 [1991] 1 AC 171; [1990] 2 All ER 513, HL; on the Court of Appeal decision see Bourn (1989) 18 *ILJ* 170; Napier (1989) 48 *CLJ* 187.
98 [1983] ICR 428; [1983] IRLR 166.
99 See Proposals of the EOC: Equal Treatment for Men and Women, p 9.
100 [1994] 1 All ER 495; [1993] ECR I-5535, ECJ; [1992] IRLR 15, CA.

differently. For example, a requirement to be clean-shaven might discriminate against Sikhs but might not affect West Indians. Therefore, if in such circumstances the applicant chose 'non-white' as his group the claim would fail. However, if he chose Sikh and non-Sikh it would be more likely to succeed. The applicant should argue all possible groups in the alternative.

The applicant must show that the group falls within the definition of racial grounds in s 3(1) of the Act which covers 'colour, nationality, ethnic or national origins' and a racial group is defined by reference to the same. Employment of the concept of ethnic origins widens the meaning of racial group and means that some religious groups may fall within it even though discrimination on the grounds of religion is not expressly covered. The leading case on the meaning of 'racial group' is *Mandla v Dowell Lee*.[101] The House of Lords had to consider whether Sikhs constituted an ethnic group and defined the term 'ethnic group' as one having a long shared history and a cultural tradition of its own, often but not necessarily, associated with religious observances. On that definition Sikhs were a racial group and fell within s 3(1). This does not mean that a purely religious group will fall within s 3(1).

Using this definition it was found in *CRE v Dutton*[102] that gypsies who have a shared history going back 700 years, may be termed a racial group and the definition was considered further in *Dawkins v Department of Environment*[103] in relation to the claim that Rastafarians constitute a racial group. It was found that the group in question must regard itself and be regarded by others as a distinct community by virtue of certain characteristics. The two essential characteristics were: a long shared history of which the group was conscious and a cultural tradition of its own including family and social customs. Lord Fraser considered that there could be other relevant but not essential characteristics such as a common geographical origin, a common language, literature and religion. It was found that Rastafarians did have a strong cultural tradition which included a distinctive form of music and a distinctive hair style. However, the shared history of Rastafarians as a separate group only went back 60 years; it was not enough for them to look back to a time when they in common with other Africans were taken to the Caribbean. That was not sufficient to mark them out as a separate group since it was an experience shared with other Afro-Caribbeans. It appears then that this first step is complex and, it might seem, not entirely free from ambiguity. The exclusion of religious groups such as Muslims from the scope of the legislation is a matter which, it is suggested, should be reviewed. Note that

---

101 [1983] All ER 1062; [1983] 2 AC 548; for comment see Beynon and Love (1984) 100 *LQR* 120; McKenna (1983) 46 *MLR* 759; Robilliard [1983] *PL* 348.

102 [1989] WLR 17; [1989] 1 All ER 306, CA.

103 (1993) *Guardian*, 1 February; (1993) *The Times*, 4 February; for comment see Parpworth, N, 143 *NLJ* 610.

religious (but not racial) discrimination in employment may give rise to liability in Northern Ireland under the Fair Employment (NI) Act 1976.

This next step according to *Perera v Civil Service Commission*[104] is for the applicant to show that an absolute condition has been applied to him or her. In *Perera* this concerned a requirement that a candidate for the Civil Service had a good command of English. This requirement was sometimes waived; it was determined that it could not therefore amount to a 'requirement or condition' for indirect discrimination purposes. As noted above in relation to indirect sexual discrimination this decision has placed a brake on claims of indirect discrimination. It was pointed out in *Meer v Tower Hamlets*[105] by Balcombe LJ in the Court of Appeal that it allows discriminatory preferences free rein, as long as they are not expressed as absolute requirements. In that case a candidate who had previous experience working in the local authority was preferred although such experience was not absolutely required and this had a tendency to debar non-British applicants. The Commission for Racial Equality has recommended that this interpretation should be abandoned so that non-absolute criteria can be considered.[106] If a condition can be identified the applicant must show that a 'considerably smaller proportion of his or her group can comply with it'.[107]

Once the applicant has established a *prima facie* case of indirect discrimination the burden of proof shifts to the employer to show that the requirement or condition is justifiable.[108] In *Ojutiku v Manpower Services Commission*[109] two African students obtained places on a polytechnic management course but were refused grants by the Manpower Services Commission since they lacked industrial experience. They claimed that this requirement was indirectly discriminatory as it was more difficult for African applicants to show that they had previous management experience. However, the claim failed on the basis that the requirement could be justified. The test for justification was determined to be somewhat short of 'necessary', connoting a belief which would be justifiable if held on reasonable grounds and this was reiterated in *Singh v British Railway Engineers*.[110] The applicant, who wore a turban in accordance with his religious beliefs, could not comply with a requirement to wear protective headgear and therefore had to take a less well-paid job. It was found that while the requirement did have an

---

104 [1983] ICR 428; [1983] IRLR 166.
105 [1988] IRLR 399, 403.
106 CRE, *Second Review of the Race Relations Act*, 1991.
107 The 'considerably smaller' test was affirmed in *Orphanos v Queen Mary College* [1985] AC 761; [1985] 2 All ER 233; [1985] 2 WLR 703; for comment on the test see Leigh (1986) 49 *MLR* 235.
108 For discussion of the justification defence see Lustgarten (1983) 133 *NLJ* 1057 and (1984) 134 *NLJ* 9.
109 [1982] IRLR 418.
110 [1986] ICR 22.

adverse impact it was justifiable, partly because the other employees would resent exceptions being made. However, the term 'justifiable' is now to be interpreted in accordance with the *Bilka* test[111] which is applicable in sex discrimination cases and should therefore, by extension, apply to the equivalent provision under the Race Relations Act according to *Hampson v DES*.[112] This accords with the ruling in *Rainey v Greater Glasgow Health Board*[113] that the *Bilka* test would be applicable in sex discrimination and equal pay cases in respect of the grounds on which differential treatment could be justified. This is an important instance of the indirect influence of EU law on national provisions against racial discrimination.

The Commission for Racial Equality has criticised the interpretation of indirect discrimination and has proposed a new definition: any practice or policy which is continued or allowed should be unlawful if it has a significant adverse impact on a particular racial group and is not necessary. It has further proposed that significant adverse impact should mean a 20% difference in impact between groups.[114]

4 VICTIMISATION

Victimisation occurs when a discriminator treats a person less favourably for taking action under the Race Relations Act – does a 'protected act'. The provisions under s 2 of the Act are almost identical to those under s 4 of the Sex Discrimination Act and have the same aim – to deter employers and others from dismissing someone who undertakes a 'protected act'. Following *Aziz v Trinity St Taxis*[115] there has to be a clear causal relationship between the action brought and the unfavourable treatment. Aziz, a taxi driver and a member of TST, thought that TST were unfairly treating him and made a tape recording of a conversation to prove it. He took his claim to an industrial tribunal but it failed. He was then expelled from TST and claimed victimisation. The Court of Appeal considered the question of causation: had TST treated him less favourably by reason of what he had done in making the tapes with a view to bringing the case or had it expelled him because of the breach of trust involved in making the tapes? It was found that the necessary causal relationship was not established; it was not apparent that TST were influenced in their decision to expel him by the fact that the tapes were made in order to bring a race relations case; they would have expelled him anyway

---

111 Above note 96.
112 [1991] 1 AC 171; [1990] 2 All ER 513, HL.
113 [1986] WLR 1017, HL.
114 See the CRE Consultative Paper, *Second Review of the Race Relations Act 1976*, 1991. The 20% notion derives from US civil rights law.
115 [1988] WLR 79; [1988] 2 All ER 860.

due to the breach of trust. This was a fine distinction to make and it is arguable that once a plaintiff has shown that unfavourable treatment has *prima facie* some causal relationship with a protected act, some causal potency, the burden of proof should shift to the employer to show that it was entirely unrelated to that act.

Under s 4(1) of the Sexual Discrimination Act less favourable treatment of someone because she has done a 'protected act' – brought an action or intends to do so or has assisted in such action under the 1975 Act or the Equal Pay Act – amounts to victimisation. The usefulness of this provision has been diminished due to the need to show that the unfavourable treatment is solely due to the protected act and not in part for some other reason.[116] It may often be hard to prove that this is the case and this is particularly unfortunate due to evidence which is beginning to emerge in both race and sex discrimination cases that employers are becoming more likely to respond to a protected act by bringing disciplinary proceedings which might not otherwise have been undertaken. This occurred when Alison Halford brought discrimination proceedings against, *inter alia*, Merseyside Police Authority and was probably a factor in her decision to settle the discrimination claim rather than pursue it to a conclusion.[117] A further barrier to victimisation claims was identified in *Wales v Commissioner of Police for the Metropolis*;[118] it was found that unless the first action complained of amounts to actionable discrimination (the action would have succeeded had it been brought) further unfavourable acts occurring due to the complaint do not fall within s 4(1). This decision may be incorrect and the decision of the Court of Appeal in *Tower Boot Co v Jones*[119] may ameliorate its impact, (since many victimisation claims could be brought as harassment claims) but it does narrow down one avenue leading to possible redress.

5 LAWFUL DISCRIMINATION

Sex

A large number of exclusions were embodied in the Sex Discrimination Act and therefore discrimination in such circumstances was lawful under

---

116 *Aziz v Trinity St Taxis* [1988] 2 All ER 860, CA.

117 A similar conclusion was reached in a race discrimination case which was settled in May 1993. Joginder Singh Prem claimed that Nottinghamshire Police had discriminated against him in failing to promote him. They responded by bringing disciplinary charges which were later dismissed. He was awarded a payment of £20,000 in respect of the discrimination and an *ex gratia* payment of £5,000 in respect of the victimisation although it was denied. See (1993) *Guardian,* 5 May.

118 [1995] IRLR 531. For discussion see (1997) 26(2) *ILJ* 158.

119 [1997] ICR 254; [1997] IRLR 168.

domestic legislation. Certain occupations were excluded under s 19 which covers employment for the purpose of organised religion and s 21 which covers mine workers. The armed forces were also excluded under s 85(4) but this exclusion was abolished under ss 21–28 of the Armed Forces Act 1996. Acts safeguarding national security were exempted (s 52) as were acts done under statutory authority (s 7 and s 51). This last provision means that the 1975 Act is of lower status than other statutes since it is unable to prevail over other statutory provisions relating to the protection of women even though they were passed before it. Thus statutes intended to enshrine discrimination in their provisions such as tax, immigration or social security statutes were not affected by the 1975 Act.[120] These exceptions have tended to be narrowed due to the impact of the Equal Treatment Directive. For discussion of lawful discrimination under EU law see below.[121]

A general exception to provisions against discrimination in the employment field also arises where sex can be said to be a genuine occupational qualification under one of the s 7 provisions.[122] This arises in a number of contexts including those where the job appears to call for a man for reasons of physiology (excluding physical strength or stamina)[123] or for reasons of authenticity in respect of plays or other entertainment or to preserve decency or privacy or where the job involves dealings with other countries where women are less likely to be able to carry them out effectively due to the customs of that other country. MacKinnon has argued that these exceptions are too broad as extending some way beyond biological differences and accepting differential treatment based solely on social categorisation,[124] and it is therefore arguable that they are due to be overhauled and narrowed down, particularly the last mentioned on the ground that the UK should not bow to discriminatory practices in other countries.

Race

Like the Sex Discrimination Act, the Race Relations Act cannot affect (a) discrimination which falls outside its scope or (b) discrimination enshrined in other statutes, even those which pre-date it (s 41(1)). In respect of (a) this includes not only racist behaviour falling outside the contexts covered by the Act but also such behaviour occurring within those contexts but unable to find

---

120 Section 51 was substituted by s 3 of the Employment Act 1989. For discussion of provisions intended to protect women, especially in relation to reproductive risks, see Kennedy (1986) 14 *IJSL* 393.
121 Pages 602–08. See particularly the discussion of *Johnston v Chief Constable of the RUC* [1986] ECR 1651.
122 For analysis of s 7 see Pannick (1984) *OJLS* 198.
123 For criticism of this provision see Pannick, D, *Sex Discrimination Law*, 1985, p 238.
124 MacKinnon, C, *Sexual Harassment of Working Women*, 1979, pp 121, 180.

a legal niche within them due to the particular wording of the Act. For example, it was found in *De Souza v AA*[125] that racial insults, as such, do not amount to 'unfavourable treatment' within employment. Similarly, one of the exceptions may apply; the Act employs the concept of a genuine occupational qualification (GOQ) but the GOQs are of much narrower scope than those arising under the 1975 Act. They come down to two. First, that for reasons of authenticity a person of a particular racial group must be employed. This might cover plays and restaurants or clubs with a particular national theme. Secondly, the services being provided are aimed at persons of a specific racial group and can most effectively be provided by persons of that same racial group. In *Lambeth v CRE*[126] it was determined that this requirement would be interpreted restrictively: a managerial position which involved little contact with the public would not fulfil it. Other exceptions in respect of small premises or partnerships with less than six partners are provided by s 10 and s 32.

6 EQUAL PAY[127]

The Equal Pay Act 1970 governs the contractual aspects of a woman's employment. It is anomalous in that it is separate from the Sex Discrimination Act; there is no good reason for having two separate instruments and it merely introduces further complexity and technicality into an already complex scheme. The Act received the royal assent in 1970 but it did not come into force until 1975; the idea was that employers would voluntarily remove sexual discrimination in pay. In fact, as the TUC warned the government would happen, employers moved women off the 'women's grade' on to the lowest grades with a view to minimising their statutory obligations and made sure that men and women were not working on comparable jobs.

The aim of the Act is to prevent discrimination as regards terms and conditions of employment between men and women and to this end it employs the device of an equality clause. If certain conditions are satisfied the terms of the woman's contract are deemed to include such a clause. Under the original provisions the equality clause only operated in two circumstances:

---

125 [1986] ICR 514; for comment see Carty (1986) 49 *MLR* 653; see also *Khan v GMC* (1993) *The Times*, 29 March.

126 [1990] IRLR 231, CA.

127 General reading: Townshend-Smith, R, *Sex Discrimination in Employment: Law, Practice and Policy*, 1989, Chap 9; Bourne, C and Whitmore, J, *Discrimination and Equal Pay*, 1989, Chap 7; Arnull 'Article 119 and Equal Pay for Work of Equal Value' (1986) Eur L Rev 200; 'Pay Inequalities and Equal Value Claims' (1985) *MLR* 560; 'Courts, Community Law and Equal Pay' [1988] *PL* 485; Edwards, M, 'Equal Pay: the European Dimension' (1990) *BLR* July 177; Bourne, C, 'Equal Pay' 140 *NLJ* 1284; Fenwick, H, 'Indirect Discrimination in Equal Pay Claims' (1995) 3 *European Public Law* 331.

that the woman was employed on like work with men in the same employment under s 1(2)(a) or on work rated by a job evaluation scheme as equivalent to that of a man in the same employment under s 1(2)(b). The latter provision was not of much value as it was voluntary and it was therefore left to the woman to persuade her employer to undertake such a scheme. In practice this meant that women were left with the like work provisions. Due to sexual segregation in the job market women were concentrated in certain occupations, such as cleaning or cooking and were unable to point to a man doing like work even where he was in the same employment.

Thus, the Act had little impact on women's lower pay since it could only be used against the most gross forms of pay discrimination. However, in 1982 the European Commission brought an action against the UK (*Commission of European Communities v UK*)[128] on the basis that the UK was in breach of its obligations under the Equal Pay Directive due to the narrow application of the equality clause. In response the UK government was forced to amend the 1970 Act in order to include the possibility of making an equal value claim. It did so very reluctantly and this was reflected in the response. The amendment (new s 1(2)(c)) was effected by statutory instrument, thereby curtailing debate on the new provisions and the new regulations were intended to operate only as a last resort: the other two possibilities had to be tried first. Moreover, an attempt was made to widen the defences available to employers by using a different wording for equal value claims.

Choice of comparator

The first step under the Act is for the woman to choose a comparator. This might have caused difficulty where the woman was employed doing like work with a few men but wanted to compare herself with a man doing work of equal value; however, the issue was resolved in favour of claimants by the House of Lords in *Pickstone v Freemans*.[129] Mrs Pickstone and other warehouse operatives were paid less than male warehouse checkers but a man was employed as an operative. The defendants therefore argued that the claim was barred due to the wording of s 1(2)(c): '... where a woman is employed on work which, *not being work to which (a) or (b) applies,* is ... of equal value ...' (emphasis added). Paragraph (a) did apply because one man was employed doing the same work and therefore it could be argued that a like work claim arose but not an equal value one. The House of Lords considered that allowing this argument to succeed would mean that Parliament had failed once again to implement its obligations under Article 119 and it could not have intended such a failure. In such circumstances any interpretation should

---

128 [1982] ICR 578; [1982] 3 CMLR 284.
129 [1988] AC 66; [1988] 2 All ER 803; for comment see: (1988) *MLR* 221; [1988] *PL* 483.

take into account the terms in which the amending regulations were presented to Parliament; in other words a purposive approach should be adopted. Using this approach the defendants' argument could be rejected on the basis that the claimant should be able to choose her comparator, rather than allowing the employer to impose one on her. This ruling put an end to what has been termed the 'token man loophole':[130] had it gone the other way employers might have been encouraged to employ one man alongside a large number of women in order to bar equal value claims.

'Same employment'

Once a claimant has chosen a comparator it must be shown that they are in the same employment. The meaning of this provision was considered by the house of lords in *Leverton v Clwyd County Council*.[131] A nursery nurse who wished to compare her pay with that of clerical staff was not employed in the same establishment as they were. Under s 1(6) 'the same employment' is defined as meaning at the same establishment *or* as by same employer and the same conditions of employment are observed. The claimant and comparators were employed by the same employer and, although there were some differences in the individual terms of employment, it was still possible for the House of Lords to find on a broad view of the agreement governing the terms of employment of claimant and comparator that they were sufficiently similar to satisfy the s 1(6) test.

Clearly it would be possible to frame legislation allowing equal value claims so that it would operate in one of three circumstances: it could apply to all employees who could point to any other employee wherever employed doing work of equal value; it could apply to employees employed by the same employer governed by roughly similar terms of service – the position taken under the UK legislation – or it could apply to employees working under the same roof as their comparators. In making it clear that a broad middle way is open to such claims the House of Lords gave encouragement to them and followed a policy which seems to be in tune with that underlying the legislation.

However, it is worth considering the advantages of the first and least restrictive method which was omitted from the legislation in order to minimise disruption to existing pay structures. If in principle a person doing work of equal value to that of another worker should be paid an equal wage if the inequality is attributable to sex discrimination, then it ought to be immaterial that the two workers are employed by two different employers. It might be said that an employer cannot be expected to take responsibility for

---

130 See 138 *NLJ* 341.
131 [1989] 2 WLR 47; [1989] 1 WLR 65, HL.

the wage policies of other concerns but can only be expected to remove pay discrimination within the sphere he or she is able to affect. However, on a broader view it might be argued that an employer has a duty to ensure that his or her own concern is not operating a discriminatory wage scheme whatever the basis of comparison. In closing off that broad possibility the legislation leaves intact the grossest pay disparities arising from establishments with low paid all-female workforces, because they cannot point to a male comparator. This aspect of the legislation may even encourage sexual segregation in employment because if no male is employed (other than those prepared to work for the same low wages as the women) – at least in any post conceivably comparable with that of the majority of the work force – equal value claims are precluded. The result in some occupations may be the encouragement of a low paid all-female-workforce overseen by a few men in managerial positions.

The term by term approach

Assuming that a claimant can point to a comparator in the same employment the industrial tribunal will appoint an independent expert in order to determine whether the two jobs are of equal value under such heads as responsibility, skill, effort, qualifications and length of training. The expert's report is not conclusive of the issue but the tribunal is unlikely to reject it. If the jobs are of equal value then a term of the claimant's contract which is less favourable than a term of her comparator's will be compared. It is now clear after the ruling of the House of Lords in *Hayward v Cammell Laird*[132] that the term by term approach – as opposed to consideration of the contract as a whole – is correct. The defendants had resisted the plaintiff's claim on the ground that her contract and that of the male comparators must each be looked at as a whole, in which case her perks such as free lunches and two additional days holiday equalled the £25 per week extra which the men received. The House of Lords found that the word 'term' in s 1(2) was to be given its natural and ordinary meaning as a distinct part of a contract and therefore it was necessary to look at one term of the claimant's contract; if there was a similar provision in the comparator's contract which was found after they had been compared to be less favourable to the woman than the term in the comparator's, then the equality clause would operate to make that term equally favourable to her.

Obviously this ruling prevented employers claiming that fringe benefits equalled pay. Such a claim might have been advantageous to an employer who might be able to provide a benefit at little real cost such as free meals for

---

132 [1988] WLR 265; [1988] 2 All ER 803; for comment see Ellis (1988) 51 *MLR* 781; Napier, 'Julie Hayward and the continuing saga of equal pay', 138 *NLJ* 341.

a cook. Moreover, previously employers might have provided a 'protective package' for female employees which included less pay but more time off or more sick benefits. All women, whether desirous of such a package or not, would receive it whether or not they would have preferred to be paid more. Employers, however, feared that the *Hayward* ruling would lead to 'leap frogging'; women would receive the male higher pay; the men would then claim the women's old fringe benefits and all employees would level up to the detriment of the company which would be faced with a great increase in costs. However, employers may be able to avoid this by gradually modifying practices on pay and fringe benefits. There would also be the possibility – mentioned only as *dicta* in *Hayward* – that certain fringe benefits might be used to found a defence to an equal value claim (see below).

The 'material factor' defence

Even if a woman is able to show that she is doing like work, work rated as equivalent or work of equal value to that of her comparator the claim will fail if a s 1(3) defence operates:

> ... an equality clause shall not operate in relation to a variation between the woman's contract and the man's contract if the employer proves that the variation is genuinely due to a material factor which is not the difference of sex and that factor:
>
> (a) In the case of an equality clause falling within subsection (2)(a) or (b) above, must be a material difference between the woman's case and the man's; and
>
> (b) In the case of an equality clause falling within subsection (2)(c) above, may be such a material difference.

This is known as the 'material factor defence'. The difference in wording for equal value claims was intended to mean that a 'material factor' could be interpreted more widely in such claims. In fact, as will be seen, the width of the interpretation given to the defence in all three types of claim means that this possibility is of less significance than was expected. The defence will operate if a material difference between the cases of the woman and the man can be identified which is *not the difference of sex* – such as additional payment for the geographical difference in the location of two parts of the same concern. As the 1970 Act must be construed in harmony with the Sex Discrimination Act the variation in pay must be genuinely due to the factor in question; otherwise it may be discriminatory and therefore in *Shields v E Coomes*[133] the difference in pay was apparently due to the protective function exercised by the male employees in a betting shop. However, not all the men discharged such a function but all received the higher pay and therefore

---

133 [1978] WLR 1408, CA.

allowing the protective function to operate as a material factor would have been directly discriminatory because a woman who exercised no protective function would not receive the higher pay while a man in the same position would.

In *Leverton v Clwyd County Council*[134] the House of Lords found that different hours and holidays could amount to a material factor under s 1(3) if pay could be broken down into a notional hourly income. If once this was done the pay of claimant and comparator was found to be equal the claim would fail on the basis that the difference in salaries was due to the difference in hours and not to the difference of sex. This point was touched on *obiter* in *Hayward* but in *Leverton* it was made clear that a s 1(3) defence might be available where a man and a woman had different contractual packages so long as the packages did not contain any element of direct or indirect discrimination. It may be noted that more than one material factor may be identified; if so it is not necessary for the employer to establish the proportion which each factor contributes to the difference in pay.[135]

The most far reaching and controversial argument under s 1(3) has been termed the 'market forces argument'[136] since it allows the employer to argue that because the market may favour some employees more than others they must be paid more and that to fail to do so would be to disrupt normal market forces.[137] In other words, if a woman is willing to work for less than a man this provides a reason for paying her less. The early cases rejected this argument;[138] in *Jenkins v Kinsgate*,[139] for example, a part time worker was paid at a different hourly rate from the full time workers. The employer tried to use the s 1(3) defence in answer to her claim for equal hourly pay in arguing that part time workers have less bargaining power and therefore the market demanded that he should pay full time workers more. The argument was that this was a genuine difference between the two cases which was not sex-related; any part time worker, male or female, would have been paid less. However, the part timers were all female and so the practice had a disparate impact on women. Construing the Equal Pay Act in accordance with the Sex Discrimination Act, the EAT concluded that a practice which had a disparate impact on women could not sustain a s 1(3) defence as to allow it to do so would be indirectly discriminatory.

---

134 [1989] WLR 47.
135 *Calder v Rowntree Machintosh Ltd* [1993] IRLR 27.
136 Townshend-Smith, R, *Sex Discrimination in Employment*, p 175.
137 The US doctrine of 'comparable worth' has also been attacked as disruptive of market forces: see eg Weiler 99 *Harvard L Rev* 1728.
138 *Clay Cross v Fletcher* [1978] 1 WLR 1429; [1979] 1 All ER 474.
139 [1981] IRLR 388 at 390.

However, this approach was not followed in *Rainey v Greater Glasgow Health Board*[140] which concerned a comparison between female and male prosthetists working in the NHS. The men were receiving higher pay but the defendants argued that this was due to the need to attract them from the private sector in order to set up the prosthetist service. This argument entailed consideration not just of factors relating to the personal attributes of the claimant and comparator, such as length of experience but also the difference in their individual positions in the market. In other words, it widened what could be considered as a material factor. The relevant circumstances were that those from the private sector had to be paid above the normal rate to attract them. However, the House of Lords held that although taking this into account as a material factor was acceptable it must be objectively justified – no element of discrimination must have crept into the circumstances. In order to ensure this the House of Lords used the same test as for justification under indirect discrimination – the *Bilka* test laid down by the European Court of Justice.[141] Here the objective was setting up the NHS prosthetist service which entailed attracting sufficient experienced prosthetists. The means chosen involved attracting persons from the private sector which involved paying them more. It was accepted that this was both appropriate and necessary. So the material factor passed the *Bilka* test and further, because this was a like work case, the factor *had* to be a difference between comparator and claimant. The difference was that she was from the public while he was from the private sector.

Thus this ruling broadened what could be termed a material factor and allowed market forces to defeat equal pay claims so long as no indirect discrimination was shown. Clearly, the danger of the market forces argument is that employers will often argue that business will suffer if a group of women are paid more. What are termed 'women's jobs' have traditionally been undervalued by the market; the equal pay legislation was specifically aimed at breaking down traditional pay hierarchies and therefore this argument, if allowed too wide a scope could completely undermine it. However, the *Rainey* ruling does appear to an extent to be trying to keep the argument in check in finding that only in objectively justified circumstances should more be paid to a certain group; this is not the same as allowing the market generally to set the rate. The effect of this argument was further curbed in *Benveniste v University of Southampton*;[142] it was found that although

---

140 [1987] AC 224; [1987] 1 All ER 65; [1987] 3 WLR 1017, HL. It may be that the reasoning in *Rainey* will be applied only where indirect discrimination can be identified affecting the factor in question: *Strathclyde Regional Council v Wallace* [1996] IRLR 672, noted (1997) 26(2) *ILJ* 171. If this is correct the factor need not be objectively justified: it need only be genuinely necessary and material, ie relevant. One problem with this approach is that it may lead to failures to recognise the existence of indirect discrimination affecting material factors.
141 In *Bilka-kaufhaus CmbH v Weber von Hartz* [1986] IRLR 317; [1986] CMLR 701. See above pp 572–73.
142 [1989] IRLR 122.

particular constraints might affect pay and might lead to a pay differential between a man and a woman, they could do so only while the constraint was in operation. Once it had ceased to apply the lower pay should be raised to the level it would have been at had it not been affected by the constraint.

A variation on the market forces argument was put forward in *Enderby v Frenchay*.[143] Speech therapists wished to compare their pay with that of clinical psychologists and pharmacists who were paid at much higher rates. The employers denied that the work of the two groups was of equal value but argued that in any event a material factor justified the difference: it had emerged as a result of different pay negotiations and, moreover, the pharmacists were in demand in the private sector and this had influenced pay. The employers further argued that the speech therapists could not assert that the material factor was tainted by indirect discrimination without first showing that a condition had been applied to employees which had an adverse impact on women. The employer thus had two arguments: first no condition could be identified which had been applied; secondly, if it had been it could be justified due to the factors mentioned: the separate pay processes in conjunction with market forces.

The claimant however argued that the salaries of the therapists were low due to the fact that the profession was predominantly female and that whether a condition could be identified or not was immaterial: in practice one type of work was largely done by women and another largely by men and although of equal value the men's work attracted a higher salary. These factors, it was claimed, gave rise to a presumption of discrimination which could not be objectively justified because the reason for the difference was that the profession in question was staffed by women. This argument, if accepted, would have distinguished the claim from that in *Rainey*.

The EAT found for the employers, ruling that the pay was the result of different bargaining processes which looked at separately were not indirectly discriminatory. Therefore, a material factor could be identified which was influenced by market forces. Further, even if the factor identified did not justify all of the difference in pay that did not matter because it was impossible to say how much was needed above normal rates to attract and retain certain staff. It was clear that the case raised difficult issues and so at the Court of Appeal stage three questions were referred to the European Court of Justice:

(1) If there is a difference in pay between two jobs assumed to be of equal value, of which one is carried out almost exclusively by women and the other predominantly by men, must the difference be objectively justified by the employer? Does this mean that all the steps needed to show indirect discrimination should be taken, including identifying a particular barrier?

---

143 [1994] 1 All ER 495; [1993] ECR I-5535, ECJ; [1992] IRLR 15, CA.

(2) Are separate bargaining processes a sufficient justification for a variation in pay if they are not internally discriminatory?

(3) If there is a need to pay men more to attract them but only part of the difference in pay is for that purpose then does that justify all of the difference?

The first question relates to the determination of a *prima facie* case of indirect sex discrimination; is it necessary to be able to identify a 'barrier' or 'condition' which it is more difficult for women to meet than men (or vice versa) in order to show indirect discrimination? The second and third questions relate to justifications for indirect discrimination. First, is the use of separate sex neutral collective bargaining systems sufficient justification for indirect sex discrimination? Second, will the more favourable market position of certain employees justify unequal pay? In other words, can the overt operation of market forces justify indirect sex discrimination?

Assuming that the jobs compared were of equal value, the Court of Justice held,[144] reiterating the well-established principle of reversal of the burden of proof in indirect sex discrimination cases (citing Case C-33/89 *Kowalska v Freie und Hansestadt Hamburg*[145] and Case C-184/89 *Nimz v Freie und Hansestadt Hamburg*[146] concerning measures distinguishing between employees on the basis of their hours of work, including equal pay cases) that '... it is for the employer to prove that his practice in the matter of wages is not discriminatory, if a female worker establishes, in relation to a relatively large number of employees, that the average pay for women is less than that for men'.

Applying these rulings by analogy to this *equal value* claim, the court concluded that there *is* a *prima facie* case of sex discrimination, where the pay of speech therapists is significantly lower than that of clinical psychologists and pharmacists and speech therapists are almost exclusively women. The 'factual' considerations as to whether the jobs are indeed of equal value and whether the statistics adduced support the required disparities are questions for the national court. At this point, the burden of objective justification shifts to the employer.

The court replied in the negative to the question whether separate collective bargaining processes, which are each, in themselves, non-discriminatory, constitute sufficient objective justification for the differences in pay. The fact that the different wages are reached by separate processes of collective bargaining does not of itself justify the discrimination, since it is a

---

144 *Enderby v Frenchay* [1994] 1 All ER 495; [1993] ECR I-5535, ECJ; [1992] IRLR 15, CA.
145 [1990] ECR I-2591.
146 [1991] ECR I-297.

merely descriptive explanation. It fails to explain *why* one process produced a more favourable result for the employees than the other. Moreover, allowing that justification would enable employers to circumvent the principle of equal pay very readily by using such separate processes.

In contrast to its answer to the second question, the court accepted 'the state of the employment market' in its answer to the third as a possible justification for indirect discrimination. The market forces concerned here were the shortage of candidates for the more highly paid job and the consequent need to offer higher pay in that job in order to attract candidates. The court repeated that it is the duty of the national courts to decide 'questions of fact' such as this and reiterated from its previous case law[147] some forms of 'needs of the employer' which may constitute justification for indirect sex discrimination.[148]

While the questions referred to the ECJ were unanswered, the issue raised in (2) was resolved in *Barber and Others v NCR (Manufacturing) Ltd*[149] using a completely different approach from that of the EAT in Enderby and one which seems to be more in harmony with the policy of the Act and with the *Bilka* test. Indirect clerical workers, who were mainly women, wanted to claim equal pay with direct clerical workers who were mainly men (the women's work was 'indirect' as not directly related to shop floor production). The direct workers negotiated a new agreement regarding hours and moved to a shorter week. Thus the hourly rates of the two groups now differed although it had been the same. The EAT considered whether the employer had established that because the difference arose from different collective bargaining agreements untainted internally by discrimination this could found a s 1(3) defence. In putting forward this argument the employers had relied on *Enderby* where the EAT had held that this was possible. The EAT said that the correct question to be asked must first be identified. It could be asked whether the cause of the variation in pay was free from sex discrimination or it could be asked whether the variation was itself genuinely due to a material factor other than the difference of sex. The second question was the right one because the cause – separate collective bargaining processes – might be free from discrimination but the *result* might not be. In this instance the evidence showed *why* the difference had been arrived at but did not show any objective factor which justified it. Thus there was a pay difference which was not based on a material factor. The equality clause therefore operated meaning that although the claimants did not obtain the same pay as the comparators due to the difference in hours, the hourly rates were equalised.

---

147 Case 170/84 *Bilka* [1986] ECR 1607, Case C-184/89 *Nimz v Freie und Hansestadt Hamburg* [1991] ECR I-297 and Case 109/88 *Danfoss* [1989] ECR 3199; [1989] IRLR 532.
148 In 1997 the government conceded the equal value issue and settled the claim: see April 1997 *IRLB* No 567.
149 [1993] IRLR 95. *Cf* the decision in *British Coal Corporation v Smith* [1993] IRLR 308.

The EAT considered that it did not need to refer to the ECJ or await the decision in *Enderby* since the proper result could be arrived at under domestic law.

This ruling was foreshadowed in *Handels-og Kontorfunktionaerernes Forbund i Danmark v Dansk Arbejdsgiverforening* (the *Danfoss* case)[150] which was a Danish reference to the ECJ. The Court did not need to consider the question as to the relevance of two separate collective agreements, one for women, one for men but when the Advocate General addressed this point he determined that the existence of such agreements would not exclude the operation of the Equal Pay Directive although it would not inevitably be unlawful to have two separate agreements; it would be the manner of the agreements which would be relevant.

This approach should prevail, it is submitted, because merely to ask whether arriving at two levels of pay was due to the operation of two different bargaining processes would be to obscure the discriminatory nature of the result.[151] It is necessary to look behind the bargaining processes and to ask why one was able to arrive at a more favourable result. This might be because unions have traditionally been more effectual in obtaining better pay for men than for women and in itself this may be due to the fact that men's work has traditionally been valued more highly by the market than women's. Thus, to use different agreements as a material factor in themselves would be to cloak the discriminatory forces which lie behind them.

The main issue in the *Danfoss* case arose because the Danfoss Company paid the same basic wage to all employees but also an individual supplement based on factors such as mobility and training. The result was that a somewhat lower average wage was paid to women and it was therefore claimed that the system was discriminatory. The Court determined that because the system lacked transparency, once a woman had shown that the average wage of women and men differed, the burden of proof would shift to the employer to prove that the wage practice was not discriminatory. It would have been unfair to expect the woman to prove that the system was discriminatory since she would not have been able to work out which factors had been taken into account. The Court considered that even if the application of criteria such as the need to be mobile worked to the detriment of women the employer could still use them in relation to specific tasks entrusted to the employee so long as the *Bilka* test was satisfied.

---

150 [1989] ECR 3199; [1989] IRLR 532.
151 For comment on this issue see 'Equal Value Claims and Sex Bias in Collective Bargaining' (1991) 20 *ILJ* 163; see also (1989) *ILJ* 63.

Conclusions

The *Enderby* approach in the European Court of Justice obviously eases the task of the claimant in showing that a material factor is tainted with indirect discrimination in order to shift the onus onto the employer and determines that asking an employee to identify a specific requirement or condition where it is alleged that a material factor is so tainted is misconceived. Sometimes it may be possible to identify a condition such as a need to be mobile in order to attract higher pay. However, and this seems to be the basis of the decision in *Enderby*, in many instances it may not be possible to identify any such condition with sufficient specificity. Instead it would seem that where two jobs are of equal value but that held by the woman attracts lower pay, the suggestion is that the market has allowed differentiation due to the traditional expectation that a woman would not be the breadwinner and would therefore work for less.

Thus the 'condition' which has been applied, in a general sense, is for a woman to work in a traditionally 'male' occupation such as lorry driving rather than in one of a traditionally 'female' nature such as cooking in order to obtain the higher pay. Obviously some women can do so but such a requirement hits disproportionately at women since in practice they will be less likely to enter the 'male' occupation due to tradition, discrimination against them, perceived and real, in such occupations and social conditioning. Identifying such a 'condition' should suffice to raise an inference of indirect discrimination which of course would be open theoretically to rebuttal by an objective justification. To go further as the EAT appeared to do in *Enderby* and require identification of some specific condition which the particular employer has imposed is to misunderstand the nature of equal pay claims and the scheme of the Act which is predicated on the assumption that it is not pure coincidence that some jobs done predominantly by women are paid less than those done predominantly by men. In other words, the 'condition' should be assumed to apply to a largely female profession; the question is whether the difference in pay can be justified and it may be argued that where a particular occupation is staffed predominantly by women and is of equal value to one staffed predominantly by men but there is a wide disparity in pay, it would be hard for the employer, if not impossible, to show that the difference arose from anything other than the mere fact that one occupation *was* female dominated. In any event it is clear that the fact of separate bargaining processes merely amounts to a smoke screen obscuring the traditional operation of market forces founding the difference in pay and therefore clearly should not be able to justify it, given that the legislation was introduced in order to interfere with, rather than bow to, market forces.

The material factor defence could potentially be seen as operating at three different levels of generality. First, it might only arise where a difference in the 'personal equation' of the man and the woman, such as length of experience or qualifications, could be identified. This was the approach rejected in *Rainey*. Secondly, a factor might be identified going beyond the personal equation of the complainant but still amounting to a non-sex-based difference between her and her comparator. At the present time this is the predominant approach. The most significant factor of this type and the one most likely to undermine the equal pay scheme is the 'market forces' factor which received some endorsement from the ECJ in *Enderby*. This factor is, however, subject to a rigorous application of the *Bilka* test; it does not mean that the laws of supply and demand can simply determine the rates of pay in question. Nevertheless, adoption of this approach may tend to undermine the aim of the Act as removing pay discrimination. Thirdly – and this defence would be available only in respect of equal value claims due to the wider wording applicable – there might be scope for a number of market based arguments *not* based on a difference between the man's and woman's case, such as using the leap frogging argument from *Hayward* as being *in itself* a material factor although arising only from the general operation of the concern in question. This possibility has not yet been put forward; it would, of course, be out of harmony with the policy of the Act and arguably could not be termed an 'objectively justified reason' under the *Bilka* test. The complexities of the second approach, which the courts are currently trying to get to grips with, illustrate the difficulty adverted to at the beginning of this chapter of ensuring that only morally justifiable differentiation occurs.

7 EFFICACY OF THE INDIVIDUAL METHOD

Remedies

The main weakness of the individual method arises from the various remedies available in both race and sex discrimination cases which (apart from an award of equal pay) are generally perceived as inadequate[152] as are the means of enforcing them. A tribunal can award a declaration which simply states the rights of the applicant and the respect in which the employer has breached the law. It can also can award an action recommendation which will be intended to reduce the effect of the discrimination. However, the EAT in *British Gas plc v Sharma*[153] held that this could not include a recommendation that the applicant be promoted to the next suitable vacancy since this would amount to positive discrimination. It has, however, been pointed out that this would merely be putting the person in the position he or she should have been in rather than giving them a special preference due to

---

152 See Lustgarten (1980) pp 225–28; Cotterrell [1981] *PL* 469, 475.
153 [1991] ICR 19; [1991] IRLR 101.

race or sex.[154] The tribunal can also award compensation which will be determined on the same basis as in other tort cases. It will be awarded for pecuniary loss and injury to feelings; exemplary damages will not be available. Awards have tended to be low[155] but they have risen since the decision in *Noone*[156] in which a consultant who was not appointed on grounds of race was awarded £3,000 for injury to feelings. In *Alexander* some guidance as to awarding compensation for injury to feelings was given by May LJ:

> ... awards should not be minimal because this would tend to trivialise or diminish respect for the public policy to which the Act gives effect. On the other hand ... awards should be restrained.

He considered that they should not be set at the same level as damages for defamation and awarded £500 for injured feelings due to racial discrimination.[157] The legislation placed an upper limit on awards which was equivalent to that payable under the compensatory award for unfair dismissal. However, the upper limit on damages in respect of sex discrimination was challenged before the European Court of Justice in *Marshall (No 2)*.[158] The ECJ found that the award of compensation in sex discrimination cases brought against organs of the state should be set at a level which would allow the loss sustained to be made good in full. Thus, the Court found that the fixing of an upper limit of this nature was contrary to the principle underlying the Equal Treatment Directive since it was not consistent with the principle of ensuring real equality of opportunity. In response to this decision the upper limits for compensation under the Sex Discrimination and Race Relations Acts were abolished (SI 1993/2798: Race Relations Remedies Act 1994). The result has been a dramatic increase in the size of awards. For example, in *Johnson v HM Prison Service and Others*[159] an award of £28,500 was upheld on appeal. It was found that the award was not excessive in the circumstances; severe victimisation on racial grounds had occurred. It may be noted that this is currently the highest UK award made in a racial harassment case. No compensation is payable in respect of indirect discrimination unless there has been an intention to discriminate; this exclusion from the compensation scheme has been much criticised[160] and may contravene

---

154 See Rubenstein, M [1991] IRLR 99.
155 Gregory notes that in 40% of cases the award was less than £200 and in only 29% it exceeded £1,000 (Gregory, *Sex, Race and the Law*, 1987, pp 80–81).
156 [1988] ICR 813; [1988] 83 IRLR 195.
157 [1988] 1 WLR 968, CA. See 144 *NLJ* for discussion of this judgment and of the general approach to the assessment of damages.
158 [1993] QB 126; [1993] 3 WLR 1054; [1993] 4 All ER 586; [1993] IRLR 445, ECJ; [1994] 1 All ER 736, HL.
159 (1996) *The Times*, 31 December.
160 See eg Townshend-Smith, R, *Sex Discrimination in Employment*, p 206.

European law.[161] It seems fairly clear that awards made at the levels mentioned prior to the *Marshall (No 2)* decision were unlikely to deter employers from discrimination and to affect deeply rooted discriminatory ideologies in institutions.

It is fairly common for the defendant to fail to comply with the award[162] and if so the applicant must return to court in order to enforce it. If an action recommendation has not been complied with the tribunal will award compensation but only if compensation could have been awarded at the original hearing. As this is unlikely to be the case in an indirect discrimination claim no remedy will be available except to apply to the CRE or the EOC alleging persistent discrimination.

Success rate of applications

The individual method has had only limited success in bringing about change. Gregory notes that in 1976 only 40% of applications in respect of sex discrimination were heard and 10% were successful, while in the same year 45% of applications in respect of race discrimination were heard and 3.4% were successful.[163] The number of applications began to decline from 1976 onwards although there is evidence that it is beginning, in the 1990s, to rise again.[164] The decline may have occurred because the success rate was so low that applicants were deterred from bringing a claim in the first place. In other words, the number of applications may have been self-limiting: only the very determined applicants would pursue cases all the way to a hearing. Of course, the decline in the rate of applications may have been partly attributable to the initial rush to attack very blatant examples of sexism and racism, which died away as employers and others began to ensure that policies enshrining such values were either abolished or made less overt.

Less than half of the applications are heard; there is obviously a strong tendency to give up a claim half way through. There may be a number of reasons why cases are not brought, why they are abandoned and why the success rate is so low. Obviously the applicant is in a very vulnerable position; the position of the parties is usually unequal especially if an applicant is bringing the claim against his or her employer. The applicant will be afraid of being labelled a troublemaker, perhaps of being sacked or of losing promotion prospects. There may be continual pressure not only on the applicant but on

---

161 In *Von Colson v Land Nordrhein-Westfalen* [1984] ECR 1891 the Court held that any sanction must have a real deterrent effect. See also *Marshall (No 2)* above note 158.
162 Leonard, *Judging Inequality*, 1987, found that almost 50% of applicants reported delay in getting the employer to pay the compensation (pp 27–29).
163 Gregory, J, *Sex, Race and the Law*, 1987, pp 87–88.
164 *The Equality Challenge*, EOC Annual Report for 1991; it showed an increase of 40% in applications in that year.

any work mates who have consented to act as witnesses in the claim and they may withdraw their consent to act. The weakness of the remedies is unlikely to encourage claims and the complexity and technicality of the substantive law may also act as a deterrent. It may do so in any event but coupled with the lack of legal aid the task facing the applicant may appear overwhelming.

These two factors are exacerbated by and also contribute to the lack of experience tribunal members have of discrimination cases. The applicant may be aided by the Equal Opportunities Commission or the Commission for Racial Equality but both have to refuse the majority of applications due to their lack of funds. This leads to a poor quality of decision-making and to the charge that the employers' lawyers may manipulate the members of the tribunal due to their lack of experience in the area. Thus a vicious circle is set up. The tribunals need more experience in these cases but do not receive it due to the factors mentioned here; when a tribunal does hear such a case it may deal with it badly, thereby having the effect of deterring future applicants and ensuring that tribunals do not gain more experience.[165]

Reform

The CRE has proposed that there should be a discrimination division of industrial tribunals dealing only with discrimination claims.[166] Such tribunals would gather expertise in such cases and could be equipped with powers to order higher levels of compensation. Legal aid could then be made available in this specialist division even though it remained unavailable in respect of other tribunal cases. The EOC has recommended that equal pay and sex discrimination provisions should be combined in one statute and that the distinction between indirect and direct discrimination as regards compensation should be abolished. Thus, where a person had acted in an indirectly discriminatory fashion, although unmotivated by sexism, compensation would still be payable. This is desirable because there is some evidence that some employers have deliberately failed to conduct a review of working practices so as to be able to put forward a convincing argument that they did not appreciate the discriminatory affect of certain practices. Both bodies have put forward proposals, which are considered below, to strengthen the individual method of challenging discriminatory practices by allowing it to work in tandem with the general, administrative method to a greater extent. Due to their levels of funding, both bodies have to refuse many applications from individuals asking for help in bringing cases; such under-

---

[165] See further on sex claims Leonard, *Judging Inequality*, Cobden Trust, 1987; on race claims Lustgarten (1986) 49 *MLR* 68. See too generally, Honeyball, *Sex, Employment and the Law*, 1991, Chap 1.

[166] *Review of the Race Relations Act 1976: Proposals for Change*, Proposal 10.

funding suggests that there is at present a lack of genuine commitment in government to ending discriminatory practices.

8 THE COMMISSION FOR RACIAL EQUALITY AND THE EQUAL OPPORTUNITIES COMMISSION

Investigative and remedial powers

Apart from the individual method of bringing about change, the Race Relations and Sex Discrimination Acts also contain an administrative method which was included with the aim of relieving the burden on individual applicants.[167] It may also represent a more coherent approach than the piecemeal method of bringing individual cases. The aim was to bring about general changes in discriminatory practices rather than waiting for an individual to take on the risk and the burden of bringing a case.

Both the CRE and the EOC have two main powers. They can assist claimants and they can issue a non-discrimination notice in respect of discriminatory practices where there may be no known victim who wants to bring a claim. This situation might arise because the company or institution had effectively deterred certain people from coming forward with applications for a job. In such circumstances if indications of discrimination became apparent – if, for example, it seemed that very few of a certain group were employed – then first a formal investigation (ss 48–50 of the Race Relations Act) would be conducted. This decision might be taken if, for example, the workforce was only 1% black although the company was in a racially mixed area in which the black group comprised about 30% of the population. It might be found that the recruiting policy was indirectly discriminatory; for example it might largely be by word of mouth and therefore the existing workforce might tend to reproduce itself. If discriminatory practices were found, a non-discrimination notice would be issued and the CRE might apply for an injunction to enforce it under s 62(1).

However, the CRE has had the use of the power to issue a non-discrimination notice curbed by the House of Lords decision in *Prestige Group plc, Re; CRE v Prestige Group plc*.[168] It was found that the CRE was not entitled to investigate a named person or company unless it already had a strong reason to believe that discrimination had occurred. This meant that where such suspicion did not exist the CRE could embark on a general investigation

---

167 For discussion of the role of these two bodies see Lustgarten, L, 'The CRE Under Attack' (1982) *PL* 229; Lacey, N, 'A Change in the Right Direction? The CRE's Consultative Document' [1984] *PL* 186; Lustgarten (1983) 133 *NLJ* 1057. For the EOC see Sacks, 'The EOC – 10 years on' (1986) *MLR* 560.
168 [1984] 1 WLR 335; [1984] ICR 473.

only, meaning that it could not subpoena evidence or issue a non-discrimination notice. Thus the CRE and the EOC are now confined to a reactive approach; they can only react to very blatant forms of discrimination rather than investigating the more subtle and insidious instances of discrimination which may be the more pernicious. After this decision the CRE had to abandon a number of investigations which it had already begun. There has therefore been a tendency for subtle institutionalised racism to continue unchecked, although more blatant racism such as the phrase 'no blacks' which used to appear in advertisements has now disappeared.

Judicial review

Although the investigative powers of the EOC have been curbed, it may be able to bring about general changes in discriminatory practices by seeking a direct change in domestic law in reliance on Community law. In *Secretary of State for Employment ex parte EOC*[169] it was found that the EOC can seek a declaration in judicial review proceedings to the effect that primary UK legislation is not in accord with EU equality legislation. Certain provisions of the Employment Protection (Consolidation) Act 1978 governed the right not to be unfairly dismissed, compensation for unfair dismissal and the right to statutory redundancy pay. These rights did not apply to workers who worked less than the specified number of hours a week. The Equal Opportunities Commission considered that since the majority of those working for less than the specified number of hours were women, the provisions operated to the disadvantage or women and were therefore discriminatory. The EOC accordingly wrote to the Secretary of State for Employment expressing this view and arguing that since the provisions in question were indirectly discriminatory they were in breach of EU law.

The Secretary of State replied by letter that the conditions excluding part-timers from the rights in question were justifiable and therefore not indirectly discriminatory. The EOC applied for judicial review of the Secretary of State's refusal to accept that the UK was in breach of its obligations under EC law. The application was amended to bring in an individual, Mrs Day, who worked part time and had been made redundant by her employers. It was found that Mrs Day's claim was a private law claim which could not be advanced against the Secretary of State who was not her employer and was not liable to meet the claim if it was successful.

The Secretary of State further argued that the EOC had no *locus standi* to bring the proceedings. However, the House of lords found that since the EOC had a duty under s 53(1) of the Sex Discrimination Act to work for the elimination of discrimination, it was within its remit to try to secure a change

---

169 [1994] All ER 910; [1994] ICR 317.

in the provisions under consideration and therefore the EOC had a sufficient interest to bring the proceedings and hence *locus standi*. The Secretary of State also argued that no decision or justiciable issue susceptible of judicial review existed. However, the House of Lords found that although the letter itself was not a decision, the provisions themselves could be challenged in judicial review proceedings. In other words, the real question was whether judicial review was available for the purpose of securing a declaration that certain UK primary legislation was incompatible with EU law and, following *Secretary of State for Transport ex parte Factortame* it would appear that judicial review was so available.

As regards the substantive issue – whether the provisions in question, while admittedly discriminatory, could be justified – the House of Lords thought that in certain special circumstances an employer might be justified in differentiating between full and part time workers to the disadvantage of the latter but that such differentiation, employed nationwide, could not be justified. Thus the EOC but not an individual applicant, was entitled to bring judicial review proceedings in order to secure a declaration that UK law was incompatible with EU law. Declarations were made that the conditions set out in the provisions in question were indeed incompatible with EU law.

This was a very far-reaching decision: it means that where UK legislation is incompatible with EU law a declaration can be obtained to that effect more rapidly than if it was necessary to wait for an individual affected to bring a case against the particular person or body who was acting within the terms of the UK legislation in question. The decision may not directly have an effect on race discrimination but it opens the possibility that the EOC may challenge other provisions of UK law and where such provisions have an equivalent under the Race Relations Act they will therefore also be affected.

Reform

The CRE and the EOC have made a number of proposals for reform which would strengthen the administrative method[170] and allow it to work more closely in harmony with the individual method. The CRE wants to try to narrow the gap between individual cases and what can be achieved by a formal investigation and has proposed that in order to do this it should be able to join in the individual's case as a party to the action so as to draw attention to the likelihood of further discrimination occurring. Thus, the individual would receive the remedy but the general effect of discrimination in the defendant body would be addressed by issuing a non-discrimination notice at the same time. This might be supported on the ground that if one

---

170 See the two CRE *Reviews of the 1976 Act 1985 and 1991*. See the EOC document *Equal Treatment for Men and Women: Strengthening the Acts*, 1988.

individual brings a successful case against an employer it is probable that discrimination in that concern is quite widespread. Both the EOC and the CRE want legislation to reverse the *Prestige* decision since they consider that they need to be able to launch investigations into a named person or company even when there is no initial strong evidence of discrimination.

9 POSITIVE ACTION[171]

The theoretical basis

A significant divergence within equality theory lies between belief in equality of outcome and belief in equal treatment. The two views appear to diverge since achieving an equal outcome may mean treating persons unequally for a time, as opposed to treating them equally even if that produces unequal results. Nevertheless, it may be argued that such divergence is to an extent more apparent than real since the underlying aim of providing equal treatment may be to ensure, ultimately, an equal outcome. The conflict between ensuring equality of treatment and furthering equality of outcome by means of positive action appears to be founded on the perception that such action means treating two likes unalike and thereby creating a denial of formal equality. In espousing a very significant principle, equal treatment of two likes or formal equality, has a clear, simple and to an extent, warranted appeal. But positive action cannot be accommodated within a formal equality model, since such a model only permits unlike (and, presumptively, unfavourable) treatment if difference is identified. In terms of pure theory positive action has no place within a formal equality model either as an aspect of the equality principle or as an exception to it. In practice an unsatisfactory compromise may be reached whereby positive action is viewed as an exception to the equality principle. Once that principle has been abandoned unequal treatment may be meted out. But, apart from the conceptual incoherence of this position, it is suggested that it is unsatisfactory in that it does not readily provide a means of recognising the *convergence* between equality of outcome and of treatment which is not apparent within the other exceptions to the equality principle.

However, it may be possible to escape from the constraints of formal equality by adopting a substantive as opposed to a formal equality model. Substantive equality recognises that men and women, whites and blacks, may be differently situated but seeks to prevent both perpetuation of such difference and disadvantage flowing from it. In particular, substantive equality recognises that merely treating like as like while ignoring the context

---

[171] For general discussion see Edwards, *Positive Discrimination*, 1987.

within which such treatment is meted out, fails to understand the disadvantages certain groups may be under due to past discrimination, social attitudes and unequal distribution of social benefits. One factor both springing from and underpinning such a situation appears to be a lack of women or blacks in more advantageous and influential employment. Thus, use of positive action may be accommodated within a substantive equality model since an outcome which both countered prior disadvantage and tended to change the context within which women or blacks take part in employment would be in accordance with such a model.

Forms of positive action and their recognition in national law

Four types of positive action may be identified:[172]

(1) reverse discrimination, which in its most absolute form would mean favourable treatment of a woman or a black on the ground of gender or race despite inferior qualification for a job or an inferior claim (in terms of criteria other than race or gender) to a facility such as housing;

(2) adopting a presumption in favour of appointing a candidate from the disadvantaged group if his or her qualifications were roughly equal to those of a person from the non-disadvantaged group;

(3) action to promote opportunities for members of the disadvantaged group in order to ensure that its members were in a strong position to compete for employment; or (in its weakest form)

(4) adoption of equal opportunities policies particularly affecting advertising and recruiting.

There is no scope for positive action in the first two forms under the Sex Discrimination and Race Relations Acts, while scope for the third form is extremely limited. Acts done to meet the special needs of certain racial groups (such as by the provision of English language classes) in regard to education, welfare and training are permissible but such provision can only be made available where there were no or very few members of the group in question doing that work in the UK at the time.[173] Also, under s 37 of the Race Relations Act employers can encourage applications from members of particular racial groups which are under-represented in the work force. Similarly, s 47(3) of the Sex Discrimination Act permits the restriction of access to training facilities to those 'in special need of training by reason of the period for which they have been discharging domestic or family responsibilities'. It should be noted that employers and others are under no duty to make such provision. But general positive action is unlawful under the wording of s 1(1) of both statutes. Thus

---

172 For discussion of forms of positive action see McCrudden (1986) 15 *ILJ* 219.
173 Sections 35–38 Race Relations Act.

employers can pursue equal opportunities policies such as stating in job advertisements that applications from certain groups will be welcomed but in general cannot appoint a less well-qualified black[174] or woman in order to address under-representation of black people or women caused by past discrimination. Nor can they import a general presumption that a woman or black with roughly equal qualifications to those of other candidates should be appointed.

A particular type of positive action known as 'contract compliance' which fell within the third and fourth forms of action identified above and had the potential to produce quite far-reaching beneficial effects, was outlawed by the Conservative government.[175] Under this method organs of the state such as local authorities produced a 'check list' of equal opportunities policies and asked the companies with which it was thinking of dealing to show evidence of compliance with such policies. If the company could not show in response that certain procedures were in place intended to combat racism or sexism it lost business. Parliament has, however, left intact a limited power to vet potential contractors as regards their race relations record,[176] presumably because the present government views race discrimination as more serious or politically contentious than gender discrimination.

Positive action favouring women under EU law

Given the recent increase in the use of positive action within some Member States of the Community and the acceptance of the need for such action by the European Council and Parliament (see Council Recommendation 84/635 EEC, below and para 26 of the Advocate General's Opinion in *Kalanke* below) and in much of the relevant literature[177] the decision in Case 450/93 *Kalanke v Freie Hansestadt Bremen* was highly significant in terms of its ability to affect an emerging tendency.

Within the Equal Treatment Directive positive action is viewed, under Article 2(4), as a derogation from the equal treatment principle which must, it seems, be looked at in the same light as the other derogations from that principle under Article 2(2) and (3). The exception under Article 2(2) is applicable to occupations in which the sex of the worker is a determining factor; Article 2(3) covers the provision of special protective measures for women, particularly those relating to pregnancy and maternity. The conceptual similarity between the derogations was confirmed and made

---

174 In *Riyat v London Borough of Brent* (1983) (cited in *IDS Employment Law Handbook* 28, 1984, p 57) it was held that discrimination in favour of black job applicants was unlawful.
175 Under s 17 of the Local Government Act 1988; for criticism see Townshend-Smith, 1989, pp 237–38.
176 Section 18 of the 1988 Act.
177 See eg Morris and Deakin, *Labour Law*, 1985, Chap 6 p 589.

explicit by the Advocate General and, to a lesser extent, by the Court of Justice in *Kalanke*; the decisions in Case 318/86 *Commission v France*[178] and Case 222/84 *Johnston v Chief Constable of the RUC*[179] on Article 2(3) and (4) are therefore relevant for comparative purposes.

The decision in Case 318/86 *Commission v France* concerned in part a quota system used to allot only 10–30% of posts to women in the French national police and prison service, regardless of their performance in the recruitment competition. The system was therefore intended to ensure that men overwhelmingly outnumbered women in these services. The French government sought to justify this policy within Article 2(2) on the ground that appointing an 'excessive proportion of women' would 'seriously damage the credibility' of the police corps since it would have difficulty in maintaining public order. The Court of Justice found that certain activities within the police service could properly be performed by men only but that this could not provide justification for a system of recruitment which left it unclear whether the quotas operating for each sex actually corresponded to the specific activities for which the sex of the person in question constituted a determining factor. The lack of transparency – the fact that no objective criteria determining the quotas laid down were available – made it impossible to verify such correspondence. This part of the Court's decision therefore left open the possibility of allocating men and women to different specific activities and thereby excluding women from certain areas of employment on grounds which, it would appear, were in themselves non-transparent, since the assumption that women police officers would be unable to carry out effectively activities intended to maintain public order was in itself untested. In effect, one non-transparent factor – the system of recruitment – cloaked another; the first such factor was rejected but the second accepted. The other part of the decision concerned direct discrimination within the system of promotion to the post of head warder within the French prison corps. The Court found that 'having regard to the need to provide opportunities for promotion within the corps of warders' (p 3580, para 17) justification for the discrimination could be found. This finding was made despite acceptance by the Court that sex was not a determining factor for the appointment of governors due to the administrative nature of the job.

A similar position was taken in Case 222/84 *Johnston v Chief Constable of the RUC* in which the Court found that Article 2(2) might in principle allow a wide derogation from the principle of equal treatment since 'in a situation characterised by serious internal disturbances the carrying of firearms by policewomen [in the Royal Ulster Constabulary (RUC)] might create additional risks of their being assassinated and might therefore be contrary to

---

178 [1988] ECR 3559.
179 [1986] ECR 1651.

the requirements of public safety' (para 16). Thus the sex of the worker could be a 'determining factor' in making appointments to posts which necessitated carrying arms. However, the national court might only rely on this derogation if it ensured compliance with the proportionality rule. It was for the national court to determine whether proportionality had been observed and therefore the Court did not give an opinion on the matter (para 9). In contrast to this stance, the Court took a narrow view of Article 2(3), finding that it would not allow a reduction of the rights of women on the basis of a need for protection 'whose origin is socio-cultural or even political' (p 1659, para 8). It thereby created an appearance of accepting substantive equality arguments but abandoned them in favour of focusing on special female vulnerability in relation to Article 2(2), readily accepting the assumption that women were more at risk than men and that women police officers could therefore be confined to other duties of a narrower, family-oriented nature. In a manner recalling the position taken in *Commission v France* the Court did not appear to recognise that there was a contradiction in rejecting a potential basis for derogation on the ground that it was founded on socio-cultural considerations but opening the way to acceptance of another which appeared to be equally open to such criticism.

The decision in *Kalanke v Freie Hansestadt Bremen* concerned a quota system which was in a sense the converse of that in question in *Commission v France* in that it ensured positive action in favour of women. In the German public services an appointing procedure had been adopted whereby women with the same qualifications as men had to be given automatic priority in sectors in which they were under-represented. In evaluating qualifications family work, social commitment or unpaid activity could be taken into account if relevant to performance of the duties in question. Under-representation was deemed to exist when women did not make up at least half the staff in the individual pay brackets in the relevant personnel group or in the function levels provided for in the organisation chart. Mr Kalanke was not approved for promotion under this procedure and sought a ruling from the *Bundesarbeitsgericht* that the quota system was incompatible with the German basic law and the German civil code. The *Bundesarbeitsgericht* considered that no such incompatibility arose since the system only favoured women where candidates of both sexes were equally qualified and, further, that the quota system was interpreted in accordance with German basic law which meant that although in principle priority in promotions should be given to women, exceptions must be made in appropriate cases. However, since the national court was uncertain whether the system was in accord with the Equal Treatment Directive, it referred to the European Court of Justice questions relating to the scope of the derogations permitted to the principle of equal treatment under the directive.

The court found that the quota system created direct discrimination within Article 2(1) but that it might be permissible under Article 2(4), basing this finding on the ruling from *Commission v France* cited by the Advocate General (para 18). It approved the finding of the Council in the third recital in the preamble to Recommendation 84/635/EEC of 13 December 1984 in relation to positive action (OJ 1984 L331 p 34) that 'existing legal provisions on equal treatment ... are inadequate for the elimination of all existing inequalities unless parallel action is taken by government ... and other bodies ... to counteract the prejudicial effects on women in employment which arise from social attitudes, behaviour and structures' (para 20). It then went on to find, citing *Johnston*, that derogations from the equality principle must be narrowly construed and that national rules which guarantee women 'unconditional priority' go beyond promoting equal opportunities and overstep the limits of the exception in Article 2(4). Although the Court found that Article 2(4) permits 'national measures relating to access to employment, including promotion, which give a specific advantage to women with a view to improving their ability to compete on the labour market' (para 19), it did not find that the promotion scheme at issue fell within the exception. This conclusion was apparently founded on the distinction it drew between equality of opportunity and equality of outcome in finding that the quota system 'substitutes for equality of opportunity the result which is only to be arrived at by providing such equality of opportunity'. It therefore found that national rules of the type in question are precluded by Article 2(1) and (4).

As this ruling and the Opinion of the Advocate General make clear, the Equal Treatment Directive encapsulates a view of equality under Article 2(1) which impliedly finds inequality of outcome acceptable so long as equal treatment is accorded. Positive action aimed at reducing such inequality must be seen as an exception to the equal treatment principle: the relationship between the two can be viewed only in negative terms under Article 2(4). The directive therefore creates a conceptual separation between positive action and the equality principle which necessitates characterising such action as direct discrimination which may be susceptible to justification only within the specified exception.[180] There is therefore, it seems, no room for an argument from principle in favour of equality of outcome as an aspect of the equality principle encapsulated under the directive. (It may be noted that this stance is out of accord with the UN Convention on the Elimination of All Forms of Discrimination Against Women 1979 Article 4(1), which provides that 'the adoption of temporary special measures aimed at accelerating de facto equality between men and women shall not be considered discrimination'.)

As the Advocate General observed, the stance of the directive under Article 2(1) reflects a formal equality position. A formal equality model only permits unlike (and, presumptively, unfavourable) treatment if difference is identified. Nevertheless, as the Advocate General pointed out, positive action may be viewed as furthering substantive as opposed to formal equality.

---

180 See Ellis, 'The Definition of Discrimination in European Community Sex Equality Law' (1994) 19 *EL Rev* 563–80, at pp 567–68; Hepple, 'Can Direct Discrimination be Justified?' (1994) 55 EOR 48.

However, the Advocate General appeared to view substantive equality measures as confined to those which would allow individual women to compete with men on a formal equality basis. He did not appear to recognise that furtherance of substantive equality demands that the context within which such competition takes place must change. As MacKinnon has argued,[181] substantive equality recognises that the context within which women take part in employment may place them under a disadvantage due to past discrimination, social attitudes and a gendered social situation. Positive action may be viewed not as compensating women for historical disadvantage but as an effective means of allowing its effects to be more rapidly overcome in future. In finding that the quota system could not fall within Article 2(4), the court and the Advocate General failed to give weight to the substantive equality argument that the social context within which women undertake employment, which is influenced by the imbalance between women and men in senior or more influential posts, tends to perpetuate inequality. Although the Court found that certain measures giving a specific advantage to women would be permissible within Article 2(4), it considered that measures used to address such an imbalance could not be seen as a means of creating a reduction in the 'actual instances of inequality which may exist in the reality of social life'. The position adopted appeared to be contradictory since it accepted that ensuring equality of 'starting points' would not lead to achieving substantive equality and yet viewed substantive equality as the ultimate objective of providing equal opportunities (para 14).

The Opinion of the Advocate General and the judgment of the Court also reveal, it is suggested, a contradiction in the application of the proportionality principle. The Court, unlike the Advocate General, did not expressly apply that principle in finding that the limits of Article 2(4) had been over-stepped. However, that finding in itself involved, it is suggested, *application* of the proportionality principle: the quota system appeared to fall within the Court's interpretation of Article 2(4) but created, in the view of the court, too great an offence to the equality principle due to its unconditional nature. In *Johnston*, in contrast, the Court found that the national court might only rely on the derogation under Article 2(2) if it ensured compliance with the proportionality rule but that ensuring such compliance was a matter for the national court to decide and therefore the Court did not give an opinion on the matter (para 9). However, it also found that in determining the scope of the derogation proportionality must be observed (para 38), implying that making such a determination would not be a matter solely within the jurisdiction of the national court. Comparing the findings within these two lines of case law, it is suggested that the point at which the Court of Justice accepts that the principle of proportionality allows a derogation to apply,

---

181 MacKinnon, *Towards a Feminist Theory of the State*, 1989; MacKinnon 'Reflections on Sex Equality under Law' (1991) 100 *Yale Law Journal* 1281.

thereby leaving the determination as to compliance with proportionality in the particular instance to the national court, is unclear; the two exercises of jurisdiction are in danger of being unclearly demarcated, laying the court open to the charge that the principle is being used to excuse either intervention or failure to intervene in national policies in a non-transparent and subjective fashion.

If the findings in *Kalanke* and *Johnston* are inconsistent as regards the demarcation between the point at which proportionality becomes a matter for the national court and the point at which it remains a matter for the Court of Justice, it is suggested that the use made of the proportionality principle in *Kalanke* to find that the derogation under Article 2(4) did not apply is also incompatible with the view taken in *Johnston* that proportionality would be sufficiently adhered to in allowing the policy in question to fall within the Article 2(2) derogation. This may also be said, it is suggested, of the ruling in *Commission v France* in so far as aspects of the systems at issue in that case were found to fall within Article 2(2). It is contended that it would have been open to the court in *Kalanke*, basing itself on the previous line of case law, to find that proportionality would be sufficiently observed in bringing the quota system within the scope of the derogation and, further, that the case for so doing was stronger than in either of the other two instances. This is contended taking into account the extent to which the policies at issue in *Johnston* and *Commission v France* created inequality of treatment and the extent to which they were found to be subject to justification

The German quota system was dependent on equality of qualifications and, according to the national court, would not be rigidly adhered to. In contrast, the policy considered in *Johnston* operated on the same basis as reverse discrimination since it was unable to take account of the fact that the qualifications of women applicants might be superior to those of male applicants. That policy created a greater affront to the equality principle than the German system in that it aimed at creating a complete imbalance between men and women in the body of police in question, thereby ensuring inequality of treatment and of outcome, whereas under the German system it seemed probable that ensuring equality of outcome would have led eventually to equality of treatment, once the imbalance in certain sectors of the German civil service had been corrected. Moreover, in contrast to the position in *Johnston* and in relation to the post of governor under the French system, the German quota rules did not preclude applications from men for the posts in question.

The justification underpinning the French public service quota system arose from the view that disorder would be less readily contained if an imbalance between men and women in the police service was not maintained, basing this view on an untested assumption regarding the possibility that the presence of a certain number of female police officers might detrimentally affect the power of the police to control disorder. This assumption was accepted by the Commission (p 3581, para 23) and the Court in relation to specific activities but it is suggested that the means adopted were not clearly an appropriate means of achieving the end in question or necessary to that end (the test for proportionality from *Johnston*, para 38). The same criticism may be levelled, it is submitted, at the justification advanced to defend the UK policy for the RUC, namely that reserving posts exclusively for men would ensure that persons in those posts would be subject to a lesser risk of assassination. In contrast, it is suggested that adoption of positive action in *Kalanke* would have been likely to contribute to achieving the desired outcome: as the Advocate General accepted, the imposition of quotas 'is an instrument which is certainly suitable for bringing about a quantitative increase in female employment' (para 9).

It is further suggested that if one applies the 'very logic underlying the derogations', which according to the Advocate General is aimed at 'ensuring the efficacy of the principle of equal treatment' (para 17) to the German quota system it may be found to cause less affront to that principle than the systems at issue in the other two rulings. As argued above, the German system was in accordance with substantive equality in that it sought to achieve an outcome which would counter past disadvantage and it recognised the real and gendered situation in which women take part in employment. In contrast, it is suggested that in both *Johnston* and *Commission v France* the Court allowed the national authorities some discretion as to permitted exceptions from the equality principle on grounds which failed to further either formal or substantive equality. Thus, acceptance of positive action could have been seen merely as a means of moving more speedily towards a desired outcome and therefore, in contrast to the position taken in both the previous decisions, the offence to the equality principle could have been viewed as less significant. By this means the Court could have recognised the distinction between the exception under Article 2(4) and the other two exceptions. Once the offence to the equality principle created by the German quota system is balanced as indicated here against the underlying justifications for it is suggested that scope can be created for finding that Article 2(4) was applicable.

However, in Case C-409/95 *Marschall v Land Nordrhein-Westfalen*[182] the Court found that a quota system allowing affirmative action was lawful on the basis that it was conditional (para 33 of the judgment). The Court said (at para 29) 'even where male and female candidates are equally qualified males tend to be promoted ... particularly because of prejudices and stereotypes concerning the role and capacities of women in working life ...'. So a rule can fall within Article 2(4) if it counteracts the prejudicial effect on women of those prejudices (para 31). But since it is a derogation it must be strictly construed and so it must contain a proviso (as did the scheme at issue) allowing men to be promoted or employed if special circumstances apply (paras 32 and 33). In

---

182 Judgment of 11 November 1997.

taking this stance the Court appears to have adopted the course the Court left open to it (as argued above) in *Kalanke*.

Article 141 of the Treaty, as amended by the Amsterdam Treaty, replaces Article 119 which provided for equal pay for work of equal value. Article 141 makes the same provision, but para 3 empowers the Council to adopt measures to ensure the application of the principle of equal opportunities and equal treatment *including* (emphasis added) the equal pay principle. Thus measures may be adopted going beyond the provision of equal pay. Paragraph 4 provides:

> ... the principle of equal treatment shall not prevent any Member State from maintaining or adopting measures providing for specific advantages in order to make it easier for the under-represented sex to pursue a vocational activity or to prevent or compensate for disadvantages in their professional careers.

This wording differs from that used in Article 2(4) of the Equal Treatment Directive since *inter alia* the word 'opportunities' which was central to the findings in *Kalanke* is not used: it speaks instead of making it easier for the under-represented sex to pursue a 'vocational activity' or preventing or compensating for disadvantages in professional careers. But the term 'specific advantages' is reminiscent of the terms used by the Advocates General in *Kalanke* and *Marschall*, and may imply that covert disadvantages are outside the scope of the provisions. Indeed, the paragraph could be interpreted simply as seeking to ensure equality of starting points in the manner of para 2(4) as interpreted in these two instances. But it seems to have been adopted in response to *Kalanke* and wording which is deliberately different from that used in Article 2(4) has been used. Thus Article 141 appears to be in accordance with the findings of the Court in *Marschall* and may even go beyond them.

Thus forms of positive action, in the sense in which that term is usually understood, are lawful in the Community so long as provisos apply. Positive action in the form of training opportunities may also be lawful within Article 2(4) but since in referring to the areas covered in Article 1(1) Article 2(4) covers training in apparent contradistinction to access to employment and promotion, it would appear that measures going beyond allowing special training opportunities should be covered. The Advocate General mentioned positive action in the form of the development of child care structures but this begs the question why such measures should be viewed as positive action, as opposed to being offered to all carers of children, men and women. Offering such measures only to women reinforces the perception not only that they are more expensive employees but also that they should shoulder the main burden of responsibility in caring for children.

The main barrier to acceptance of positive action within the Equal Treatment Directive is created by its restrictive approach which allows such action to be scrutinised only as an exception to the equality principle.

Nevertheless, adoption of a broad approach to Article 2(4), similar to that taken in relation to Article 2(2) in *Johnston* and *Commission v France*, allowed the accommodation within the directive of forms of positive action in *Marschall*. Such an approach can be justified in relation to Article 2(4), although not in relation to Article 2(2), on the basis that it provides a means of recognising the limitations of the formal equality approach.

CHAPTER FOURTEEN

THE CRIMINAL LAW AND THE CRIMINAL JUSTICE PROCESS; DISCRIMINATION ON GROUNDS OF SEXUAL ORIENTATION

1 RACIAL DISCRIMINATION

Criminal law

The criminal law does not overtly enshrine discrimination on grounds of race as it does on grounds of sex or sexual orientation. Instead it contains some specifically anti-racist measures – although not many – intended to combat expressions of racial discrimination largely arising in the public order context. In general, however, it has only a very narrow role to play in fighting racial discrimination due to the policy decision taken when the relevant legislation was being drawn up to leave the individual to pursue his or her individual remedy by means of a tort action. Even gross racial discrimination evinced by an employer, including racial harassment or absolute segregation, can be addressed only by a civil remedy if the individual chooses to seek it – unless it falls within the ambit of one of the general offences such as assault.

Thus racial harassment of individuals in certain areas of the UK can be addressed only by the normal criminal measures; the offences in question do not exist in an aggravated form because there is an added element of racism, although it is arguable that an assault which is clearly racially motivated should be classed as an aggravated assault. At present there seems to be no prospect of creation of a specific offence of racial attack. The case for creating such an offence and perhaps a general offence of racial victimisation, is quite strong, given that it could be worded in such a way that it did not collide with other civil liberties as the incitement to racial hatred provision does.[1]

Criminal justice

A degree of official recognition has been given to fighting or preventing racial as opposed to sexual discrimination in the criminal justice system, at least at the investigation stage. Section 101(b) of the Police and Criminal Evidence Act 1984 (PACE) provides for regulations to make racially discriminatory behaviour a specific disciplinary offence. Whether this provision will deter the use of racist remarks or racial harassment of offenders is open to doubt especially in the face of some evidence that officers may display racism to

---

[1] See Chap 5 pp 225–27. For discussion of these possibilities see Hare, I (1997) 17(3) *OJLS* 415.

their own black colleagues.[2] Guidance is given under the PACE Codes of Practice as to interviewing practices to be adopted with detainees not proficient in English. Code A of PACE enjoins officers not to stop and search on the basis of a person's colour,[3] and by implication this may also apply to arrests. It is unclear whether this has had any effect on the arrest rates of blacks who have been found in various studies to be over-represented in each offence group.[4] One possible conclusion which could be drawn is that the police are more ready to arrest blacks due to a stereotypical assessment of their propensity to commit offences but doubt has been cast on this assumption recently in a study[5] by Jefferson and Walker which suggested that when blacks were compared with whites living at a similar level of social deprivation as opposed to comparing them with the white population generally, the difference in arrest rates between the two groups largely disappeared. The study also found a wide variation in the experience of blacks and Asians in the criminal justice system, blacks having consistently a less favourable attitude to the police[6] while Asians had a more favourable attitude than whites.

Evidence as to discrimination at the court hearing and in the outcome of arrests is mixed despite quite a large body of work in the area.[7] The Jefferson and Walker study found that although the cautioning rates of Asians and blacks differed significantly, it was not possible to find a clear difference in sentencing policy.[8] A study of contested bail applications found no racial bias in the remand decisions of magistrates[9] although some difference as to conditions of bail was found between Afro-Caribbean and white defendants.[10]

Although the evidence of racial bias seems to be inconclusive, it would seem appropriate to try to remove any appearance of unfairness from the

---

2   On 4 May 1993 Joginder Singh Prem was awarded £25,000 damages for racial discrimination and victimisation in settlement of his claim after the force had admitted discrimination (see (1993) *Guardian*, 5 May).
3   Paragraph 1.7; see further Chap 11 p 398.
4   Crime statistics from the Metropolitan Police District by ethnic group for 1987, victims, suspects and those arrested: *Home Office Statistical Bulletin* 5/89. Blacks comprised 16% of those arrested in 1987 but only 5% of the population of London.
5   See Jefferson and Walker, 'Ethnic Minorities in the Criminal Justice System' [1992] *Crim LR* 83.
6   *Op cit* p 92.
7   McConville and Baldwin, 'The Influence of Race on Sentencing in England' [1982] *Crim LR* 652–58; Crow and Cove, 'Ethnic Minorities and the Courts' [1984] *Crim LR* 413–17; Walker, *The Court Disposal and Remands of White, Afro-Caribbean and Asian Men*, 1983; Brown and Hullin, 'The Treatment of Ethnic Minority and White Offenders' (1992) 32 *Brit J Criminal* 41–53.
8   *Op cit* p 90.
9   Brown and Hullin, 'Contested Bail Applications: The Treatment of Ethnic Minority and White Offenders' [1993] *Crim LR* 107 at p 111.
10 *Op cit* p 110.

criminal justice system and to this end it may be argued that certain practices should change; for example juries should contain some members from ethnic minority groups in cases where this was particularly appropriate. However, it seems clear that the Race Relations Act cannot be used to change practices in the criminal justice system except in the areas it specifically covers.

The decision in *Farah v Commissioner of Police of the Metropolis*[11] makes it clear that racial bias in policing decisions will fall within the Act. Farah, a Somali citizen and refugee who was 17 at the time, was attacked by a group of white teenagers who set a dog on her and injured her. She summoned police help by telephone, but when the police arrived they made no attempt to arrest her attackers but arrested her and charged her with affray, assault and causing unnecessary suffering to a dog. No evidence was offered when she appeared to answer the charges and she was acquitted. She brought an action for damages against the Commissioner of Police of the Metropolis, alleging false imprisonment, assault and battery and malicious prosecution. She included in the statement of claim an allegation that the conduct of the police officers amounted to unlawful racial discrimination. Judge Harris refused to strike out the allegation of racial discrimination. He also allowed her to amend that part of her claim, so that she alleged that the officers were acting as the commissioner's agents and had discriminated against her on grounds of race in both failing to afford her the protection which would have been afforded to white victims of crime and in bringing the proceedings against her. The commissioner appealed against the refusal to strike out the allegation of racial discrimination.

The Court of Appeal found that two important issues fell to be determined. First, whether a police officer came within s 20 of the Race Relations Act 1976 which prohibits racial discrimination in the provision of services and secondly, if he did, whether his Chief Officer of Police would be answerable in law for any breaches of the Act he might have committed. The court held that an officer providing protection to a citizen was providing a service within the section. Policy reasons against such a conclusion, including the possibility that the police would have to face numerous claims of race discrimination, were rejected as outweighed by the need to provide a remedy for a citizen who had suffered discrimination in a situation where she was in dire need of protection. Moreover, nothing in the Act made police officers immune from claims of racial discrimination. However, the court found that the commissioner was not vicariously liable for the acts of the officers. Section 53 appeared to deny vicarious liability except in so far as provided for by the Act. Her claim against the individual officers for discrimination was out of time. The appeal was allowed and therefore her claim of discrimination would have to be struck from the statement of claim. This decision is partly to be welcomed as making it clear that the possibility of compensation for

---

11 [1997] 1 All ER 289.

racially discriminatory police actions and decisions is available. However, it also hedges this possibility around with restrictions since it denies the possibility of vicarious liability.

Other discriminatory practices within the criminal justice system fall outside the Act. For example, racial discrimination in a prison resulting in refusal of employment would be covered[12] but an application from a black to have black jury members resulting in a multi-racial jury would not and, moreover, would not, according to the ruling in *Ford* (1989),[13] be available under any residual discretion of the judge. This decision of the Court of Appeal brought an end to the practice of some judges who had managed to achieve a racially mixed jury in certain cases.[14] An appearance of unfairness in the criminal justice system and perhaps the reality of it may also be created by the lack of black judges (in 1991 1% of judges were black) and exacerbated by the failure of the law society to adopt an anti-discriminatory practice – both matters which have recently been the subject of concern.[15]

2 GENDER DISCRIMINATION

Criminal law

Until the late 19th century and in one respect until 1991, the criminal law enshrined and perpetuated gross sexual discrimination. Violent or indecent behaviour in the form of assault, battery, procuring sexual intercourse by threats, false imprisonment, indecent assault or rape was, it seems, lawful[16] if perpetrated against a married woman by her husband. The respect in which such discrimination survived was until very recently to be found in the law of rape: wives were deemed to have given an irrevocable consent to sexual

---

12 Part II of the RRA; in *Alexander v Home Office* [1988] 1 WLR 968, CA (the plaintiff, a prisoner, was refused work in prison kitchen due to racial stereotyping).
13 [1989] QB 868, CA. The Society of Black Lawyers in 'A Time for Freedom and a Time for Justice' has suggested that the practice of allowing a racially mixed jury in certain cases should be enshrined in statute. See 143 *NLJ* 837 (editorial).
14 For example, Bansal [1985] *Crim LR* 151.
15 See 141 *NLJ* 1692 and 143 *NLJ* 1376. It should be noted that s 64(1) of the Courts and Legal Services Act 1990 made special provision for amending the Sex Discrimination and Race Relations Acts in order to ensure that discrimination against barristers fell within their ambit.
16 Until *Jackson* [1891] 1 QB 671 it was thought that a husband could forcefully imprison and (probably) chastise his wife in order to enforce the right to cohabitation. See *Atwood v Atwood* Finch's Chancery Precedents 492 and *Re Cochrane* 8 Dowl 630 in which Coleridge J said 'the husband may keep her by force ... and may beat her'. Under s 3 of the Criminal Law Amendment Act 1885 a husband who forced his wife by threats to have sex with another incurred no liability. As late as 1984 in *Caswell* [1984] *Crim LR* 111 it was found that a husband could incur no liability in respect of what would otherwise have been an indecent assault on his wife. Marital rape was lawful until 1991, below note 17.

intercourse within marriage. Hale's law on marital rights[17] is credited with creating immunity for a husband from a rape conviction and therefore the law was that by marrying her a man acquired the right to rape a woman without being convicted of rape. Hale also considered whether concubines should be able to withdraw consent to sex and determined that they should,[18] a liberal view at that time which ran counter to the previous position.[19] The marital immunity was favoured in some quarters because it was thought that the criminal law should not violate the privacy of the home as it might endanger the continuance of family life. However, the argument that wives must not have the full protection of the criminal law because if they invoke it the marriage is unlikely to survive,[20] fails to recognise that in itself it is helping to perpetuate their suffering by refusing to offer a sufficient deterrent to their husbands. It seems reasonable to assume that the 'ordinary raping husband'[21] was encouraged to rape by an exemption which declared, in effect, that he had a right to do so.

The marital immunity created some interesting anomalies such as that found in the ruling of the Court of Appeal in *Kowalski*.[22] A husband who forced his wife to have oral sex with him as a preliminary to forced sexual intercourse was convicted of indecent assault although no liability could arise in respect of the sex act itself. It also seemed that a husband could be liable as an accessory to rape[23] but not as a principal.

The House of Lords in *R*[24] finally swept away the marital exemption. However, it is still possible that husbands will be sentenced more lightly than other rapists because some judges appear to see cohabitation as a mitigating factor. In *Berry*[25] a man raped his former cohabitee after some years had passed; the factor of cohabitation played a part in the decision to award a sentence of four years. That this policy may be pursued after the decision in *Billam*[26] that a sentence of five years would normally be appropriate for a rape without aggravating or mitigating features, is suggested by the decision of the

---

17 Chief Justice Sir Matthew Hale, *History of the Pleas of the Crown*, 1736.
18 1 PC 628–29.
19 In the 13th century it seems to have been the case that if a man had had consensual sex with his victim previously he would be acquitted of rape. *Crown Pleas of the Wiltshire Eyre 1249*; Stenton, *Rolls of the Justice in Eyre for Yorkshire, 1218–19*.
20 Put by Glanville Williams, 142 *NLJ* 11. For reply by the author see 142 *NLJ* 831–32, 870–71.
21 (1991) *NLJ* 206.
22 (1988) 86 Cr App R 339.
23 *Cogan and Leake* [1976] QB 217.
24 [1991] 4 All ER 481; [1991] 3 WLR 767; [1992] *Fam Law* 108; [1992] *Crim LR* 207. For comment see 55 *MLR* 386.
25 [1988] *Crim LR* 325.
26 [1986] 1 All ER 985.

Court of Appeal in *AG's Reference No 7 of 1989*[27] in which again a sentence of four years as opposed to five was awarded, possibly, although this was not made explicit in the judgment, because the man had cohabited with his victim. The ruling in *Stockwell*[28] suggests that the length of cohabitation will also be considered relevant; in reducing a sentence of three years to two the Court of Appeal took into account the 10 years that the wife and husband had lived together. However, if a judge is able to look at all the circumstances of a rape without being expected to give the factor of cohabitation undue prominence, the domestic and stranger rapist will be punished on roughly the same scale bearing in mind the specific circumstances of each case. This is not merely a matter of proper sentencing policy but of a declaration that women have the right to full protection from violation whatever the status of the attacker.

A number of areas of criminal law remain enshrining gender-based differentiation on grounds which, it is submitted, are not objectively justifiable. These include the anomalous defence of coercion available to married women under s 47 of the Criminal Justice Act 1925, which assumes that wives are under the subjection of their husbands and the offences relating to abduction of a woman under the Sexual Offences Act 1956 – in particular the offence under s 19 of abducting a girl under 18 (whether or not with her consent) which assumes that such girls are to a greater extent than boys in the possession of their parents. The offences relating to prostitution under the 1956 Act and the Sexual Offences Act 1985 are, it is suggested, unnecessarily sexually segregated; if such offences are to exist there seems to be no good reason why all of them should not apply equally to women and men.

Criminal justice

There is quite a large body of literature postulating and analysing institutionalised sexist ideologies in the criminal justice system[29] but this does not seem to have brought about sweeping changes, although it is fair to say that in one area – the management of a rape allegation – there have been improvements at the investigation stage, such as the introduction of 'rape suites' and questioning by female officers. Only the barest indication of the findings of this body of work can be given here but it is clear that it has been wide ranging, considering the perceptions of female offenders held by magistrates, judges, police officers, prison officers and probation officers. A

---

27 (1990) 12 Cr App R (S) 1.
28 (1984) 6 Cr App R (S) 84.
29 See Edwards, *Policing Domestic Violence*, 1989 and *Female Sexuality and the Law*, 1981, especially Chaps 2 and 5; Dunhill, ed, *The Boys in Blue: Women's Challenge to the Police*, 1989; Gelsthorpe, *Sexism and the Female Offender*, 1989 (which criticises the other writings but seems to arrive at similar conclusions regarding the institutions under scrutiny).

common theme seems to be that the treatment of female offenders may be affected by the private sexist ideologies of such persons, male or female but that this factor is not as significant as the effect of such ideologies enshrined in the administrative and organisational context of the occupations in question.

A recurring theme concerns the treatment of victims of rape. Disquiet as to their treatment in the 1970s led to the setting up of the Heilbron Committee in 1975 whose recommendations were in part enshrined in the Sexual Offences (Amendment) Act 1976. This provides under s 2 that the victim should not be questioned as to her sexual experience except at the judge's discretion. It seems that a judge will not allow a complainant to be cross-examined as to sexual experience in order to suggest that for that reason alone she should not be believed,[30] but if her past sexual experience can be made to relate in some way to the issue of consent leave should be given to cross-examine her on it.[31] Rape is the only crime in which a corroboration warning has to be given before allowing the jury to rely on the adult victim's evidence. Thus the possibility of casting serious doubt on the credibility and veracity of the victim[32] and of indirectly blackening her character has subsisted into the early 1990s although at the time of writing it is due for abolition.

Policies and perceptions underlying investigation, prosecuting policy, sentencing and judicial pronouncements in passing sentence in rape and indecent assault cases are still, it is submitted, a matter of concern in so far as they reflect a perception that women are not all equally worthy of protection by the criminal law.[33] Prostitutes, promiscuous women, women who are out on the streets at night or who accompany a man to a house after an evening out may be seen as to different degrees blameworthy[34] and this may be reflected in the nature of the sentence and in the likelihood that the allegation of rape will be rigorously pursued. It seems that factors such as being out on the street at night tend to be seen as of less relevance in relation to male victims of serious crime.

---

30 *Viola* (1982) 75 Cr App R 125.
31 *SMS* [1992] *Crim LR* 310.
32 Judge Sutcliffe gave this corroboration warning in 1976: 'It is known that women in particular and small boys are liable to be untruthful and to invent stories', Old Bailey 18 April 1976.
33 See the analysis of the response of the criminal justice system to the rape victim by Temkin, J, *Rape and the Legal Process*, 1987, Chap 1.
34 In a 1986 case the Court of Appeal drastically reduced the sentences of a group of men convicted of indecent assault, Watkins LJ commenting that the victim was 'dissolute and depraved': (1986) *The Times*, 28 February. It may be of interest to note that in less liberal countries than Britain, such as Turkey, it is official policy to sentence rape of a prostitute much less heavily than rape of other women.

3 DISCRIMINATION ON GROUNDS OF SEXUAL ORIENTATION[35]

Employment and education

At present a person who is refused promotion, dismissed from a job or refused an offer of housing on grounds of sexual preference is in the same position as a woman so treated would have been before 1975. If a lesbian or homosexual has been employed for at least two years before dismissal, the provisions against unfair dismissal under the Employment Rights Act 1996 (previously contained in the Employment Protection (Consolidation) Act 1978) may offer some protection, although a dismissal will be fair if it is for 'some other substantial reason of a kind to justify dismissal', provided that the employer acts reasonably. Where dismissal is on grounds of sexual preference it seems that a wide interpretation will be given to the meaning of 'reasonable'. In *Saunders v Scottish National Camps*,[36] the applicant, who was employed as a maintenance handyman at a boys' camp, was dismissed on the grounds of homosexuality although his duties did not ordinarily bring him into contact with the boys. His dismissal was nevertheless held to be fair on the ground that many other employers would have responded in the same way. The decision is clearly open to attack on the ground that even when his duties brought him into contact with the boys there would have been no more reason to believe that they would have been in danger from him than would girls from a male heterosexual. Similarly, it has been found that the dismissal of a homosexual from GCHQ as a threat to national security was not unreasonable despite the fact that he had been open about his homosexuality and therefore could not be blackmailed.[37] It is clear that a homosexual applicant cannot fall within the Sex Discrimination Act unless he or she can show that someone of the opposite sex would have been treated more favourably. In the UK courts it has also been found that applicants treated unfavourably due to their sexual orientation are not covered by the Equal Treatment Directive.[38]

---

35 Reading: see Cane, *Gays and the Law*, 1982; Feldman, D, *Civil Liberties in England and Wales*, 1993, pp 525–29; Hewitt, P, *The Abuse of Power*, 1982, Chap 9; Wintemute, R, *Sexual Orientation and Human Rights: The US Constitution, the ECHR and the Canadian Charter*, 1995; Hervey, T and O'Keeffe, D, eds, *Sex Equality Law in the European Union*, 1996, Chap 17; Wilkinson, B, 'Moving Towards Equality: Homosexual Law Reform in Ireland' (1994) 45 NILQ 252; Wilets, *The Human Rights of Sexual Minorities*, 1996; Heinze, E, *Sexual Orientation: A Human Right: An Essay on International Human Rights Law*, 1995; Wintermute, R (1997) 60(3) MLR 334; Bamforth, N, *Sexuality, Morals and Justice*, 1997; Skidmore, P (1997) 26(1) ILJ 51. For discussion from a non-liberal standpoint see Stychin, C, *Law's Desire: Sexuality and the Limits of Justice*, 1995.

36 (1981) EAT 7/80, judgment delivered 14 April 1980; for criticism see quoted comments of Levin, B, in Beer *et al*, *Gay Workers, Trade Unions and the Law*, NCCL, 1981, p 27. See to similar effect *Boychuk v Symons Holdings Ltd* [1977] IRLR 395 but *cf Bell v Devon and Cornwall Police Authority* [1978] IRLR 283.

37 *Director of GCHQ ex parte Hodges* (1988) COD 123; (1988) *The Times*, 26 July.

38 *Smith v Gardner Merchant* [1996] ICR 790; [1996] IRLR 342, noted [1996] 67 EOR 48.

In the UK homosexuals are barred from the merchant navy forces, where homosexual acts are classed as 'disgraceful cond the armed forces in Belgium, Denmark, France, the Netherlands and Spain a._ all open to homosexuals. The legality of the policy of the Ministry of Defence in maintaining the ban was challenged in *R v Secretary of State for Defence, ex parte Lustig-Prean, Smith and Others*.[40] The applicants, homosexuals who had been dismissed due to the existence of the ban, applied for review of the policy; their application was dismissed at first instance in the Divisional Court and the applicants appealed. Rejecting the argument of the MOD that it had no jurisdiction to review the legality of the policy in question, the court applied the usual *Wednesbury* principles. This meant that it could not interfere with the exercise of an administrative discretion on substantive grounds save where it was satisfied that the decision was unreasonable in the sense that it was beyond the range of responses open to a reasonable decision maker. But in judging whether the decision-maker had exceeded that margin of appreciation the human rights context was important: '... the more substantial the interference with human rights, the more the court will require by way of justification before it will be satisfied that the decision was reasonable.'[41] Applying such principles and taking into account the support of the policy in both Houses of Parliament, it could not be said that the policy crossed the threshold of irrationality, although it was criticised. The European Commission on Human Rights has rejected a challenge to the provision relating to the army as inadmissible on the argument that there is a special need to prevent disorder in the armed forces.[42] The *Smith* case has been referred to the European Commission. The court may be inclined to find that the proportionality test under Article 8 is not satisfied where an applicant not on active service is dismissed due to homosexuality.

A large number of posts in the Home Civil Service[43] are subject to positive vetting. In 1982 the Security Commission recommended[44] that male homosexuality should be dealt with on a case by case basis in relation to PV clearance but that it should be refused if the individual's practise of his homosexuality placed any doubt upon his discretion or reliability. PV clearance for the Diplomatic Service or armed forces will be automatically refused.

---

39   See s 66 of the Army Act 1955; ss 1(5) and (2) of the Sexual Offences Act 1967.
40   [1996] 1 All ER 257; [1996] ICR 740. Noted: Skidmore (1995) 24 *ILJ* 363, (1996) 25 *ILJ* 63. For discussion see: Rubin, G, 'Section 146 of the Criminal Justice and Public Order Act 1994 and the Decriminalisation of Homosexual Acts in the Armed Forces' [1996] *Crim LR* 393; Skidmore, P (1997) 26(1) *ILJ* 51.
41   *Ibid* p 263.
42   *B v UK* 34 D and R (1983); (1983) 6 EHRR 354.
43   In 1982 PV covered 68,000 posts (Cmnd 8540, p 5).
44   Cmnd 8540, 1982.

Discrimination against homosexuals in the field of education is enshrined in s 28 of the Local Government Act 1988; it prohibits the promotion of homosexuality or the teaching of 'the acceptability of homosexuality as a pretended family relationship'. Thus local authorities may still fund certain groups so long as this is aimed at benefiting the group rather than at promoting homosexuality. Robertson argues that s 28 will not have a significant effect in schools as local authorities do not directly control the curriculum[45] (and this is particularly the case under local management of schools). However, s 28 may serve to ratify and legitimise intolerance of homosexuals in education and outside it. In opposition, the Labour party pledged to abolish s 28.

There is a growing recognition in Europe that such discrimination amounts to a general problem which should be addressed. A report compiled for the Commission of the European Communities in May 1993[46] on discrimination against homosexuals found that the UK was one of the worst offenders and was one of only four Member States which provided no legal protection against discrimination. The report also criticised the Commission which has argued that homosexuality is a matter to be left to individual governments. It recommended that human rights for homosexuals should be enshrined in European Community law.

In 1997 it appeared that the weak position of homosexuals who are dismissed from employment or otherwise detrimentally treated might be about to change under the influence of EU law. In Case 13/14 *P v S and Cornwall CC*[47] P was dismissed from her employment on the ground that she was a transsexual. Her application under the Sex Discrimination Act 1975 failed as it was found that transsexuals were outside the terms of the Act. It was argued that her case fell within the Equal Treatment Directive. The decision of the European Court of Human Rights in *Rees*[48] was relied upon by the European Court of Justice in deciding that transsexuals fall within the Equal Treatment Directive. This was found on the basis that the Directive is simply the expression of the principle of equality, which is one of the fundamental principles of European Union law. If transsexuals are within the directive it is probable that it also covers homosexuals. The words 'on grounds of sex' within the directive may be found to mean *inter alia* 'on grounds of the sex of the partner'. In other words, if discrimination occurs due to the fact that a person's partner is or is potentially of the 'wrong' gender the directive should in principle cover such a situation. However, the Court did not confine its ruling to the expression of a sexual orientation. It found that discrimination

---

45 Roberson, *Freedom, the Individual and the Law*, p 382.
46 By Peter Ashman, Director of the independent European Human Rights Foundation.
47 Judgment of 30 April 1996; [1996] ECR I-2143; [1996] IRLR 347.
48 (1986) 9 EHRR 56.

based on the orientation itself is within the Directive since a state of mind linked to sex is the cause of the discrimination. This latter argument was considered in *R v Secretary of State for Defence, ex parte Perkins*[49] which also concerned the ban on homosexuals in the armed services and it was determined that due to the *P v S* decision the case must be referred to the ECJ. In Case 249/96, *Grant v South West Trains Ltd*,[50] which was before the court at the time of publication, it was argued that a refusal to allow a lesbian partner the same employment perks as those which would be allowed to a heterosexual partner is discrimination. The Advocate General gave his Opinion that discrimination contrary to the Equal Pay Directive and Article 119 had occurred. However, the Court failed to decide in the same way, with the result that lesbians and homosexuals are unable to claim in the domestic courts any pay or fringe benefits currently only available to heterosexuals. Thus the Court refused to take this step forward in terms of outlawing discrimination on grounds of sexual orientation. Currently, the most pressing need is to outlaw discrimination on grounds of sexual orientation within decisions as to dismissal and appointment. The Amsterdam Treaty Article 6a signed by the Member States on 19 June 1997 provides that the Council can adopt provisions intended to combat discrimination on grounds of sexual orientation.

The criminal process

Studies of discrimination against homosexuals in the criminal justice system have tended to concentrate on the investigation stage and methods of enforcing certain areas of the criminal law such as s 32 of the Sexual Offences Act 1956.[51] This provides that it is an offence 'for a man to persistently solicit or importune in a public place for immoral purposes'. research suggests that this section is used by police officers engaged in surveillance in public lavatories to trap gay men into some behaviour which might be said to come within the terms of the section. It seems that almost any behaviour, 'any physical gesture or words' in context may fulfil its terms. Thus homosexuals can be criminalised in respect of trivial behaviour which would not have occurred had a police officer not trapped them into it. Judgments under this section appear to reflect the bare tolerance of homosexuality mentioned above since in determining what is meant by the term 'immoral' as used in the section the assumption has been made that a jury would inevitably decide that

---

49 [1997] IRLR 297.
50 (1996) unreported.
51 See Cane, *Gays and the Law*, 1982; Campaign for Homosexual Equality: evidence to the Royal Commission on Criminal Procedure 1981 Cmnd 8092; 'Soliciting by Men' [1982] *Crim LR* 349; Power, H, 'Entrapment and Gay Rights' 143 *NLJ* 47–49 and 63.

homosexual behaviour is immoral[52] and therefore there is nothing to encourage police officers to adopt different investigative methods. Such assumptions made by judges imply that the homosexual way of life is contemptible and mean that the coercive force of the law may be used to impose a view of 'normal' behaviour on a minority, thereby failing to treat a group of citizens with equal concern and respect.

The European Convention on Human Rights

The European Convention on Human Rights offers further potential as a means of improving the position of homosexuals in the criminal justice system and also in a number of the contexts considered in this chapter but that potential has not yet been realised. Article 14, which provides a guarantee of freedom from discrimination, appears to cover discrimination on grounds of sexual orientation due to its use of the words 'without discrimination on any ground such as ...'.[53] Therefore a number of possibilities are open. Article 2 of the First Protocol might be used to argue that education in accordance with one's own philosophical convictions must include the need to allow some teaching about the homosexual way of life. Article 6 might be used where a homosexual was refused a hearing in, for example, a child care or adoption case where a heterosexual would not have been so refused. Article 8 has already shown its potential in this area read alone but there might also be instances in which, although an invasion of privacy grounded on homosexuality fell within one of the exceptions, it could nevertheless be established taking Article 14 into account due to its discriminatory nature. Article 10 read in conjunction with Article 14 might offer protection to expressions of the homosexual way of life such as the wearing of badges or even some physical gestures.[54] All these possibilities will offer homosexuals avenues of challenge to discrimination practised against them by public bodies once the Human Rights Act is in force.

---

52 For example, *Gray* [1981] 74 CAR 324; *Kirkup* (1992) *Guardian*, 10 November; for comment see Power *ibid*.

53 In *Dudgeon* (1981) 4 EHRR 149 the European Court of Human Rights was asked to consider the application of Article 14 read in conjunction with Article 8. It appeared to assume that Article 14 did cover discrimination on grounds of sexual preference although it found that it did not need to consider the application of Article 14 in the instant case since a breach of Article 8 had been found.

54 In *Masterson v Holden* [1986] 3 All ER 39; [1986] 1 WLR 1017 the Divisional Court found that magistrates were entitled to view the behaviour of two homosexuals in kissing and cuddling as insulting for the purposes of s 54(13) of the Metropolitan Police Act 1839. This approach might also be taken under s 5 of the Public Order Act 1986 but such a wide interpretation of 'insulting' could allow many restrictions on the public expression of homosexuality which might be in breach of Article 10, either read alone or in conjunction with Article 14. It appears that Article 10 does not cover homosexual intercourse *per se* but may cover the physical as well as verbal expression of homosexual love: *X v UK* (1981) 3 EHRR 63.

APPENDIX

THE HUMAN RIGHTS ACT 1998

1998 CHAPTER 42

ARRANGEMENT OF SECTIONS

Introduction

1 The Convention Rights.
2 Interpretation of Convention rights.

Legislation

3 Interpretation of legislation.
4 Declaration of incompatibility.
5 Right of Crown to intervene.

Public authorities

6 Acts of public authorities.
7 Proceedings.
8 Judicial remedies.
9 Judicial acts.

Remedial action

1 Power to take remedial action.

Other rights and proceedings

11 Safeguard for existing human rights.
12 Freedom of expression.
13 Freedom of thought, conscience and religion.

Derogations and reservations

14 Derogations.
15 Reservations.
16 Period for which designated derogations have effect.
17 Periodic review of designated reservations.

Judges of the European Court of Human Rights

18 Appointment to European Court of Human Rights.

Parliamentary procedure

19 Statements of compatibility.

Supplemental

20 Orders etc. under this Act.
21 Interpretation, etc.
22 Short title, commencement, application and extent.

SCHEDULES

Schedule 1 – The Articles.
Part I – The Convention.
Part II – The First Protocol.
Part III – The Sixth Protocol.
Schedule 2 – Remedial Orders.
Schedule 3 – Derogation and Reservation.
Part I – Derogation.
Part II – Reservation.
Schedule 4 – Judicial Pensions.

An Act to give further effect to rights and freedoms guaranteed under the European Convention on Human Rights, to make provision with respect to holders of certain judicial offices who become judges of the European Court of Human Rights; and for connected purposes.

[9th November 1998]

BE IT ENACTED by the Queen's most Excellent Majesty, by and with the advice and consent of the Lords Spiritual and Temporal, and Commons, in this present Parliament assembled, and by the authority of the same, as follows:

The Human Rights Act 1998

Introduction

The Convention Rights

1 – (1) In this Act 'the Convention rights' means the rights and fundamental freedoms set out in:

(a) Articles 2 to 12 and 14 of the Convention,

(b) Articles 1 to 3 of the First Protocol, and

(c) Articles 1 and 2 of the Sixth Protocol,

as read with Articles 16 to 18 of the Convention.

(2) Those Articles are to have effect for the purposes of this Act subject to any designated derogation or reservation (as to which see sections 14 and 15).

(3) The Articles are set out in Schedule 1.

(4) The Secretary of State may by order make such amendments to this Act as he considers appropriate to reflect the effect, in relation to the United Kingdom, of a protocol.

(5) In subsection (4) 'protocol' means a protocol to the Convention:

(a) which the United Kingdom has ratified; or

(b) which the United Kingdom has signed with a view to ratification.

(6) No amendment may be made by an order under subsection (4) so as to come into force before the protocol concerned is in force in relation to the United Kingdom.

Interpretation of Convention rights

2 – (1) A court or tribunal determining a question which has arisen in connection with a Convention right must take into account any:

(a) judgment, decision, declaration or advisory opinion of the European Court of Human Rights,

(b) opinion of the Commission given in a report adopted under Article 31 of the Convention,

(c) decision of the Commission in connection with Article 26 or 27(2) of the Convention, or

(d) decision of the Committee of Ministers taken under Article 46 of the Convention,

whenever made or given, so far as, in the opinion of the court or tribunal, it is relevant to the proceedings in which that question has arisen.

(2) Evidence of any judgment, decision, declaration or opinion of which account may have to be taken under this section is to be given in proceedings before any court or tribunal in such manner as may be provided by rules.

(3) In this section 'rules' means rules of court or, in the case of proceedings before a tribunal, rules made for the purposes of this section:

(a) by the Lord Chancellor or the Secretary of State, in relation to any proceedings outside Scotland;

(b) by the Secretary of State, in relation to proceedings in Scotland; or

(c) by a Northern Ireland department, in relation to proceedings before a tribunal in Northern Ireland:
   (i) which deals with transferred matters; and
   (ii) for which no rules made under paragraph (a) are in force.

Legislation

Interpretation of legislation

3 – (1) So far as it is possible to do so, primary legislation and subordinate legislation must be read and given effect in a way which is compatible with the Convention rights.

(2) This section:
   (a) applies to primary legislation and subordinate legislation whenever enacted;
   (b) does not affect the validity, continuing operation or enforcement of any incompatible primary legislation; and
   (c) does not affect the validity, continuing operation or enforcement of any incompatible subordinate legislation if (disregarding any possibility of revocation) primary legislation prevents removal of the incompatibility.

Declaration of incompatibility

4.– (1) Subsection (2) applies in any proceedings in which a court determines whether a provision of primary legislation is compatible with a Convention right.

(2) If the court is satisfied that the provision is incompatible with a Convention right, it may make a declaration of that incompatibility.

(3) Subsection (4) applies in any proceedings in which a court determines whether a provision of subordinate legislation, made in the exercise of a power conferred by primary legislation, is compatible with a Convention right.

(4) If the court is satisfied:
   (a) that the provision is incompatible with a Convention right, and
   (b) that (disregarding any possibility of revocation) the primary legislation concerned prevents removal of the incompatibility,
it may make a declaration of that incompatibility.

(5) In this section 'court' means
   (a) the House of Lords;
   (b) the Judicial Committee of the Privy Council;
   (c) the Courts – Martial Appeal Court;
   (d) in Scotland, the High Court of Justiciary sitting otherwise than as a trial court or the Court of Session;
   (e) in England and Wales or Northern Ireland, the High Court or the Court of Appeal.

(6) A declaration under this section ('a declaration of incompatibility'):
- (a) does not affect the validity, continuing operation or enforcement of the provision in respect of which it is given; and
- (b) is not binding on the parties to the proceedings in which it is made.

Right of Crown to intervene

5 – (1) Where a court is considering whether to make a declaration of incompatibility, the Crown is entitled to notice in accordance with rules of court.

(2) In any case to which subsection (1) applies:
- (a) a Minister of the Crown (or a person nominated by him),
- (b) a member of the Scottish Executive,
- (c) a Northern Ireland Minister,
- (d) a Northern Ireland department,

is entitled, on giving notice in accordance with rules of court, to be joined as a party to the proceedings.

(3) Notice under subsection (2) may be given at any time during the proceedings.

(4) A person who has been made a party to criminal proceedings (other than in Scotland) as the result of a notice under subsection (2) may, with leave, appeal to the House of Lords against any declaration of incompatibility made in the proceedings.

(5) In subsection (4):

'criminal proceedings' includes all proceedings before the Courts – Martial Appeal Court; and

'leave' means leave granted by the court making the declaration of incompatibility or by the House of Lords.

Public authorities

Acts of public authorities

6.– (1) It is unlawful for a public authority to act in a way which is incompatible with a Convention right.

(2) Subsection (1) does not apply to an act if:
- (a) as the result of one or more provisions of primary legislation, the authority could not have acted differently; or
- (b) in the case of one or more provisions of, or made under, primary legislation which cannot be read or given effect in a way which is compatible with the Convention rights, the authority was acting so as to give effect to or enforce those provisions.

(3) In this section 'public authority' includes:
- (a) a court or tribunal, and
- (b) any person certain of whose functions are functions of a public nature,

but does not include either House of Parliament or a person exercising functions in connection with proceedings in Parliament.

(4) In subsection (3) 'Parliament' does not include the House of Lords in its judicial capacity.

(5) In relation to a particular act, a person is not a public authority by virtue only of subsection (3)(b) if the nature of the act is private.

(6) 'An act' includes a failure to act but does not include a failure to:

    (a) introduce in, or lay before, Parliament a proposal for legislation; or

    (b) make any primary legislation or remedial order.

7 – (1) A person who claims that a public authority has acted (or proposes to act) in a way which is made unlawful by section 6(1) may:

    (a) bring proceedings against the authority under this Act in the appropriate court or tribunal, or

    (b) rely on the Convention right or rights concerned in any legal proceedings,

but only if he is (or would be) a victim of the unlawful act.

(2) In subsection (1)(a) 'appropriate court or tribunal' means such court or tribunal as may be determined in accordance with rules; and proceedings against an authority include a counterclaim or similar proceeding.

(3) If the proceedings are brought on an application for judicial review, the applicant is to be taken to have a sufficient interest in relation to the unlawful act only if he is, or would be, a victim of that act.

(4) If the proceedings are made by way of a petition for judicial review in Scotland, the applicant shall be taken to have title and interest to sue in relation to the unlawful act only if he is, or would be, a victim of that act.

(5) Proceedings under subsection (l)(a) must be brought before the end of:

    (a) the period of one year beginning with the date on which the act complained of took place; or

    (b) such longer period as the court or tribunal considers equitable having regard to all the circumstances,

but that is subject to any rule imposing a stricter time limit in relation to the procedure in question.

(6) In subsection (l)(b) 'legal proceedings' includes:

    (a) proceedings brought by or at the instigation of a public authority; and

    (b) an appeal against the decision of a court or tribunal.

(7) For the purposes of this section, a person is a victim of an unlawful act only if he would be a victim for the purposes of Article 34 of the Convention if proceedings were brought in the European Court of Human Rights in respect of that act.

(8) Nothing in this Act creates a criminal offence.

(9) In this section 'rules' means:

(a) in relation to proceedings before a court or tribunal outside Scotland, rules made by the Lord Chancellor or the Secretary of State for the purposes of this section or rules of court;

(b) in relation to proceedings before a court or tribunal in Scotland, rules made by the Secretary of State for those purposes,

(c) in relation to proceedings before a tribunal in Northern Ireland:

   (i) which deals with transferred matters; and

   (ii) for which no rules made under paragraph (a) are in force, rules made by a Northern Ireland department for those purposes,

and includes provision made by order under section 1 of the Courts and Legal Services Act 1990.

(10) In making rules, regard must be had to section 9.

(11) The Minister who has power to make rules in relation to a particular tribunal may, to the extent he considers it necessary to ensure that the tribunal can provide an appropriate remedy in relation to an act (or proposed act) of a public authority which is (or would be) unlawful as a result of section 6(1), by order add to:

(a) the relief or remedies which the tribunal may grant; or

(b) the grounds on which it may grant any of them.

(12) An order made under subsection (11) may contain such incidental supplemental, consequential or transitional provision as the Minister making it considers appropriate.

(13) 'The Minister' includes the Northern Ireland department concerned.

8 – (1) In relation to any act (or proposed act) of a public authority which the court finds is (or would be) unlawful, it may grant such relief or remedy, or make such order, within its powers as it considers just and appropriate.

(2) But damages may be awarded only by a court which has power to award damages, or to order the payment of compensation, in civil proceedings.

(3) No award of damages is to be made unless, taking account of all the circumstances of the case, including:

(a) any other relief or remedy granted, or order made, in relation to the act in question (by that or any other court), and

(b) the consequences of any decision (of that or any other court) in respect of that act,

the court is satisfied that the award is necessary to afford just satisfaction to the person in whose favour it is made.

(4) In determining:

(a) whether to award damages, or

(b) the amount of an award,

the court must take into account the principles applied by the European Court of Human Rights in relation to the award of compensation under Article 41 of the Convention.

(5) A public authority against which damages are awarded is to be treated:
  (a) in Scotland, for the purposes of section 3 of the Law Reform (Miscellaneous Provisions) (Scotland) Act 1940 as if the award were made in an action of damages in which the authority has been found liable in respect of loss or damage to the person to whom the award is made;
  (b) for the purposes of the Civil Liability (Contribution) Act 1978 as liable in respect of damage suffered by the person to whom the award is made.

(6) In this section:

'court' includes a tribunal;

'damages' means damages for an unlawful act of a public authority; and

'unlawful' means unlawful under section 6(1).

Judicial acts

9 – (1) Proceedings under section 7(1)(a) in respect of a judicial act may be brought only
  (a) by exercising a right of appeal;
  (b) on an application (in Scotland a petition) for judicial review; or
  (c) in such other forum as may be prescribed by rules.

(2) That does not affect any rule of law which prevents a court from being the subject of judicial review.

(3) In proceedings under this Act in respect of a judicial act done in good faith, damages may not be awarded otherwise than to compensate a person to the extent required by Article 5(5) of the Convention.

(4) An award of damages permitted by subsection (3) is to be made against the Crown; but no award may be made unless the appropriate person, if not a party to the proceedings, is joined.

(5) In this section

'appropriate person' means the Minister responsible for the court concerned, or a person or government department nominated by him;

'court' includes a tribunal;

'judge' includes a member of a tribunal, a justice of the peace and a clerk or other officer entitled to exercise the jurisdiction of a court;

'judicial act' means a judicial act of a court and includes an act done on the instructions, or on behalf, of a judge; and

'rules' has the same meaning as in section 7(9).

Remedial action

Power to take remedial action

10 – (1) This section applies if:
  (a) a provision of legislation has been declared under section 4 to be incompatible with a Convention right and, if an appeal lies:

(i) all persons who may appeal have stated in writing that they do not intend to do so;

(ii) the time for bringing an appeal has expired and no appeal has been brought within that fume; or

(iii) an appeal brought within that time has been determined or abandoned; or

(b) it appears to a Minister of the Crown or Her Majesty in Council that, having regard to a finding of the European Court of Human Rights made after the coming into force of this section in proceedings against the United Kingdom, a provision of legislation is incompatible with an obligation of the United Kingdom arising from the Convention.

(2) If a Minister of the Crown considers that there are compelling reasons for proceeding under this section, he may by order make such amendments to the legislation as he considers necessary to remove the incompatibility.

(3) If, in the case of subordinate legislation, a Minister of the Crown considers

(a) that it is necessary to amend the primary legislation under which the subordinate legislation in question was made, in order to enable the incompatibility to be removed, and

(b) that there are compelling reasons for proceeding under this section,

he may by order make such amendments to the primary legislation as he considers necessary.

(4) This section also applies where the provision in question is in subordinate legislation and has been quashed, or declared invalid, by reason of incompatibility with a Convention right and the Minister proposes to proceed under paragraph 2(b) of Schedule 2.

(5) If the legislation is an Order in Council, the power conferred by subsection (2) or (3) is exercisable by Her Majesty in Council.

(6) In this section 'legislation' does not include a Measure of the Church Assembly or of the General Synod of the Church of England.

(7) Schedule 2 makes further provision about remedial orders.

Other rights and proceedings

Safeguard for existing human rights

11 A person's reliance on a Convention right does not restrict:

(a) any other right or freedom conferred on him by or under any law having effect in any part of the United Kingdom; or

(b) his right to make any claim or bring any proceedings which he could make or bring apart from sections 7 to 9.

Freedom of expression

12.- (1) This section applies if a court is considering whether to grant any relief which, if granted, might affect the exercise of the Convention right to freedom of expression.

(2) If the person against whom the application for relief is made ('the respondent') is neither present nor represented, no such relief is to be granted unless the court is satisfied:
- (a) that the applicant has taken all practicable steps to notify the respondent; or
- (b) that there are compelling reasons why the respondent should not be notified.

(3) No such relief is to be granted so as to restrain publication before trial unless the court is satisfied that the applicant is likely to establish that publication should not be allowed.

(4) The court must have particular regard to the importance of the Convention right to freedom of expression and, where the proceedings relate to material which the respondent claims, or which appears to the court, to be journalistic, literary or artistic material (or to conduct connected with such material), to:
- (a) the extent to which:
    - (i) the material has, or is about to, become available to the public; or
    - (ii) it is, or would be, in the public interest for the material to be published;
- (b) any relevant privacy code.

(5) In this section

'court' includes a tribunal; and

'relief' includes any remedy or order (other than in criminal proceedings).

Freedom of thought, conscience and religion

13.– (1) If a court's determination of any question arising under this Act might affect the exercise by a religious organisation (itself or its members collectively) of the Convention right to freedom of thought, conscience and religion, it must have particular regard to the importance of that right.

(2) In this section 'court' includes a tribunal.

Derogations and reservations

Derogations

14 – (1) In this Act 'designated derogation' means:
- (a) the United Kingdom's derogation from Article 5(3) of the Convention; and
- (b) any derogation by the United Kingdom from an Article of the Convention, or of any protocol to the Convention, which is designated for the purposes of this Act in an order made by the Secretary of State.

(2) The derogation referred to in subsection (1)(a) is set out in Part I of Schedule 3.

(3) If a designated derogation is amended or replaced it ceases to be a designated derogation.

(4) But subsection (3) does not prevent the Secretary of State from exercising his power under subsection (1)(b) to make a fresh designation order in respect of the Article concerned.

(5) The Secretary of State must by order make such amendments to Schedule 3 as he considers appropriate to reflect

- (a) any designation order; or
- (b) the effect of subsection (3).

(6) A designation order may be made in anticipation of the making by the United Kingdom of a proposed derogation.

Reservations

15.– (1) In this Act 'designated reservation' means

- (a) the United Kingdom's reservation to Article 2 of the First Protocol to the Convention; and
- (b) any other reservation by the United Kingdom to an Article of the Convention, or of any protocol to the Convention, which is designated for the purposes of this Act in an order made by the Secretary of State.

(2) The text of the reservation referred to in subsection (l)(a) is set out in Part II of Schedule 3.

(3) If a designated reservation is withdrawn wholly or in part it ceases to be a designated reservation.

(4) But subsection (3) does not prevent the Secretary of State from exercising his power under subsection (l)(b) to make a fresh designation order in respect of the Article concerned.

(5) The Secretary of State must by order make such amendments to this Act as he considers appropriate to reflect:

- (a) any designation order; or
- (b) the effect of subsection (3).

Period for which designated derogations have effect

16.– (1) If it has not already been withdrawn by the United Kingdom a designated derogation ceases to have effect for the purposes of this Act

(a) in the case of the derogation referred to in section 14(1)(a), at the end of the period of five years beginning with the date on which section 1(2) came into force;

(b) in the case of any other derogation, at the end of the period of five years beginning with the date on which the order designating it was made.

(2) At any time before the period

- (a) fixed by subsection (l)(a) or (b), or
- (b) extended by an order under this subsection,

comes to an end, the Secretary of State may by order extend it by a further period of five years.

(3) An order under section 14(1)(b) ceases to have effect at the end of the period for consideration, unless a resolution has been passed by each House approving the order.

(4) Subsection (3) does not affect:
- (a) anything done in reliance on the order; or
- (b) the power to make a fresh order under section 14(1)(b).

(5) In subsection (3) 'period for consideration' means the period of forty days beginning with the day on which the order was made.

(6) In calculating the period for consideration, no account is to be taken of any time during which
- (a) Parliament is dissolved or prorogued; or
- (b) both Houses are adjourned for more than four days.

(7) If a designated derogation is withdrawn by the United Kingdom, the Secretary of State must by order make such amendments to this Act as he considers are required to reflect that withdrawal.

Periodic review of designated reservations

17 – (1) The appropriate Minister must review the designated reservation referred to in section 15(1)(a):
- (a) before the end of the period of five years beginning with the date on which section 1(2) came into force; and
- (b) if that designation is still in force, before the end of the period of five years beginning with the date on which the last report relating to it was laid under subsection (3).

(2) The appropriate Minister must review each of the other designated reservations (if any):
- (a) before the end of the period of five years beginning with the date on which the order designating the reservation first came into force; and
- (b) if the designation is still in force, before the end of the period of five years beginning with the date on which the last report relating to it was laid under subsection (3).

(3) The Minister conducting a review under this section must prepare a report on the result of the review and lay a copy of it before each House of Parliament.

Judges of the European Court of Human Rights

Appointment to European Court of Human Rights

18 – (1) In this section 'judicial office' means the office of:
- (a) Lord Justice of Appeal, Justice of the High Court or Circuit judge, in England and Wales;
- (b) judge of the Court of Session or sheriff, in Scotland;
- (c) Lord Justice of Appeal, judge of the High Court or county court judge, in Northern Ireland.

(2) The holder of a judicial office may become a judge of the European Court of Human Rights ('the Court') without being required to relinquish his office.

The Human Rights Act 1998

(3) But he is not required to perform the duties of his judicial office while he is a judge of the Court.

(4) In respect of any period during which he is a judge of the Court

  (a) a Lord Justice of Appeal or Justice of the High Court is not to count as a judge of the relevant court for the purposes of section 2(1) or 4(1) of the Supreme Court Act 1981 (maximum number of judges) nor as a judge of the Supreme Court for the purposes of section 12(1) to (6) of that Act (salaries etc.);

  (b) a judge of the Court of Session is not to count as a judge of that court for the purposes of section 1 (1) of the Court of Session Act 1988 (maximum number of judges) or of section 9(1)(c) of the Administration of Justice Act 1973 ('the 1973 Act') (salaries etc.);

  (c) a Lord Justice of Appeal or judge of the High Court in Northern Ireland is not to count as a judge of the relevant court for the purposes of section 2(1) or 3(1) of the Judicature (Northern Ireland) Act 1978 (maximum number of judges) nor as a judge of the Supreme Court of Northern Ireland for the purposes of section 9(1)(d) of the 1973 Act (salaries etc.);

  (d) a Circuit judge is not to count as such for the purposes of section 18 of the Courts Act 1971 (salaries etc.);

  (e) a sheriff is not to count as such for the purposes of section 14 of the Sheriff Courts (Scotland) Act 1907 (salaries etc.);

  (f) a county court judge of Northern Ireland is not to count as such for the purposes of section 106 of the County Courts Act Northern Ireland) 1959 (salaries etc.).

(5) If a sheriff principal is appointed a judge of the Court, section 11(1) of the Sheriff Courts (Scotland) Act 1971 (temporary appointment of sheriff principal) applies, while he holds that appointment, as if his office is vacant.

(6) Schedule 4 makes provision about judicial pensions in relation to the holder of a judicial office who serves as a judge of the Court.

(7) The Lord Chancellor or the Secretary of State may by order make such transitional provision (including, in particular, provision for a temporary increase in the maximum number of judges) as he considers appropriate in relation to any holder of a judicial office who has completed his service as a judge of the Court.

Parliamentary procedure

Statements of compatibility

19 – (1) A Minister of the Crown in charge of a Bill in either House of Parliament must, before Second Reading of the Bill:

  (a) make a statement to the effect that in his view the provisions of the Bill are compatible with the Convention rights ('a statement of compatibility'); or

(b) make a statement to the effect that although he is unable to make a statement of compatibility the government nevertheless wishes the House to proceed with the Bill.

(2) The statement must be in writing and be published in such manner as the Minister making it considers appropriate.

Supplemental

Orders etc under this Act

20 – (1) Any power of a Minister of the Crown to make an order under this Act is exercisable by statutory instrument.

(2) The power of the Lord Chancellor or the Secretary of State to make rules (other than rules of court) under section 2(3) or 7(9) is exercisable by statutory instrument.

(3) Any statutory instrument made under section 14, 15 or 16(7) must be laid before Parliament.

(4) No order may be made by the Lord Chancellor or the Secretary of State under section 1(4), 7(11) or 16(2) unless a draft of the order has been laid before, and approved by, each House of Parliament.

(5) Any statutory instrument made under section 18(7) or Schedule 4, or to which subsection (2) applies, shall be subject to annulment in pursuance of a resolution of either House of Parliament.

(6) The power of a Northern Ireland department to make:

(a) rules under section 2(3)(c) or 7(9)(c), or

(b) an order under section 7(11),

is exercisable by statutory rule for the purposes of the Statutory Rules (Northern Ireland) Order 1979.

(7) Any rules made under section 2(3)(c) or 7(9)(c) shall be subject to negative resolution; and section 41 (6) of the Interpretation Act Northern Ireland) 1954 (meaning of 'subject to negative resolution') shall apply as if the power to make the rules were conferred by an Act of the Northern Ireland Assembly.

(8) No order may be made by a Northern Ireland department under section 7(11) unless a draft of the order has been laid before, and approved by, the Northern Ireland Assembly.

Interpretation, etc

21 – (1) In this Act:

'amend' includes repeal and apply (with or without modifications);

'the appropriate Minister' means the Minister of the Crown having charge of the appropriate authorised government department (within the meaning of the Crown Proceedings Act 1947);

'the Commission' means the European Commission of Human Rights;

'the Convention' means the Convention for the Protection of Human Rights and Fundamental Freedoms, agreed by the Council of Europe at

Rome on 4th November 1950 as it has effect for the time being in relation to the United Kingdom;

'declaration of incompatibility' means a declaration under section 4;

'Minister of the Crown' has the same meaning as in the Ministers of the Crown Act 1975;

'Northern Ireland Minister' includes the First Minister and the deputy First Minister in Northern Ireland; 'primary legislation' means any(a) public general Act; (b) local and personal Act;

(c) private Act;

(d) Measure of the Church Assembly;

(e) Measure of the General Synod of the Church of England;

(f) Order in Council:

   (i) made in exercise of Her Majesty's Royal Prerogative;

   (ii) made under section 38(1)(a) of the Northern Ireland Constitution Act 1973 or the corresponding provision of the Northern Ireland Act 1998; or

   (iii) amending an Act of a kind mentioned in paragraph (a), (b) or (c);

and includes an order or other instrument made under primary legislation (otherwise than by the National Assembly for Wales, a member of the Scottish Executive, a Northern Ireland Minister or a Northern Ireland department) to the extent to which it operates to bring one or more provisions of that legislation into force or amends any primary legislation;

'the First Protocol' means the protocol to the Convention agreed at Paris on 20th March 1952;

'the Sixth Protocol' means the protocol to the Convention agreed at Strasbourg on 28th April 1983;

'the Eleventh Protocol' means the protocol to the Convention (restructuring the control machinery established by the Convention) agreed at Strasbourg on 11th May 1994;

'remedial order' means an order under section 10;

'subordinate legislation' means any:

(a) Order in Council other than one

   (i) made in exercise of Her Majesty's Royal Prerogative;

   (ii) made under section 38(1)(a) of the Northern Ireland Constitution Act 1973 or the corresponding provision of the Northern Ireland Act 1998; or

   (iii) amending an Act of a kind mentioned in the definition of primary legislation;

(b) Act of the Scottish Parliament;

(c) Act of the Parliament of Northern Ireland;

(d) Measure of the Assembly established under section 1 of the Northern Ireland Assembly Act 1973;

(e) Act of the Northern Ireland Assembly;

(f) order, rules, regulations, scheme, warrant, byelaw or other instrument made under primary legislation (except to the extent to which it operates to bring one or more provisions of that legislation into force or amends any primary legislation);

(g) order, rules, regulations, scheme, warrant, byelaw or other instrument made under legislation mentioned in paragraph (b), (c), (d) or (e) or made under an Order in Council applying only to Northern Ireland;

(h) order, rules, regulations, scheme, warrant, byelaw or other instrument made by a member of the Scottish Executive, a Northern Ireland Minister or a Northern Ireland department in exercise of prerogative or other executive functions of Her Majesty which are exercisable by such a person on behalf of Her Majesty;

'transferred matters' has the same meaning as in the Northern Ireland Act 1998; and

'tribunal' means any tribunal in which legal proceedings may be brought.

(2) The references in paragraphs (b) and (c) of section 2(1) to Articles are to Articles of the Convention as they had effect immediately before the coming into force of the Eleventh Protocol.

(3) The reference in paragraph (d) of section 2(1) to Article 46 includes a reference to Articles 32 and 54 of the Convention as they had effect immediately before the coming into force of the Eleventh Protocol.

(4) The references in section 2(1) to a report or decision of the Commission or a decision of the Committee of Ministers include references to a report or decision made as provided by paragraphs 3, 4 and 6 of Article S of the Eleventh Protocol (transitional provisions).

(5) Any liability under the Army Act 1955, the Air Force Act 1955 or the Naval Discipline Act 1957 to suffer death for an offence is replaced by a liability to imprisonment for life or any less punishment authorised by those Acts; and those Acts shall accordingly have effect with the necessary modifications.

Short title, commencement, application and extent

22 – (1) This Act may be cited as the Human Rights Act 1998.

(2) Sections 18, 20 and 21(5) and this section come into force on the passing of this Act.

(3) The other provisions of this Act come into force on such day as the Secretary of State may by order appoint; and different days may be appointed for different purposes.

(4) Paragraph (b) of subsection (1) of section 7 applies to proceedings brought by or at the instigation of a public authority whenever the act in question took place; but otherwise that subsection does not apply to an act taking place before the coming into force of that section.

(5) This Act binds the Crown.

(6) This Act extends to Northern Ireland.

(7) Section 21(5), so far as it relates to any provision contained in the Army Act 1955, the Air Force Act 1955 or the Naval Discipline Act 1957, extends to any place to which that provision extends.

SCHEDULES

Schedule 1

THE ARTICLES

PART I

THE CONVENTION

RIGHTS AND FREEDOMS

ARTICLE 2

RIGHT TO LIFE

1   Everyone's right to life shall be protected by law. No one shall be deprived of his life intentionally save in the execution of a sentence of a court following his conviction of a crime for which this penalty is provided by law.

2   Deprivation of life shall not be regarded as inflicted in contravention of this Article when it results from the use of force which is no more than absolutely necessary:

   (a) in defence of any person from unlawful violence;

   (b) in order to effect a lawful arrest or to prevent the escape of a person lawfully detained;

   (c) in action lawfully taken for the purpose of quelling a riot or insurrection.

ARTICLE 3

PROHIBITION OF TORTURE

No one shall be subjected to torture or to inhuman or degrading treatment or punishment.

ARTICLE 4

PROHIBITION OF SLAVERY AND FORCED LABOUR

1   No one shall be held in slavery or servitude.

2   No one shall be required to perform forced or compulsory labour.

3   For the purpose of this Article the term 'forced or compulsory labour' shall not include:

(a) any work required to be done in the ordinary course of detention imposed according to the provisions of Article 5 of this Convention or during conditional release from such detention;

(b) any service of a military character or, in case of conscientious objectors in countries where they are recognised, service exacted instead of compulsory military service;

(c) any service exacted in case of an emergency or calamity threatening the life or well-being of the community;

(d) any work or service which forms part of normal civic obligations.

ARTICLE 5
RIGHT TO LIBERTY AND SECURITY

1   Everyone has the right to liberty and security of person. No one shall be deprived of his liberty save in the following cases and in accordance with a procedure prescribed by law:

- (a) the lawful detention of a person after conviction by a competent court;
- (b) the lawful arrest or detention of a person for non – compliance with the lawful order of a court or in order to secure the fulfilment of any obligation prescribed by law;
- (c) the lawful arrest or detention of a person effected for the purpose of bringing him before the competent legal authority on reasonable suspicion of having committed an offence or when it is reasonably considered necessary to prevent his committing an offence or fleeing after having done so;
- (d) the detention of a minor by lawful order for the purpose of educational supervision or his lawful detention for the purpose of bringing him before the competent legal authority;
- (e) the lawful detention of persons for the prevention of the spreading of infectious diseases, of persons of unsound mind, alcoholics or drug addicts or vagrants;
- (f) the lawful arrest or detention of a person to prevent his effecting an unauthorised entry into the country or of a person against whom action is being taken with a view to deportation or extradition.

2   Everyone who is arrested shall be informed promptly, in a language which he understands, of the reasons for his arrest and of any charge against him.

3   Everyone arrested or detained in accordance with the provisions of paragraph 1 (c) of this Article shall be brought promptly before a judge or other officer authorised by law to exercise judicial power and shall be entitled to trial within a reasonable time or to release pending trial. Release may be conditioned by guarantees to appear for trial.

4   Everyone who is deprived of his liberty by arrest or detention shall be entitled to take proceedings by which the lawfulness of his detention shall be decided speedily by a court and his release ordered if the detention is not lawful.

The Human Rights Act 1998

5   Everyone who has been the victim of arrest or detention in contravention of the provisions of this Article shall have an enforceable right to compensation.

ARTICLE 6

RIGHT TO A FAIR TRIAL

1   In the determination of his civil rights and obligations or of any criminal charge against him, everyone is entitled to a fair and public hearing within a reasonable time by an independent and impartial tribunal established by law. Judgment shall be pronounced publicly but the press and public may be excluded from all or part of the trial in the interest of morals, public order or national security in a democratic society, where the interests of juveniles or the protection of the private life of the parties so require, or to the extent strictly necessary in the opinion of the court in special circumstances where publicity would prejudice the interests of justice.

2   Everyone charged with a criminal offence shall be presumed innocent until proved guilty according to law.

3   Everyone charged with a criminal offence has the following minimum rights:

   (a) to be informed promptly, in a language which he understands and in detail, of the nature and cause of the accusation against him;

   (b) to have adequate time and facilities for the preparation of his defence;

   (c) to defend himself in person or through legal assistance of his own choosing or if he has not sufficient means to pay for legal assistance, to be given it free when the interests of justice so require;

   (d) to examine or have examined witnesses against him and to obtain the attendance and examination of witnesses on his behalf under the same conditions as witnesses against him;

   (e) to have the free assistance of an interpreter if he cannot understand or speak the language used in court.

ARTICLE 7

NO PUNISHMENT WITHOUT LAW

1   No one shall be held guilty of any criminal offence on account of any act or omission which did not constitute a criminal offence under national or international law at the time when it was committed. Nor shall a heavier penalty be imposed than the one that was applicable at the time the criminal offence was committed.

2   This Article shall not prejudice the trial and punishment of any person for any act or omission which, at the time when it was committed, was criminal according to the general principles of law recognised by civilised nations.

ARTICLE 8

RIGHT TO RESPECT FOR PRIVATE AND FAMILY LIFE

1   Everyone has the right to respect for his private and family life, his home and his correspondence.

2   There shall be no interference by a public authority with the exercise of this right except such as is in accordance with the law and is necessary in a democratic society in the interests of national security, public safety or the economic well – being of the country for the prevention of disorder or crime, for the protection of health or morals, or for the protection of the rights and freedoms of others.

ARTICLE 9

FREEDOM OF THOUGHT, CONSCIENCE AND RELIGION

1   Everyone has the right to freedom of thought, conscience and religion; this right includes freedom to change his religion or belief and freedom either alone or in community with others and in public or private, to manifest his religion or belief, in worship, teaching, practice and observance.

2   Freedom to manifest one's religion or beliefs shall be subject only to such limitations as are prescribed by law and are necessary in a democratic society in the interests of public safety, for the protection of public order, health or morals, or for the protection of the rights and freedoms of others.

ARTICLE 10

FREEDOM OF EXPRESSION

1   Everyone has the right to freedom of expression. This right shall include freedom to hold opinions and to receive and impart information and ideas without interference by public authority and regardless of frontiers. This Article shall not prevent States from requiring the licensing of broadcasting, television or cinema enterprises.

2   The exercise of these freedoms, since it carries with it duties and responsibilities, may be subject to such formalities, conditions, restrictions or penalties as are prescribed by law and are necessary in a democratic society, in the interests of national security territorial integrity or public safety, for the prevention of disorder or crime, for the protection of health or morals, for the protection of the reputation or rights of others, for preventing the disclosure of information received in confidence, or for maintaining the authority and impartiality of the judiciary.

ARTICLE 11

FREEDOM OF ASSEMBLY AND ASSOCIATION

I   Everyone has the right to freedom of peaceful assembly and to freedom of association with others, including the right to form and to join trade unions for the protection of his interests.

2   No restrictions shall be placed on the exercise of these rights other than such as are prescribed by law and are necessary in a democratic society in the interests of national security or public safety, for the prevention of disorder or crime, for the protection of health or morals or for the protection of the rights and freedoms of others. This Article shall not prevent the imposition of lawful restrictions on the exercise of these rights by members of the armed forces, of the police or of the administration of the State.

ARTICLE 12

RIGHT TO MARRY

Men and women of marriageable age have the right to marry and to found a family, according to the national laws governing the exercise of this right.

ARTICLE 14

PROHIBITION OF DISCRIMINATION

The enjoyment of the rights and freedoms set forth in this Convention shall be secured without discrimination on any ground such as sex, race, colour, language, religion, political or other opinion, national or social origin, association with a national minority, property, birth or other status.

ARTICLE 16

RESTRICTIONS ON POLITICAL ACTIVITY OF ALIENS

Nothing in Articles 10, 11 and 14 shall be regarded as preventing the High Contracting Parties from imposing restrictions on the political activity of aliens.

ARTICLE 17

PROHIBITION OF ABUSE OF RIGHTS

Nothing in this Convention may be interpreted as implying for any State, group or person any right to engage in any activity or perform any act aimed at the destruction of any of the rights and freedoms set forth herein or at their limitation to a greater extent than is provided for in the Convention.

ARTICLE 18

LIMITATION ON USE OF RESTRICTIONS ON RIGHTS

The restrictions permitted under this Convention to the said rights and freedoms shall not be applied for any purpose other than those for which they have been prescribed.

PART II

THE FIRST PROTOCOL

ARTICLE 1

PROTECTION OF PROPERTY

Every natural or legal person is entitled to the peaceful enjoyment of his possessions. No one shall be deprived of his possessions except in the public interest and subject to the conditions provided for by law and by the general principles of international law.

The preceding provisions shall not, however, in any way impair the right of a State to enforce such laws as it deems necessary to control the use of property in accordance with the general interest or to secure the payment of taxes or other contributions or penalties.

ARTICLE 2

RIGHT TO EDUCATION

No person shall be denied the right to education. In the exercise of any functions which it assumes in relation to education and to teaching, the State shall respect the right of parents to ensure such education and teaching in conformity with their own religious and philosophical convictions.

ARTICLE 3

RIGHT TO FREE ELECTIONS

The High Contracting Parties undertake to hold free elections at reasonable intervals by secret ballot, under conditions which will ensure the free expression of the opinion of the people in the choice of the legislature.

PART III

THE SIXTH PROTOCOL

ARTICLE 1

ABOLITION OF THE DEATH PENALTY

The death penalty shall be abolished. No one shall be condemned to such penalty or executed.

ARTICLE 2

DEATH PENALTY IN TIME OF WAR

A State may make provision in its law for the death penalty in respect of acts committed in time of war or of imminent threat of war; such penalty shall be applied only in the instances laid down in the law and in accordance with its provisions. The State shall communicate to the Secretary General of the Council of Europe the relevant provisions of that law.

Schedule 2

REMEDIAL ORDERS

Orders

1 – (I) A remedial order may:

    (a) contain such incidental, supplemental, consequential or transitional provision as the person making it considers appropriate;

    (b) be made so as to have effect from a date earlier than that on which it is made;

    (c) make provision for the delegation of specific functions;

    (d) make different provision for different cases.

(2) The power conferred by sub-paragraph (1)(a) includes:

    (a) power to amend primary legislation (including primary legislation other than that which contains the incompatible provision); and

(b) power to amend or revoke subordinate legislation (including subordinate legislation other than that which contains the incompatible provision).

(3) A remedial order may be made so as to have the same extent as the legislation which it affects.

(4) No person is to be guilty of an offence solely as a result of the retrospective effect of a remedial order.

Procedure

2. No remedial order may be made unless:
   (a) a draft of the order has been approved by a resolution of each House of Parliament made after the end of the period of 60 days beginning with the day on which the draft was laid; or
   (b) it is declared in the order that it appears to the person making it that, because of the urgency of the matter, it is necessary to make the order without a draft being so approved.

Orders laid in draft

3.– (1) No draft may be laid under paragraph 2(a) unless
   (a) the person proposing to make the order has laid before Parliament a document which contains a draft of the proposed order and the required information; and
   (b) the period of 60 days, beginning with the day on which the document required by this sub – paragraph was laid, has ended.

(2) If representations have been made during that period, the draft laid under paragraph 2(a) must be accompanied by a statement containing
   (a) a summary of the representations; and
   (b) if, as a result of the representations, the proposed order has been changed, details of the changes.

Urgent cases

4 – (1) If a remedial order ('the original order') is made without being approved in draft, the person making it must lay it before Parliament, accompanied by the required information, after it is made.

(2) If representations have been made during the period of 60 days beginning with the day on which the original order was made, the person making it must (after the end of that period) lay before Parliament a statement containing
   (a) a summary of the representations; and
   (b) if, as a result of the representations, he considers it appropriate to make changes to the original order, details of the changes.

(3) If sub-paragraph (2)(b) applies, the person making the statement must:
   (a) make a further remedial order replacing the original order; and

    (b) lay the replacement order before Parliament.

(4) If, at the end of the period of 120 days beginning with the day on which the original order was made, a resolution has not been passed by each House approving the original or replacement order, the order ceases to have effect (but without that affecting anything previously done under either order or the power to make a fresh remedial order).

Definitions

5   In this Schedule:

'representations' means representations about a remedial order (or proposed remedial order) made to the person making (or proposing to make) it and includes any relevant Parliamentary report or resolution; and

'required information' means:

(a) an explanation of the incompatibility which the order (or proposed order) seeks to remove, including particulars of the relevant declaration, finding or order; and

(b) a statement of the reasons for proceeding under section 10 and for making an order in those terms.

Calculating periods

6   In calculating any period for the purposes of this Schedule, no account is to be taken of any time during which:

(a) Parliament is dissolved or prorogued; or

(b) both Houses are adjourned for more than four days.

Schedule 3

DEROGATION AND RESERVATION

PART I

DEROGATION

The 1988 notification

The United Kingdom Permanent Representative to the Council of Europe presents his compliments to the Secretary General of the Council, and has the honour to convey the following information in order to ensure compliance with the obligations of Her Majesty's Government in the United Kingdom under Article 15(3) of the Convention for the Protection of Human Rights and Fundamental Freedoms signed at Rome on 4 November 1950.

There have been in the United Kingdom in recent years campaigns of organised terrorism connected with the affairs of Northern Ireland which have manifested themselves in activities which have included repeated murder,

The Human Rights Act 1998

attempted murder maiming, intimidation and violent civil disturbance and in bombing and fire raising which have resulted in death, injury and widespread destruction of property. As a result a public emergency within the meaning of Article 15(1) of the Convention exists in the United Kingdom.

The Government found it necessary in 1974 to introduce and since then, in cases concerning persons reasonably suspected of involvement in terrorism connected with the affairs of Northern Ireland, or of certain offences under the legislation who have been detained for 48 hours, to exercise powers enabling further detention without charge, for periods of up to five days, on the authority of the Secretary of State. These powers are at present to be found in Section 12 of the Prevention of Terrorism (Temporary Provisions) Act 1984, Article 9 of the Prevention of Terrorism (Supplemental Temporary Provisions) Order 1984 and Article 10 of the Prevention of Terrorism (Supplemental Temporary Provisions) (Northern Ireland) Order 1984.

Section 12 of the Prevention of Terrorism (Temporary Provisions) Act 1984 provides for a person whom a constable has arrested on reasonable grounds of suspecting him to be guilty of an offence under Section 1, 9 or 10 of the Act, or to be or to have been involved in terrorism connected with the affairs of Northern Ireland, to be detained in right of the arrest for up to 48 hours and thereafter, where the Secretary of State extends the detention period, for up to a further five days. Section 12 substantially re – enacted Section 12 of the Prevention of Terrorism (Temporary Provisions) Act 1976 which, in turn, substantially re – enacted Section 7 of the Prevention of Terrorism (Temporary Provisions) Act 1974.

Article 10 of the Prevention of Terrorism (Supplemental Temporary Provisions) (Northern Ireland) Order 1984 (SI 1984/417) and Article 9 of the Prevention of Terrorism (Supplemental Temporary Provisions) Order 1984 (SI 1984/418) were both made under Sections 13 and 14 of and Schedule 3 to the 1984 Act and substantially re – enacted powers of detention in Orders made under the 1974 and 1976 Acts. A person who is being examined under Article 4 of either Order on his arrival in, or on seeking to leave, Northern Ireland or Great Britain for the purpose of determining whether he is or has been involved in terrorism connected with the affairs of Northern Ireland, or whether there are grounds for suspecting that he has committed an offence under Section 9 of the 1984 Act, may be detained under Article 9 or 10, as appropriate pending the conclusion of his examination. The period of this examination may exceed i2 hours if an examining officer has reasonable grounds for suspecting him to be or to have been involved in acts of terrorism connected with the affairs of Northern Ireland.

Where such a person is detained under the said Article 9 or 10 he may be detained for up to 48 hours on the authority of an examining officer and thereafter, where the Secretary of State extends the detention period, for up to a further five days.

In its judgment of 29 November 1988 in the Case of Brogan and Others, the European Court of Human Rights held that there had been a violation of Article 5(3) in respect of each of the applicants, all of whom had been detained under Section 12 of the 1984 Act. The Court held that even the shortest of the four periods of detention concerned, namely four days and six hours, fell outside the constraints as to time permitted by the first part of Article 5(3). In addition, the Court held that there had been a violation of Article 5(5) in the case of each applicant.

Following this judgment, the Secretary of State for the Home Department informed Parliament on 6 December 1988 that, against the background of the terrorist campaign, and the over-riding need to bring terrorists to justice, the Government did not believe that the maximum period of detention should be reduced. He informed Parliament that the Government were examining the matter with a view to responding to the judgment. On 22 December 1988, the Secretary of State further informed Parliament that it remained the Government's wish, if it could be achieved, to find a judicial process under which extended detention might be reviewed and where appropriate authorised by a judge or other judicial officer. But a further period of reflection and consultation was necessary before the Government could bring forward a firm and final view.

Since the judgment of 29 November 1988 as well as previously, the Government have found it necessary to continue to exercise, in relation to terrorism connected with the affairs of Northern Ireland, the powers described above enabling further detention without charge for periods of up to 5 days, on the authority of the Secretary of State, to the extent strictly required by the exigencies of the situation to enable necessary enquiries and investigations properly to be completed in order to decide whether criminal proceedings should be instituted. To the extent that the exercise of these powers may be inconsistent with the obligations imposed by the Convention the Government has availed itself of the right of derogation conferred by Article 15(1) of the Convention and will continue to do so until further notice.

Dated 23 December 1988.

The 1989 notification

The United Kingdom Permanent Representative to the Council of Europe presents his compliments to the Secretary General of the Council, and has the honour to convey the following information.

In his communication to the Secretary General of 23 December 1988, reference was made to the introduction and exercise of certain powers under section 12 of the Prevention of Terrorism (Temporary Provisions) Act 1984, Article 9 of the Prevention of Terrorism (Supplemental Temporary Provisions) Order 1984 and Article 10 of the Prevention of Terrorism (Supplemental Temporary Provisions) (Northern Ireland) Order 1984.

These provisions have been replaced by section 14 of and paragraph 6 of Schedule 5 to the Prevention of Terrorism (Temporary Provisions) Act 1989, which make comparable provision. They came into force on 22 March 1989. A copy of these provisions is enclosed.

The United Kingdom Permanent Representative avails himself of this opportunity to renew to the Secretary General the assurance of his highest consideration.

PART II

RESERVATION

At the time of signing the present (First) Protocol, I declare that in view of certain provisions of the Education Acts in the United Kingdom, the principle affirmed in the second sentence of Article 2 is accepted by the United Kingdom only so far as it is compatible with the provision of efficient instruction and training, and the avoidance of unreasonable public expenditure.

Dated 20 March 1952

Made by the United Kingdom Permanent Representative to the Council of Europe.

Schedule 4

JUDICIAL PENSIONS

Duty to make orders about pensions

1 – (1) The appropriate Minister must by order make provision with respect to pensions payable to or in respect of any holder of a judicial office who serves as an

(2) A pensions order must include such provision as the Minister making it considers is necessary to secure that

   (a) an ECHR judge who was, immediately before his appointment as an ECHR judge, a member of a judicial pension scheme is entitled to remain as a member of that scheme;

   (b) the terms on which he remains a member of the scheme are those which would have been applicable had he not been appointed as an ECHR judge; and

   (c) entitlement to benefits payable in accordance with the scheme continues to be determined as if, while serving as an ECHR judge, his salary was that which would (but for section 18(4)) have been payable to him in respect of his continuing service as the holder of his judicial office.

Contributions

2   A pensions order may, in particular, make provision

   (a) for any contributions which are payable by a person who remains a member of a scheme as a result of the order, and which would otherwise be payable by deduction from his salary, to be made otherwise than by deduction from his salary as an ECHR judge; and

   (b) for such contributions to be collected in such manner as may be determined by the administrators of the scheme.

Amendments of other enactments

3   A pensions order may amend any provision of, or made under, a pensions Act in such manner and to such extent as the Minister making the order considers necessary or expedient to ensure the proper administration of any scheme to which it relates.

Definitions

4   In this Schedule:

'appropriate Minister' means:

(a) in relation to any judicial office whose jurisdiction is exercisable exclusively in relation to Scotland, the Secretary of State; and

(b) otherwise, the Lord Chancellor;

'ECHR judge' means the holder of a judicial office who is serving as a judge of the Court;

'judicial pension scheme' means a scheme established by and in accordance with a pensions Act;

'pensions Act' means:

(a) the County Courts Act Northern Ireland) 1959;

(b) the Sheriffs' Pensions (Scotland) Act 1961;

(c) the Judicial Pensions Act 1981; or

(d) the Judicial Pensions and Retirement Act 1993; and 'pensions order' means an order made under paragraph 1.

INDEX

Abortion,	37, 69, 389	Anti-discrimination legislation	
Access to a court,	534–35	*See* Discrimination	
Access to legal advice,	56, 58, 469	*Anton Piller* orders,	375
Code of Practice,	441,	Appeals,	55, 56
	443–49, 453	asylum,	533
confessions,	446,	contempt of court, and	152
	474, 477–79,	deportation,	542
	483–84, 487–89	freedom of movement,	528–36
denial of,	442–43	illegal entry,	538
detention,	440–55	immigration,	525, 527, 528
duty solicitors,	441, 446, 453	Appropriate adult,	427–28, 430, 439,
encouragement to			457, 465, 483
defer decision,	444–45	Armed forces	
encouragement to		homosexuals in,	102, 617, 619
forego advice,	445–48, 454	sex discrimination,	578
exclusion of evidence,	469	Arrest,	393, 405–16
Home Office circulars,	448, 453	arrestable offences,	366,
improving,	453–55		406–07, 412
interrogation,	426, 431,	breach of the peace,	406
	436, 437–38,	Code of Practice,	409
	440–55, 457	common law,	405–06, 414–15
notification of right,	443–44, 454	conditions,	407–09
PACE,	440, 443,	detention,	47–50, 417
	453–54	European Convention	
quality of advice,	454, 455	on Human Rights,	418
right to silence,	441, 450–53,	false imprisonment,	405, 416
	458, 460	firearms,	417–18
Royal Commission on		illegal entry,	537
Criminal Procedure 1993,	454	obstruction of a	
serious arrestable offences,	441, 442	police officer,	419–20
solicitors' clerks,	448–49	PACE, under	405–15, 417–18
vulnerable suspects,	443–44, 445	powers of entry,	366
Administration of justice,	147–79	procedural elements,	414–16
Admissibility of evidence		racial discrimination,	610
See Exclusion of evidence		reasonable suspicion,	366, 407–13
Admissions,	441, 495,	reasons, for,	50–51, 415–16
	493–95	right to liberty,	48–49, 50–51
Affirmative action		serious arrestable	
See Positive discrimination		offences,	407, 414,
Affray,	311–12		421, 441, 442
Agents provocateur,	490	stop and search,	401
Aliens,	49–50, 80	terrorism,	50–51, 412, 413–14
Amsterdam Treaty	110, 607–08, 619	use of force,	417–18
Annan Committee,	211	warrant,	413
		without,	406–12

Wednesbury unreasonableness,	411–12
Assault,	418–21
Assembly *See* Freedom of Assembly, Freedom of Association	
Asylum	
access to courts,	534
appeals,	533
deportation,	545–46
destitution,	534–35
European Convention on Human Rights, and	536
European Union, and	536
fast track procedure,	533
freedom of movement,	528–36
illegal entrants,	529
inhuman or degrading treatment,	42–43
judicial review,	531, 534
persecution,	529, 531–33
racial discrimination,	536
reform,	535–36
sex discrimination,	532
third country rule,	534, 535–36
UN Convention Relating to the Status of Refugees,	528–34
Wednesbury unreasonableness,	530
white list,	533
Autonomy	
bodily,	377–81
freedom of expression,	137–38, 143
medical treatment,	379–81
moral,	143, 184, 187–88, 224, 319, 553
personal,	318
pornography,	184, 187–189
privacy,	318, 319
sexual,	138
Bail,	52, 300–06
Banning orders,	295–99
BBC Governors,	206, 207
Bentham, Jeremy,	6, 113
Bias of judges,	119–22, 173–75

Bill of Rights for UK,	1, 87–145
Bentham,	113
Conservative Party support for,	90–91
democratic process,	93–112, 114–18
Dicey,	98–106, 113, 133
discrimination, and	100
Dworkin,	93, 114
elections,	116
emergencies,	95
enforcement,	133–36
entrenchment of,	114–16, 118, 125–26, 129, 132–33
European Convention on Human Rights,	87–93, 101, 103, 118, 123–36
European Union, and	103, 107–12
freedom of expression,	100–01
history of debate,	89–93
interception of communications,	95, 97, 98
interpretation,	117–18
judges, and	98–106, 113–14, 117–22, 123–24
judicial review,	101, 103–06, 116, 133–34
Labour Party position,	92–93
Liberals,	91
miner's strike,	99
national security,	94, 101
'notwithstanding' clause,	126, 128, 130, 131
official secrets,	94, 95
prisoners' rights,	99–100
privacy,	117
proportionality,	105, 134
protecting freedoms common law inefficacy,	109–10
Parliamentary inefficacy,	129–33
repeal,	125, 127–29, 132–33
remedies under,	133–35
role of judiciary in relation to,	98–106, 113–14, 117–22

Index

scrutiny,	135–36	preserving confidentiality,	330
second chamber,	96–97	prior restraints,	252, 256
statutory interpretation,	98–106	privacy,	323–331
terrorism,	95, 114–15	public domain,	324–26
Wednesday unreasonableness,	102–03, 105, 134	public interest defence,	134–35, 250–57, 324, 330–31
Bills of Rights,	1, 116, 127, 130, 143, 144	*Spycatcher* litigation,	99, 251–56
		United States,	255–56
See also Bill of Rights for the UK		Younger Committee,	323
		Breach of the peace,	300–06, 315, 406
Binding over,	300–06	British citizenship,	509, 511, 517, 519–20
Blasphemy			
abolition of,	217, 219, 221–24	British Board of Film Classification,	212, 213
discrimination,	218–19	Broadcasting	
European Convention on Human Rights Article 10,	109, 216–20	Annan Committee,	211
		BBC Governors,	206, 207
		bias, in	207
extension of,	217, 221–24	Broadcasting Complaints Commission,	334–35
freedom of expression,	215–24		
incitement to racial hatred,	218	Broadcasting Standards Commission,	210, 335
margin of appreciation,	219, 220	Broadcasting Standards Council,	210
reform,	217, 219–24		
seditious libel,	218	cable,	226
Bodily integrity,	377–81	censorship,	206, 208, 210–11
Breach of confidence,	250–57	European Convention on Human Rights Article 10,	208–09
commercial information,	324, 326		
contempt of court and,	178, 256–57	European Union,	211
data protection,	358	films,	190, 205–06, 212–13
European Convention on Human Rights,	252, 254	freedom of expression,	66, 67, 205, 206–211, 215
freedom of expression,	67, 69, 252, 254	government control over,	206–11
freedom of information,	258, 267	incitement to racial hatred,	226
gagging orders,	252	Independent Television Commission,	207, 210, 211
injunctions,	252		
interim,	250, 251–52, 254–57, 316, 325–28	Internet,	206, 213–14, 215
		judicial review,	209
permanent,	250, 251, 253–54, 316	media ownership,	206
		obscenity,	211
national security,	254	political control,	206–09
official secrets,	134–35, 228–30, 235, 240, 247, 250, 253	pornography,	211

651

Programme Code,	210, 211	interrogation,	426–29, 430
radio,	207, 211	marriage,	72
satellite,	211	privacy,	333, 360
taste and decency,	210–11	Cinema,	190, 205–06, 212–13
terrorism, and	208, 209		
videos,	213	Citizen's Charter,	266
Buggery,	382–85	Citizenship,	509, 511, 517, 519–20
Bugging devices,	62, 76, 95, 97, 343, 349–56		
		Civil liberties	
		definition,	3
Calcutt Committee,	334, 335, 337, 339, 340–41	Parliamentary sovereignty and,	1, 129–30, 132
Canada		Closed shop,	278–80
Bill of Rights,	130–31	Commercial information,	324, 326
freedom of expression,	121–22	Commission for Racial Equality,	559, 566–67, 575, 576, 594
freedom of information,	264		
judges,	119–20, 121–22		
state surveillance,	354	Communitarians,	7
Capital punishment,	37, 42, 74	Compensation, *See also* Damages	33, 53
Cautions,	403, 426, 433, 437	Complaints against police,	469, 503–06
Censorship		Confessions,	469–91, 496–500
British Board of Film Classification,	212, 213	access to legal advice,	446, 474, 477–79, 483–84, 487–89
broadcasting,	208, 210–11		
films,	190, 205–06, 212–13	appropriate adult,	483
freedom of information,	258	bad faith,	475, 482, 489
pornography,	181, 183, 188	breach of rules,	481–90
reform,	214	substantial or significant,	482–83
taste and decency,	210–11	causation,	478–79, 484–85, 487, 489
theatre,	190, 198		
Children		children,	427, 483
access,	389	Code of Practice,	477–78, 481–85, 487–90
legal advice, to,	445		
appropriate adult,	427–28, 430, 439, 457, 465, 483	exclusion of evidence,	469–91, 496–97
confessions,	427, 483	fabrication,	436, 488
detention,	49	fairness test,	480–90
education of,	74	Home Office circulars,	482
immigration,	519, 526	identification,	496
indecency,	200	mentally disordered suspects,	428
Internet,	213–14		
information relating to upbringing,	360–61	Notes for Guidance,	482–83
		oppression test,	473–75, 478–79

Index

PACE, under	474–90
physical evidence,	472
reliability,	476–78
right to silence,	450, 451–52, 458, 480, 484, 487
unfairness,	485–88
vulnerable suspects,	477, 479, 499
Confidential information	
See Breach of confidence	
Conspiracy to corrupt	
public morals,	202, 203–04
Contempt of court	
actus reus,	148, 150, 168, 173
active period,	163, 173
anonymity,	162–63
appeals,	152
Bill of Rights in UK, and	99
breach of confidence,	178, 256–57
civil proceedings,	148, 152
common law,	148–51, 173
comparison with CCA 1981,	169–70
Contempt of Court Act 1981,	151–70, 177
criminal,	147, 148, 152, 153
disclosing sources,	177–79
European Convention on Human Rights Article 10,	60, 150–51, 157, 168–72, 176, 178–79
fair trials,	147, 161
freedom of expression,	65–70, 143–77
gagging writs,	152
injunctions,	150–51, 178
interfering with the course of justice,	171–72
journalists,	177–79
judiciary,	150–51, 161–62, 173–75
jury deliberations,	176–77
media,	143–77
mens rea,	170, 172
names, prohibiting publication of,	162–63
Phillimore Committee,	149, 150, 151
photographs,	155
prejudicing proceedings,	148–70, 172

prejudgment test,	150
Prevention of Terrorism Act 1989, and	179
proportionality,	150–51
public interest,	147, 159, 161, 162–63, 176–77, 178
reform,	149, 177
scandalising the court,	170–75
serious prejudice,	152–56
Spycatcher case,	164, 167
strict liability,	148, 152, 157, 159, 165, 173
sub judice,	148–49, 152, 165–66
United States,	
comparison with,	175
witnesses, victimising,	175–76
Corporal punishment,	41, 378
Correspondence, respect for,	64
Criminal proceedings	
breach of confidence,	250
contempt,	147, 148, 152, 153
criminal justice system,	609–12
fair trials,	54, 55, 57–59
freedom of assembly,	289
marches,	306–15
meetings,	306–15
official secrets,	231, 237–44, 247, 249
public order,	306–15
retrospective legislation,	59–61
sex discrimination,	612–15
sexual orientation,	619–20
Critical Legal Studies,	8
Crown privilege,	259–60
Custody officer,	425–26, 427–29
Custody records,	431, 436, 439, 455–58
'D' notices,	258
Damages	
defamation,	69–70
injured feelings,	592
police powers,	469

racial discrimination,	558	marriage,	539, 540
sex discrimination,	592–93	national security,	542–43
state liability,	135	political activities,	540–41
Data protection,	266, 338–39, 342, 357–60	right to liberty,	47, 49–50
		sex discrimination,	539
breach of confidence,	358	Detention,	393, 417, 421–24
inaccurate information,	359	access to legal advice,	440–55
medical records,	362	aliens,	49–50
national security,	359	arrest,	48–49, 417
privacy,	338–39, 357–58	charges,	421, 422
Death penalty,	37, 42, 74	Code of Practice,	417, 422
Defamation		compensation,	53
blasphemy,	216, 217	consensual,	417
damages,	69–70	conviction, after,	47
freedom of expression,	69–70, 139, 140–42	custody officers,	425–26, 427–29
		deportation,	49–50
government bodies of official secrets,	230	European Convention on Human Rights Article 5,	47–50, 422–23
privacy,	332–33	exclusion orders,	514
Defence		*habeas corpus*,	422
See National security		helping police with their enquiries,	417
Democracy		internment,	48
Bill of Rights in UK, and	93–112, 114–18	minors,	49
definition,	141	non-criminals,	49
freedom of assembly, and	285, 286	obligations, to fulfil,	47–48
minority interests,	5	PACE, under	417, 421–22
protection for rights in,	6	remand,	52
sexual orientation,	5–6	review of,	52–53, 422, 423
Demonstrations,	226–27, 275, 289, 294	searches,	378–79, 423–24
		serious arrestable offence,	421
Deportation		terrorism,	48–49, 50–51, 422–23
appeals,	542		
asylum,	544, 545	time limits,	421–22, 423
conducive to public good,	540–45	Devlin, Lord,	182
conviction, after,	539–40	Dicey, AV,	98–106, 113, 133
detention,	49–50	Disciplinary procedures	
EU nationals,	523	fair trials,	55
EEA nationals,	523	police powers,	504, 565–67
European Convention on Human Rights, and	544–45	stop and search,	404
exclusion orders,	514	Discrimination,	547–608
freedom of movement,	538–45	*See also* Positive discrimination, Racial discrimination, Sex discrimination	
inhuman or degrading treatment,	43		
judiciary,	545	aliens,	80

654

Index

assimilationism,	551–52
Bill of Rights in UK, and	100
blasphemy, and	218–19
contract compliance,	600
definition,	547
direct discrimination,	552
employment,	548–49
European Convention on Human Rights Article 14,	76–78
family life,	77
formal equality,	548–49
history,	549–50
inhuman or degrading treatment,	42
liberalism,	548
reverse,	599
sexual orientation,	384, 550–51
age of consent,	383–84, 550
transferred discrimination,	559, 566
Domestic remedies,	75–76, 612–13
Domestic violence,	320, 612–13
Drittwurkung,	28, 117
Drugs,	60, 399
Duty solicitors,	441, 446, 453
Dworkin, Andrea,	185
Dworkin, Ronald,	3, 5–6, 9–11, 13–14, 93, 114, 137, 183–84, 189
Education,	74, 550–51, 616–19
EEA nationals,	518, 521–23
Elections,	74, 116, 288
Emergency situations	
Bill of Rights in UK,	95
European Convention on Human Rights,	78–80, 82
war,	79
Employment	
equal pay,	548–49, 556, 557, 558
forced labour,	44–45
harassment,	568–69
immigration,	525–26, 527
positive discrimination,	599–607
pregnancy,	562–66
racial discrimination,	567, 577, 579
sex discrimination,	548–49, 556, 557, 558, 560–73, 577–78, 591–97
sexual orientation,	550–51, 616–19
work permits,	527
Entrapment,	490–91
Entrenchment, of Bill of Rights	114–16, 118, 125–26, 129, 132–33
Entry to Premises *See* Powers of entry	
Equal Opportunities Commission,	593, 594, 595–98
Equal pay,	548–49, 556, 579–91
collective bargaining,	587–89
comparators,	580–83
equal value claims,	581, 586–87
equality clauses,	579–80, 588–89
European Union,	586–91
like work,	580, 583
market forces,	585–86
material factor defence,	583–89, 590–91
'same employment',	581–82
segregation,	582
term by term approach,	582–83
Equal treatment,	78, 111, 547–48, 563, 578
See also Discrimination, Equal pay	
European Commission on Human Rights	
admissibility conditions,	20–21, 27–30
creation,	20
decisions,	32
European Convention on Human Rights, relationship with,	19–20
European Court of Human Rights,	21, 32
merger with,	20, 22

exhaustion of domestic remedies,	26, 29	blasphemy,	109, 216–20
		bodily integrity,	377–78
filtering process,	20–21, 32	breach of confidence,	252, 254
individual applications,	25–34	broadcasting,	208–09
inter-state applications to,	25	Committee of Ministers,	21, 24–25, 31–32, 34
manifestly ill-founded applications,	30	common European standard,	40, 83, 84, 125
members,	21		
merger,	20, 22	compensation under,	33, 53
merits,	30–31	complaints,	25–34
petitioning,	25	contempt of court,	60, 150–51, 157, 168–72, 176, 178–79
registration of complaints,	27		
role,	20–22, 30, 32–33	data protection,	338
European Convention on Human Rights,	1, 11, 17–86	decisions,	31–34
		deficiencies of,	85–86
admissibility,	26–30, 81, 85	delay,	19
aliens,	80	deportation,	544–45
applicant must be victim,	25–26	derogation from,	78–80
arrest,	418	destruction of Convention rights,	81
Article 1,	107		
Article 2,	35–40, 83	detention,	422–23
Article 3,	40–44, 83	discrimination,	76–78
Article 4,	44–45	*Drittwurkung*,	28, 117
Article 5,	45–53	elections,	74
Article 6,	53–59	emergencies,	78–80, 82
Article 7,	59–61	enforcement,	19, 20, 85
Article 8,	61–64, 81–82, 83	entrenchment,	114–16, 118, 125–26, 129, 132–33
Article 9,	64–65, 81–82, 83		
		European Court of Human Rights,	17–18
Article 10,	13, 65–70, 81–82, 83	exclusion of evidence,	494, 495
Article 11,	70–71, 81–82, 83	exclusion orders,	515–16
Article 12,	71–73	exhaustion of domestic remedies,	26, 29
Article 13,	75–76		
Article 14,	76–78, 125	fair hearings,	18, 53–59
Article 15,	78	filtering process,	20, 27
Article 16,	80	forced labour,	44–45
Article 17,	28, 125	freedom of assembly,	70, 71, 275
Article 19,	20	freedom of association,	70, 71, 275
Article 24,	25	freedom of expression,	65–70, 143–45, 214
Article 25,	25, 28		
Article 26,	29	freedom of information,	361
Article 27,	29–30		
Article 53,	34	freedom of movement,	74, 391, 509–10
Article 64,	81		
asylum,	536	freedom of religion,	64–65
Bill of Rights in UK,	87–93, 101, 103, 118, 123–36	freedom of thought,	64–65
		friendly settlement,	17–18, 30
		guarantees,	75–76, 82

Index

Human Rights		Protocols,	19, 26, 73–75, 124
Commission,	135–36	public order,	290, 296,
immigration,	525–26		298, 301, 303–06
incorporation into		remedies,	75, 135–36
UK law,	89, 91–92, 103,	repeal,	125, 127–29, 132–33
	107–08, 123–33,	reservations,	81
	209, 621–39	respect for the home,	363
indecency,	204–05	restrictions of rights	
individual applications,	25–34, 89,	and freedoms,	78–85
	103, 107,	retrospective legislation,	59–61
	124, 128	right to education,	74
influence in domestic law,	107–10	right to life,	35–40
influence on EU law,	110–12	right to liberty and	
inhuman or degrading		security of person,	45–53
treatment,	40–44	right to marry and	
interpretation of,	17, 24, 107–08	found a family,	71–73
inter-state applications,	25	right to privacy,	61–64
judges,	123, 124–25	right to silence,	459–60, 464–65
judgments,	34	settlement,	17–18, 30
judicial review,	75	sex discrimination,	557
legal aid,	136	sexual orientation,	383–84, 387,
marches,	290, 296,		388, 617, 620
	298, 301,	slavery,	44–45
	303–08	statutory interpretation,	107–08, 127
margin of appreciation,	18, 82–85, 86	substantive rights	
meetings,	290, 296,	and freedoms,	35–75
	298, 301,	supervision,	20–34, 34
	303–08	surveillance,	344–45, 349,
merits test,	30–31, 34		350–51, 356
national courts,	107	telephone tapping,	62, 76
national security,	83–84	torture,	11, 40–44
'necessary in a		trade unions,	279–83
democratic society',	81–82	United Nations	
obscenity,	197–98	Declaration of	
official secrets,	229	Human Rights,	17
police powers,	495	European Court of	
positive obligations under,	84	Human Rights	
'prescribed by law',	81–82	admissibility,	24, 32
privacy,	317, 318–19,	adverse rulings,	17–18, 112
	321, 377	approach to,	23
proportionality,	81–82, 103	compensation,	33
Protocol 1,	19, 26, 28, 73–75	European Commission	
Protocol 4,	19, 74–75	on Human Rights,	32–33
Protocol 6,	19, 74–75	merger with,	20, 22
Protocol 7,	19, 74–75	freedom of expression,	13
Protocol 8,	26	individual standing,	19, 23–24,
Protocol 9,	23		32–33
Protocol 11,	23–24,	interpretation of ECHR,	17, 24
	74–75, 112		

judges,	22–23, 24, 32–33	admissions,	493–95
		agents provocateur,	490
judgments,	33	arrest,	416
jurisdiction,	25	Code of Practice,	469–70, 491–92
membership,	22	common law,	498
procedure,	32–33	deception,	491–93
settlements,	17–18, 24, 33	definition of	
utilitarianism,	10	excluded material,	371
violations,	86	entrapment,	490–91
European Economic		European Convention	
Area nationals,	521–23	on Human Rights,	494, 495
European		identification evidence,	496
Social Charter 1961,	18	Notes for Guidance,	395–96
European Union,	14–15	PACE,	469–73, 491, 494–98
See also Equal pay		physical evidence,	472–73, 497
asylum,	536	police powers,	469–98
Bill of Rights in UK, and	103, 107–12	privacy,	494–95
data protection,	338	privilege against	
deportation,	523	self-incrimination,	492
direct effect,	111	right to silence,	471
equal treatment,	111	secret recording,	490–95
European Convention		searches,	371–72, 375, 404, 471
on Human Rights, and	110–12		
free movement		stop and search,	404
of workers,	522	truth of charges,	470
freedom of movement,	510, 521–23	tricks by police,	490–95
harassment,	569–70	undercover work,	490–95
internal market,	521–22	unfairness,	491–93
judicial review,	596–97	United States,	471
national laws, conflict with,	1	Exclusion orders,	511–16
Parliamentary sovereignty,	129–30	Expression	
positive discrimination,	600–08	*See* Freedom of Expression	
pregnancy, discrimination	562–66	Expulsion,	509–10
proportionality,	523	Fair hearings	
racial discrimination,	559, 576	access to courts,	55–56
satellite broadcasting,	211	access to legal advice,	56, 58
sex discrimination,	557, 596–97	appeals,	55, 56
sexual orientation,	383, 616–18	civil trials,	54, 55, 57
Evidence		contempt of court,	147, 161
See also Confessions,		criminal trials,	54, 55, 57–59
Exclusion of evidence,		cross-examination,	59
Identification		delay,	51–52, 56–57
interrogation,	438	disciplinary	
police powers,	395–96	procedures,	55
powers of entry,	375	European Convention	
Exclusion of evidence		on Human Rights	
See also Confessions		Article 6,	53–59
access to legal advice,	469		

Index

freedom from self-incrimination,	57–58
freedom of expression,	12, 147
guarantees,	54, 56
judges,	122–23
legal aid,	55, 56
legal representation,	58–59
presumption of innocence,	57–59
proportionality,	12
regulatory offences,	55
right to liberty,	51–52
right to silence,	484
False imprisonment,	405, 416, 500
Family	
See also Children	
discrimination,	77
freedom of movement,	509–10
marriage,	71–73
privacy of,	61, 320, 388
Feminism	
anti-assimilationism and,	551–52
pornography,	142–43, 181, 184–89
Films	
censorship,	212–13
classification,	212, 213, 215
distribution,	212
freedom of expression,	190, 205–06, 215
videos,	213, 215
Finger printing,	468
Force, use of	
See Use of force	
Forced labour,	44–45
Forfeiture,	196–97
Franks Committee,	236
Freedom of assembly,	284–306
See also Public order	
bail conditions,	300–06
banning power,	295–99
binding over,	300–06
breach of the peace,	300–06
criminal law,	289
democracy,	285–86
demonstrations,	275, 284, 289
European Convention on Human Rights Article 11,	70–71, 275–76
freedom of expression,	284, 288
highways,	288–89, 299–300
incitement to racial hatred,	225
legal recognition of,	288–89
marches,	284, 288, 290–98
meetings,	284, 288, 289
miners' strike,	99, 303–04, 306, 308
nuisance,	299–300
permits,	70
police,	287
prior restraints,	287
processions,	290–91, 293
protests,	275, 285–88, 290–98
riots,	286–87
subsequent restraints,	287
trespassory assembly,	289
Universal Declaration on Human Rights,	275
Freedom of association,	275–83
Civil service unions and proscription,	280–83
definition,	71
European Convention on Human Rights,	70, 71, 275–76, 278
proscription,	277–78
quasi-military organisations,	276–77
terrorist groups,	277–78
trade unions,	71, 84, 278–84
uniforms associated with political object,	278–84
Universal Declaration of Human Rights,	275
violent groups,	276–78
Freedom of conscience,	64–65
Freedom of expression,	65–70, 137–227
See also Freedom of assembly, Freedom of information, Official secrets	
abortion, and	69

659

administration of justice,	147–79	outraging public	
argument from truth,	138–40	decency,	215
autonomy,	137–38, 143	Phillimore Committee,	149
Bill of Rights in UK,	100–01	political ideas,	66–67, 140–42
Bills of Rights,	143, 144	pornography,	142–43,
blasphemy,	215–24		181–89, 214
breach of confidence,	67, 69, 252, 254	prior restraints,	144, 159
broadcasting,	205, 206–11, 215	privacy,	140
Canada, in	121–22	protection of morals,	143–44,
censorship,	205, 214		189–204
common law,	145	public interest,	140–41, 149
confidentiality,	67, 69	public order,	309
contempt of court,	65–70, 147–77	racial hatred,	225
defamation,	69–70, 140	racist speech,	66
democracy,	139, 140–42	Rawls,	137
Dworkin,	137	religion, and	64, 68–69
European Convention		religious hatred,	224–27
on Human Rights		role of judiciary in	
Article 10,	65–70, 143–45,	relation to,	144–45
	149, 214	seditious libel,	218
European Court of		sex establishments,	215
Human Rights, and	13	statutory interpretation,	144
exceptions,	67–70	subsequent restraints,	144, 159
fair trials,	12, 147	Thalidomide litigation,	149
films,	205, 212–13, 215	United States,	143
forfeiture,	215	Universal Declaration	
freedom of assembly,	275–76,	of Human Rights,	67
	284, 288	videos,	213, 215
freedom of association,	275–76	Williams Committee,	205, 214
freedom of information,	67, 69, 229	Freedom of information,	258–73
freedom of thought,	65	abroad,	264
gagging writs,	149	breach of confidence,	258, 266–67
indecency,	198–205,	Campaign for Freedom	
	206, 214	of Information,	265–66, 268
individual self-fulfilment,	142–43	Canada,	264
injunctions,	149	categories of information,	231
Internet,	206,	censorship,	258
	213–14, 215	Citizen's Charter,	266
journalists,	140	Code of Practice on	
judges,	121–22, 144–45	Access to Government	
marches,	309	Information,	265–72
media,	145, 338	commercial information,	264
self regulation		'D' notices,	258
proposals,	338–39	European Convention	
meetings,	309	on Human Rights,	361
Mill,	6, 138–39	freedom of expression,	67, 229
obscenity,	68, 190–98,	future of, in UK,	232, 272–73
	206, 214		

Index

Information Commission, 272–73
injunctions, 258
Labour Government, and 272–73
maladministration, 269
manual files, 360–62
media, 338
New Zealand, 269, 271
ownership, 228–30
Parliamentary
  Ombudsman, 266–71
personal information, 265–66, 271
present policy on, 272–73
privacy, 230
public interest
  immunity, 259–63
  Matrix Churchill, 261–63, 271
  Scott Report, 263, 271–73
public records, 264–65
right to know, 231–32, 271–73
Security Services'
  exemption, 266–67, 272–73
Spycatcher, 258
statutory, 272–73
United States, 264, 265
voluntary open
  government, 265–73
Freedom of movement, 509–45
asylum, 528–36
British citizens, 509, 511, 517, 519–20
deportation, 538–45
EU nationals, 510, 521–23
EEA nationals, 518, 521–23
European Convention
  on Human Rights, 74, 391, 509–10
exclusion orders, 511–16
expulsion, 509–10
families, 509–10
illegal entrants, 537–38
immigration, 509, 516–22
International Covenant on
  Civil and Political Rights, 510
passports, 511, 521
right of abode, 516–22
right of entry, 523–36
royal prerogative, 511
temporary entrants, 525–28
travel abroad, 510–11

Freedom of religion, 64–65
Freedom of speech
  See Freedom of expression
Freedom of thought, 64–65

Gagging orders, 149, 152, 252
Gender
  See Sex discrimination
GCHQ, 105, 280–83, 355
Government information
  See Freedom of information,
  Official secrets
Gypsies, 63

Habeus corpus writ, 422
Hacking, 359–60
Harassment
  employment, 568–69
  European Union, and 569–70
  media, 334, 340
  public order, 308, 309
  racial, 225, 227, 568–70, 609
  reporters, 340
  sexual, 568–70
  telephone calls, 364, 365
Hart, HLA, 4, 182
Highway
  elections, 288
  freedom of assembly, 288–89
  obstruction, 289, 299–300
  public order, 298–300
Hohfeld, Wesley, 14–15
Home Office circulars, 396, 419
Homosexuality
  See Sexual orientation
Hostages, 36, 39
Human Rights Act 1998 125–36, 621–39
  See also European
  Convention on Human
  Rights, Bill of Rights for UK

Human rights
See also European
Commission on Human
Rights, European
Convention on Human
Rights, European Court of
Human Rights, Rights
concept of, 6
Human Rights Commission, 135–36

Identification, 465–68
  appropriate adult, 465, 468
  children, 468
  Code of Practice, 465, 466–67
  confessions, 496
  confrontation, 466
  consent, 465
  exclusion of evidence, 496
  fingerprints, 468
  group identification, 466, 467
  identification officer, 466, 467
  parades, 466
  racial discrimination, and 467
  safeguards, 467
  samples, 465, 468
  terrorism, 465
  video film, 466, 467
  vulnerable groups, 465
  witnesses, by, 466–67
Illegal entry, 529, 537–38
Immigration
  acquired rights, 518–19
  appeals, 525, 527, 528
  British citizens, 517, 518, 519–20, 521
  certificate of entitlement, 520–21, 527
  children, 519, 526
  Commonwealth, 516, 518, 519
  EEA nationals, 518, 521–22
  EU nationals, 521–22
  employment, 525–26, 527
  entrants intending to remain, 525–28
  European Convention on Human Rights, and 525–26
  freedom of movement, 509, 516–22
  Home Office guidelines, 524
  illegal entry, 537–38
  marriage, 520, 525–26, 527
  naturalisation, 520
  primary purpose rule, 525, 526
  racial discrimination, 517
  refusal of entry, 527–28
  relatives, 526–27
  right of abode, 516–22
  rights of entry, 523–36
  sex discrimination, 526
  sexual orientation, 525
  temporary entrants, 525–28
  terrorism, 517
  work permits, 527
Immunities, 14
Implied repeal, doctrine of, 125, 127–29, 132–33
Imprisonment
  See Prisoners' Rights
Incest, 381
Incitement to racial hatred, 224–27
Incitement to religious hatred, 218, 224–27
Indecency
  artistic expression, 201
  children, 200
  common law, 201, 202–05
  conspiracy to corrupt public morals, 202, 203–04
  corrupt and deprave test, 199
  customs, 200–01
  definition, 199–200
  European Convention on Human Rights, 204–05
  freedom of expression, 198–206, 214
  obscenity, 192, 196, 198–99, 201, 202–05
  outraging public decency, 202–03
  pornography, 201
  post, material sent through the, 220, 201
  public displays, 198, 200, 203
  reform, 214
  statutory provisions, 200–01

Index

theatre, 201
Independent Television Commission, 206–07, 210, 211
Inhuman or degrading treatment
  asylum seekers, 42–43
  common European standard, 40
  corporal punishment, 41
  death penalty, 42
  definition, 41
  deportation, 43
  discrimination, as 42
  European Convention on Human Rights Article 3, 40–44
  medical treatment, 40
  solitary confinement, 41
  self-defence, 41
Injunctions
  breach of confidence, 250–54, 325–28
  contempt of court, 150–51, 178
  freedom of expression, 149
  freedom of information, 258
  interim, 250, 251–52, 254–57, 325–28
  permanent, 250, 251, 253–54
  privacy, 340–41
  public order, 316
  surveillance, 340–41
Internet, 206, 213–14, 215
Interception of communications, 343–49, 356
  admission of evidence Bill of Rights in UK, 95, 97, 98
Interfering with the course of justice, 171–72
International Covenant on Civil and Political Rights 1966, 18, 20, 224, 280, 510
Interrogation, 424–65
  See also Confessions
  access to legal advice, 426, 431, 436, 437–38, 440–55, 457
  appropriate adult, 427–28, 430, 439, 457
  arrest, 438
  blind suspects, 429
  cautions, 426, 433, 437
  children, 426–29, 430
  Code of Practice, 424–40, 457–58
  custody officers, 425–26, 427–29
  deaf suspects, 429
  evidence, 438
  hearing impaired suspects, 429
  Home Office circulars, 431
  interpreters, 429
  interviews, 431–39
  intimate searches, 430
  Judges' Rules, 430
  medical treatment, 430
  mentally disordered suspects, 426–30
  national security, 438–39
  non-interviews, 431–35, 439
  Notes for Guidance, 431, 436, 438
  notification of rights, 426, 427–28
  PACE, 424–31, 457–58
  physical treatment, 429–30
  police station,
    inside, 425–30, 435–39
    outside, 435–39
    volunteers at, 437–38
  records, 431, 436, 439, 455–58
  right to silence, 426, 457, 458–64
  Royal Commission on Criminal Procedure 1992, 426, 456
  Runciman Commission, 428, 437, 457
  safeguards, 430–40
  tape-recording, 431, 436–40, 455–56
  techniques, 455–58
  terrorism, 425, 438–39
  use of force, 429
  video-recording, 455–57
  vulnerable groups, 426–29
Interviews with police See Interrogation
Intimate samples, 378–79, 430, 465, 489

Journalists
   data protection, 338
   freedom of expression, 140
   investigative, 342
   official secrecy, 242–43, 248
   privacy, 342
   protection of sources, 177–79
   public interest, 342
   stalking, 340
   surveillance, 346–47

Judges
   bias, 119–22, 173–75
   Bill of Rights in UK, 98–106, 113–14, 117–22, 124–25
   Canada, 119–20, 121–22
   contempt of court, 150–51, 161–62, 173–75
   deportation, 545
   European Convention on Human Rights, and 119–20, 123
   European Court of Human Rights, in 22, 24, 32–33
   fair trials, 122–23
   freedom of expression, 121–22, 144–45
   margin of appreciation doctrine, 120

Judgments
   European Convention on Human Rights, 34
   European Court of Human Rights, 33
   supervision, 34

Judicial review
   asylum, 531, 534
   Bill of Rights in UK, and 101, 103–06, 116, 133–34
   European Convention on Human Rights Article 13, 75
   European Union law, and 596–97
   illegal entry, 538
   legislation, 1
   locus standi, 596–97
   proportionality, 134
   remedies, 134
   sex discrimination, and 596–97
   trade unions, 281, 282

Jury deliberations, 176–77

Juveniles
   See Children

Legal advice
   See Access to legal advice
Legal aid, 55, 56, 136
Legal positivism, 6, 9, 10
Legal privilege, 461
Legal rights, 8–11

Lesbian and gays
   See Sexual orientation

Libel
   See Defamation

Liberal concept of rights, 6–8
Life, right to, 35–40

MacKinnon, Catherine, 185–87
Mail intercepts, 343–50
Maladministration, 269
Malicious falsehood, 332–33
Malicious prosecution, 500
Marches, 284, 288–98, 301

Marriage
   chastisement of wife, 386
   children, 72
   cohabitation as, 613–14
   criminal law, and 612–15
   deportation, 539, 540
   divorce, 72
   domestic violence, 320, 612
   European Convention on Human Rights
      Article 12, 71–73
   family life, and, 71–73
   immigration, 520, 525–26, 527
   marital discrimination, 558
   marital immunity, 613
   prisoners, 73
   privacy, 613
   rape, in 320, 613–14
   right to, 71–73
   sex discrimination, 558, 612–15
   transsexuals, 72

Index

Maternity rights, 563, 565–66, 600
Marxism, 7
Matrix Churchill, 168, 261–63, 271
Media
  See also Journalists, Official secrets
  Calcutt Committee, 334, 335
  Broadcasting Complaints Commission, 334–35
  Broadcasting Standards Commission, 335–36
  code of conduct, 334–35
  contempt, 143–77
  freedom of expression, 145, 338
  freedom of information, 338
  harassment, 334, 340
  intrusion, 323–42, 363
  ownership, 206
  Press Complaints Commission, 334–35
  Press Council, 334
  privacy, 323–42
  public interest, 334
  self-regulation, 333–35
  Younger Committee, 334
Medical records, 361–62
Medical treatment
  autonomy in, 379–81
  inhuman or degrading treatment, 40
Meetings, 284, 288, 290–98
Mentally disordered suspects, 499
Mill, JS, 6, 138–39, 183
Miners' strike, 99, 303–04, 306, 308
Minors
  See Children
Miscarriages of justice, 394, 507
Moral rights, 8–11
Motor vehicles, 400, 401

National security
  Bill of Rights in UK, and 94, 101
  breach of confidence, 254
  deportation, 542–43
  data protection, 359
  European Convention
    on Human Rights, and 83–84
  exclusion orders, 514–15
  interrogation, 438–39
  official secrecy, 231, 237–42, 246, 248–49
  privacy, 62
  sexual orientation, and 616
  surveillance, 344, 346, 353–55
Natural law, 9
Natural rights, 6
Naturalisation, 519, 520
New Zealand
  Bill of Rights, 127
  freedom of information, 269, 271
Newspapers
  See Media
Nuisance, 299–300, 364

Obscenity
  common European standard, 198
  contempt of court, 173
  defence of 'public good', 194–96
  'deprave and corrupt' test, 191–94, 197
  European Convention on Human Rights
    Article 10, 197–98
  forfeiture proceedings, 196–97
  freedom of expression, 68, 190–98, 206, 214
  indecency, 192, 196, 198–99, 202–05
  Internet, 214
  pornography, 190–91, 195, 197
  protection of morals exception, 197–98
  reform, 214
  satellite broadcasting, 211
  'significant proportion' test, 193

statutory, 190–98
telephone calls, 365
United States, 191
Williams Committee, 194
Obstructing a constable, 418–21
Official secrets, 229–49
  See also Freedom of information, Privacy
  accountability, 231
  authorised disclosures, 244
  Bill of Rights in UK, 94, 95
  breach of confidence, 134–35, 229–30, 235, 240, 247, 250, 253
  categories of information covered, 244
  Civil Service Conduct Code, 231
  Code of Practice on Access to Government Information, 265–73
  criminal law, 231, 237–44, 247, 249
  defences, 244–47
  democracy, 230
  European Convention on Human Rights Article 10, 229
  foreign countries, in, 231–32
  Franks Committee, 236
  harm tests, 245, 246, 247–48, 267
  history of, 23–33
  information published abroad, 247
  journalists, 242–43, 248
  mens rea, 232–33, 236–37, 242–43, 248
  national security, 231, 237–42, 246, 248–49
  non-Crown servants, 248
  Official Secrets Act 1911, 232–36
  Official Secrets Act 1989, 236–49
  open government, 265–73
  other statutory provisions enforcing secrecy, 249
  personal information, 265–66, 271
  prior publication, 246
  public interest defence, 231, 237, 245–47
    lack of, 134–35

  receiver of information, 237, 242
  reform, 266
  'right to know', 231–32
  Spycatcher case, 235–36, 249
  strict liability, 233
  United States, 246
  whistle-blowing, 246
Outraging public decency, 202–03, 215

Parliamentary
  Ombudsman, 266–71
  sovereignty, 1, 129–30, 132
Passports, 511, 521
Personal information, 323–62
Phillimore Committee, 149, 150, 151
Photographs, 155, 364
Police powers, 393–507
  See also Arrest, Confessions, Detention, Identification of suspects, Interrogation by police, Stop and search
  access to legal advice, 469
  accountability, 372, 374–76, 503
  admissions, 495
  assault on officer in execution of duty, 420–21
  breach of PACE, 395
  bugging devices, 62, 76, 95, 97
  Codes of Practice, 394–507, 610
  complaints, 469, 503–06
  damages, 469, 500–03
  deception, 493
  disciplinary procedure, 504, 505–07
  entrapment, 490–91
  European Convention on Human Rights, 495
  evidence, 395–96
    exclusion, 396, 469–98
  false imprisonment, 500
  hearing impaired suspects, 429
  helping police with their enquiries, 417
  Home Office circulars, 396, 419
  impropriety, 468–506
  intimate searches, 378–79
  malicious prosecution, 500
  mentally disordered and handicapped suspects, 499

Index

miscarriages of justice,	394, 507	sex discrimination,	185–87
Notes for Guidance,	369, 395–96	sexual offenders,	188
obstruction of officer in		therapeutic effect,	195
execution of duty,	418–21	Williams Committee,	181, 183
PACE,	393–507, 610	Positive discrimination,	549–50, 598–608
personal information,	356	advertising and	
powers of entry,	365–76	recruitment,	599
privacy, and	494–95	contract compliance,	600
public interest immunity,	505	employment,	599–607
public order,	291–95,	equal opportunities,	599–601
	301–03, 315–16	European Union, and	600–08
racial discrimination,	609–12	formal equality,	598–99, 603
right to silence,	507	forms,	599–600
Royal Commission		maternity,	600
on Criminal		pregnancy,	600
Procedure 1981,	393–94	proportionality,	600–01, 604
Runciman Commission,	394, 505–06	quotas,	601–06
secret recording,	490–95	racial discrimination,	599–600
searching of premises,	365–76	recognition,	599–600
seizure of material,	365, 367,	reverse discrimination,	599
	369–72	sex discrimination,	599–607
stereotyping,	610	terrorism,	601
surveillance,	340–41,	theoretical basis,	598
	343–62, 619	Positivism,	6, 9, 10
terrorism,	393	Powers of entry	
tortious remedies,	500–03, 507	accountability,	374–76
tricks,	490–95	*Anton Piller* orders,	375
undercover work,	490–95	arrest,	366
use of force,	420	code of practice,	372–76
Wednesbury		common law,	369
unreasonableness,	501	evidence,	375
Pornography		information to	
autonomy,	184, 187–89	be conveyed,	373–74
censorship,	181, 183, 188	legal advice,	372–73
conservative position,	182	Notice of Powers	
Devlin,	182	and Rights,	373, 374
Dworkin, Andrea,	185	PACE 1984,	365, 366,
Dworkin, Ronald,	183–84, 189		367, 374–75
feminist position,	181, 184–189	police,	365–76
freedom of expression,	142–43,	privacy,	375, 376
	181–89, 214	surveillance,	367
Hart,	182	terrorism,	366–69, 374
indecency,	201	United States,	365
Internet,	214	warrants,	374
liberal position,	181, 183–84	without,	366–68
MacKinnon,	185–87	Pregnancy,	561–56, 600
Mills,	183	Prejudice to proceedings,	148–70
obscenity,	190–91, 195, 197		
satellite broadcasting,	211		

Press
  See Media
Presumption of innocence, 57–58
Prevention of Terrorism
  provisions
  See Terrorism
Prisoners' rights
  See also Detention
  Bill of Rights in UK, 99–100
  correspondence, 64
  life imprisonment, 85
  marriage, 73
  racial discrimination, 612
  religion, 65
Privacy, 317–21
  access to personal
    information, 356–62
  autonomy, and 318, 319, 379–81
  Bill of Rights in UK, 117
  breach of confidence, 323–31
  bodily privacy, 377–81
  Calcutt Committee, 336–37
  children, 333, 360–61
  civil liability, 339–43
  concept of, 317–18
  confidentiality, 62
  corporal punishment, 378
  correspondence, 64
  criminal liability, 339–42
  data protection, 338–39, 357–58
  defamation, 332–33
  definition, 317, 377
  domestic violence, 320
  European Convention
    on Human Rights, 61–64, 317,
     318–21, 377
  exclusion of evidence, 494–95
  exposing crime, 342
  family life, 61, 320–21, 388
  freedom of expression, 140
  freedom of information, 230
  gypsies, 63
  harassment, 340
  homosexuality, 62–63, 319
  injunctions, 340–41
  intimate searches, 378–79
  journalism, 342
  malicious falsehood, 332–33
  manual files, 359, 360–62
  media,
    intrusion, 323–42, 363
    self-regulation, 333–35
  medical records, 361–61
  national security, 62
  personal information, 323–62
  photographs, 364
  police powers, 494–95
  powers of entry, 375, 376
  prisoners' correspondence, 64
  private life, 61–63
  property, intrusion onto, 363–65
  public interest, 337
  remedies for intrusion,
    proposals, 340–42
  respect for the home, 63–64, 363
  security services,
    intrusion, 363
  self-determination in
    relation to medical
    treatment, 379–81
  sexual life, 62–63
  sexual orientation, 62–63, 319,
     319, 383, 387
  surveillance, 340–41, 342–62
  telephone tapping, 62, 343–49
  tort of invasion of
    privacy, proposals, 336–38
  United States, 336
  Younger Committee, 336
Privilege against
  self-incrimination, 57–58, 459,
     464, 465, 492
Processions, 290–91, 293
Proportionality
  Bill of Rights in UK, and 105, 134
  contempt of court, 150–51
  European Convention
    on Human Rights, 81–82, 103
  European union, 523
  fair trials, 12
  judicial review, 134
  positive discrimination, 600–01, 604
  right to life, 38–40
Prostitution, 614, 615
Protests, 275–76,
     285–86, 287

Index

Public interest
  breach of confidence, 250–57, 324, 330–31
  contempt, 147, 159, 161, 162–63, 176–77, 178
  data protection, 338–39
  freedom of expression, 140–41, 149
  freedom of information, 259–63, 271–73
  immunity, 168, 259–63, 505
  journalists, 342
  Matrix Churchill, 168, 261–63, 272
  media, 334, 337
  official secrets, 231, 237, 245–47
  police powers, 505
  Scott Report, 233–34, 263, 271–73

Public nuisance, 299–300

Public order, 286–88
  See also Freedom of Assembly
  advance notice of marches, 290–98
  affray, 311–12
  bail conditions, 300–06
  banning orders, 295–99
  binding over, 300–06
  breach of the peace, 300–06, 315
  civil remedies, 316
  criminal law, 306–15
  criminal trespass, 289, 312–15
  disorderly behaviour, 310
  European Convention on Human Rights, 290, 296, 298, 301, 308–10
  football matches, 227
  freedom of expression, 309
  harassment, 308, 309
  highways, 298–300
  incitement to racial hatred, 224–27
  injunctions, 316
  marches, 290–98, 301
  meetings, 290–98
    conditions, 291–95
    private premises, 315–16
  miner's strike, 303–04, 306, 308
  obstructing the highway, 298–300
  organisers, 290–91
  police, 291–95, 301–03, 315–16
  power to impose conditions on assemblies, 291–95
  power to impose conditions on marches, 291–95
  processions, 290–91, 293
  public nuisance, 299–300, 364
  racial discrimination, 609
  right of access, 298
  riot, 286, 311–12
  threatening, abusive, or insulting behaviour, 306–07, 309
  violent disorder, 311–12

Public records, 264–65

Quasi-military organisations, 276–77

Queen's peace, preserving
  See Public Order

Racial discrimination, 550, 558–59
  arrest, 610
  assimilationism, 551–52
  asylum, 536
  burden of proof, 567, 575
  Codes of Practice, 610
  Commission for Racial Equality, 559, 566–67, 575, 576, 595–98
  contract compliance, 600
  criminal justice system, 609–12
  criminal law, 609
  damages, 558, 592–93
  detriment, 568, 569
  direct discrimination, 559, 566–70
  defences to race discrimination claims, 576, 578–79
  employment, 567–69, 577, 579, 595
  European Union, 559, 576
  exceptions, 559
  freedom of expression, 66
  genuine occupational qualifications, 579
  harassment, 225, 227, 568–69, 609

669

identification,	467	discrimination,	574–76
immigration,	517	religious hatred,	218, 224–27
incitement to racial hatred,	218, 224–27, 609	Remand,	52
		Remedies,	75–76
indirect discrimination,	559, 573–76	Bill of Rights in UK,	133–35
individual methods,	591–608	European Convention on Human Rights,	75, 135–36
injured feelings,	592	judicial review,	134
judicial review,	596–97	police powers,	500–03, 507
lawful,	578–79	public order,	316
non-discrimination notices,	595, 597–98	racial discrimination,	591–93
PACE,	610	sex discrimination,	591–93, 595–98
police,	609–12		
positive discrimination,	599–600	Retrospective legislation,	59–61
prisons,	612	Reverse discrimination,	599
public order,	609	Right of abode,	516–22
racial abuse,	569	Right of entry,	523–36
racial groups,	226–27	Right to liberty and security of person	
reform of law relating to remedies,	594–95, 597–98	arrest,	48–49, 50–51
religious groups,	574–76	bail,	52
remedies,	591–93	compensation,	53
segregation,	559, 567, 609	deportation,	47, 49–50
stereotyping,	398, 402, 610	detention,	47–50
stop and search,	398, 401–02, 610	aliens,	49–50
		arrest, after,	48–49
success rate of applications,	593–94	conviction, after,	47
transferred discrimination,	559, 566	non-criminals,	49
		obligations, to fulfil,	47–48
victimisation,	576–77, 592, 609	review,	52–53
Radio,	207, 211	European Convention on Human Rights Article 5,	45–53
Rape		internment,	48
anonymity of victims,	119–20, 163	minors,	49
Canada,	119–20	remand,	52
marriage,	320, 613–14	terrorism,	48–49, 50–51
sex discrimination,	612–15	trials, delay in,	51–52
sexual history of victims,	615	Right to life	
		abortion,	37
Rawls, John,	3, 4–5, 7, 10–11, 137	death penalty,	37
		European Convention on Human Rights Article 2,	35–40
Refugees			
See Asylum, Immigration		exceptions,	37–38
Religion,	64–65, 68	hostages,	36, 39
See also Blasphemy		proportionality,	38–40
autonomy,	224	self-defence,	38
definition,	224	use of force,	38–40

Index

Right to marry,	71–73	Sado-masochism,	385–88
Right to silence,	426, 457, 458–64, 507	Samples, intimate and non-intimate,	378–79, 430, 465, 468
abolition,	459	Satellite television,	211
access to legal advice,	441, 450–53, 458, 460	Scandalising the court,	170–75
adverse inferences,	426, 459–62	Scott Report,	233–34, 263, 271–73
cautions,	459		
Code of Practice,	459–60, 463	Searches,	365–76
confessions,	450, 451–52, 458, 480, 484, 487	*See also* Stop and search	
		accountability,	372, 374–76
European Convention on Human Rights, and	459–60, 464–65	code of practice,	372–76
		detention,	378–79, 423–24
		evidence,	371–72, 375
exclusion of evidence,	471	exclusion of evidence,	471
fair hearings,	464	illegal entry,	537
legal professional privilege,	461	information to be conveyed,	373–74
PACE,	450, 462	intimate,	378–79, 430
privilege against self-incrimination,	459, 464, 465	legal advice,	372
		Notice of Powers and Rights,	373, 374
Royal Commission on Criminal Justice,	451	personal,	378
Runciman Commission,	458–59	police,	372–76
serious fraud,	463–64	powers of entry,	365–76
Rights		privacy,	375
competing,	12	privilege,	371–72
core,	12	property,	365–76
derivation,	3–8	seizure,	365, 367, 369–72
legal,	8–11		
liberties and, distinguishing,	13–15	terrorism,	371
meaning of,	8–15	voluntary,	369–70
moral,	8–10	warrants,	368, 371, 374
nature of,	1–15	Secrecy in government	
overriding,	11, 12	*See* Official secrets, Privacy	
protection for in UK,	1–2	Serious fraud,	463–64
risk to society,	13	Seditious libel,	218
strength,	10–13	Segregation,	559, 567, 582, 609
Riot,	286, 311–12		
Royal Commission on Criminal Justice 1993,	177, 451	Seizure of property,	365, 367, 369–72
		Self-defence,	38, 41
Royal Commissions on Criminal Procedure,	393–94, 426, 454, 456	Self-incrimination privilege,	57–58, 459, 464, 465, 471
Runciman Commission,	394, 428, 437, 457–59, 505–06	Serious arrestable offences,	407, 414, 421, 441, 442

671

Servitude,	44–45	pluralist approach,	556, 570
Sex discrimination,	550, 555–58	pornography,	185–87
See also Equal pay		positive discrimination,	599–607
armed forces,	578	pregnancy,	561–66, 600
assimilationism,	551–52	rape,	612–15
asylum,	532	reform,	594–95, 597–98
burden of proof,	561	remedies,	591–93, 595–98
comparable man,	560, 564	sexual harassment,	568–70
continuous employment,	561–62	sexual orientation,	382
contract compliance,	600	success rate of	
criminal justice system,	614–15	applications,	593–94
criminal law,	612–14	victimisation,	576–77
damages,	592–93	Sex offenders,	188, 190, 381–85
defences,	572–73, 577–78	Sexual expression and identity,	381–88
deportation,	539	*See also* Sexual orientation	
direct,	560–66	Sexual orientation	
domestic violence,	612–13	age of consent,	383–84, 550
EU Code of Practice on sexual harassment,	569–70	armed forces,	102, 617, 619
employment,	548–49, 556, 557, 558, 560–73, 577–78, 591–97	buggery,	382–85
		Bill of Rights in UK,	102
		criminal law,	382–85, 619–20
		discrimination,	384, 550–51, 616–20
Equal Opportunities Commission,	593, 594, 595–98	employment and education,	550–51, 616–19
Equal Treatment Directive,	563, 578	European Convention on Human Rights,	383–84, 387, 388, 617, 620
European Convention on Human Rights Article 14,	77, 557	European Union,	383, 616, 618
		immigration,	523
European Union,	557, 596–97	margin of appreciation, and	385
female offenders,	614–15		
formal equality,	556, 560	national security,	616, 617
genuine occupational qualifications,	578	privacy,	62–63, 319, 383, 387
harassment,	568–70	promotion of homosexuality,	618
history,	555–56		
indirect,	570–73, 592	sado-masochism,	385–88
immigration,	526	sex discrimination,	382
judicial review,	596–97	surveillance,	619
lawful,	577–78	transsexuals,	618–19
marital status,	558, 612–15	Silence	
maternity rights,	563, 565–66, 600	*See* Right to silence	
		Slavery,	44–45
non-discrimination notices,	595	Social Charter,	18
		Social contract,	3–4, 5

Index

Solitary confinement,	41
Speech	
See Freedom of Expression	
Spycatcher,	99, 164, 167, 235–36, 249, 251–56, 258
Stalking,	340
State surveillance	
See Surveillance	
Statutory interpretation	
Bill of Rights in UK,	98–106
European Convention on Human Rights,	107–08, 127
freedom of expression,	144
Stereotyping,	398, 402, 610
Stop and search,	366, 394–95, 397–405
anticipated local violence,	399–402
arrest,	401
breach of rules on,	404–05
cautions,	403
Code of Practice,	398–405
disciplinary action,	404
drugs,	399
effect of power,	397, 401–03
exclusion of evidence,	404
PACE,	397–404
procedure,	402
racial discrimination,	401–02, 610
records,	402, 404
reasonable suspicion,	398–400
stereotyping,	398, 402
supervision,	400–01
terrorism,	399–402
vehicles,	400, 401
voluntary,	402–03, 404–05
vulnerable groups,	403
Sub judice rule,	148–49, 152, 165–66
Surveillance,	343–62
bugging devices,	62, 76, 95, 97, 343, 349–56
Calcutt Committee,	340–41
Canada,	354
detection of crime,	351–52
European Convention on Human Rights,	344–45, 349, 350–51, 356
GCHQ,	355
injunctions,	340–41
interception of communications,	343–49, 356
journalists,	346–47
mail intercepts,	343–50
national security,	344, 346, 353–55
nuisance,	364
police,	340–41, 343–62, 619
powers of entry,	367
privacy,	340–41, 343–62
sexual orientation, and	619
telephone tapping,	62, 76, 343–51
warrants,	344, 346, 347, 349, 362, 354–56
Younger Committee,	340, 349
Tape-recording,	431, 436–40, 455–56
Telephone tapping,	343–51
European Convention on Human Rights,	62, 76
privacy,	62
terrorism,	76
Terrorism,	
arrest,	50–51, 412, 413–14
Bill of Rights in UK,	95, 114–15
broadcasting controls,	208–09
contempt of court,	179
detention,	422–23
exclusion orders,	511–15
freedom of association,	277–78
identification,	465
immigration,	517
interrogations,	425, 438–39
police powers,	393
positive discrimination,	602
powers of entry,	366–69, 374
Prevention of Terrorism Act 1989,	179, 277–78, 366–67, 399–400, 511

public interest,	179	contempt of court,	175
right to liberty,	48–49, 50–51	exclusion of evidence,	471
stop and search,	399–403	freedom of expression,	143
telephone tapping,	76	freedom of information,	264, 265
uniforms,	278	immunities,	14
Thalodomide litigation,	149	official secrets,	246
Theatre censorship,	190, 198	pornography,	191
Torture		powers of entry,	365
definition,	41	Universal Declaration of Human Rights,	67, 275
European Convention on Human Rights Article 3,	11, 40–44	Use of force	
Trade unions,	71, 84, 278–84	arrest,	417–18
closed shop,	278–80	interrogation,	429
European Convention on Human Rights,	279–83	police powers,	420
freedom not to join,	278–79	right to life,	38–40
freedom of choice,	279–80	Utilitarianism,	5–7, 10–11, 114
freedom to join,	280–83		
GCHQ,	280–83	Victimisation,	576–77, 592, 609
International Covenant on Economic, Social and Cultural rights,	280	Vehicle searching,	400, 401
		Video films,	213, 215, 466, 467
judicial review,	281, 282	Video-taping of interrogations,	455–57
Transsexuals,	72, 111, 120, 388, 618–19	Violent disorder,	311–12
Trespass,	289, 312–15, 339–40, 363–64	War,	79
Trials		*Wednesbury* unreasonableness,	102–03, 105, 134
See Fair hearings		arrest,	411–12
		asylum,	530
Undercover work,	490–95	Bill of Rights in UK,	102–03, 105, 134
Uniforms, prohibition on,	278	police powers,	501
United Nations Convention Relating to the Status of Refugees 1951,	43, 528–34	Whistleblowing,	246
		Williams Committee,	181, 183, 194, 205–06, 213, 214
United Nations Declaration on Human Rights,	17	Witnesses	
		contempt of court,	175–76
United States		victimisation,	175–76
Bill of Rights,	116		
bodily autonomy,	379	Younger Committee,	323, 334, 340, 349
breach of confidence,	255–56		